STORIES ABOUT THE PARTITION OF INDIA

Stories About the Partition of India

VOLUMES I-III

Edited by

ALOK BHALLA

MANOHAR
2026

First published by Indus in 1994
Reprinted 2026

ISBN 978-81-7304-934-7 (Set)
ISBN 978-81-7304-935-4 (Vols. I-III)

Published by
Ajay Kumar Jain *for*
Manohar Publishers & Distributors
4753/23 Ansari Road, Daryaganj,
New Delhi 110 002

Printed and bound in India

VOLUME I

CONTENTS

Acknowledgements

Editorial Note

Introduction

Syed Mohammad Ashraf
Separated From the Flock 1

Salil Choudhary
The Dressing Table 25

Jamila Hashmi
Exile 39

Rajinder Singh Bedi
Lajwanti 55

Mohan Rakesh
The Owner of Rubble 67

Intizar Husain
A Letter From India 79

Saadat Hasan Manto
Cold Meat 91

Saadat Hasan Manto
Compassion 97

Saadat Hasan Manto
Sorry 99

Umm-e-Ummara
More Sinned Against Than Sinning 101

S.H.Vastsayan 'Ajneya'
Getting Even 119

Manik Bandyopadhayay
Childishness 127

Lalithambika Antharjanam
A Leaf in the Storm 137

Bhisham Sahni
The Train Has Reached Amritsar 147

CONTENTS

Ahmad Nadeem Qasmi
Parmeshwar Singh 159

Ramlal
A Visitor From Pakistan 179

Shaikh Ayyaz
Neighbours 187

Yaspal
A Holy War 193

Kulwant Singh Virk
Weeds 203

Satinath Bhaduri
The Champion of the People 209

Notes on the Authors 229

Glossary 233

ACKNOWLEDGEMENTS

I would never have succeeded in editing this three-volume anthology of stories about the Partition of India without the help, generosity and support of a large number of people. First and foremost, I should like to thank my uncle, Vishwamitter Adil, who worked with me in the true spirit of an intellectual adventurer. Not only did he hunt down stories about the Partition written in Urdu, he also worked hard on translating many of them with me.

I need to offer my special thanks to Asif Aslam Farrukhi, the young Pakistani writer in Karachi, who was not only the first one to respond to my initial inquiries, but was also kind enough to present me with a copy of Mumtaz Sherin's excellent anthology of Urdu stories about the Partition.

There are many other friends and scholars whose kindness I wish to acknowledge here: Mubarak Ali, Masud Ashar, Iqbal Khan, Tahir Kamaran, Aga Sohail, Ahmad Nadeem Qasmi and Intizar Husain; Bernd Siebers, Saeeda Gazdar, Hajira Masroor, Ahmad Ali Khan, Khalid Ahmad and Seema; Tejwant S. Gill and Gurupdesh Singh; Mihir Bhattacharya, Tutun Mukherjee, Julu Sen, Sukanta Choudhuri and Swapna Mazumdar; Girdhar Rathi and Alok Rai; Digish Mehta and Bholabhai Patel; Sudhakar Marathe, G.P. Pradhan, Ravi Kant, Adil Mehdi and Gyan Pandey; Muralidharan, C.M.Mohanan, Mohammad Umar Memon and Tanvir Mokammel.

I should also like to thank Peter Bumke, Director of Max Mueller Bhavan, Hyderabad, who was generous enough to let me use the resources of his institute while I was working on this anthology. He made it possible for me to go to Pakistan and find the kind material I would never have come across without making that trip.

Anna Kurien, Santosh James and Satish Podwal were kind enough to read through the proofs of these volumes.

This manuscript was typed and processed on a computer by Herbert Harry, R. S. Manian, Naseeruddin and Josephine. I must thank them for their patience and efficiency.

My finest debt is, however, to my family. My daughters have, however, made me promise that I shall not take so much time away from them, and work under such intense pressure, in the future — a promise which I shall have to keep for my own good.

Alok Bhalla

EDITORIAL NOTE

The stories in these three volumes have neither been arranged chronologically nor according to the original languages in which they were written. I have chosen, instead, to let a variety of different voices and the complexity of experiences which they narrate, resonate in each volume.

Every effort has been made to ensure that the translations are not only readable, but are also accurate renderings of the original texts.

Alok Bhalla

INTRODUCTION

By

Alok Bhalla

I was born a Hindu, no doubt. No one can undo the fact. But I am also a Muslim because I am a good Hindu. In the same way I am also a Parsi and a Christian too.

Mahatma Gandhi, May 30, 1947.

A friend sent me a harsh letter asking me if I must persist in my madness. "In a few days you will be leaving this world," he says, "Will you never learn?...You talk like the foolish sadhu who again and again tried to save a scorpion from drowning while it went on stinging him. If you cannot give up your refrain of ahimsa you can at least allow others to take the path of their choosing. Why do you become a hindrance?"...

The example of the sadhu and the scorpion is a good one. When some person without faith asked him why he was set on saving the scorpion, whose very nature was to sting, he answered: "If it is in the nature of the scorpion to sting it is in the nature of man to put up with the sting. If the scorpion cannot give up its nature, how can I give up mine? Do I have to become a scorpion that stings and kill it?"

Mahatma Gandhi, June 13, 1947.

To India came caravans from all over the world,
Each found a home here and so India was made.

Firaq Gorakhpuri.

The Partition of the Indian subcontinent was the single most traumatic experience in our recent history. The violence it unleashed was unprecedented, unexpected and barbaric. Provoked by the hooligan actions of a few, the vengeance that ordinary Hindus, Muslims and Sikhs wrecked on each other coarsened our social sense, distorted our political judgements and deranged our understanding of moral rightness. The memory of those days is branded so deeply in our souls that it still provokes us into irrational behaviour and careless thought.

The real sorrow of the Partition was that it brought to an abrupt end a long and communally shared history. The relations between the Hindus and the Muslims were not, of course, always free from suspicion, distrust or the angry rejection by one group of the habits and practices of the other. Occasionally the conflicts were even harsher and fell below the realms of mere nastiness and stupid abuse into murder and arson. But such moments of active malevolence and communal frenzy were rare and transient. The experience of a life lived together was sufficiently secure and rooted to enable the communities to have evolved mechanisms for containing tensions and even outrage. So that even if there were disruptions, the rich heterogeneity of the life of the two communities was never seriously threatened — the Hindus never ceased from paying homage at dargahs, the Muslims continued to participate in Hindu festivals, traders of both the communities carried on with their usual exchange of goods and services in the bazaars, learned men sought each other out to gather information and knowledge about the best of both the traditions, and princes never stopped to consider the religion of the mercenaries they recruited into their armies.

Had there been a history of irreconcilable hatred or non-negotiable aversion between the Hindus and the Muslims, it would have been reflected in the cultural and social practices of the two groups. The pain of living together would have been extensively recorded in popular kissas and tamashas or chronicles and songs. While popular lore did talk about Muslim conquests and destruction or about Hindu intolerance and retaliation, there are hardly any accounts of conflagrations between the two communities in their ordinary lives which were so serious as to have threatened the very structure of a life of interdependencies in the various regions of the subcontinent. In order to make a contrary case, one could, of course, point to the later writings of Sir Syed Ahmad Khan and the romances of Bankimchander Chatterjee as articulations of the feeling that the identity and interests of the Hindus and the Muslims were so utterly different as to make it impossible for them to coexist with each other. Both of them, however, were rather late in historical time and were themselves so fraught with ambiguities that their writings can hardly be used to construct a theory of communal hatred. Besides, they were both seriously challenged from within their own communities. Thus, Tagore thought that Bankimchander's claims of imaginary glory or complaints of imaginary humiliations were useful for spinning fine fables, but were not the best guides for our understanding of a multi-ethnic and multi-religious society.. Ghalib, on the other hand, refused to write an introduction to Sir Syed's edition of *Ain-i-Akbari* because he neither thought that the "worship of the past" was a "useful past-time" nor did he want to encourage a "wise man" in the "constitution of hypocrisy." Sir Syed was also declared a heretic by the more orthodox of the Muslims because they saw the Aligarh School as a threat to traditional Islamic feelings and thought. Indeed, one can assert with confidence that the dominant concerns of the Hindu and the Muslim intellectuals throughout the 19th century and till about 1935, were more with creating free spaces for enlightened thought than with confining people within their narrow religious identities. Organizations which nurtured violent hatred towards each other and incited communal passions did exist, but at the very margins of the functioning social and cultural order. People who commanded respect were the ones who acknowledged the dependence of the Hindus and the Muslims on each other and encouraged acts of 'well-doing.' How else would one explain the fact that Raja Rammohan Roy, whom many thought was more inclined towards Islam, edited the first Persian newspaper in 1822 (*Miraatul Akhbar* — 'Mirror of News') and Munshi Sade Sukh the first Urdu newspaper in 1823 (*Jaame Jahan Numa* — 'Crystal Cup Showing the World'); or that Hindu and Muslim soldiers fought the British together in 1857; or that Zakaullah taught with Hindu colleagues in Delhi College; or that Premchand wrote movingly about the duty of Hindu and Muslim friends towards each other and the country in *Karambhumi* (1932); or that Iqbal opened his *Bal-i-Jibril* (1935) with a couplet from Bhartrihari; or that there was an essential sympathy of interests between Tagore, Nazrul Islam and Hasrat Mohani; or...One could add endlessly to the catalogue of people who thought that the notion of a unified state, with its multiplicity of religious, social or moral ideals, had legitimacy, not only because it made good sense, but also because it was derived from a long practice of living together. It is perhaps the fact that the daily life of the Hindus and the Muslims, at the ordinary and the local levels, even as late as 1946, was so richly interwoven as to have formed a rich archive of customs and practices, that explains why there is a single, common note which informs nearly all the stories written about the Partition and the horror it unleashed — a note of utter bewilderment. It is as if the separation and the carnage were so completely without any historical or social reason that most of the writers could only watch as the place they had called 'home' or 'basti' was reduced to rubble, and the memories of their collective rites and traditions, stories and songs, names of birds and trees were permanently tinged with the acrid smell of ash, smoke and blood.

My concern with the Partition is an old one and is connected both with the recollections of my family and my first confrontation with horror. As with almost everyone of my generation from the northern or the eastern parts of India, my childhood consciousness was scarred by the cruelties I saw during the riots of 1947-48 and the lamentations I heard. For me they were forewarnings about the world beyond the secure walls of my home as a place where grim death lay in wait for those who were unlucky. I have put together this anthology of stories about the Partition not in order to exorcise the past, but in the hope of initiating an ethical inquiry into the history of my age and place.

My earliest memory is of a hot summer day in Delhi in 1948. It was like any of the other and usual summer days in the north. The sun was harsh and indifferent; the dust was full of the dry buzz of flies and the smell of the tar and flint of the streets. The courtyard of our small house was surrounded by a high wall which was washed with white lime so that it could absorb the glare of the sun and resist the hot winds. The entrance to our house was through a small green door with a black chain-lock. A few discoloured steps led down from the door to the level of the road and its burden of leaves outside. The details are important; they are necessary both as evidence that the events I recall really happened and as boundaries against the phantasmogoric.

I remember that as I unlocked the door to our house, I saw, stretched out on the steps below, the body of a man. He was lying face down. His bag had fallen near his feet; it was open and a few common household things had scattered out of it. The man's limbs were in disarray, his clothes were soaked in blood and the sun had begun to darken his skin. There was no one in the street, not even the usual garbage dog. My father had heard the sound of the chain on the door and had hurried out. Later he told me that the man, marked with so many wounds, had earlier in the day sought shelter in our house. He was a Muslim trader who had been chased into our locality by violent men seeking revenge for blood spilled in Pakistan. We were Hindus and he had stayed with us in security for a few hours. Near noontime my father had gone out to see if the streets were safe. The man was obviously anxious to get back to his family. My father had looked about the street carefully and had thought that the man could negotiate his way back to his own neighbourhood without fear. Too late had my father realized that he had failed to notice one of the shadowy corners of the wall beyond the grounds of old St. Stephen's College in Kashmiri Gate. The man had turned back and had tried to reach our house once more.

My father had forgotten his name. There were too many of those who had been killed.

I have never since forgiven that day. It taught me that a group of people — any people — in their religious passion or tribal pride can always go mad; and that after a time they can relapse into madness again. I became conscious of the fact that the world which most of us had chosen to create, and in which I would have to grow up, was neither safe nor brave. The Partition had broken the covenant that men must make with men, castes with castes, religions with other tolerant religions, without which our survival is always precarious and our enslavement by some barbarian is certain. All that men of good sense could do in the fragments of nations which had come into being was to endure, console and be generous.

Over the years, I came to realize that my recollections of those days were not private obsessions with the horrific. Similar incidents were known to others and had become a part of their experiential world. My own memories began to acquire a density and a detail from the narratives of a variety of different people. My aunts told me of properties burnt, my grandfather about friends lost; one spoke to me about a massacre witnessed, another about the mutilations of women. There were a few, of course, who also talked with nostalgia and with tears in their eyes, about acts of kindness and decency, courage and selflessness — about acts which, being free always from prejudices of race and religion, suggested modes of behaviour which we had failed to transform into qualities of our ordinary culture during the time of the Partition. And I grew up trying to understand the problem of evil and to explore the possibilities of magnanimity in such a world as ours.

Now a generation later, whenever I think about the Partition, I am confronted by a series of doubts and questions. Unfortunately, however, even though the Partition was a decisive event (a *kairos*) in our social and political life, it has yet to become a central part of our nationalist discourse. There are hardly any chronicles of those days, written with any degree of objectivity and trustworthiness, which can serve as aids to reflection and offer a reliable set of explanations.

Most of the available histories of the Partition (the new investigations of Bipin Chandra and Ayesha Jalal, Sudhir Chandra and Gyanendra Pandey are exceptions) are written either by the apologists of Pakistan or by its bitter opponents; the former invariably begin by talking about Muslim apprehensions of Hindu thralldom and intolerance and go on to prove their charges through repetition, while the latter speak with rising stridency about Muslim collaboration with the British and treachery. If the first set of histories read like incantations, the second work like old demonologies. Neither are required, by the very simplicity of their forms, to carry the burden of proof or be cluttered with facts — indeed, they are effective precisely because they are free of both. Their pathos and melodrama reminds me of Burke's response to such myth-makers — "I do not know the method of drawing up an indictment against a whole people."

Thus, Choudhary Rahmat Ali, whose Cambridge pamphlet of 1923 outlining the idea of Pakistan was immediately dismissed by the Muslim League representative to the Joint Committee of the British Parliament as "only a student's scheme...chimerical and impracticable," declares that the Muslims should struggle for their "social liberation," "economic liberation," "national liberation"and "spiritual liberation" from the "barbaric influences" of "Indianism." For good measure, he calls upon the other "races" which were also "oppressed" by "Indianism", like the Dravidians, the Sikhs, the Rajputs and the Marathas, to join the battle. Like all the other supporters of the Pakistan movement who were to follow, Rahmat Ali collapses the distinctions and antagonisms between the various sects of Islam in India and between the Muslims who may have defined themselves either as members of a specific region or a craft guild. Similarly, K.K. Aziz, a respected historian of Pakistan, writing as late as 1968, begins his version of the events leading upto the Partition by reasserting that the "Indian nationalism" espoused by the Congress was, from its very inception, a "Hindu nationalism in essence," which the Muslims couldn't possibly have supported. He quotes with approval a statement by Ameer Ali, published in 1906 when the Congress was not yet in complete control of the national movement, urging the Muslims not to join the Congress, for otherwise, "tied to the wheels of the Juggernauth of majority they would in the end be crushed out of the semblance of nationality." Since this declaration has little historical substance and can only be proved by repetition, Aziz goes on to do so by evoking the authority of an article by Maulana Shaukat Ali published in the *Empire Review* in 1931. In this article Maulana Shaukat Ali calls upon the Muslims to place their faith in the British because the Hindus were trying to coerce them into accepting a subordinate position in the nation. After this conventional call to the faithful to be vigilant against Hindu subversion, Maulana Shaukat Ali's argument, which Aziz accepts without a murmur of dissent, becomes a little baroque. Unlike the Hindus who are used to being subjects, Maulana Shaukat Ali says, the Muslims are remarkably free from servility and know how to maintain their poise and dignity in adversity. The Muslims, being a constitutionally minded people should trust the British because they have made fair laws and treated them justly. Moreover, Hindu agitational politics, as advocated by the votaries of Satyagraha, is not only unconstitutional, it is also against the Islamic injunctions about obeying the rulers. Indeed, it is reasonable for the Muslims to try to establish closer ties with the British, with whom they have greater social, intellectual and spiritual affinity than with the "idol worshipping Hindus." The most bizarre part of this argument is that since the British had established the "greatest 'Muslim' Empire in the world," and had "intimate relations with all the independent Muslim states," it was to be expected that the Indian Muslims would wish to remain within the security of the Empire for their own well-being. Given this kind of thinking, it is not surprising to find that people like Aziz regard the Partition as 'azadi' from the 'fasadat' (riots) caused by the Hindus — for them the creation of Pakistan becomes a vindication of their presuppositions, history becomes a tautology instead of an explanation.

If the historians of the Pakistan movement manipulate facts to justify the existence of a separate Muslim consciousness which 'naturally' constitutes a nation, the historians of the Hindu Rashtra conjure up a past in order to accuse the Muslims of desecration and betrayal, as well as, to assert the presence of a Hindu brotherhood which has a primal right to the inheritance of India. But their construction of a fundamental entity called a 'Hindu', who could become the basis of a new collectivity of true believers, turns out to be as confusing and mythical as that of Islamic nationhood. Thus, Bharatendu Harishchandra, who wasn't perhaps a communal thinker but was passionately concerned with the shape of the Hindu civilization, in a lecture in 1884, defines the 'Hindus' as people who lived in Hindustan and includes the Jains, Buddhists, Sikhs, Brahmos and Muslims in his sweep. In order to give substance to such a meta-religious category, Bharatendu translated parts of the *Koran* into Hindi(1884), wrote brief biographies of the Prophet, Hassan and Hussain(1875) and a long poem praising Kabir, Tansen and Pirzadi Bibi (it is worth noting here that Sir Syed Ahmad Khan also described the 'Hindus' in a lecture in 1884 in precisely the same terms as Bharatendu and included the Muslims in his definition). By 1924, however, Lala Lajpat Rai and Swami Shradhanand began to speak forcefully about the old antagonism between the Hindus and the Muslims, and even urged the formation of two distinct religious nations for the sake of peace. As the years went by, the term 'Hindu' became sharper and harder, and Gandhi, who was one of the finest witnesses to the possibility of a Hindu spiritual and democratic life in modern times, was ruthlessly eliminated for having tarnished the glory of Hinduism. The 'Hindu' came to be defined, by the more communally committed historians, as one who was first an unrelenting enemy of Islam and only after that as someone who had a particular set of ideals and practices. The Partition was offered as yet another example in a long sequence of Muslim faithlessness, instead of being an exceptional moment of disorder in a continuing history of a life lived together in all its complex variety.

Contrary to the communal histories, the stories about the Partition have more to do with the actualities of human experience in barbaric times than with ideologies, and seem to be bound together by one common thread — they find the notion that there was always hatred between the Hindus, Sikhs and Muslims in ordinary life, completely incomprehensible. I hope that the stories collected in these volumes will help one to find some coherent explanations for the irrational passions that erupted so violently amongst us that, forgetting our humanity, our religious faith and our cultural pride, we began to stalk and kill each other. Why did we not, as a people, resist? Why did we not follow Gandhi, as we had done often before, on his pilgrimage to Noakhali and gather around him at Srirampur to pledge to uphold the peace? How did the complex weave of works and deeds and words that the communities had woven together come apart so suddenly? Why did we become so self-enchanted as to believe that our sublime feelings about our particular faiths alone would lead us to social justice? How did those who were decent, who refused to give into rage, deal with the blank spaces left in their lives by those who were abducted, killed or sold? How did the ones who had killed so much or raped so many, continue to live afterwards — with guilt, remorse or continuing exultation? How should we now remember this past so that, overcoming anger and grief, we may now begin to work towards a new civilized order?

The stories about the Partition can, I think, be divided into the following categories, each reflecting the ways in which the writers tried to make sense of events which were otherwise unimaginable.

1. Stories which are communally charged.
2. Stories of anger and negation.
3. Stories of lamentation and consolation.
4. Stories of the retrieval of memories.

The stories in the first category of my classification, which are extremely rare (I have included only three, Ahmad Nadeem Qasmi's, "Parmeshwar Singh," Gulam Abbas's, "Avtar: A Hindu Myth" and Krishna Sobti's, "Where is My Mother?"), are communal narratives because they deny the claim to holiness of all religions, except the one to which the authors themselves belong. They also present all those who belong to the same religious community as the story-tellers as unsuspecting victims of atrocities by members of others communities, without mentioning what their own communities did during those hooligan days. They are simple stories because they suppress historical facts. They are also graceless stories because they claim sympathy only for the sufferings of one community, while demanding that it be withheld from others equally distraught. So, instead of upholding the basic ethical principle that correct remembrance alone can be the basis of a just society in the future, they perpetuate codes of fraud.

Thus, Ahmad Nadeem Qasmi's, "Parmeshwar Singh," tells the story of a Muslim boy who, while chasing butterflies, gets separated from the caravan of refugees heading towards Pakistan. The child, Akhtar, knows his prayers and rituals, and is set-up as a brave and innocent representative of the Muslims going towards their new homeland. For Qasmi, he is innocent because he is a Muslim, and not because he is, like all other children, a "moralist with no pretence" (Robert Coles). The Sikh children in the story, with whom he plays, are brutes.

Akhtar, as he looks for his mother, is surrounded by a mob of frenzied Sikhs who threaten to kill him. Parmeshwar Singh, who is a bit dim-witted, and who babbles about the fact that all human beings are created by God, comes to his rescue and persuades the other Sikhs to let him adopt Akhtar. Parmeshwar's ferocity is tamed and humanized by his encounter with Akhtar's natural religiosity. Parmeshwar's family, however, which now lives in a house once owned by Muslims, continues to be fearful and superstitious. They are terrified when they hear Akhtar recite a few verses from the *Koran*, unable to recognize holiness. They, instead, think that the corners of the house are still haunted by the spirits of its former Muslim owners. At the end of the story, Akhtar walks towards Pakistan, in the direction from which the morning azan rises into the sky — his mother, his nation and his true spiritual home await him there.

Qasmi's story is not only a bit disingenious, but is also cynically manipulative. The last gesture of humanity by the child, when he runs towards Parmeshwar after he is injured by the border police, merely adds to the halo sorrounding him. Parmeshwar, on the other hand, remains a caricature throughout, and the sarcasm directed towards him, given his name, is always a little heavy handed. His wife and daughter are hysterical representatives of their tribe who not only find Islam incomprehensible, but are hostile to it — they are refractions, Qasmi wants us to believe, of the ancient antagonism between the Sikhs and the Muslims.

It is apparent that by making the child an embodiment of Islam and then having him waylaid by fanatical and murderous Sikhs, Qasmi not only wants to evoke sublime pathos for the Muslims as victims of an unthinking faith, but he also wants to conceal facts. Qasmi refuses to acknowledge that in the 1930's and 40's inhumanity wasn't the exclusive right of any one community. He should know this well, since he was the first editor of the progressive Urdu journal *Savera* and had written angry editorials against the Partition. Immediately after the Partition he changed his stance and wrote a poem entitled "Battle Cry of the Kashmiri Freedom Fighter." In any case, the last image of the morning prayer, echoing in the sky over Pakistan, is offered in perverse refusal to accept the fact that corpses also littered the landscape from Rawalpindi to Lahore and that the air was filled with smoke. Muslim hordes were equal accomplices in the crimes of the period. Qasmi's deliberate evasion of facts doesn't give one the confidence to believe that his interpretation of those days can help one to re-establish the norms by which the rightness of acts can be judged.

Similarly, in Gulam Abbas's, "Avtar: A Hindu Myth," and Krishna Sobti's, "Where is My Mother?" sympathy for the victims of one's own religion replaces accuracy of observation and political sanity. Like Qasmi, both of them use helpless children to make their tale of betrayal more terrifying and plaintive. Neither of them have the kind of compassionate imagination which can see that the innocent, the helpless and the good of both the religious communities were equally the victims of venal religious politics, and that often both the Hindu and the Muslim killers thought that they were fulfilling a divine injunction. Abbas and Sobti, like wounded and resentful nationalists everywhere, rely upon a "retrospective mythology" (E.J. Hobsbawm) in order to suggest that the hatred between the two communities was so fundamental as to have made it 'naturally' impossible for them to have ever had anything to do with each other in the private and the social space (analogies with Nazi Germany and present day Bosnia are obvious). Abbas invokes Hindu myths to suggest that since the Hindus had over millenniums betrayed their gods by indulging in the most reprehensible forms of killings, their gods had now decided in disgust to abandon them and send a new avtar on earth in a Muslim household. There is, of course, no hint of the history of massacres by the Muslims.

Sobti, on the other hand, plays upon the popular Hindu fear of the Pathan (which Tagore, the sane nationalist, had once demystified for us in "Kabuliwala") as a mindless killer in order to weave her tale of sorrow. I am not questioning the veracity of her narrative, but her mode of presentation and her use of common prejudices without interrogation. Her narrative structure, however, doesn't permit us remember the fact that one of the gentlest of Gandhi's disciples was Khan Abdul Gaffar Khan, a Pathan and a Muslim. She is, instead, sure that a large majority of communally insecure Hindus amongst her readership will accept, without making a critical demand for social analysis or psychological justification or historical discrimination, the fact that a Pathan would have instinctively killed a Hindu in those times.

Neither Qasim, nor Abbas and Sobti, ever pause to consider that people during the Partition killed not because they were

Muslims or Hindus who couldn't have done anything else when confronted with each other, but perhaps because in liminal times they were tempted by the ease of loot and cowardice (at least that is one explanation Gandhi gave repeatedly — "we have been cowards and slaves so long that we are unable to resist the temptation to do ignoble acts," and, "We have not lived and toiled in vain all these years that we should become barbarians as we appear to be becoming, looking at all the senseless bloodshed in Bengal, Bihar and the Punjab. But I feel it is just an indication that as we are throwing off the foreign yoke all the dirt and froth is coming to the surface. When the Ganges is in flood the water is turbid. The dirt comes to the surface. When the flood subsides, you see the clear blue water which soothes the eye." — June 10 and May 28, 1947.) Their victims, of course, deserve our sympathy, not because they belonged to one community but because they were human beings with hopes and dreams — the children more so, because they still had their lives ahead of them.

I have deliberately excluded from this anthology other communal stories. Thus, Sobti's well-known story "Sikka Badal Gaya" (The Coin Was Transformed) merely replaces the figure of a the lost child with that of an abandoned and lonely old Hindu woman in order to arouse our feelings. When the old woman is persuaded to leave her rich ancestral home and migrate, there is not one amongst her Muslim neighbours, whom she had helped in the past who sheds a tear as she walks towards the army truck. They merely wait like vultures to claw through her property and grab what they can in their greed. Other stories like Azeez Ahmad's "Kaali Raat" (Dark Nights), Hayat Ullah Ansari's "Shukar Guzar Ankhien" (Grateful Eyes) and Premnath Dar's, "Akh Thu" (I Spit On It All), are much too hypnotized by scenes of carnage to produce anything other than disgust in the reader. The pile of bodies, they seem to suggest, is a sufficient proof of the demented hatred between the Hindus and the Muslims.

The largest number of stories included in these volumes belong to the second group in my classification and are marked by a sense of rage and hopelessness. Stories by Saadat Hasan Manto, Ibne Insha, Ibrahim Jalees, S.H. Vatsayan, Kamleshwar, Umm-e-Ummara, Kulwant Singh Virk, Sant Singh Sikhon and others appalled witnesses to an age of genocide. They are terrifying chronicles of the damned which locate themselves in the middle of madness and crime and can see nothing but an endless and repeated cycle of more madness and crime. Unlike the communal narratives, which require perpetual belligerence towards beliefs that are different from one's own and silence over the atrocities by members of the religion to which one belongs, these stories are written by people of conscience who know that, during the days of the Partition, the monstrous was a part of all the communities. Touched by annihilating violence and death, all that these writers can do is watch with dismay as the familiar social and religious space, which had once sustained them, is shredded by knives and goons. They record with shock as people in an obscene world become either predators or victims, as they either decide to participate gleefully in murder and loot or find themselves unable to do anything but scream with pain as they are stabbed and burnt or raped again and again. Without sentimentality or illusions, without pious postures or ideological blinkers, they describe a vile and grotesque time in which the sustaining norms of the society as it had existed are erased, and no moral and political reason is available.

Since these stories offer no historical explanation for the carnage and see no political necessity for the suffering, they are brutally ironic in tone and fragmentary in form. Each story is an instance of violence in an unending series; savagery is random and capricious; anyone can become a beast and each one can be destroyed. It is as if the Partition had not only shattered the narrative continuity of the traditions of the nation in which the Hindus, the Sikhs and the Muslims had defined their individual and communal identities, but it had also ensured that it will never again be possible for anyone to imagine a community in which serious moral and political choices which are valid for all can be made.

Thus, the two short, fragmentary and ironic pieces by Ibne Insha included in this anthology are taken from a book entitled *Urdu Ki Akhari Kitab* (The Last Book in Urdu). The title signals the death of the culture out of which Urdu and its rich literary tradition had emerged and to which both the Hindus and the Muslims had made their contributions. Ibne Insha's parodies of history and political thought negate Pakistan's pretence to being, as a Muslim state, the only inheritor of that tradition, as well as, the attempt by the Hindu nationalists to deny that they were ever a part of it. In order to appreciate the bitter truth behind Ibne Insha's sardonic tales about the absurdity of constructing fundamental entities called the Muslims or the Hindus who could easily be separated into distinct nation states, one has only to place them besides the slogan "Hindi, Hindu, Hindustan," by the proponents of a Hindu Rashtra on the one hand, and Jinnah's statement, "made in the clearest language," before a huge crowd of Bengali-speaking Muslims in Dhaka on March 21, 1948 that "the State Language of Pakistan is going to be URDU and no other language." The subsequent history of language riots in India, and of the break-up of Pakistan, show the difficulty of forcing people into narrow definitions by suppressing the other varieties of ways in which they have always defined themselves in the subcontinent over the years. Ibne Insha's point is that in a region where people defined themselves either as Muslims and Bengalis or as Hindus and Sindhis or in any other set of differing religious, linguistic and provincial combinations, only a secular state can accommodate the plurality of selves in a non-antagonistic way. His sardonic humour becomes even more raucous when one recalls Jinnah's speech to the first constituent assembly of Pakistan in Karachi on August 11, 1947. In that speech, Jinnah suddenly called upon all those gathered there to struggle for the creation of a secular state in which the minorities would have equal rights — this was declared by a man who had fought so hard for the creation of a separate Muslim state and in the midst of religious massacres all round, and much after people of good-will had tried, without any success, to bring all the religious groups in India together to work out the constitution of a secular society precisely of the kind called for by him. As far as Ibne Insha is concerned, the formation of Pakistan was a mistake, but one whose consequences have been so horrendous that they can never be atoned for.

Manto's stories about the Partition are more realistic and more shocking records of those predatory times. They are written by a man who knows that after such ruination there can neither be any forgiveness nor any forgetting. Those who have seen the carnage can only stand and wait for death like Toba Tek Singh, the Sikh from the lunatic asylum, who stands in the no man's land between two 'pious' nations and calls down curses upon both — except that since there seems to be no God who can carry them out, the interdictions are uttered with ferocity and threaten to turn us all into absurdities, "Oper di, gur gur di, anex di, bay dhania di, mung di daal di of Toba Tek Singh and Pakistan!" In this last incantation are encoded all the slogans which were use to beguile and befool a people into believing that they had religious identities which were also national identities. In the story itself one of the lunatics, Muhammad Ali, thinks of himself as Jinnah and another as Master Tara Singh. At the end, one sympathizes with the death of Toba Tek Singh because one senses that he was the last man in whom one could still have recognized some of those values which once belonged to a compassionate humanity.

In his stories, Manto is not interested in offering the kind of banal sermons about the "glimmer" of humanity and the tenacity of hope, even as people commit the most heinous of crimes, that some of his critics seem to want him to look for (e.g. Leslie Fleming). Stories like "Thanda Gosht" (Cold Meat) and "Khol Do" (Open It) rather suggest that the inhumanity of the Partition has so obliterated the moral realm that there is nothing left to retrieve and nothing to hope for; people are now so degraded that they can only act as beasts. 'Hope' is a word one can utter if there is a legitimate authority which owes its legitimacy to binding truths and if there is a shared language with which people can establish relations with each other. But in Manto's stories, language betrays, and ordinary people, in whose restraint and decency others had placed their faith, become ruthless killers. Thus, when the old man, Siraj-ud-din in "Open It," asks eight young volunteers in a refugee camp in Pakistan to find his daughter, who has been left behind in India, they pick her up, rape her and then abandon her. Later, she is brought to the doctor's tent in the camp. On hearing male voices, she, like a battered animal, lowers her pyjama and opens her legs as the doctor and her father watch in horror. Similarly, in "Cold Meat," Ishwar Singh (note the bitter pun on his name) rapes a dead girl and is later stabbed to death by his mistress in a fit of jealousy. In all these stories, horror is unflinchingly observed and recorded, not in order to help us find some ersatz moral which will make the world endurable, but to make us understand that we are all accomplices in the making of a barbarous world and that now nothing can save us. "Alas," Manto seems to say with Euripedes, "We look for good on earth and cannot recognize it/ When met, since all our human heritage runs mongrel."

Similarly, in stories like Vatsayan's, "Getting Even," Ibrahim Jaleez's, "Grave Turned Inside-Out," Umm-e-Ummara's, "More sinned Against Than Sinning," or Salil Choudhary's, "The Dressing Table," intelligence and moral imagination are defeated as they confront the massive dislocation of people from their familiar surroundings caused by the Partition. Each of them is concerned with the sorrow of migration, with uprooted people who find that they have nowhere to go. In none of them is the exodus of the Hindus, the Muslims and the Sikhs understood as a temporal re-enactment of one of the sacred events from their religious traditions. The pain of the present migration, a result of unique historical circumstances, is not lessened by references either to the wanderings of Rama and the exile of the Pandavas, or to the hijrat of the Prophet Muhammed from Mecca to Medina. No attempt is made to find in the fate of the migrants a universal pattern of sufferings leading to salvation. The migrants, in these stories, are not religious people who have read so profoundly into their holy texts as to recognize in the effacement of their habitual world another chance to be "filled with grace," and to rejoice in the Partition as "the telos of a burgeoning historical expectation" (see Mohammed Umer Memon). They are, instead, all too human and are bewildered and hurt by the annihilation of a world which had sustained them. They only understand that they have been forcibly separated from their homes and from that "secret life" of their small communities (a notion I have borrowed from Vaclav Havel) which had flowed through time even as the world outside had fought its political battles and spoken on their behalf — a secret life in which they had, each one of them, learnt slowly about the definitions of things. The Partition, they know, has forced them to leave behind a human world and has given them in return only an empty allegory of a religious community.

The incident recorded in Vatsayan's "Getting Even," for example, takes place on a train. Two Sikhs (father and son), who have fled from Pakistan and don't know where to go, find refuge on a train which happens to be going to Aligarh. The train is, in this and other stories (e.g. Bhisham Sahni's, "The Train Has Reached Amritsar" and Krishan Chander's, "Peshawar Express), a fitting symbol of liminal spaces and the death of old structural certainties. On the train they meet two frightened Muslim women who are, given the times, suspicious of them. Soon, however, when some Hindus,who have not suffered any loss, enter the compartment and begin to give a vivid account of the atrocities in Delhi, the elder Sikh chastises them and promises safety to the women. The Sikh refugees and the Muslim women, who have evidently chosen not to migrate, understand the anxiety of each other and establish a temporary community. At the end, however, nothing is resolved; the gesture of humanity, full of remembrances of a different past, carries no suggestion that it can become the model of a humane future. The Hindus on the train remain unashamed, and the Sikhs carry on travelling in search of a place where they can begin their lives again.

Ibrahim Jaleez's tale is more brutal. It describes the fate of some Bihari Muslims who migrate to East Pakistan in the hope of finding there a new world of Islamic brotherhood and economic equality — they remember that such a world is what the Qaid-i-Azam had promised to all the Muslims. In Dhaka, however, they find themselves once again in the same narrow lanes as the ones they had left behind. They learn Bengali and become a part of the poverty of their new country. After the formation of Bangladesh, however, they discover that as Bihari Muslims they are not subject to the same protection of the law as the Bengali Muslims. They become the victims of hoodlums. Ayesha's husband is killed and her daughter is abducted, even as the Pesh Imam watches from the tower of the mosque across from her house. Ayesha finally arrives in Karachi, after a long detour through Kathmandu, accompanied by her 'new husband' whose real plans are to use her as a prostitute. Immediately afterwards, she is raped by the goons who supervise the slum for Bihari migrants from East Pakistan, killed and buried in the earth where she had hoped to find her economic and spiritual home.

Umm-e-Ummara's story, too, is about the devastation of the hopes of the migrants from Bihar to East Pakistan. They fail to trust the rich 'inwardness' of their lives in Bihar where they had lived for generations; they only recall it with nostalgia later in Dhaka (there is no suggestion in the story that they leave Bihar because of the ferocity of the riots there). Entrapped by the logic of exclusive nationalism, they learn too late that neither the community of religion nor the shared idioms of language can offer a sufficiently secure guarantee of a just society and so become the basis of a firm identity. Religious and linguistic definitions, they realize with horror, succeed only in establishing shifting grounds for the inclusion of some and making all others expendable. There is an essential whimsicality in these definitions which can be manipulated for the purposes of political power by the unscrupulous. At the end they can do nothing but watch as the earthly kingdom, which they had hoped to pass on to their children as their real inheritance, is reduced to ash.

The third set of stories — the stories of lamentation and consolation — are primarily concerned with the survivors of those genocidal days. Stories like "Exile," by Jamila Hashmi, "Lajwanti," by Rajinder Singh Bedi, "I Shall Live," by Vishnu Prabhakar, "Separated From the Flock," by Syed Mohammed Ashraf," "Weeds," by Kulwant Singh Virk, "A Leaf in the Storm," by Lalithambika Antharjanam and "A Visitor From Pakistan," by Ramlal are troubled attempts to find out if, after having suffered so much, it is possible for the survivors to cease to "dwell in grief" and learn to live in kinder days; if they can accept the fact of having been permanently 'marked' by violence and yet resist the temptation to retaliate; if they can mourn for those who were killed and still urge forgiveness. They are, of course, full of incomprehension and grief, because without lamentation for the dead and sympathy for the survivors, our sorrow would turn once again into rage, and evil would seize us in its bloody claws. But these stories are also about people who refuse to give into rage and struggle to discover ways of living which could restore us to sanity and redeem us.

In Jamila Hashmi's "Exile," the narrator tells her own story of abduction, rape and marriage. The narrator uses the story of Sita's exile, abduction, rescue and final rejection in order to understand her own predicament, as well as, to draw attention to the fact that a society whose epic celebrates the defeat of evil every year has succumbed to evil. The story opens on Dassera day and deliberately locates itself within a sanctified space. But the modern Rama and Laxmana are greasy and tinsel-crowned actors. This enables the narrator to counter-pose the public remembrance of the acts of Rama, both to those of her Sikh husband who now urges her to forget the past, as well as, to those of her brothers in Pakistan who refuse to come to her rescue. The failure, thus, is not only of the Hindus and the Sikhs to remember that evil can only be defeated by one who has a firm grasp over righteousness, but also of her Muslim brothers who suspect her purity and reject her. She sees herself as a modern day Sita (it is significant that though she is a Muslim, she draws upon the mythic traditions of the Hindus and so points to the fact that these myths were the common heritage of both the communities — a point which is underscored in the stories of Ashfaq Ahmad and Intizar Husain also) who has to suffer, as always in times of crises, the ancient and repeated humiliation of women.

Yet, she refuses to dwell upon those aspects of her life that are too painful, and by deciding to nurture her daughter, she resolves "not to breed sorrow from sorrow" (Sophocles). Further, she lives her life with such scrupulous regard to her 'duty' as a 'wife' that she soon comes to be praised as the 'devi' of the family by her former tormentors. While she scorns at the term, she also knows that it has disarmed and humanized the father of her children and has helped her recover her sense of herself as a human being. Her life becomes a challenge to those who had abused and rejected her to live upto the ideals they celebrate only during public festivals every year. I read here a Gandhian conviction that it is only in acts of "well-doing," even as the world goes mad, that true religion resides.

Syed Mohammad Ashraf's "Separated From the Flock," tells the story of two old friends who meet by chance as they go duck-shooting on a lake in Pakistan much after the Partition. They exchange tales about their childhood in a village in Uttar Pradesh and fondly recall old friendships, dreams, fields, lanes and songs. They also tell each other about the women they had loved, and who were lost or killed during the Partition. But it is their memory of a very personal past, which is prior to the Partition and far removed from politics and sorrow, which seems to them to be more worthy of their better selves and more representative of a good society. As they talk, they become aware of their presence amidst migratory birds in the lake whom they had come to hunt for their sport, and they instinctively lower their guns in a gesture of renunciation of violence. Here suffering is not forgotten, for it can never be, but what is aroused is a new awareness of the gratuitous infliction of pain on the unsuspecting creatures of the earth by hunters like themselves, and of their responsibility in ensuring that the long enduring patterns of life are never again destroyed. Their own loss does not have to be repeated.

Lajwanti, the woman in Rajinder Singh Bedi's story, is abducted and raped by Muslims during the Partition. Later she is rescued and returned to her husband. Babu Sunderlal, who was once a lusty and violent husband, is now the main spokesman for the local committee for the rehabilitation of women. He leads morning processions of fellow workers urging people to treat women who had been abducted as they had always treated them, instead of rejecting them as defiled women. The sight of his genuine personal suffering at the loss of Lajwanti (her name means 'bashful' and 'chaste') always silences the morally self-righteous and the priest-beguiled critics of the committee. His concern and gentle regard for these women, whom the others refuse to acknowledge, is not hypocritical. But just as his earlier violence had denied Lajwanti the right to a life of kindness, his new solicitude fails to satisfy her desire for affectionate regard. He begins to regard her as a devi. She, on the other hand, longs to cease lamenting for the past, to be accepted as a victim of historical circumstances, to be treated as a human-being with flesh and blood who has endured a lot but will not wither when touched, and above all to be embraced as a woman who is physically alive and longs for the generosity of love.

Vishnu Prabhakar narrates the tale of woman who loses her child as she flees from Pakistan. On the way, she find a baby who has been left behind in a train and decides to bring him up as her own. She also meets a man who supports her during those difficult days and begins to live with him. As the years pass, she learns to take some measure of her grief and learns to live a reasonably contented life. Chance, however, has other tests for her. The parents of the abandoned child come back to claim him. Her second 'husband' urges her not to aggravate suffering in a society which has endured enough and to return the child. Later, her first husband finds her and wants her to return. Sure that the only way to heal past wounds is in doing one's duty, her second 'husband' persuades her, with dignity and respect, to consider returning to her family. It is significant that the experience of evil doesn't so paralyse either the woman or the people who have suffered that they fail to realize what right actions must be performed to prevent the world from sliding further into ruin.

What happens to the woman in Lalithambika Antharjanam's "A Leaf in the Storm," is typical of what many women had to suffer during the Partition. Still tormented by her experiences, her rage is intense. She understands the bitter irony of the fact that during the Partition, as during all processes of 'ethnic cleansing', the bodies of women have become the contested sites for men of the warring communities to prove that they have the proper claim to be called God's own people and, hence, the right to possess or to kill the women whom they find in their Kingdom. After all, it was 'natural' for men of distinct religions to claim the women of 'enemy' Gods — they could violate them to prove their own religious faith, sell them to establish their own purity, or put them in brothels as examples to other heretics.

The woman, who is also the narrator of the story, is justifiably horrified when she realizes in the refugee camp that she is pregnant. At first she wants to abort the child (as many women in such camps were advised to do by the social workers), both to avoid social stigma and to seek revenge. But the moment the child is born, she is filled with enormous compassion for the life she is carrying and the responsibility she has to sustain it. In a moment of visionary understanding, she decides to nurture and nourish it and so ensure the ongoingness of the earth. There is no forgiveness in this decision, but there is an awe-inspiring sense of sympathy for those who are more helpless and a refusal to inflict further wounds. Instead of thinking endlessly about days under the curse of evil, she realizes that, the longer she lives in the world, the more profoundly is the sense of its immortality aroused in her (see Robert Lifton's work on the sense of the self which survivors of horror develop); the more 'natural' it is for her to love the child.

Life for the survivors after the carnage of the Partition was hard won. Many of the stories deal with their struggle for coherence and with their determination to avoid facing anything which could remind them of the blind forces unleashed by jingoism, hateful invective, chauvinistic nationalism and religious pride. In stories like "A Visitor from Pakistan," by Ramlal, "Roots", by Ismat Chugtai, "A Sacred Trust," by Sant Singh Sikhon, people who are threatened, instinctively seem to be able to act correctly, according to the norms of a humane social order so as to ensure that all that had brought them face to face with the monstrous does not happen again.

The writers in the fourth set of my classification accept without ambiguity the fact of the Partition as an irreversible part of our geopolitical reality and place it at the centre of their concern for the fate of the civilization of the region. Yet they draw upon their historical, cultural and personal memories to organize their narratives in the hope that such recollections would humanize us and so persuade us to find a way out to a different future. The past which writers like Intizar Husain, Qurratulain Hyder, Asif Aslam Farrukhi, Aga Sohail, Maheep Singh, Ashfaq Ahmad or Narendranath Mitra appeal to, is not only elegant but is also honourable. Writing for them means, as it does for the great poet of exiles, Edmund Jabes, "a passion for origins." Their struggle to retrieve the past has nothing to do with nostalgic evasion, it is rather the key to the discovery of a habit of thought and a mode of living which may provide one with ideas and examples sufficient to resist the drummed-up enthusiasms of crowds. Beside, they fear that to speak only about the atrocities during the Partition may make us all vulnerable to enchantment by Medusa once again and turn all our affective and political reasoning to stone.

Intizar Husain, for instance, doesn't think that there was anything either "historically inevitable" about the creation of

Pakistan or "natural" about its emergence. Instead, he has said repeatedly, that to assert that the Muslim identity in the Indian subcontinent has always been utterly distinct from Hinduism and has been formed in antagonistic relationship with it, making the formation of Pakistan a political necessity and a logical outcome of cultural differences, is not only bad history but is also bad metaphysics. Such poor faith towards the past, such thoughtless disregard for the long history of daily and peaceful intermingling of communities which worshipped different gods, he believes, always leads to disaster.

"I have no idea what a purely Islamic culture is," Intizar Husain said to me when I met him in Lahore in 1992. The best of the Muslim minds, like the best minds of any community, were in love with the 'good'. They realized that in a place like India before 1947, where there were a plurality of gods and a plurality of 'truths', ethicality and religiosity were not the exclusive preserves of any single community or sect. The only logical and workable political and social consequences of this recognition was that they made extensive and unanxious use of the myths of the other religions of India to give to their own formulations about personal and public conduct, rights, dignity, justice or benevolence, a richness of tone and a clarity of perception. Intizar Husain in his various interviews recalls the names of Nizamuddin Auliya, Amir Khusrau, Abul Fazl and Dara Shikoh, and asserts that such self-understanding alone would enable us once again to articulate the conditions which would make a good society and discover the political means necessary to achieve it in our present circumstances. Maybe Gandhi's ahimsa failed during the Partition, told me, but immediately afterwards he added that the religious prophets never killed, that the sufis were men of peace and tolerance, and that the ecstatic songs of Kabir and Mirabai should be sung once again to remind us all of the fact that the grace and the delight of life are a part of our real heritage.

Given the sense Intizar Husain has that "our experiences are so knotted up," that they neither permit easy analysis nor offer simple answers, it is not surprising to discover that stories like "An Unwritten Epic," "City of Sorrow," and "A Letter from India" are complex, difficult, ambiguous and sometimes perplexing. He cannot, he insists, write linear narratives about the Partition like the progressive writers of the 1930's and 40's (see Krishan Chander's, "Peshawar Express," and K.A. Abbas's, "The Death of Sheikh Burhanuddin"). Unlike them, he has never been able to presuppose the existence of a rationally comprehensible or a metaphysically coherent world-view which can enable him to make sense of the human tragedy which confronted him when India was partitioned. The Partition disrupted his life and shaped his creative self. He still finds it difficult to make sense of the brutal, degrading, shameful and gruesome acts which accompanied it. Those acts still haunt him; he sees them not only as enactments of his own fears and nightmares, but also as examples of how atrocious our lives can always become when our social, moral and religious imagination fails. In stories like "An Unwritten Epic," "A Letter From India" or "The City of Sorrow," he has set upon himself the profoundly difficult task of retrieving all that was good in life in India before the Partition, while at the same time analysing the causes of evil which lie both in the soul of man and in the social circumstances in which he finds himself. He tells stories in order to understand and at the same time repudiate hatred; to turn the accuser away from seeking revenge and to win his trust once again in the ordinary and daily kindliness which also make up our lives; to heal wounds; to find consolation in memories for the loss of yellow mustard fields, harshringhar, trees crowded with parrots and other emblems of innocence and joyous creativity; to notice the world again with all our empathy and imaginative resources; and to discover the minimum ethic by which we can live. Like all fine writers, he wants to give back to us a world in which we can cultivate our reason and our moral goodness; but like all fine writers, he also knows how difficult that task really is and how often we fall into evil.

Thus, in the complex story, "An Unwritten Epic," much of which is in the form of diary enteries by a writer who has migrated to Pakistan and is struggling to write a new epic, the hero is a local bully who is enthusiastic about the idea of Pakistan, but doesn't know where it is. He fights the Hindus, not because he wants to help the Muslim League, but because he wants to prove that he can weild the club better than the Hindus. He is convinced that Qadirpur, given its name, must naturally belong to Pakistan. He even tries to plant a Pakistani flag on the peepul tree near the idgah. Intizar Husain deliberately locates the peepal tree, sacred to the Hindus, next to a Muslim shrine.

Whe Pachhwa finally reaches Pakistan, he discovers that he no longer has the status he once had. The new heroes are the manipulators of the political system. Frustrated and nostalgic, he returns to Qadirpur, only to discover that it has been erased from the new map and replaced by Jatunagar — the city of the Jats. He is killed and his head is stuck on the peepul tree. The cycle of degradation set off by the Partition is completed, when the writer compromises with the local bosses and gets them to allot him a flour-mill which had been abandoned by its Hindu owners. While the narrator himself gives up the struggle for humane and literary values, Intizar Husain sees in the very persistence of memories the possibilities of a different future.

Even in the bleak story, "The City of Sorrow," written after the 1971 war in East Pakistan, Intizar Husain doesn't abandon his sense of a past when social and moral values guided behaviour. The story itself seems to be a hermetically sealed nightmare without hope of change or escape. Three men, without names or faces, describe how each of them had raped and killed endlessly and without shame. Now they have become horrors to themselves; they can neither find a place in any society, not a spot on earth in which they can bury their own corpses. Yet, their recollections of a time before the Partition, lie outside the structure of the present and exist as moments "which Satan cannot find" (William Blake). Memory offers a vision which can counter violence.

Similarly, the memory of a functioning Indo-Muslim culture forms a part of the texture of Asif Aslam Farrukhi's story, "The Land of Memories." It torments his characters even years after the Partition and becomes subversive of the politics of separatism and hate. The story itself uses a theme which is common to many of the stories written about that period. A man longs to see his native place and returns to India for a few days. Initially, he is disturbed by the fact that the old streets, houses and trees by which he had once oriented himself have disappeared. But, soon, he meets a childhood friend who becomes his guide through the lanes and through the history of old friendships. Eventually, he meets his Muslim relatives who did not migrate. Asif Farrukhi places value on people who don't forget, who fondly remember friendships, bazaars, tongewallas, tea-stalls and debates. In contrast to the old man, are his children, who trail behind their father singing American songs, eating chewing-gum and longing to be with their cousins in Canada. They are amnesiacs who don't have to overcome anything, and so see nothing and hope for nothing.

Gani Miyan, the main character in Mohan Rakesh's "The Owner of Rubble," returns after many years to the lane in

Amritsar where he had once built a house and where his family had been killed in 1947. He goes back, not to repossess the house, but out of a non-egotistical longing to see again the place where his life had once had its anchoring. He first realizes that the older sense of fellow feeling, which he remembers had governed life in the public space and had given him personal confidence, has vanished, when his former neighbours fail to recognize him and regard him with suspicion as a kidnapper. The Partition, it is clear, has broken all the affective and communal bonds which had once existed between different communities.

Gani Miyan seeks out Rakkha Pahlwan, who had once been his son's friend. He doesn't know that Rakkha was the one who had killed his family and had taken possession of his house. Gani Miyan's house now lies in ruins and no one can approach the heap of rubble without Rakkha's permission. The relation between the personal, the local and the political is obvious. The new bully-boys who control the nations after the Partition are the kings of rubble.

There is a series of fine ironic reversals, however, the moment Gani Miyan finds himself standing before Rakkha. The hooligan is unable to face the frail old man who, speaking as the voice of the past, wonders why Rakkha had failed to protect his friend Chiragdin (the name is interesting for it signifies the light of day, just as Rakkha contains in it a pun on rakh — ash). Rakkha, the wrestler, is reduced to a crouching figure, unable to move before such trusting innocence. Later, when Gani Miyan, still ignorant of the truth, blesses him, Rakkha is not only disarmed, but he is also reduced to an absurd and helpless figure who is chased away from 'his rubble' by a mongrel dog. Wrath is defeated by pity. Memory, which offers a vision of a past life, becomes the source of dignity in the present. Gani Miyan walks out of the lane as a figure of awe. The history of atrocities is not forgotten, but neither is the memory of a life of connectednesses. The archives of memory are used, not only to explore the life of greed and violence, but also as a source for a life of communal togetherness again.

In Ashfaq Ahmad's story, "The Shepherd," memory is not a source of estrangement, but an acknowledgement of the presence of a society in which notions of morality and religiosity were arrived at together by the best representatives of the Hindus and the Muslims out of mutual regard for each other. The story is an investigation of the constituents of the 'good' — of all that could be regarded as moral life and moral action in society — at a time in the 1920's and 30's when life in India was increasingly becoming a trap. Its concern is not with what could be regarded as the right action within a given situation, but with the right action in any situation and by anybody — an acknowledgement of the absolute moral demands men must quietly make upon themselves out of love for the earth.

Dauji, its main character who is a Hindu, understands that the worship of one god, one text and one ritual may lead to catastrophe, not because the god, the text and the ritual are false, but because they may require the sacrifice of other gods, texts and rituals, and so result in evil. The intuitive sense he has that there are different ways in which people ground that which is 'good' without changing its essence, is later confirmed for him by his Muslim teachers who have a reverence for the learning and the customs of the Hindus. Dauji's presence honours his Muslim teachers, just as their knowledge enobles and enlightens him. Both know, and repeatedly affirm in their daily practices, that one always lives, and must always do so, "in one's brother's eyes" (William Blake). Dauji is a Hindu, but he knows (just as Gandhi did) that the recitation of the Kalma always resonates with the power of truth and holiness, and the reading of the *Koran* is unambiguously a good act in itself. He fulfills (as do his teachers) Walter Benjamin's definition of a righteous man as the one who is "the advocate of all created things and at the same time their highest embodiment."

After the Partition, as people leave their homes in fear, Dauji refuses to go, and so puts into practice the Gandhian demand for courage in demented times. Gandhi, it needs to be remembered, urged people repeatedly not to run, to stay where they were, and force their leaders to fulfill their pledges to protect the minorities and give justice to all. Dauji is surrounded by a revenge maddened crowd of Muslim refugees, beaten by goondas who cut off his tuft of hair, and forced to recite the Kalma. As Dauji recites the Kalma with deep reverence, he seems to the narrator, who is his student and a Muslim, to be surrounded with radiance. The word of God not only protects Dauji from evil, but also makes him one with the ancient prophets.

If all religions are one, as visionary poets and enlightened prophets tells us, and if god resides in the human heart and if the assertion of anything else is dangerous vanity, then why did religious conflicts destroy the communal life of the subcontinent? Why did we, as Gandhi wondered, "meet madness with madness?" The stories collected in these volumes don't, of course, give us answers. They are rather witnesses to a period in which we fell out of a human world of languages, customs, rituals and prayers into a beastial world of hatred, rage, self-interest and frenzy. The writers of these stories frame the events in a variety of ways and read them according to their own sense of the multi-religious and multi-cultural past of the Indian subcontinent. How we, in turn, read these stories, based upon our own presuppositions, will determine the kind of politics we choose to practice in the future.

25 December, 1993.

SYED MOHAMMAD ASHRAF

SEPARATED FROM THE FLOCK

A thick layer of mist, shimmering with starlight, lay across the sky on that winter night in early January. Occasionally a star twinkled brightly through the haze. Two broad beams of light pierced the night as the jeep sped forward. Darkness had enveloped everything. There was nothing but silence all around, except for the dull throb of the jeep's engine and the whisper of trees shivering in the cold night. Suddenly a sharp and biting gust of wind swept through the jeep. I placed my gun on my lap, tightened the belt of my hunting jacket and wrapped a scarf around my neck. The night had become colder. The moment the wind dropped, I took a cigarette out of my pocket and lit it.

We had left the boundaries of Lahore far behind.

"Gulam Ali," I called out to the driver.

"Ji huzoor."

"Is Shahganj much further?"

"Oh, perhaps another twenty or thirty miles, Sahib."

"I hope the ducks won't fly away before we reach Shahganj."

"What's the time now, Sahib?" Gulam Ali asked as he stepped on the accelerator.

I took a long puff and, in the dull glow of the cigarette, looked at my watch.

"It's past four-thirty."

"Then there's nothing to worry about, Sahib. We'll be there by five or six — the sun doesn't rise before seven — and the birds begin to stir only after that."

There was silence once again.

"How far is Shahganj from your house?"

"Before Shahganj, there is a masjid by the roadside built by some Mughal King. Behind it is a dirt road. If you go straight down the road for about two miles you can see my village."

"What's the name of the village?" I asked, merely to continue the conversation.

"Kharan-wallah."

What more could I have asked that Punjabi driver —?

Silence descended over everything once more.

In the middle of that cold winter night, the shadows of old, gnarled trees seemed to have got entangled with each other. The silence became heavier — so heavy that I felt I could reach out of the jeep and touch it — I took one last puff of my cigarette and flicked it outside. It traced an arc of light in the air and scattered into glowing embers when it hit the ground. Countless sparks lit up the darkness and then vanished.

"Sahib, since when have you been interested in hunting?"

"Since my childhood, Gulam Ali."

"Is duck shooting allowed in India?" he asked me without looking back at me.

"Yes, bhai. At least it used to be forty-seven years ago. Now I don't know."

I don't even know if the walls, surrounding the place where I grew up, are still standing or have crumbled into ruins.

"You once lived in U.P., didn't you, Sahib?"

"Hmm," I mumbled.

I wanted to tell Gulam Ali to stop asking me questions which would remind me of my past. But I kept quiet. I didn't want to reveal my weakness to anyone. Otherwise — Gulam Ali — I would have discussed the word "lived" with you for hours. I no longer have any relationship with that part of the earth where my childhood was spent listening to my mother's lullabies, where, as a boy, all the small things I beheld were dear to me — and where, in my youth, I first felt life's upsurge and learnt to test my wings.

But how could I tell him all that — how could Gulam Ali possibly understand it? Leave aside Gulam Ali, even I don't understand everything — how could I? The hard, deep lines of the Partition have erased the signs of all other feelings — feelings which belong intimately to that place where a human being first opens his eyes on earth and catches a glimpse of the sky.

The wind grew stronger. But the mist was as heavy as before.

"So, you never went back to India, Sahib?" Gulam Ali asked me — the silences on the road begged the whispering trees to be quiet. But when those who are living have become insensitive, how can one expect trees, which have no feelings, to respond with sympathy. "Government servants can't go back so easily. The Government wants to know the names of people one wants to meet."

"So you have no relatives left back there?"

"No. They were all cowards. They came and settled here. I too was a coward, but a 'minor' coward — perhaps I was not even eighteen years old then — yes, I was eighteen."

"Why do you call them cowards, Sahib. Instead of living there, they came here." It was as if Gulam Ali was trying to comfort me. But there is nothing which can console me.

"It's a difficult philosophic issue, Gulam Ali. You won't understand it."

He fell silent, as if I had insulted him. A little later he said, "My wife's parents too are from India. She has often begged me to take her there at least once. When I applied for a permit, I was asked to give the names of our relatives there... She has no relatives left back there, Sahib, but she does remember the name of her village and of her district."

We were once again lost in silence.

"Gulam Ali," I called again.

"Yes," he turned back to look at me.

"Where is your wife from?" I asked without looking at him.

"Hardoi district, Sahib."

"Hmm. Then she too is from U.P.?"

Even in the darkness, I sensed that he was smiling.

"I know why you are smiling, Gulam Ali."

"Sahib, can I tell you something? My wife knows that you belong to U.P. The other day she said to me — I know that your Sahib is from U.P., my native place. Take me to see him. He will get me a permit — So, Huzoor, she knows that you are going duck shooting today and that you will stop at our house. If she asks you, please tell her bluntly that you can't get her a permit."

"Why, Gulam Ali? Why should I tell her that? It's easy enough for me to get her a permit."

"I am not concerned about the permit, Sahib. It's not the only problem a man faces in his life, Sahib! It's merely a whim — the visit to India. To satisfy that whim, I'll have to waste four to five hundred rupees."

"Hmm..." I didn't know what to say — Gulam Ali took advantage of my silence.

"Sahib, I have a friend, Vaziruddin. His wife was also born in India. By hook or by crook, she got a permit made. And then she sold her ear-rings and asked her husband, Vaziruddin, for permission to go. At first he was surprised, then he lost his temper. Later, he pretended to give her his consent. At night, however, he stole her permit and burnt it. When she woke up the next morning and saw that the permit had disappeared, she kicked up a shindy and accused Vaziruddin of having stolen it. At first Vaziruddin tried to make excuses — then he picked up his stick and went after her, shouting — Haramzadi, will your mother cook for me while you are away for three to four months?"

Gulam Ali looked back at me, as if he wanted me to applaud his friend's wisdom and courage.

I kept quiet. He couldn't see me in the darkness and, perhaps, thought that I had dozed off. He turned away to watch the road again and pressed the accelerator a bit more. As the speed of the jeep increased, the wind became sharper. I felt that the wind sweeping across the road and over the trees was stronger — and that the mournful rustle of the leaves made everything more mysterious. Compared to the noise outside, the silence in the jeep was ominous — like the silence of a lonely ship whose crew has been butchered by pirates, floundering in the midst of angry waves. I shuddered at the thought — and said to myself: Gulam Ali — you are both mean and a fool — you and your friend will never understand what happens to a man who has been separated from the place where he was born, where he was suckled by his mother, and where he felt his father's affectionate hand ruffle his hair. You won't understand how strongly attached a man is to the place, where he has spent his childhood surrounded by daily acts of kindness and joy; you can never feel, Gulam Ali, how precious those moments of innocence are, how one nurtures them with one's blood, how they are a part of everything that one has become. You will never understand. Stick to the steering- wheel of the jeep for your brains are addled. At that moment, I hated Gulam Ali intensely.

But then a voice within me whispered, "It's not Gulam Ali that you hate. You hate anyone who reminds you of the past which you long to recover; anyone like Gulam Ali who adds another small brick to the mausoleum of lost desires. Poor fellow. How can you blame him? He only told you about his wife and his friend's wife — that's all. You can't hate him because, unwittingly, he made you conscious once again of the fact that you will never be able to go back — that you will continue to long to return to India forever. It's your own sorrow, your own sense of helplessness that made you lose your temper at him."

There is a part of me which has begun to feel more hopeless, more despairing, especially after the wars of 1965 and 1971. Frenzied like a convict who hears that he has been sentenced to death, it asks irrational questions for which I have no answers. Indeed, how can I answer them? There is nothing left for me to say. I feel that everything I had once known, I had once thought about, has vanished — has flown away like the birds from the surface of the lake.

I rested my head on the seat of the jeep.

"Sahib," Gulam Ali whispered apprehensively. His voice was so soft that had I dozed off, I wouldn't have heard what he said — perhaps that's what he intended.

"Hmm..." I felt as if a stranger had answered him.

"Were you asleep, Sahib?" he asked.

"No...What is it?"

"Nothing much, Huzoor — Have you noticed that since the last war ended people from both sides can cross the border more freely? Those who want to go to India can easily do so, and visitors from there are welcomed in Pakistan. The border was thrown open a long time ago, yet the surge of people crossing it from both sides hasn't subsided."

Silence. Did I keep quiet because I was afraid that if I uttered a single word I would break down and weep?

"Sahib...Sahib! Did you hear what I said?"

I continued to stare out of the jeep in silence. It was dark and desolate outside. As the jeep sped through the night, I thought — Gulam Ali, you have just given me more proof of your meanness. You know quite well that my job is such that I shall never be allowed to cross the border even in peace time. You are deliberately trying to scratch open old wounds.

Disappointed by my refusal to respond, Gulam Ali continued to drive in silence.

Why are there so many restrictions on the wives of Gulam Ali and Wazir Ali? Why can't they go back to the lands where they were born — dream about places without which their lives will always remain unfulfilled?

Gulam Ali, you may be quiet now, but I know that you are not as innocent as you pretend to be. Thrice a year you ask me for leave so that you can visit your parents in Karachi. And yet you tell me that you can't afford to go to Hardoi? Hardoi is as far from Lahore as Karachi is. Don't you spend money to go to Karachi? Or are you allowed to travel free? — But who am I to ask you these questions? What right have I? No...I can't even ask you what prevents you from eating in a restaurant for three or four days so that your wife, aching to stand once more on that part of the earth where she was born, can at least go back again — to feel once again the spirit of the place where her mother used to sing her lullabies, to walk once again in the warmth of the village where she had flung her arms out in gladness to welcome her youth? Don't I have the right to ask you these questions, Gulam Ali? In any case, I do not have any answers. I have wrestled with them for the last thirty years. While I understand the finer nuances of all the possible answers, I also know that each answer is always incomplete, is always false. Besides, Gulam Ali, I don't ever want to find out the correct answer, for the moment I do, I shall lose this easy luxury of asking questions. Sometimes when I suspect that the answer stands in front of me in all its terrifying clarity, I immediately seek refuge behind other questions, till the answer loses its outlines once again, becomes hazy and vanishes. I am afraid of the right answer...

"Sahib, we are approaching the mosque," Gulam Ali said, "It is still dark. There is enough time to stop at my house, otherwise Jameela will be disappointed."

"All right, if there is still time, let's go...And yet, why don't we go to the lake first and to your house on our way back?"

All of a sudden, Gulam Ali hit the brakes and the jeep screeched to a halt. It was cold, though the wind had dropped. There was a deep silence all around.

Through the night's haze, I saw the faint outlines of the mosque. Next to it there was a small fire burning. Three men stood in its circle of light — I looked at them carefully — two had guns slung over their shoulders — they had turned around to look at us.

Gulam Ali got down muttering angrily to himself. He always got angry when he came across other hunters.

I picked up my gun and got down from the jeep. The night was so cold and damp that I was chilled to the bone. The three men moved to one side, as if they were silently inviting us to join them and share the warmth of the fire. I signalled to Gulam Ali to follow me and walked upto them.

Their jeep was parked nearby. One of them was in a driver's uniform, while the other two were wearing hunting-jackets. They stood so very close to the fire that their faces sparkled in its light. One of them seemed familiar. Imperceptibly, a face resembling his floated upto the surface of my memories. But it was unclear, indistinct like one's handwriting in one's primary-school notebooks which one can neither recognize when one grows up nor ever forget. I looked at the face again. It shone brightly in the golden light of the fire. I was convinced that I had seen the face before. That man too stared back at me. My eyes were transfixed on his face. He rubbed his hands in front of the fire and then warmed his face with them. Suddenly, the frozen regions of past recollections thawed — the many-mirrored room of memories lit up. In a flash, I travelled back thirty years — I saw before me, as if by magic, scenes from my childhood and youth — many shapes and outlines in gorgeous, exhilarating colours — a small village in U.P. between the Ganga and the Jamuna, mosques, temples, narrow and meandering lanes, small houses and mud-huts, a primary-school, faces of those I had loved...alas, those who were still alive were only shadows and no longer my affectionate companions...

Then in another flash I saw...two boys with air guns in the mellow light of a summer evening. The cry of partridges in a garden of wild berries. One boy entered the garden and returned a few minutes later triumphantly holding a dead partridge. The other stood patiently with his hands behind his back. And then, he startled his friend by dangling in front of his face a ritually slaughtered rabbit — Both laughed happily. Their hunt had been a success...

My memory threw up other images — The boys were older and had rifles in their hands. After their Ramzan meal before sunrise, they had set out with their friends for a hunt. Their mothers had stuffed their bags with food so that they could break their fast in the evening. The boys were, of course, thrilled at the chance of cheating their parents by not keeping the holy fast. The night was cold and the moon shone brightly. Each one secretly prayed that he should shoot the maximum number of ducks — As they walked down the embankment towards the pond, they made plans for the hunt...tried to guess where the ducks were, argued about who should fire first — the sun rose, the morning light spread over the waters, the sky lifted the veil of mist off its face — there were no ducks on the lake. They accused each other... "Didn't I tell you there were no ducks here?...What you heard was the cry of a group of egrets..." Then they shot at random in the air and brought down egrets and doves...

On their way back home in the evening, they rubbed their lips with clay so that their lips would seem parched and their parents would believe that they had kept their ritual fast. They were so excited that they chattered meaninglessly. As they approached the boundary of their village one of them had a bright idea...They plucked the birds they had shot so that they could tell their elders that they had hunted them...

Other scenes too threw their reflections on the surfaces of my memory.

"Sahib — lets go to the village now?" Gulam Ali's voice fell like a stone on my house of mirrors and shattered it.

I took no notice of Gulam Ali. I tried hard to see if the man standing before me was the one my memories had evoked. He again warmed his hands at the fire and rubbed them against his cheeks. Nawab too used to do that — Now I was sure that the boy I had seen in the mirrors of my memory was now standing before me — thirty years later.

The wind suddenly dropped and the night became very still. The dry twigs crackled in the fire and sparks flew all around. From the other shore of the sleepy lake came the cry of an egret.

I walked slowly towards the fire...looked into the eyes of the man and asked," You...aren't you Nawab?"

He narrowed his eyes, nodded his head. A smile flicked across his face — and then his eyes filled with tears which flowed down his face. In the bright light of the fire, his face seemed to glow with intense emotions like a burning coal — He took the gun off his shoulder and handed it over to his companion, walked around the fire, came up to me and hugged me. Unable to utter a single word, we looked at each other for a long time...

"You don't have to tell me who you are." After thirty years I recognized the voice which I had heard everyday for the first sixteen years of my life.

"No, I won't tell you who I am," I held him tightly in my embrace. God knows how long we stood like that.

The fire died down. Half-burnt leaves and ash scattered into the night. The fog began to lift a little — Gulam Ali and Nawab's two companions stood around us like statues and watched us with surprise. An infinite range of tender and loving emotions swept through the two of us. After sometime, I took his head in both my hands and kissed his forehead, as if I was kissing a sixteen year old boy.

— "Gulam Ali, there is hardly any time left now to go to your village. Let's go to the lake first...We can go to your house afterwards."

I told Nawab that Gulam Ali was my driver. Gulam Ali bowed and greeted him respectfully.

Nawab informed me that one of his companions was his driver and the other was the manager of his factory. His name was Salimullah — I stepped forward and shook the latter's hand. He was a handsome young man around thirty years of age.

— We drove towards Shahganj lake.

— Nawab told me about how he had to struggle for a living after he migrated from India — how he finally set up a rubber chappal factory — then he told me that a few days ago he had learnt that I had been promoted as the Superintendent of Police and had been transferred to Lahore.

"Why didn't you come to see me then?" I asked.

"I wasn't sure if it was really you. Someone had merely mentioned the name of the new Superintendent."

As he said that it occurred to me that our identities had become so indistinct that our names could no longer be connected to a person with a recognizable face. I couldn't, of course, blame Nawab alone for being so unsure. I too had been startled when I had seen an advertisement for "Nawab and Sons" in some paper, but had hesitated to meet him because I wasn't confident that it was the same Nawab whom I had known in my childhood — We were equally guilty and had no right to ccuse each other...

"Did you come all the way from Karachi only to hunt ducks?" I asked him.

"Oh, no — I came to Lahore on some work connected with the factory. I have a ticket for tomorrow's flight. Since I had a day off, I said to myself — why not go duck-hunting?"

Beyond the jeep, wheat and sugar-cane fields were stretched as far as the eye could see. Though there was now a faint morning light, the horizon was still shrouded by the mist. At the far edges of the fields one could see the outlines of trees and herds of sheep grazing under them. Soon we heard the first faint sounds of birds and guessed that we were approaching the lake. As I looked up ahead, I saw beyond the cane-fields a vast stretch of water shimmering in the mellow, hazy light of the morning. I couldn't have guessed that there were ducks in that part of the lake. We would be able to see them only after the sun had scattered the mist and lit up the waters of the lake.

— Gulam Ali stopped the jeep.

— "Huzoor, if we drive any further, the sound of the jeep would alarm the birds and they would fly away."

"Of course," Nawab agreed, and jumped down from the jeep. I followed him.

As I got down, I thought to myself — We have met again after thirty years. This time I hope that we are not disappointed and that there are ducks on the lake! I smiled as I recalled our old misadventure.

— "Listen," Nawab said, as he turned to me, "Do you remember the day we went hunting like this and the lake fooled us — when the sun rose we realized that the sounds we had heard were not of ducks but of..." He couldn't complete the sentence and looked at me intently — Perhaps, he had realized that I too was thinking of the same thing. He wrapped his muffler tightly around his neck, loaded his rifle, came up very close to me and said in a soft whisper, "So, you too remember those days!"

I slowly nodded. Both of us understood at the same time what we had lost. Memories raged within me like uncontrollable, wild fires.

The second jeep drove up and stopped behind us. Salimullah got down with his gun.

— "One can hear the cries of a lot of birds," he said, as he gazed towards the mist covered lake.

— Gulam Ali walked towards the edge of the cane-field, tried to guess where the ducks could be and then came back to us.

"This is a very big lake, Sahib. There are ducks here all day. There are more in the morning though. They feed at this time and are unsuspecting," Gulam Ali said, in order to impress us with the wealth of information he had.

I looked towards the far shore of the lake. Spots of sunlight had now begun to sparkle over those parts of the lake which were still covered by mist. We should be able to start hunting soon, we thought. We selected our places. Nawab and I, without removing our boots, waded upto our knees in the muddy water and then climbed onto a dry embankment near the shore of the lake. The lake was surrounded by cane-fields on three sides. Salimullah picked up his gun and walked towards the other shore of the lake. Gulam Ali, holding his gun by its barrel, walked away in the opposite direction.

Nawab and I sat quietly on the embankment for a while. There was no point in making any move till the fog lifted completely. One could shoot only after the sun rose. Long streaks of crimson-coloured light slowly crept across the eastern sky. The sun was about to break through.

"How good a shot is Salimullah?" I asked, as I lit a cigarette.

"Very good. He is an experienced hunter," Nawab said, taking the packet of cigarettes from me.

Suddenly the cranes on the other side of the lake raised an alarm and began to shriek loudly. All the small birds stopped chirping and the ducks fell silent.

I loaded my gun. "Nawab," I whispered.

"Yes," he said and looked towards me.

I didn't say anything.

"Yes...you were going to ask me something."

"Yes, I was going to ask you if, after migrating to Pakistan, you had ever thought of going back home?"

— At that moment the silence between us was like a deep chasm — He didn't say a word — I felt as if there were cranes shrieking hundreds of miles away. The waters of the lake were still and the wind was absolutely silent.

— I said to myself, Nawab, you are nervous...I have asked you a very awkward question...and I know that any attempt to answer it would make the bitterness you feel even more unbearable...But I want an answer...I am trapped and can't go back, but what prevents you?... Have you really forgotten that land...those lanes, houses, fields, fairs...your school?...Don't you remember anything? Has the memory of those ponds, where we hunted in our childhood , become dry? Have those trees burnt to ash?...I continued to gaze at him, but he turned his face away and refused to look at me.

Finally, with a great effort, he said, "A day out of Karachi means a loss of two thousand rupees for me. A trip to India would cost me forty to fifty thousand."

As he spoke he seemed to gain in self-confidence. He looked at me challengingly, and I guessed that he wanted to ask me in return — Well, my dear friend! Why didn't you give up your job and go to India? Why? Come, tell me!

"It is my turn now to ask you embarrassing questions."

I didn't dare to look into his questioning, mocking eyes. It seemed as if they wanted to pierce through to the inner-most secrets of my soul and discover all that lay hidden there, all that I am afraid of revealing.

But Nawab didn't say anything. I had not shown him any mercy, but he had forgiven me, had treated me with kindness, taken pity on me and given me a reprieve.

It occurred to me that neither of us had any control over our lives; that we were helplessly trapped by circumstances over which we had no influence; that we were utterly defenceless...If I were to resign my job and go to India, how would my family survive; and, Nawab, if you were to neglect your factory and leave Pakistan, who would compensate you for your loss of forty to fifty thousand rupees? Yes, both of us are paralyzed, are unable to make a move...

A yellow circle of light filtered through the fog in the horizon. Then slowly, very slowly, the red disk of the sun broke free from the shadows of the night and hung above the distant shore of the lake beyond the sugar-cane fields.

I felt as if all the birds in the trees standing by the shore of the lake had suddenly begun to sing together — "Look, the sun has risen!" Somewhere far away, a village dog, who had kept vigil all night, barked loudly to welcome the dawn. Silhouettes of birds flew across the sun...Morning hours are neither sad nor depressing, but that day, the dawn failed to make us feel glad...Our sorrows are not determined by the changing moods of the day; they depend upon what the heart knows and feels — that day our hearts were heavy.

Once the mist was scattered and the surface of the lake was clear, I saw a flock of ducks floating near the place where Salimullah was hiding. From where I stood they looked like clods of mud scattered in a field. Near them were a few sandpipers and groups of small birds hovered above them. A bit further away a crane stood quietly in the water. Suddenly the birds became restless and alarmed. Their sharp, shrill cries shattered the silence...Gulam Ali fired the first shot. The ducks panicked, flapped their wings frantically, churned up the still surface of the lake with their feet and flew up into the air. Salimullah fired twice and two ducks dropped like stones into the lake. A few egrets, screaming with terror, spread out their long, ribbed wings and flew in circles above them. A flock of silver cranes flashed past over the lake and then vanished like smoke. The sky was full of thousands of birds, but they were all beyond the range of our guns.

"If only that stupid fellow, Gulam Ali, had not opened fire in a hurry, we could have had a shot at the ducks," I said angrily.

"No," smiled Nawab, "The ducks were about to fly away in fear, that's why he fired at them. In any case, they were in the middle of the lake and outside our range...It's lucky that Salimullah managed to shoot two ducks."

Then I saw Salimullah upto his waist in the water. With one hand he held his gun above his head and with his other he paddled through the waters as he moved rapidly towards the ducks. At that moment he looked like a huge giant.

Gulam Ali also plunged into the water and moved towards the ducks from the opposite side to help Salimullah.

"I am coming Sahib...Keep your eye on them, make sure they don't fly away, we have them cornered..." Gulam Ali shouted.

"Don't worry...their wings are broken...they'll never be able to fly again..." Salimullah's voice, rising above the sound of the splashing waves, was terrifying.

— I saw that the ducks were frantically beating the water with their broken wings and were desperately trying to get away from the hunters. Suddenly I felt as if a deep and deathly hush had fallen over everything...Salimullah lunged forward and grabbed the ducks. Nawab and I turned to look at each other... A vision flashed before our eyes... We saw thousands and thousands of birds — rows upon rows of them — innocent, gloriously plumaged birds — flying across India, China, Mongolia, Siberia and beyond — flying over open wheat fields, over lands covered with translucent snow, over herds of antelopes — innocent birds absorbed in the round of daily activities — nuzzling their heads together in affection, dancing as if in some elaborate ritual of their own — then we saw the snow fall and ice-cold winds blow over the plains, flocks of ducks bury their eggs in the snow, bid farewell to a part of themselves which they had hidden there, and fly south — fly to their summer home in search of the sun and warmth — some birds lost their way as they flew towards their new home, got separated from their flock — but they flew on towards their destination, continued to look for the sun and the warmth necessary for their survival — And we saw them again, in a later season, when the snow had melted in the sun, make their journey back to plains they had left behind, fly over the fields and the ice and the antelopes...

Salimullah stood before us holding up the ducks. Their wings were broken. I saw in their innocent eyes reflections of dreams which were more luminous than the snow covered plains, deeper than the waters of lakes, more vibrant than the colours of their wings — their eyes, which were about to close forever, were searching for something far away — I saw, in those round, still eyes which were about to shut forever, a vision. — An infinite number of blue and yellow and green birds singing and playing in sheer delight amongst giant pine trees covered with snow — in love with themselves and the world around — a vision of exultation and joy...I said to them in sorrow — Farewell, innocent ones, farewell — Forget your friends and companions, forget all those whom you loved once — stop grieving for those you will leave behind — those eggs buried in snow — forget everything — your wings are broken, you'll never, never be able to fly again — never return — never...

Gulam Ali joined Salimullah. Together they uttered the prescribed holy verses and ritually slit the necks of the birds. I noticed that Nawab had turned his face away.

"Sahib, we can come back here in the afternoon. Now the ducks have flown, but they will return later and land again on the lake — come to my house for a while. You can rest there and have something to eat."

— I looked back towards the lake once more. The water was very still — silent and somber like a white shroud —

— There was silence all around as we drove back. No one uttered a word on the way. After a short drive we reached Gulam Ali's house.

"Sahib, this is my hut," Gulam Ali said, as he leapt out of the jeep.

It was an old, brick house with a front porch made of clay.

I suddenly saw two legs draped in a large, baggy salwar standing behind the door. Gulam Ali went in and came back with a cot which he placed on the porch. He asked us to make ourselves comfortable. Then he went back again and returned with a few more things. I was so absorbed in my own thoughts that I forgot to request him not to make elaborate arrangements for us.

Then Gulam Ali said to me, "Sahib, could you come inside for a few moments please. My wife, Jameela, insists that she must meet you..."

I informed Nawab that Gulam Ali's wife was from Hardoi and that she had found out that I too was from U.P. — "She wants me to get her a visa to India."

— Nawab looked at me, but didn't say anything.

— I opened the door, walked in and found myself in an open courtyard.

Gulam Ali called his wife. She was a slim, fine featured woman of about thirty-five years of age. She was wearing a baggy salwar typical of these parts — Gulam Ali, I said to myself, has made her into a Punjabi!

— She came out without any hesitation and sat on the ground next to me. I was taken aback by her innocent confidence.

"Bhaiya, salaam," she said. I felt as though a sister of mine had addressed me.

"So... you are Jameela," I said, as I returned her greetings.

"Yes," she said, proud and happy that I, a Police Superintendent, knew her name. But when I looked at her, I felt ashamed of my own meanness. She was excited because, despite he wall that divided us, I was still her countryman, someone who had once lived in the land where she was born.

"Bhaiya, get me a permit — I want to go to Hardoi once, see my old house again. When I asked my husband to get me one, he said that he had no influence. I told him that I'd talk to you directly, that you would help me."

She said all this in one breath like an excited little girl who asks her father to get her trinkets from the city. I looked at Gulam Ali. His eyes made the same plea which he had made to me the previous night in the jeep — "Sahib," he seemed to be saying, "Please tell her bluntly that she can't get a permit. Otherwise, I'll lose all that I have saved, merely to satisfy a whim of hers — She being unreasonable, Sahib..."

— His wife sat next to me like a beggar with a bowl.

I was confused — Did I have the right to be cruel to her? — ould my conscience permit it?

Gulam Ali again looked at me pleadingly.

"Listen, Jameela," I said to her, "I can't help you get a passport You will not be able to visit your native place."

I felt as if my entire inner being had shattered into small ›ces of sharp edged glass... Thousands of shadows flickered over neela's face.

"Why...why not, Bhaiya? Why can't I get one?... Can't you get or me, Sahib?...Sahib, you are a big police officer."

Instead of addressing me as her brother, she had suddenly 'ome formal. It was as if in an instant I had become a stranger.

"Well...your Sahib may be a big officer, but he can't get a sport even for himself, how can he then help you?" As I said t I felt mean and vile. I clenched my teeth so hard that my jaws t.

"But Vaziruddin's wife got one made for herself," she said as ıe was making one last helpless plea on her own behalf.

"Yes," I said, mutilating my conscience again, "She may have, but it wasn't legally valid. That's why her husband burnt it."

That simple woman had placed all her trust in me as a brother and I had betrayed her. She shed her last tears for her home and for her dreams.

Gulam Ali was about to say something harsh when I stopped him — Let her cry, I thought, let her weep for the last time — A little later when she looked up, I gently pushed her hair back in place with both my hands, and then thrust a ten rupee note in the hand of her small son who had come out to watch us.

After a long silence, I told Nawab about all that had happened inside. He listened to me quietly. When I had finished, he smiled, not as one who smiles at human beings and their actions, but mockingly, bitterly. It was as if he was pained at the thought of a society where relationships were always unequal — How can a man live with so much bitterness? I couldn't bear to look at him. He turned his face away. The others were busy eating and hadn't noticed anything. I felt as if Nawab's mocking smile had stabbed me in the back.

I said to myself — Nawab, you may think of yourself as a brave man, a hero, but what would you have done in my place? Would you have let your subordinate's wife squander away her husband's hard earned money just to satisfy a whim? — I looked up at him. Nawab sat motionlessly. His face was blank. Had he also become aware of my dilemma?

We got into our jeeps again and started out towards the lake. Many villagers had come to see us...Gulam Ali waved to them patronizingly as if to say — Don't think that I am an ordinary man like you. The Superintendent of Police comes to my house for breakfast — I too smiled at them.

When I looked back, I saw her standing on the roof of Gulam Ali's house — a woman from Hardoi who had migrated here and now wore a big, baggy salwar. Her hair was dishevelled and her dupatta fluttered wildly in the wind.

I looked at Nawab. Both of us thought of those ducks with broken wings..."O Birds, your wings have been broken. Now you cannot return to those fields of snow!"

— "Goodbye, sister. You'll never again see that land where you grew into consciousness — hear its songs, swing from its trees on rainy days, play hide-and-seek in its chicken coops, dye your dupatta there in rainbow colours, collect flowers with your childhood friends — never again will you see the place where you gathered tenderness in your hands and pressed it against your heart — Forget that place, sister. Don't grieve for it anymore. Let the tears you just shed be the last. There are others who share your sorrow. Don't waste your tears anymore — Why thrash your wings about in vain, a hunter hidden in the shadows of the lake broke them a long time ago — There is nothing left now." —

I put my head down on the seat in front. The jeep was travelling over a broken unpaved road and had left a cloud of dust behind.

"Did you ever get married? I forgot to ask you," I heard Nawab's whisper above the noise of the jeep's engine.

For some unknown reason, I felt afraid. I pressed his hand and nodded.

"How many children do you have?" he asked again.

"Three," I said.

— I know what you are going to ask me next, Nawab. Go ahead, ask without any hesitation, ask whatever you want freely so that there are no secrets left between us —

"Did you ever get a letter from her?" Nawab asked.

— Well done, my friend — may you live long — there are some wounds which have still not healed. You have just opened them!—

"A letter from whom?" I opened my eyes and looked at Nawab who stared at me in disbelief in the same way as a policeman looks at a thief. He was about to say something when I placed my hand on his arm and stopped him — I couldn't look straight into his eyes because I felt guilty...

Everything around us was now brightly lit and the wheat and cane fields looked golden and lovely. I shut my eyes and felt the warmth of the sun on my eyelids — and then like a glorious revelation, I saw a scene from the past fill with radiance the mirror-house of my memories. It is difficult to describe it in words, and to paint it in all its magnificence I will have to mix the colours with my blood... The image of the woman I had once loved stood before me. She was sublimely beautiful —

It was a hot summer afternoon, one of those days when the wind carries fire in its cloak. A young girl, wildly sensual like the waves of the Brahmaputra, self-possessed and proud like the Himalayas, stood in the middle of a clay courtyard of a lovely house surrounded by open fields; next to her, leaning against the brick-wall stood a young man. She had just managed to untie the charming knots of childhood and had taken her first, bold and free steps into the exciting realms of adolescence; he was as audacious as a young man is expected to be.

"So, Bhai, it seems that your lordship is in love with me!" the young woman teased him.

The young man did not say anything.

"Since when have you been so kindly disposed towards me?"

He still did not answer.

"Hmm...Do you know that I am older than you are?" she asked.

"These things are not in one's control..." the young man stuttered.

She smiled at the simplicity of his logic.

The wind outside stopped blowing. It was as if it was fascinated by the scene and was watching it keenly.

Who knows why that girl, who had the reputation of being so proud and vain but whose soul was untainted, stepped forward as if to say to the young man that he should take her in his arms — to hold her divine body, sinuous like the Brahmaputra and noble like the Himalayas, with all the strength of his love. The young man also stepped forward. Put his arms around her as if he had never before touched a body which was so fresh and soft and lovely and he kissed her lips with all the veneration in his heart.

They spent a joyous year together full of love for each other — tender, innocent, playful love.

Then came 1947 — growling, gnashing its teeth, holding the order of the Partition in one of its claws. And they heard voices calling for terrible sacrifices rumble down the mountains — screams of Ya Alahi rent the sky. The young man met that girl the day he was leaving his native land for an unknown country. He was calm, his feelings were under control, his heart did not beat faster than usual; his feet were restless to carry him away from the place, to walk thousands of miles away to an unknown destination without any hesitation.

"So you are off?" she asked.

The young man wanted to say lots of things, but he did not have the courage to utter a single word.

"You don't have to look sad like Majnu or Farhad. Marry a girl of your parent's choice...Do you understand? That would be the best thing for you."

The young man tried to say something, but the girl urged him to be brave. Trying to console him and to keep back her tears, she said, "Come back after three or four years, marry me and take me away with you."

Both knew how impossible that was, yet both tried to convince each other that they would meet again.

— And then, it so happened that it started snowing. Snow flakes covered the scene. Cold winds began to blow. It became unbearably cold — flocks of birds, in order to survive flew off to warmer lands and left behind, buried in the snow, precious parts of themselves in delicate eggs, in the hope of returning to them some day...

The girl never heard from him because the customs of their families were such that it was forbidden for an unmarried girl to receive letters from a young man — especially from one in a foreign country.

After migrating to Pakistan, the young man often sat by the banks of the river which flowed through both the nations and built castles of sand which were always swept away by the powerful and careless currents of the river which had its source in another land — I am sure that there were other young men who sat on the banks of the same river in the other nation and built similar sand castles which were destroyed by the flow of the river; I am sure they too said that the waters were hostile because they came from another land —

That young man built many castles of sand over the years, but they were all washed away by the river — It had erased the dreams even of the bravest, how could the longings of an ordinary young man survive? Besides, sand castles are made of sand and cannot last!...

"What are you thinking about?" Nawab's voice shattered his reverie.

"Nothing," I said and opened my eyes.

Nawab smiled as if to say that he understood why I had lied and that he sympathized.

I got lost in my dreams again.

Twenty years after I had migrated to Pakistan, I learnt that Begum, the young girl whom I had so desired, had been married to a drunkard and a consumptive. Girls from respectable families which had been crushed by misfortune still had to be married with pomp and show!

"Listen," I heard Nawab call me again.

"Hmm," I said.

"Begum is now a widow. Her husband had tuberculosis and was also an alcoholic...Didn't you know that?" His words whizzed past me like thousands of sharp, steel tipped arrows.

I looked around. We were approaching the lake. The sun shone over the wheat fields. The wind howled like a ghoul through the trees. Everything seemed ominous.

— "Oh God, why is everything so gloomy today...?" I asked Him who never condescends to give answers to ordinary human beings like me. He speaks only to prophets...

"Nawab — is Begum really a widow now?" I asked the question in such a way as if I actually wanted to know why Begum had become a widow.

"Didn't you know? Her husband died many years ago...You may have heard that my Ghazala died."

— Oh Nawab, why must you torment me today, as if the news about Begum was not enough. But I don't want to know how Ghazala, who was as gentle and frolicsome as a dove died. Nor do I want to know how Begum has survived. Who knows how many more poisoned arrows lie in your quiver.

The jeep stopped. The two of us were the last to get down.

Gulam Ali came and said, "This time the birds are on this shore and some are in the middle of the lake. You must make the best of this chance."

The bright and clear blue sky was reflected on the surface of the lake and the rays of the sun made the colorful wings of the ducks more resplendent.

"I will take my place in that cane field. Nawab, you go and hide behind those bushes. And Salimullah Sahib, you go with

Gulam Ali to the other shore and fire from there. When the birds take wing, they will fly towards us and we'll shoot them down —." I gave these instructions and took up my position.

Gulam Ali and Salimullah walked to the other shore. They whispered conspiratorialy to each other as they went. I hid at one end of the cane field. Nawab loaded his gun with shining new cartridges and moved towards the bushes.

The ducks didn't suspect anything and continued to swim peacefully in the lake. I loaded my gun and got ready. All of a sudden I heard the sound of the flapping of wings overhead and I saw the wing of a duck fall into the water with a loud splash. There were ripples on the surface of the lake, then it became as still and silent as before.

I recalled the eyes of the ducks who had been shot that morning — their wings had been broken, they had the same dreams as those two women —

The reeds on the far shore rustled mysteriously. Gulam Ali and Salimullah were moving stealthily towards the ducks.

I looked at the lake. Sometimes it seemed to me that its water was very still, at other times it seemed that the ducks were motionless — that there was no difference between stillness and movement. This happens when one looks at lakes and rivers for a long time — everything seems the same, all differences are obliterated. That day as I sat by the shore of the lake, I felt that it wasn't only the water which was silent and still, but that the entire universe was quiet and without any movement. Only the dreams in the eyes of those trusting and astonished birds still stirred. If there was any life, it was in their hopes of returning home; if there was any warmth, it was in their passionate desire to go back to those snowy fields; if there was any vitality, it was in their fervent longing to find again those eggs in which they had buried the most precious parts of themselves...

— Nawab, at this moment you are sitting far away from me. Later I shall tell you what I think we are — we are birds with broken wings and we can never fly back to those fields of desire — we are more helpless and defenceless than those birds because once their wings are broken they are ritually slaughtered — but people like us — our torment never ends, we die slowly, we are tortured at every moment of our lives, we are hunted without mercy and we can only beat our wings in the throes of death, but we can not die — Yes, I shall tell you all this later.

Then a shot rang out from the opposite side of the lake. I shuddered. I thought that the sun and the lake had turned red; that the whole universe had been splattered with blood — who knows how many wings had been broken and how many birds were writhing in pain in the lake?

The ducks flew up and scattered in the sky. A small group flew within the range of my gun. I raised my gun and then noticed that there was blood on my hands...It was the blood of the dreams I had seen in those tired and sleepless eyes, it was the blood of those longing to return to the snow covered fields, it was the blood of that love I had seen in the mating dance of birds...

— God knows when I lowered my gun.

— I heard the sound of wings fluttering above Nawab's head.

— Gulam Ali was shouting, yelling at us, "Fire, Huzoor, fire, they are flying over your head, right over..."

— I looked again at my blood covered hands and addressed them, "Tell me, whom should I ask about Begum — how she lives now — where she lives shrouded by her desires, in what coffin of hopes? Who will tell me how Ghazala died? How will I ever find out about my friends who are now lost in the dust of time? — Is that house still standing or is it in ruins, that house where she and I had built the Taj Mahal of our dreams?..."

When I looked again there was no blood on my hands!

I saw a flock of ducks in the east vanish like smoke.

I spoke to them ardently — You have escaped. Your wings are not broken. As you fly over India, grieve for those who had migrated from there and had to find another home in a strange land — And remember, if you fly in the other direction, towards Germany, mourn for the people there also for they suffered a similar fate as ours — You have seen us, we are not the only ones who have endured pain. There are people with broken wings everywhere — like Gulam Ali's wife and Vaziruddin's wife and — Nawab. Each one still dreams of those fields beyond the mountains — Go, go back to the snow covered lands, fly over the pine trees, the wheat fields and the open spaces where the antelopes run — May God be with you and may He guide your flight — Farewell —

The last flock of birds seemed like a faint wisp of translucent smoke in the horizon.

I saw Gulam Ali and Salimullah coming towards us. They were arguing about something and gesticulating wildly — their voices sounded like buzzing flies.

I stepped out of the field where I was hiding and stomped the mud off my shoes.

Nawab walked towards me and asked from a distance, "Why didn't you fire?"

At once everything around us became preternaturally quiet — The leaves stopped rustling, the wheat fields stopped swaying in the wind — the pair of cranes near the shore became very still — the soft ripple of water became inaudible —.

"Oh — Nawab — these cartridges are old — they cheated me — they didn't fire —" I lied.

"But, listen ..." I said.

"What?" He looked sheepishly at me.

"Why didn't you fire? You could have shot a few birds down — they flew right over your head."

He was silent, so silent that I became apprehensive. Then he came up close to me and, choosing every word carefully, whispered, "I too suffered as much as you did."

Suddenly four shots rang out at the same time from our two guns — the pair of cranes flew up into the sky — Gulam Ali and Salimullah ran towards us shouting and wailing.

— Nawab's driver, who had been startled by the firing, took our guns away from us.

— Nawab and I gazed at each other in recognition and then embraced each other in silence for a very long time — We did not weep and felt a certain joy in restraining our tears — No one said a word — Soon the wind started blowing more strongly. The waves of the lake began to beat quietly against the shore.

Original in Urdu.
Translated by Vishwamitter Adil
and Alok Bhalla.

SALIL CHOUDHARY

THE DRESSING TABLE

Almost every letter, Nanda had written to me after our marriage, had a note at the end. She would invariably scribble "P.S." and then add in her crooked handwriting:

"If you rent a house, don't forget to buy a dressing-table for me — and make sure that the mirror is large and clear."

When I used to visit Nanda's house before we got married, the first thing I always noticed was a cracked mirror which hung on the wall opposite the front door. How it used to distort my face when I stood before it! It would elongate the upper half of my face and shrink the lower half. From my forehead down to the tip of my nose, my face seemed to be longer than the palm of my hand, while the area from my lips down to my chin seemed no more than half an inch. And if I dared to make the slightest move my reflection in the mirror seemed to make faces at me!

That sight would dampen my spirits. But Nanda would laugh and say, "Never mind! Buy me a good mirror when I come to live with you."

Later in life, I had to face many critics. They held up before me an image of myself in the mirror of their criticism. At those moments I would be reminded of the mirror which used to hang on the wall facing the front door of Nanda's house. But, I am afraid I have begun to digress from the real story.

The incident I want to describe happened soon after our marriage. At that time I was hoping to get a job with one of the leading newspapers of the day. I was sure that I would get a job merely for the asking and that a letter of appointment would be issued at once.

We decided that Nanda should continue to stay with her father till I got a job. She was to join me in Calcutta the moment

I got one. We discussed our plans at length. We decided how we would decorate our home, where we would keep our furniture, etc.

I reached Calcutta with the detailed plans of our house in my head. Nanda stayed back in her village with her father.

Now, if you could only listen to all that actually happened to me over the next six months! But, I must resist the temptation to lament over my fate for that will unnecessarily consume a lot of space in this story.

The story that I want to tell you is not really about myself. Still, I should let you know that I did get a job. You may otherwise think that I am hinting at the problem of unemployment. I did not, however, get the kind of job I had hoped for. On the contrary, I had never even dreamt of the kind of job I finally managed to get. I began my career as a salesman in a shoe-store. I rented a small, two-room house with a tin-roof beside a muddy pond in the very heart of Kasba. I shared the house with a cousin of mine. Nanda joined me soon afterwards.

We were quite happy. Nanda had a wonderful capacity to adjust to all circumstances. It is a gift which, perhaps, all women possess. I never saw unhappiness cast its shadow on Nanda's face. It was as if Nanda had always dreamt of renting a house with a tin-roof in Kasba. But, after we had moved into our new home, Nanda never again talked about her dream of buying a dressing table. I, too, almost forgot about it.

One Saturday afternoon, however, something strange happened. I was returning home from the shoe-shop with sixty, fresh and crisp, one rupee notes in my pocket. As I walked along, I looked at the shops on both sides of the road. I fancied that I could, if I wanted to, buy any of the lovely goods on display. I felt as if I were an emperor. Such is the magic of money in one's pocket. It makes one feel good!

Suddenly at the cross-roads of Kasba I saw it! A beautiful dressing-table on the pavement for auction. There were many other pieces of furniture along with it for sale at throw-away prices. The dressing-table was in almost perfect shape. The mirror had a small crack in one corner. The highest bid till then had been only thirty rupees. Can you imagine that! So, impulsively, ignoring all the problems which would inevitably have followed at the disappearance of half my salary, I bought the dressing-table, hired a porter to carry it on his head, and walked home. On the way I calculated, "Fifteen rupees for house rent. That means we shall have only fifteen rupees for all other expenses this month!" But then Nanda's face appeared before my eyes. I thought of all the dreams and hopes she had cherished when she had fallen in love with me. I hadn't fulfilled a single one of them! If I could fulfill at least one, then the thirty rupees would have been well-spent. I wasn't going to be sorry for having done so.

Nanda was, of course, very surprised when she saw me walk into the house with the dressing table. But her surprise immediately gave way to joy. Another woman in her place would have counted the money I had spent and nagged me, but Nanda was different. She was generous and large hearted like the ocean. Though not a poet herself, she was certainly fit to be a poet's wife!

She spent the entire afternoon in front of the mirror. She combed her hair in different styles, changed her saree, put a bindi on her forehead, covered her head with one end of the saree and shyly smiled at her reflection a number of times. I lay in bed and gazed at her in rapture. I don't know when I fell asleep watching her happy face.

While I slept, I dreamt of the days of our courtship. Life had seemed to overflow with joy then.

I woke up with a start. Nanda was calling me. I looked at her and was amazed. Why were her eyes swollen? Why? What had happened? Tears were streaming down her face! Her entire body was trembling with emotion.

"What's wrong, Nanda? Why are you weeping so bitterly?"

"Please return that dressing table. I don't want it." Nanda buried her face in the pillow and started crying again.

I thought, she felt insulted because the dressing-table was old and used.

But a new dressing-table would have cost a lot. More than I could have afforded. How could she be so unreasonable? And, besides, the dressing-table was almost new!

"No, Nanda! Listen to me. Please."

"No, no, no. I don't want it. Please return it at once."

I was stunned by her behaviour. Was she really so arrogant, so conceited about her status? Didn't my feelings have any value for her?

"Alright. As you wish. I'll return it to the shop."

Slowly, Nanda got up from the bed and left the room, only to return immediately afterwards. She dropped a bundle of letters in my lap and said, "Read these letters."

There were four letters in blue envelopes written in clear Bengali script.

"Whose letters are these? Where did you find them?"

"In the drawer of the dressing table."

I opened the letters and sat down to read them one by one. My hands trembled in anticipation. Who knew what they would reveal? I arranged the letters in chronological order. The first letter read as follows :

First Letter

Bagerhat

Dearest,

I reached here at midnight yesterday. It already seems as if I have been separated from you for a very long time. I just can't believe that only yesterday, at this very hour, you were so very near!

This place is a bit far from the town. Do you remember my friend, Amal? He is teaching here in a college. I'll stay with him from tomorrow. I am very tired, though the journey was quite comfortable. I had a funny experience on the train. A middle-aged gentleman, his wife, their little son and two daughters occupied the seats opposite mine. They were a courteous, small and happy family — three healthy children, a good-hearted, middle-aged husband and father, beaming with a generous smile, and a real Bengali mother. I was happy to see them.

I opened my sketchbook so that I could capture that family group for my future reference. One of the girls, however, noticed that I was making a sketch of the family. She told her sister, who told her mother and the mother passed the information on to the father. The middle-aged man was elated when he learnt that I was a painter.

"Really? Show me your sketch of my family. Oh! My, my! It is wonderful! You, sir, are a magician!"

The entire family, then, showered attention on me. They offered to share with me the food they had bought at the station. My protests were in vain.

"Listen, sir, do you know why the Bengalis are in such a sorry state today? It is because they have forgotten to honour their artists. I, too had an artistic streak in me once. I had even made a name for myself amongst the singers and the musicians...Eat this. Please! Don't feel shy."

I had to eat what they offered. The curious thing about the gentleman was that he never expected an answer from his listener. He was so confident of himself that he didn't believe that anyone would dare to contradict his beliefs and statements, even if they weren't based on facts.

"You are a bachelor, aren't you? Very good! Don't ever make the mistake...Just look at me...Ha, ha! If you get married, everything will be ruined!"

I was about to tell him that I was married, but he didn't give me a chance to open my mouth. He continued to talk instead.

"Why don't you teach my daughter drawing? I shall pay you whatever you ask for. You shouldn't have any problems doing so since you live in Calcutta. I live on Bidon street. You must come home. Promise me that you will do so. Oh Hashi! Oh Khushi! Are you happy now? You must thank your stars! How lucky you are to have found a drawing teacher while travelling in a train. Ha, ha, ha!"

He didn't give me a chance to reply.

His daughters asked me, "Will you really come?"

"Oh yes! I shall," I replied helplessly.

While we were talking, the little boy, who had been looking through my bag, managed to pull out my album. He started turning its pages after wetting his fingers with saliva.

The mother scolded him mildly, "That's bad manners, son! Please put it back."

"No. mother! He gave me permission to look at it. Didn't you, sir? Please, tell my mother that you had asked me to look at your album."

"O yes, yes! I asked him to." I could see that all of them were of the same kind.

The family had to get off at Ranaghat. So I offered them some of the puris you had made. "You must share these with me," I insisted. I gave some to the little boy, who shared them with his sisters. We began to discuss the various problems of the day — the condition of the country, the Tenancy Act, the Commonwealth, etc. Then they got off at Ranaghat. The train was about to start when the gentleman suddenly remembered, "Oh God! I forgot the most important thing. I haven't taken down your name and address. Tell me quickly!"

He took out his pen and a piece of paper. I told him my name, but he didn't hear it clearly. I repeated it.

"Rahimuddin Choudhury."

"What!"

"Rahimuddin Choudhury."

"Oh! I see."

He wrote it down, but his hands shook. He said, as if he was swallowing a lump in his throat. "Right. It doesn't matter. It's alright. Everything is fine. I really failed to identify you. You could easily pass for a Bengali. Isn't that so, wife?"

You could easily pass for a Bengali! Isn't that so wife! I wanted to scream at him, "So where do you think I am from? From Punjab?" But I couldn't utter a word. I was so completely nonplussed.

The two sisters tried to make light of the entire incident. They smiled and said, "Don't forget. You must come. Bidon street."

I tried to smile back.

The train started moving. I saw the boy's mother snatch the puri you had made from her son's hand and throw it on the platform. A delicious puri, made so lovingly by you, lay on the platform. I felt like crying. I wanted to turn to the other passengers in the compartment and shout, "Come and see the injustice! I have been very unjustly treated!" But I restrained myself and no one heard my complaint. I sat quietly. The entire day had been ruined for me.

I don't remember all the details now, nor do I want to remember them. The words of the two sisters, however, still ring in my ears, "Don't forget. You must come. Bidon Street." I want to tell them, "No, I shall not forget the two of you, because you are the pioneers of a new Bengal. Our hopes live in young people like you, otherwise we would have died by now. How can I ever forget you?"

Please do write back soon.

Yours,

Rahim.

The envelope bore the following address :

Amina Choudhury
Ujanipura
Howrah.

Second Letter

Bagerhat

Wife,

I reached Amal's house today. On my way I saw people fleeing from this place, deserting their homes. The whole town is as silent as a graveyard. People are even scared to talk loudly. You can well imagine my condition. I find myself, quite unexpectedly, in a place where things have taken a bad turn. Before I could even understand what was going on, Amal told me that he had resigned his job. His wife and he are busy packing their belongings and will leave for Calcutta in a day or two. They plan to go to Pakistan from there. They never expected me to come in such difficult times. Amal's wife greeted me with a nervous smile.

"What's the matter? What's going on, Amal? Have the two of you also decided to leave the country at last?"

Amal's wife tried to smile, "But we no longer have a place in your country, brother-in-law."

"Your country! What do you mean by 'your country'? Amal's country is Khulna and mine is the 24 Parganas. In fact, you are coming to my country, aren't you?"

"Things have changed. Now the Muslims belong to Pakistan and the Hindus to Hindustan."

Amal turned to his wife and said, "Why don't you go and finish your work."

She went inside to finish packing. I sat quietly, staring at Amal. His child had just learnt to crawl. A lovely child — I could see his two little teeth. The child cried as it fell to the floor with a thud while trying to stand up holding onto his father's leg. But Amal didn't pay him any attention.

"Look here, Rahim. I've got to tell you something."

"Tell me. What is it?" I picked up the child from the floor. He was still crying.

I am giving you only a gist of what Amal said. Recently, there had been a terrible riot in a scheduled-caste village a few miles from the town. The scheduled-caste villagers were either farmers or fishermen. They were, by and large, poor people. They had been trying for a long time to unite so as to fight the injustice and the brutality of the zamindars. The police issued a warrant for the arrest of two of the leaders of the rebellious villagers. One of them was a Hindu and the other a Muslim. When the police entered the village in search of the two leaders, the villagers asked the police to leave the place. But when they failed to persuade the police to do so, they beat them up and pushed them out of the village.

That incident was responsible for setting into motion all that followed. One day, a number of armed policemen, accompanied by a gang of hooligans, attacked the village. Brutality, in its most horrendous form, was unleashed upon the villagers. The policemen didn't differentiate between men and women. Village after village was burnt and looted. The inhabitants fled from their homes. The sky and the air were rent with the screams of the victims. In the meantime, some people began shouting that the Hindus were enemies of Pakistan. Slogans like "Throw the Hindus out," were raised.

Taking advantage of the confusion created, a few goondas in the town looted and then set fire to some shops owned by the

Hindus. Hindus, walking down the main roads, were threatened in broad daylight.

Do you remember Anwar, that scoundrel who had once passed a crude remark about you while we were still at college? He ran away to Pakistan after cheating someone of all his money by promising to work with him as a business partner. I am told that Anwar is now the leader of a large gang of goondas. It seems he is one of the main organizers of the riot.

My blood has been boiling ever since I heard that. If I ever come across that rascal, I shall lynch him. Believe me! I shall certainly do that. Amal and his family are planning to leave either tomorrow or a day or two later. How can I console them? What can I tell them? My heart is being torn apart by shame and grief. I feel that I must do something, but I don't know what. If Amal feels that he must leave his place of birth, what reason do I have to stay on? The very thought of doing so depresses me.

I don't know anyone intimately here. I met an old student of mine by chance. He told me that they were trying to establish a peace committee.

Nearly all the offices are closed. I am planning to leave for the Deccan in a day or two. I think it is still possible to get a few assignments there.

Please don't lose heart. These days one can't delude the people for very long. We must have faith in our hearts and continue to hope that one day humanity will win. Inform all our friends at home of the actual incidents that are taking place here.

Yours,

Rahim.

Third Letter

Dhaka,

Wife,

Received your letter. It has made me even more worried than I was. If the Calcutta newspapers have started distorting the Khulna incident then the results will be disastrous. The monster they are arousing, out of greed for money, will destroy them in the end. They do, however, seem to know that they can start a riot or end it to suit their own convenience. The local newspapers here are playing the same dirty game. More and more people are becoming suspicious of each other, losing faith in each other's integrity.

Anticipating the worst, pessimistic people can be seen spreading rumours everywhere. If only there was a force which could raise the flag of humanity high in the sky and trample all that is foul and ugly under its feet! It's not only me, but almost everyone, who feels the need for such a force today. But where is it?

I have to visit Government offices almost everyday in search of assignments. I have almost forgotten the fact that I am a Bengali.

You know that I have spent a lot of time learning Urdu. I love Urdu literature. But when it is used as a scythe by a tyrant, threatening to chop off one's neck, or is used to strangle one's culture, one's heritage, then one is justified in disowning it. That is why I now answer all queries in simple Bengali. I don't care if they don't understand it. You can easily imagine that my hopes of getting a job are rather remote.

I felt very sad when I heard that you had stopped attending Rabindra Sangeet classes. At least I am convinced that those who turned their faces away from you, have no right to learn Rabindra Sangeet. But don't ever lose your faith in the truth that people are basically good. It is impossible to abandon them and move forward alone. It is our bad luck that the country is still under a curse. O my wife, how can we alone escape its evil spell? But when our humanity is being so grievously abused, I want to burn down this rotten, stinking, foul and cursed society.

The other day, I heard that a few road-side heroes gathered on the main road and insulted the pundit of a local college in a manner which cannot be described in words. They cut off his tuft of hair and forced beef into his mouth. I told the local V.I.P.s, "Shameful incidents take place in your presence, before your very eyes everyday and you don't protest. Are you sure that you are still alive?"

They replied, "What can we do? We are utterly helpless. They carry guns and have the support of the police. Whoever tries to interfere or protest is condemned as an enemy of Pakistan."

They burn down the houses of those who protest and, sometimes, even kill them. There are times when I think the entire race is crooked and deformed. Otherwise, it is difficult to believe that a few poisonous weeds can't be uprooted. Or is it that the weeds are far more numerous than in the past. I think, however, that the truth is far harsher and we shall have to accept it.

O my dear, I can't stay here any longer. Coming over to this side was a mistake. Now, I can't stay away from you even for a moment longer...Let work go to hell! I shall leave within a day or two.

Amal has written to me. They will leave tomorrow. He says that they will meet you when they reach Calcutta. Invite them to stay with you. We shall somehow manage.

Yours,

Rahim.

The next letter was written about twenty days later. It seems that there was another letter before that one. For some reason, it wasn't in the bundle of letters in the dressing-table.

Fourth Letter

Dear Amina,

I am sure that I will lose my mind. I haven't slept a wink over the last seven days. I wander about in the town like a mad man. People seem to have lost even the last drop of humanity. Bestiality, in its most terrifying form, has been unleashed upon the town. The entire town is filled with screams, wails and fiendish laughter. On top of all this, there have been no letters from you for the last eight days!

Thousands of refugees have been pouring into the city every day. They say that not a single Muslim has been left alive in Calcutta. I am going mad with uncertainty. I can't decide whether I should believe them.

Where are you, dear? Are you still alive? These days I don't seek an answer from human beings. I ask the sun and the trees. I ask them again and again, "How is my Amina? Where is she?"

I received a letter from Amal. They were beaten up at the border and all their belongings were snatched from them. Sister-in-law has been abducted. Amal has somehow managed to reach Ranaghat with his little son. Amal writes, "It's better not to describe my condition. I still have enough reason left to know that news about what happened to me must not reach the Calcutta newspapers. Do what you think is right. I am mentally and physically paralysed. I plan to leave this place at once. If I remain here even for a few more hours, I will commit suicide. I must find my wife. I would have felt a little stronger mentally if I had heard from you. I don't know when I shall see you again. I don't even know if I shall ever meet you again!"

Please forgive my weakness. I was proud of my people and my country. Today that pride has been shattered. I always praised man for his humanity, but I forgot his capacity for bestiality. Now it is the beast in man which has begun to prowl.

Wherever you are, in whatever condition, please take care of yourself. I cannot bear to lose you, my dear wife. I just cannot do that. Nor do I want to be tested to see if I am as strong as Amal. I am a very ordinary human being...

Yours,

Rahim.

There were no other letters. After reading them, I went to Ujanipura, Howrah, in search of the couple. I asked the people in the area for the house of the artist, Rahimuddin. One said, "I don't know." Another said, "No, sir. There are no mullahs in our locality anymore."

Finally, a paanwallah directed me to a single storyed house. Rahimuddin's family had rented two rooms in that house.

It was a dilapidated house. The doors were broken and the windows had no frames. Only a jute curtain hung from the door.

I called out repeatedly, but no one answered. After sometime, I pushed the jute curtain aside and went into the house. I discovered that there were at least twenty people inside. Some of them were sitting with their babies, and some lay on the floor. They were startled to see me. The condition of the women seemed to be worse than that of the building.

"Does Rahimuddin Choudhury live here?" I asked.

But no one had even heard of his name. They had taken shelter in that house only that morning because it was unoccupied. They were refugees from East Bengal.

I learnt that they had already been threatened four times, and had been told to vacate the place by nightfall.

A middle-aged woman, sitting in a corner, started vomiting. The others in the room watched her indifferently.

At that very moment, two boys walked in with a basket of puffed rice and corn. The boys, it seems, were two school students. They had persuaded the refugees to take shelter in that house and were looking after them.

I asked them about Rahimuddin. One of them knew Rahim and Amina. Rahim used to teach the elder sister of one of them drawing. He used to visit Rahim's house with his sister. I learnt about their fate from him.

He said, "I have heard that he is in Pakistan, but that Amina didi may not be alive. One day, at midnight, the house was locked from outside and set on fire. We tried hard to put out the flames and rescue the refugees, but in vain. There was a lot of firing, bullets were flying all around and it was impossible to step outside." The boy's eyes became misty with tears.

I looked at the house. The walls had been blackened by smoke. The neem tree next to the house was scorched and had shrivelled. It was obvious that the house had been set on fire.

I didn't tell Nanda anything about my visit to Howrah, Ujanipura, for I still had a slight doubt in my mind about Amina's fate. If Amina had been burnt in the fire, how had her dressing-table escaped from being singed by it!

The student had told me, "The dressing-table was kept in the smaller room."

Perhaps, Amina, too, was in the same room that night, But, then, where did she go after that?

Nanda is convinced that if Amina's story is published in the newspapers, she will come back to claim her dressing-table. I have written this story in that very hope. Nanda has wrapped up the mirror in a piece of cloth.

The Epilogue

My story ends here. But it wouldn't be out of place to describe another incident for my readers. This incident may not have any link with the story I have narrated, but it seems to have a curious bearing on it.

On the 1st of April, a Bengali newspaper published the following news item:

"Yesterday, the police arrested a man whose movements around Howrah station had aroused their suspicion. He was carrying a bag which had a few paint brushes and a few sketches. The police suspect that he was drawing the plans of the Howrah station and the Howrah bridge. When he was asked to give his name, he pretended to be mad and replied: 'A human being'."

The news item carried the following headline :

"A Pakistani Spy Arrested."

Original in Bengali.
Translated by Julu Sen.

JAMILA HASHMI

EXILE

The birds had spread their wings and flown home. The yellow light of the setting sun lay on the village pond and the golden dome of the gurudwara sparkled and shimmered. The crowd at the fair on the other side of the pond had begun to disperse. A few moments later the huge effigies made for Dussera were set on fire. People shouted, and ran in fear in all directions. In the evening mist, sparks scattered across the dim blue sky like a garland of flowers. The flames blazed for a long time afterwards. In the glow of the fire, the faces of the people who had gathered there, seemed hideous. It was as if each of them had assumed the shape of Ravana, and had come there to see with delight, Sita weep as she was exiled once more.

Exile is terrible. But there is nothing in this world which is entirely under one's control. No one really wants to suffer.

Bhai used to say, "Bibi, why do you dream all the time? This love that surrounds you, this gaiety that you see, will slowly fade away. Time erodes everything. But the desolation it causes is so slow that we don't notice it; indeed, we become used to it."

Where is Bhai today? If the wind from my native town could travel like a spy and find him, I would ask Bhai, "Why does anguish never diminish? Why do human beings continue to dream even after they have endured so much sorrow, traversed over such difficult paths? Why do they continue to long for happiness?"

Why did Sita pray, even after she had endured a long exile, that she be granted one last meeting with Ramchandra? Doesn't misfortune so disillusion human beings that they cease to hope for better days? Why don't they learn to love darkness more? Why not?

The pear tree in the courtyard has blossomed every year since Munni was born. When the seasons change, its branches become so heavy with flower and fruit that they bend to the ground. The bond between the tree and the earth is strong. The roots of the tree burrow even deeper into the ground. No one can break that bond.

Today, Badi Ma told Gurpal, "Son, take Bahu and the children to the Dussera fair. She hasn't been out of the village for years."

Gurpal had shot back, "Ma, have you ever asked me to take her out? Is it my fault that she hasn't gone out for years?"

How can I blame anyone? When someone calls me Bahu, I feel as if I am being abused. I have heard myself being called Bahu for years. Ever since that night when Gurpal pushed me into the courtyard and proclaimed, "Look Ma, I have brought you a Bahu. She is tall and good looking. Of the girls who fell into our hands tonight, she was the prettiest."

His mother had raised the flame of her lamp and walked upto me. My eyes were dazed with hunger and fear. After having walked barefoot for miles, I had no strength left in me to even lift a finger. I fell at her feet in a heap. The cows and the buffaloes, who were chained in the courtyard, stopped eating their fodder and turned to look at me in surprise.

Once Badi Ma had scrutinized me from head to foot, she turned to her son and said, "If you had behaved more responsibly in the past, I wouldn't have had to suffer now. I have been almost blinded by the smoke from the angeethi. All the maid servants have stopped working in the house because we can't give them grain during the harvest season. Tell me, how much longer can I run this house alone? I would be happier if you began to cultivate your land again."

Gurpal had pleaded, "At least look at her. You won't have to put up with the insolence of maid servants any more. She will be your slave. Order her to grind corn, fetch water. As far as I am concerned, you can ask her to do anything you wish. I have brought you a Bahu!"

Many wives were brought to Sangraon during those days. No one had greeted them with music. No one had beaten the drums or sung lusty songs. No dancers had swirled through the night, or swayed their hips and made outrageous demands.

No one had greeted me at the door of the house with a handful of rice and corn; or anointed my dust covered hair with oil; or adorned me with jewels and fine clothes; or put mehndi on my hands and sindhoor in the parting of my hair. But I had become a bride.

Badi Ma had looked at me as if her grandson had kidnapped me only to add to the troubles of her life. She had turned her back on me and walked away to the kitchen. She hadn't bothered to say a word to me. That is how she had welcomed her new Bahu into the house.

At the fair, those who owned the swings were busy dismantling them, smoking bidies and cursing each other. They placed heavy loads on the backs of their donkeys as if those animals were made of wood. The raths used for the Ramlila performance were parked on one side and the youngsters who had acted in it, seemed to have forgotten their bright and glittering costumes, and were greedily eating kulfis and spicy pakoras. The chutney stains on their colourful dresses looked like leprous patches.

Munni stood and gazed at them. She was oblivious of the possibility that she could get lost. Does knowledge of the danger help? Those who are fated to disappear, vanish even if they are in a room full of people.

Gurpal pulled Munni away. My two sons were tired and had begun to demand, with tears in their eyes, that I buy them some fruit from the vendors.

In a fair, mothers are often separated from their children. Little children, who are lost, run fearfully from one place to another, gaze apprehensively at every face they meet and weep loudly. Can those who are lost in a fair, ever be found again? The very fact of separation stands like a wall between people who once loved each other. Once separated they are fated never to see each other's faces again. The paths they travel over are obliterated behind them like the tracks made on water by small insects. They can never retrace those paths again. They can never return to their past again. The crowd at a fair always moves forward.

Time lost can never be recovered. Whenever I didn't pay attention to my studies, or spent my time decorating my doll's house or playing with my friends, my brother used to say, "Bibi, each moment of time that is not used, is erased. It mingles in the dust."

That doll's house had been given to me as a present by my father. He had bought it at some exhibition.

Munni stood holding a large cloth doll in her hands. Every now and then she bent over it and gazed at it with shy affection. It was an ugly doll with a broad face, and clumsily stitched eyes and nose. It had a nose ring. With its head covered with a gold-fringed chunni and its skirt, it looked like a cheap dancing girl. Yet, Munni loved it.

Gurpal stood watching the crowd for a while. My two sons stood beside him, holding small images of Ravana in their hands, gazing at every face that passed by.

The road back to Sangraon meandered past Uchchal's pond and cut across some fields. The caravan of life moves on forever. Even if one has no fixed destination, one must keep walking, over straight and winding paths, across confusing and bewildering ways. Keep walking. Always. Even if one's feet are bruised and one's heart is empty.

It grew darker and the evening mist surrounding us became thicker. In the empty sky above, a single star trembled like the flame of an earthen lamp. I don't know why evenings always make me feel sad.

In the wilderness of my house, I am like that lonely tree which neither blossoms nor bears fruit.

That star reminded me of the ship in which my brother had crossed the seas. The day he was to leave and was busy packing his luggage, my mother's voice had been choked with grief. Yet, with a great show of courage, she had continued to help him and had said her prayers quietly. My father had busied himself outside with other necessary arrangements. Bhai had looked despondent. And Appa had walked up and down the house without uttering a word. I, on the other hand, had scampered through the house shouting with excitement. After all, one can never know how much a wound hurts, until one is injured oneself.

We had gone to the port to see him off. Bhaiya had taken charge of Bhai's luggage and was guiding it across the gangway. I had leaned over the guard-rail, gazed into the muddy water and asked Bhai, "Why is the water so dirty? Why do boats have oars? Why do they need anchors? When the boats rock violently in the sea, aren't people afraid?"

Tired of my questions, Bhai had replied, "You will understand everything when you grow up."

I have grown up since then and have begun to understand things. I know that a boat without oars sinks; that a boat can sink near the shore; that a single wave can smash it. Unfortunately, Bhai is not with me.

When we heard the siren of the ship, father put his arms around Bhai, placed his hand on his head and prayed, "May God look after you." Bhaiya flung himself on Bhai. Appa, who was sentimental and cried on every occasion, wept uncontrollably. Bhai said to her, "Look at Bibi, how happy she is. Why are you crying? I'll be back in two years. I am not going away forever." Then he embraced me and said, "Bibi, I'll bring back presents for you from Paris. Write to me regularly." I nodded my head enthusiastically.

When he heard the final whistle, he turned away and walked upto the deck so casually that it seemed as if he was going somewhere nearby. We continued to wave our handkerchiefs till we lost sight of the ship.

The sun set. The bright lights of the port shimmered in the restless waters of the sea. The light of the ship trembled in the distance like a lonely star for a while, and then disappeared. With it, all the lights of my life were extinguished forever. Since then, no ray of light has gleamed in the wilderness that surrounds me.

I remember throwing myself on my mother's shoulders and weeping. A voice within me whispered, "You will never see that face again. You will never meet your Bhai again." I trembled with fear like a lonely star in the blue sky.

Darkness had slowly begun to spread its wings over the fields. Gurpal lifted his two sons onto his shoulders, and began to walk ahead of us, on a gleaming white path which wound its way through the fields. He said that he would wait for us on the other side of the fields and, on the way, tell his sons the story of Ravana. He didn't realize that Sita was following him and that he himself was Ravana.

Munni,who was walking wearily beside me, asked "Ma, Swaroop's Mama has sent her colourful clothes for Dussera. They are made of silk. It feels good to touch them. Don't I have a Mama who will send me pretty gifts? Why don't you say something, Ma? Didn't you like the fair? Are you tired?"

"Yes, Munni, I am tired. I have grown old. I have travelled far."

"You aren't old," Munni said firmly as she looked at me. "You are like the image of a goddess. Even Badi Ma says so."

How could Munni have understood the distances I had travelled? The spaces that separate one life from the next are immense. When human beings lose hope, their bodies become hard and brittle. Then they look like gods ready to be worshipped. I have waited for so long on the roads of Sangraon, for those who had been separated from me, that my eyes have turned to stone. My heart has become empty. I have become Lakshmi. Yet those old bonds, strengthened by sorrow, have not snapped. In fact they have become deeper and stronger. How can I ever forget my past?

Munni asked once more, "Ma, don't I have a Mama?"

What could I tell her? How could I answer her questions? I stood at the cross-roads for a while, lost in thought.

Bhaiya had been dear to me. But I had also been afraid of him. Whenever he walked into the house, I used to immediately cover my head with a chunni, lower my voice and try to suppress my laughter. Standing beside him, I felt that there was no other human being in the world who was as tall as him. He walked gracefully and talked elegantly. His handwriting was neat and straight. His pages never got smudged and his fingers were never stained with ink. He always said to me, "Bibi, when you grow up, you too will write like me — in a neat hand and without smudges."

What would he say if he saw me now? The page on which my life story has been written, is so smudged with black ink, that it is difficult to find a single straight line on it. I never did learn how to write neatly.

In those days, I used to play with my doll's house and think, "We can all live here — Ammi and Baba, Bhaiya and Bhabhi. All of us. Life is a happy song. We lack nothing. There is no need for anything more."

When Bhaiya had got married, I had said, "Our house is Paradise itself. A real place of bliss." In those days, if I raised my hands in prayer, I didn't know what to ask for. Till this day, I have never asked God for anything. The wheel of life revolves between happiness and suffering.

After Bhai went abroad, my world of dreams was shattered into bits like a house of glass. Its splinters scattered all around me and their sharp edges still cut my feet, still cause me pain. Now I am too weary to walk anymore. Besides, the road to the other land is desolate and passes through a burial ground. There is no one there who waits for me. Whoever paid attention to Sita's lament? Loneliness is hard to endure. Life is difficult.

Gurpal called out to us from a distance. We continued to walk slowly. There was only dry stubble in the cotton-fields. People had already picked all the flowers. The fields of wheat had yet to ripen. The wind swept over the tender plants and bent them to the ground. When the wind blows everyone has to bend. Everyone has to bend before the wind, every one has to bend.

I was sure that Badi Ma would be restless. I don't know why she is so anxious about me. Some unknown fear troubles her these days. She doesn't understand that I can no longer walk across to the other country. Besides, I have travelled far with Gurpal and I no longer have the strength to go any further. After all, how long can one keep walking? In any case, there is no other place to which I can go. Where else can I go after so much suffering? Who will accept a woman who has been despoiled? Besides, Munni is now with me. She now stands as an obstacle between me and my relatives on the other side. The distance between them and us is very great.

Soon we heard groups of singers and the beating of drums behind us. The people at the fair had dispersed in all directions. Labourers, talking loudly and laughing, walked past us. They were followed by women who wore beautiful clothes and whose faces were partially covered with veils. They walked by briskly, holding their crying children with one hand, and a packet of sweets bought at the fair with the other. They walked barefoot; they had tied their chappals to one end of their dupattas and had flung them over their shoulders.

There is a profound relation between human beings and the earth. Why should a veil hide them from each other?

A sadhu, playing a single-stringed instrument, walked past us on the path to Sangraon. His song was full of sorrow. He sang of our longing for light even when there is no sign of light, no hope of it. After a while only a few words of his song, carried by the wind, reached my ears.

"Ma, why are you so quiet? Talk to me. I am afraid," Munni said, as she clutched my hand more tightly and tried to hold her doll in the other hand. Then she began to sob and couldn't ask me anymore questions.

I said to myself, "When Munni grows up, she will realize how futile it is to be afraid of the dark. One can do nothing before its magic."

Bhai used to tell me, "Bibi, water has its own force. It always finds its own path." At that time I hadn't understood what he had meant. Now I know that circumstances force us to find our own paths.

These days, whenever Badi Ma calls me, I cover my head with an embroidered cloth and softly whisper, "Yes." I do everything quickly and efficiently so that I am always busy and have no time to think about my loneliness.

When I had the time, I had nothing to think about; now that I understand some things, I don't have the time to think. There is always something lacking in our lives, something which is always missing.

Today, when I closed my eyes, my heart whispered, "They will all come soon." And that, as soon as Bhaiya sees me, he will say, "Why are you dressed like that, Bibi? That embroidered cloth covering your head, doesn't suit you at all. Throw it away. Stop all your work. Come and sit with us. See what I have brought for you. My vacations are always very short and they end much too soon. When I come home, spend all your time only with me."

During the vacations we always gathered together in the sitting-room, sat on the sofa, looked through the photographs, talked, drank tea, warmed ourselves before the fire and laughed a lot. Mother invariably called out to us in a drowsy voice and said, "You can talk in the morning, children. Now go to sleep." Bhaiya would shout back, "Amma, we are away throughout the year and sleep so as to forget our sadness and our loneliness. What's the hurry? We'll go to sleep."

For a long time, I thought that these memories would vanish like dreams, crumble into dust. That the paradise of affections we had built would be overtaken by terrible storms of dust and destroyed. My memories are like the photographs on the walls, shadows of reality. I have always been a foolish woman and my imagination has always been unconventional.

I still have strange dreams and my heart still beats with excitement. A voice within me says, "Dream, if you want to dream. And besides, what's wrong with the dream that one day, those whom you long to see, will walk in through the open door?"

I reply, "There is nothing but darkness left for me."

The voice says, "It's a sin to give up hope."

But what should I hope for?

Munni tugged at the end of the my chunni and said, "Ma, tell me, why can't we go and see Mama during Diwali? All the other girls are going. Ma, I don't like this village anymore. I didn't like the fair either. I feel sad. I want to go to my Mama's place."

To whom should I turn for information about my Mamas? All villages outside Sangraon look like dolls' houses to me. They don't seem to be real. Sangraon, too, is nothing more than a shadowy village. Everything around me is illusory.

Yet, I don't know why my soul wanders restlessly in search of things which never existed; why it longs to hear voices which it will never hear again?

I don't know why my heart has been pounding so strangely for the past few months? Often when I carry a basketful of cow dung or milk the cows, or burn uplas, I suddenly catch a familiar fragrance in the wind, or hear a familiar tune near me. They make me forget myself. But now I have understood the truth about them. They are from a country which lies forever beyond my reach. Like the roads to Sangraon, all the other roads also get entangled with each other and make one lose one's way. Why should I search for the city of my dreams?

I saw rooms lit with flickering lamps through open doors. They seemed like fairy lands.

Gurpal and the boys, Munni and I, walked side by side. The soft reeds swayed in the gentle breeze and brushed against my hair.

A journey with companions is easy.

Munni said, "Ma, I am exhausted. I can't walk anymore." The boys began to cry. They were so sleepy that they couldn't keep their eyes open nor could they hold onto their small images of Ravana. We stepped off the track and sat down to rest for a while on an embankment.

Gurpal said, "Women are stupid. Lots of children got lost at the fair today. When women go to a fair, they forget themselves. Entranced by the Ramlila, they forget their children and get separated from them."

"Children get separated from their mothers even outside fairs," I said, without looking at him and caressing Munni's head.

"Can't you ever forget that incident? Those days were different. Times have changed," Gurpal said softly.

How could I have explained to Gurpal that times never change? That human beings are forever doomed to suffer pain because they can never forget. I can still recall those days vividly. Everything around us was in flames. The country had become independent and had been divided. My mother and father had said, "These people, who are running away out of fear, are mad. After all, we live in the midst of our brothers and sisters. Who can hurt us?"

How innocent my father and mother were! It's those who are close to us, who make us suffer. The wounds that strangers inflict on us are unreal.

Life soon lost all its charm, and everything which was familiar, was drowned in a tide of blood. Those who had once been ready to die for their mothers and sisters, now began to play cruel games with the honour of women. The bonds of brotherhood that people had established over generations were broken and lay trampled in the dust under the feet of marauding hordes.

Amma told my father, "Let's take our daughters away. I am terrified. It is useless to trust anyone these days."

Trying to comfort her, father had said, "Don't lose your nerve like everyone else. Who will hurt us? Partition was inevitable. This unrest will soon subside. Don't worry, everything will be alright. Everything."

Normally Amma would have been reassured by such an answer. But that day she had said, "It isn't our lives alone which are in danger. Our honour too is threatened. We have grown up girls. Take my advice and send us to my brother's place."

My father had replied, "The roads are swarming with hooligans from the villages. They attack trains and kill everyone they can find. It's even more unsafe to travel than to stay here. You'll be safe here. God will protect us."

My father was certainly perturbed, but instead of seeking help, he placed all his trust in God alone. He didn't realize that it was already too late. His mistake was that he placed his faith in the life and values of the past. He had to pay a cruel price for it. When Gurpal dragged me out of the house, I saw my father's body lying in a gutter and his grey head outside it. With his eyes shut and his head soaked in blood, he seemed to be praying. Till the end he had believed that prayers could still be heard in those merciless times. Amma's heart had been pierced by a gleaming spear. She had fallen at the very spot where she had prayed to God for our safety and honour. Sometimes, when the winds are strong, I can still hear her screams. I was as helpless then as I am now. What could I have done? My head was not covered with a chunni when I was dragged away by Gurpal, and I had no hope of meeting Bhaiya on the way. Had Bhaiya been with us, no one would have dared to touch me. No one would have been able to drag me, with my head uncovered, through the dust of the land where I had been born and which I had loved. Where is that country now, whose earth is soaked with my father's blood? Where is that dust in which his old head had rolled? If I could only touch that soil once more, I would bow down and touch it reverentially with my forehead, because that soil is more fortunate than I am.

I still had a lot to say to my father. I hadn't yet teased my mother enough or troubled my bothers to my heart's content. My body had been dragged to Sangraon without ceremony. Unlike a traditional bride, I never had the chance to weep on my mother's shoulder. No one sang songs about the sorrow of leaving the home of one's parents, no one bade me farewell.

If those who suffer have some hope that their present pain would end someday, they can endure their suffering.

In the beginning, I had endured Badi Ma's beatings and Gurpal's abuses, because I was sure that Bhai and Bhaiya would come to Sangraon soon to look for me. Then, I had thought, I would smile at Badi Ma, and without even glancing at Gurpal, go away with my brothers. That day the wind would dance playfully in the neem leaves and the entire village would rejoice. I don't know why human beings think that they are the centre of attention of the entire universe? I don't know why. As long as one's eyes don't get used to the dark, they continue to strain after light. Dreams and hopes, like aimless wanderers,weave circles around the heart.

Once Munni was born, however, my dreams loosened their hold over me. The hopes which had encircled my heart scattered. I began to pay more attention to the world around me. Occasionally my voice could even be heard in the songs of Sangraon.

When Gurpal heard that the two countries had made an agreement with each other to maintain peace, he became sad and anxious. I often saw him and Badi Ma sit together and carry on a conversation in frightened whispers. Neither of them told me what they talked about. Those were the days when Munni had just learnt how to walk and to lisp a few words. All sorts of rumours swirled around me for a while and then suddenly subsided like dust storms. No army came to rescue me.

Sometime later, I heard that some soldiers from the other country had come to a village nearby, and had taken away many of the women who had been abducted. Where had they taken them? To which country? To whom? Even I had begun to hope that Bhaiya and Bhabhi would come looking for me. I had thought that, having waited outside the gates of the city of magic for me to return, they would finally come themselves to take me away. Everyday, ready with my bundle of hopes, I sat outside the door of the house and stared longingly down the lane.

In the winter of that year, soldiers finally came to Sangraon to take me back. But I realized that, apart from being a sister, I was also Munni's mother. I asked myself, "Who are those soldiers? Which country have they come from?" For the first time in my life, my faith was shaken. The city of dreams, which I had built, crumbled into dust and vanished. My life had taken roots in Sangraon, and the roots had spread wide and deep. Who wants life to wither and die? After all, every girl has to bid farewell to her parent's house and go to her husband's place. Every bride has to leave her childhood home after marriage. So what if my brothers had not been present at my wedding? Gurpal had after all spread a carpet of corpses for me. He had painted the road red with blood and illuminated it by setting villages on fire. People had celebrated my wedding with screams and lamentations. According to the changed customs of the times, the air was filled with the bitter smell of smoke, fire and singed flesh. He had carried me to Sangraon; taken me to a small mud house surrounded by wheat fields. I had to spend the rest of my days there.

Once, when Gurpal had brought a book of alphabets for Munni, I had stared at it for a long time. Its letters brought back old memories. I remembered the stories Bhaiya and Bhabhi used to tell me and then add, "Bibi, there are even more interesting stories in other books. You'll read them when you grow up."

When the army came to rescue me like a princess in a fairy-tale, I hid myself. How could I have gone with strangers? Why hadn't Bhaiya and Bhabhi come with them? I was angry with them. I haven't forgiven them till this day.

Munni asked me again, "Ma, why don't you go to your brother's house for Diwali? Ma, why doesn't anyone send us sweets?"

Your Mama never came in search of you, Munni. He never came to take me away. Who has the time to look for anybody? After sometime people find other things which give them support. Bhaiya's children must be as old as Munni. I am sure that whenever they ask about their Mama, their parents don't have to either change the subject or divert the attention of the children.

There are times when, instead of talking about my past, I have to keep quiet. When the women of the neighbourhood sit under a neem tree and sing, I remain silent. Their songs are full of joy. Seasons change. Year after year, either their parents or their brothers come to take them home. Then Asha, Rekha, Pawan and Chandra seem to walk on air. They embrace everyone before they go to their mothers' homes. Their words sound musical. Seasons change.

When young girls of the village climb upto the terraces of their houses, to discover from the flight of crows,the direction from which their future husbands would come, my heart beats so violently that I think it will burst. As time went by, Badi Ma became fond of me. When I broke my links with the past, my bonds with her became stronger and deeper. Now she looks upon me as Lakshmi and proudly shows everyone she meets, the cloth I weave. When other women praise their daughters-in-law, she speaks so glowingly of me that they are envious.

I still dream of a day when a young man will dismount from a horse, and I will call out "Bhaiya" in ecstasy and embrace him. That day the air will be filled with the fragrance of ripe corn, the sky will sparkle with stars and the waters of the canal will sing songs. Oh, why do I stand waiting at the door? For whom? How much longer will I have to carry this dead corpse of my hopes? Why do my eyes fill with tears when I find that the lane outside is desolate? If these tears fall on Munni she will wake up with a start and ask, "Why are you crying, Ma?" How will I ever be able to explain to her the cause of my sorrow?

What answer could I have given Munni, when on the way back from the fair, she asked, "Why do you cry even on Dussera? Are you tired?"

Gurpal lifted both the boys onto his shoulders. Munni and I followed him to Sangraon. Instead of going into exile for a second time, it seemed as if Sita has accepted Ravana's home. How will I ever have the strength to leave again, without the certainty of support?

We left the city lights far behind.

I felt that I had left behind all that could have illuminated my life. But I still haven't learnt to love darkness. I don't know why?

We continued to walk, even though we were tired.

I must keep on walking. Fatigue, like sorrow, has become a part of my body. Like everyone else in this caravan of life, I have to keep on walking. As I take one weary step after another, I wonder if Bhai and Bhaiya ever think of me and feel sad?

It is Munni that I am most afraid of. I know that tomorrow she will ask me questions again, and I will be unable to answer them. Nor, perhaps, will Gurpal and Badi Ma be able to answer them.

Why are some questions so difficult to answer?

In the winter, when the nights are long and cold, sorrow lights a fire and recalls old dreams and tales. Can stories ever be true? The heart is very stubborn. I don't know why it refuses to forget the past.

Are there anxieties beyond Sangraon?

Small streams of cow dung and urine, mingled with the strong odour of ripe wheat, flow through the narrow and muddy lanes of the village. Life too flows on, carrying with it, as it always does, the smell of death.

Yet another day has ended. Slowly, days sweep past me like gusts of wind. I don't know when my journey will ever end.

Original in Urdu.
Translated by Alok Bhalla.

Rajinder Singh Bedi

LAJWANTI

Do not touch lajwanti
For she will curl up
and die.

A Punjabi folk song.

The carnage of the Partition was at last over. Thousands of people joined hands, washed the blood off their bodies, and turned their attention to those who had not been physically mutilated, but whose lives had been shattered and souls had been scarred.

In every lane, in every locality, "Rehabilitation" committees were set-up, and in the beginning there was a lot of enthusiasm for programmes like "Trade for the Displaced," "Land for the Refugees," and "Homes for the Dispossessed." There was, however, one task which was neglected by everyone. That was the programme for the rehabilitation of women who had been abducted and raped. Its slogan was "Honour them. Give them a place in your hearts." This programme was opposed by the priests of Narain Baba's temple, and by all those good and orthodox people who lived in its vicinity.

A committee was formed to campaign for the implementation of the programme by the residents of 'Mohalla Shakoor,' a locality near the Narain Baba's temple. Babu Sunderlal was elected its secretary by a majority of eleven votes. According to Sardar Sahib, the lawyer, the old petitioner of Chauki Kalan and other well respected people of the locality, no one could be trusted to do the job with greater zeal and commitment than Sunderlal, because his own wife had been abducted. Her name was Lajo — Lajwanti.

Every morning Sunderlal, Rasalu, Neki Ram and others, took out a procession through the streets of the city. They sang hymns and folk songs. But whenever they started singing, "Do not touch lajwanti/for she will curl up/and die," Sunderlal's voice would begin to choke with tears. He would continue to follow the procession in silence and wonder about Lajwanti's fate, "Where is she now, how is she, does she ever think of me, will I ever see her again...?" Walking on the hard and stony streets, his steps would falter.

But soon there came a time, when he ceased to think about Lajwanti with so much sorrow. To ease his pain, he began to sympathize with the sufferings of others. He immersed himself in the service of others. But, even though he devoted himself to giving solace to those who needed it, he could not help wondering how fragile human beings really were. A careless word could hurt them. They were delicate like the lajwanti plant, the mere shadow of a hand could make them tremble and wither... And how often had he mistreated Lajwanti himself. How frequently had he thrashed her because he didn't like the way she sat or looked, or the way she served his food!

His poor Lajo was a slender, naive, village girl; she was supple and tender and fresh, like a young mulberry bush! Her skin had been tanned by the sun; she was full of joyous vitality and restless energy. She moved with the mercurial grace of a drop of dew on a large leaf. When Sunderlal first saw her, he thought that she wouldn't be able to endure hardships. Sunderlal himself was tough and well-built. But soon, he realized that she could lift all kinds of heavy weights, bear a lot of suffering, and even tolerate the beatings he gave her. He began to treat her even more cruelly, and lost sight of the limit, beyond which the patience of any human being breaks. Lajwanti herself was, perhaps, responsible for the blurring of these limits. For even after the severest of beatings, she would begin to laugh happily if she saw a faint smile on Sunderlal's face. She would run upto him, put her arms around his neck and say, "If you beat me again, I shall never speak to you..." It would be obvious that she had forgotten the thrashing. Like the other girls of the village, she knew that all husbands beat their wives. Indeed, if some men let their wives show independence and spirit, the women themselves would turn up their noses in contempt and say, "What kind of man is he! He can't even control a woman...!" The fact that husbands were expected to beat their wives was a part of their folk songs. Lajo herself used to sing, "I shall never marry a city boy/He wears boots and my back is slender..."

Nevertheless, when Lajwanti saw a city boy, she fell in love with him. His name was Sunderlal. He had come to her village with the bridegroom's party to attend Lajwanti's sister's wedding. When he saw Lajwanti, he had whispered in the bridegroom's ear, "If your sister-in-law is so spicy yar, your wife must be really hot...!" Lajwanti had overheard Sunderlal. She did not notice that his boots were large and ugly, and she forgot that her back was slender.

Whenever Sunderlal heard that song about lajwanti being sung by the processionists in the morning, he would feel tormented by memories of his wife and he would swear to himself, "If I ever find her again, if I ever again do...I shall honour her and give her a place in my heart...I shall tell everyone that the women who were abducted are innocent. They are victims of the brutality and the rapacity of the rioters...A society which refuses to accept them back, which does not rehabilitate them...is a rotten, a foul society, which should be destroyed..." He would spend long hours pleading with people to take such women back into their homes, to give them the respect due to a mother, daughter, sister or wife. He would exhort people, "Never remind them, either by word or gesture, of the humiliations they have suffered; don't ever reopen their wounds. They are gentle and fragile like the leaves of the lajwanti...if you touch them they will curl up and die..."

In order to make the work of the Committee for the Rehabilitation of Women more generously and widely acceptable, Sunderlal had organized many processions through the city streets. The processionists sang hymns and folk songs. The best time for such processions was around four or five in the morning. Then there was neither the chatter of people nor the noise of traffic. Even the watchful street dogs slept quietly near the warm tandoors. When people, wrapped in their quilts and sleeping comfortably, heard the singers, they would mutter drowsily, "Oh those singers again." Children would open their eyes, listen to the chorus chanting, "Honour them, give them a place in your hearts," and be lulled back to sleep.

People listened to Sunderlal's sermons and pleas, sometimes with patience and sometimes with barely concealed irritation. The most intolerant, however, were those women who had come safely across from Pakistan and were now as complacent as large cauliflowers. Their husbands, who stood around them like stiff and proud sentinels, often turned away from Sunderlal and the processionists with a curse.

But words heard in the morning are not easily forgotten. Even if one doesn't understand them, one repeats them like a futile argument, collides with them, hums them as one goes about the tasks of the day. It is because such words had left their mark on some people that, when Miss. Mridula Sarabhai arranged for the exchange of abducted women between India and Pakistan, some families from Mohalla Shakoor agreed to take them back into their homes. Their relatives went to the outskirts of the town near Chauki Kalan to receive them. For sometime, the women who had been rescued and their relatives, stared at each other like awkward strangers. Then, with their heads hanging in shame and sorrow, they went back to their ruined homes, to try to rebuild their lives. Rasalu, Neki Ram and Sunderlal, encouraged them with slogans, "Long Live Mahinder Singh," "Sohanlal Zindabad"...They shouted slogans till their voices became hoarse.

There were some amongst these abducted women, whose husbands, parents, brothers and sisters refused to recognize them. "Why didn't they die? Why didn't they take poison to preserve their virtue and honour? Why didn't they jump into a well? Cowards, clinging to life! Thousands of women in the past killed themselves to save their chastity!..." Little did they understand the courage of these women, the awesome strength with which they had faced death, but had chosen to carry on living in such a world — a world in which even their husbands refused to acknowledge them.

One woman, whose husband turned away from her, sadly repeated her name again and again, "Suhagwati...Suhagwati..." Another, when she saw her brother in the crowd, cried, "O Bihari, even you refuse to recognize me? You played in my lap as a baby!" Bihari wanted to reach out to her, but stood rooted in his place, paralyzed by the look in the eyes of his parents. His hard-hearted parents turned towards Narain Baba for instructions, he stared up at the sky, as if searching for an answer from the heavens — but the heavens up there are no more than an illusion created by our fearful imagination, and the sky is only the furthest limit to which our eyes can see.

Sunderlal watched the last woman step down from the trucks Miss Sarabhai had brought from Pakistan. Lajo was not in any of them. With patience and quiet dignity, Sunderlal again immersed himself in the work of the committee. Now the committee members had begun to take out processions in the morning and in the evening. They had also started organizing small meetings. At these sessions, the old and asthmatic lawyer, Kalka Prashad, would first make a speech full of Sufi sayings, while Rasalu would stand dutifully beside him with a spittoon. During Kalka Prashad's speech, the loudspeaker would hiss and sputter with strange sounds. Then Neki Ram, the pleader, would get up to say something. But the longer he talked and the more he quoted from the *Shastras* and the *Puranas*, the more he ended up making a case against the cause he meant to plead for. Watching him make a mess of the argument and lose ground, Babu Sunderlal would intervene to say something. But after only a few sentences, he would stop. His voice would choke. Tears would begin to flow down his face and, overcome with emotion, he would be forced to sit down. A strange hush would descend upon the audience. However, the few broken sentences by Sunderlal, spoken from the depth of his sorrowing soul always made a far greater impression than the Sufi sermons of Kalka Prashad. But the effect would never last long. People would shed a few tears, feel morally cleansed and uplifted, and then return to their homes, as unconcerned as ever about the fate of the abducted women...

One evening, the processionists found themselves in the vicinity of a temple, which was located in the stronghold of the traditional and the orthodox. Sitting on a cement platform under a peepal tree, was a crowd of the faithful and the devoted, listening to the *Ramayana*. Narain Baba was reciting that section in which a washerman, having thrown his wife out of his house, had said that he wasn't Raja Ramchandra, who could take Sita back, even after she had lived with Ravana for years. Stung by the rebuke, Ramchandra had ordered Sita, who was virtuous and faithful, out of his palace, even though she was pregnant at that time. Commenting on this incident, Narain Baba said. "That was Ram Rajya! In it even the word of a washerman was respected."

The processionists stood and listened to the *Ramayana* and the commentary. The last sentence provoked Sunderlal and he said, "We don't want such a Ram Rajya, Baba!"

"Shut up!...Who are you?...Quiet... the people in the audience shouted at Sunderlal.

Sunderlal stepped forward and said, "No one can stop me from speaking."

There was another angry chorus of protests, "Silence...We will not let you speak!" From one corner of the crowd someone even shouted, " We will kill you!"

Gently, Narain Baba said, "Sunderlal, you don't understand the sacred traditions of the *Shastras*!"

Sunderlal retorted, "But I do understand that in Ram Rajya, a washerman's voice can be heard, but not the voice of Sunderlal."

The same people, who a moment ago had threatened to kill him, now made space for him under the peepal tree, and said, "Let him speak... let him speak..."

As Rasalu and Neki Ram urged him on, Sunderlal said, "Shri Ram was our God. But, tell me Baba, was it just that Ram accepted the word of a washerman as the truth, and doubted the word of his great and honourable Queen?"

Playing with his beard, Narain Baba answered, "Sita was his wife, Sunderlal! You won't understand the importance of that fact!"

"Yes, Baba," Babu Sunderlal replied. "There are many things in this world which are beyond my comprehension. Yet, I believe that in Ram Rajya, a man cannot commit a crime against his own self. To inflict pain on oneself is as unjust as it is to hurt someone else... Even today, Lord Ram has thrown Sita out of his home because she was forced to live with Ravana...Did Sita commit any sin? Wasn't she, like our mothers and sisters today, a victim of violence and deceit?... Is it a question of Sita's truthfulness, faithfulness or is it a question of Ravana's wickedness? Ravana was a demon...He had ten human heads, but his largest head was that of a donkey!...Once again, our innocent Sitas have been thrown out of their homes...Sita...Lajwanti..."

Sunderlal broke down and wept. Rasalu and Neki Ram picked up their red banners with slogans, which had been pasted on them that morning by school-children, and started yelling,"Sunderlal Zindabad!" Somebody from the procession shouted, "Mahasati Sita, Zindabad!" And someone else cried, "Shri Ramchandra..."

There was pandemonium. Many voices shouted, "Silence! Silence!" But it was too late. What Narain Baba had achieved, after months of careful teaching, had been undone in a few moments. Many people who had been with him, joined the procession led by Kalka Prashad and Hukum Singh, the writer of petitions from Chauki Kalan. These two old people tapped their sticks hard on the ground and raised slogans...Sunderlal walked along with them. There were tears in his eyes. Today he felt his loss even more painfully...The processionists sang with great enthusiasm:

> Do not touch lajwanti
> For she will curl up
> and die.

The people sang lustily; their song filled the air. The sun had not yet risen. The widow in house number 414 of Mohalla Shakoor, stretched her limbs and shifted uneasily in her bed. At that moment Lal Chand, who was from Sunderlal's village and whom Sunderlal and Khalifa Kalka Prashad had helped to set up a ration shop, came running upto Sunderlal. He was excited, and he cried out breathlessly, "Congratulations Sunderlal!"

Sunderlal put some tobacco in his chillum and said, "Congratulations for what, Lal Chand?"

"I just saw Lajo Bhabhi!"

The chillum fell from Sunderlal's hand and the tobacco scattered on the floor. "Where did you see her?" He took Lal Chand by the shou der, and when he didn't answer quickly enough, shook him hard.

"At the Wagah border."

Sunderlal let go of Lal Chand and said despondently, "It must have been someone else."

"No, Bhai," Lal Chand said, trying to convince him, "I did see her...I saw Lajo."

"How could you recognize her?" Sunderlal asked as he gathered the tobacco scattered on the floor and rubbed it on his palm. "All right, tell me what are her identifying marks?" he asked, as he filled Rasalu's chillum with tobacco.

"A tattoo mark on her chin...another on her cheek..."

"Yes...yes...yes..." Sunderlal cried excitedly, "And a third one on her forehead." He didn't want to have any doubts.

Suddenly he recalled all the tattoos marked on Lajwanti's body; she had them painted on her body when she was still a child. They were like the soft green spots on a lajwanti plant which disappear when its leaves curl up. Whenever he tried to touch them with his fingers, Lajwanti would curl up with shyness...would try to hide the tattoo marks on her body, as if they were some secret and hidden treasure, which could be despoiled by a predator and a thief...Sunderlal trembled with fear and hope; his body began to burn with a strange longing and a pure love.

He again put his hand on Lal Chand's shoulder and asked, "How did Lajo reach Wagah?"

Lal Chand replied, "There was an exchange of abducted women between India and Pakistan."

"What happened then?" Sunderlal asked, as he kneeled on the floor, "Tell me, what happened after that?"

Rasalu got up from his cot and, wheezing like a tobacco smoker, asked, "Is it true that Lajo Bhabhi has come back?"

Lal Chand, sticking by his story, said, "At the Wagah border, Pakistan returned sixteen of our women in exchange for sixteen of theirs...But there was some argument...Our volunteers objected that most of the women the Pakistanis had sent back were old, middle-aged and utterly useless. A large crowd gathered and heated words were exchanged. Then one of their volunteers pointed at Lajo Bhabhi and said, 'Is this one old? Look at her...Look...Have you returned any woman who is as beautiful as she is?' Lajo Bhabhi stood there trying to hide her tattoo marks from the curious gaze of people. The argument got more heated. Both sides threatened to take back their 'goods'. I cried out, 'Lajo...Lajo Bhabhi...' But our own policemen beat us with their canes and drove us away."

Lal Chand bared his elbow to show the mark of a lathi blow. Rasalu and Neki Ram continued to sit in silence, and Sunderlal stared vacantly into space. Perhaps, he was thinking about Lajo who had returned and yet was so far away...He seemed like a man who had undergone an ordeal and didn't have the strength left to ask for help. The violence of the Partition, he felt, still continued. It had only taken a new form. The only difference was that now people felt no sympathy for those who had suffered. These days if you asked someone about Lahna Singh and his Bhabhi, Banto, who used to live in Sambharwal, he would curtly answer, "They are dead," and walk away as if nothing serious had happened, nothing out of the ordinary.

There were even more cold-blooded people around now — people who traded in flesh, in living and suffering human beings. They treated women like cows in a cattle-fair. At least, the slave-traders in the past had some conventions and courtesies, and they settled their terms of sale in private. Now the buyers and the sellers had given up the formalities of the old slave-traders. They bargained for the women in the open market-place. The Uzbek buyer stood before rows of naked women and prodded them with his fingers...The women, he rejected, stood before him sobbing helplessly, clutching their garments and hiding their faces in shame.

Sunderlal was getting ready to go to the Wagah border, when he heard about Lajo's return. The news was so sudden that at first he was confused. He couldn't decide what to do. He wanted to go to her at once and yet was afraid to meet her. He was so bewildered that he wanted to spread out all the banners and the placards of the committee on the floor, sit in their midst and weep. But then he pulled himself together and slowly, with measured steps, he made his way to Chauki Kalan where the abducted women were being exchanged.

Suddenly Lajo was standing in front of him and was trembling with fear. She alone knew Sunderlal as no one else knew him. He had always mistreated her, and now that she had lived with another man, she dared not imagine what he would do to her.

Sunderlal looked at Lajo. Her head was covered with a red dupatta like a typical Muslim woman, and one end of it was thrown over her left shoulder. She had learned to imitate the women she had lived with in the hope of evading her captors someday. But recently, events had moved so fast, and she had thought of Sunderlal so desperately, that she had neither the time to change her clothes nor think about the way she had worn her dupatta. She was in no condition to think about the basic differences between Hindu and Muslim culture or worry about whether her dupatta had to be thrown over her left or her right shoulder. She stood before Sunderlal trembling with hope and despair...

Sunderlal was shocked. Lajo looked healthier than before, her complexion looked clearer, her eyes brighter and she had put on weight... She looked different from what he had imagined. He had thought that suffering and sorrow would have reduced her to a mere skeleton, that she wouldn't have the strength to utter even a few words. He was startled to see that she had been well treated in Pakistan. He was puzzled. "If she had been comfortable and happy there why did she agree to return?" he wondered. "Perhaps she has been forced to return by the Indian government..." He didn't, however, say anything to her because he had sworn not to chastise her. It was clear that he had failed to read the signs of pain and humiliation in her face. He didn't notice that the brightness of her face was feverish and that her body had lost its youthful tautness. For Sunderlal, the thought of confronting his wife, who had been abducted and raped, was strangely disturbing. But he did not flinch from doing his duty, and behaved in a manly and courageous manner.

There were many other men at the police station with him. One of them even shouted, "We don't want these sluts...they were defiled by Muslims." But that voice was drowned by slogans being shouted by Rasalu, Neki Ram and the old lawyer of Chauki Kalan. Cutting through all the noise was the harsh and grating voice of Kalka Prashad. He was coughing and shrieking into the loudspeaker about the need for a new *Shastra* and a new *Veda,* which would help people understand the new world confronting them...While people continued to shout slogans, make speeches and scream abuses, Sunderlal took Lajo by her hand and began walking back towards his home. The scene was a re-enactment of the old story about Ramchandra leading Sita back to Ayodhya after years of exile. As in the past, there was rejoicing and sadness, celebrations welcoming the couple home and a sense of shame at the sufferings they had endured.

Even after Lajwanti's return, Sunderlal continued to work with devotion for the Rehabilitation Committee. He fulfilled his pledge both by word and deed, and those who had earlier mocked him as a sentimental idealist, were now convinced of his sincerity. Many people were happy that his wife had returned. There were, however, some who were annoyed at the turn of events. The widow who lived in house number 414 wasn't the only woman who kept her distance from the house of Babu Sunderlal, the social worker.

But Sunderlal ignored all those who either praised him or abused him. The queen of his home had returned and had filled the emptiness of his soul again. He enshrined Lajo like a golden idol in the temple of his heart and guarded her like a jealous devotee. Lajo, who had once trembled before him, was touched by the unexpected kindness and generosity of Sunderlal, and slowly began to flourish and blossom.

Sunderlal no longer called her Lajo. He addressed her as "Devi." Lajo was deliriously happy. She had never known such joy before. She wanted to tell Sunderlal, with tears in her eyes, all that she had suffered so that she could feel clean again. But Sunderlal always shrank away from hearing her story, and Lajo always felt apprehensive about her new life of love and kindness. Sometimes at night, when Sunderlal slept, she would lean over him and gaze at his face. If he ever caught her doing so and asked her for an explanation, she would merely mumble a vague reply, and Sunderlal would fall back into exhausted sleep...

Of course, soon after her return, Sunderlal had asked Lajwanti about those "dark days."

"Who was he?"

Lajwanti had lowered her eyes and said, "Jamal." Then she had raised her eyes apprehensively and looked at Sunderlal. She had wanted to say something more, but the look in his eyes was so strange that she had lowered her eyes in silence once again.

"Did he treat you well?" he had asked as he played with her hair.

"Yes."

"He didn't beat you, did he?"

Lajwanti had leaned back, rested her head against his chest and replied, "No." After a pause, she had added, "He didn't beat me, but I was terrified of him. You used to beat me, but I was never afraid of you...You will never beat me again, will you?"

Sunderlal's eyes had filled with tears and, in a voice full of shame and remorse, he had said, "No, Devi...I shall never beat you again...never..."

"Devi!" Lajwanti had softly echoed and had begun to sob.

At that moment, Lajwanti had wanted to tell him everything, but Sunderlal had said, "Let us forget the past! You didn't do anything sinful, did you? Our society is guilty because it refuses to honour women like you as goddesses. It ought to be ashamed of itself. You shouldn't feel dishonored."

And so, Lajwanti's sorrow had remained locked up in her breast. Helplessly, she had gazed at her body and had realized that, since the Partition, it was no longer her own body, but the body of a goddess. She was happy, ecstatically happy. But she was also apprehensive. She was afraid that her dream world would suddenly be shattered one day, that she would hear the sound of the footsteps of a stranger...

Slowly, happiness was replaced by suspicion. This was not because Sunderlal had begun to mistreat her once again, but because he continued to treat her with excessive kindness. Lajo didn't expect him to be so gentle...She wanted to be Lajo again, the woman who could quarrel with her husband over something trivial and then be caressed. These days the question of a fight didn't even arise. Sunderlal made her feel as if she was something precious and fragile like glass, that she would shatter at the slightest touch...Lajo began to gaze at herself in the mirror and came to the conclusion that she would never be Lajo again. She had returned home, but she had lost everything... Sunderlal had neither the eyes to see her tears nor the ears to hear her sobs...He went out every morning with the procession through Mohalla Shakoor and joined Rasalu and Neki Ram in singing:

Do not touch lajwanti
For she will curl up
and die...!

Original in Urdu.
Translated by Alok Bhalla.

MOHAN RAKESH

THE OWNER OF RUBBLE

They had returned to Amritsar from Lahore after seven-and-a-half years. The hockey match was only an excuse; they were more keen to see the houses and the bazaars which they had known seven-and-a-half years ago and which now belonged to the strangers. Groups of Muslims could be seen strolling down every street of the city. Everything in it caught their attention. For them Amritsar was not just an ordinary city, it was a place of wonder and surprise.

As they walked through its narrow bazaars, they reminded each other of the past, "Look Fatehdina, how very few misri shops are left in Misri Bazaar!...A panwallah now sits at the corner where Sukhi used to light her bhati...Ah, Khan Sahib, this is Namak Mandi! The girls of this lane were really so namkin that...!"

It was after a long time that these bazaars had seen red turkish caps and turbans with well-starched tassels. In the group that had come from Lahore, there were quite a few Muslims who had been forced to leave Amritsar during the Partition. Some of them were surprised at the changes that had taken place there during the last seven-and-a-half years, while others were saddened — "Allah! How did Jayamal Singh acquire so much land ? Were the houses on this side burnt down?...Wasn't this Hakim Asim Ali's shop? Has it now been taken over by a cobbler?"

Some of them could be heard exclaiming, "Wali, that masjid is still standing! These people didn't convert it into a gurudwara!"

The people of the city watched these groups of Pakistanis walking through the city with eagerness and curiosity. There were, of course, some who were still so suspicious of the Muslims that they turned away when they saw them on the road, but there were many others who walked up to them and embraced them. Most people who met the visitors assailed them with a variety of questions — "What is Lahore like these days? Is Anarkali still as bright and gay as it used to be? We hear that the bazaar of Shah Alami Gate has been completely rebuilt. Krishna Nagar couldn't have changed much, could it? Was Rishwatpura really built from money taken in bribes?...They say that the burqa has disappeared from Pakistan, is that really true? — These questions were asked with such sincerity and concern that it seemed as if Lahore wasn't merely a city, but a person who was related to thousands of people who were anxious about its well-being. The visitors from Lahore were treated as the guests of the whole city and most people were delighted to talk to them.

Bansan Bazaar is a poor and run-down locality of Amritsar where lower-class Muslims used to live before the Partition. Most of the shops there used to sell bamboo and wood. They had all been burnt down. The fire in Bansan Bazaar had been the worst of the fires in Amritsar and for sometime it had threatened to send the entire city up in flames. Indeed, the fire had burnt down many of the areas in the neighbourhood of Bansan Bazaar. Somehow it had been brought under control, but for every Muslim house burnt, four or five Hindu homes had also been reduced to ash. Now, seven-and-a-half years later a few structures had been rebuilt, but there were still piles of rubble strewn everywhere. These new buildings, standing in the midst of ruins, presented a strange sight.

As usual, there wasn't much activity in Bansan Bazaar that day, because most of the people who had once lived there had perished along with their homes, and those who had fled, didn't have the courage to return. That day, however, one old and frail Muslim did venture into the deserted bazaar, but when he saw the new buildings standing next to ruins, he felt as if he was lost in a labyrinth. He reached the lane which turned to the left, but instead of entering it, he stood outside it, perplexed. He couldn't believe that it was the lane he wanted to take. On one side of the lane a few children were playing hopscotch, and a little further up two women were screaming and cursing each other.

"Everything has changed except the curses!" the old Muslim mumbled to himself as he stood there resting on his cane. His legs were bent and his pyjamas were a little torn. His sherwani, which didn't reach upto his knees, was patched in several places.

A child came running out of the lane crying. The old man called out to him in a kind voice, "Come here, son! Come, I'll give you something nice, come." He put his hand in his pocket and began searching for something to give to the child. The child stopped crying for a moment, but then pouted and began to weep again. A young girl of about sixteen or seventeen years came running after him, caught him by his arm and started dragging him back into the lane. The girl picked him up, put her arms around him, kissed him and said, "Stop crying, you little devil! If you don't, that Muslim will catch you and take you away! So stop crying!"

The old Muslim put the coin, he had taken out to give to the child, back into his pocket. He took off his cap, scratched his head, and then put the cap under his arm. His throat was dry and his legs were shaking. He supported himself against the porch of a closed shop in the street and then put his cap on again. There was now a three-storey house in the open yard across from the entrance to the lane, where there used to be a shed for logs of wood in the past. Two well-fed kites were sitting absolutely still on the electric wires running past the house. There was a patch of sunlight near the lamp-post. The old Muslim stood quietly for a while in the sunlight and watched the dust being raised by the wind. Then, almost involuntarily, he sighed, "Ya Mallik!"

A young man came towards the lane swinging a bunch of keys on a chain. Seeing the old man standing there, he asked, "Miyan, why are you standing here?"

The old man felt his heart beat a little faster and a slight tremor of excitement ran through his body. He moistened his lips, looked at the young man curiously and asked, "Son, aren't you Manori?"

The young man stopped swinging the key chain around, clutched it in his hand and asked with surprise, "How do you know my name?"

"Seven-and-a-half years ago you were only this tall," the old man said, as he tried to smile.

"Did you come from Pakistan today?"

"Yes! We used to live in this lane once," the old man said. "My son, Chiragdin, was your tailor. Six months before the Partition, we had built a new house for ourselves here."

"Oh, Gani Miyan!" Manori said, as he recognized him.

"Yes, son, I am Gani Miyan! I know that I shall never meet Chirag, his wife and his children in this life again. But I thought that I should at least see our house once again." The old man took his cap off, scratched his head, and wiped his tears as they flowed down his face.

"You had left this place long before the Partition, hadn't you?" Manori asked with sympathy in his voice.

"Yes, son, it was my misfortune that I escaped alone before the Partition. If I had stayed here, then along with them, I too would have..." As he said that, he felt that he ought to be more discreet. He stopped himself in mid-sentence, but he let the tears flow from his eyes.

"Forget the past, Gani Miyan, what's the use of thinking about it now?" Manori reached out and held Gani Miyan's arm. "Come, I'll show you your house."

In the meanwhile, a rumour had spread through the lane that a Muslim standing at the entrance of the lane had tried to kidnap Ramdasi's son...His sister had rescued him in time, otherwise the Muslim would surely have carried him away! As soon as they heard this news, the women, who were sitting on low stools in the lane outside, picked up their stools and shut themselves in their houses. They also called indoors, all the children who were playing in the lane. By the time Manori and Gani walked into the lane, there was hardly anyone to be seen there, except for a single street-hawker, and Rakkha Pahlwan, who was sleeping comfortably under a peepal tree near the well. Of course, there were lots of curious faces peeping out into the lane from behind the windows and the doors of the houses. When they saw Gani walking with Manori, they began to whisper together. Despite the fact that his hair was now completely white, they had no difficulty in recognizing Abdul Gani, the father of Chiragdin.

"Your house was there," Manori pointed to a heap of rubble in the distance. Gani stared in astonishment in that direction. He had reconciled himself to the death of Chirag, his wife and children a long time ago. But he wasn't prepared for the shock he received, when he saw the ruins of his house. His mouth became parched, his knees became weak.

"That heap of stone and ash?" he asked in disbelief.

Manori noticed that the colour had drained from the old man's face. He held him a little more firmly and told him as if he was narrating a distant event, "Your house was burned down during the riots."

Supporting himself on his cane, Gani somehow walked upto the spot where his house had once stood. All that remained there now was a heap of dust and ash with a few broken and burnt pieces of brick. Things made of iron and wood had been picked out of the rubble a long time ago. By some strange chance, the charred frame of a door still stood in the middle of the rubble. Beyond it were two almirahs which had been blackened by smoke. After gazing at the heap of rubble for sometime, Gani whispered to himself, "Is this all...is this all that is left?" He staggered a little, and had to hold onto the charred door-frame for support. A moment later, he sat down and rested his head against the door-frame. Then he began to moan quietly, "Oh, my Chiragdin!"

The door-frame, which had stood like a proud relic for seven- and-a-half years in the middle of the heap of rubbish, was so badly seared that it had begun to crumble. The moment Gani leaned his head against it, small bits of it disintegrated and scattered on the ground around him. A few pieces of wood and ash fell on his cap and on his white hair. Along with the cinders, a long worm also fell out of the wooden door near his feet. It raised its head a few times, slithered here and there looking for some hole to hide in, and then wriggled desperately towards a brick-lined drain that ran past the spot.

By now many more people were staring out of their windows. They were sure that something dramatic was about to happen — "Chiragdin's father, Gani, is here," they whispered. "He will find out what happened seven-and-a-half years ago" — They felt that the rubble-heap would reveal the whole story — That evening Chiragdin was eating his dinner upstairs, when Rakkha Pahlwan shouted for him from the street...asked him to come down for a minute. In those days, Rakkha was the uncrowned King of the lane. Even the Hindus were afraid of him; Chirag was a Muslim. Chirag got up without finishing his food, and went downstairs to meet him. His wife, Zubaida, and his two daughters, Kishwar and Sultana, watched from the windows upstairs. The moment Chirag stepped out of the door, Rakkha grabbed him by his shirt-collar, threw him down in the street and sat on his chest. Chirag caught Rakkha's hand in which he held a knife and screamed, "Rakkha Pahlwan, don't kill me! O God, help...save me!" Zubaida, Kishwar and Sultana screamed helplessly and ran downstairs wailing. One of Rakkha's disciples pushed Chirag's arm aside, while Rakkha pressed his knee down on his thighs and shouted, "Don't scream, you sister-fucker...You want Pakistan, don't you! I only want to send you there! Now go!" By the time Zubaida, Kishwar and Sultana reached the door downstairs, Chirag had already been dispatched to Pakistan.

By then all the windows in the neighborhood had been shut. Those who had witnessed the murder, had shut their doors and had refused to get involved. Even behind shut doors, they could hear the screams of Zubaida, Kishwar and Sultana for a very long time. Rakkha and his companions had arranged to have them sent to Pakistan too that very night, but by a different and longer route. Their bodies were later discovered, not in Chirag's house, but in the canal nearby.

For two days, the house was raided and completely ransacked. After everything had been looted, someone set the house on fire. Rakkha Pahlwan swore that if he ever caught the person who had lit the fire, he would bury him alive in the earth. He had killed Chirag because he wanted to grab that house. He had even bought all that was necessary to perform the purification rituals. But he was never able to discover who had burnt the house down.

Over the last seven-and-a-half years, everyone had accepted the fact that Rakkha was the owner of the rubble that had been left behind. He would neither allow anyone to tie a cow or a buffalo there, nor let anyone put up a temporary shed. No one ever dared to take even a small piece of brick from the rubble-heap without his permission.

People looking out of their windows were sure that Gani would discover the entire story — that he would be able to read the history of his family's fate in the pile of rubbish. They watched as Gani sat in the middle of the rubble, scratched ash from the rubble with his nails and scattered it over his head. Then he put his arms around the door-frame and wailed, "Speak to me, Chirag! Say something! Tell me where you are? O Kishwar! O Sultana! My children! O God, why is Gani still alive!"

The fragile door-frame crumbled a little more, and pieces of charred wood fell to the ground and scattered.

Rakkha Pahlwan, who had been sleeping under the peepal tree, woke up or was woken up by someone. When he learnt that Abdul Gani had returned from Pakistan and was sitting on the debris of his house, his mouth went dry. He cleared his throat and spat on the ground near the well. When he looked towards the rubble-heap, his heart beat faster and his lower lip became a little more pendulous.

"Gani is sitting in the middle of the ruins of his house," Laccha Pahlwan, one of his disciples, informed Rakkha as he came and sat down next to him.

"The ruins of his house? That rubble is mine!" Rakkha said in a hoarse voice.

"But he is sitting there," Laccha said and looked at him meaningfully.

"Let him sit there. Go and get my chillum!" Rakkha said, as he stretched out his legs and massaged his naked thighs.

"Suppose Manori tells him ...?" Laccha asked, as he got up to fill the chillum.

"Does Manori want to get into trouble?"

Laccha left to get the chillum.

Dry leaves from the peepal tree had scattered around the well. Rakkha picked them up one by one and crushed them with the palms of his hands. After Laccha had wrapped a cloth filter around the chillum and had handed it to Rakkha, he took a long puff and asked, "Has Gani talked to anyone else?"

"No."

"Here, take it," Rakkha said as he coughed and passed the chillum to Laccha.

Manori helped Gani off the pile of rubble and supported him as he walked towards the well. Laccha crouched on the ground and puffed hard on the chillum. He watched Rakkha's face and also kept his eye on Gani.

Manori walked a little ahead of Gani, as if he wanted to make sure that Gani walked past the well without noticing

Rakkha. But Gani had already seen Rakkha and had recognized him from the way in which he was sitting with his legs stretched out on the ground. As soon as Gani came near the well, he stretched his arms out and said, "Rakkha Pahlwan!"

Rakkha looked up, squinted a little and stared at Gani. Then he grunted, but didn't utter a word.

"Don't you recognize me?" Gani asked, as he dropped his arms. "I am Gani, Abdul Gani, Chiragdin's father!"

The people at the windows continued to gossip — "Now that they have come face to face, they are bound to talk about what happened...Maybe they'll abuse each other...Now Rakkha can't touch Gani. The times have changed...He thought that he was the owner of that rubble!...That heap of rubbish belongs to neither of them. The government owns the ruin!...That bastard doesn't even let anyone tie his cow there!...Manori is a coward. Why didn't he tell Gani that it was Rakkha who had killed Chirag, his wife and his children?...Rakkha is not a human being, he is a wild bull. He roams the streets all day long like a bull!...Look how thin poor Gani is! His beard is completely white..."

Gani sat down by the side of the well and said, "Look at my fate Rakkha! When I went away, I had a fine and happy household, and now there is nothing left but that heap of dust! The only sign of a house which was once inhabited! To tell you the truth, I don't want to leave that pile of rubble behind." His eyes filled with tears.

Rakkha pulled his legs in and sat cross-legged. Then he picked up his towel which was lying on the parapet of the well and wrapped it around his shoulders. Laccha pushed the chillum towards him and he started puffing on it.

"Tell me, Rakkha, how did it happen?" Gani asked as he wiped his eyes. "You were friends. You loved each other like brothers. Couldn't he have hidden in your house? He was bright enough to have thought of that."

"I don't know," Rakkha replied, but he sounded strangely unconvincing. His mouth was dry. There were drops of sweat on his moustache, and they trickled down to his lips. His forehead felt heavy, and his back ached for support.

"What is it like in Pakistan?" Rakkha asked. His voice was tense and the veins on his neck were throbbing. He used his towel to wipe the sweat under his armpits, and then he cleared his throat and spat into the lane.

"What can I tell you, Rakkha?" Gani said as he leaned with both his hands on his cane. "Only God knows how I live. If Chirag had been with me, the story would have been different...I tried to persuade him to go with me. But he was determined not to leave his newly built house...This is our lane, he said obstinately, there is no danger here. Like an innocent dove, he didn't consider the threat from outside. All four of them gave up their lives trying to protect that house!...Rakkha, he depended on you. He used to say that, as long as Rakkha was around, nobody would dare to hurt him. But when death finally came, even Rakkha couldn't help."

Rakkha tried to stretch his back because it had begun to ache badly. His sides too had begun to pain severely. He couldn't breathe with ease. He felt as if he had stomach cramps. He was perspiring badly and his feet seemed to be full of thorns. He saw flashes of bright light burst like fireworks before his eyes. He could neither open his mouth nor utter a word. He wiped his face with one end of his towel. And then, quite involuntarily, he whispered to himself, "Oh dear God, have mercy on me, have mercy on me!"

Gani noticed that Rakkha's lips had become dry, and there were deep and dark circles under his eyes. He placed his hand on Rakkha's shoulder and said, "What happened was fated, Rakkhiya. There is no use moaning about the past! May God bless the virtuous, and may He forgive those who have sinned! Now that I have met all of you, I feel as if I have seen Chirag again. May Allah keep you in good health." And then, with the help of his cane, he stood up. As he started to leave, he said, "Allow me to take my leave, Rakkha Pahlwan."

Rakkha tried to say something. He folded both his hands. Gani looked around at the neighborhood once more with regret and longing, and then walked slowly out of the lane.

The people at the windows started whispering once again — "Once outside the lane, Manori will tell Gani the entire story... Rakkha didn't dare to say anything to Gani...Now he won't dare to stop us from tying our cows in that area...Poor Zubaida! She was such a fine woman! Rakkha neither has a home nor a family, how can he respect the wives and sisters of others?..."

After sometime the women came out of their houses into the lane. The children began to play gilli-danda. Two teenage girls began to argue with each other about something and then came to blows.

Rakkha continued to sit by the well till late into the evening smoking his chillum and coughing. People who passed by that place, asked him, "Rakkhey Shah, I hear that Gani came from Pakistan today."

"Yes, he came," Rakkha would answer every time.

"What happened?"

"Nothing happened. He went away."

When night fell, Rakkha went to the shop on the left side of the lane as usual, and sat on the porch. Everyday, he used to greet his acquaintances as they passed by, and tell them about the secrets of the lottery or give them remedies for good health. But that day, he told Laccha about the pilgrimage he had made fifteen years ago to Vaishno Devi. When he went back into the lane after sending Laccha home, he saw that Loku Pundit had tied his buffalo near the ruins of Gani's house. Instinctively, he picked up his stick and drove it away,

"Tat, tat, tat...tat, tat...!"

Then he sat down to rest for a while near the charred remains of the door-frame in the middle of the rubble. Since there was no street-light nearby, it was dark there. He could hear the soft sound of water running through the drain nearby. The silence of the night was pierced by all sorts of sounds rising from the mound of dust and ash...chick, chick, chick...kirrr-rrrr-ki-ki-ki... Suddenly a crow, who had lost his bearings, fluttered around, and then came and sat on the door-frame. The wooden frame crumbled a little more, and pieces of burnt wood fell here and there. As soon as the crow settled down on the door-frame, a dog, who had been sleeping in one corner of the rubble, got up and started barking at it loudly — Bow-wow-wow-wow...bow-wow-wow-wow. At first the crow stayed where it was, but then it flapped its wings rapidly, and flew upto the peepal tree near the well. After chasing away the crow, the dog turned towards Rakkha Pahlwan and began to growl at him. In order to chase away the dog, Rakkha shouted at him, "Go away, shoo, shoo..."

But the dog became more aggressive and began to bark at Rakkha more loudly — Bow-wow-wow-wow...

"Hat-hat...durr-durr-durr...!"

"Bow-wow-wow-wow...bow-wow-wow-wow...!"

Rakkha picked up a stone and threw it at the dog. The dog moved away a little, but didn't stop barking. Rakkha called it a son of a bitch, got up and slowly walked upto the well and lay down on the platform. As soon as he left, the dog followed him and continued to bark after him. After sometime, when the dog saw no one moving about in the lane, it twitched its ears and went back to the rubble. It then sat down in a corner and continued to growl.

Original in Hindi.
Translated by Alok Bhalla.

INTIZAR HUSAIN

A LETTER FROM INDIA

My dear Kamaran,

May God bless you and may you live long. May you continue to be a man of lofty ideals. You are dearer to me than my own life. You cannot imagine how I yearn to see you again and how anxious I am to receive a letter from you.

I have often tried to get news about you from others and have often attempted to send you letters from here. Unfortunately, however, I have always failed. I addressed a letter to you and sent it to Ibrahim's son, Yousuf, and begged him to forward it to you at Karachi. I also requested him to send me your letter in reply as soon as he received it. He is, as you know, in Kuwait and has a good income. That seems to have gone to his head and has made him forget his duty. He did not even bother to inform me if he had posted my letter to you and whether he had received a letter in reply. When Sheikh Saddique Hasan's son was going to England, I gave him yet another letter addressed to you and requested him to post it to you from London. But that haramzada too did not inform me whether he had posted it or not.

I am very worried about Imran Miyan. I do not know if he reached Karachi. He should, at least, have informed us if he had. Imran Miyan passed through this place two or two-and-a-half months after the war. Winter had just set in. I had pulled my cot from the verandah back into the room. Late one night there was a knock on the door. Puzzled and anxious, I wondered who had come knocking at my door at that hour and what he could possibly want? I opened the door and examined the man standing there from head to toe. At first I didn't recognize him. But then I realized that he was my own flesh and blood, even though he had changed beyond recognition. I embraced him and said, "Son, we didn't send you to Pakistan in this shape. What have you done to yourself?" But immediately afterwards, I regretted what I had said. Was it not enough that the one whom God had entrusted in our care, had been returned to us? A man should thank God in all circumstances. He must never utter a word of complaint lest it becomes, like the word of an infidel, a curse and rebounds on him. Men of weak faith have done such deeds that there is no room left for complaint. We should silently endure everything and be afraid of the anger of the wise and almighty God.

When your Chachi saw Imran Miyan, she was astonished. She hugged him and wept. I had resolved not to question him about anything, but she could not restrain herself and asked, "Why didn't you bring your wife with you? Where have you left your children?" Those questions unnerved Imran Miyan and he turned pale. Your Chachi and I were concerned. Then we decided that we would not bring up the painful matter again.

Imran Miyan stayed with us for three days. How strange those three days were! He neither talked nor laughed. He merely sat lost in thought. On the third day he decided that he wanted to visit the grave of Miyan Jani. I blessed him and said, "Son, you should of course read a prayer on your grandfather's grave. It has been more than twenty-five years! But it is not advisable to go there in the daytime. You were born here and are a part of this soil. You will be easily recognized." He laughed bitterly, and said, "Chachajan, I walked through the basti before I came to your house. Even the soil did not recognize me." Well, I took Imran Miyan to the graveyard in the evening. I showed him all the new graves of the family. He recognized the old graves without my help. As it got darker, it became difficult to make out the graves clearly. When we reached Miyan Jani's grave, Imran Miyan was overcome with emotions. I, too, had tears in my eyes. That grave is old and in disrepair. The harshringar tree, which used to grow by its side, withered some time ago. You may remember that Miyan Jani used to be very fond of harshringar. He had planted many harshringar trees in his garden and used to look after them with great care. The trees always gave so many flowers that the girls of the family used them throughout the year to dye their dupattas and the cooks to flavour the biryani made for every party. Even then lots of flowers used to be left over. But a harshringar tree needs to be tended carefully. And I can no longer look after everything by myself. The tree next to Miyan Jani's grave was the last one remaining in the graveyard. It fell in the rains before the war.

Now there are no harshringar trees left either in our garden or in the graveyard. By the grace of Allah, we still retain the garden. We do so only because it is next to the graveyard and is regarded as a part of it. Over the last twenty-seven years so many trees have fallen, and with them so many memories have been buried, that one should now consider the garden to be an extension of the graveyard. The few trees that still remain in it are like tombstones on the graves of days long dead. Anyway, Imran Miyan knows what state the garden is in. If he reached Karachi, he must have told you about it.

Imran Miyan left early next morning. He had spent the night beside Miyan Jani's grave. I, too, sat with him. At dawn, when the birds began to chatter, he stretched himself, stood up and begged me to give him permission to leave. I was concerned and said, "Why do you want to go away? Now that you have returned, why don't you stay?" In a dry voice, he replied, "No one recognizes me here any longer." I said, "Son, your safety lies in your not being recognized." He wasn't convinced. He had decided to leave. I asked, "Where will you go, son?" He said, "Wherever my feet carry me." I sensed, however, from what he told me, that he was first planning to go to Kathmandu and that he would then try to get to Karachi. I was sad. But his insistence and my concern for him if the news of his presence got out, made me give him permission to leave. I untied an amulet from my arm and tied it on his. I recited a prayer for his safety. Before he left, I implored him to send me news about himself as soon as he crossed the border. Since that day, however, I haven't heard from him.

Here one rarely ever gets news from Pakistan. And I don't feel like believing the news that does get across. One day, Sheikh Saddique Hasan told me that everyone in Pakistan had become a socialist and that onions were being sold there for five rupees a seer. When I heard that news my heart sank. But then I told myself that since Sheikh Sahib was an old Congressee, he couldn't possibly give me any other kind of news about Pakistan, and that I shouldn't believe what he says. A few days later, I heard something which contradicted the bad news. I was told that Pakistan had declared that the Mirzayis were non-Muslims. When I passed on that information to Sheikh Sahib he was unable to come up with anything to counter it. May Allah have mercy on Pakistan and reward it for its goodness. We live amongst infidels. We follow un-Islamic rituals and practices here and can't raise our voices in protest. Non-believers have built a masjid near our haveli. When they proclaim the ameen loudly, we have to keep quiet.

Oh yes, Sheikh Sahib once brought me news about you too. He told me that you had built a house. That there was a sofa-set in your sitting room and a television. I was happy to hear that news. Thank God that everything you longed for here and didn't have, had been granted to you there.

The haveli is in disrepair. The wooden beams supporting the roof, which were already sagging, have begun to sag some more after the last rains. The diwankhana is in such a bad condition that if you look up towards its ceiling you can catch a glimpse of the sky. As you well know, our financial situation is rather bad. If you can send me some money, I can use it to repair Jani Miyan's grave and have some clay plastered on the ceiling of the diwankhana. There is no need to undertake any more repairs at present. The court case regarding the haveli has yet to be settled. My late and respected brother had placed all the papers regarding the case in my custody before he left in 1947. With God's help, I have thus far handled all the appearances in court satisfactorily and have always hired competent lawyers. God willing, the case will be decided soon and in our favour. But who can predict the arrival of the angel of Death? He may come at any time. I am very concerned about who will continue to fight the case after I am gone.

In whichever direction I cast my eye, I see only darkness. My son Akhtar — what can I tell you about his character! He has changed his name to Premi, and he goes to the radio station to take part in dramas! Khalida, the daughter of my younger brother, Marhoom, has married a Hindu lawyer! Now she wears, without any sense of shame, a saree and puts a bindi on her forehead! You can, of course, shed more light on the state of our family in Pakistan than I can. But I hear that Appajan's daughter, Nargis has married someone of her own choice, and that the one she has married is a Wahabi! I also hear that Appajan herself sits in her son's car without a veil covering her face, and that she bargains, publicly and without shame, with all the cloth merchants!

Alas, I am the one who has been spared death to witness all this and write about it. My late and respected elder brother and my younger brother passed away at the right time. When I go to the graveyard to read a prayer over the graves of Miyan Jani and my younger brother, I always remember my elder brother and say a prayer for him too. What times we live in! These days none of us can go and read a prayer over Miyan Jani's grave! The graves of our family — our family which had lived in one place and whose dead had been buried under the same soil — are now scattered across three different lands. I had respectfully urged my elder brother to go to Karachi — "Since you are determined to leave us, go and live with Kamaran Miyan. That would be the proper thing to do." But his love for his youngest son drew him to Dhaka. His untimely death was a great shock to all of us. But I now believe that his death was an act of mercy by God. He was a good soul. And God did not wish that he should live to witness these days of evil and suffering. It is only a sinner like me who has been condemned to see such days.

Now that the protective shadow of our elders has been lifted from over our heads, and now that our family has been divided and scattered over Hindustan, Pakistan and Bangladesh, and now that I am standing at the edge of my grave, I think that the history of our family, which had been given to me as a sacred trust, should be passed on to you because you are now the eldest member of the family after me. But the history entrusted to me can only be told to you orally and from memory. My elder brother had taken the memories of the family and the history of its lineage with him to Dhaka. When the members of his family were killed in Dhaka and buried there, the memories of the family were also buried with them. Imran Miyan came back here empty handed. The biggest calamity for our family is that its history has been lost. Our forefathers, who were the descendents of Saadat-e-Azam, had preserved that history even when the times were bad and they had to suffer a lot of pain and torment. We, however, have to bear the shame and sorrow of losing the history of our family and forgetting our lineage. These days we are a family which has been afflicted by misfortunes. Now we have neither a place which is our own nor a history to remember. We are the victims of a time when everything has fallen apart. Some members of the family died in Hindustan, some disappeared in Bangladesh, and some wander from place to place in search of a home in Pakistan. Our faith has been corrupted. It has been polluted by un-Islamic rites and customs. Some of us have married outside our community or into different sects. If this continues much longer, our lineage will be completely wiped out and there will be no one left to remind us about who we are and who our ancestors were.

Let me, therefore, tell you, my son, that we are the descendents of the holy and renowned Sayyids. Our family can be traced back to Hazrat Imam Musa Karzan. But, al-hamdulillah, we are not Rafzis. We are Sahihul Aqeeda Hanafi Muslims. The true followers of Ashab-e-Kabar, followers of Ahele Bait. Miyan Jani's practice was to keep a fast of Ashoora and sit on the prayer mat for the entire day. Our family was in possession of holy-beads which used to turn a deep red on Ashoora. Miyan Jani used to tell us that the beads had come from the place where our forefather, Sayyidana Hazrat Imam had first got down from his horse and set foot on earth. As the beads turned red, our grandfather would go into a trance, but he never beat his breast or wept. He thought that it was not proper to do so. However, large pots of khichdi were always cooked and distributed amongst the poor and the needy. After the Partition, we were left with only one large pot. Last year, we lost even that. We could only afford to make a small pot of channa and have it distributed amongst the poor. Allah alone knows what our condition will be next year. Things are becoming more and more expensive and our existence is becoming more and more precarious. We know the price of onions in Pakistan. But, son, always remember this. Once prices rise, they never fall, in the same way, as once our standards of morality decline, they can never be raised again. Pray that you may be spared from witnessing the days when prices begin to rise and morals begin to decline. When such a time comes, those who truly believe in God should do penance and recite the *Koran*. There are many signs that such a day will be upon us soon, and the wise know how to read them.

Anyway, I was going to tell you the history of our family — the family which I had known when it was together and which is now scattered. Miyan Jani summoned the three of us when he was at his death bed and pleaded with God that his grave should always be scattered with the sweet smelling flowers of harshringar. He told us that his father Sayyid Hatim Ali had told him, when he was himself at his death bed, that his father, Sayyid Rustum Ali had orally passed on to him the entire history of their family. The written documents concerning our family were partially lost in the tumultuous times of 1857, when our forefathers had to leave their home in Bayees Khala and wander for years from place to place without any shelter. It is out of respect for our ancestors that I want to tell you that we originally came from Isphahan. The exiled Emperor Humayun, when he was gathering his forces together to regain his lost dynasty, had invaded Isphahan. Our ancestor, Meer Mansoor Muhammad, was in those days a date merchant. He was known as an ocean of learning. When he came to Hindustan, he was acknowledged as the light of faith. His grave in Akbarabad is still a place of pilgrimage. The grave is now covered only with dust. When unmarried girls pick up dust from it and put it in the parting of their hair, it turns into red sindhoor within a year; and when childless wives carry away a bit of that dust in their saree, they always return with a child to give their thanks and cover the grave with a cloth. During the reign of Shahjahan, the descendants of our worthy ancestor left Akbarabad and settled in Jahanabad. During the troubles of 1857, however, they had to flee from their homes. Our ancestor, Rustum Ali, didn't take a single coin with him. He did, however, tie the parchment, on which the family tree was drawn, to his waistband and clutch the bundle of papers containing the history of the family under his arms as he ran. On the way he was, unfortunately, attacked by dacoits. In the ensuing fight, the papers were scattered. He could only gather together a few of them, the rest were lost. By the grace of God, the paper containing the family tree was saved and not a single word on it was defaced.

After wandering like haunted fugitives across dusty lands, they passed through this settlement. They found this piece of earth hospitable and decided to build their home on it. As one knows, when the earth is kind, it is soft and gentle like the bosom of a beloved and is generous like the lap of a mother. When it becomes cruel, however, it behaves more cold bloodedly than an Emperor and more callously than a hard-hearted miser. The truth is that this earth treated our family generously for a long time. It nurtured our family at its bosom, and watched it grow and prosper like a jealous mother who hugs all her children in her embrace and does not let them out of her sight. Before the Partition only three members of the family had left home. Bhai Ashraf Ali, Bhai Farrukh and Pyare Miyan. Bhai Ashraf Ali, was the son of my chachajan and was one year older than Kibla Bhaisahib. He was, therefore, your taya. By the grace of God, he became a Deputy Collector and was posted in different districts. However, all the gifts and tributes that used to be offered to him he used to send here. Bhai Farrukh, who was his younger brother, was of the same age as myself. He was in the forest department and spent his youth in the Central Provinces. All the wooden furniture that you saw in our haveli had been made and sent by him. Both the brothers were the pride of the family. They spent their youth outside, but they spent their last days in the comfortable embrace of this earth.

Pyare Miyan was the favourite son of our Phuphi Amma. He had been so spoilt by the love and affection showered on him that he grew up to be an undisciplined man who couldn't refrain himself from indulging in all the seven deadly sins. He was the first one in our family to see the biscope. Once, he even enticed me from the path of duty. After I saw Madhuri, my heart was perturbed for sometime, but I controlled myself and never again accompanied him. Pyare Miyan was already addicted to the theatre. But after the biscope came to town, he became its ardent disciple.

He was so smitten by Sulochana in *Bombai Ki Billi* that one day he stole Phuphi Amma's gold ear rings and ran away to Bombay. Miyan Jani sent word to him that he was no longer welcome back — "Sahibzade, don't ever come back home." In Bombay, a dancing girl duped him into believing that she would help him to meet Sulochana. She didn't of course introduce him to Sulochana, but ensnared him into marrying her. He spent his youth in Bombay. When he got the news of Phuphi Amma's death, he came back home. By then he was old. He had a long, white beard and a string of beads in his hand. He wept a lot for his mother. All of us urged him to stay back. But he said that he couldn't possibly do so without Miyan Jani's permission. Unfortunately, however, Miyan Jani had already departed from this earth. So, who could give him permission to stay back? He decided to return to Bombay. That was in the year 1947. Trains were being attacked and looted. We tried to persuade him not to travel at that time, but he didn't listen to our advice. He got into a train. He never reached Bombay. Who knows what happened to him on the way?

Pyare Miyan was our family's first offering in the riots of forty-seven. I have made a list of all the names and collected the figures of our family members who have died since then. Thirty-one were embraced by God, twenty-one were murdered, five died naturally, seven were martyred by the Hindus in Hindustan, and fourteen were sent to God by their Muslim brothers in Pakistan. Out of the last fourteen, one was shot by Ayub Khan's henchmen during the elections for supporting Motrima Fatima Jinnah. Ten died in East Pakistan. In this count, I have not included Imran Miyan. A man should never despair of God's mercy. Deep in my heart, I feel that Imran Miyan, who is a part of my flesh and blood, is alive and if he hasn't yet reached Karachi then he is still in Kathmandu.

Kathmandu reminds me — Bhaiya Farrukh's son, Sharafat, had also passed through this place. He had escaped from Dhaka and was on his way to Kathmandu when he decided to stop here for a while. He is the exact replica of Pyare Miyan. Calamity has had no effect on him. During his stay here he went fearlessly to see the biscope everyday. When it was time for him to leave, he packed up to go to Bombay instead of Kathmandu. When I asked why he had decided to go to Bombay, he said that he wanted to meet Rajesh Khanna. I said, "You idiot, is Rajesh Khanna, E. Bellimoria or A. Bellimoria, that you should be so anxious to meet him?" But, he turned a deaf ear to what I said and left for Bombay. Later, he sent me a letter from Sri Lanka to inform me that he was well. I don't know what misfortunes drove him there. When I saw Sharafat, I thanked God. But his behaviour didn't please me.

I have heard that after going to Pakistan, the girls of our family have become more independent. Each one of them, I believe, has married a man of her own choice. Before the Partition, there was one such incident which could have brought a bad name to our family. But it was tactfully dealt with. One day, a kite fell on the roof of our younger Phupha's house. Now, as you know, it's not a good sign when a kite flutters over the roof of a house where a young girl is growing up or when a pebble falls into its courtyard. In those days, younger Phupha's daughter, Khatija, was coming of age. The younger Phupha went and reported the matter to Miyan Jani. She also placed before him the note which had been tied to the kite. Miyan Jani boiled with rage. He shouted and screamed, "How dare Raza Ali's son drop a kite on our roof!" But, after our younger Phupha explained the entire matter to him in detail, he cooled down. He had no choice but to get Khatija married to that ruffian and send her to her new home. Raza Ali had never even dreamt of getting a girl from our family in marriage for his son. He agreed at once. But at the last moment he insisted that the sighah had to be read at the ceremony. Miyan Jani had to swallow his pride and accept his condition. But the result of that affair has not been happy. Half of Khatija's children are teetars and half are batters. One son takes care of the niaz of the Gyarveen Sharif, and the other does azadari at Moharrum. Anyway, now our entire family is divided into teetars and batters.

Our family tree has been lost and our lineage has been sullied for ever. How will our family be recognized as a distinctive one in the future? Indeed, I feel that our family members are like the falling leaves of a tree which are scattered by the wind and crumbled into dust.

Azeez, I am now the only one left to mourn over scattered leaves. I remember those days when this family was prosperous and flourishing, and we could count the leaves which had been blown away.

I have records not only of those who have died. My records also contain the names of those who are still alive and work somewhere. I have kept a list of their names and addresses, and I have followed the history of those who went away to other countries and wander in other lands. I shall soon send you that document because it is full of revealing details. Who knows what the future has in store for me. I am like a fading lamp in the morning light. The flame has begun to die and my eyes have begun to close. You are the new light of this ill-fated family. It is your duty to light the path of those who wander in darkness. Of course, I know that experience teaches us that leaves which have once been scattered can never be gathered again. A family which has once broken apart can never be united again. But it is man's duty to try. So, try to be a guide to this family of wanderers. Find those who have strayed off the path. The borders are now open once more, do visit us at least once. Show us your face, have a look at us. Your Chachi's command is that you should bring your wife with you. Yes, Miyan, don't come alone. That will give us a chance to see your children too — look at their faces, note who is fair and who is dark. And one more thing. There have been many additions to the family in Pakistan. I have tried to include their names in my family history — noted their dates of birth. Of course, I couldn't record what they look like.

There are still a lot of blank spaces left which only you can help me to fill. So please send me a list of all those who were born and all those who died in Pakistan during the past three or three-and-a-half years. I can't write separate letters to every family member. There is no censorship of letters these days, but an ordinary post-card is so expensive that it costs as much as a telegram. By the way, is it true that Khatija's youngest daughter has divorced her husband and taken up a job in the Population Control office? She has, of course, ruined her own life, but why must she interfere in the marriages of others? Yes, Miyan, I am now convinced that our family's lineage has been lost forever. But I hear that other families are even worse off. The other day someone told me that Ibrahim had made so much money by adulterating wheat flour that he has constructed another mill. And Miyan Faizuddin, who used to walk about in rags here, has accumulated enough black money to build a number of houses. I wonder if all the families in Pakistan have lost their family heritage. It must be a strange and peculiar country! We had spent generations in the land of Hind. We saw here good days and evil days. By the grace of God, we ruled over it and were also slaves in it, but we never forgot the proud and honourable lineage of our family. But in Pakistan people seem to have lost all sense of self-respect and forgotten the entire history of their families in just a quarter of a century. Well, anyway — I hope they are happy.

There is so much to tell you and so much to write about, but I hope that the little I have written is sufficient for now. Let us know how you are and inform us about your plans to visit us. I must now end this letter because the time for saying the namaz is at hand. I still have to put all the legal documents in order because our case is to be heard in court tomorrow. It will be the four hundred and twenty-seventh hearing. Insha Allah-al-Aziz, even that one will be handled with the usual care. Sometimes, I feel that I am still alive for the sake of this case alone. Otherwise, there isn't much left in this old body of your chacha's — not even the desire to live. I have lived through a lot since my birth.

From your distant Chacha,
Kurban Ali.
Dated : 28 Ramzan-ul-Mabarak, 1394 Hijri
Mutabiq: 15 October, 1974 A.D.

Original in Urdu.
Translated by Vishwamitter Adil and Alok Bhalla.

SAADAT HASAN MANTO

COLD MEAT

The moment Ishwar Singh entered the hotel room, Kulwant Kaur rose from the bed. She looked at him with alert and apprehensive eyes, and quickly locked the door behind him. It was midnight and an ominous silence had descended over all the lanes of the city.

Kulwant sat cross-legged on the bed. Ishwar Singh stood quietly for a while with a dagger in his hand. He seemed haunted by some guilty and horrifying thoughts. There was silence in the room for a while. Unable to sit still for too long, Kulwant swung her legs over the edge of the bed. Even then Ishwar Singh didn't say anything.

Kulwant Kaur was strong and well-built. She was a woman with large and heavy hips, exceptionally big breasts, bright eyes, thick lips and a hint of a moustache. The shape of her chin indicated that she was strong-willed.

Ishwar Singh continued to stand with his head down.

His turban was loose. The hand in which he held the dagger was trembling. It was, however, obvious from his height and build that he was the right kind of man for Kulwant Kaur.

After a few more moments of silence, Kulwant guessed that something was wrong, but with a twinkle in her eyes, she called out, "Ishwar Singh..."

Ishwar Singh lifted his head, but unable to deal with the fire and passion in her eyes, turned his face away.

Kulwant nearly screamed, "Ishwar Singh." But she controlled herself at once and asked quietly, "Where were you all these days?"

Ishwar Singh moistened his dry lips and replied, "I don't know."

Annoyed, Kulwant Kaur retorted sharply, "That's no fucking answer!"

Ishwar Singh flung his dagger aside and threw himself on the bed. It seemed as if he had been unwell for a few days. Kulwant felt sorry for him. She touched his forehead and asked kindly, "Jani, what's the matter?"

Ishwar Singh, who had been staring at the ceiling, slowly turned and stared at Kulwant Kaur's familiar face. "Kulwant!" he exclaimed as if he was in agony.

"Yes, Jani!" Kulwant Kaur replied and put one end of her saree in her mouth.

Ishwar Singh took off his turban. He looked helplessly at Kulwant Kaur, then he slapped his thigh hard, shook his head violently and exclaimed, "I am going mad!"

His hair became undone. Kulwant Kaur ran her fingers through it and asked sweetly, "Ishwar Singh, where were you all these days?"

"Fucking the mother of my enemy," Ishwar Singh replied as he stared at her. Then he began to fondle her breasts violently and said, "I swear by Waheguru that you are a gorgeous woman."

Kulwant Kaur pushed his hand aside with a coquettish gesture and said, "Tell me honestly, where were you? Did you go to the city?"

"No," Ishwar Singh replied, knotting up his hair.

Irritated, Kulwant Kaur said, "I am sure you went to the city to loot — and you have hidden all the money."

"Am I a bastard that I should lie to you?"

Kulwant Kaur kept quiet for a while, but then exploded angrily, "I still don't understand what happened to you the other night. You had made me wear all the jewellery you had stolen from the city and were making love to me. You were sucking my breasts, when you suddenly got up, put on your clothes and left."

Ishwar Singh turned pale. The moment Kulwant Kaur noticed the change in him, she said, "See, what I mean. You are pale. Ishwar Singh, I swear by Waheguru that something is wrong."

"I swear upon your life that there is nothing wrong," Ishwar Singh replied. But there was no conviction in his voice.

Kulwant Kaur became convinced that her hunch was right. She bit her lower lip and, emphasising every word, said, "Ishwar Singh, what is the matter? You have changed during the last eight days."

Ishwar Singh sat up quickly as if someone had attacked him. He took Kulwant Kaur in his strong arms, hugged and kissed her violently, and said, "Jani, I haven't changed...Hug me till the warmth of your body seeps into me..."

Kulwant Kaur didn't resist him, but she continued to ask him accusingly, "Why did you leave me that night?"

"The mother of my enemy was getting married."

"Why don't you tell me?"

"There is nothing to tell."

"May you cremate me with your own hands if you tell me a lie."

Ishwar Singh put his arms around her and kissed her lips. His moustache tickled her nostrils and she sneezed. Both began to laugh.

Ishwar Singh took off his shirt and looked lustfully at Kulwant. "Let's play cards," he said.

Sweat trickled down Kulwant's face. She looked coyly at Ishwar Singh and said, "Go to hell."

Ishwar Singh pinched her breast hard. Kulwant Kaur cried out in pain and jumped aside, "Don't, Ishwar Singh, that hurt!"

Ishwar Singh moved towards her, took her lower lip between his teeth and begun sucking it. Kulwant Kaur melted in his arms. Ishwar Singh took off the rest of his clothes, flung them aside and said, "It's time to play my trump card..."

Kulwant Kaur's lips began to tremble. Ishwar Singh caught the hem of her shirt and, just as a butcher skins a goat, pulled the shirt off her body and threw it aside. He stared at her naked body, pinched her arm as hard as he could and declared, "I swear by Waheguru, you are a delicious woman, Kulwant Kaur."

Kulwant examined the red welt on her arm and said, "You are a bastard, Ishwar Singh."

Ishwar Singh smiled through his thick and black moustache. "Let me be a bastard today," he said and begun making violent love to her.

He bit her lower lip, sucked the lobes of her ears, squeezed her big breasts, smacked her large hips, kissed her cheeks, and licked every part of her body. Kulwant Kaur began to writhe and groan with passion. Ishwar Singh, however, despite all his efforts, couldn't get an erection. He tried every trick he knew, but felt helplessly inadequate, like a wrestler who knows he'll be defeated. He still couldn't get an erection.

Kulwant Kaur, who was humming like a well-tuned instrument, got irritated at the delay and said, "You have shuffled enough, Ishwar Singh. Now throw your trump card."

Ishwar Singh felt as if someone had knocked the entire deck of cards from his hands. He broke into a cold sweat and lay down panting besides Kulwant Kaur's body. Kulwant Kaur tried very hard to arouse him, but failed. Till now neither of them had said anything. Kulwant Kaur, whose physical passion had been cruelly frustrated, suddenly jumped out of the bed, quickly covered herself with a sheet and screamed at him, "Ishwar Singh, tell me the name of that bitch who has sucked you dry?"

Ishwar Singh lay panting on the bed and didn't reply.

Kulwant Kaur, bursting with rage, said, "Who was that witch...who was that thief...who was that creature from hell?"

Exhausted, Ishwar Singh said, "There was no one, Kulwant, no one."

Kulwant Kaur put her hands on her large hips and said, "Ishwar Singh, I want to know the truth. Swear by Waheguru, that you weren't with another woman."

Ishwar Singh tried to say something, but Kulwant Kaur interrupted him and said, "Before you take an oath, remember that I am the daughter of Sardar Nihal Singh. If you dare lie to me, I'll cut you into pieces. Now swear by Waheguru that you weren't with another woman."

Guiltily, Ishwar Singh shook his head. Kulwant Kaur lost her head. She snatched the dagger lying in a corner, pulled it out of its scabbard and lunged at Ishwar Singh.

Blood began to spurt out of the wounds. Still unsatisfied, Kulwant Kaur began to claw at his face like a mad cat and to curse the nameless woman.

After sometime, Ishwar Singh begged, "Please, Kulwant, let go now. Please." His voice seemed to be full of grief.

Kulwant stepped back.

Blood had drenched Ishwar Singh's beard and chest. There was pain and gratitude in his eyes. He said, "Jani, you acted in haste...But what you did was just..."

Kulwant again lost her temper and screamed, "Tell me who she was? Your mother?"

A thin stream of blood trickled into Ishwar Singh's mouth. When he tasted it, a shiver ran through his body. "I...I...I killed six men, with that dagger."

But Kulwant Kaur was obsessed with that other woman, "Who was that bitch?"

Ishwar Singh's eyes began to close. He forced them open for a moment and said, "Don't curse that poor woman."

Kulwant screamed, "Who was she? I want to know."

In a tearful voice, he said, "I'll tell you." He ran his hand over his throat. When he saw blood on his hand, he smiled and said, "Man is a strange mother-fucking creature!"

Impatient for an answer, Kulwant Kaur said, "Answer my question, Ishwar Singh."

Ishwar Singh grinned and said, "That's what I am trying to do. You have slit my mother-fucking throat. I can only talk slowly."

When he began telling her the story, his forehead was covered with cold sweat, "Kulwant, my love, you won't believe what happened to me...Man is a strange animal...When people began looting the city, I joined them. I gave you all the money and gold I could lay my hands on...There was, however, something I didn't tell you about..."

Ishwar Singh began to groan with pain. Without paying him any attention, Kulwant Kaur said brutally, "Tell me now."

Ishwar Singh tried to wipe the blood that had dried on his moustache, and said, "The house I broke into...There were seven...seven people in it...six men...I killed them...with the dagger with which you...let that be...Listen...there was a beautiful girl...I took her with me..."

Kulwant heard him in silence. Ishwar Singh once again wiped the blood from his moustache, and said, "Kulwant my love, I can't tell you how beautiful she was...she was...I could have killed her, but I didn't...I said to myself...Ishwar Sian, you enjoy Kulwant Kaur everyday, taste this delicacy also..."

Kulwant Kaur merely said, "Yes..."

"I carried her over my shoulder...on the way...What was I telling you?...Yes, on the way...on the bank of the canal...I laid her down behind some bushes...First I thought I should shuffle her a bit, but then I decided against that..." His voice sank.

Kulwant Kaur moistened her lips and asked, "What happened after that?"

Ishwar Singh whispered, "I...threw my trump card...but...but..." His voice sank once more.

Kulwant Kaur shook him violently and asked, "What happened after that?"

Ishwar Singh could barely keep his eyes open. He looked at Kulwant Kaur. She was trembling. "She...was dead...a lifeless corpse...a cold, lifeless corpse...Jani, give me your hand..."

Kulwant Kaur placed her hand in his hand, which was colder than ice.

Original in Urdu.
Translated by Alok Bhalla.

SAADAT HASAN MANTO

COMPASSION

"Please don't kill
my young daughter
before my eyes..."

"Alright, let's do as he says...
Strip her
and drag her away..."

Original in Urdu.
Translated by Alok Bhalla.

SAADAT HASAN MANTO

SORRY

The knife
ripped through the stomach
reached down to the penis.
The cord of the pyjama was cut.
The man with the knife
exclaimed
with surprise,
as if he was reading the kalma to ward off evil,
"Chi, chi, chi...I made a mistake."

Original in Urdu.
Translated by Alok Bhalla.

Umm-e-Ummara

MORE SINNED AGAINST THAN SINNING

1

It was a cold and misty morning. When I opened my eyes and heard the shouts of coolies and the sleepy sounds of vendors, I realized that the train had stopped at some station. I, carefully, raised the glass shutter of the window and looked outside. It was a large railway junction. A gust of cold wind suddenly blew in through the open window. I quickly pulled the shutter down, climbed back into my berth and tried to sleep.

"Don't lie down again. We have arrived," my mother said, as she gently ran her hand over my head.

I had never been on a train for so long. Nor had I ever travelled without my father. He used to live in a city somewhere far away and my mother was responsible for looking after the household. My mother ran everything efficiently. She sent all her children to the best of schools, cultivated the fields, and had an ever expanding net-work of friendships and relationships. No one ever had an occasion to complain against her.

In the absence of our father, Amma treated us children so well that we never missed his presence. She loved us so much that we worshipped the very ground she walked on and hurried to obey every command of hers. And, thus, the members of the family continued to live and prosper without much concern for their future happiness, confident that they were well on their way to success. Our father came back home to visit us once a year, after travelling through many cities. When he saw his family growing and blooming, his heart was always filled with joy.

We were fond of our father. His presence always added to our store of happiness, though we were also a bit scared of him. When he was at home, Amma seemed as if she was drunk. She followed Baba about and continuously told him stories about everything and everyone. Baba also never tired of listening to her. She had an opinion about everything and Baba respected her judgments. Whenever he was perplexed by something, and his own reason failed to provide him with an answer, he used to turn to Amma for a solution and always followed her advice. He had complete faith in her; she was his guiding spirit and he was sure that her reason would never lead him astray. Amma was the dominant presence in the house. Everyone in the family respected her intelligence.

This time, however, when Baba returned from Bengal and announced his decision, Amma lost her nerve and her intelligence failed her. She paced up and down the house like a disturbed spirit, repeatedly felt each door and wall of the haveli; caressed each brick as if she was touching something which she loved dearly. Often, she went back to Baba's room to argue with him and to try to reason him out of his decision. This time, however, Baba refused to take her advice. Instead, he chanted over and over again that he could no longer live in this place; that he could no longer send us money from the new country where he worked; that if he couldn't send us money, we could no longer receive an education; that illiterate children were good for nothing. His real argument, however, was that the future of his children in the country in which they lived at present was very bleak. He, therefore, had to insist on their leaving, since his children were his real wealth and the source of all his happiness and he was concerned with their well-being alone.

"What about our fields, our haveli, our village, our people..." Amma asked, as her voice faltered and was then drowned in a flood of tears. She knew that she would have to leave behind forever all her brothers and sisters.

"Why don't you try to understand? We can no longer do anything here. These children are our treasure. Even if you want to stay here, they have no future here. These fields will not yield anything more for you. This earth no longer belongs to us, we are aliens in this country. I can no longer live here." Baba announced his decision and left.

That was perhaps the first and the last time Amma had failed to have her own way. We saw that Amma was sad and unhappy. She began packing her things, but every few moments her eyes brimmed over with tears. When I saw how depressed

Amma was, I couldn't understand why Baba thought that his own home was a place of exile.

Amma was very proud of that haveli, with its open courtyard, which was so long that one got tired as one walked from one end of it to the other, its tall and strong neem and peepal trees under whose shade we used to play marbles, its broad gates which were very impressive. Often, Amma used to say, "It was through those gates that I came into this house as a newly wedded bride. If God so wills, it will be through those gates that my coffin will be carried out. That, after all, must be the wish of every woman who has been happily married."

I was puzzled and anxious. I wondered how a world which was so familiar had suddenly become a world of strangers. After all Amma hadn't changed, the house hadn't changed, the city hadn't changed! Besides, how had the place where Baba lived, and which we had never seen, become our country? I couldn't understand anything. The more I pondered over the matter, the more entangled my thoughts became. Finally, I admitted defeat and went upstairs to the terrace and slept. My brothers and sisters, however, had no such anxieties. They were busy with the packing, dreaming of a bright future and talking about the happy days that lay ahead of them. Neither of them thought about me and left me alone to sleep in comfort. Only after sometime did it occur to Amma that she had not seen me around. In a frenzy, she roused everyone and they searched for me in every corner of the house and in every house in the neighbourhood. Later, when everyone was exhausted and despairing, it occurred to Amma that I might be up on the terrace, which she knew was my favourite place. My elder brother and she found me sleeping there. In those days everyone was worried about each other.

I, on the other hand, was only concerned about one thing, and that was whether Baba's house in the new country had a terrace. When Baba had come to visit us, I had asked him if his house had a terrace. Instead of answering me, he had merely smiled. I wondered why he had evaded my question. I was convinced that his house didn't have a terrace. I was puzzled by that and tried to figure out what a house without a terrace would be like. Thus, my last days in our old house were spent in doubt and anxiety. Amma, however, spent them in weeping and making preparations for our departure. One day we found ourselves at the railway station ready to leave the country which had become strange to us. Two days later, after a long journey, we were at the large railway station in our new land.

At the station, while the coolies pushed and shoved, my eldest brother, along with an orderly from my father's office, took charge of the luggage and organized everything. We had a lot of luggage with us. It seemed as if Amma had brought the entire household with her. After the luggage had been collected, our caravan began to move. I, however, refused. It was bitterly cold and my feet were frozen. It was difficult for me to take even two steps. "Bade Bhaiya, why don't you hire a rickshaw?"

A coolie, who was passing by, replied, "There are no rickshaws here, Bibi. You can hire a tumtum."

"Fine, let's hire a taxi, Bade Bhaiya," I said, for I didn't like the look of the tumtums.

"You surprise me, Bitiya. There are no rickshaws here and you want a taxi," the orderly said in reply.

"How can I walk? My feet are numb with cold," I said, and looked up helplessly at my eldest brother.

"Come, Munni, let me carry you," Bade Bhaiya said, as he hugged me.

"No, am I a child?" I broke free from his embrace.

Ever since my elder sister had got married, I had begun to consider myself a grown up woman. If someone took me for a child and ignored me, I reacted violently and made him become aware of my sense of hurt.

"In which case, there is only one thing you can do, Bitiya. Walk as fast as I do. Then your feet won't get cold," the orderly said, as he walked past me at a fast pace. My elder brother too followed him. I decided to imitate them and walked behind them as fast as I could.

As I stepped off the platform onto the metalled road, I was surprised by the softness of the tar on the road.

"Why did Baba tell us a lie," I wondered. "He told us that the streets here were so beautiful and they glittered so much that one could see one's reflection in them. But this road..." We did not know then that love can change dust into gold and stones into mirrors. Nor did I realize how much my father loved that soil. At that moment I was satisfied with the thought that sometimes even Baba told lies. It was an important revelation and added to the sum of my knowledge.

I really enjoyed my first experience of walking on a metalled road. I still love metalled roads because I associate them with that misty morning. That day, as I walked on the ground, I had a strange feeling of freedom. Back in my own town, I had always gone from one place to another in a palanquin and the roads were always crowded with rickshaws. The feelings of liberty which had smouldered in my heart that day as I had walked on the metalled road, I still feel burning within me. Everything around me, the soft mist, the gentle perfume of the wet earth, the dew that clung to my feet, felt lovely. A little later, I felt a wave of joy rising within my heart as I saw Baba helping the coolies unload the luggage. Wrapped in a Kashmiri shawl, he looked tall, handsome and very impressive.

"It's me, Baba," I said, and flung myself on him.

"My daughter," Baba exclaimed and knelt down to hug me. "Where have you left Amma and your brothers and sisters?"

"They are following behind. I ran ahead so that I could see you," I said, as I looked around happily.

Baba gave the orderly instructions about the luggage and then got absorbed in a discussion with Bade Bhaiya.

I looked carefully at the house before which I was standing. It was very different from the haveli we had left behind. The house was built in the latest style. It was very high and was surrounded by a large open ground. There were verandahs in the front and the back, but nothing which could be called a courtyard. The open ground was surrounded by a barbed wire.

Our old haveli had a courtyard with neem and peepal trees, and with sweet-smelling guavas. In the open space in front of the new house, mango, jamun and jackfruit trees swayed next to coconut and betel-nut trees. The humid air was filled with the smell of wet earth. When I took a deep breath, my entire being was overcome by the fragrance of harshringar. In the cold light of the morning when I looked at the house again, I realized that, whereas our old house was a haveli, our new residence was Bungalow Number 3/80.

"Baba, Baba," I ran to my father, who was standing with his arms around my younger brother and was busy talking to Amma.

"Baba, see even here...well...the air is fragrant," I said with delight.

"Yes, that is the fragrance of harshringar. It is called shaoli in this region."

"Why shaoli, Baba? Why not harshringar?"

"Because each region has its own language, and in this region of your country, harshringar is called shaoli."

2

Harshringar or shaoli, what difference did it make? The story of the transformation of harshringar into shaoli, however, was a long one.

I never stopped asking, "Why shaoli, why not harshringar?"

"That is because in this sacred land of yours harshringar is called shaoli," Bade Bhaiya used to reply, with irritation in his voice, "You will have to accept that harshringar is known as shaoli here, because you have chosen to live and die on this land. Harshringar was a part of your past. It is called shaoli in your present place. It is here that you will have to build a bright future. Therefore, Munni Bitiya, my advice to you is that you forget your past and begin to give greater importance to your future."

"Listen, Bade Bhaiya, I can't accept your logic. How can one have any relationship with the present or dream of the future, by forgetting the past? If you don't remember your past, you will never learn to love your present and..."

"Stop. Your brain is filled with straw. The fact is that you are merely prejudiced," Bade Bhaiya said, accusingly.

"How can you accuse me of being prejudiced? Surely it is not a crime that I don't speak Bangla? It's only that I can't forget my own language."

"I don't understand what you mean."

"I mean, Janab Bade Bhaiya Sahib, that if I can get by with Urdu, I see no reason why I should spoil a beautiful language like Bengali by speaking it in a garbled way. No, I can't bring myself to speak a language incorrectly and soil my soul," I said with a laugh.

"What about English? Is it your mother-tongue that you pursue it so diligently?" Bade Bhaiya asked peevishly. "Why must you speak it all the time, even when you can't make head or tail of it?"

"God forbid that I should ever regard English as my mother-tongue. I work at it because I don't want highly educated people like you to mock me and regard me as an illiterate. And as far as speaking it incorrectly is concerned, I shall ruin it to my heart's content. After all, it's not a sign of our independence. In fact, it is a memorial of our enslavement and surely no one should remember it fondly. Do you now understand what I mean, Bade Bhaiya?" I looked at him ironically.

"I don't think it is right not to learn the language of the place where you live."

"But who said that I don't want to learn it. All I said was that I wasn't interested in speaking it like a boor..."

"What about the bits and pieces of Urdu that I have begun to speak? Why should I bother to speak it?" Bade Bhaiya's wife, Pakhi, suddenly asked.

"That is because Urdu is my language," Bade Bhaiya answered mischievously.

"You do have illusions about yourself, don't you?" Pakhi replied with an arch smile.

"Will you dare to admit that Urdu is not the language of love?" Bade Bhaiya asked happily.

"But does Munni Bitiya think that my language is so much worse than English that her soul would be stained if she spoke it?" Pakhi asked because she felt insulted.

"No, Pakhi, I never said that. How could I have? With freedom, your language came to us as a gift. Who are we in comparison to what your language has to offer us? We love it as the language of our liberty," I said in my defence.

"And what about me..."

"You are inimitable, Pakhi Rani! Have I, like you, taken the vows of love!" I said and laughed.

"I don't like that, Munni Bitiya. Instead of appreciating my efforts, you make fun of me."

"But, Pakhi, it is your duty to admire..."

Pakhi's admiration for her husband was so deep that, without even making a special effort, she adopted the language and customs of our family. Instead of *pakh,* she first learnt to say *pirni,* and finally *phirnee. Sharm ata hai* soon transformed itself into *sharm ati hai.* When Bade Bhaiya took her to Patna, showed her his past haunts and introduced her to the entire family, she came back completely changed. She declared that everyone there had taken a liking to her, and began to speak about, "Our house in Patna...my in-laws...When we went to Allahabad we saw the confluence of Ganga and Jamuna. They fall into each other in the same way as our Sheetha, Alakhiy and Dhaneshwari do..."

"Or, the same way as you fall into my arms," Bade Bhaiya laughed and said. Pakhi looked away shyly.

It was strange to see her smile shyly, because here even newly wedded women don't feel coy and shy.

Bade Bhaiya's prediction that we'll slowly begin to like the place had turned out to be a hundred percent correct. In the course of time things did turn out well.

Pakhi had not only married him, but had also adopted his language, his habits, his rites and rituals. And Bade Bhaiya was so charmed by her that he had forgotten his real circumstances. Pakhi added one child after another to the family.

In the beginning Amma and Baba had merely tolerated her presence in the house as an unpleasant duty, but her fecundity had completely won their admiration. The house which had once seemed spacious, began to feel cramped. Out of the five rooms in Bungalow Number 3/80, Pakhi had captured two outright and her children had the freedom to run through the other three rooms. The one room, which was called a drawing-room, was only so in name. In fact, it was always strewn with nipples and milk-bottles. One of her children used the room to recite the alphabet, while the other used it as a playing-field, and yet another as a place where books could be crumpled with delight. Whenever my younger brother came home from Dhaka during the vacations, the children would tear his books and papers into shreds.

I, who had once been a small and dark girl, and who had felt lonely and ignored even though I was surrounded by my family, was now in love with life and longed for joy. In my own estimate, I was a courageous girl who could face and conquer a mountain range, but I felt myself unable to confront Bade Bhaiya, Pakhi and their children who were no less formidable than any mountain range with small peaks. Before them I had to admit defeat.

Bade Bhaiya, whom I had once loved dearly, had changed considerably. He was the one who, in the goodness of his heart and purity of spirit, had taught me to love life, to turn away from the darkness of the past and look at the brightness of the days to come; who knew how to keep his word and, once he accepted something, to give his life for it. The same brother had now sacrificed everything for Pakhi. I thought that the best thing I could now do was to find a corner for myself to hide in.

I took matters into my own hands and decided to occupy the small room next to the verandah in which Amma used to store all sorts of odds and ends. I spent days cleaning it. The day I occupied it and sat in it quietly weaving a fabric out of my thoughts and dreams, Pakhi dropped in to chat with me about various things.

After a while she suddenly became anxious and said, "Don't you feel suffocated in here, Munni Bitiya?"

Like my eldest brother, she too had started calling me Munni Bitiya even though it was I who had introduced her to my brother and she had been my friend before her marriage. But could her friendship with me now have the same intensity as her bond with my brother? Even today when I think about the past, I am shocked by the changes that my brother underwent.

When I was a child, I used to hear a song whose refrain was, "Beware of the women of Bengal, they are sorceresses." Pakhi had shown me the magic spell the women of Bengal could cast over men.

"You seem to be lost in dreams, Munni Bitiya. Where are you? What did I ask you?" Pakhi asked, as she shook me by my shoulders.

Puzzled, I looked at her in silence.

"I asked you if you don't feel suffocated here in this closed room?" She repeated her question loudly.

At that moment it occurred to me that there wasn't much difference between that closed room and the oppressiveness I had felt in the large house.

In a toneless voice I said, "This closed room is...."

Yes, the women of Bengal knew how to weave magic circles. Without completing my sentence, I continued to stare at Pakhi as if she had hypnotized me. Pakhi, who was now the mother of a number of children, seemed to have blossomed into a beautiful woman. Her hair had grown longer and reached below her waist, she wore a saree like her mother-in-law and covered her head. She seemed to me like someone whom I had not seen before.

"Why do you want to stay in this suffocating room, Munni Bitiya? Have you decided to renounce the world and become an ascetic?" Once again, she held me by my shoulder and shook me.

"So now you have learnt how to ask questions, have you?"

"Yes, of course. After all my children's..." Pakhi suddenly yawned loudly, "Allah, I feel faint in this heat."

I suddenly understood what Pakhi was saying. I started at her and said, "You are amazing, Pakhi. You are going to have your eighth child! Let me tell you clearly for the last time that I shall not vacate this small room for you."

I also understood what Amma had meant yesterday when she had approvingly said, "It's good that you have cleaned this room. It's out of the way and will be useful when the time comes."

Pakhi's yawns had made Amma's meaning clear. I knew what she meant by saying "useful when the time comes." I thought it was best to put a stop to all such hopes right then, otherwise I would be pushed out once again. At that very moment, however, Bade Bhaiya arrived and said, "There is no need for you to worry, Munni Bitiya. 'People with foresight will establish new cities...'"

"How will they do that, Bhaiya?"

"They will do so by going away to Phoolbari. We have been in this region for too long. It's time to go and inhabit a village," Bade Bhaiya declared with calm resolve.

Amma and Baba were very upset by my elder brother's decision to go away.

"Why do you want to leave, Miyan? Who can live in a place like that? The education of your children will suffer. There isn't even a decent school in that village."

"What are you talking about, Baba? That place has two High Schools. One for boys and the other for girls."

"But son, the medium of instruction there is Bangla. That would mean that your children will not..."

"So what, Baba? If we have to live here we must become a part of this very soil, only then will we be able to strengthen our roots," Bade Bhaiya said, interrupting Baba.

"You can say that, son. But my experience has taught me that even if we take root in this soil, we will always be regarded as transplants. A grafted tree can never be regarded as anything else."

My younger brother suddenly intervened and said, "No, Baba, you are mistaken. How can you even think like that?" He had recently returned from Dhaka and was staying at Santahar. That was in 1958-59 when people were being quietly arrested everywhere. He had thought it wiser to return home. That way he could keep his family happy and also evade danger.

"Can anyone imprison thought and sit guard over it, son? If that were possible wouldn't I have controlled you? You seem to be determined to wipe-out all traces of our traditions. Our future generations will never know that..."

"But, Baba, you don't have the right to talk like that," my younger brother said confidently. "We had pleaded with you not to bring us here. It was your decision. You betrayed your traditions. What traditions are you now talking about? You uprooted a flourishing tree and tried to replant it here. Why do you now feel so alienated from this place?"

"Why I feel alienated is my business. As far as the question of coming here is concerned, I don't think I have ever made a better decision in my life. I couldn't have lived in peace with myself if I hadn't done everything to ensure the future of my children. And you will have to admit, son, that none of you has suffered any loss by living here. That light that burns inside you, that hope and belief, that determination to win an argument, are a testimony of the freedom you found here in this country. Freedom which is only in name is not worth much. Think about your past. Back there your relatives, despite their abilities, have been unable to find a way out of their narrow confines. Here each one of you has used the abilities you possess to make a success of your lives..."

"You merely choose to deceive yourself, Baba. In this repressive country, it is not even possible to speak freely. Is this what you mean by freedom?" My younger brother retorted angrily. "What do you think of the orders issued by the army?"

"Who has asked you to obey those orders? If you have the courage and the ability, why don't you seize power? What prevents you?" Baba was unwilling to hear even a word against the government and its orders.

"It's futile to argue with you, Baba. What you want me to do is to snatch sugar-cane away from an elephant. What can one possibly do when one isn't even allowed to open one's mouth?"

"Instead of worrying about what is possible and what isn't, it would be better if you kept your mouth shut. That would be in the interest of all of us," Baba said angrily.

"Even if I keep quiet, do you think others will not raise their voices? Even if all the lips are sealed, the bricks in the walls will speak."

"I think you should keep your mouth shut. Do you want to go back to jail?" Amma said, as she looked at my younger brother anxiously.

"People are being arrested everyday. Yesterday they arrested Pakhi's brother. It may be my turn today. In these times the only one who has the courage to speak is Mansoor, he is a messiah."

"There is no need to say anything. I don't need a Mansoor or a messiah in this house. You have ruined our reputation. No member of the family had ever been to jail before. Pakhi's brother is used to handcuffs. In our place only goondas go to prison." In her rage, Amma revealed all that had been smouldering inside her.

"Excuse me, Ammaji," that was the first time Pakhi had dared to contradict my mother. "Maybe there are goondas in your place. But here the story is different. We have the courage to speak the truth even if our hands are in chains. Without it there may soon come a moment when the storm that is gathering will sweep you away with it." Amma had after all insulted her brothers who were respected political workers.

"Pakhi, are you less dangerous than a storm? You are taking away with you everything we have," I said, trying to restore a delicate balance in the discussion.

The argument ended there. A few days later, Bade Bhaiya gathered his family together and left to create a wonderful new garden in the wilderness.

After Bade Bhaiya's departure, Amma started hating the house. She heard voices arising from every nook and corner. By then Baby and Rani had passed their Matriculation examinations. Baba could have sent them to a hostel. But he couldn't afford to keep three of his children there. It was, therefore, decided that the family move to Dhaka.

In 1960-61, I joined the University after graduating from college. I saw that my younger brother, who was still a child in Baba's eyes, was looked upto with respect in the University. He was a popular and an important person in the University, and everyone admired his courage and his ideological positions. During those days no one asked who was an outsider and who was a Bengali. People were only concerned with the fruit and not with the tree.

When I was in college, I was confident that the roots of the tree of hatred were shallow and weak, that it really didn't have the sap to blossom and bear fruit. I was sure that the basic faith people had in life itself, and the trust that guided their relations with each other, would root out the tree of hatred once and for all. I was certain that a life of decency and reason would establish itself, and that the differences between natives and outsiders would vanish. The example of my younger brother was always before me. He spoke a faltering Bengali and English, for his mother-tongue was Urdu, but he spoke passionately, with sincerity and feeling, and had been accepted without prejudice as an important member of the University. By the time I entered the University, he had already left it, but people still remembered his commitment and his style, and whenever they got stuck on a difficult issue, called upon him to help them resolve it. I found myself repeating over and over again, "The walls of hatred will soon break." Indeed, I had begun to feel that people had started coming closer to one another. Even I, who had once been ashamed to speak in Bengali with Pakhi, had begun to speak it, though haltingly.

When Bade Bhaiya came to attend Amma's funeral, I noticed that he was no longer as smartly and fashionably dressed as he used to be. Instead of being the model of taste and elegance for the rest of the family, he was dressed like a Bengali, in loose and baggy trousers, and his hair was long. He had also begun to speak Urdu as if it was alien to him.

When Amma died, her only regret was that both her sons had been swallowed up by Bengal. One had been so charmed by its magic that he had forgotten that he was also someone's son. The other was so determined to disentangle its knotted problems that he spent six months a year in jail. Of course, Amma counted herself amongst those few fortunate ones who had lived a full and happy life. But her dreams for her sons had not been fulfilled. As she lay dying, she didn't have even one of them with her to give her two spoons of water.

Bade Bhaiya arrived after Amma's death. He wept profusely and without restraint. When I saw the state he was in, I stopped weeping. Bade Bhaiya, whose Urdu was once so graceful and pleasing that it was held up as an example by our teachers, had now begun to make elementary mistakes. He spoke in fluent Bengali with his children because it was, he insisted, their mother-tongue. He had erased his past self completely and had become a part of the very soil of this new country. I couldn't help wondering why he spoke Bengali, why he had forgotten his old roots, but I too spoke without any self-consciousness, in my faltering Bengali, to Pakhi and her children. The children smiled at my Bengali and Pakhi joked about it and said, "Why must you speak Bangla? I can speak Urdu."

I was surprised to see that Pakhi spoke Urdu better than Bade Bhaiya. When I asked her about it, she replied, "Why not, it is the language of my children's father." Pakhi's kind response made me resolve to go with Bade Bhaiya and live in his village for a while.

Because of a strange series of coincidences, Amma had never been able to take me with her to Phoolbari. Sometimes, I had exams and at other times, I was required at home to look after Baba and my younger brother. Now, finally, I got the chance to go. Amma was dead and Baba had at last recognized that Rani and Baby were no longer little girls. He decided to leave them in the care of my younger brother and go to Phoolbari. I too had no excuse to stay in back in Dhaka. I had passed my Masters examination and was looking for a job.

I wanted to visit Phoolbari because I had heard stories about it from Rani and Baby. They had often told me about the fragrance of the motiya and the kindness of Pakhi. Whenever they came back from Phoolbari, the only song they sang was about Bade Bhaiya's life of quiet comfort, the smell of hilsa cooked by Pakhi and the fragrance of motiya. Bade Bhaiya had encouraged me to cultivate flowers. There is an incident from the past which has been a part of my conscious being throughout my life. One day, back in Patna, Bade Bhaiya had brought cuttings of bela from his school. It was a sunny day. Bade Bhaiya and I had dug beds to plant them. The day had been hot and humid, but we had worked all morning to plant them. The cuttings had taken root. Soon they had green leaves, and one day I saw a small bud peep out from under the leaves. Wild with excitement, I had run to tell Bade Bhaiya. I have never forgotten that day. When I gave Bade Bhaiya the news, he too shouted with glee. That night I talked for a long time about the flowers and looked at them repeatedly. At that moment, I felt waves of fragrance rise from the flowers, touch my forehead and recede. I don't know when I fell asleep still dreaming of bela.

I remember also that when I opened my eyes the next morning, I heard a lot of voices coming from the courtyard. I caught hold of my younger brother and asked him, "What's going on?"

"A wedding party will stay in the courtyard tonight." After giving me that information in a toneless voice, he went away carrying his books under his arm.

Because our house was large, the neighbours used it as a guest house. That night the wedding guests came and departed like waves, but they also carried away all the flowers with them. Those uncouth, uncultured people had dug up the courtyard to make latrines for themselves. The tall and rooted plants had withered. I had wept loudly. Bade Bhaiya was also shocked. But Bade Bhaiya could take the blow because he was older and a man. I, on the other hand, wept so loudly that Amma, in sheer frustration, had slapped me a few times.

Bade Bhaiya had hugged me and said, "Let it be, Munni Beti, I'll plant a garden of bela for you."

I have never forgotten that incident. We had left the old house behind, our past world had vanished from our sight, everything had changed utterly. I never got a chance to plant bela again. But in Phoolbari I noticed that Bade Bhaiya had converted the courtyard into a small garden. His life was happy and contended; he was surrounded by the laughter of children and the perfumes of flowers. During my stay there I failed to notice that the direction of the wind blowing over our world had changed, and I didn't hear the wings of the approaching storm Pakhi had once talked about in Santahar.

During my final days at the University, I had felt that the gulf separating people had begun to widen and that evil had begun to encircle and entrap good. My younger brother, whose life and actions had guided people, seemed to have lost heart. The fire of youth in him had begun to grow dim. Despite his honesty, people had begun to drift away from him. Cracks of suspicion had begun to appear in the trust people had built in each other. On the chess-board of life there was no longer a clear demarcation between black and white. As time passed, the temptation of power, its intoxication, persuaded people to make compromises, choose separate paths.

I felt as if someone had mingled poison in the air; as if someone had placed boulders in the river of life so as to obstruct its smooth flow, to change its direction. Water cannot be stopped from flowing. It always seeks new paths. So I saw the river, which once seemed to flow towards honesty, light and life, seep past the obstacles and trickle in countless small rivulets in different directions. Each trickle slowly lost its force, sank into the ground, turned into a small, stagnant pool and became a breeding place for worms and maggots. The souls of men were corrupted. Eyes, filled with greed, lost their life-inspiring glow.

At Bade Bhaiya's place, I was so absorbed in the laughter of children and the perfume of flowers that I forgot that a happy life must always be guarded against the evil eye, that flowers fade and perfume dissolves in the air. That was a foolish mistake.

Evil finally strangled good. The enemy attacked with all its force and fury, and man lost all traces of his humanity. Phoolbari was set on fire. Poor Pakhi, with her hair dishevelled, ran from one singed flower to the next like a frightened bird. But before she regained her senses, her Phoolbari had been burnt to ashes. She tried to bury herself in the ash.

When I looked into Bade Bhaiya's eyes they had no life in them — those eyes which had always glowed with the joy of life, where there had been confidence and love; those eyes which had deliberately refused to look at the past and had dreamt only of a bright future. Now there was nothing but blank surprise in them.

I looked towards Baba. He had thought that his children were his life and future. At Amma's grave he had appealed to God to grant him one last wish — that his body not be buried under the earth in this place. Baba had prayed for that at the edge of Amma's grave as he had watched with horror her grave slowly fill with water and the body of the woman with whom he had spent a life-time, float on it. God had chosen a strange way to grant him his wish. Not only was his body not buried, it was not even enclosed in a coffin.

Pakhi's lovely body was reduced to ash and her flower-like children were burnt to death.

And I...I didn't have the courage to die. I drank the poison of life.

Original in Urdu.
Translated by Vishwamitter Adil
and Alok Bhalla.

S.H. VATSAYAN 'AJNEYA'

GETTING EVEN

Hurriedly shoving her things into the unlit compartment, depositing little Abid on a seat through one of the windows and helping her elder daughter, Zubeida, into the carriage, Suraiya herself barely managed to clamber aboard the train as it was starting to pull out. She heaved a sigh of relief, and had only just bethought herself of the Pure and Merciful One, when she noticed the two forms, all wrapped up in blankets, in the far corner of the compartment. And they weren't her Muslim brethren — they were Sikhs! In the intermittent light that shone in the dark of the compartment as the train moved past successive lights on the station platform, she noticed something inhuman in their pitiless, unblinking eyes. As if their sight were not a whit impeded by the fact of her body, but went clear through it; and in them she noticed a cold hostility, as if beyond all human appeal, so sharp it seemed that it would draw blood from anyone who sought to touch it in any way. Although the light was hardly sufficient to actually see all this, Suraiya imagined she saw clearly that their eyes were bloodshot and...and...a fearful tremor passed through her. But the train had picked up speed by then, it was no longer possible to move to another compartment. She would have considered jumping out of the running train, children and all, but then, she thought, being thrown out by one's fellow-passengers couldn't be that much worse, could it? Immersed in these thoughts, and keeping a sharp eye on the handle of the alarm chain dangling above, she sat, uncertain...but she'd do something about it at the next station...there shouldn't be anything to fear in just one stop...at least there had been no incidents on this stretch so far...

"How far will you be going?"

Suraiya was startled. The older Sikh was asking her something. And what a deep voice he had! Though he might very well kill her and throw her out of the train after a couple of stops, yet he was speaking to her with such elaborate courtesy now — Suraiya reflected upon the irony of this, and so forgot to reply to his question.

The Sikh asked again, "How far will you be going?"

Suraiya had unveiled her face, but she drew her veil back on, and replied, "I am going to Etawah."

The Sikh thought for a moment, "Is there no one else with you?"

Suraiya speculated about the moment's hesitation that had preceded that last question, "He is calculating how much time he'll need for killing me...O Lord, please send some more passengers at the next stop...and I must surely tell him I have someone with me — that might frighten him a little! Though what good is a travelling companion these days if he isn't in the same compartment...if you should happen to get stabbed. Just hang on till the next stop — someone will come to the window and ask you if there is anything you need..."

She said, "There's my brother...in the next compartment."

Little Abid piped up smartly, "What are you saying, Ma! Mamu has gone to Lahore..."

Suraiya rebuked him sharply, "Keep quiet!"

After a little while, the Sikh asked again, "Do you have a family in Etawah?"

"Yes."

The Sikh remained silent for a while. Then he said, "Your brother should have been in the same compartment with you. Nobody sits apart from one's near and dear ones these days."

Suraiya wondered if the old rascal had guessed that there was really no one with her!

The Sikh said, almost as if to himself, "But no one can be depended upon when things begin to fall apart...it's everyone for himself..."

The train had slowed down. It was a small station. Suraiya was unable to decide whether she should move to another compartment, or stay where she was? Two more passengers entered the compartment. Suraiya quickly sized them up — "Hindus" — and then she really got afraid, and started to gather her things.

The Sikh asked her, "Are you planning to get down here?"

"I thought, I might go and sit with my brother..." What strange creatures we are that we try and shelter behind lies even in such situations...and then, such flimsy lies...for wouldn't her brother have come himself to help her move? But how could he come, since he wasn't there at all?

The Sikh then said to her, "Stay where you are. You have nothing to fear here. You are like a sister to me, and these children are as my own. I will see you safely upto Aligarh. There is little danger beyond that point, and anyway some of your own people will also be entraining there."

One of the Hindus spoke up, "Sardarji, let her go if that's what she wants. What is it to you?"

Suraiya was unable to decide what to make of this exchange between the Sikh and the Hindu, but the train decided the issue by moving off again. She sat down.

The Hindu asked "Sardarji, do you come from Punjab?"

"Yes."

"Where is your home?"

"Used to be in Shekhupura. Now it might as well be here."

"Here? What do you mean?"

"Wherever I happen to be, there's my home! One corner of a railway compartment."

The Hindu checked his tone somewhat, and then, as if his voice were a glass and he were stirring a generous dose of sympathy in it before offering it to the Sikh; he said unctuously, "Then you are a refugee..."

The Sikh replied dryly, as if declining the proffered glass, though the Hindu gentleman quite missed the subtle resonance of his tone, "Yes."

The Hindu gentleman turned to him with somewhat greater interest, "Terrible things must have happened to your family members —"

There was a flash of anger in the Sikh's eyes, but he did not fall for the bait. He kept quiet.

The Hindu looked in Suraiya's direction and went on, "They say that in Delhi terrible things have been done to Hindus and Sikhs. Such things people recount, I tell you, one is ashamed even to talk about such things. They stripped the women naked and..."

The Sikh turned to the wrapped up figure sitting beside him, and said, "Kaka, go and sleep on the upper berth." He was obviously the older Sikh's son and, when he got up and stretched his slim young body, the light in the old man's eyes, as he looked up towards the upper berth was unmistakably paternal. The young boy climbed onto the upper berth and lay down, and the old Sikh stretched his legs on the lower one and began staring out of the window.

The Hindu gentleman's recital had been interrupted, and he started again, "Right in front of their fathers and their brothers, young girls were stripped naked and..."

The Sikh said, "Babu Sahib, why tell me about things that I have seen myself anyway..."

This time the sharp dryness in the tone was even clearer, but the Hindu gentleman missed it again. As if encouraged, he started again, "You are quite right...How can we ever begin to understand your sorrow. We can but sympathize, and yet what is that sympathy worth which cannot even gauge the depth of another's pain! Just think, how can I even comprehend what those Sikhs went through, before whose very eyes their wives and daughters were..."

The Sikh could barely control his voice, "All people have wives and daughters, Babu Sahib."

The Hindu gentleman was arrested briefly by something incomprehensible in the Sikh's tone, but not for long. "Well, now Hindus and Sikhs have also woken up. Of course it's wrong to take revenge, but how long can one be tolerant? In Delhi they have rallied strongly, and in places they have even retaliated in kind, an eye for an eye...Really speaking, there is no other option. I heard that in Karol Bagh, a Muslim doctor's daughter was..."

This time it wasn't any longer a dry and subtle resonance in the Sikh's voice, it was a manifest and grating harshness, "Babu Sahib, a woman's dishonour is a matter of shame for all men. And sister — " he said, turning towards Suraiya, "I apologize to you for your having to hear all this."

The Hindu gentleman was taken back, "What, what, what was that about? I haven't said anything to this lady." And then, getting a grip on himself, he said with a hint of deliberate rudeness, "Is she — she with you, then?"

The Sikh replied even more harshly, "Yes! I am escorting her till Aligarh."

"This poor man," a voice spoke up inside Suraiya's head, "this poor, good man is going to Aligarh, Aligarh..." She made so bold as to ask him, "You will get down at Aligarh?"

"Yes."

"Do you have anyone in Aligarh?"

"I have no one anywhere. My son's with me."

"What is taking you there? Will you be staying for some days?"

"No, I return tomorrow."

"So...you are going for the fun of it."

"Fun!" The Sikh repeated in a lost sort of voice, "Fun!" Then he controlled himself and said, "No, we're not going anywhere really — we're still thinking about where we might go. And when nothing is stable any longer, the only place where one can think at all is in a moving train..."

Again a voice prompted inside Suraiya's head, "Aligarh...Aligarh...He is a decent sort..."

She spoke out, "Aligarh...it is not such a good place. Why are you going there?"

The Hindu gentleman also spoke up, as if taking pity on someone obviously deranged, "Just imagine!"

"Good place or bad, what difference can it make to me?"

"Even so — don't you feel afraid? Suppose you get stabbed at night..."

The Sikh smiled and said, "Have you ever considered that someone might even welcome that as a deliverance?"

"But that's absurd!"

"And why not? So, who will kill me? It could be a Muslim, or a Hindu: If a Muslim kills me, I will only go and join up with the other members of my family, wherever it is that they have gone before me. And if a Hindu should get me, I will console myself with the thought that even this last has been accomplished. The disease which has gripped the whole country has reached its climax — and we can at last start on the road back to health and sanity."

"But why will a Hindu kill you? A Hindu may well have a million defects, but he will never do such a thing..."

Suddenly, the Sikh lost his temper. He said contemptuously, "Go on, Babu Sahib! Only just now you were relating the Delhi incidents with such obvious relish. Now, if you had a knife, and there was no danger to yourself — would you have spared your fellow-passengers...these people...and if I should have dared to intervene, me as well?"

The Hindu gentleman made as if to say something, but the Sikh restrained him with a commanding gesture, "Since you apparently wish to know about it, prepare to listen well. You presume to give me sympathy because I am a refugee. Sympathy is a big thing, and I would have considered myself fortunate indeed if you had been capable of true sympathy. But how can you even begin to understand my anguish, when in the very same breath you speak of the Delhi happenings with such heartlessness. If you had been capable of giving me sympathy — if you had so much heart, your tongue would have stuck to the roof of your mouth, it would have frozen with shame before you could begin to utter one syllable regarding the things that you were so keen to gossip about — your head would have bowed with shame. A woman's dishonour is a woman's dishonour — it is not a Hindu's shame or a Muslim's shame, in her the mother of all mankind has been dishonoured. Whatever happened to me in Shekhupura...happened. But I know that I can never take revenge for that, because there can be no adequate vengeance for all that took place there! I can only get even after a fashion — so that whatever happened to me should never happen to another. And that is why I escort people back and forth between Delhi and Aligarh. It helps to pass the days, and I am able to get even just a little. And in this way if someone should happen to kill me some day, the account will at last be closed — it matters little whether the killer is a Muslim, or a Hindu! My only aim is that no one — Hindu, Sikh or Muslim — no one should ever have to see what I have seen. And whatever befell my family members before they died, may it not be the fate of anyone's wives and daughters ever to have to behold!"

For sometime after this, there was complete silence in the compartment. When the train slowed down as it approached

Aligarh, Suraiya desperately wanted to say some words of gratitude to the Sikh, but she was unable to make a sound.

The Sardar roused himself and turning towards the upper berth, said, "Up, Kaka, we're at Aligarh." Then he turned to the Hindu gentleman and said, "You must forgive me, Babu Sahib, if I have inadvertently said some harsh things to you. After all, we're your refugees now!"

It was clear from the Hindu gentleman's expression that if the Sikh had not been disembarking there, he himself would have moved to another compartment.

Original in Hindi.
Translated by Alok Rai.

MANIK BANDYOPADHAYAY

CHILDISHNESS

The divide didn't last. A narrow, blind passage, about three feet wide, separated the front part of the two houses; their front doors also faced each other across this passage. At the back, under a single continuous roof, the space was divided by a man-high wall. An adult could see above it by climbing onto a stool or chair.

The divide didn't last. How much after all was the difference in lifestyles — in joy and sorrow, laughter and tears, hope and happiness, detestation and love? Tarapada and Nasiruddin both went to work in the morning and came home exhausted at the day's end. The same blighted dreams and eager imaginings piled up day by day in both their hearts, the same anger against the same forces grew intenser every day. Indira and Halima spent the same captive life: cooking and serving, scrubbing the pots, dreaming their dreams and silently bearing the unmerited blows of a cruel, callous dispensation. One day Gita came to fill Indira's lap. The next year, reliving exactly the same pains, Halima brought Habib into the world.

Even if the division might have lasted, two naughty children now shatter it with their denial of any unnatural man-made remoteness. They draw the two families together, bring about intimacy between Indira and Halima.

One day, two children of the neighbourhood are married at an auspicious hour. It's a new game for Gita. She puts on her mother's sari, folded to a manageable size, draws clumsy patterns in sandalwood-paste on her cheeks and forehead, pins on her father's red tooth-brush as a tiara to become Habib's bride. It is she who dresses Habib as the groom, smearing sandal-paste on his forehead and draping a towel round his neck in lieu of body-wrap. Both, Indira and Halima, have to act as mothers-in-law. Indira must greet her son-in-law with joyful ululation, and Halima her daughter-in-law. They must bring out food and offer it with due solicitude to the young couple, feeding them with their own hands; apparently newly weds don't eat any other way. From time to time, the mothers burst out laughing. Incensed at this, Gita suddenly forgets her bridal reticence and begins crying and writhing on the floor. After that the mothers laugh furtively, stuffing their sari-ends in their mouths.

Then Gita calls to Habib, as she has heard her mother do, "Listen! Are you listening, son-in-law? Son-in-law, I'm calling you."

"Uh?" says Habib.

"What's that — Uh? Don't say uh. Say 'What, my dear?'"

Halima and Indira fall over each other laughing.

But Indira's aunt-in-law looks stern. As soon as Halima has left, she asks, "What's all this, niece-in-law?"

"What's what, Aunt?"

"It's all right giving her tea. But she touched that cup with her lips — how could you just rinse it and put it away with all the other crockery? Couldn't you at least sprinkle it with Ganga water? Why don't you keep a separate cup for her? Really, this is the end of our caste and our faith!"

"I have washed it in Ganga water," Indira lies easily.

In the other house, Nasiruddin's mother is also glum. "Why don't you go and live in their house? You're going too far. Who knows whether they like it either!"

Halima smiles and says, "They wouldn't let me go without a cup of tea. That's what made me late."

"And you happily drank their tea! Try offering them some one day."

"They do drink our tea."

All the housework is lying undone; it hasn't started on time. That, Halima knows, is really why Nasir's mother is angry, so she sets to work even as she replies. She doesn't have to hear much more on the subject.

An hour later, Nasiruddin's mother can be seen standing at the front door, holding her youngest granddaughter, talking over things good and bad with Tarapada's aunt, who has her little great-nephew on her lap.

The divide doesn't last.

It doesn't even last that afternoon when Halima comes over after her chores, looking rather guilty. "Something awful has happened, sister," she says a little uncomfortably.

"O my mother! What is it?"

"Your daughter's eaten a little beef. You know, we have to have some today. Habib had sat down to eat. I wasn't giving her any, but the naughty girl kept insisting — and then she suddenly snatched a bit from the plate and put it in her mouth."

"Will anything happen to her?" asks Indira, alarmed.

She then breaks out laughing on seeing Halima's face. "Really, what am I saying! If it doesn't harm Habib, why should it harm her? What does it matter if she's eaten some — a tiny girl like her! But don't tell anyone, sister."

"How could I?" says Halima, relieved. "Dear father! Don't I know? The other day Ali Sahib and his wife came to give us such a talking-to. Somebody's sneaked to them that Habib had offered flowers and eaten prasad at your Saraswati Puja."

"Just listen and I'll tell you what happened." There's no-one in the room, yet Indira moves closer and lowers her voice. "Wasn't Aunt angry that Habib had offered flowers! Finally my husband opened the almanac and reeled off some Sanskrit nonsense, and told his aunt, 'There's no harm done if it's Saraswati Puja — that's what it says in the scriptures.' Then Aunt cooled down and said, 'Oh, is that so?'"

The afternoon is peaceful. The pedlar goes down the lane crying "Saris, petticoats and blouses!" The two of them sit down to play noughts and crosses with chalk on the floor. But they begin to yawn; their eyelids droop. They smile weakly, tiredly, as they catch each other's eyes. Then spreading their sari-ends, they lie down side by side — two wives, two mothers, two cooks, two slaves.

But they cannot sleep. That luxury can be theirs only when the days become longer in the summer. Now they only have leisure to drowse a little. The scattered sounds of the quiet afternoon penetrate their drowsy senses. Clearest among them is Habib and Gita's clatter on the rooftop.

The divide didn't last. So they couldn't understand why it should suddenly rear its head in such ugly shape, why there should be so much fighting and killing all round. They were bewildered and terrified; their hearts quavered. Earlier, during the Japanese air-raids, their hearts had quaked at the sound of the siren, the terror of an alien threat blown on the winds from far away. But now, here was a wider, more terrible calamity rising from the nation's own breast — across the city, in their very quarters, at their own doors. The heart's loud flutter found no pause; it rose and fell, fell and rose.

The saving grace was that theirs was a mixed locality. They kept saying this to themselves, not so much helplessly as desperately. This was what gave them a measure of hope amidst the endless blows — direct, roundabout and hidden — of destructive terror, rumour and incitement. They also had a more concrete resort in the form of a Joint Peace Committee. The way this was born gave cause for hope rather than mischief. Instead of setting the meeting afroth with great idealistic outpourings, singing victory-hymns to unity in the hope of thereby ensuring it, stress was laid on the simple material truth that any violence in the area would be equally dangerous for all. It was a mixed locality.

Perhaps there wouldn't be any havoc in this neighbourhood. Who could tell? Everything around was in flames; even the blistering wind blowing from there made the soul smart. Near and dear ones — destitute, grief-stricken, confounded — came mouthing curses, crying, "Kill, cut them up, butcher them, finish them off." People kept coming to explain that the only way to live was to kill.

The inhabitants had lived side by side, mixed together, for a long time. Perhaps they hadn't all mixed intimately, but that was really because this was a city. They had all had their wings clipped; it was the whim of their owners to keep them like poultry. They could only flutter along the path of life.

"Are we no better than birds? That's what I'd like to know," says Halima across the facing windows. "Are we going to be driven around — here today, there tomorrow? Are we going to nest in trees?"

"Let's not talk about it, sister," says Indira. "My head's in a whirl these last few days. What goings-on! Uh — what have you cooked today?"

But it isn't as frank a chat as it had been a few days ago. There is a mild embarrassment in both voices. They cautiously open a single shutter to talk, avoiding each other's eyes as though they are doing something wrong. They have already stopped visiting each other — not only because both houses are full of sudden sheltering guests, but because the people at home have forbidden their friendship, their mixing together — at least for the time being.

"I wonder what's going to happen."

"They say the milkmen are poisoning the milk. I boil it and first feed a little to the cat. The children are hungry and keep crying, but I'm forbidden to give them any. They have it only after we've watched the cat for half an hour. My man's even stopped buying bread — it seems most of the bakers are your people. There used to be a piece of bread with the morning tea; now it's only a little tea with molasses till one or two o'clock."

"All these extra people in the house! One day I'm left only with a speck of dal and vegetables, next day perhaps nothing at all. Even the rice gives out."

"Today I only had dry rice and salt. There isn't even any molasses."

They look into each other's eyes for a while, heads lowered. Slowly the two shutters close.

There are more children too in both the houses. They have come with the adults, driven out of other areas. The grown-ups don't even know one another's faces, but who can keep the children apart? Their urge to mix together knows nothing of politics, of agreements and permissions, caste and religion. They have no school, no studies, no pleasure-trips; they are forbidden to leave the house. The grown-ups go about with sour faces, the house is as sombre as when somebody's dying and doctors keep going in and out.

What can the children do? They contrive to play together under Habib and Gita's leadership. There's no space in the houses, so they build their own playroom. It isn't difficult; they simply drive a nail into either wall of the passage outside and hang up a piece of cloth. The end of the passage thereby becomes a small enclosed room. They get together a little rice and dal, with some leaves and stalks. Gita has brought along the little portable stove and some oil and spices. Everyone keeps grumbling about the lack of vegetables, so Habib smuggles out potatoes, onions and a whole aubergine. There is a fierce debate as to whether it should all be made into a big khichdi, or whether khichdi, fries and curry should be cooked separately. The task of cooking is shouldered by Meher. At the age of nine or ten, she has to help the grown-ups with real cooking; the others bow to her experience without protest.

But they can't even light the fire or start to cook. The grown-ups from both houses find out and come yelling. Nurunnisa, Meher's father's wedded wife, catches her daughter by the plait and gives her a tight slap. Pushpa's aunt cuffs her niece on the lip and draws blood. Gita thrashes about to free her ear and lands Tarapada a kick in the stomach. Habib bites Nasiruddin's hand. The children's cries and adults' shouts create a great clamour. The neighbours turn this into a real commotion as they rush out to see what's wrong. Quite a little crowd gathers in the lane, at the entrance to the passage, brandishing sticks, bricks and iron rods.

A few moments more — just a few moments, and the fate of the mixed neighourhood would have been decided for good; peace preserved, or causeless ruin called down on its head. Forgetting their tears, the children look wide-eyed at the folly of their elders.

The two Joint Secretaries of the Peace Committee narrowly avert violence by running up with a team of volunteers. They explain things. The crowd begins to break up; the volunteers clear the place in a few minutes.

The Joint Secretaries then confer and send volunteers round the neighbouring quarters to announce what really happened. People's minds have grown so sensitive that even a trifling business like this might flare up into a dangerous rumour.

That afternoon, a truck comes round with a little band of soldiers and policemen. Everything was quiet by then. For a while, they pace up and down in their noisy boots, banging on this door, entering one shop or the other to find out where the trouble had been. The reply is amazing, incredible — there has been no trouble at all. They seem angry and dissatisfied; have they come for nothing? A picket of four armed soldiers is left on a charpoy outside Nitai's shop; the truck carries the rest away. A new fearful unease spreads across the mixed neighbourhood. Shops close before lighting-up time; people retreat into their holes; the roads are empty.

Anything said in one house can be heard in the other, but there is no exchange of talk any more. The facing shutters don't even open secretly for a moment or two. Each house thinks the other responsible for bringing the military into the neighbourhood; who knows what might happen now? The children are forbidden to go out. They are prisoners in the home gaol.

"Come over, Habib!" calls Gita across the wall dividing the roof.

"They'll beat us if we do."

"No, we'll play quietly in Great-Aunt's room."

"She'll scold us."

"No. It'll be afternoon before she's finished cooking and bathing."

For a long time now, Aunt has occupied a long, narrow cubby-hole at the bend of the stairs leading to the roof, just above the first- floor washroom. A tall man could touch the ceiling if he stood here. The cubby-hole was full of Aunt's very own pots and pans, wooden boxes, quilts and bedclothes. She would say her prayers here, seated on a rush mat. Once she'd entered the fish- kitchen downstairs, she wouldn't return to this room before cleansing herself with a bath.

But what could they play here secretly? With Habib around, they couldn't call the other children in the house, or bring over the ones from next door. They must invent a new game.

"Let's play at Riots," says Gita.

"Where are the knives and sticks?" asks Habib.

"Just wait," says Gita.

She quietly fetches weapons: Tarapada's razor and a knife. The razor is an old one; it isn't used for shaving, only to cut paper and string or sharpen pencils. Gita latches the door with great effort, standing on tiptoe; she is a little taller than Habib.

"You're Akbar and I'm Padmini. Come on!"

Just a game, a child's game. One of them gets a slight, careless wound from the other's weapon.

"You've hit me!"

Hurt and angry, the child attacks the other in revenge. Two obstinate, unruly children begin stabbing and lunging at each other with a blunt knife and a blunt razor, crazed by pain, rage and resentment. At the same time, they keep sobbing with terror at the tops of their voices. Indira, the Aunt and all the others run up clamouring; so do Halima, Nurunnisa and the rest from next door. They rush up the stairs and crowd round the door to Aunt's cubby-hole; Tarapada and the other men of the house have to stand around at the foot of the stairs.

From the front door, surrounded by the menfolk of the other house, Nasiruddin calls, "Tarapada!"

Aunt's room has but a small aperture with two bars across it, only one person can look in at a time. Indira takes a glance and begins screaming: "He's killing her! He's killing my girl!"

She too bangs on the door and shouts, "Open up! Open the door! That killer boy has locked the door and is murdering my girl! Open the door!"

Halima too takes a look and screams in just the same key, "She's killing him! She's killing my boy!"

She too bangs on the door and shouts, "Open up! Open the door! That killer girl has locked the room and is murdering my boy! Open the door!"

Aunt screams, "Oh, oh, oh! He's touched and soiled everything!"

Nasiruddin shouts from below, "We'll enter your women's quarters, Tarapada! I'm warning you."

Pushing Aunt aside, Indira and Halima press forward like madwomen to look through the opening at the same time. Their heads knock together. They look at each other with savage eyes, like two tigresses about to attack.

Meanwhile, inside, the weapons have dropped from Gita and Habib's hands. The commotion outside has silenced them. But they haven't stopped fighting; neither will yield to the other. They wrestle noiselessly on the floor, biting each other. Aunt's pots and pans are shattered to pieces.

"Oh, oh, oh! Everything's gone, everything's ruined!"

Tarapada calls Nasiruddin upstairs. It's Nasir who kicks down the door — or rather doesn't quite kick it down, only dislodges the latch.

There are a lot of skin-deep wounds, a quantity of blood. Indira and Halima clutch their offspring to their bosoms and scan their bodies with agonized eyes. Then, almost at the same instant, they look up at each other, an unspeakable ferocity burning in their eyes; as though each is amazed at seeing the listless child on the other's lap, as though each has realized after a period of long oblivion that the other too was a mother, that the other child too had blood in its veins.

A crowd had gathered outside. A clash seemed imminent. The Peace Committee couldn't possibly have warded off a calamity, if they hadn't brought out the heads of the two households, Tarapada and Nasiruddin, side by side.

Habib and Gita were treated with iodine and bathed and fed and made to lie down in their respective houses. It was a holiday; the household work would have dragged on through the afternoon in any case, the more so now with all the extra people around. It was almost evening, before the two households began to miss the two children.

Neither can be found.

Again they searched through and through the house, in every nook and corner, under the beds. Gita isn't at home. Habib isn't at home.

Both houses grow dark with foreboding. The stillness resounds for a time, then a hubbub breaks out.

The people of this house cry out, beating their breasts, "They've had their revenge. They've lured the child over and holed her up, or else — "

The people in the other house echo the cry, banging their heads on the floor.

Tarapada says, "Nasir, Gita must be in your house."

Nasiruddin says, "Tarapada, you must have holed Habib up."

This time, there is no way to stem the tide; rumour and tension begin to spread like fire. All these days, for all their efforts, the provocators haven't been able to show their fangs in the neighbourhood. They must have been waiting for just this chance, and now they spring. In a trice, two bands of demented men gather in front of the two houses. This lot wants to attack that house, that lot this. But as there are two groups, neither can reach its target without first defeating the other in a street battle.

Everybody can tell there's going to be a fight. It would have started already, only the Peace Committee was staving it off for a few minutes.

"We'll search the houses," says the Joint Secretary.

The crowd refuses to listen. The volunteers are abused, some are even beaten up as they try to pacify them. They keep on trying nonetheless. The four militiamen sit silently at the corner of the lane.

Then someone calls out, "There's Habib! There he is!"

"And there's Gita!" shouts another.

Everyone's eyes had been rivetted downwards, no one had looked up. No one had seen that from the room on the roof of Nasiruddin's and Tarapada's house, a boy and a girl had been peering out side by side for some time, watching the goings-on below.

The two houses had a single common room on the roof, crowning the two staircases, straddling the partition wall. They had climbed there unobserved at some point to find a safe shelter to play in. Looking up now, a few people begin clamouring, "They've been found! They've both been found!"

Maybe even the appearance of the two lost children, safe and alive for all to see, could not have prevented a fight. For many of those who had flocked there, out of their minds with homicidal rage, didn't even know these t o were the cause of the trouble. But as a few people on both sides begin shouting and cheering at the bizarre turn of events, it sets off a wave of curiosity among the crowd. The Joint Secretaries of the Peace Committee put this to use, to deflect the course of events.

Well after the crowds have melted away, a truckload of soldiers comes round again.

They carry out a long search in Nasiruddin and Tarapada's houses for the two abducted children. Nestling close to Halima and Indira, Habib and Gita watch them with frightened eyes.

Original in Bengali.
Translated by Sukanta Chaudhuri.

LALITHAMBIKA ANTHARJANAM

A LEAF IN THE STORM

1

She was certainly the most emaciated of the women reclaimed from that obscure village in western Punjab; and the most outraged of them all, too.

She didn't bother to tell them her name or caste. Perhaps she even hesitated to accompany them to the refugee camp. She realized that she would be one of the many to be given in exchange. Fifty bonded girls were to be given away for the fifty 'reclaimed'. The exchange took place on the border, black bundles of rags crawled up and down, like ghosts let loose from the sepulchres. She was the last to come. She halted. She wasn't too sure...

"From one prison to another?..."

The transport was ready. The police and the army personnel would accompany them too. The social service volunteers were generous in their consolation. Still, someone had to gently force her into the vehicle bound for the camp.

The women were looked after well in the camp. They rejoiced as though they had been reunited with their lost children. The relatives of some of those women joined them in the camp. Some asked after their kinsfolk. Only one of them sat quietly, all by herself, in a corner. She did not lift her veil. As the lady volunteer approached her with some food, she exploded, "Damn your crumbs of bread; I want a gun. Or a dagger. Wouldn't mind a little poison either. It's that I want...first and last..."

The lady volunteer stood aghast. This woman must have gone mad. Well, who wouldn't under these circumstances? What is indeed amazing is that she is alive. A good many of these women keep crying. Some of them recount their baneful lives. That old woman there — is the mother of nine children, who in turn have given her fifty children of their own. She has indeed been a mother to the whole village, to both Hindus and Muslims. The family decided to stay on because of their mother's insistence that she should breathe her last in her own village. Today, she alone remains. Her children were killed. The girls were abducted. Her house was gutted. And there she stood, in the courtyard, supporting herself on a stick, watching her house burn down to ashes. Yet, she lives on...She eats, sleeps, and talks...Hope, passion for life..

There you see another woman, now at her breakfast, chewing hard at dirty bits of chapati. Her cheeks and breasts are swollen. Her clothes are torn. She had been married to a big officer in Sindh. She set out with her three children as soon as the people had been warned of the revolt. Tragedy overtook her car and waylaid her. She was violated in front of her husband's body which lay ripped open and scattered. She could only see the blood-stained hands of her children. Someone reclaimed her body, more dead than alive, from the railway tracks. Alas, she hasn't yet died.

On the other side of the hall, a Sikh girl is consoling a Hindu child. Another child has now dozed off, crying. Loud wails, everywhere, after one's parents. No one answers — Where are those parents?

Among them are people who ran for life, for several miles. Many have arrived with bruised feet, broken limbs and withered bodies. Not to speak of their fear of fever and epidemics. Despite all this, they seem to have got used to this way of life.

She observes everything about her. She doesn't cry now. But her eyes are dim with pity and despair. At times her eyes reflect the hate and cynicism of one who despises the whole world. Her belly remains big even though she hasn't had food for four days. She clenches her fist, aims it at her belly. But, now the occupants of the camp have begun to notice this small woman, good looking and noble, and perhaps born into a well-to-do family. Her frail body evidently cannot stand such torture — the four-day fasting and much else besides. Maybe she was the darling of her parents, the beloved of her husband...By now, inevitably, the report of her condition must have reached the camp doctor.

The doctor coaxed her to drink milk. He begged her, "Won't you drink this milk, for me sister? Why don't you realize that this life is also valuable for our beloved country?"

"One life...one life!" She broke into tears and said, "Why one life? How many lives have we lost now? Look at me! I am damned too...You want me to live on still, and sow the seed of damnation?"

She continued sobbing, "My life...doctor...may I ask you something? Tell me, are you able to destroy something which must be destroyed, just as much as you can preserve something you think must be preserved? Now this life bred of damnation — conceived in consequence of inhuman rape and ignorance — tell me doctor, can you destroy this, save another life...? Can you do that?"

She raised her eyebrows in question. The doctor turned pale. He wasn't quite prepared to answer something like this when he came to the camp. He was a disciple of the supreme master of ahimsa. It was at his master's instance that he had given up a well-paying job to serve the refugees here.

Her demand was loud and clear. Further, he was trained and adequately equipped for the task. But, still...But, would it be proper? He was stricken with a kind of moral cowardice. Breaking an egg, and wringing another's neck are taking away lives, in different ways...

He spoke like a vedantin, "Sister, who are we to fight the decree of destiny? Look, I'm a doctor. I have no moral right to take away someone's life; I can only redeem it. Look at the lakhs of people in this camp; there are many more like them in other camps too. We will overcome this storm that rages over the east and west of our land. Bharat will endure; are you not a woman of India? Cheer up; here, drink this milk..."

She said nothing in return. She drank the milk, however. It does not matter whether it was the doctor's sermon or her zest for life that eventually prevailed upon her desperate obstinacy. Since then she has been eating regularly.

The camp register entered her name as 'Jyoti'. It was a Sikh woman who told us that her name is 'Jyotirmoyi Devpal'. We began to hear more and more about her presently — that Jyoti's mother and the Sikh lady came from the same village; that even after coming of age, Jyoti had gone about refusing to veil her face; that she had spurned the proposal for marriage from a zamindar, true to her self-assertive nature, and so on. The women in her village were rather amazed at this girl's independent ways. Maybe now she is paying too high a price for such indulgence!

The crowd in the refugee camp grew day by day. Different costumes...different languages...Men, women, children. The young and the old. And the number swelled. And new stories; loud clamour as never before. And in the midst of all these no one bothered about Jyoti. In that ocean of mass movement she was but a wave. She witnessed many births in the camp. More deaths than births. In the camp one could witness all the scenes of human life.

At sunset people gathered under the big leafy tree at the backyard of the camp. They were villagers, who knew little of national politics. They all belonged to that beautiful land of five rivers and sugar-cane fields, the land where the wheat fields swayed in laughter as the breeze blew over them, where the buffaloes grazed in the fields...Far away, in the desert, a caravan of camels crawled towards the adjacent village. On many evenings like this one, these men had returned home, humming tunes, their work-tools balanced on their shoulders. And those houses...They have been hounded out of those houses — those ancestral homes they had inherited, and which, they would have passed on to their progeny. They have been driven away from them like stray dogs...hunted out of them like wild hen. How did this happen? Who was at fault?

They cursed all the well-known leaders. They gnashed their teeth in vengeful rage. Some of them blamed even the "toothless grandsire" of Indian politics — that kindly soul! Poor people. They were not amongst those who made others suffer, but those who suffered themselves.

In the camps across the border, do the people have the same feelings of outrage?

Jyoti listened to everything. She moved about slowly, trying hard to contain her swollen belly within the folds of her sari. Only a few people knew her secret; that she was pregnant and unmarried, and had been 'reclaimed' by the camp. Her burden grew heavier as the days passed. Those first imperceptible pulsations grew into swollen coils within her, threatening a revolt that might stifle her. What moved within her was a challenge to every cell of her being. It symbolized everything womanhood and humanity found despicable in nature. And that it should grow within her, drawing on her life-blood! It moved and drew breath from her life-breath. One day, it will emerge — this "cosmic shape" — biding no one's time, seeking no one's permission. Come out it must, willy-nilly.

Pressing her big belly hard against the floor, she bore her pain. What else could she do?

The next day something unusual happened. There lay in the toilet the lifeless body of a child, new born and deserted. A beautiful child it was, round and gleaming, like a thick clot of blood. Its fair skin was like that of an inhabitant of the territorial border. It had brown hair. On its neck was a thick bluish mark resembling a crescent. The scavenger dragged its still warm body away, and put it into his garbage bin. No girl shed a tear. There was no case against anyone.

Jyoti stood and watched all this. She wondered how courageous these people were in practical life — people one could easily mistake for cowards and slaves! They had no qualms. No indecisiveness. Nor did they turn to anyone for advice. Whatever the obstacles, they swept past them and went on ahead.

Faster than those tremors within her belly rose her heart-throbs. So, that's very easy...and equally trivial...It shouldn't take more time than it would in nipping off a blade of grass. A second? Maybe, a minute at the most — at midnight she could wipe herself clean of her filth and come out — into a new world of hopes...!

During the day she wandered about in the open and desolate space outside the camp. At night she preferred to be left alone in a corner. One day, at supper she felt a terrible pain in her back and felt dizzy. The people around had to lift her up and lay her on the cot. Jyoti was worried and anxious. She did not know anything. Was this a prelude to that momentous happening? Ayyo...and then?

But nothing happened. No one was suspicious either. It was quite normal for some people in the camp to feel sick.

Weeks passed by.

That day, a distinguished guest arrived. Everyone had heard about him. In fact, the message he brought them was well known and appreciated by them all. The guest addressed the people under the shade of the big tree in the backyard of the camp. "Young men should be prepared to accept abducted women as their mothers, sisters, and even as their wives — Those children..." Jyoti pricked up her ears, "those children are indeed the citizens of India, the first citizens of a free India..."

Her face glowed. "How ironical that would be! Are they citizens of India alone? That is, of India as we conceive of her today? They will grow up...these children...as they begin to comprehend the reality, as they come of age...that blood...No! The source of that blood is hate, not love... would it not run amok, driven by the intense desire for vengeance? Even break past the borders?..."

When Jyoti came to herself, she noticed that there was nobody around her? Perhaps the guest had left. And so had every other listener. It was late night.

She got to her feet hoping to go into the camp from the open yard which was steeped in darkness. It was cold. She couldn't walk, her body was shivering. She felt helpless and weak...A pain, with the speed of a thousand bolts of lighting, invaded her brain. The overwhelming travail of creation...She stood clinging to the branch of the big tree, trying to endure the pain. For how long? She couldn't remember. In the meanwhile, hazy memories thronged her mind...

Far away, in one of those prosperous villages in the Punjab — in a well-to-do household — a mother was in labour...There, the doctor and the nurses waited at hand...Her relatives were anxious. The master of the house sat on the bed, his eyes fixed on the clock. They were waiting for the fruit of prolonged medical treatment and their virtuous deeds.

The girl who was born that day was the darling of her kinsfolk and neighbours. She grew up in perfect happiness. No one had faulted her for anything. She joined college, despite the initial objections of her parents whom she won over by her charm. She shocked her people when she decided to give up her purdah. They chose to ignore such aberrations in her. She loved her freedom. That explained her refusal to settle for a marriage, which others considered desirable. The freedom she had earned was not only for herself. It was also the freedom from slavery for her community, indeed for the whole human race. She wanted to free the bonded, those who were enslaved by convention. She wanted to make them happy and contented.

She hoped in vain that she could knit together a net of silver threads.

Her dreams had landed her in prison. In her fight to uphold her ideals she had to suffer police brutality. For days she had gone about without food or rest. Ignoring all warnings, she had dedicated herself to the uplift of women. "I trust my brothers," she used to say, when others tried to dissuade her venturesome spirit. And now...this reward!

Oh my mother!

During those periodic bouts of excruciating pain, she shuddered. Her legs grew weaker and weaker. Her whole body was perspiring. Was she about to throw up? Resting her head against the trunk of the tree, she took a deep sigh. She was utterly exhausted.

Memory...frightening scenes from memory again...

2

Fifteen woman wearing ghoshah veils were confined in a room, far inside the lady's wing of the palace, in her neighbourhood. The master of that house, Qasim, was a good friend of her father. And Ayesha was her bosom friend. Ayesha had given them refuge. Only Ali, Ayesha's brother, thought otherwise, "Damn them! Our land will yield gold only when it is soaked by the blood of these kafirs!"

Ayesha tried hard not to rouse suspicion even in her brother. She had concealed those ghoshah ladies with great care. Her plan was to send them across the border when her father's bullock cart went on its usual trip. The refugee camp across the harbour would take care of them. Qasim Sahib's cart had been on its regular trips across the border for fifty years. No one would suspect that it carried women. And no one would stop it on the way.

That night, the miserable journey inside the iron-cage: one felt choked amidst violent bumps and jerks. Loud slogans rent the air...The air was full of the smell of flesh burning...the heat of flames...Qasim Sahib periodically hollered, ignoring other voices, "Pakistan Zindabad...Allah-ho-Akbar!"

The travellers thought for a while that they were out of danger. Then suddenly a big row erupted. The cart stopped. Someone pulled out the bundles of hay from the cart, ignoring Qasim Sahib's swearing and protests. Loud, thunderous laughter. Wild shouts. From among the bundles of hay fifteen women were dragged out. One by one, those flowers fell...

Oh...how cruel life's traffic is! Overwhelming pain! What could it be — the agony of life, or death?

It seemed her mother, now returned from the dead,was speaking to her — "Jyoti, I too went through this. My mother and mother's mother...In fact, all mothers..."

No woman can evade the tax levied on her life. Suddenly, she thought of the prison in which she had lain unconscious. An awful lot of men must have come into that cell. Those devilish faces...reddened by fanatic hate and frenzy! To which one of those faces does this bear a resemblance?

Jyoti felt a deep convulsion from within. She felt hot...and thirsty. She breathed hard and her body shook in agony...

Ho! And so it ends. Was it really the end?

The lamps had gone out in the camp sheds. Here and there the sick groaned. The children cried. No one, however, would really know about this.

She lay on her back on the lawn, a triumphant soldier, fallen in exhaustion on the battlefield. The stars had dimmed in the sky. The young one of a bird cried "kee...kee," and fluttered its wings on the tree.

Her first instinct was to close her eyes, grope her way about, and choke it to death with her hands. With that, she might bury the bundle of her misery and shame which she had borne all these months...there; bury it under that tree, forever...She wouldn't let the scavenger drag it away. One must carry one's cross oneself.

Jyoti got up and stretched her hand. She felt that mass of flesh..."O, how warm it is! Did my body give it so much warmth? I hope its looks are like mine...Perhaps I should look at it, its small eyes, once...once only!"

"Oh! it is seeking refuge, stirring its little feet." That voice didn't resemble hers; in fact it wasn't like anything she had heard so far. Its voice resounded like the assertion of a right, an appeal to nature.

"Perhaps the voice has woken up the camp. The whole universe and its creatures might wake up, hearing this voice. It is so compelling. And so tender!"

She tried to cover its parted lips, to hush its voice. How ticklishly smooth they felt, like the tender leaves. More than compassion, fear overcame her. As though someone had forbidden her, and said, "No don't stifle that voice! It is not the voice of an individual, but that of the whole world!"

Jyoti drew back with a shudder. She was confused. "Why not run away from this place of conflicting emotions, of fear and suspicion, and go into hiding? But where? The place doesn't matter...to the utmost boundary of this earth, or hell... wherever...Will this voice haunt me there too?

Let the child be, amidst the green grass, in the light of the stars. I have heard it said that babes deserted by their mothers are tended to by goddesses. Someone will surely spot the child in the morning. Perhaps, one of those mothers without children..." And then a doubt crossed her mind — did she have children?

Jyoti was confused. It was rather difficult to sever life's bonds so easily. The scar would remain. The world would suppurate and continue to afflict one's life till the very end. Jyoti returned slowly. The child was still crying. Its voice grew hoarse. Its limbs began to grow limp. There was no time to wait.

The mother swooped the child up into her arms. She warmed its forehead by caressing it gently. Her life-blood flowed like fresh milk.

As the mother walked slowly towards the camp, the stars beamed from heaven. Maybe they had resolved a complicated puzzle.

Original in Malyalam.
Translated by Narayan Chandran.

BHISHAM SAHNI

THE TRAIN HAS REACHED AMRITSAR

There were very few passengers in the compartment. The Sardarji, sitting opposite me, had been telling me stories about the war. He had fought on the Burmese front, and every time he talked about the white soldiers, he laughed at them derisively. There were also three Pathan traders in the compartment. One of them, who was dressed in green, lay stretched on the upper berth. He was a jovial man who had joked throughout the journey with a frail-looking Babu. That Babu seemed to be from Peshawar, because at times they talked to each other in Pushto. On the berth opposite me and to my right, sat an old woman whose head and shoulders were covered. She had been telling the beads of her rosary for quite sometime. There may have been other passengers in the compartment, but I can't remember them anymore.

The train moved slowly, the passengers gossiped with each other, the wheat fields outside swayed gently in the breeze, and I was happy because I was going to Delhi to watch the Independence Day celebrations.

When I think back on those days they seem to be shrouded in mist. Perhaps, the past always seems hazy. And as the future opens up before us, the past becomes even more indistinct.

The decision to create Pakistan had just been announced, and people speculated about the shape of things to come. But no one could foresee the future clearly. The Sardarji, sitting opposite me, asked me repeatedly whether I thought Jinnah Sahib would continue to live in Bombay or move to Pakistan. My answer was always the same, "Why should he leave Bombay? What would be the point? He can always go to Pakistan and come back." There was speculation about which side of the border Lahore and Gurdaspur would find themselves. Nothing had changed in the way people talked to each other or joked together. A few people had abandoned their homes and run away, while those who had chosen to stay back had merely laughed at them. No one knew what to do, what steps to take. Some people rejoiced at the creation of Pakistan, others rejoiced at India's Independence. There had been riots in a few places, but there were also preparations being made for the celebration of freedom in other places. Given the history, everyone felt that after Independence the riots would automatically stop. The golden glow of freedom was surrounded by uncertainty and darkness. Only occasionally did one catch a glimpse of the future through the surrounding haze.

Soon after we crossed the Jhelum, the Pathan sitting on the upper berth, untied a bundle, took out chunks of boiled meat and nan, and offered them to the passengers. In his usual jovial way, he invited the Babu sitting next to me to share them with him, "Here Babu, eat. You will become strong like us. Your wife will be pleased. Eat it, dalkhor, you are weak because you only eat dal."

Everyone in the compartment laughed. The Babu smiled, shook his head and said something in Pushto.

The other Pathan joined in the teasing and said, "O zalim, if you don't want it from our hands, pick it up yourself. I swear it's only goat's meat and nothing else."

The Pathan sitting on the upper berth chuckled, and added, "O son of a swine, no one will know. We won't tell your wife. If you share meat with us, we'll 'drink' dal with you."

Everyone laughed. The Babu smiled, shook his head and said something in Pushto again.

"How can we let you sit there and stare at us, while we eat? It's not courteous." The Pathans were in a good mood.

"He doesn't want to take food from you because you haven't washed your hands," the fat Sardarji said and tittered at his own joke. He was reclining on the berth and half his belly had spilled over the seat. "The Babu doesn't want to accept meat from your hands, because you have just woken up and have begun eating. There is no other reason." As he said that he looked at me, winked and tittered.

"If you don't eat meat, you should travel in the ladies compartment. Why sit here?" Again, the whole compartment laughed.

There were other passengers in the compartment, but a sort of informality had grown between those of us who had been together since the beginning.

"O zalim, come and sit, sit with me. Let's tell each other stories," one of the Pathans said.

The train stopped at a station and lots of new passengers pushed their way in.

"What station is it?" someone asked.

"Wazirabad, I hope," I replied, looking out of the window.

The train didn't stop there for long. But before it left, there was a minor incident. A man had got down from the next compartment to get some water. He had just begun to fill his pot, when he suddenly turned around with a start and ran back. Some water spilled out of his pot. But the manner in which he had been startled was revealing in itself. Others who were standing around the tap also ran back towards their compartments. I had seen people run in fear like that before. Within a few seconds, the platform was deserted. Inside our compartment, however, people were still laughing and joking.

"Something is wrong," the Babu sitting next to me muttered.

Something was certainly wrong. But none of us was able to find out what had happened. Since I had seen many riots, I could sense the slight change in the atmosphere. The sound of doors shutting, people standing on roof-tops and an eerie silence — they were all the signs of a riot.

Suddenly, there were some altercation at the door opposite the one that opened onto the platform. Some passengers were trying to get in.

"There is no place in here. Don't try to force your way in," someone shouted.

"Shut the door. Can't you see there is no place. People think they can push their way in..." Many passengers shouted at the same time.

As long as a passenger outside tries to force his way in, people inside oppose him. But the moment he gets in, all opposition subsides and he becomes a part of the inner world of the compartment, and at the next station begins to shout and scream at other passengers trying to get in — "There is no place here, go to the next compartment...People think they can walk in..."

The commotion at the door increased. A man, with a drooping moustache, wearing tattered clothes, was trying to squeeze his way into the compartment. From his filthy clothes, it appeared that he worked in a halwai's shop. Without paying attention to the protests of the other passengers, he turned around and began pulling in an enormous black trunk.

"Come on, climb in," he shouted to someone behind him. A thin, frayed woman climbed up, followed by a young, dark girl of sixteen or seventeen. People continued to scream at them. The Sardarji had to get up and sit upon his berth.

"Shut the door...People barge in as if they are walking into their father's house...Don't let anyone else in...What are you doing...Push him out..." Everyone shouted at the same time.

The man continued to pull his trunk in, while his wife and daughter stood against the toilet door.

"Couldn't you have found another compartment?...Did you have to bring women in here too..."

The man was breathless and his clothes were soaked through his sweat. Having pulled in the trunk, he began hauling in a bundle of wooden legs for his cot.

"I have a ticket. We are not travelling without tickets. I was lucky to reach the station." Suddenly all the passengers fell silent.

But the Pathan sitting on the lower berth yelled, "Get out of here! Can't you see there is no room?" Blind with rage, he suddenly got up and tried to kick the man. But, unfortunately, he missed him, and the kick landed on his wife's stomach. She screamed with pain and collapsed on the floor.

That man had no time to argue with the passengers. He was much too busy collecting his luggage. But an ominous silence descended on the compartment. The man began pulling in large bundles packed with his things. Seeing that, the Pathan sitting on the upper berth lost his patience, and yelled, "Throw him out. Who does he think he is?" The Pathan sitting on the lower berth, got up and threw the man's trunk out of the door of the compartment. It fell at the feet of a coolie in a red uniform.

No one interfered, only the old woman sitting in a corner muttered, "Have some pity. Be kind to them and let them come in. Come, child, come and sit next to me. We'll somehow manage! Leave them alone, you scoundrels, let them in."

Before that man could pull all his baggage in, the train began to move.

"My luggage! My luggage has been left behind!" he screamed in despair.

"Father, our luggage is still outside," the girl standing against the toilet door said, as she trembled with fear.

"Get down, down," shouted the man in despair. He threw the rest of his luggage out and, holding the iron-bars of the door, jumped down himself. His terrified daughter and his wife, who was still groaning with pain, followed him.

"You are cruel people, that was an awful thing to have done," the old woman protested loudly. "There is no pity left in your hearts. He had a young daughter. You are cruel, pitiless people, you pushed them out."

The train sped past the deserted platform. There was an uneasy silence in the compartment. No one had the courage to defy the Pathans.

Just then, the frail Babu sitting next to me, touched my arm and whispered, "Fire. Look something is burning."

The train had left the city behind. We saw flames leaping out of the clouds of smoke which rose above the city.

"A riot. That is why people were scared at the platform. There has been a clash somewhere."

The city was in flames. The passengers in the compartment rushed to the windows to catch a glimpse of the fire.

After the train left the city far behind there was silence in the compartment. When I turned around to look at the passengers, I noticed that the Babu's face was pale, and that his forehead was covered with sweat. He looked deathly pale. I realized then that each passenger was nervous and suspicious about his neighbour. The Sardarji got up from his seat and sat down next to me. The Pathan on the lower berth climbed up to join his two companions on the upper berth. Perhaps, the condition in the other compartments was also the same. Everyone was tense. The lights had been turned off. The old woman was telling her rosary. The three Pathans on the upper berth quietly watched everyone down below. The passengers were alert to everything around them.

"What station was that?" someone asked.

"Wazirabad," another person replied.

The name produced a strange reaction amongst the passengers. The Pathans became less tense, the silence amongst Hindus and the Sikhs became more ominous. One of the Pathans took some snuff out of a small box and sniffed it. The other Pathans did the same. The old woman continued to tell her beads over and over again and mutter something in a hoarse voice.

There was an ominous silence at the next station where the train stopped. Not even a bird was in sight. A mushqee, however, walked across the deserted platform with a bag full of water on his back, offering some to the passengers. "Water, come and drink water," he cried. The women and children sitting in the ladies compartment, stretched out their hands for water.

"There's been a communal riot here. Many people have been killed." It appeared as if he was the only man who had stepped out to do a good deed.

As soon as the train began to move, people pulled their windows down. One could hear, over the clatter of the wheels, the loud rattle of windows being pulled shut in compartments far away.

The Babu, sitting next to me, was so terrified that he jumped up from his seat and lay down flat on the floor. His face was tense with fear. Seeing him thus, one of the Pathans on the upper berth, mockingly said, "O coward, are you a man or a woman? Don't lie there on the floor. You are a disgrace to all men." Then he added something in Pushto and laughed. The Babu lay on the floor without saying anything in reply. The other passengers sat in tense silence. The atmosphere in the compartment was charged with fear.

"We won't let a coward stay in our compartment. O Babu, get down at the next station and go sit in the ladies compartment."

The Babu's lips were dry. He stammered something and then fell silent. After sometime he got up, dusted his clothes and sat on his seat again. I didn't know why he had decided to lie on the floor. Maybe, when he heard the sound of the shutters being pulled down, he thought that people outside were either throwing stones or firing at the train.

I was confused. It was possible that one person had, in panic, pulled the shutters of his window down, and others had instinctively followed his example.

Tense and nervous, we continued on our journey. The night outside grew darker. The passengers watched each other suspiciously. If the train slowed down they stared at each other apprehensively. If it stopped the silence inside became unbearable. Only the Pathans seemed to be unconcerned. After sometimes, however, they too stopped gossiping because no one was in the mood to talk to them.

A little later the Pathans began to doze, while the other passengers continued to stare anxiously into nothingness. The old woman covered her head, folded her legs up on the seat and went to sleep. One of the Pathans, climbing onto the upper berth once again, pulled out his rosary and began counting the black beads mechanically.

The moon had appeared in the sky by then, and the world outside seemed even more mysterious and even more threatening. Sometimes, in the far distance, we saw flames leaping up into the sky. Cities were burning all around us. There were times when the train screamed through the night; at other times, however, it crawled slowly for miles.

Suddenly the Babu, who had been looking out of the window, shouted excitedly. "We have crossed Harbanspura!" All the other passengers were startled by his shrill voice. They turned to look at him.

"O Babu, why are you screeching?" the Pathan with the rosary asked in surprise. "Do you want to get down here? Shall I pull the chain?" He continued to make fun of the Babu. It was obvious that he had neither heard of Harbanspura nor was he aware of its importance for the passengers.

The Babu didn't say anything in reply. He merely shook his head, looked at the Pathan and turned around to look out of the window again.

Everyone in the compartment was silent. The engine blew its whistle and slowed down. There was a loud clatter of the wheels. Perhaps, the train had changed tracks. The Babu continued to lean out of the window and stare ahead.

"We have reached!" he shouted again in excitement. "We have arrived at Amritsar!" He leapt up, whipped around to face the Pathan and began shouting, "Come down you bastard. You son of a bitch...May your mother..."

The Babu began to hurl filthy curses at the Pathan. The Pathan with the rosary in his hand, turned to look at the Babu and said, "O Babu, what's the matter? What have I said?"

Seeing the Babu so agitated, the other passengers sat up.

"Come down, you son of a bitch...You dared to kick a Hindu woman, you bastard..."

"O Babu, stop cursing and screaming. I'll cut your tongue out, you son of a pig."

"You dare to abuse me! May your mother..." the Babu shouted as he stood on his seat. He was trembling with rage.

"Enough, enough," the Sardarji said, "Don't fight. We don't have far to go now."

"I'll break your legs. You think the train belongs to you?" the Babu continued to shout.

"O Babu, what have I said? Everyone wanted to throw them out, I pushed them. Why curse me alone? If you don't stop, I'll cut out your tongue."

The old woman pleaded, "Please sit down and be calm. Please, in the name of God, be calm."

The Babu seemed as if he was possessed and was muttering something incoherently. He continued to shout, "You pretend to be brave like a lion in your own backyard. Now talk, you son of a bitch."

The train slowly pulled into the Amritsar station. The platform was crowded. The people, who peered into the compartment, wanted to ask only about one thing, "What's happening back there? Where have the riots broken out?"

The entire platform was buzzing with talk about the riots. The passengers in the train had pounced upon the few hawkers on the platform. They were hungry and thirsty.

A few Pathans appeared at the window of our compartment. The moment they spotted the other Pathans inside they began talking to them in Pushto. I looked around for the Babu. He was nowhere in sight. I was disturbed. He had been trembling with rage. I didn't know what he would do. The Pathans in our compartment collected their bundles and left with the other Pathans to sit in a compartment up ahead. The segregation, which had taken place earlier in our compartment, was now taking place in the entire train.

The crowd around the hawkers began to thin out. People started walking back towards their compartments. I suddenly saw the Babu. His face was still pale and a lock of hair had fallen across his forehead. As he came closer, I noticed that he was carrying an iron rod in his hand. I didn't know where he had found it. Before entering the compartment, he hid the rod behind his back, and as he sat down on the seat next to mine, he slipped it under the berth. When he raised his eyes, he was startled to find that the Pathans were no longer sitting on the upper berth.

"The bastards have run away. The sons of bitches...they have all escaped." He stood up and started shouting angrily, "Why did you let them escape? You are all impotent and cowardly."

The train was very crowded. Many new passengers had boarded it. No one paid him any attention.

The train began to move and, once again, he sat down on his seat next to me. But he was very upset and was continuously muttering something to himself.

Slowly the train lurched forward. The passengers who had travelled with us, had eaten as many puris as they could have and had quenched their thirst. The train was now passing through a region in which there was no danger to the lives and property of the passengers.

The new passengers were gossiping. The train had begun to move at a steady pace. Soon the passengers began to doze. But the Babu continued to stare into empty space. Repeatedly, he asked me to tell him where the Pathans had gone after getting down from the compartment. He seemed to be possessed.

Soon even I was lulled to sleep by the rhythmic movement of the train. There was no space to lie down in the compartment. I slept where I sat, and my body swayed with the train. Sometimes when I woke up, I heard the Sardarji lying on the opposite berth snoring comfortably. He looked like a corpse. Indeed, I felt, looking at the awkward postures people were reclining in, that I was travelling in a train full of dead bodies. The Babu, however, was restless. He sometimes leaned out of the window and sometimes sat still, with his back erect against the wall.

If the train stopped at a station and the clatter of its wheels ceased, a deep silence fell over everything. In such a silence even the sound of something falling, or the footsteps of someone getting down, startled me out of my sleep.

Once when I woke up, I noticed that the train was moving slowly. It was dark inside the compartment. All the lights had been switched off. I looked out of the window and saw the red light of a signal glowing somewhere far behind. We had recently passed a station, but the train had still not picked up speed.

I heard a vague sound outside the compartment. Then, still half asleep, I saw the shadow of something moving. I stared at it for a while and then forgot about it. It was nearly dawn.

Suddenly, I heard someone outside bang at the door of the compartment. I turned around to look. The door was shut. I again heard someone bang at the door. It seemed as if someone was hitting the door with a stick. When I leaned outside the window, I saw a man on the foot-board of the compartment. He had a lathi in his hand and a bundle over his shoulder. His clothes were dirty and he had a beard. When I looked down, I saw a woman running barefoot alongside the train. She was carrying two bundles in her hands. Because of their weight, she couldn't run fast. The man standing on the foot- board urged her again and again, "Come on, climb up!"

The man banged at the door with his lathi and called out, "Open the door. In the name of Allah, open the door."

He was breathless, "In the name of Allah, open the door. There is a woman with me. She'll be left behind..."

Suddenly I saw the Babu jump up from his seat, rush to the window and ask, "Who is it? There is no place in here."

The man outside pleaded, "For the sake of Allah, she'll be left behind..."

The man pushed his hand in through the window and groped for the latch.

"There is no place in here, get down from the train," the Babu screamed, and the next instant pulled the door open with a jerk.

"Ya Allah," I heard the man exclaim with relief.

At that very instant, I saw the iron rod flash in the Babu's hand. He gave the man a sharp blow on his head. I was so shocked that I couldn't move. At first I thought that the blow had no effect on the man. He still held onto the bars of the door. The bundle had slipped down his shoulder and hung on his arm.

Suddenly, two or three thin streams of blood began to flow down the man's face. In the faint light of the morning, I saw the man grimace with pain. He uttered "Ya Allah" a few times, groaned and staggered. He looked at the Babu with eyes which were barely open as if they were trying to ask his assailant what crime he had committed. The shadows of the night scattered. I saw terror on the man's face.

The woman, who was running along the track, was shouting and cursing. She didn't know what had happened. She thought that her husband had staggered under the weight of the bundle he was carrying. Running beside him, she kept trying to place his feet back on the foot-board of the compartment again.

Suddenly, the man's grip on the door-handles loosened and he fell to the ground like a tree which had been chopped down. As soon as he fell, the woman stopped running, as if both of them had reached their journey's end at the same time.

The Babu stood at the door like a statue. The iron bar was still in his hand. His arm didn't seem to have the strength to throw it away. I was still afraid and sat hidden in my corner staring at him.

After sometime the Babu stirred. A strange impulse made him lean out of the door and look back. Somewhere far behind, next to the railway tracks, he saw a dark heap. The train continued on its journey.

The Babu roused himself out of his trance. He threw the iron rod out of the door. Turned around and cast his eyes over the passengers. They were all asleep. He didn't notice me.

Then he closed the door shut. Examined his clothes carefully, checked both his hands and sniffed them to see if they smelled of blood. After that he walked quietly across and sat down on his seat.

Slowly, the morning sun dispelled the darkness. Bright and clear light spread over everything. No one had pulled the chain to stop the train. The body of the man who had fallen had been left miles behind. The wheat fields swayed gently in the breeze.

The Sardarji woke up and scratched his body. The Babu sat quietly with his hands behind his head and stared into space. There was a shadow of a beard on his face.

Seeing the Babu sitting opposite him, the Sardar laughed and said, "You look frail, Babu, but you are brave. You showed real courage back there. The Pathans got scared of you and ran away. If they had stayed here, you would have smashed the heads of each of them."

The Babu smiled in reply — it was a terrifying smile. He continued to stare at the Sardar's face for a long time.

Original in Hindi.
Translated by Alok Bhalla.

AHMAD NADEEM QASMI

PARMESHWAR SINGH

Akhtar was suddenly separated from his mother. He was beside her a moment ago and a moment later he had vanished — like a coin which falls out of the pocket of a running man and disappears. A hue and cry was raised. People searched for him, but only within the circle of the plundered and disheartened caravan. The commotion was like foam in soapy water — it rose suddenly and just as suddenly subsided. "He must be around somewhere. He'll find us," someone said. "There are thousands in this caravan." And Akhtar's mother, supporting herself on the strength of such a hope, continued to drag herself towards Pakistan. "He will follow us," she reassured herself. "He must have run after a butterfly...O, how he must miss me and weep!... I am sure he is close by and is following us. He is a clever boy. He's more than five years old. He'll make his way to Pakistan. Once I settle down in peace, I'll look for him and find him."

About fifteen miles from the border, Akhtar had got separated from the caravan. It is possible that he had, just as his mother had thought, run-off either to catch a butterfly or to break some sugar-cane, and had then wandered further and further away into the surrounding fields. Anyway, as he ran around aimlessly, waving his arms and shouting, he was suddenly surrounded by a group of Sikhs. At first, Akhtar threatened them angrily — "I shall shout Allah-ho-Akbar" — but then he was frightened.

Except for one Sikh, all the others burst out laughing. That Sikh was named Parmeshwar Singh. A few dishevelled strands of hair hung freely out of his turban, which was loosely tied. The bun of hair on his head was uncovered.

He said, "Don't laugh, yaroon. This child was created by the same Waheguruji as the one who created you and your children."

A young Sikh, who had by then pulled out his kirpan, said, "Wait a moment, Parmeshwarji, let this kirpan first fulfil its sacred duty, then we shall talk about our religion."

"Don't kill him, yaroon," Parmeshwar Singh pleaded. He was panting with excitement. "He is so small and he was created by the same Waheguruji as the one..."

"Let's ask him," said another Sikh. Then he walked upto the frightened boy and said, "Tell me. Who gave birth to you — Khuda or Waheguruji?"

Akhtar felt his mouth go dry. He moistened it. When he blinked his eyes, he felt as if they were filled with sand. As he looked towards Parmeshwar Singh he thought he was looking at his mother. He spat out the tears which had tickled down into his mouth and sobbed, "I don't know."

"There, did you hear that?" Somebody said and cursed him.

Akhtar, who had not yet completed his sentence, continued, "My mother says that I was found in hay in a small barn."

The Sikhs began to laugh, but were taken aback when they saw that Parmeshwar Singh was sobbing like a child. Then he wailed, "All children are alike, yaroon. My Kartara also used to say the same thing. He too had been found by his mother in hay in a small barn."

The Sikhs sheathed their swords and moved aside to whisper among themselves. Then one Sikh walked upto the whimpering Akhtar, took him by his hand, and leading him upto Parmeshwar who was crying softly, said, "Here Parmeshwarji, take care of him. Let him grow his hair long, name him Kartar Singh, treat him like your son. Here, take him."

Parmeshwar Singh gathered Akhtar into his arms so quickly that his turban came undone and his long hair fell loosely over his shoulder. He hugged Akhtar tightly, kissed him like a man who was possessed, and then, looking deep into his eyes, saw so many of his old dreams that his face began to glow with joy. Suddenly, he turned and looked back at the place where the other Sikhs were standing, put Akhtar down, rushed towards them, ran past them and began to leap and dance like a monkey in the bushes. The Sikhs watched him with utter amazement. Soon he came back with both his hands cupped together. There was a smile on his lips which were covered by his sweaty beard, his eyes were glittering with excitement and he was breathless.

He went upto Akhtar, knelt in front of him and asked, "What is your name?"

"Akhtar," the boy replied. This time his voice didn't tremble with fear.

"Akhtar, my son, would you like to see what's in my hands?"

Akhtar leaned forward slightly with curiosity. Parmeshwar Singh opened his cupped hands a little and then closed them again.

"Aha!" Akhtar clapped his hands with delight, smiled through his tears, and then, placing his hands over Parmeshwar Singh's, exclaimed, "A butterfly!"

"Want it?" Parmeshwar Singh asked.

"Yes," Akhtar replied and rubbed his hands together in excitement.

"Take it," Parmeshwar Singh said and opened his hands.

Akhtar tried to catch the butterfly, but it flew away leaving a thin film of colourful powder on his fingers. He felt sad.

Parmeshwar Singh turned to the other Sikhs and said, "Why are all children alike, yaroon? Kartar also became sad when he couldn't catch a butterfly."

"Parmeshwar Singh has lost his mind," said a young Sikh contemptuously.

The entire group got ready to leave. When Parmeshwar Singh lifted Akhtar onto his shoulders and followed the other Sikhs, Akhtar began to weep bitterly, "I want my mother. I want to go to my mother." Parmeshwar Singh caressed his head and tried to console him. But Akhtar pushed his hand away angrily.

Then Parmeshwar Singh said, "Alright, alright son, I'll take you to your mother." That comforted Akhtar a bit and he sobbed only once in a while. Grudgingly, he let Parmeshwar Singh caress him.

Parmeshwar Singh took him back to his house. Till very recently it was the house of a Muslim family. When Parmeshwar Singh had come to zilla Amritsar from zilla Lahore, after having lost everything he owned, the villagers had allotted him this house. When he had first walked into the house, he was taken aback. With fear and astonishment in his eyes, he exclaimed, "There is someone reading the *Koran* in here!"

The village granthi and the other villagers had laughed at him. His wife had already told them that ever since Kartar Singh's disappearance, her husband had lost his wits.

"I don't know what's wrong with him." She had said, "May Waheguruji not let me tell a lie! Back there he used to thrash Kartar Singh as if he was a donkey. Since Kartarey's disappearance, I have wept and suffered and reconciled myself, but he continues to moan for him. Back there I could never have dared, even once, to look angrily at my daughter, Amar Kaur. If I did, he would lose his temper and say, don't you ever say a word against your daughter, because a daughter is an innocent traveller, a wayfarer in your house. She has come to live in comfort for a while. When the time comes she will go away. Now, if Amar Kaur makes even the slightest mistake, he loses control over himself. He even goes to the extent of saying that he has heard of wives and daughters being abducted, but that he hasn't heard of small boys of five and six years of age being kidnapped."

Though Parmeshwar Singh had been living in this house for over a month, he still slept fitfully. Often he would mumble incoherently in his sleep, and would sometimes wake with a start and whisper fearfully to his wife, "Listen, there is someone reading the *Koran* in here!"

His wife would turn her back to him and go to sleep. But Amar Kaur, awakened by his whispers, found it impossible to sleep again. Throughout the night, she would imagine that she could hear all sorts of shadows reading the *Koran* around her. At the break of dawn, she would sit up in her bed with her hands pressed against her ears. Their house in Lahore zilla was near a mosque and the azan at dawn had sounded delightful. It seemed to her as if the morning light spreading in the east was singing. But ever since the day her neighbour, Pritam Kaur, had been raped by a few young men and then cast away like a torn rag on a garbage heap, she heard screams even in the muezzin's call. The very mention of the azan now filled her with dread. She would forget that there was no mosque in their neighbourhood now and that she didn't need to sleep with her hands covering her ears. Because she often lay awake at night, she slept late in the morning. Parmeshwar Singh now got angry with her because of this and often cursed her, "She sleeps late because she is a lazy, good for nothing, useless creature. All girls are good for nothing.

By this time of the day a son would have done a lot of work, yaroon."

That day Parmeshwar Singh walked into the courtyard of his house with a strange smile on his face. His long hair was open and hung over one of his shoulders. His comb was still stuck in it. Akhṭar was sitting on his other shoulder and Parmeshwar Singh was fondling him lovingly. His wife was sitting in one corner and sieving flour through a cane basket. When she saw him, her hands stopped in mid-air and she stared at him in disbelief. Then she leapt over the basket, ran to Parmeshwar Singh and asked, "Who is he?"

Parmeshwar Singh smiled and said, "Don't be afraid, you fool. He talks just like Kartarey. His mother also found him in hay in an old shed. He, too, loves butterflies. His name is Akhtar."

"Akhtar!" His wife screamed angrily.

"You can call him, Akhtar Singh," Parmeshwar Singh explained patiently. "And don't worry about his hair, it will grow long in no time. Then the comb will stay in place with ease. We can give him a steel bracelet and a long underwear straight-away."

"But whose son is he?" The wife inquired.

"Whose?" Parmeshwar Sing said, as he put Akhtar down and caressed his head, "He is Waheguruji's son, yaroon. Like our own Kartarey, he has a small black mole on his forehead. Kartarey's was a little bigger. I used to kiss it often. Akhtar's ear-lobes are like rose-petals. Don't you remember that Kartarey's ear-lobes were similar? Perhaps, his were a bit thicker than Akhtar's. But..."

Akhtar, who had till then been so frightened that he hadn't uttered a sound, couldn't control himself any longer and started shouting, "I won't stay here. I want my mother. I want my mother."

Parmeshwar Singh took Akhtar by his arm and, pushing him towards his wife, said, "There, take him, he wants to go to his mother."

"Leave him alone," his wife shouted. There was the same look of terror in her eyes, which Parmeshwar Singh had also experienced back in the fields, a terror which he had overcome and left behind.

"Look at this brave hero!" she exclaimed, "He had gone out to become a great dacoit, but all he could find was this little runt, this puny brat! If he had kidnapped a grown-up girl, we could have sold her, maybe not for a thousand rupees, but we would have got at least a few hundred for her! Enough to furnish this empty house. Idiot! What's wrong with you? Can't you see that he is a mussalla? Take him away and dump him where you found him. I'll be damned if he steps into my kitchen!"

Parmeshwar Singh pleaded, "Don't you understand that Kartarey and Akhtar were created by the same Waheguruji?"

"No," his wife shrieked, "I don't understand and I don't want to. I'll cut his throat at night. I'll cut him into small bits. Who knows where you have picked him up from? Take him away! Throw him out!"

"Why shouldn't I throw you out?" Parmeshwar Singh said, losing his temper. "Why shouldn't I cut your throat?" And when he advanced towards his wife, she ran out beating her breasts, wailing and howling. Amar Kaur came running back from the house next door. Men from the neighborhood gathered around Parmeshwar Singh's wife and saved her from getting a thrashing.

Everyone tried to reason with Parmeshwar Singh. His intentions were noble, they agreed. In olden times, he would have been regarded as a saint. But now it wasn't easy to teach a Muslim to become a Sikh. His wife was emboldened by their talk. Amar Kaur, however, continued to sit in a corner with her head on her knees and weep.

Suddenly, Parmeshwar Singh let out such a loud cry that everyone got scared. "Where has he gone?" he screamed. "Where is he? Tell me. I hope one of you hasn't butchered him, yaroon? Akhtar! Akhtar!" He searched every nook and corner of the house, and then, calling out for the boy, he ran out into the streets. Fascinated and curious, the children of the neighbourhood followed him. The women climbed upto the terraces of their houses to watch. Parmeshwar Singh ran through the village and out into the fields.

"O, I would have taken him back to his mother, yaroon. O, where has he gone? Akhtar! Akhtar!"

"I will not come back," Akhtar shouted. He stood crying at the bend of the path which encircled Gyan Singh's sugar-cane fields, "You are a Sikh!"

"Yes, son, I am a Sikh," Parmeshwar Singh said, in a resigned tone, as if he had acknowledged his crime.

"Then I shall not go with you,," Akhtar said, as he wiped the traces of old tears from his face only to make room for more tears.

"So, you won't come," Parmeshwar Singh said. This time there was an edge to his voice.

"No,"

"Sure, you won't come."

"No, no, no."

"Just try," Parmeshwar Singh said. Then he caught Akhtar by the ear and, biting his lower lip, gave him a resounding slap. "Come along," he growled.

At first, Akhtar was so pale with fear that it seemed as if all the blood had drained out of his body. Then, he suddenly threw himself on the ground, started kicking up dust and crying bitterly, "No, I won't come. You are a Sikh. I won't go with a Sikh. I want to go to my mother. I'll kill you."

Now it was Parmeshwar Singh's turn to be frightened. It seemed as if all the blood had been drained out of his body. He clenched his teeth, his nostrils flared and trembled. Then he began to wail so loudly that even the children and the neighbours, who had followed him, and were standing on the field's embankment at some distance, got frightened. Parmeshwar Singh knelt before Akhtar and began pleading and sobbing like a child. "Forgive me, Akhtar. I swear by your God that I am your friend. If you go away from here by yourself, someone will kill you. Then your mother will come from Pakistan and kill me. I'll take you to Pakistan myself and leave you there. And listen, if you find a boy named Kartar Singh there, send him back to my village. Is that a deal?"

"It's a deal," Akhtar said, as he wiped his eyes with the back of his hand and made his bargain with Parmeshwar Singh.

Parmeshwar Singh lifted Akhtar onto his shoulder and started walking back to his village. But he stopped after taking a few steps. His path was blocked by his neighbours and the numerous children who had watched the entire scene.

A middle-aged neighbour said, "Why are you crying, Parmeshwar ? It's only a matter of a month or so. By then his hair will grow long, and he'll look like Kartara."

Without replying to him, Parmeshwar Singh quickly walked past the group. Then he suddenly stopped, looked back at his neighbours, and said, "How can you be so cruel, yaroon? You want to make Akhtar, Kartara, but supposing someone were to make Kartara, Akhtar? You'll call him evil, won't you?"

After a pause, he roared with anger, "No, this boy will remain a Muslim. I swear by Darbar Sahib. I'll take him to Amritsar and get his hair cut in the English style. What do you take me for? I am a Khalsa. The heart of a lion beats in my breast, not the heart of a chicken."

When Parmeshwar Singh reached his house, he ordered his wife and daughter to take care of Akhtar.

Soon the village granthi, Sardar Santo Singh, walked up to his house and called out to him, "Parmeshwar Singh."

"Yes." Parmeshwar Singh said. When he came to meet him, he saw that the granthi was accompanied by his neighbours.

"Listen," Granthiji ordered. "From tomorrow, he will tie his turban like a Khalsa, wear a bracelet, come to the dharmshala and share the prashad. No scissors will touch his hair. If you cut his hair, you will have to vacate this house at once. Do you understand?"

"Yes," said Parmeshwar Singh quietly.

"Now, make sure that you obey," Granthiji said angrily, once again.

"So it shall be, Granthiji," Parmeshwar Singh's wife said. "As such, he hears someone reading the *Koran* in the corners of this house at night. I am sure he was a mussalla in his previous birth. Ever since that mussalla has entered our house, my daughter, Amar Kaur, has not stopped weeping. She sits in a corner and says that some new calamity is sure to befall us. If Parmeshwar Singh doesn't listen to your advice then Amar Kaur and I will move into the dharmshala. Then he can keep the boy if he wants. He is such a rotten fellow that he doesn't even respect Waheguruji."

"Who doesn't respect Waheguruji, you stupid donkey," Parmeshwar Singh shouted at his wife, though he was angry at the granthi. He continued to mutter abuses at her for a while. Then he got up and went up to the granthi. "Alright, that's enough," he said with such anger in his voice that the granthi and the neighbours got up at once and left the house.

After a few days, it was difficult to tell the difference between Akhtar and the other Sikh boys. He wore the same kind of turban wound tightly down to the ear-lobes, the same steel-bracelet, and the same long underwear. Only when he took his turban off at home, would one have known that he was not a Sikh. His hair was growing fast. Parmeshwar Singh's wife used to feel happy when she touched his hair.

"Come here for a moment, Amar Kaurey. See how well his hair is growing. One day, he'll be able to tie it in a bun and put a comb in it, then we'll name him Kartar Singh."

"No, mother," Amar Kaur replied without moving from her place, "Just as there is only one Waheguruji, only one *Granthsahib* and only one moon, there is only one Kartara, my younger brother!" Then weeping bitterly, she whispered, "No, I won't be consoled by this toy. I know he is a mussalla, mother, and Kartara can never be replaced by a mussalla!"

"Am I saying that he is the real Kartara? My beloved son was like the moon." Having said this, Parmeshwar Singh's wife also began to weep.

Both of them would then leave Akhtar alone, sit in a corner together and cry for a long time. They would console each other, and then begin to wail loudly for Kartar Singh once more.

Akhtar wept for his mother for a few days. Soon, however, he cried for something else. Whenever Parmeshwar Singh would bring back rations and cloth from the Panchayat's office for the Rehabilitation of Refugees, Akhtar would rush upto him, cling to his leg and, with tears in his eyes, beg, "Tie a turban around my head. Let me grow my hair long. Buy me a comb."

Parmeshwar Singh would hug him and say sorrowfully, "Everything will take care of itself, son. Everything. Your hair will grow long. But as I promised Waheguruji, you'll not become a Sikh. That will never happen. I'll never allow that. Do you understand?"

Akhtar now hardly remembered his mother. As long as Parmeshwar Singh stayed at home, Akhtar clung to him. Whenever he was away, Akhtar would look at Parmeshwar Singh's wife and daughter, as if he was begging them for a few shreds of love. Parmeshwar Singh's wife would bathe him. But Amar Kaur continued to treat him with contempt and would turn away if he looked at her. In the beginning, she often slapped him. Once Akhtar complained to Parmeshwar Singh about it.

Parmeshwar Singh shouted at Amar Kaur, abused her, and would have thrashed her and thrown her over the wall of the house, out into the street, had his wife not intervened and fallen at his feet. "Bitch," he had thundered. "I had heard that they were kidnapping girls, but this whore continues to be with us. The one who was kidnapped was a five year old boy — too young to even wipe his own nose — what a calamity, what strange and dark times, yaroon." After that incident, Amar Kaur never dared to lift her hand at Akhtar, but she began to hate him even more intensely.

Akhtar had a very high fever one day. Parmeshwar Singh went to consult a vaid. After he had left, his wife went to her neighbour's house to borrow some ground ajwain. Akhtar felt thirsty.

"Water," he called out aloud. He opened his blood-shot eyes and looked around him. "Water," he sobbed involuntarily. He threw his blanket aside and sat up. Amar Kaur was sitting at the threshold of the door and weaving a cane basket. "Give me some water," Akhtar ordered her. Amar Kaur made a face, glared at him and continued working. Akhtar shouted, "Will you give me some water or no? Give me water, otherwise I'll hit you." This time Amar Kaur didn't even bother to look at him and said, "Try to hit me. Are you Kartara that I should tolerate your beating? I'll chop you into pieces."

Akhtar started weeping helplessly. Once again, he recalled his mother. By the time Parmeshwar Singh came back with the medicine, his wife also returned with the ajwain powder. In their absence, Akhtar had been weeping and complaining, "I want to go home to my mother. This Amar Kaur, this daughter of a Sikh, doesn't even give me water. I want my mother, I want my mother."

Parmeshwar Singh looked angrily at Amar Kaur. She was crying and telling her mother, "Why should I give him water? Somewhere Kartara must also be begging for water from someone, and if no one takes pity on him, why should I take pity on this fellow — tell me?"

Parmeshwar Singh went up to Akhtar and, pointing to his wife, said, "Son, she too is your mother."

"No," Akhtar shouted angrily, "She's a Sikh. My mother reads the namaz five times a day and when she gives me water she says bismillah."

Parmeshwar Singh's wife, without saying anything, filled a cup of water and brought it to Akhtar. He flung the cup against the wall and shouted, "I'll not take water from you."

"This man is the father of a bitch like me, " Amar Kaur taunted Parmeshwar Singh.

"Let him be," said Parmeshwar Singh, "How does it concern you?"

Conflicting emotions flickered across Parmeshwar Singh's face — he smiled at Akhtar and felt sad at what he had said. Then he gave Akhtar water, kissed his forehead and caressed his back. He persuaded him to lie down on the bed and slowly massaged his forehead. Only by late evening did Akhtar's fever subside and after that he slept peacefully.

That night, after a long time, Parmeshwar Singh got up with a start, woke up his wife and whispered, "Listen. Can you hear something? There is someone reading the *Koran* in here."

At first, his wife thought that he was merely reliving an old fear, and tried to ignore him. But then she suddenly sat up with fear, leaned across to Amar Kaur's bed and shook her awake. She whispered softly, "Daughter."

"What is it, mother?" said Amar Kaur in surprise.

Her mother whispered, "Listen quietly. There really is someone here reciting the *Koran*."

There was a fearful moment of silence. Then Amar Kaur screamed with terror. Her scream was followed by an even more terrifying scream from Akhtar.

"What's the matter, son?" Parmeshwar Singh asked anxiously and went up to Akhtar's bed. He hugged him and said, "Did something scare you, son?"

"Yes," said Akhtar, peeping from under his quilt, "Someone screamed."

"Amar Kaur screamed," Parmeshwar Singh said, "We all thought that someone in the house was reciting the *Koran*."

"I was reciting it," Akhtar replied.

A muffled scream escaped from Amar Kaur's mouth.

Parmeshwar Singh's wife quickly lit a lamp and sat down on Amar Kaur's bed. Both of them stared at Akhtar, as if he would turn into smoke and, escaping from under the door, say to them in a terrifying voice, "I am a jinn. I'll come again tomorrow night and recite the *Koran.*"

"What were you reciting?" Parmeshwar Singh asked.

"Would you like me to recite it again?" Akhtar asked.

"Yes, yes," Parmeshwar Singh said lovingly.

Akhtar began to recite, "Qul huwallah-ho-ahad." Then he recited upto, Kufuvan ahad, and as prescribed by ritual, blew into his gareban. He turned to Parmeshwar with a smile and asked, "May I blow down your gareban also?"

"Yes, yes," Parmeshwar opened the top button of his gareban and Akhtar blew down it.

This time Amar Kaur had difficulty in stifling her cry.

Parmeshwar Singh asked Akhtar, "Couldn't you sleep?"

"No," said Akhtar, "I keep remembering my mother. My mother says that if one can't sleep, one should recite 'Qul huwallah-ho-ahad' thrice. That will help one to sleep. I was about to sleep when Amar Kaur's shriek frightened me."

"Recite it again and go to sleep," said Parmeshwar Singh, "Recite it every day. Loudly. Never forget to do so, otherwise your mother will thrash you. Now go to sleep."

He persuaded Akhtar to lie down on his bed and covered him with a quilt. But when he tried to blow the lamp out, Amar Kaur shouted, "No, no, father, don't blow it out. I am afraid."

"Afraid?" Parmeshwar Singh asked with surprise," Afraid of what?"

"Let it burn, what's the harm?" Parmeshwar Singh's wife asked.

But Parmeshwar Singh blew the lamp out and laughingly said, "Donkeys."

In the darkness of the night Akhtar recited "Qul huwallah-ho-ahad...Qul huwallah-ho-ahad," quietly to himself. After sometime he began to snore gently. Parmeshwar Singh also went to sleep, so did his wife. But Amar Kaur was anxious and awake for the rest of the night. She kept on imagining that the muezzin was calling the faithful to prayer from the mosque in the neighborhood.

Soon Akhtar's hair grew quite long. A comb could be stuck in it. Like the other villagers, Parmeshwar Singh's wife too began to call him Kartar Singh and started treating him well. But Amar Kaur continued to regard Akhtar as a changeling who would, at any moment, cut his hair, take off his turban and throw it away, and then disappear reciting, "Qul huwallah-ho-ahad."

One day, Parmeshwar Singh came home running. He was panting with excitement as he asked his wife, "Where is he?"

"Who, Kartara?"

"No." Then after a moment's hesitation, he said, "Yes, yes, Kartara"

"He has gone out. He must be playing in the street outside."

Parmeshwar Singh ran out of the house again. He ran through the streets looking for Akhtar and then, when he reached the open fields, ran faster. Far away, in Gyan Singh's sugar-cane fields, he spotted a few children playing kabbadi. As he approached them, he saw that Akhtar had pinned another boy down to the earth and was kneeling on his chest. Blood was trickling out of the boy's mouth, but he was still muttering, "Kabbadi, Kabbadi." Finally, the boy conceded defeat and when he freed himself from Akhtar's grip, he asked him, "Hey Kartaron, why did you hit me on the mouth with your knee?"

"I am glad, I did," Akhtar replied arrogantly, as he tied his loose hair into a bun and stuck his comb into it.

"Has your rasool taught you only this?" the boy taunted him.

Akhtar was puzzled for a moment. Then, after a little thought, he retaliated, "And what has your guru taught you?"

"Mussalla," the boy abused him.

"Sikhra," Akhtar said, abusing him in return.

All the boys pounced on Akhtar. But, as soon as they heard Parmeshwar Singh's loud roar, they scattered in all directions and left the field empty. He tied Akhtar's turban, took him aside and said, "Would you like to live with me or go back to your mother?"

Akhtar couldn't make up his mind at once. He stood looking into Parmeshwar Singh's eyes for a long time and then finally said with a smile, "I would like to go to my mother."

"And you wouldn't like to stay with me?" Parmeshwar Singh's face became red and it seemed as if he was about to cry.

"I'll stay with you too!" Akhtar said, resolving the dilemma.

Parmeshwar Singh picked him up and hugged him, and those tears of disappointment which had collected in his eyes, flowed down as tears of joy. He said, "Listen, son, today an army convoy is coming here. These army men are coming to snatch you away from me. Do you understand? Go and hide somewhere. After they have left, I'll come and take you back."

At that very moment, Parmeshwar Singh saw a cloud of dust rising in the distance. He climbed the mud embankment of the field and carefully watched as the dust-cloud became bigger and bigger. Then he announced excitedly, "The army lorry is here."

He jumped down from the mud embankment and walked around the sugar-cane field.

"Gyaney, O Gyan Singh," he shouted. Gyan Singh emerged from the field of sugar-cane. He held a sickle in one hand and a bundle of grass in the other. Parmeshwar Singh took him to one side and explained the situation to him. Then both of them walked up to Akhtar. Gyan Singh broke a stick of sugar-cane from his field, cleaned it with his sickle and, giving it to Akhtar, said, "Come Kartarey. Sit with me and chew this sugar-cane till these faujis leave. They have come to grab such a well-trained Khalsa like you. Let's see!"

Then, Parmeshwar Singh asked Akhtar for permission to go, "Can I go now?"

Akhtar, with a piece of sugar-cane held tightly between his teeth, tried to smile at him. Having been granted permission, Parmeshwar Singh ran back to his village.

The cloud of dust was rapidly approaching the village. When Parmeshwar Singh reached his village, he tried to explain the situation to his wife and daughter. Then he rushed to see the granthi. After talking to him, he explained the situation to the other villagers.

The army trucks stopped in the fields beyond the dharmshala. The army men, accompanied by the villagers, went to the granthi's place. The numberdar of the area accompanied them. The army men made inquiries about the presence of

Muslim girls in the village. The granthi swore by the *Granthsahib* that there were no Muslim girls in his village.

"Boys are a different matter," someone whispered into Parmeshwar Singh's ear and smiled conspiratorially at him.

The army officer then addressed the villagers and laid great stress on the sacredness of motherhood, and talked at length about the deep scar left on the hearts of those women who had lost their daughters. He drew a frightful picture of those brothers and husbands, whose sisters and wives had been snatched away from them.

"What is religion, my friends?" He said. "Every religion of the world teaches us how to become more humane. But you, in the name of religion, make man more inhuman. You steal his humanity from him, trample on his dignity, and then proclaim that you are Sikhs or that you are Muslims, that you are the followers of Waheguruji or the slaves of Rasool!"

After the speech, the crowd dispersed. The army officer thanked the granthi, shook hands with him and got into the truck.

Soon after the truck left, it was the granthi who was the first to congratulate Parmeshwar Singh. Other people also surrounded Parmeshwar Singh and offered him their congratulations. However, Parmeshwar Singh, who had looked utterly bewildered before the truck had arrived, now looked as if he had lost everything he had. He left the village and went back to Gyan Singh's fields. He lifted Akhtar on to his shoulders and brought him home. After feeding him, he hugged and caressed the child so affectionately that Akhtar was lulled to sleep. Lost in thought, Parmeshwar Singh sat by Akhtar's bed for a long time. He was scratching his beard and looking around absent-mindedly, when he saw a little boy, on the terrace of his neighbor's house, suddenly clutch his foot, stagger and howl, "O, there is a long thorn in my foot. The whole thing has gone in." The boy's mother rushed up the stairs without pausing to cover her head. She called down to her daughter, asked her to fetch a needle, dug the thorn out of her son's foot and kissed him wildly. Later, she leaned down from the terrace and shouted, "Aye, throw me my dupatta. How shamelessly did I rush up the stairs!"

Parmeshwar Singh was startled by that scene. Later he asked his wife, "Listen, do you still long for your Kartara?"

"Just listen to him!" his wife said, and then suddenly burst out crying, "Kartara is that wound in my heart which will never heal."

The moment Amar Kaur heard Kartara's name, she came and sat by her mother's feet and began to weep.

Parmeshwar Singh jumped up with such a start that it seemed as if he had heard someone drop a tray full of glasses on the floor.

Later, he took Akhtar by his hand, walked out into the courtyard and said, "Did you sleep well, son? Let's go for a walk. It's a moonlit night."

Akhtar readily agreed. Parmeshwar Singh wrapped him in a blanket and lifted him onto his shoulder. When they reached the field, he said, "Look at that moon in the east, son. When it reaches over our heads it will shine as brightly as the morning sun."

Akhtar looked at the moon.

"That moon shines over your mother's country too."

This time Akhtar leaned down to look at Parmeshwar Singh.

"When the moon is right above our heads, it will also shine above your mother's head."

Akhtar asked, "Is my mother too watching the moon?"

"Yes," said Parmeshwar Singh in clear voice. "Would you like to go back to your mother?"

"Yes," replied Akhtar. "But you refuse to take me to her because you are very bad. You are a Sikh."

Parmeshwar Singh said, "No, my son, I will certainly take you back to her today. I got a letter from your mother. She says that she is very sad without her son."

"I too am sad," said Akhtar as if he had suddenly remembered something which he had long forgotten.

"I am going to take you to your mother now."

"Really," Akhtar began to jump up and down on Parmeshwar Singh's shoulder, and cried excitedly, "I am going to see my mother! Parmo is taking me to my mother! I am going to see my mother! I shall write a letter from there to Parmo."

Parmeshwar Singh wept silently. He dried his tears, cleared his throat and asked Akhtar, "Would you like to hear a song?"

"Yes."

"But first you must recite the *Koran* for me."

"Alright," said Akhtar and he began to recite "Qul huwallah-ho-ahad." When he reached "Kufuvan ahad" he blew ritually into his gareban and said, "Come, let me blow into your gareban also."

Parmeshwar Singh stopped, opened the button of his gareban and looked up. Akhtar leaned down, blew into his open gareban and said, "Now it's your turn to sing."

Parmeshwar Singh shifted Akhtar onto his other shoulder. He didn't remember any children's songs. So he began to sing all sorts of songs and continued to walk fast. Akhtar heard him in silence.

Banto's head is like a forest.
Banto's face is like the moon.
Banto's waist is like a river.
Hey, look folks,
Banto's waist is like a river.

"Who is Banto?" Akhtar asked, interrupting Parmeshwar Singh.

Parmeshwar Singh laughed. After a pause, he said, "You know, my wife, Amar Kaur's mother — her name is Banto. Amar Kaur's name is also Banto. Your mother's name is also Banto."

"Why?" Akhtar asked angrily. "Is she a Sikh?"

Parmeshwar Singh fell silent.

The moon was now shining brightly overhead. The night was silent. Every now and then a jackal would howl near the sugar-cane fields and then there would be silence again. At first, Akhtar was frightened by the howling of the jackals. But Parmeshwar Singh had reassured him and calmed him down. After a long period of silence, he asked Parmeshwar Singh, "Why aren't the jackals howling now?"

Parmeshwar Singh laughed. He then recalled a story. It was a story about Guru Gobind Singh. With great tact, however, he substituted the names of the Sikhs with Muslim names. Akhtar kept on asking, "Then what happened...then...then..."

The story had not ended, when Akhtar suddenly exclaimed, "Look, the moon is above our heads!"

Parmeshwar Singh stopped and stood on a mud embankment for a long time. Suddenly, he heard the sound of the azan from somewhere far away and Akhtar jumped up with joy. Parmeshwar Singh had a difficult time controlling him. He lifted Akhtar down from his shoulder and sat down on the ground. Then placing his hands on Akhtar's shoulder, who was standing before him, he said, "Now go son. Your mother is calling you. Go straight towards that sound."

"Shhh," Akhtar said, as he put his finger to his lips. "One shouldn't speak during azan."

"But I am a Sikh, my son," Parmeshwar Singh said.

"Shhh." This time Akhtar glared at him angrily.

Parmeshwar Singh took him into his lap, caressed his forehead lovingly, kissed him repeatedly and after the azan was over, wiped his eyes on his shirt-sleeve and said in a tearful voice, "I'll not come any further. Only you..."

"Why? Why not?" Akhtar asked.

"Your mother's letter said that Akhtar should come alone."

Parmeshwar Singh tried to soothe and comfort him, "Now, walk straight ahead in that direction. You'll reach a village. Give them your name. Not Kartar Singh but Akhtar. Tell them your mother's name and the name of your village. And look, write me a letter once you get there."

"I'll write," Akhtar promised.

"And listen, if you find a boy named Kartar Singh there, send him across to this side. Alright."

"Alright."

Parmeshwar Singh kissed Akhtar's forehead once more and fighting back his tears, said, "Now go!"

Akhtar took a few steps, and then looked back. "Why don't you come too?"

"No," Parmeshwar Singh said. "Your mother didn't ask me to also come in her letter."

"I am afraid," said Akhtar.

"Why don't you recite the *Koran*," Parmeshwar Singh advised.

"Alright," said Akhtar, and began repeating the verse "Qul huwallah-ho-ahad." He walked towards the village.

In the horizon, the first soft light of dawn struggled to break free of the darkness. In the dim, misty light, the little boy Akhtar, walking down the dirt path, seemed like a tall and brave Sikh.

Parmeshwar Singh continued to sit on the mud embankment, his gaze fixed on the receding figure of Akhtar. He sat there till Akhtar became a small dark speck in the distance and then disappeared from sight.

Akhtar had hardly reached the village when two soldiers leapt towards him, caught and asked him, "Who are you?"

"Akhtar," he said, as if the entire world ought to have known his name.

"Akhtar!" Both the soldiers looked in turn at his face and at his turban which was tied like a Sikh's.

Then one of them stepped forward and snatched his turban away.

Akhtar's long hair opened and scattered down his head.

Furious, Akhtar snatched his turban back from the soldier, and then, reaching for something on his head with his other hand, lay down on the ground and wailed, "Where is my comb? Give me back my comb. You have stolen my comb. Give it back or I'll beat you."

Suddenly, both the soldiers dropped to their knees, hoisted their guns onto their shoulders and took aim at something.

"Halt!" one of them shouted and waited for a reply.

Then in the growing light of dawn, both the soldiers looked at each other in surprise. One of them opened fire. At first, Akhtar was paralyzed with fear at the sound of the gun. Then, when he saw the soldiers run towards something, he too ran after them shouting and crying.

By the time the soldiers reached him, Parmeshwar Singh had already bandaged his thigh with his turban, though blood was still oozing out of his wound. He said, "Why did you shoot me? I had forgotten to cut Akhtar's long hair. I came to give him back his religion, yaroon."

In the distance, he saw Akhtar running towards them, his loose and dishevelled hair streaming in the wind.

Original in Urdu.
Translated by Viswamitter Adil and Alok Bhalla.

RAMLAL

A VISITOR FROM PAKISTAN

Munni and Meesha were playing in the sunlit courtyard. Saraswati quickly collected some hot water, a towel, soap and some clothes so as to give them a bath in an area which had been marked off in a corner of the courtyard by a low wall. "Munni, Meesha," she called, "Come, let me bathe you. I won't have the time later. Didn't you hear me?"

The children were busy playing. She caught hold of them by their arms and said, "Damn you. You play in the dust all the time. Can't you walk properly? Have you broken your legs?"

When she finally managed to drag them to the bucket which was full of water, they began to splash the water all around in glee. She snapped at them angrily, "Can't you stand still for a minute without being mischievous?" Her dupatta got caught in their wildly flaying arms and fell to the floor. She quickly snatched it up and flung it over the bathroom wall.

The woman bathing the children was tall, healthy and beautiful. The children had splashed water on her shirt and salwar and wet them completely. Soap got into the eyes of the children and they screamed loudly. She gave each of them a slap and said, "Your father will soon be here. It's time for his lunch. The poor man must be hungry. He supervises labourers all day at the government site. You, on the other hand, munch on something throughout the day."

At that very moment there was a knock on the door.

"There, didn't I tell you that he'd be here soon?" Still sitting on the bathroom floor, she turned towards the door and shouted, "Wait, let me finish bathing the children."

Meesha saw her chance and splashed her mother with water once more.

"Damn you," she said and picked up both the children and put them down on the cot lying outside in the courtyard. Since the children were dripping wet, her shirt got even more wet and clung to her body. She threw a towel towards the children and said, "Dry yourselves. I'll be back."

As she walked towards the door to open it, she called out, "I knew you'd be here soon. You must be famished. That's what I was telling the children. I've cooked the mushroom curry you wanted..."

Unlatching the door, she pulled both the flaps open. But instead of her husband, she saw a stranger standing before her. She was so surprised that she stopped talking in mid-sentence. In fear and astonishment she stepped aside. She didn't have a dupatta to cover her head. She ran to pick it up and covered her head. The children, who had been sitting on the bed and snatching the towel from each other, stared at the stranger with curiosity — "Who was he?"

The man was tall and well-built. His hair was a bit curly, and his trimmed moustache was covered with dust. He wore a striped shirt, a salwar and a pair of thick-soled peshawari chappals. He tried to smile and then pursed his lips. He held a leather bag in one hand and a blanket in the other.

"Don't you recognize me?" The stranger asked anxiously and then tried to smile again.

Saraswati had looked at him carefully. She stood with her head bowed and her eyes fixed on the ground. Her forehead was covered with sweat.

The stranger spoke again, "I am Baldev, Saraswati. Don't you remember me?"

Saraswati looked at him once more, lowered her head without uttering a word and turned to walk towards the children. From the slow, faltering and anxious steps she took, it was obvious that she did remember him. She remembered every single moment. The anxiety on her face showed that she had certainly not forgotten him. She had recognized Baldev the moment she had opened the door.

The children moved closer to their mother. Still apprehensive and nervous, Saraswati wiped her children with a towel. Hesitatingly and slowly, Baldev walked into the house. He went and stood next to the cot on which she was sitting. He stared at Saraswati and her children. Countless emotions passed over his face. It was obvious that a storm of emotions raged within him.

Saraswati realized with a start that she hadn't yet asked Baldev to sit down. She quickly pulled down the cot which was leaning against the wall and dragged it out into the sunlight. Baldev put his bag and blanket down on the cot and asked, "Are they your children?"

Saraswati didn't say anything in reply. Oblivious of everything around her, she continued to pull a thread out of the towel she was holding in her hand. Baldev walked upto the children and ruffled their hair. There were tears in his eyes. With a heavy voice, he said, "I was sure you had got married again. And why not? But when I heard that you were still alive, I left home at once to meet you. Shafi cried a lot and tried to stop me. Do you remember Shafi, the daughter of our mason, Miyan Sharif? When you last saw her she was still a child. She is now grown up. She comes upto my shoulders."

Baldev's eyes were fixed on Saraswati. That beautiful woman with intoxicating eyes, heavy lips and a youthful body, had once been his. She had been his wife. He looked at her with infinite love and tried hard to suppress the storms of desire rising up within him. Saraswati blushed with shame, turned pale and sorrowful. A lock of hair, which had escaped from behind her ear, fluttered across her face. Her eyes were filled with tears, which flowed down her face and fell on her shirt.

Baldev stood absent-mindedly drawing circles and lines with his toe on the dust in the courtyard and then rubbing them off. After sometime he said, "I have come from Pakistan."

When Saraswati heard his voice, she looked up with a start. Baldev smiled and said, "Yes, from Pakistan. From our town, Miyanwali. But now I'll stay here. Shouldn't I?"

Suddenly, an elderly woman walked in. She had been laughing when she entered, but when she saw Baldev she looked at him open mouthed. She blinked her eyes a few times as if in disbelief, and then walked up to him and asked, "Aren't you Baldev?"

Baldev stood up, touched her feet and said, "Yes Amma, at least you have recognized me."

"Why shouldn't I have recognized you? But...but, we didn't

know that you were still alive. We thought that...?

She suddenly stopped mid-sentence, looked at her daughter and said, "Why are you sitting here? Have you no sense of shame? Go in at once."

Feeling hurt and humiliated, Saraswati tried to cover herself with her dupatta and, dragging her children with her, went inside. Her mother sat down on the cot next to Baldev and said, "I thank God a thousand times that you are alive. May evil never touch you again. But what will happen now? We thought that you were...O no, I must never utter that word again. May hot coals burn my tongue. The very thought of that word terrifies me. But...but what will we now do?"

She got up, walked towards the room inside and said, "What will happen now, Saraswati? Tell me for my mind refuses to work." But before Saraswati could reply, she retraced her steps. She made a move to go out of the house to summon someone.

But Baldev stood in her way and prevented her. He put his arms around her, persuaded her to sit down on the cot again and said, "Amma, why are you so upset? Aren't you happy to see me?"

Saraswati's mother clutched her dupatta in both her hands, buried her face in it and wept, "My daughter's life is ruined. Her reputation lies in mud...She has two husbands now. Hai, hai...Why don't you kill yourself, Saraswati? Why doesn't the earth open up and swallow you? You escaped from Pakistan with your honour intact. But now death is the only solution left!"

She continued to weep and moan loudly. Baldev stood with his head bowed, unable to say a word. After sometime when he did get a chance, he said, "Ma, I was convinced that all of you had been killed. I had seen Saraswati's Chacha's body with my own eyes in Bhola's house. I had also seen Ramchand and his sons lying dead in front of their house. Navneet and Lajwanti were thrown down from their terrace before my eyes. Those weren't days of minor skirmishes. Those were cataclysmic days. There was terror on both sides of the border. I was told that all of you had been murdered. That none of you had been left alive. I believed what I had been told."

"But why? Why didn't you make any attempt to find us? Answer me," she screamed like a wounded lioness.

"What could I have done, Amma? When I was convinced

that all of you were dead, why should I have searched for you?"

"That's what we had also concluded about you. We are not guilty. We didn't want you to be killed so that we could marry our daughter to someone else. Parents are never so mean. No, son, never," she said, as she continued to weep and wring her hands helplessly. "No one told us about your fate. Saraswati and I searched for you everywhere, in every refugee camp. We waited for you at every station, looked into every train. We called your name and wept. When we heard the news that your parents and brothers had been slaughtered, how could we have assumed that you alone had survived? Whether we live or die depends upon God, my son. The same God who cast a veil over our eyes."

"But couldn't you have waited for me, Amma?"

"Waited? I would have waited till the day of my daughter's death. I wouldn't have allowed them to light her pyre, if I had learnt that you were alive. She almost died when a bullet pierced her shoulder. Indeed, it would have been better if she had died. Sunderdas carried her back bleeding to our camp. He risked his life for us again and again. Since our arrival in India, he has continued to be our saviour."

Baldev showed her the marks of wounds on his shoulders, and said, "Because of these wounds, I lay in a faint on the terrace of my house, otherwise I would have come to your aid."

By then some other people arrived. Saraswati's aged father, her aunt and some men and women of the neighbourhood. Each of them looked at Baldev in wonder. They were puzzled. No one said anything for a while. Then Saraswati's mother screamed, "Don't you recognize him? He has returned to dishonour my daughter. Now the whole world will laugh at us."

Saraswati's father stepped forward. The others stood rooted where they were.

"Are you really Baldev?" Lala Bodhraj asked in a trembling voice, which emerged from somewhere behind his white moustache.

"Yes, Lalaji," Baldev replied, as he bent down to touch his feet.

"But where were you for so long?"

"In Pakistan. In my own house, Lalaji."

"In Pakistan? But what have you been doing there all this time?"

Baldev bit his lower lip and said, "What I have always done; looked after my small shop."

"You are a strange creature. Why didn't you come to India?"

"I thought there was no point in migrating since none of my relatives were alive."

"Oh, I see. Wasn't your life in danger there?"

Baldev laughed and said, "They killed me in their own way. When the bodies of thousands of refugees started arriving in Pakistan, it became impossible for me to live there. But, by God's grace, I was saved by my neighbours and friends, Miyan Sharif and the Head-master, Malik Khudadad. They helped me in every possible manner. They saved me and protected me from the rioters. It is because of them that I am alive today, and that my house and shop are safe."

But Baldev's reply did not satisfy Lala Bodhraj. Disturbed and anxious, he asked, "Have you married someone else there?"

"Married?" Baldev exclaimed and looked at everyone gathered there with a pained expression. They were all standing around him in a circle, waiting for an answer to that question. That was, indeed, the only question they wanted to ask. Perhaps, even Saraswati, who was hiding behind the door of the inner room, was waiting to hear his answer to that very question. What answer did they hope to hear? Saraswati's mother who was trembling with anxiety, her poor old father whose eyes were wet with tears and wrinkled face was pale with shame. What other truth did they want to know?

Suddenly another man walked in through the front door, pushing a bicycle. He was wearing khaki shorts and a white shirt. His clothes and hair were covered with layers of dust. He was surprised to see so many people gathered in the courtyard. He leaned his bicycle against the wall, stamped his feet on the ground to get rid of the dust that had gathered on his boots, wiped the sweat off his face and hands with a handkerchief, walked upto the group and asked, "What's the matter? What has happened?"

The people made way for him and he walked into the middle of the circle. Baldev was sitting on the cot surrounded by the group. The man looked at Baldev with surprise, but didn't recognize him. Realizing Baldev was the centre of attention, he looked at him curiously. Baldev too stared back at the man. Baldev's attention was caught by the long scar that ran down the man's face. He stood up and said to Lala Bodhraj, "Is he Sunderdas? I know him!"

"Yes," Lala Bodhraj replied and put his arms around Sunderdas's shoulders. "He is the Sunderdas I told you about. He saved us, shared our sufferings in the refugee camp through winter and summer. He helped us sort out our problems regarding our claims and the property we had left behind. This lion-hearted man saw us through our trials and enabled us to resettle here. This small house is his. He built it out of his hard-earned money, and made it habitable for a small family of his own, for his wife and his two innocent children, a family of love and affection.

He is the idealistic young man who agreed to marry our daughter when he learnt that she had been left a widow at a very young age. What other alternative had we, except to give the hand of our daughter in marriage to him? We didn't know where you were. Everyone advised us to accept his offer of marriage. How else could we have protected the honour of a poor, young girl?"

As he spoke, Lala Bodhraj's voice choked. Tears began to flow down his face. But Baldev continued to stare hard at the scar which ran down Sunderdas's face. That deep, red scar brought back memories of a story which was fifteen years old — a tale of hatred and jealousy. It was the sign of a free-for-all fight during a municipal election. Even Saraswati knew about that incident, but she had never dared to ask Sunderdas about it. Circumstances had snatched her away from Baldev and offered her to Sunderdas. Otherwise, Sunderdas would never have even dared to think about taking her away from Baldev.

Sunderdas was flushed with jealousy and anger. He clenched his jaws, suddenly pushed the people around him away and went inside. Everyone turned to look in the direction he had gone. Baldev, too, stared at the shut door of the room. Saraswati's mother began to cry inconsolably. Her face was stained with tears. A few moments later, Sunderdas returned, with his hands in his pockets and stood deep in thought. He stood like that for a while. Then he looked up, turned towards Baldev and said in a quiet and decisive voice, "You can appeal to the court if you like."

Everyone heaved a sigh of relief. It was as if that was what they were hoping for. They waited for Baldev's reply. They were all on one side, and Baldev was on the other, silent and alone. After having endured silence and loneliness for ten years, he was still silent and alone. His face reflected his silence and loneliness. Without making a response, he continued to look at Sunderdas for a while. Then he turned to look towards the half open door of the room inside. The door seemed to shake slightly as if it was being clutched tightly by someone. He cleared his throat and said, "Saraswati is my legal wife and she can never forget that I love her. Instead of giving her back to me, for she is rightfully mine, you want me to go and knock at the doors of the court for justice. I am sure the courts will be just. But the process will take long. I don't know how many years will pass by. I shall, instead, knock at the door of another court, at this very moment, now. I have full faith in that court and know that I shall be dealt with justly."

As he spoke his voice became heavy with emotion. He couldn't continue to speak. His eyes brimmed over with tears. He looked at the half-open door of the inner room, cleared his voice and asked, "Saraswati, give me an answer. I don't want to ask anyone else. I want an answer from you and only you."

Suddenly there was a loud scream from the room. Saraswati broke down and wept. The women who were gathered in the courtyard, too, had tears in their eyes.

At that very moment, another man appeared at the front door. He had a brown government envelope in his hand. He came in and asked, "Is there a visitor from Pakistan in this house?"

Baldev took the envelope from his hand. After reading the paper in it, he returned it and said, "Yes, he is here, but he will return to Pakistan today."

He wiped his eyes on his shirt sleeves, picked up his bag and his blanket, and slowly walked out of the house.

Original in Urdu.
Translated by Alok Bhalla.

SHAIKH AYYAZ

NEIGHBOURS

While Khanu, the barber, was cutting hair, the National Guard was on parade: left-right, left-right. The khaki uniforms of the young men were drenched with sweat. They were proud, strong and carefree. After his hair-cut, Seth Shyam Das watched the young men marching for a while. He seemed despondent, afraid and contemptuous at the same time.

"Khanu, who is that man — the one who is carrying the flag with the crescent moon and stars, and is leading the others?" Seth Shyam Das asked. There was anxiety in his voice.

"He is Salar Khan Mohammed."

The Seth, who had full faith in Khanu, asked, "What are they saying, Khanu? Are they trying to start a riot?"

Khanu, who was a member of the Muslim league and proud of his Islamic heritage, replied with his usual courtesy and respect, "Sethji, how can they start any disturbances? They are only on parade."

"But, my friend, they could as well do their military exercises at Rama Musti or Wahid Baksh. Why must they do this left-right, left-right business in the middle of this street? I am leaving with my wife and children for Jodhpur tomorrow."

Khanu had been hearing people say that sort of thing for the past three or four days. He had read about the disturbances in Bengal and Bihar in the *Alabhid* and *Sansar Samachar;* dreadful tales of murder and brutality. People seemed to have lost their humanity. Women were being mutilated and raped, children were being dispatched to the valley of death, brothers were playing holi with the blood of their brothers. The same was happening at Lahore, Bombay and at other places near the borders. He had seen horrifying photographs in the newspapers. He had often thought about the cruelties committed by the Hindus of Bihar on the Muslims. They had shed the blood of men of his faith and community. They had insulted women who had never come out of purdah. He wondered if the riots would start in his city too, after the second of June. Are we going to avenge the killings of Bihari Muslims? Should I, for example, cut the throat of this Seth with my razor? His heart trembled at the thought.

Although Khanu was a barber, when he went for a stroll to the Lakdi Darwaza in the evenings dressed in his palm-beach pants, no one could have guessed that he was an ordinary barber. Most of the college students in Shikarpur were friendly towards him. He kept the journals of all the colleges of Sindh in his shop. He also subscribed to a good number of Hindi and Urdu magazines. His shop was decorated with photographs of Ashok Kumar and Prithviraj Kapoor. He could hold his own in any discussion on literature and film. He also had a stock of many different kinds of fancy powders and oils, which always attracted a number of school boys. Khanu was friendly with the college boys, as well as with the uneducated sons of Hindu seths and Muslim zamindars. These boys wore pants and talked about film actors. They were also interested in hunting and wandering from one place to another.

There were, however, a few amongst them who believed in Bolshevism. They often came to Khanu's shop, but rarely ever paid any attention to him. They talked mainly amongst themselves. Yesterday they had been there for a hair-cut.

"Sindh belongs to the Sindhis," one of them said. "The identity of the Sindh nation is in danger. These Punjabis, Gujaratis and Biharis want to destroy our culture and language; they also want to take over our business and our land. It is our duty to prevent that from happening immediately. The Gujaratis are in command of the Sindh Congress. And the Muslim League is busy distributing free meals to the Biharis and the Punjabis. Neither of them is concerned with the hungry and the dying Sindhis."

Another man, who was a Hindu, said, "I would rather die with my Muslim brothers in Sindh, than go and live in Udaipur or Jodhpur. My soul is attached to this country. The roads, the gardens, the people of this place are a part of my soul. Out of Sindh, I would die."

That was the first time Khanu had come across such a large-hearted Hindu. He had listened to him carefully. That Hindu lad was excited and had shouted, "Jai Sindh." In the past, when Khanu had heard the slogan "Jai Hind," it had reeked of Hinduism, and he had always felt as if someone had slashed him with a razor. But now when he heard the slogan "Jai Sindh," he felt as if someone had sprinkled his body with rose water and his entire body had been perfumed by it.

"What will I do if disturbances break out in Sindh tomorrow?" Khanu wondered. "Will I cut the throat of this Seth with my razor? Sethji's son goes to a local college and also comes here for a hair-cut."

Khanu had met these people at the Sindhu river during the Navroz celebrations. They had asked Khanu to come over and sit with them. There was a lot of activity all around. The Sindhu river was full of water, the waves splashed against the banks and everyone was thrilled with joy. That day, Khanu had put his hand on his ears and sung, "Hey you, young girl in a kurta..." The atmosphere was filled with love. There was no difference between the Hindus and the Muslims. Everyone had enjoyed the enchanting music and had kept time with it. Later everyone had gone for a swim in the river. While swimming they had eaten mangoes.

Khanu remembered that day, and said to himself that the water of the Sindhu river did not know the difference between the two sects. It was not as if the water would let the Hindu drown and the Muslim swim across. Besides, the same sun shone on the heads of both the communities. Both the communities took a dip in the same water to cool off when it got too hot. It wasn't as if the sun gave shade to the Muslim and burnt the Hindu. If nature did not differentiate between the Hindus and the Muslims, who was he to differentiate between the two? Was he the creator of the universe? And when the Lord Himself didn't treat people differently, how could he do so? He wondered how, after having lived with the Hindus and their children for so long, he could possibly kill them?

Whenever Khanu went to Shahi Bagh with his Hindu friends to hear folk songs, or to watch a play or a dance, or whenever Bhagat sang, "If I die take my body to my country, mother." He felt as if he could die blissfully at that moment. He wished that the leaves of the large bargat tree would rustle forever in the breeze; that his grave would be dug beneath that tree and its leaves would fall on his grave; that the cool breeze of Shahi Bagh would gently scatter them; that Bhagat's soft voice would sing on forever; that he would escape from heaven to hear it. Khanu was not the only one who felt that. Whoever heard Bhagat sing, whether a Hindu or a Muslim, was moved in the same way. How could the Hindus dream of leaving Sindh? Who would sing the songs of Shah Latif to them? How could they ever forget the sweet smell that rose from the soil of Sindh?

Khanu had heard the same songs on the radio. He hated them, they sounded as if they were being sung by ghosts. How can anyone love a foreign language? We have always loved the poetry of Sindhi Shah and have always lived besides the Sindhu river, how can we go away and begin life again somewhere else?

He knew that the lives of the Hindus and the Muslims were so intimately woven together that they were a part of the same cloth. Sindh was one nation with one culture. These thoughts made Khanu's brain work as quickly as his hair-cutting scissors. In the evening when Khanu was returning home after closing the shop, he saw a number of carriages going towards the railway station. These people were leaving their native land and going to places far away. Places which did not have Shah Latif, Sami, Zinda Pir, Bhaga or the fair of the twelfth day, or the raag of the chaudhavin. They were going to unknown places where the languages, customs and dresses were unfamiliar.

But, Khanu thought to himself, only a couple of rich seths can hope to go away. They have their bungalows in Jaipur and Udaipur. They have money. But what about the clerks, the accountants and the teachers?

What will they do?

The next morning when Khanu was brushing his teeth, he heard the fisherwomen. His wife went out to buy some fish. At the same time Pesu Ram's mother came out and said, "Jeebal, buy a whole piece. We will share it."

While Jeebal was watching it being cut into two, Pesu Ram's mother said, "I have heard that there is a lot of hatred being spread. Muslims are going to start a riot. If this happens, I will come and live with you, Jeebal."

Khanu said teasingly, "I belong to the Muslim League and I wear a Jinnah cap. You should be afraid of me."

"Do not talk like that, Bhaiya. You will always remain Khanu Bhai for me. How can you kill us? You often say that neighbours are like our own fathers, mothers, brothers and sisters. You always send us Phiru on Id and share our sweet bread during Sheetla. How can you forget all this? But even if I die at your hands, I will be happy and satisfied." Pesu Ram's mother also reminded him of the famous line said during a fight between a brother and a sister, "You can kill me, my brother."

Khanu wondered — Can I kill this woman? She is asking for refuge. Can I kill her? No. Never. It cannot be. If the Hindus in Bihar have killed the Muslims, Pesu Ram's mother has nothing to do with it. She has always been our neighbour. Both of us have played together in our childhood. Both of us have always used the same tap for water. How many times had I helped her pick up her pitcher of water...How many times had my kite fallen on her roof and how many times had she come running with it to return it...Besides she had helped Jeebal during childbirth. How can we kill her? No. No. Never. We cannot have any rioting in the country of the sufis. Someone whispered in his ears, "Jai Sindh."

Who can be so cruel as to kill a neighbour and a helpless person?

Suddenly the fog in his mind lifted — like a clean shave!

Original in Sindhi.
Translated from Hindi
by Saroj Vashistha.

YASPAL

A HOLY WAR

Profound darkness and the deep silence of a city under curfew!

Not a ray of light filtered through the cracks in the doors and windows of the two or three storied houses on either side of Gangu-ki-Gali. There was no sign of life in any house. Four days ago, a fire in the Gali had destroyed all the electric wires and the street-lamps. Now, only fear haunted the abandoned and ruined houses here and made the darkness more terrifying and unbearable. Darkness and silence also lay along the entire length and breadth of Sayyidmittha Bazaar which ran perpendicular to the Gali. The few street lights that still burnt in these deserted streets only made the desolation and the sadness more oppressive.

A city of beautiful gardens and bustling crowds, Lahore, after the Partition of the country, was paralyzed by fear and mutual hatred amongst the communities. Communal frenzy had spread devastation and destruction all around. The government had imposed a curfew so as to stop the destruction.

The curfew had made the night even more gloomy and suffocating. The dark clouds above the still and silent city had closed it in so firmly that even the breeze could not stir in it.

By the 13th of August, all the Hindu families living in Gangu-ki-Gali had run away; the old woman, Moolan Tai, was the only one who had stayed behind. Those Muslims who used to sit out on the platforms in front of the small shops in the bazaar — Niyamat, the tailor, Rashid, the metal-worker, Nazzu, the lace-maker, and Latif, the printer, had not entered the lane out of fear since the beginning of August. Only Fazzay, the dyer, who had a shop at the corner of the lane and the Bazaar, and his son, Nasru, had stayed behind out of desperation. This shop, which was six feet long and four feet wide, was also their home.

There were many ropes tied on the roof of Fazzay's low and narrow shop. Now these ropes were unused. In better times, Fazzay and Nasru would, during the course of the day, dye turbans, sarees and chunnies, put mica on them and starch them, and then hang them up separately on these ropes to dry. In their cell-like room there was a cupboard without doors. They kept small packets of colour and boxes of powdered mica in it. In one corner of the room lay all the wealth that father and son possessed — an aluminium pot with a long and narrow spout, a cooking pan, a plate and a cup which lay next to a few clothes piled on a mat. The three earthen pots for mixing colours and the vessel for making starch were kept at night under a bench on the platform in front of the shop. An earthen pitcher full of water was always left against the wall outside the shop. The weather of Lahore was such that Fazzay and Nasru needed to sleep in their small room either when the nights were freezing in winter or when it was raining. Otherwise, Fazzay would sleep on the platform next to the shop and Nasru would lie on a mat which he would spread out in the street, leaving some space for people to walk past. Often he sat late into the night singing *Heer* and folk songs.

Nasru and Ramesh were great rivals when it came to singing folk songs and reciting *Heer*. Ramesh's family used to live on the second floor of a house a few blocks away from Fazzay's shop. Whenever Ramesh sat at his window, put his hands on both his ears and sang loudly, Nasru would take his place on the mat in the street, cover his ears with his hands, look up towards Ramesh's window and sing equally loudly in reply. Sometimes, they would both sit on the balcony in Ramesh's house and sing together.

By the end of July 1947, the Hindus had established their control over Sayyidmittha Bazaar. The few Muslims who used to live there had been killed. And now since the Muslim customers no longer came there, the Muslim shopkeepers in Gangu-Ki-Gali had abandoned their businesses. Only Fazzay and Nasru had refused to leave Gangu-Ki-Gali. Pretending that he was not afraid, Fazzay hoped that Allah, Ram and all the other Gods would protect him. He was confident that the respect he had earned during the forty years he had lived in the lane would help him. After all the children, the young men and the young women of the lane had called him Mama for years. And the wives and daughters of the neighbourhood had often come to his shops, without bothering to cover their heads or veil their faces, to give him sarees, chunnies and turbans to dye. They would even quarrel with him if they thought that the colour was a shade less bright or the mica powder was too little. The boys would sneak upto his shop and steal a bit of starch to fix their torn kites and then run away.

Fazzay would scream loudly — "Nasru, catch those thieves. Damn these..." But by the time he picked up the long stick which he kept to pull down the clothes left to dry on the ropes strung high above the roof of his shop, the children would escape cackling with delight. He knew the names of all the children, of all the old men and women, of all the wives and daughters who lived in the Gali. Where could he go now? Where else did he really belong?

The Hindus regarded the flight of the Muslim shopkeepers from Gangu-Ki-Gali as their victory, but saw in Fazzay's refusal to run away from his shop, a challenge to their authority. Karamchand, proudly twirling his moustaches which had only recently sprouted, confronted Fazzay one day and asked threateningly — "So Miyan, what are your plans?"

Fazzay folded both his hands before him and replied — "Badshahoh, maliko, I'll follow your advice, obey your orders. I have lived here in this lane for forty years and have no other home. If you throw me out, I won't resist. But where can I go! Badshahoh, such sudden storms often seize and sweep over the affairs of men. Why should we unnecessarily add to our miseries?"

The merchant, Harcharan, intervened and said, "Leave him alone! Leave him alone! He hasn't harmed anyone. If he leaves, who will dye the sarees and the chunnies for our wives and daughters?" But Karamchand's younger brother, Dharmchand, who was seven years old, and Ramesh's younger brother, Rajesh, couldn't control their religious fervour. They threw pebbles at the earthen pitcher lying outside Fazzay's shop and smashed it. If such an incident had occurred in the Gali a fortnight ago, the children would have been properly scolded. But that day no one said anything to them.

Nasru wasn't a calm person. His blood boiled when they broke the pitcher. He couldn't bear an insult by the kafir Hindus. In his heart, he wanted to do what the other Muslims of the city were doing. He also longed to participate enthusiastically in the holy war for the creation of Pakistan, but was constrained by the sheer obstinacy of his father. How could he leave his poor and old father alone in the stronghold of the Hindus? Only a few days ago, he had pleaded with him to leave the Gali. After the threat by Karamchand and the incident with the water-pitcher, he had turned angrily upon his father and said, "May pigs get the mothers of these kafirs...It's impossible for us to live here any longer. If we can't find a room of our own anywhere, we'll take refuge in a mosque or a dargah."

Fazzay scolded him in a suppressed whisper — "Shut up. You stupid son of a pig! Don't show-off like Durray Khan! People always peck and claw at each other...So don't talk nonsense...This shop was set-up by your father. You were born in this room. It's the women of this lane who had looked after your mother. She had died in this very room. It is this Gali which has given us shelter and helped us earn our bread. Wait patiently, things will settle down."

After the second week of August there was a dramatic change in Sayyidmittha Bazaar. It had been attacked twice by hordes of Muslims. Many of the houses and shops owned by the Hindus had been burnt. All the houses in Gangu-Ki-Gali were still occupied by the Hindus, even though thousands of Hindu families had already fled Lahore. When they heard about the exodus from the other parts of the city, the Hindus of Gangu-Ki-Gali at first proclaimed their determination to stay on — "Even Aurangazeb and Nadir Shah didn't scare us, Jinnah and the Muslim League are nothing in comparison! We will never change our religion or abandon our homes!" But after more incidents of burning, looting and killing in Sayyidmittha Bazaar, many Hindu families quietly slipped away, and others began to plan anxiously to leave as soon as they could. Only Moolan Tai got left behind.

Moolan Tai had been widowed twenty-six years ago. God had blessed her with three daughters. Moolan's husband had divided the family's inheritance with his brothers. When the Hindus of the Gali began to leave, Moolan Tai was unable to tear herself away from her greedy attachment to her house and the wealth she had secretly hoarded. She cared for no one. Other than Thakurji, she regarded no one as her own in the world. She was suspicious of everyone. Her eccentricities used to surprise all her neighbours who always wondered — "What will this old woman do with all her money? Perhaps, she wants to build a temple or a dharmshala to be named after her." During those days of grave danger, no one came forward to help the old woman through her difficulties. Moolan Tai was left alone in her house, in that desolate lane, with only the Thakurji to protect her, just as Fazzay has been left alone in his shop at the corner of the Gali with only his son Nasru as his support.

Before the riots began, Fazzay had always maintained some sort of relationship with every family which lived in Gangu-Ki-Gali. After the marriage of her third daughter, the only contact Moolan Tai had with Fazzay was that of a landlady who collected rent from her tenant at the beginning of each month. There were always some months when Fazzay had to be reminded to pay his rent. Whenever Moolan Tai had to do so, she would take her idol of Thakurji out onto the balcony facing Fazzay's room, sit in front of Thakurji and, while pouring water over Him and praying to Him, add a few irritated sentences about people who didn't pay their rent on time.

When Fazzay saw his neighbours gather their belongings and abandon their homes, he sighed, "Yah Allah! what a catastrophe! After all these people leave, how will I carry on in this desolate lane! How will I live in this ghost-haunted place!"

But when the youthful Nasru saw the kafirs run away from the lane, he felt elated. He clenched his teeth in anger and said, "Let the kafir bastards go to hell! Pakistan doesn't need kafirs!"

Everyday, Fazzay made a count of the families which had escaped and made a note of those which were still in their homes. On the morning of 13th August, after Sadhuram and Jamunadas also departed with their families, he looked at his son and said sadly, "Now only that old woman, Moolan Tai, is still here."

Nasru grimaced and said contemptuously, "Where will that old witch go! She will guard all that gold and silver, she has buried, like a snake! That mother...where will she go!"

That day hordes of Muslim goondas, excited by communal hatred, came from the direction of Hira Mandi and attacked Sayyidmittha Bazaar. The Hindu shopkeepers had put big locks on their shops. The people in the crowd shouted slogans, "Pakistan Zindabad! Allah-ho-Akbar! Saltanat-Islami Zindabad!" Then they broke open the shops and looted them. Some grabbed bales of silk, cotton and muslin from the cloth-merchant's shop. Others smashed into the shops of the food merchants and carried away sacks of almonds, raisins, dry apricots, flour, sugar and sooji. A shop full of aluminium vessels was stripped bare.

When they heard the commotion, Fazzay and Nasru came to the corner of the lane to see what was happening. Nasru's mouth began to water with greed and he asked, "Abba, can I also get a few bales of cloth or a few sacks of sugar and flour?"

Fazzay shouted at him in rage, "Shut up, you son of a pig!"

Nasru tried to argue, "Why, everyone is looting. They say they are collecting the just rewards of a holy war."

Fazzay became even more angry and shouted, "You are the son of a pig. Are smashing locks, breaking into homes and looting sanctioned in a holy war? The offerings of a holy war! They are the turds of pigs!"

Nasru's religious passion was, however, so inflamed by now that his father's chastisement had no effect on him. He ran to join the crowds and followed them towards Lohari Mandi. His religious frenzy became wilder when the procession passed by the mutilated bodies of three Hindus on the road. Like a man intoxicated, he longed to participate in the holy war. The rioting and the killing became so vicious in the bazaars of Lahore that, in order to control the situation, the government sent in contingents of soldiers in military trucks. The bazaars began to resound with the sounds of gun-fire. Soldiers opened fire without hesitation, whenever they came across mobs of people.

Fazzay sat on the platform outside his shop and watched all that was happening in the main bazaar. A man carrying a large aluminium plate ran through the Gali towards him. Suddenly, the man let out a scream and fell down. At the same time, the entire lane was filled with the echo of gunfire and the clanking sound of the metal plate falling on the ground. Fazzay became numb with fear, "O God, Nasru!"

Soldiers with rifles were stationed all along the bazaars of the city. A curfew had been imposed. More than three people weren't allowed to gather at any place. The following order had been announced — "Anyone found walking in the streets after sun-down and after the street-lamps have been switched on, would be shot at sight."

Because of the curfew, Nasru couldn't get back home. Anxious and afraid, Fazzay waited for him with tears in his eyes.

He muttered to himself and cursed his son's folly, "Idiot...He has lost his head. What's gone wrong with him?"

When, at last, Nasru did manage to reach home before sun-down, Fazzay heaved a sigh of relief. Scolding his son, he said, "Get inside at once. And don't you dare to step out again! If the soldiers shoot you down like a mad dog, all your religious talk will ooze out of your..."

Nasru answered nonchalantly, "Why are you so worried? Now the army is ours and the soldiers are our Muslim brothers. All the kafirs have run away. People have collected tons of gold and filled their houses with food."

Nasru's heart was dancing with joy at the victory of his religion. He had even picked up a knife at Lohari Mandi. Because he didn't want his old father to feel disturbed, he had hidden it in the folds of his tehmad.

When Fazzay and Nasru heard the siren for the curfew at seven in the evening, they went into their room. Fazzay didn't feel like making food. Nasru also didn't seem to want any. Both of them lay down side by side on the mat on the floor of the room. It was pitch dark in the lane outside and it was even darker inside the room. The night was absolutely still and silent. The sky was covered with heavy, rainless clouds. It seemed as if the clouds had lidded the new city so tightly that its brick houses didn't have the chance to cool down. That made the night even more warm and humid. The old city lay as if it was stunned. There wasn't a whiff of breeze anywhere.

Lying in that closed and narrow room, both Fazzay and Nasru were drenched with perspiration. Fazzay had taken off his kurta and tehmad and was lying in his langot. Nasru had also taken off his kurta. In order to prevent his legs from getting sticky, he had rolled his tehmad upto his waist. Irritated by the curfew, the heat and the humidity, both lay without uttering a word. They had a fan made of palm leaves with them. Fazzay used it to fan Nasru and himself. When his arms got tired, he threw it down on Nasru's chest. Nasru then fanned his father and himself. Irritated by the situation, irritated with each other, they continued to fan each other in silence. Only sleep could have calmed them. But in that heat neither of them could sleep. That made them even more anxious and restless. The fearful silence of the bazaar, broken only by the sharp clatter of the steel-tipped boots of the armed soldiers who patrolled the streets, made them feel even more apprehensive, helpless and bitter.

One quarter of the night had passed. Neither Fazzay nor Nasru had managed to go to sleep. Nasru got more and more annoyed as his back, soaked with sweat, got stuck to the woven mat. Finally, he handed the fan to his father, and in order to catch a bit of fresh air, went and crouched next to the door of the room.

Nasru was startled by the soft sound of footsteps in the Gali. He turned and stared in the direction of the sound. He caught sight of Moolan Tai, wrapped in a bed-sheet, stealing away quietly towards the bazaar. Nasru turned to his father and whispered, "Look, that old woman, Moolan, is trying to run away."

Fazzay continued to fan himself and replied casually, "Let her...Living alone, she must have got scared. Only Allah can help us."

Nasru carefully watched the old woman moving towards the bazaar. "That kafir is running away with all her wealth tied in her bundle..." As those words escaped his lips, he felt all his religious zeal rekindle.

"Let her, why should you care? May Allah protect her," Fazzay said, his voice filled with compassion.

By the time Fazzay, staggering on his aged legs, managed to reach the bazaar, Nasru had not only caught up with the old woman near a street-lamp, but had also stabbed her with his knife and snatched away her bundle.

Trembling with rage, Fazzay dragged his son back to their room.

Elated by his success, Nasru exclaimed, "That kafir woman thought she could could get away with everything." He quickly began to open the bundle.

Fazzay, still gasping for breath, sat with his head in his hands. He didn't have the strength to utter a word. Nor did he have the strength, to prevent his son from opening the bundle of the old woman he had murdered, and to force him to throw it away.

Nasru opened the bundle and then lifted the lid of the box in it, "Bitch...the kafir was running away with the stone idol of her God." He laughed derisively.

Fazzay's eyes were burning with rage. When he realized that his son was safe, he cursed him angrily, "May a pig...your mother. May you burn in Hell for murdering an innocent old woman. The kafir was running away with the stone idol of her God. She should have smashed your head with her stone idol. You are really a great Ghazi, you have saved your God!"

Original in Hindi.
Translated by Alok Bhalla.

KULWANT SINGH VIRK

WEEDS

This is a story about Pakistan. Pakistan had only been created about three or four months before. Every town there seemed desolate and ruined. In the police stations and in the public squares of each town lay piles of all sorts of things — trunks, cots, stools, tables, sofa-sets, almirahs, pictures. They had all been snatched out of their usual places and had been dumped outside police stations or piled-up in public squares. It was very strange to find them there. Once upon a time each thing must have had a special place in a house. Each owner must have thought that if a particular chair or picture was not in its proper place it would have looked ugly and destroyed the symmetry of the house. Now those cherished items lay in undistinguished piles in public places. Household vessels, almirahs, cots had travelled through a variety of streets and wandered past different localities, only to lie in piles in front of police stations or out in public squares. They had neither been cleaned nor dusted, neither polished nor used. No human hands had touched them for the last few months.

All the towns and villages in Pakistan seemed desolate and forlorn. Its ruined and burnt houses were now inhabited by people who had been uprooted from their own homes elsewhere. They often sat at the doors of their new houses and looked out at the world with despair and sorrow in their eyes; and when they walked, they placed their feet upon alien soil with fear and apprehension. In those strange, confused times only the earth still seemed to have stayed firmly in its place. Everything else was out of joint.

The refugees, who had been uprooted and thrown out of their native lands, were forced to move from one place to another. When they were pushed out of the big refugee camp at Vaghey, near the border, they had to drag themselves from zilla to zilla, crawl from village to village, till they could find a hovel somewhere which would give them shelter.

Even those who hadn't been forced out of their homes, felt as if they had lost their bearings. Communities had been scattered, friends had lost each other, factories had been abandoned by their owners, labourers had run away. Now there were new people everywhere, each place was occupied by strangers. To those who had lived in a place for a long time, these new people seemed strangely different — they were dirty and stupid, they seemed lost and bewildered. They couldn't get along with the older inhabitants of a place, didn't understand its local customs. Lacking the easy confidence of those who had lived for a long time in a place, they couldn't say salaam-alekhum, sit down next to their neighbour or begin a conversation. When asked a question, they could only stand and stare silently. These people had disturbed the traditions of the villages and of the towns, shaken them to their very roots. Even the older residents had begun to feel alien, for they could no longer recognize the places where they had been born and had grown up. The old havelis were now occupied by strangers, the rivers and the canals which flowed past their towns and villages were polluted. Indeed, they had not been able to perform their daily rituals in the rivers and the canals, because for days the water flowing through them had been reddened by blood and befouled by the bodies of men and women who had been mutilated and killed. They even prevented strangers from bathing in these rivers and canals.

Life in every village and town had been turned upside down. Each town and village was trying to find some way of re-discovering its old rhythms of life, rebuilding itself, becoming stable again.

"This country is ruined," said a young Jat to his old father as he looked at the devastation all around.

"No, there is no need to despair," his father replied. "If you look carefully, nothing much has happened! The population of the world has always wandered from one place to another and then found a place to rest. Everything will soon find its proper place and then life will settle down once more."

"Those are just words! Where will these poor people settle? They don't even have the strength to lift a morsel of food to their mouths."

"Don't be silly. It only seems as if they are lost. Look at those weeds. When the sowing and planting season begins, the farmer ploughs the field and pulls them up by their roots. He gathers them together with all the other wild plants and throws them away. But after a few days the weeds sprout again. A month later, it seems as if the field had never been ploughed."

There seemed to be some truth in what the old man had said. Those migrants who had got a small piece of land settled down. They found solace in what had been temporarily allotted to them. They had built a wall around their piece of earth, tied their buffaloes to long nails and dug pits to light their fires. They had even found the time to sit down and smoke a hookah together. For some, the nostalgia for the past and the strangeness of their present place had already disappeared.

Now, whenever a tahsildar or any other official came to visit these people, there were already some amongst them who were willing to set themselves up as leaders. They would make it their business to speak about the problems of resettlement of each of the members of the group to the tahsildar. When with the officials, they would make everyone in the group sit down, and repeat again and again, "Let only one man speak at a time." They would also make sure that the officers were neither hungry nor thirsty, and thus, having drawn attention to themselves, establish their control over the groups. It is such people who always assured us that, no matter how grim the tragedy, the human spirit can never be extinguished.

It is to one such desolate and ruined village that I came as a liaison officer appointed by the Government of India. My mission was to trace those women and children who had been abducted; to find those families who had been forcibly converted to Islam, and help them to return to India. A unit of the Indian army and a few officers from Pakistan's special police force were assigned to help me. The task of discovering and helping women who had been abducted was awkward and difficult, though surprisingly, at times, it was also easy. Sometimes one found such women without much difficulty. There were times, however, when even after an extensive search one couldn't discover where they had been hidden and rescue them. The Pakistani police would offer help only after one had been tipped off about the places where these women could be found, they would rarely give us the addresses themselves. When they did work sincerely the task of finding these women was much easier.

This story is about a woman whose address was given to me by the thanedar of the area to which the woman had been taken.

He also told me that the woman concerned had been the wife of the numberdar of the village.

No metalled road went past the village we had to go to. We walked through fields and stumbled over broken and uneven dirt paths for a long time. When we reached the village, the important people of the village got together to receive us and help us.

Government officers had a lot of power in Pakistan in those days. When the thanedar inquired about that woman, the choudharys of the village quickly showed us the house in which she was being kept. The house was at the edge of a large, open field. The thanedar and the villagers stayed outside, while I went in alone to see the woman. The house was three storeys high and was built of bricks and mud. On one side of the courtyard, there was a small room in which there were a few metal plates, a few bowls and glasses, and some firewood. On the other side lay a mattress and a few other things. The woman was lying on a cot. She had been ill for the last few days. One hand was bandaged. It seemed as if a boil had become infected. She seemed very weak. She spoke slowly and softly. I sat down on a cot next to her.

"How are you?" I asked as if I had only come to enquire after her health.

"I have been running a temperature for the last few days."

"Isn't there a woman here to look after you?"

"No. No one who is related to me."

Her way of handling herself was very different from that of all the other abducted women I had met till then. They were never alone. There were always people around them who insisted that they were either the sisters or the wives of someone. I had never been left alone with them.

I felt as if this woman was utterly alone in the house; as if she had been left to her fate, though it was also obvious that the villagers had helped her in the past.

I had already learnt about how the people of her village and the members of her family had been slaughtered. There was no point in asking her to tell me about it again. I was more concerned about her present state.

"How long have you been living here?"

"Since the day the village was destroyed."

"Who gave you those cooking vessels?"

"You really are foolish and naive."

I understood. She wasn't living alone nor did the things in the house belong to her. However, the man who was the master of the house, of all the articles in it and of her body was at that moment nowhere to be seen.

How easy it is for me to write all this! At that time, however, I was shocked and disturbed by what I had seen and heard. The helpfulness of the policemen and of the villagers which had made me think kindly of mankind once again, vanished at that moment. I couldn't deal rationally with the bitter and stark reality of life before me. In that house made of brick and mud, the abducted wife of another man lay helplessly before me on a cot. I couldn't think of an uglier image of man's inhumanity to man. Abducted, raped and humiliated, she lay quietly and still. There was no one from her caste, community, religion or village with her. No one had told her that she could once again be with the people who were dear to her. Perhaps even if someone had told her, she would have refused to believe him. After all, how could anyone rescue her from such a big and strong country like Pakistan? It was foolish even to dream of such an attempt.

Given her physical condition, the question of taking her to India didn't arise. She was much too ill and the winter was severe. Besides, the people of the village couldn't hide her from us again. They knew we could force them to tell us of her whereabouts.

"Alright bibi, I'll come back later." I meant that I would return in a few days so that I could take her away with me. She, however, didn't think that such an escape was even possible in her dreams.

"Are you leaving? Please stay for a bit longer. I want to say something to you. Please listen to me."

I sat down on the cot near her bed again.

"I want to ask you for a favour. Will you help me? I want you to do something for me."

"What is it?"

"You are my Sikh brother. I was also a Sikh once. Now I am a Muslim. At the moment there is no one in the world whom I can call my own. I am in great trouble. You can help me.

There is a sister-in-law of mine in a village nearby. She is very young. She was abducted by the scoundrels when they attacked our village. Their gang was the largest and the cruellest. I am sure they are the ones who abducted her.

Please. Help me. I need your help desperately.

Bring her back to me.

Everyone defers towards you. Even the policemen listen to you.

Give her my regards. I am her eldest sister-in-law. I raised her and looked after her as my own daughter. If she comes to live with me, I will find someone for her. My health, my position here, too, will improve. At last, I will be able to call someone my own."

I recalled what that old Jat had said. "Look at those weeds. When the planting season begins, the farmer ploughs the field and pulls them up by their roots. He gathers them together with all the other wild plants and throws them away. But after a few days those weeds sprout again. A month later it seems as if the field had never been ploughed."

Original in Punjabi.
Translated by Alok Bhalla
and Gurupadesh Singh.

SATINATH BHADURI

THE CHAMPION OF THE PEOPLE

Between the police districts of Gopalpur in Purnea and Sripur in Dinajpur runs the Nagar. The mountain stream here is not that wayward. That is why the wobbly wooden bridge still stands over it with almost rude indifference to the river's endless advances. The bridge spans the path taken in earlier times by troops dispatched from north Bengal to places in north Bihar. The road remains at both ends of the bridge, but its best days are gone. Only the nearby market at Aruakhoa in Gopalpur has been flourishing in the last few years, thanks to the traffic in contraband which started with the war. The weekly market is just to the west of the bridge. A second road starting in Malda skirts the market, cuts through the districts of Purnea and Jalpaiguri, and stretches right upto the town of Siliguri. Countless loaded bullock-carts converge near the bridge from the three directions of Malda, Dinajpur and Jalpaiguri. Before Bakri Id last year, when the S.D.O. came to get an undertaking for peace from the ijaradar of the market, his car got stuck on the way. Since then, the potholes have been filled.

The railway station of Sudhani, which links the place with the outside world, is sixteen miles away. From Aruakhoa, the heart of the black-market, cows, buffaloes, sugar and ghee cross the bridge; from Bengal, come paddy and husked rice.

The place has a mixed population of Hindus and Muslims. Most of the Hindus are Rajbanshis. The twisted rumours spread from Calcutta, Bihar and Noakhali last year had cut deep, but the scars were soon covered over. The compulsions of habit and livelihood were beginning once again to pull their patchwork lives together. But suddenly, along the old cracks, the ruin set in.

Munim Sahib, the local agent of Johurmal Dokania, who owns the Sudhani depot, is taking his cart to the market in

Aruakhoa one Saturday night. A stretch of canvas has been spread over the sacks of sugar. To take the cart out after dinner means reaching Aruakhoa the next morning. After the last puff, he hands the end of the bidi to Bilat, the carter. Bilat is instantly pleased.

"Won't you lie down, Munimji? No use getting up before Aruakhoa. Two miles to the hour is the most you can get out of this cart on a long trek. Throw in an extra hour for the dark. Which means you won't get to wash yourself at Aruakhoa before sunrise."

Munimji is in a good mood today. Everyone will ask him about the latest turn of events in the country the moment he arrives. Those who meet him on the way, including the teacher of Consi L.P. School, want to know the news. As it is, he is the munim of such a big depot, a man who can read and write. On top of that, his employer's house has that machine which brings the news by "electric." Even the Viceroy speaks to Dokaniaji on that machine. So many people send Dokaniaji so many messages on it, so many women sing and play to please him. Munimji's words, therefore carry a lot of weight with the local men.

"If someone asks at night what we are carrying, remember to say potatoes. Have you put the sack of potatoes in front?"

"Ji."

"I had better stretch out on the sacks of sugar at the back. It would have been an easier ride had the sugar been stacked in front."

"Ji."

"Watch out when we get to Mirpur. The secretary of the Village Advisory Committee there is a rascal. Every fool is a jumped up secretary these days. If anyone questions you there, just wake me up. And when you are passing through the village, keep singing at the top of your voice. They'll be suspicious if we are silent. It's a stupid waste of money. Ten rupees for a secretary on an average. The Mirpur one won't cost less than fifty. Be careful."

"You don't have to tell me that, huzoor. You get some rest. I'll take care. No bumps on the way."

But Munimji is too excited to sleep. The news he is carrying will startle the whole market place. The people of these parts have not had such important news for ages...Damn these ants, the creatures won't let anyone sleep. Didn't that idiot, Bilat, dust the sacks before loading?

"Hey Bilat, are you dozing off?"

"No huzoor, it's just that my eyelids were getting heavy."

Munimji knows that Bilat will now look for ways to get a bidi out of him. Poor man, has to sit up all night after all. One only hopes that he won't go round spreading the half-heard rumours along the way.

"Here, keep the bidi and the light. And don't repeat to anyone what we heard at Sudhani today."

Bilat had not thought about the news at all. Now he tries to recall what he had heard.

"You can count on me, Munim Sahib. All these years I've eaten your salt. Have I ever blabbed? We're poor people, what good will the news do us?"

He takes the bidi and the light with pleasure. Twisting the tail of the bullock to the left, he starts on another series of curses on the creature's nearest female kin.

It is almost ten in the morning when the cart reaches Mushar Sao's store.

"Ram Ram, Munimji."

"Jaigopal, Jaigopal."

Mushar Sao and his son unload the sacks of sugar and take them into the courtyard. Others are sure to drop in soon.

"Only four sacks?"

"Have you any idea how tough it gets everyday? It was trouble enough getting that lot through. Times are nauseating. One has to put a plain sack over the one branded at the mill, and lug the stuff inside double sacks."

Saoji does not bother to take the sack of potatoes inside. "Now let's hear what's going on."

Munimji looks grave. He asks for his tooth-cleaner without answering the question. It must be important news, Saoji thinks. One by one the men begin to gather. They are mostly stall-keepers of the market, only a few have come with their rice-laden carts from distant villages. Munimji concentrates on scrubbing his teeth with the twig. The way he nods to acknowledge the many greetings of "Ram Ram, Munimji" suggests a weary disillusionment with the world. He takes his time rinsing his mouth as everyone waits for a couple of precious words he might let drop. Now he is wiping his face...he isn't going to ask for his bath-oil next, is he?

On any other day, Saoji might have suggested a bath. Today, avid for news, he lets it pass. Munimji gives money to Bilat to get curd and crisped rice for the two of them.

"Get some good jaggery too. No use looking for sugar. You can't get a pinch since the day the Congress ministry took over."

Munimji tucks the remaining small change in his girdle and says without looking up, "Well, Dinajpur is to become a district of Pakistan." His tone suggests a matter-of-factness, as if districts are in the habit of turning into Pakistan every other day. He finds time at last to look at the faces around him, radiating the confidence worthy of an important political leader addressing a press conference.

For a moment no one knows what to say. The heavens tumble around Darpan Singh, the Rajbanshi from Sripur. Others hold their breath; who knows what has happened to their districts. Is Munimji going to mention their villages too? Saoji has turned pale — what is to become of his shop, his wife and son, his household? Summoning up courage, he asks, "And Aruakhoa?"

"Aruakhoa is in Purnea district. Hindustan. After all, this isn't Bengal, this is Bihar. They won't dare try any of their tricks here."

The shop-keepers sigh in relief. Munimji does not let go of all the news at one, he squeezes it out in little doses. So many eyes are fixed on him in consuming anxiety. To them, his words are as momentous as the Viceroy's broadcast. It is hard not to indulge in such a luxurious sensation of power.

The rice-sellers from far-off villages are usually the first to arrive. A few of them are among the listeners.

"Where does Mirpur go, huzoor?" asks Achhimaddi.

"Which district is it?"

"It's Harischandrapur thana," replies Achhimaddi, voice choked with fear.

"That's Malda district," Saoji tells them.

"Malda has gone to Pakistan."

Over-whelmed by this evidence of Allah's endless mercy, Achhimaddi is unable to find his voice.

Pora Gossain of Bajargaon fights his way to the front. He is the priest of the Rajbanshis. There are quite a few of his clients in the area. Saoji makes room for him on the cot, but he seems not to notice. Walking straight up to Munimji, he asks, "And Bajargaon, Titlia thana, Jalpaiguri district?"

"Babaji, you rest in peace. By the grace of Ramji, Jalpaiguri falls in Hindustan."

"And why shouldn't it? We've been in Bajargaum since my grandfather's days. It can't just go over to Pakistan like that. The holy land of Jalpeshwar, the kingdom of Mahakaal, go over to Pakistan! The Viceroy is a wise man, thank heavens. Narayan, Narayan."

While invoking the deity, he shoots a burning glance in the direction of Achhimaddi. In their anxiety they had all forgotten his existence. Now the man shrinks under the glare of so many eyes. Except Qasim, everyone there seems to find him guilty. Asghar Ali, who has the lease of his village, must have pulled strings to take it to Pakistan.

Achhimaddi's offence is that the news has made him happy. He senses that he is unwanted here. Taking Qasim by the hand, he leads him away. Once they are near his cart, Achhimaddi says with a broad smile, "He's a true son of his father, Asghar Ali, the pattanidar; he kept his word. Let's get rid of this lot of grain. Never mind the price. We must thank the pattanidar when we get back."

"Why not leave right away?" asks Qasim. "Today, these people here make me nervous."

"How will you buy the medicine if you don't sell the paddy? You have already spent two rupees for each maund you got past the police in two districts. To take the stuff back you've got to bribe them again. And not a paisa earned yet. Haji Sahib is the ijaradar here, he has the lease on this market. What are you so scared about? If there's trouble, his goons will bludgeon the life out of this lot."

Qasim picks up courage to go to Haji Sahib's office — the ijaradar is a Muslim after all. He would never have dared before, but ever since the events in Bihar last year, a Muslim never thinks twice before walking up to a fellow Muslim. Qasim finds that there is already a crowd there. All of them are hurling threats at the ijaradar. Haji Sahib tries to calm them down. He tells those who have come from far to start back immediately. "There are Hindu settlements all around. Watch your step. Take turns sitting up during the nights. They won't just walk away with the Kishangunj sub-division into Hindustan. I'll see to that. We don't have the facts yet. One can't trust that munim's words."

Qasim and Achhimaddi feel a stab of panic at the last remark. They object in chorus, drawing murderous glares from the others. The two quickly ask Haji Sahib to buy their grain — at whatever price. The ijaradar has no need for the stuff. Yet he asks one of his men to make the deal for the sake, he says, of these poor men of the faith. "Fix the rate, Masum. Do you get me?" An old hand, Masum gets his master's hint alright.

Haji Sahib continues placating the crowd. "Don't worry Miyan, even the Viceroy might change his tune if he is pushed. I am going to town tonight. They took a subscription of twenty-five rupees for the District Pakistan Conference, the Sudder Sahib gave so many assurances, they can't just turn around and say this district will go to Hindustan. There will be some extra expenses, that's all."

The market could not warm up today. The news brought by Munimji spreads quickly. Soon Saoji's store is spilling over with people. The munim is pelted with questions: all of them want the news from the horse's mouth. The Hindu traders from Dinajpur and Malda come in a group for his advice. He asks Saoji to clear the shop of outsiders — one never knows if a Muslim is sulking in the crowd. With the Hindus from Dinajpur and Malda he goes into a long huddle. Munimji's instant support at this hour of crisis gives them confidence. Those places are no longer safe for their families; they must move out. They want to return home even before the trading begins. Munimji, his voice dripping concern, urges them not to waste a minute. At their own entreaties, he buys up all the rice they have on them at sixteen rupees a sack. The price last market-day was nineteen rupees; yesterday at Sudhani, it was twenty two.

A while later, a messenger arrives from Haji Sahib to say that the ijaradar would like a word with Munimji. Haji Sahib takes him to a separate room as soon as he arrives. "This market of mine is finished this time," says Haji Sahib, after a brief exchange of radio news. "Anyway, one can't fight fate. It seems all this will go on for some time. Better talk business. How many sacks of sugar have you brought?"

"Four. One goes to Saoji, three for you. It's seventy rupees a maund this time."

"Never! All this time it was sixty. You can't push up the price just like that. And why a full sack for Saoji? Give him half a sack, three and a half for me. The last lot you brought was damp."

"Saoji gets only one sack, and you must have your share of Pakistan parcelled out from even that! That can't be. We must give him a full sack. A word once given cannot be broken. As for the sugar, how could it be wet, it was covered with canvas? And what about the two sacks of jute you are getting free? You expect me to pay for that from my pocket, I guess? Damp sugar indeed! In any case, Malda and Dinajpur are soon going to be in Pakistan. It will be party time for your people there for a few days. They will also start stocking up for Id from now. You will easily get two rupees fifty for a seer."

The stream of Haji Sahib's arguments loses its way in this verbal deluge. He can manage only a feeble protest. "How can you say that, Munimji? Where would Muslims get money?"

"Oh alright, knock two rupees off the price. But you will have to do something, Ijaradar Sahib. You'll have to fix a few carts for me. I have to take the rice to the Sudhani depot. There's no room for all of it here. Can't leave it in the open like this, not when the monsoons are on. You have quite a few carters at your beck and call."

"Okay, that can be arranged. You'll be leaving before dawn, I take it?"

Masum comes in to say that the traders are furious. There is already a mob inside the premises. They want Munimji back. They have been told that Haji Sahib won't let him off alive.

A big uproar can be heard outside.

"Have they all gone mad?" Haji Sahib's face turns white with fear.

The two come out of the room together. On seeing Haji Sahib, the regular stall-keepers push the traders from outside forward; after all, the man is their landlord. Munim Sahib calms the belligerent crowd. To the ones nearest him, he says in a lowered voice, "How could you think he would dare touch me? Why are you not home yet? It's not wise to stay away from your homes for too long these days. You know very well how bad things are. What new counsel can I give? Talk to the headmen of your villages and decide for yourselves. The women are a cause for worry. Be careful. We didn't push our luck with the women even in Sudhani; we took them all to Rajputana this month. You can't trust them with those talking machines. If the stupid Viceroy had mentioned 'Purnea' even by mistake, it would have been a fine mess by now. One can't be too careful."

The narrow eyes of the Rajbanshis dilate with terror. The Polia women begin to wail.

"There's-no time to buy salt."

"Hey Bachhidai, where are you? Come along quick."

"Hurry up and move, you son of a nawab. This is no time to dawdle."

"Don't want the money today. Just weigh and keep the stuff with you."

"Will Munimji please take the cash deposit? I am too scared to carry it."

The panic in the air could make even the strongest of minds unsure of himself. After the brief surge of feverish activity, the place is quiet.

From the very next day, Aruakhoa wears a changed look. It used to host a market only once a week; now there is a miserable crowd of terrified men and women at all hours of the day and night. Cart after cart trundles across the bridge from the direction of Sripur. Droves of women, children, cattle and goats come on foot. Even a little boy carries a pile of pots and pans on his head. A man struck by kala-azar staggers along, gasping for air, a cat held in his scraggy arms. An asthmatic crone goes wheezing past, about to cough up her life, it seems, in her desperation to escape Pakistan. All this time the world of these people was small. Today, however, some of them will move on like hunted deer to an uncertain address, after a brief halt at the market place. Some will stay back, in the hope of finding work in the fields. There is no dearth of food along the way; the palms ripen around this time.

Neither of the two District Boards of Purnea and Dinajpur is willing to pay for the upkeep of the bridge over the Nagar. The shaky woodwork has been taking quite a strain the last few days. Camps have been set up on both sides. Munimji has talked a relief society from Calcutta into opening a camp for the refugees at Aruakhoa. He has also got the Local Board to send a doctor. The whole show is being run with his support.

A stream of people throng Munimji's camp to unburden their worries. He reassures some of them, asks some to pray to Ramji or to be patient, and to some others he deplores the pussy-footing of the Congress government. While making out the relief tokens for curd and crisped rice, he asks, "How many? Five and a child? Right, get this stamped from the tent with the flag over there and go over to Saoji's shop. Everything will be fine." The refugees are filled with gratitude. Not many people have kind words for them in their moment of distress.

On the railing at the far end of the bridge, the Muslim League's green flag with the crescent and the star is put up; the Congress tricolour flies at this end. Over there they shout, "We have wrested Pakistan, see what's left of Hindustan"; a group on this side shouts back, "Bande mataram, jai Hind."

The air grows bitter and tense in no time. Things threaten to go out of hand any moment. The men across are planning to set fire to the bridge, whispers someone, to stop goods from being brought over. The reaction is instant and loud. "We'll burn it down first. We won't let them have our cattle go over any more." Munimji pacifies the people here; Haji Sahib, at his end. What will happen to the market if the bridge is gone?

Munimji reasons with his men. "Give it a couple of days. Wait and watch. Do you think Mahatmaji will let them get away with this? He has got the Viceroy to form a Commission. The Viceroy is no riff-raff. He has pedigree, royal breed."

The word spreads. Very soon it is on everyone's lips. "Commission," one hears it mouthed everywhere, "Commission."

Chualal Rajbanshi of Sripur is known to be a clever man. It is felt that Munimji never tells the whole story, so they put Chualal on a rice-laden cart and send him to Sudhani station to find out more about the Commission. Chualal is not one for shifts and sleights; he walks straight up to the pointsman and asks him about the Commission. The pointsman is surprised. Didn't Chualal know that the Commission's report was out, that wages were going up? The people back at Sripur do not know what to make of this.

"Commission?" Israel, the old guard of the ijaradar strikes the ground with his stick. "Commission is what you pay at the depot, it's called the faith-tax. No Muslim is going to pay it any more. They can go and stuff their Commission. We'd like to see how they get the market into Hindustan!"

Darpan Singh's father slaps his wizened old thigh. "None of you are to pay any toll to a Mussalman ijaradar from now on. We've left our hearth and home, land and chattel to come to Hindustan. And for what? I have heard they are not going to let Hindus live there with their wives and daughters. And are we to pay tax to a Muslim here as well?" He would have said more, but Darpan's mother pulls him away. Why tempt the trouble-makers?

From that day, the stall-keepers stop paying the toll.

"Have you noticed," the munim asks Saoji, "the ijaradar doesn't spend the nights this side any more? Is he paying for the camps on his side?"

"No, he is running it on subscriptions. He has raised quite a sum. Says it's needed to bribe the Commission so that Gopalpur can go to Pakistan."

Munimji's eyes light up — perhaps in envy, or is it admiration?

"Well, Munimji," Saoji, carries on, "why don't we raise some money as well, to save Gopalpur? Haji Sahib is the foxy sort; who knows, he might buy the Commission over. You are the man to save us. Purnea too might be saved."

Munimji has already been weighing the possibilities. He cannot afford to go wrong. The risks at the moment are not worth the gains. One thing could be done, however. Raise the money and lie low. If the place goes to Pakistan, pay it back and say the magistrates were stiff. If not, keep the cash and say that it's been fed to the Commission. No, it's too dicey. Go for the bird in hand.

"No Saoji, I don't want to get mixed up in all that. There's the Congress government, there's Mahatmaji, there's my boss. They are the ones to take care of such things. Let's talk instead of what we can do about the goods blocked up at both ends of the bridge. It's a monsoon river. We might have done something had it been some other time."

"And the rice-searchers on both sides are suddenly acting pious. The policemen today let through hundred and fifty cows and buffaloes on their way to Mymensingh from Muzaffarpur; that should have been a hundred and fifty in hush money on other days. The officer of the rice-watch on that side too has lost his appetite over the last few days. This way the market will fold up in no time. No wonder Haji Sahib has given up his habit of spending the nights here."

"Maybe they fear a magistrate's visit or something. Take it easy, it will be fine in a couple of days. The relief is being run from your store. What's your worry? We are men of business. We'll manage."

Saoji nods in agreement, but it is clear from his expression that he is not reassured. Four annas out of every rupee he makes in relief profits, will go to Munimji — not an awful lot to put by.

"The jute had grown to a man's height, you know."

"My son-in-law stayed back, the stubborn fool."

"Life won't be easy for that wretched girl."

"Didn't leave even at the time when cholera nearly emptied the village."

Different voices, different accents intone the same litany of woes.

Darpan Singh tries to console his father. The honour of the women at least is safe. The old man bursts into tears. "Irfan, my servant, will lord over my sixty-bigha estate. And that's supposed to be God's justice!"

Haji Sahib can see the Congress flag from his office, fluttering in the morning breeze, its three colours shedding the poisons of despair, hatred and fear. He longs to go over to the camp near the green flag across the bridge. A short distance, and yet, how great the difference! One of the flags is his own. Below it dwell peace, pleasure, unblemished joy — the safety under the crescent, in the shadow of al hilal. But if he were to be scared away from his own fief by these Rajbanshis, could a single paisa be raised in toll-tax in the future? No one can say what the Commission will decide. It will be as God wills.

"You spent a day there after it became Pakistan. Tell me, did the air smell of garlic being fried?" Saoji's mother asks Darpan Singh's wife, "Did those creatures force you to eat meat that night? The rascals must have started their low-born tricks, I'm sure."

Darpan's wife has no proper answers to the questions. She goes on mumbling to herself. "Couldn't ever find the heart to slice a stalk off that lovely pumpkin plant. And I cut it off at the root before coming away. God knows what the pair of bullocks sensed; they sniffed and turned away from the pumpkin leaves I gave them to chew. I smashed the oven too. It was a beautiful smooth clay oven that I had built. God knows what filth Irfan's aunt will now cook on it. And what am I to do with this image of the Lord? We had worried so much about it. But the Lord takes care of Himself; we worry because we are ignorant fools. Let's see now what the priest has to say about it. There's such a mishmash of castes in this place. The Lord has left no way I can get a proper bhog cooked for him."

She was about to lift her joined hands in prayer when she realized that Saoji's wife, forgetting the circumspection typical of her trading caste, has gripped them unawares. Darpan's wife does not feel any desire to free her hands of that warm touch, not even in order to raise them to God. Burying her face in the bosom of the woman she has known for only three days, this wife of a shop-keeper from far-off Balia, Darpan's wife sobs out her sorrows.

For the first few days, the suddenness of the calamity had left the people stupefied. A little more time, and the uncertainty becomes a way of life, the keen edge of fear gets blunted. Cart-fares and food-prices, after having doubled, come down again. The policemen get over their righteous fit in three days. Soon carts heaped with rice begin to arrive from across the bridge; thousands of cows and buffaloes are herded over to the other side.

In spite of the hectic days, people are still anxious about the Commission. Everyday numerous carts carry to Sudhani the rice Munimji had bought up at the first go. Munimji is a special case, so he pays a lower freight. People feel so grateful to him that had he asked for free transport, the carters would probably still have felt themselves honoured.

"Oh no, Munimji is no fake. He is a Hindu. And not one of your fish-eating ones. He is from Rajputana, the land of heroes — they never cringed before the Muslims even for a day. He can't take your cart for free; only a Muslim ijaradar might do that. Munimji will pay you a fair rate."

"Don't we know that, Saoji? When will the Commission's report be out?"

"Who knows? Within a couple of days, I believe. Munimji was saying that even there, the Muslims are kicking up trouble."

"Saoji, let me carry Munimji's letter today."

"You carried it the day before yesterday, Sukdev. Let me have it today, Saoji."

Every carter covets the privilege of carrying the letter. Munimji writes everyday to Sudhani for news of the Commission.

Sirilal wants to know if all the Viceroy's news that comes on the machine at the Sudhani depot is taken down in a cash-book. "When I gave the men at the depot Munimji's letter the other day, they copied something out from it in a book, and they also scribbled something from the book on the reply I brought back."

"Could be. That's a large warehouse. Small fish like us have no use for the customs of those big places. We are happy if we can serve you and get by, Ramji willing. Anyway, Misrilal will carry the letter today. And listen, Sirilal. Munimji will be going to Sudhani himself tomorrow. Can't you manage a covered seat on your cart? Okay, I will get you one. Haji Sahib is dying to lend Munimji his own covered cart. But Munimji is not the sort to take even a small favour from the ijaradar, he is a man of honour. We need a reliable carter tomorrow. There's still some money left after buying rice from the deposits people had left with Munimji. All that public money will have to be put away safely at the depot. This place is full of crooks — you can't have so much money lying about. Later, when all this fuss is over, everyone will get his full deposit back, not a paisa less. It's one of those shady places. Even the Viceroy knows about Dokaniaji's depot."

Wherever one goes, one hears the name of Munimji on everyone's lips. He has scarcely time to eat or wash. Tireless, he works round the clock with the sole aim of making life a little easier for the helpless refugees.

To Darpan Singh's father, Munimji has promised an advance. The old man had wanted to teach Irfan a lesson. The wretch has some cheek — wants to marry a Rajbanshi girl! In spite of all the risks, the munimji has promised to buy the old man's sixty bighas, just so that Irfan should know his place. And he has assured Darpan fifteen bighas out of the depot's estate — after the Commission's verdict, of course.

The government officials of Bihar and Bengal are impressed with Munimji's efficiency, the relief society in Calcutta is full of praise; the Hindus are grateful to him, the Muslims are not altogether lacking in esteem.

"Hindustan is going to be free on the fifteenth of August," Munimji informs the stall-keepers.

"And Pakistan?"

"Oh yes, Pakistan will be free on the same day."

"Can't that be stopped?" the hundreds gathered there would have liked to ask. As if in answer to their speechless query, Munimji says, "Take it or leave it." He would have added, "You won't wait long to regret it," but a sudden rush of commiseration for the Muslims checks his tongue.

Shadows of dread darken across the faces of the refugees from Dinajpur and Malda.

"And the Commission?" they ask almost in a chorus. "What about its decision?"

"That will be known a few days later. But it's certain now that the district of Purnea, which means Aruakhoa, isn't going to Pakistan."

"Gandhiji ki jai!" The cheers come from the people of Purnea, especially from the stall-keepers of Aruakhoa. Umbrellas, slippers, handkerchiefs fly in the air. Dancing with joy, Jadu, the panwallah, gifts away his whole stock.

A number of people from Malda and Dinajpur bring up the subject of renting land from Munimji in Purnea.

Malaria and kala-azar infest this part of Purnea. Acres on acres lie untilled; capital is scarce, so is labour. Now there will be so many eager tenants, even prepared to pay high salamis. Most of the land is for sharecropping or peasant freehold. That is a blessing, for they say that the ministry is going to abolish zamindari very soon. Munimji has clear visions of prosperous days ahead. He does not reply to the men's entreaties, his studied indifference making it plain to the supplicants that they can take the land or leave it — he has nothing to say on the matter.

"We can see to the land later. But there is something else for the present. Now that the refugees have brought all the cattle with them, the cattle can't go on grazing just anywhere. The local people are not going to stand this nuisance for ever. I can arrange for grazing plots at a cheap monthly rate, but you must pay cash."

At the glimpse of this solution to at least one problem, there is an immediate rush of eager men, each wanting his rights settled first.

All this cheering and excitement stir those on the other side of the bridge. "What's up? Must be something big. Don't panic."

Iqbal takes up the tin speaking-trumpet. "Nara-e-takbir!" The rest say, "Allah ho akbar!"

"Are you dead or something? Can't you speak up? We've got to drown the din there."

Hanif, Iqbal, and a few others troop out to investigate the cause of all this rejoicing.

"Keep it up. Don't trail off while we are away, get me?"

"Who goes there in the cart?"

"The daughter and son-in-law of Darpan Singh of Sripur."

"Search them. See that they don't smuggle anything out of Pakistan."

Irfan arrives quickly on the scene. "Is that Didimoni? Jamaibabu? Why are you running away? We are here, aren't we? How Khokababu has grown! He looks as if he is scared of me. What are you afraid of, Didimoni? See your parents and come right back. Why are you turning tail, Jamaibabu? I thought you were a man."

Jamaibabu fumbles for words. Irfan puts a paper flag of the League into the hand of their little boy. "Lovely isn't it, Khokababu?"

Then he sees the cart safely across the bridge. "The ruler on foot," he says with a broad grin to Darpan's son-in-law before parting, "the ruled in a carriage."

As soon as they are told the news, the Muslims from Purnea accompanying Iqbal grow furious with the ijaradar. "That subscription was a fiddle. We've got to teach the crook a lesson. He must be in Aruakhoa now. You think the Hindus could have greased him to tip the verdict their way? Just let him show his face tonight."

The news brought by Munimji creates a great sensation on both sides. Even Darpan Singh's old father tries to smile. How long can one sustain the forlorn hope that Sripur will be returned to Hindustan? A life of pain and want stretches inescapably ahead, having begun the day they trekked across the bridge. The memory of the long years of plenty lies strewn on that far side. Can one start afresh now, at this age? And in this place? All their lives, they had scorned the land west of the Nagar as a malarial pit. It seems ridiculous now to hail this place as part of "golden Hindustan". In the worldly-wise judgment of the old man, the inconsistency rankles. He cannot understand why this should have happened.

Even at the time when the Nagar had swept away their homes, they had spent nights on high makeshift platforms on the road above the embankment. Never for a moment had they thought of crossing over. Then the old man remembers Irfan, and immediately reason gives way to impotent rage.

In all this excitement, people forget to ask Munimji what he has brought for them in six loaded carts.

The munim has ordered that there are to be no more squabbles between the people on the two sides of the bridge. Whatever has happened is now in the past. On the fifteenth, there are to be hearty celebrations on both sides.

Munimji goes across himself to talk to the people on the other side. All this time he had not stepped beyond the no man's land in the middle of the bridge. Now he walks right up to their camps. Everyone agrees that the man has real nerve.

Munimji soon mediates a pact — both sides are to stop shouting slogans threatening "death" to each other. "And do you have Pakistan's new flag? No, not this one. This is the old flag, the League's. Haven't you heard about the new one? Let me know if you need it. Flags are available at prices which suit everyone."

After all this time, Munimji breaks the news to the people on this side: Hindustan, too, has a new flag.

"Where will we get it?"

"Haven't I taken care of that? Flags are available at prices which suit everyone."

No wonder people go overboard in their praise. The right thing at the right time — you name it, and Munimji has it ready.

The atmosphere near the relief camp has turned festive. Bilat's brother works in a jute mill in Calcutta. They are expecting riots on the fifteenth, so he has come away with his ten-year old son. Father and son have been working for the relief society camps for the last two days. Being from the city, Bilat's brother has a good time bossing over the wide-eyed boys of the village. He has been teaching them a new game, although it is the relief workers from the town who have really brought it in. The game has Hindu ghosts in one team, and Muslim ghosts in another. The first group is the Bel-tree side; the second, the Graveyard side: a bamboo-splinter is used to draw a dividing line on the ground between the two. Those killed in Noakhali are bemmodottis; those in Bihar, mamdos. If a player nears the graveyard side, the mamdos shout in a spooky nasal chorus: "Look, he's come from Bihar!" And if anyone gets close to the Bel-tree end, the boys ask, "Are you from Noakhali?" One is expected to answer, "No, from Chitpur."

The boys come up with strange distortions of the place-names. The grown-ups watch the fun, and roll in laughter.

Munimji tells the boys off. "What's going on here? You want trouble again? Beat it. If I catch anyone at it again, I'll drop him into the river from the bridge."

Then he turns to the relief workers. "One would have expected responsible behaviour from you at least."

They are embarrassed.

Within a couple of days, the flags are sold out at a high price. Haji Sahib fled to escape the wrath of his clan. His guard says he has gone to Patna.

On the fifteenth of August, people celebrate Independence Day with great enthusiasm. The flag of Hindustan is raised on this side of the bridge; that of Pakistan on the other side. Showered with rose petals and attar, the bridge looks unreal — part of it in Pakistan, part of it in Hindustan, part of it suspended over an undefined space. It is of the bridge that Darpan Singh thinks in the midst of all this flutter. He is now in Aruakhoa, but his heart is with his estate in Sripur. The bridge remains the one link between his soul and his body. It is because of the bridge that he could escape in time; he might yet go back to his own country, God willing. Or is it will of the Commission? Could the Commission be mightier than God?

In the middle of the bridge, the relief workers from the city are allowed by the people on both sides to perform a charade of dead flags. A group of boys draped in the dead Union Jack pass by wiping their tears. They are followed by two more tearful groups wrapped in the flags of the Congress and the League, who sing the Muharram dirge. Then come boys carrying the 'live' new flags of Hindustan and Pakistan. As they hug one another, even Darpan Singh's father is unable to hold back a smile.

Just when it seems that all but the refugees have forgotten the Commission, Munimji makes the sudden announcement, "The Commission's verdict is out."

People come running.

"Sripur has been given to Hindustan."

Darpan Singh flings his arms round the munim. No one can say what his mother makes of the news, but she breaks into a loud sob. His father bows low to God and the Commission. The Commission has at last heard their prayers.

"Haripur thana goes to Pakistan."

"And Malda?"

"Your end is in Hindustan, Sukdev. You've made it."

Pora Gossain, holy smear on forehead, comes rushing.

He tries a joke even before getting his breath back. "Just in. When getting off the cart, I saw this word 'Capstan' painted on the wall outside Siri Sao's shop. For a moment, I thought it was 'Pakistan', written, you know,in that wrong-side-up way of Urdu. Then they told me it was a brand of cigarettes. Well Munimji, what news?"

Munimji ignores him. The Rajbanshis are surprised that he should choose to snub their priest.

In the end, however, he is forced to break the bad news. "The Titlia thana of Jalpaiguri has gone to Pakistan."

"Never! It can't happen just like that!"

Leaning on his stick, Pora Gossain slumps heavily down on the cot. "Oh God, did you have to do this to me? Now I am going to be buried when I die. They won't even let me go to the temple. Was it in my stars?"

For most of the refugees, it is the end of a bad dream. The same scenes again. The relief camps are dismantled within a day. Carts, people and cattle return from far-flung places in a steady stream. The tricolour flies on the carts. Some of the people carry the flag of Hindustan; their faces glow with the pride of conquest. The women are delirious at having returned from the tiger's jaws.

The world moves fast. Those who ran it all these years never imagined a pace as breathtaking as this. Nor did they dare to trifle with the minds of so many people with such abandon. The thought crosses Iqbal's mind as he pulls down the flag of Pakistan from the bridge. There was no need for this farce, for this cruel mockery. It took two hundred years to pull down the flag of the English; it didn't take more than three days to remove the one he had put up. One can stomach the disappointment, the pain — but where does one hide from the shame? A whole line of refugees on the bridge, a market full of people — they all watch the fun. Iqbal feels his face burn; he longs to dissolve into the sand of the riverside, to fling himself into the water. With what emotions he had raised this flag! "The beggar's three-day pipe-dream is over," Ramji Sao's taunt cuts him to the quick. They will fly Hindustan's tricolour here. Was it for this that we stood below the flag and shouted "Long live Pakistan" till our voices cracked? Tomorrow the boys from Sripur will perhaps wrap themselves with this and play out the charade of the dead flags. Whom can he blame when the whole world has turned against him?

Without looking up, Iqbal puts the lowered flag on its pole across his shoulder and starts walking — towards the north where the flag is not yet dead.

Hanif had lit a bidi to flaunt his apathy. He now drops its burning end on the bridge and hopes that it will start a fire. It would be great — Aruakhoa and Sripur would be separated for good. He knows it is a fantastic thought, but it pleases him.

Munimji occupies the camps of the ijaradar on the other side.

The boys drag out a family hiding in the fields. Who knows, they may have been planning to set fire to the jute.

"Hey, it's Achhimaddi."

Achhimaddi starts to cry. "We were running away towards Haripur. Mirpur has been Hindustan for the last two days. They say, we'll be forced to pray facing east,that they won't let us kill chicken. So we cleared out leaving everything behind. Thought we'll hide in the jute-fields all day and start at sundown..." Howling, he grips the munim's feet.

"Let him go. I know the man."

"Huzoor is so kind."

"Victory to Munim Sahib! Victory to Mahatma Gandhiji!" The air rings loud with the cheers.

"You must get rid of the Pakistani flags by morning," Munimji explains to the people on the other side. "You can give them to me. I'll deposit them with the government. It's against the law to have Pakistani flags in Hindustan."

The flags he had sold are handed back to him.

Tomorrow these need to be taken to Titlia, Munimji tells himself. He will stop at Pora Gossain's empty house, will have a good look around at the land the priest owns. The Pakistani flags will have to be sold there, and the Hindustani flags taken back. The same goods are to be sold twice. He tries to reckon what his profits will add up to. The Commission has given a lot to some people; from others, it has taken away a great deal. But it has not failed him; he has extracted his fair share from its verdict. He got the Commission right; there was no mistake.

Shouts of "Victory to Munim Sahib" can still be heard outside. A nagging doubt bothers Munimji. Perhaps it would have paid to buy a khadi cap beforehand, perhaps it would have helped in the reckoning, perhaps he has made a small mistake after all. Forget it. A man should be happy with what Ramji chooses to grant him.

Munimji sits down with his pocketbook and, in the age-old code of the merchant-venturer, makes up his accounts.

Original in Bengali.
Translated by Swapan Chakravorty.

NOTES ON THE AUTHORS

Lalithambika Antharjanam: Born in 1909, she was amongst the first women to begin writing in Malayalam. Her novel *Agnisakshi* won the Sahitya Akademi Award in 1963. She wrote a number of novels, collections of short stories and essays. She died a few years ago.

Syed Mohammad Ashraf: He studied at the Aligarh Muslim University, and later joined the Indian Administrative Services.He has, thus far published a few stories in Urdu in various journals. The story included here was first published in Urdu in the Aligarh University Journal.

Shaikh Ayyaz: Popularly known as "Sindh jo Awaz" (The Voice of Sindh), he is considered to be the greatest Sindhi poet after Shah Latif Bhitai. Born in 1923 in Shikarpur, he achieved fame at a very young age. He spent most of his life in Karachi, where he worked as lawyer. He was a Sindhi nationalist to the core and was imprisoned several times. He wrote more than thirty books of poetry and prose.

Manik Bandyopadhyay: A major Bengali writer. He was born in 1908, in Dhaka. His collected works in Bengali run into sixty volumes. His most famous novels are *Padma Nadir Majhi (The Boatmen of the Padma)* recently made into a film by Gautum Ghose, and *Putul Nacher Itikatha (The Puppet's Tale)*. He died in 1956.

Rajinder Singh Bedi: A highly respected Urdu writer. He was born in 1920. His novel, *Ek Chadar Maili Si* (translated into English as *I Take This Women*), won the Sahitya Akademy Award. He also wrote a number of film-scripts and short stories. He died in 1984.

Satinath Bhaduri: An important Bengali writer, he was born in 1906, in Purnea district in Bengal. He studied at the University of Patna, and made a name for himself with *Jagari*, a novel about the Quit India Movement of 1942 (translated into English as *Vigil*). He died in 1965.

Salil Choudhary: A musician, who has made his reputation in films. He has written a few short stories, poems and songs in Bengali.

Jamila Hashmi: She was born in Lyallpur, Punjab in 1929. She did her M.A. in English Literature from the Punjab University, Lahore in 1954 and then taught for a few years in a school. Her first novel, *Talash-e-Baharan* (In Search of Spring) was given Adamji Literary Prize. Her most famous book was *Atash-e-Rafta* (The fire of the Past) about rural Punjab. Her historical novels describing Qurratulian Tahira, the Iranian poetess, and Mansoor Mallaji, are highly regarded. She spent most of her life in Lahore. She died in 1989.

Intizar Husain: Born in the 1920's, in U.P., India. He migrated to Pakistan after the Partition. Considered to be one of the most important writers in Urdu, he has, thus far, published six collections of short stories, three novels (*Basti* is considered to be a classic), and a volume of essays. Recently, he was given the first Yatra Literary Award.

Saadat Hasan Manto: Born in 1912 in Ludhiana, he migrated to Pakistan in 1947. Considered to be one of the greatest Urdu short story writers, his writings have been recently collected in five volumes. Apart from writing short stories, he has written film-scripts, radio plays and essays. He died in 1955 in Lahore.

Ahmed Nadeem Qasmi: Born in 1916, he has written stories and poems in Urdu and Punjabi. His writings have been collected in twelve volumes. His best-known collections of stories are *Neela Pathar* and *Aas Paas*. At present, he lives in Lahore, and is the Director of the Urdu Academy.

Mohan Rakesh: Born in Amritsar in 1925. He studied at the Oriental College, Lahore, and taught at Elphinstone College, Bombay, and D.A.V. College, Jullunder. Associated with the "Nayi Kahani" in Hindi, he published two highly acclaimed novels (*Adhe Adhure* is regarded as a classic), plays (*Ashard Ka Ek Din* has been performed repeatedly) and a few collections of short stories. He received the Nehru Fellowship and the Sangeet Natak Akademi Award. He died in 1972.

Ramlal: Born in Mianwali, in Pakistan, in 1923. He has, thus far, published in Urdu, fourteen collections of short stories, six novels and many radio plays.

Bhisham Sahni: He was born in 1915, in Rawalpindi, Pakistan. He studied at the Government College, Lahore. After 1947, he taught in a college in Delhi. Thus far, he has published numerous volumes of short stories, novels and plays in Hindi. *Tamas*, his novel about the Partition, won the Sahitya Akademi Award in 1971.

Umme-e-Ummara: Born in Bihar, she migrated to East Pakistan after Independence. Later she left Dhaka and migrated to Karachi after the Bangladesh war. A highly respected writer of Urdu fiction, her best-known work is a collection of short stories entitled, *Agahi-ke-afsane*.

S.H. Vatsayan 'Ajneya': A celebrated Hindi writer, he was born in 1911, in Kusinagar, Uttar Pradesh. He published four novels (of which *Shekhar: Ek Jeevani* is the most famous), collections of short stories and more than twelve volumes of poems. He won the Jnanpith Award in 1978. He died in 1989.

Kulwant Singh Virk: Born in 1920, in Shekhupura district, is a Punjabi writer of distinction. He has published more than six novels and many collections of short stories. In 1968, he was given the Sahitya Akademi Award.

GLOSSARY

Abba	Father
Abbajan	Father
Ajwain	Oregano
Al-Hamdu-lillah	Praise be to God
Ameen	Amen
Amma	Mother
Ammi	Mother
Angeethi	Stove
Azadari	To mourn for the martyrdom of Imam Hussain during Moharram
Azadi	Freedom
Azan	Call for prayers
Babu	Respectful term of address for a man
Bade Abba	Grandfather
Badi Amma	Grandmother
Bade Bhaiya	Elder brother
Bahen	Sister
Bahu	Daughter-in-law
Baisakhi	Harvest season
Basti	Town
Batter	Quail
Behist	Paradise
Bhai; Bhaiya	Brother
Bhati	Oven
Bhog	Food offered to a diety
Bigha	A measure of land
Bismillah	In the name of Allah
Chacha	Father's brother
Chachi	Father's brother's wife
Chandan	Sandal-wood powder or paste
Chillum	Earthen pot of a hookah in which tobacco is burnt
Chorbazaar	Thief's market

Chunni	Cloth draped by women over their heads and shoulders
Daal	Lentils
Daalkhor	Derogatory term used for vegetarians
Didimoni	Sister
Diya	Earthen lamp
Dharmshala	Public inn for pilgrims
Fauji	Soldier
Gali	Lane
Gareban	Collar; also shirt
Gilli-danda	Children's game
Goonda	Hooligan
Granthi	Priest in a gurudwara
Gyarveen Sharif	Date of birth of Sheik Abdul Qadir Jeelani
Hanafi	Sunni Muslim
Hilal	Crecent moon
Houri	Celestial nymph
Ijaradar	One incharge of land allotment
Jagir	Inheritance
Ji	Yes
Kafir	Infidel
Khalsa	Sikh
Khichdi	Dish of rice and lentils; also means, hotchpotch
Khokha	Brother
Khuda	God
Kulfi	Frozen milk sweet
Kufuvan ahad	None comparable to Him(God)
Lajwanti	Touch-me-not plant
Langot	Loin cloth
Mama	Mother's brother
Mandi	Market
Maulvi	Muslim religious teacher
Mehndi	Henna
Misri	Sugar
Miyan	Respectful way of addressing a Muslim man

Mushquee	A water-carrier
Mussalla; Mussalli	Abusive way of referring to Muslims
Namak	Salt
Namkin	Salty
Niaz	Ritual offering
Nara-e-takbir	Call the name of God
Navroz	Parsi new year's day
Pakora	Fried savoury
Paan	Betel-leaf
Paandan	Box for keeping betel-leaves
Paanwallah	Seller of betel-leaves
Pattanidar	Landlord
Phuphi	Father's sister
Phoolbari	Garden of flowers
Prashad	Offering in a temple
Purdah	Veil
Qul huwallah-ho-ahad	Say God is one
Raag	Musical composition
Rafzi	Shia Muslim
Rajya	Kingdom
Rasool	Messenger of God
Rath	Chariot
Sadhu	Ascetic; mendicant
Salaam	Greetings
Salwar	Loose pyjama
Seth	Rich businessman
Sherwani	Long coat
Sighah	Marriage rites
Sindoor	Vermillion
Sooji	Cream of wheat
Tahsildar	Officer of a district
Taya	Father's younger brother
Tehmad	Lungi
Thana	Police station
Thanedar	Policeman
Tonga	Horse-driven carriage
Tongawallah	Driver of a horse-driven carriage

Teli	Oil-seller
Tumtum	Horse-driven carriage
Upla	Cow dung cake used for burning
Vaid	Doctor
Waheguru	God of the Sikhs
Ya Mallick	O Lord
Yar	Friend (user colloquially)
Zalim	Evil man
Zamindar	Landlord
Zindabad	Long live

VOLUME II

CONTENTS

Ashfaq Ahmed
The Shepherd 1

Narendranath Mitra
The Four-Poster Bed 41

Saadat Hasan Manto
Open It 69

S.H. Vatsayan 'Ajneya'
The Refuge 73

Intizar Husain
The City of Sorrow 85

Attia Hosain
After the Storm 101

Ibne Insha
Our Country 105

Ibne Insha
Pakistan 107

Suraiya Qasim
Where Did She Belong? 109

Mohan Rakesh
God's Dog 119

Ramesh Chandra Sen
The White Horse 127

Krishna Sobti
Where is my Mother? 135

Ibrahim Jalees
A Grave Turned Inside-Out 141

Saadat Hasan Manto
Mozel 153

Kamleshwar
How Many Pakistans? 173

Syed Waliullah
The Story of the Tulsi Plant 191

CONTENTS

Lalithambika Antharjaṇam
The Mother of Dhirendu Muzumdar 199

Vishnu Prabhakar
I Shall Live 207

Narain Bharati
The Claim 219

Khwaja Ahmed Abbas
The Death of Sheikh Burhanuddin 223

Masood Ashar
A Very Old Story 235

Notes on the Authors 243

Glossary 247

ASHFAQ AHMED

THE SHEPHERD

1

It was a long, cold, winter night. I was sleeping comfortably in a warm bed, with my head under a quilt, when someone shook me roughly and woke me up.

"Who is it?" I screamed.

A heavy hand struck my head in reply and a voice in the dark said, "The police have arrested Rano."

"What?" I said, as I tried to push the hand away from me, "What is it?"

The ghostly voice, rising from the surrounding darkness, repeated, "The police have arrested Rano — translate that into Persian!"

"Damn you, Dauji," I groaned, "You harass me even in the middle of the night...Go to Hell...I won't stay in your house any longer. No...I will not study...Damn you, Dauji — you are a dog..." Then I started weeping.

Dauji kissed me, and said, "How will you pass, if you don't study? And, how will you grow up to be a great man, if you don't pass? How will people come to know about your Dauji?"

"May Allah destroy everyone. Even you and all those who know you...Even me...even me —" The vision of early death so disturbed me that I began to weep bitterly and couldn't speak any more.

Dauji caressed my head tenderly and said, "Enough...now stop crying. You are a brave boy...you are my darling son...Translate that sentence and I shall not wake you up again."

I couldn't stop the tears which were streaming down my face. I said angrily, "The bastards arrested Rano today. Tomorrow they will arrest someone else, and your translations..."

"No, no," he said, interrupting me. "I promise, I shall never wake you up like this again and ask you questions. Come, be a good boy and translate...The police have arrested Rano."

Still sulking, I said, "I can't."

"At least try," he said, removing his hand from my head.

"I won't," I replied angrily.

He laughed and said, " 'Karkunane germakhana Rano taukeef kardand,' means that the police have arrested Rano. Don't forget the new words and their usage. Now repeat them ten times."

I knew he would cling to me like misfortune if I didn't repeat them. Helplessly, I began to recite the Persian conjugations of those words. After I had gone over them ten times, Dauji said, apologetically, "Now repeat the sentence five times." And after I had repeated that cursed sentence five times, he helped me back into my bed, covered me with the quilt and said, "Don't forget it. I'll ask you to repeat it as soon as you wake up in the morning."

Then he left my room.

2

Every evening, on my way back home from the maulvi, who taught me how to read the *Koran,* I used to pass through a narrow lane. All sorts of people lived in that lane, but I was only familiar with the fat water-carrier whom we used to jokingly call, " 'Kaddu Karela dhai anney.'" Next to the water-carrier's house, there was an enclosure for goats. There were mud houses on three sides of the enclosure, and the fourth side was fenced in by dry twigs of different shapes and sizes, and by thorny bushes which grew haphazardly. On the other side of the enclosure was an open and rectangular field; beyond that lay the house of the lame potter and a small cemented house with red coloured windows and a door with metal handles. After that the lane became narrower, and as one walked further down it, its two sides seemed to meet each other. It was, perhaps, the longest and the loneliest lane in our locality. That is why, whenever I walked down it, I felt as if I was passing through the barrel of a gun, and that as soon as I emerged from its muzzle, I would hear the deafening noise of a bullet being fired and would die. But in the evenings, I always came across someone else in the lane and heaved a sigh of relief.

Amongst those I sometimes walked past in the lane, I came across a tall man with a white moustache, who bore an uncanny resemblance to the 'barah mah wallaha Milkhi'. He used to stoop a little, wear a large muslin turban, a loose khaki coat, narrow khaddar pyjamas and flat, thick-soled boots. He was often accompanied by a boy of about my age who used to be dressed just like him. The man, with his head bowed, his hands in his coat pocket, often talked softly to the boy. Whenever they walked past me, the boy looked up at me and I stared back at him. Though curious about each other, we never stopped, but continued to go our way.

One day, after trying to fish unsuccessfully in one of the ponds near the village, my brother and I were returning home, when we came across that man sitting on the canal bridge with his turban in his lap. His white chutiya seemed to be pasted on his bald head like the feather of a hen. As we approached him, my brother raised his hand to his forehead and said, "Dauji, salaam."

The man nodded and replied, "May you live long."

I was delighted to discover that my brother knew the man and, I too, squeaked. "Dauji, salaam."

"May you live long, may you live long," he responded, raising both his hands in blessing.

My brother, however, gave me a resounding slap and screamed, "You are a cocky bastard. Why did you have to imitate me and greet him again? Why must you meddle in everything? Idiot — Do you even know who he is?"

"Dauji," I whimpered.

"Who is Dauji?" my brother asked angrily.

"The man sitting there," I replied, as I wiped my tears.

"Don't talk nonsense," my brother retorted, as he glared at me, "You imitate everything I do, you cocky bastard."

I didn't say anything in reply, but continued to walk in silence. I was, however, pleased that I had finally been introduced to Dauji. I wasn't bothered about the fact that my brother had slapped me. He did that often. He was older than me and loved to show off.

Anyway, Dauji and I had finally become acquaintances. Thereafter, I tried to be in the lane at the time he usually walked through it. It was always a delight to greet him and it was even pleasanter to receive his blessings in return. He said "May you live long," with such love that I always felt as if my life was suddenly filled with the bright radiance of two moons and that I was walking on air, a few feet above the ground.

We continued to greet each other like that for about a year, during which time I found out that Dauji lived in the house with the red windows, and that the young boy with him was his son. I longed to know more about him, but my brother was a hard-hearted fellow who always got irritated if I asked him any questions. He had two standard answers for every question I asked him — "Why do you want to know?" and, "Don't be stupid." But, by the grace of God, my curiosity about Dauji was soon satisfied.

After I had passed the fourth standard from the Islamia Primary School, and was admitted into the fifth standard in the M.B. High School, I discovered that Dauji's son was my class-fellow. No longer dependent on my brother, I soon found out from Dauji's son that he was a khatri, and that he worked as a writer of applications in the local Munsif's office.

Dauji's son was called, Aminchand, and he was the brightest student in our group. He wore the largest turban in class, but his face was small like that of a cat. Some boys had nicknamed him "miaoon," while others called him "mongoose." Out of respect for Dauji, however, I always addressed him by his real name. That is why he became my friend. We even exchanged gifts and promised to remain friends for life.

3

A week before the summer vacations, I went to Aminchand's house for the first time. It was a very hot afternoon. But I had wanted to borrow from Aminchand some stories of Sheikh Chilli which I read obsessively, and went straight from school to his house, without being bothered either by the heat or by hunger.

Aminchand's house was quite small. But it was clean and bright. Beyond the door with the metal bolts, was a small porch which opened onto a rectangular courtyard. Facing it was a verandah which was painted red and behind it was a room of the same size. In one corner of the courtyard there was a pomegranate tree, a few plants of akeek and a small bed of coriander. On the other side was a broad staircase with a small kitchen in its niche. The red windows I had seen from the outside, opened into the sitting room, which was next to the porch.

When we walked through the front door, Aminchand shouted, "Bebe, namaste." He left me standing in the courtyard and disappeared into the sitting room. His mother was seated on a mat in the courtyard and stitching on a sewing machine. The girl sitting next to her, was cutting cloth with a large pair of scissors. Bebe muttered something in reply and continued to sew on the machine. The girl looked up, and then turned to her mother and said, "Bebe, I think the Doctor Sahib's son is here." The machine stopped whirring.

"Yes, yes, of course," Bebe said, as she smiled and beckoned me towards her. Hesitatingly, twisting the strap of my bag around my fingers, I went and stood next to the pillar in the verandah.

"What is your name?" Bebe asked gently. I lowered my eyes in embarrassment and told her my name.

"Doesn't he resemble Aftab?" the girl asked, as she put her scissors down.

"Of course. After all, he's Aftab's brother," Bebe replied.

"What about Aftab?" someone asked from the room inside, "What about Aftab, my child?"

"Aftab's brother is here, Dauji," the girl answered after a pause. "He has come with Aminchand."

Dauji came out. He had rolled his pyjamas upto his knees and had taken his kurta off. But he was still wearing his turban. Carrying a small bucket of water, he came upto me, examined me carefully and said, "Yes, he certainly resembles Aftab, but Aftab was rather lean, while he is plump." Then he put the bucket down, placed his hand affectionately on my head, dragged a wooden stool out and sat down beside me. He lifted his feet off the ground, dusted them and then soaked them in the bucket of water.

"Does Aftab write home?" he asked, as he poured a handful of water over his legs.

"Yes, he does," I replied. "We got a letter the day before yesterday."

"What does he say?"

"I don't know. Only Abbaji knows."

"I see," he said. "You should ask Abbaji. Those who don't ask questions, never learn anything".

I kept quiet.

After a while, as he continued to pour water over his legs, he asked me, "Which part of the *Koran* are you reading these days?"

"The fourth," I replied confidently.

"What's the third part called?" he asked.

"I don't know," I said. I felt ashamed.

"Tilk-ar-Rasool," he said, as he took his hands out of the water. He shook his hands in the air to dry them. Bebe continued to sew on the machine. The girl got up and began to serve food on the low table in the verandah and I stood twisting the strap of my bag around my fingers. Aminchand was still in the sitting room, while I was trying to merge into the shadow of the pillar.

Suddenly, Dauji turned towards me and said, "Recite the Sura Fatiha."

"I don't know it," I replied shamefacedly.

He looked at me with surprise and exclaimed, "You don't even know the al-hamdulillah!"

"I know the al-hamdulillah," I replied quickly.

He smiled and muttered, "It's the same thing, the same thing."

He then nodded his head and said, "Recite it."

When I began to recite it, he rolled the ends of his pyjamas down, and covered his bare shoulders with the loose end of his turban. When I recited upto Walad-waleen, he repeated ameen after me. I thought he would get up and give me a present. Because, when I had recited alhamd for my grandfather, he had also repeated ameen after me and had given me a rupee as a gift. But Dauji continued to sit still. It seemed as if he had been turned to stone.

Soon Aminchand came back with the book I had come to borrow. Before leaving, out of habit I said, "Dauji, salaam." With his usual kindness, he replied, "May you live long." Bebe stopped her sewing machine and added, "Come and play with Aminchand sometimes."

"Yes, yes, do come again," Dauji said as if he had been suddenly reminded of something. "Aftab also used to come here." He bent towards the bucket and added, "We miss Aftab." Then he recited a Persian couplet.

That was my first meeting with Dauji. I came away with the impression that he was a miser, a reticent man, and perhaps a little deaf.

That evening I told my mother that I had been to Dauji's house and that he had enquired after Aftab Bhai. She scolded me and said, "You should have taken my permission. Aftab used to take lessons from Dauji and had a lot of respect for him. But your Abbaji doesn't talk to him anymore. They have quarrelled over something, and they are still angry with each other. If he finds out that you have been to his house, he will get angry." Sympathizing with me, Amma added, "Don't tell Abba about your visit."

Of course, I didn't tell my father, but I continued to visit Dauji's house and talk to him like a grown up about everything. If I saw him sitting on a mat reading, I would sneak up and stand behind him. He would shut his book and say, "Ah, Golu, I am glad that you have come..." Then he would turn towards me, smile and say, "What's the latest gossip?" I would make up a story and he would laugh heartily with me so as to please me. I now realize that what I often told him was neither interesting nor clever.

He would tear a sheet of paper out of his register and say, "Here, solve this equation." That always made me lose my nerve, but his proposition, that if I solved one problem I could gossip for another fifteen minutes, was always very tempting. I would invariably agree and try to answer his question. But sometimes his questions were so complicated that I never got a chance to gossip. If, however, I succeeded in solving the problem quickly enough, he would point to the mat and say, "What is this?"

"Mat," I would say confidently.

"No," he would shake his head, and add, "What is it called in Persian?"

I would retort, "Do you think we are taught Persian at school?"

"But I can teach you Persian. Why don't you let me, Golu? It's called boriya in Persian and haseer in Arabic."

I would mischievously fold my hands before him, and say, "Please have mercy upon me, please. I don't want to learn either Persian or Arabic. Leave me alone."

He would pretend that he hadn't heard me, and say, "Boriya in Persian and haseer in Arabic." After that it would be impossible to keep his voice out of my ears, even if I could have stuffed them with crushed glass.

4

Aminchand was a bookworm. He sat and read all day. Dauji rarely ever interrupted him, but he would not hesitate to challenge him whenever he got the chance. If Aminchand ever got up to drink water from the pitcher outside, Dauji would look up from his book and ask, "Tell me, son, what is the past tense of 'do'?"

Aminchand would murmur "did," as he drank water from the glass, quickly put the glass down on the bench and run back to the safety of the sitting room. Dauji would turn back to read his book again.

Dauji was very fond of his daughter. We used to call her Bibi. Dauji had named her Qurrat. Often he would call her and say, "Qurrat Bitiya, when will you get rid of those scissors?" She would merely smile and keep quiet.

Bebe was allergic to the name Dauji had given to his daughter. "By calling her Qurrat," she would complain, "you have doomed her to stitch qurratas for the rest of her life." Then she would suddenly lose control over herself and start screaming abuses and curses. Bibi would burst into tears, but Dauji would console her and say, "The wind must blow, my child, and bullets must fly. Never try to stop them." After that he would gather his books, roll up his favourite mat, and quietly go upstairs.

5

In the ninth standard, I acquired a bad habit for which I had to pay dearly. Hakim Ahmed was the only hakim in our town. He wasn't really interested in his medical practice, but he could narrate wonderful stories. Tales of adventure, stories about fairies and ghosts, the dastans of Hazrat Suleman and Mallika Saba were a part of his pharmacopoeia. In his small dispensary there was nothing more than a few boxes of powder, about ten bottles of sharbat and two reflecting glasses. Apart from giving out medicine from those two bottles, he used to treat his patients by entertaining them with stories of magic and romance, and with amulets made especially by Hazrat Suleman. People would come to listen to his stories from distant villages and go back cured.

Within a week or two of our acquaintance, both of us came to an agreement with each other. I would steal empty bottles from my father's dispensary for him, and he would give me *Dastan-e-Amir Hamza* to read in return.

Those books were so fascinating that I would hide under my bedsheet and secretly read them late into the night. Of course, the result was that I slept well into the morning. My mother was very annoyed by my behaviour. My father was worried about my health, but I assured him that I would risk my life to pass the tenth class examination. Thus, my nights were spent in the magical palaces of *Tilisme Hosh Ruba,* and my mornings standing on the bench in the class-room. I nearly failed my first term examinations. I fell ill during the second term exams and was passed in the final exams because Hakim Ahmed used his influence on my behalf with the teachers.

In the tenth standard, *Sandalinamah* and *Afsana-e-Azad* were my constant companions and I used to hide them in my room at home. I kept *Alif Laila* locked in my desk at school. I always sat on the last bench in class, and instead of reading my geography book, I read books of romance, and wandered with Sindbad across the seas.

Well, at ten in the morning of the twenty-second of May, the results of the examination conducted by the University reached M.B. High School. Aminchand stood first, not only in our school, but in the entire district. Twenty-two students passed and six failed. Hakimji's magical powers had no effect on the University. My name was included by Punjab University amongst the six who had failed. That evening my revered father thrashed me with a cane and threw me out of the house.

I spent the entire night sitting near a well, wondering what I should do next and where I should go. God's country wasn't small and I was familiar with the tricks of Umaro Ayyaar and knew how to navigate Sindbad's ship! But even then I couldn't figure out what to do. I sat near the well for more than three hours thinking about the various paths open to me. My mother, who had been wandering through the night wrapped in a white sheet, came to my rescue. She promised to make my father forgive me and persuaded me to return home.

I was not interested in my father's forgiveness. I was only interested in spending one more night at home, for I had decided to leave early the next morning. I spent that night sleeping comfortably in my bed. The next day, I found two of the other students who had also failed, Khusia Kodu and Desu Yabyab, sitting on the hillock behind the mosque. They were planning to go to Lahore and start some business of their own. Desu Yabyab assured me that there were many business opportunities in Lahore, and that he had often heard from his uncle about his friend, Fatehchand, who had done so well that he had bought two cars in one year. When I asked Desu Yabyab what kind of business Fatehchand had, he said that there was so much work in Lahore that all we had to do was to open a shop and put up a sign board in front of it. People would come to us on their own and offer us work. He was full of fantastic dreams about the money we would make. When I asked him once again about the kind of work we could expect in Lahore, Khusia Kodu flared up and said, "Yar, Desu knows everything. Tell us, do you want to come with us or no?"

Then he turned towards Desu and asked him, "We'll set up our office in Anarkali, isn't that so?"

Desu thought for a while and said, "Either in Anarkali or outside Shah Almi. Both are nice places."

I said, "Anarkali would be better because it is more famous. All the advertisements in newspapers give Anarkali, Lahore, as their address."

Finally we decided that we would leave for Lahore the following day by the afternoon train. I went back home and started packing for the journey. While I was polishing my shoes, our servant came and said, "Come with me, Doctor Sahib has summoned you."

"Where?" I asked, as I put the brush down.

"He is at the hospital," he said spitefully and grinned at me. He had been a witness to the thrashing I had received the other day.

Afraid of what was in store for me, I climbed up the stairs next to the verandah. When I slowly opened the door and stepped into my father's room, I saw Dauji sitting there. Still apprehensive, I greeted Dauji and heard his familiar and sad voice bless me in reply, "May you live long."

"Do you know him?" my father asked me in a stern voice.

"Of course," I replied, like a confident salesman.

"Damn you, you bloody brat, I'll..."

"No, no, Doctor Sahib," Dauji intervened with his hands upraised, "He is a good child, he..."

My father interrupted him, and said sharply, "You don't realize, Munshiji, that this idiot has ruined my reputation."

"Don't worry," Dauji replied, with his head lowered, "He is brighter than Aftab, and one day..."

At that my father really lost his temper, banged his fist on the table and thundered, "You don't know what you are talking about, Munshiji. He's not even as good as the dust on Aftab's shoes."

"He will succeed one day, Doctor Sahib, he will," Dauji said, trying to pacify my father. "Stop worrying about him."

Then he got up from his chair, put his hand around my shoulders and said, "I am going for a walk. Come with me, we'll talk on the way."

My father continued to sit and turn the pages of his register angrily. I started walking out of the room slowly. When I opened the door, Dauji turned to my father and said, "Doctor Sahib, please don't forget to send everything soon."

As we walked through the town, Dauji told me the Persian names of the trees we came across. Soon we reached that bridge over the canal where I had first met him. He sat down on his favourite spot, took off his turban and placed it in his lap, rubbed his shaven head, and asked me to sit facing him. Then he closed his eyes and said, "I shall teach you from today, and I assure you that even if you don't stand first in your class, you will certainly get a first division. Each of my decisions is made with the help of God and he has always treated me with mercy..."

"I don't want to study," I said rudely.

"Then what will you do, Golu?" he asked with a smile.

"I'll do business, earn money, and when I come back in my car you..."

Dauji interrupted me and said very affectionately, "May God give you ten cars, but I will not sit in the car of an illiterate. Nor will Doctor Sahib."

I retorted angrily, "I don't care. May Doctor Sahib live happily in his house, and I in mine!"

Surprised, Dauji said, "You don't care for me either!"

I was about to say something, when he added, "Don't you care for me either, Golu! Really, Golu!"

I was touched by the tone of his voice and muttered softly, "I do care for you, but..."

It seemed, however, that he hadn't heard me, "Had I spoken like that before my Master, had I uttered a blasphemous word, then...then...?" He quickly picked up his turban, placed it on his head once more, and folding his hands in prayer, said, "I, who am a humble dog in the Prophet's durbar; I, who am no better than the dust under the feet of Hazrat Maulana would have said to my Master, 'Put a chain of slavery around my neck'." Then he put his hands on his chest and said, "I was born a goatherd. My father was a milkman from Mundasi. I am the child of ignorance, born in the home of the ignorant. But a single gesture of Hazrat Maulana's transformed Chintu into Munshi Chintu Ram. People call me Munshiji. But I say that I am a lowly servant of Rehmatulla and I am only fit to carry his shoes...People think..." Then Dauji folded his hands, bowed his head, kissed his fingers, touched his eyes, and continued to recite Persian couplets.

Disturbed and puzzled, I touched his knees and pleaded with him, "Dauji, Dauji!" But, without paying any attention to me, he continued to chant over and over again, "O my Akka, my Maula, my Mursheed."

After sometime he came out of his trance, looked at me and said quietly, "How lovely this season is! It is sunny and warm throughout the day, and cool in the evenings." Then he stood up and said, "Let's go. I have to buy a few things from the market."

If I had been rude and insolent earlier, now I was chastened and repentant. He bought the things he needed at the store owned by Desu Yabyab's father, put them in his bag and started walking towards his house. Repeatedly, I thought of asking him to let me carry the bag, but didn't have the courage to do so. I don't know why I hesitated, but I felt a strange sense of shame which I couldn't explain. I was still feeling embarrassed and ashamed of myself when we reached his house.

It was only then that I realized that, henceforth, I was expected to sleep and study at Dauji's house. My bedding and a hurricane lamp had got there even before me.

It seemed as if I was not destined to become a businessman and drive my own car. Even my friends who had fled, were brought back from Lahore by their parents three days later. But perhaps, if I had gone with them we would have had an office in Anarkali and a rapidly growing business.

6

Dauji made my life hell. He ruined it. Destroyed it. My mornings were spent listening to rubbish at school and nights — the brief nights of summer — answering his questions. He would pull his cot next to mine on the terrace and ask me questions about the canals at Moong, Rasool and Marala. If I answered them correctly, he would ask me about them once again. And, if I answered them correctly again, he would repeat his questions once more. If I got irritated and said angrily, "I don't know, I won't answer," he would sit quietly for a while and sigh. I would shut my eyes and try to sleep, but would soon feel remorseful and sit up.

Then I would call him softly, "Dauji."

"Yes," he would reply sadly.

"Dauji, please ask me another question."

" 'Bahut be abaruh hokar terey kuche se hum nikley' — scan the line."

I would try to evade the task by saying, "That's a long line. I'll write it down in the morning and then try to scan it. Ask me something else."

He would look up towards the sky and say, "My Golu is a good boy. Translate it."

I would think about the sentence for a while and begin to translate it into Persian. I would, of course, soon make a mistake and he would say, "Janpidar, you must conjugate masnad first. I have told you that often."

Trying to escape from his clutches, I would ask him, "Why do you call me janpidar? Why don't you call me janey dau?"

"Excellent," he would exclaim with delight. "I wish you would ask me such questions more often. The word jan is from Persian and dau is a dialect. The two cannot be joined. Those who do so when they write or speak, commit a serious error. That is why..."

Only then would I realize that my trick had landed me into more serious trouble. I would yawn and say plaintively, "Dauji, I am very sleepy."

"Is that another excuse?" he would ask at once.

After that even if I tried a hundred thousand excuses, even if I tried to divert his attention by telling him thousands of stories, he would continue to sit on his cot and ask me questions. If it got late, he would pick up his turban which lay on a chair and put it on his head again. No matter what subterfuge I tried, I had to answer his questions.

After Aminchand went away to college, I moved into the sitting room which he used to occupy. Later I even replaced him in Dauji's affections. I too became fond of Dauji. But I never did approve of the manner in which he treated me. I still don't. Perhaps, I don't approve of it because I am now a learned man with modern ideas, while he was a man full of old fashioned learning. The worst thing about him was that he always asked questions. Moreover, he forbade me to play. He wanted me to study all the time. I am sure that he would have been happy if I had died on a heap of books. He had only one prescription for physical fitness — a long walk, and that too early in the morning. He would come into the sitting room about two hours before sunrise and wake me up. Shaking me by the shoulder, he would say, "Wake up Golu, otherwise you'll grow fat."

All over the world, parents wake up their children telling them that the sun has risen, but Dauji used to taunt me and say, "If you become flabby, how will you ride through your district on a horse when you become a Collector?" Refusing to stir out of my warm bed, I would fold my hands together and plead, "Please, for God's sake, Dauji, don't wake me up so early in the morning. Kill me instead. Take my life." This last entreaty never failed to hurt him. He would at once pull the blanket back over my head and leave the room.

7

It seemed that Bebe, for some reason, which only God knows, had an ancient enmity with Dauji, and that he was mortally afraid of her. She would spend the day stitching clothes for the neighbourhood and cursing Dauji. I always got angry with her when she lost control over her tongue. But those who live in a river can't afford to be at war with the crocodile. Sometimes, when she showered abuses on him and called him filthy names, he would seek refuge in my room. He would sit quietly for a while with his hands covering his ears. Later he would say, "I know it is a sin to speak ill of someone behind her back, and may God forgive me, but your Bebe is a demon and in her house, Qurratulain and I, and perhaps even you, live like helpless travellers who have been trapped."

Bebe did, indeed, look like a demon. She was very dark, her teeth were white, her forehead jutted out and her eyes were narrow. She walked (may God forgive me too) like a cat and carried tales from one person to the next. She always said such awful things to poor Bibi that she wept for days. Bebe got along only with Aminchand. Perhaps that was because Aminchand looked like her or because he didn't love Dauji as much as Bibi did.

I liked Bibi, but I didn't get along too well with her. If I sat on the terrace doing my work, and Dauji was in the verandah down below reading, Bibi would come upstairs to spy on me and then shout, "Dauji, instead of studying, he is weaving a cot out of twigs." Like an angry child, I would make faces at her and say, "Mind your own business. Shut up, spy." Dauji would call out to me from below and say, "No Golu, you shouldn't fight with your sister." I would retort, "She is a liar. I am studying."

Dauji would slowly climb up the stairs and on seeing me sitting on my bed with my note books, he would say, "Why do you tease him, Qurrat? It's been tough controlling this wild spirit. If he goes out of hand again, I'll never succeed in disciplining him."

Bibi would say, "Pick up his notebooks, then you'll see what dreams he has been weaving."

I would glare at Bibi, but she would quietly walk down the stairs. Defending her, Dauji would say, "Bibi wants you to do well. Why should she bother otherwise? Why should she care whether you pass or fail? She has your best interest in mind, she wants you to do something useful." I could never understand how someone could complain about me, betray me, in order to do me a favour.

During those days, the routine was that I would leave Dauji's place before ten in the morning, eat breakfast at my own house and then go to school. Lunch would be sent to the school. After school, I would go back home, fill a lantern with oil and go back to Dauji's place. My mother would send my dinner to Dauji's.

When Dauji wasn't required to fill applications at the court, he would wait for me in the school yard and we would walk back together. All the way home, he would shower me with questions and ask me in detail about what I had been taught at school. He would escort me upto my house and go for his evening walk. In our region a munsif was required only for ten days in a month; during the other twenty days Sahib Bahadur's court was held in the district headquarters. During those ten days, Dauji sat faithfully outside the court. He usually got a few applications to fill and earned a few rupees. Thank God, for otherwise he would have kept up with his questions even during those days!

Bebe earned enough to run the house. She stitched well and had the support of the neighbourhood. But because it was her income which covered the daily expenses, she treated Dauji with contempt.

One day, contrary to my daily routine, I went to the court to meet Dauji. The court had been closed by then and Dauji was sitting under the thatched roof of Nanbai's shop drinking tea with jaggery in it. I sneaked upto him, picked up his bag, put my arms around him and said, "I came to fetch you today." Without looking towards me, he gulped down his tea. Took an anna out of his pocket, gave it to Nanbai, and without uttering a word started walking back home with me.

Mischievously, I said, "When we get home, I'll tell Bebe that you were drinking tea."

Trying to hide his embarrassment, Dauji smiled and said, "Tea here is good, and tea with jaggery gives one energy. A full glass of tea only costs one anna. But please don't tell Bebe. She'll merely pick up a quarrel with me." Then he sadly added, "She can't go against her nature."

That day I felt very sorry for Dauji. I wished I could have helped him. I did, however, please him by promising not to tell Bebe anything. After I narrated that incident to my mother, she began sending some milk, fruit or sugar everyday to Dauji's house either with me or with the servant. Her generosity, however, did Dauji very little good. It did, on the other hand, make Bebe treat me with a little more respect and kindness.

I remember carrying a jug of milk to Dauji's house one morning. Bebe wasn't at home. She had gone with her friends to bathe in Baba Sawan's pond. Dauji and Bibi, however, were at home. When Dauji saw the jug of milk he said, "Good, let's make tea. I'll get some jaggery from the shop. You boil some water on the fire." Bibi quickly lit the fire. I fetched some water in a pot and, both Bibi and I sat down in the kitchen to gossip. When Dauji returned, he said, "Why don't you go do your work, I'll make the tea." Bibi went back to her sewing machine and I to my grammar exercises. Dauji tended the fire and, as was his habit, continued to instruct me in a loud voice, "Repeat after me — Galileo said, the earth revolves around the sun. Galileo proved, the earth revolves around the sun!" Soon the water began to boil. Dauji was ecstatic. He was so happy that he began to dance to a song he made up, "O Golu, Galileo said, don't forget what Galileo said, O Golu!" Then he put some tea leaves in the boiling water. Like a little boy, Dauji began to dance and sing to the tune of boiling water, "Golu Galileo, Golu Galileo." I laughed happily as I watched him. Bibi smiled quietly, but continued with her stitching. The three of us were a small happy family. Indeed, it seemed as if all the joys of the neighbourhood — no, of the entire village — had descended into our midst like fairies with large and colourful wings.

Suddenly the front door of the house opened and Bebe walked in. Dauji turned around when he heard the door and the blood drained from his face. A bright column of steam rose from the pot of tea behind him. In the silence, only the sound of the water bubbles crashing against the sides of the pot could be heard. The old man had been caught at play. Bebe took a few steps towards the fire. Dauji stood up and said apologetically, "I was making tea."

Bebe thumped him hard on his back and said, "You old fool, aren't you ashamed of yourself? Damn you. May death take you away. You actually want to drink tea at your age. I wasn't at home, so you decided to indulge yourself. I know you want me to die. May your wishes come true. May your hopes be fulfilled. Cursed be the woman who gave birth to you. Damn the line of fate which bound me to you. Why don't you die? If only you would die..." As she screamed curses, she leapt towards the fire like a wild wolf, picked up the pot of tea with a cloth and flung it on to the floor. Boiling tea splashed on Dauji's legs and feet, and he ran out of the kitchen muttering like a child, "May God help you, may God have mercy on you..."

Bibi and I thought that the scene was so funny that we couldn't suppress our laughter. We cackled so loudly that the entire house echoed with the sound of our delight. I somehow escaped Bebe's wrath, but she caught Bibi by her hair and screamed, "Tell me why you hate me? What is your relation to that old man? Why did you give him tea leaves? Tell me, otherwise I'll kill you."

When Bibi began to sob loudly, I escaped into the sitting room. Dauji was sitting in his favourite chair and was rubbing his feet. I don't know why, but when I saw him sitting like that I couldn't contain my laughter. I hid my face behind the almirah so that I could laugh without being observed. With a wave of his hand he called me to his side and said in Persian, "Thank God that though I am in trouble, I have committed no sin."

Then after a pause, he said, "I am humbler than the dog of that holy person of Mecca on whose sacred head an unfortunate old woman used to throw dust."

When I looked bewildered, he said, "If a humble slave of Akka-e-Namdar laments and weeps because a few drops of boiling water splashed on him, then his life is truly cursed. May God save me from the fires of Hell. May the God of Abraham give me strength; may the God of Ayub give me patience."

I asked, "Dauji, who was Akka-e-Namdar?"

Dauji was upset by my ignorance. But with his usual kindness he replied, "Don't you know, my dear son? Your question will hurt the soul of my master, my spiritual teacher, Hazrat Maulana. He was my Lord, my master and my father. He was your spiritual father...your true teacher..." Then he placed both his hands on his chest respectfully.

That was the first time I heard about Akka-e-Namdar from Dauji. He took a long time to tell me about him. After each sentence he would stop and recite a series of verses in praise of the Prophet and repeatedly call upon the soul of his teacher to have patience.

After he had finished his paean of praise, I courteously asked him, "Dauji, even if your teacher was such a great soul, why do you fold your hands and call yourself his humble servant?"

Dauji smiled and said, "A man who can transform a humble donkey like me into Munshi Chintaram, who is respected by everyone, is really a Messiah, is really an Akka."

I slowly sat down in the middle of my bed, wrapped a quilt around me and stared at Dauji. He was sitting with his head bowed and was slowly massaging his feet. Every now and then he would laugh softly and then sit silently again. After a while, he said, "Who was I, what have I become today? Well, Hazrat Maulana was the first one to notice me. He looked at me with his gracious eyes and said, 'Chaupalzade, come here.' I went and stood next to him, leaning on my staff. Boys from Chhattapattar and Deegar districts were sitting around him in a semi-circle. It was like a durbar. No one had the courage to look up. When I stood next to him, that gracious man said, 'Bhai, I see you herding goats everyday. Why don't you let them graze on their own and come and study with me here?' Then, without waiting for an answer, he asked, 'What is your name?' Like a village bumpkin,

I said, 'Chintu.' At that, Hazrat smiled — even chuckled a bit — and then asked, 'What is your full name?' But without waiting for an answer, added, 'It must be Chintaram.' I nodded my head. By then his students had worked up enough courage to look at me. I was wearing a long khadi shirt, and instead of a pyjama, I had a loincloth on. On my feet, I wore heavy soled shoes and my head was wrapped in a bright red cloth."

Interrupting him, I asked, "Were you really a shepherd, Dauji?"

"Yes, yes," he smiled and said with pride, "I was a shepherd and my father owned twelve goats."

My mouth fell open in surprise. In order to get to the bottom of the story, I quickly asked him, "And you used to herd goats near the school?"

Dauji pulled his chair upto my bed, put his feet on it and said, "My dear son, in those days there were no schools even in the cities. Who had heard of M.B. High School seventy-four years ago? It is just that my master was fond of teaching. Children from the neighbourhood used to come to him to learn how to read a few words. His family was an ornament of learning and was spiritually very rich. His father was the only hakim in the district as well as a preacher of great distinction. His grandfather was the Head Munshi of the Maharaja of Kashmir. The house was a place of learning. Persian, Arabic, mathematics, astronomy, medicine and culture were like the servants of the family. I never had the good fortune of meeting my teacher's father, but I did hear stories about his learning. He was also a friend of Shaiftah and Hakim Momin Khan Momin. And the Mufti Azurda himself honoured him with the title of Maulvi."

Afraid that Dauji would soon digress from his main narrative, I asked him, "So you began studying with Hazrat Maulana?"

"Yes," he said, as if he was talking to himself. "His conversation was hypnotic, his eyes were irresistible. His knowledge transformed ordinary men into learned souls; he could infuse dust with living fire. I laid my staff on the ground and sat down next to him. He said, 'Sit with your brothers on the mat.' I replied, 'I have spent eighteen years of my life sitting on the ground. What difference would it make now?' He smiled, pulled an alphabet book out of his bag and said, 'Alif, be, pe, te,'" Dauji recited the alphabet as if he was in a trance.

After sometime he pointed towards the right and said, "On that side there was a well and next to it was a fish pond." Then he waved his left hand and said, "On that side were the houses of the peasants. My master's garden was in the middle and his magnificent haveli was across from the garden. His school was in the garden. Its gates were always open. Everyone was welcome there. Religion was no bar; faith was no obstacle."

After a long pause, and after constructing the sentence carefully, I asked, "What was the great Hazrat Maulana's name?"

First he corrected my sentence and then said, "Hazrat Ismail Chisti Rehmatullah Alaih used to say that his father used to call him Janejahan."

I wanted to hear more about his interesting life history, but Dauji suddenly stopped and asked, "What was the Subsidiary System? May all the Britishers be damned! They pretended to be merchants of the East India Company or the representatives of Queen Victoria, but they interfered with everything here."

Anyway, I repeated the entire structure of the Subsidiary System in the same way as I used to repeat the multiplication table. Then he picked up the book of grammar lying on the table and said, "Go and see if Bebe's anger has cooled down." Pretending that I needed to fill my ink-bottle with water, I went out and saw Bebe working at the sewing machine and Bibi cleaning the kitchen.

Bebe was the one person, Dauji was really afraid of in his life. But whenever he saw that she didn't have a scowl on her face and the atmosphere in the house was pleasant, he would say, "Come, all of you recite a couplet each." Invariably, I would be the first one called upon and I would at once recite the following lines:

"You should have watched the road
for my return for a few days more,
But having forsaken me,
forsake me for a few days more."

He would clap his hands in delight and say, "Good, but I want to hear new verses. I don't want to hear couplets in Urdu, nor do I want to hear a long nazm."

I would protest and say that I needed time to think. In the meantime, Bibi would recite a couplet. Often, she too would begin with well-known lines:

"I heard that when Shahpur died,
showing for the living no mercy,
Khusro put a line across her name
Showing her no signs of mercy."

Dauji would applaud her and ask her to recite more couplets. Bibi would put her scissors down and recite:

"The noise of the world woke me
from my dream after death.
But the turmoil of the world sent me
back to eternal death."

Dauji would praise her, but add, "My daughter, you have recited that couplet often in the past." Then he would turn to Bebe and say, "Today even Bebe will recite a couplet."

But Bebe would dryly retort, "I don't know any."

Dauji world persist, "Alright, sing us some marriage songs. Sing us those songs you sang at your son's wedding."

That would tempt Bebe to part her lips in a smile, but she would only end up looking more hideous. Dauji would then begin to sing marriage songs and as he sang, he would sometimes add Aminchand's name and sometimes mine. At the end he would say, "I will wear a bright red turban when Golu Molu gets married. I will walk in his barat with Doctor Sahib and sign my name as one of the witnesses on the marriage certificate."

I would, as I was expected to, look down shyly, and he would add, "I am sure that somewhere in the country there is a small little girl studying in the fifth or sixth standard, who will be the daughter-in-law of this house. Girls are taught how to do household work at least once a week. She must have learnt to cook many things by now. She is, I am certain, a clever student. Unlike this fool who doesn't know if 'maadiyan' refers to a horse or a hen. She, on the other hand, recites everything quickly. I will teach her Persian. First, I will teach her calligraphy. I shall, then, teach her different styles of writing. Girls are usually not taught how to write beautifully. But I'll teach my daughter-in-law — Oh, but listen Golu, then I'll have to live with you. She and I will speak to each other in Persian, and you will look at us like an idiot!..." Dauji would continue to talk in that vein for a long time. Poor Dauji would sit on his mat, imagine a beautiful little world of his own, and speak about it as if it would soon become real.

"Just as I know that God will grant you an obedient wife and me a courteous daughter-in-law, I pray that He grant a good wife to my Aminchand also. I am not at all happy with him these days. I don't like deception and violence, or parties which want to dig up everything; I don't like the Seva Sangh, the Muslim League and the Belcha Party. Aminchand has begun to learn the use of lathis. He, of course, doesn't listen to me. Yes, if God, in his kindness, gives him a pious Momin wife, may be she will bring him back on to the right path."

I was disturbed by his desire for a Momin daughter-in-law, but I didn't say anything. I kept quiet, because I was sure that if I said anything, he would have been hurt. I don't know what Aminchand would have thought.

Anyway, Bibi actually got married on the twelfth of January. Dauji had already told us that her husband, Rampratap, was a very fine man. He seemed to fulfill Dauji's expectations and praise. What had pleased Dauji even more was that Rampratap's father was a teacher of Persian and a member of the Kabir Panthi sect.

On the evening of the twelfth of January, when it was time for Bibi to depart, the house was thrown into turmoil. Bibi wept inconsolably. Aminchand couldn't restrain his tears. The women of the neighbourhood whispered loudly amongst themselves. I stood against a wall, and Dauji, who stood beside me with his hand on my shoulder for support repeated again and again, "The earth seems to shake under my feet today. I don't seem to have control over myself."

When the bridegroom's father came and said, "Munshiji, please give us permission to leave now," Bibi fainted and fell to the ground. She had to be carried to a cot. While the women surrounded her and fanned her, Dauji, still leaning on me for support, walked upto her, helped her sit up and said, "Come now, Bitiya. Get up. This is the first hour of your new and independent life. Don't spoil it."

Bibi fell on Dauji's shoulder and began to weep bitterly. He caressed her head and said, "Qurratulain, I am a sinner. I am sorry that I couldn't educate you; I am ashamed that I couldn't give you knowledge and culture as a part of your dowry.

Perhaps you and Rampratap will forgive me, but I will never be able to forgive myself. I have sinned and I bow my head before you in shame."

When Bibi heard that, she began to cry even more loudly. Even Dauji's eyes brimmed over with tears and they flowed down his face profusely.

Rampratap's father came upto him and said gently, "Please don't worry, Munshiji. I assure you, I'll teach her how to recite the Kalima."

Dauji turned to him with folded hands and said, "She knows how to recite the Kalima. But my dream of educating her hasn't been fulfilled."

Rampratap's father laughed and said, "I still haven't read the whole of the *Gulistan*. I have always skipped the parts written in Arabic."

Dauji stood quietly with his hands folded.

Bibi pulled her hands out from under the bright red chaddar she was wearing, and first touched Aminchand's head in blessing, and then touched mine. After that she walked out with her friends to the front door of the house. Still leaning on me, Dauji followed her. He hugged me tightly and said, "Even you are crying. You are supposed to give me support, Golu...What's come over you...Why are you..." His voice choked and my eyes filled with tears.

8

Rano, who lived in our mohalla, was a nasty man. Evil and malice had been pounded and mixed into his very being. He had about thirty goats and cows. All day long he sat and sold milk in the open space next to the lane through which I had to pass everyday. Nearly everyone in the mohalla bought milk from him and was afraid of his wicked ways. Whenever he passed by our house, he would mischievously bang his lathi on the ground and loudly greet Dauji, "Pundita, jai Ramji ki." Dauji had often tried to tell him that he wasn't a pundit, but an ordinary man. He was, however, unsuccessful in convincing Rano that only an educated and wise man could be called a pundit. Rano would merely chew his mustache and reply, "Arrey Bhai, the one who has a bodi on his head is called a pundit."

The thieves and the goondas of the locality were Rano's friends. They gathered at his place every evening to gamble and conduct a mushaira of filthy jokes and vile curses.

The evening after Bibi's departure, when I went to Rano's house to buy milk, he narrowed his eyes, laughed mockingly and said, "Why do you continue to live in that house; the peacock has flown." When I didn't say anything, he stirred the froth in the milk can and said, "Tell me truthfully, did you get a chance to take a dip in the Ganga that used to flow in that house?" I got angry and flung my milk-pail at his head. He didn't bleed, but I must have hit him hard enough, because he fell down and fainted. I ran back to Dauji's house and narrated the entire incident to him. Then I ran to my place and told my father the whole story. Because of my father's influence, Rano was taken to the police station and was let off with a stern warning from the Station Officer.

From that day onwards, whenever Rano passed by Dauji's house he abused and cursed him. Dauji's bodi became the special target of his jokes. It is true that Dauji's bodi, which used to lie flat against his head, was rather ugly. But Dauji always said, "This is the last sign of my dear mother, and I love it like my own life. She used to place my head in her lap and anoint my bodi with curd and oil before washing it, till it glittered. Though I had never dared to remove my turban in front of Hazrat Maulana, he knew about my bodi. When I came back to the village during the vacations, after spending a year at Dayal Singh Memorial High School, Huzoor had asked me, 'I hope you didn't remove your choti in the city?' When I told him that I had not, he was delighted and said, 'Very few mothers are fortunate enough to have a son as worthy as you are, and very few teachers can feel as proud as I do of a student like you.' I touched his feet and said, 'Don't make me feel ashamed. I am like the dust on your feet.' He laughed and said, 'Please don't touch my feet. Why offer homage that I cannot feel?' My eyes filled with tears and I said, 'If I knew what medicine would help, I would cross the seas to get it for you. I would lay down my life for your health. But I am helpless.' He was silent for sometime. Then he looked up and said, 'Everything depends on God's will. May you live long. Thanks to your strong shoulders, I have been able to see most of my village.'" Soon Dauji was lost in his reminiscences.

"Every morning, I would go to the front door of the haveli and cry — 'Your slave has come.' The women of the house would go into purdah, and Huzoor would invite me in and praise his good fortune. With folded hands, I would approach him, touch his feet and wait for his orders. He would bless me. Ask about the well-being of my family. Enquire about the village and say, 'Come Chintaram, lift this bundle of sins.' I would lift him up like a basket full of flowers, place him on my shoulders and carry him out of the haveli. He would sometimes say, 'Take me to the garden,' and at other times say, 'Take me to the well.' Once in a while he would request me, in a gentle voice, 'Chintaram, if it won't tire you, could you take me to the mosque?' I would reply, 'I have told you, I can easily carry you upto the mosque everyday.' But he would reply, 'No, I'll request you only when I really want to go there.'

I would help him sit on the platform in the garden, take off his light shoes and sit leaning against the wall. Huzoor used to drag himself across the platform to sit on a mat. I watched him do that once, but never after that. After helping him take off his shoes, I would sit with my face covered and look up only after he would call my name. When we got back to the haveli, after slowly walking through the meandering lanes of the village, he would say, 'Chintaram, I know that you take the long way back home to please me. But it pains me to see you do so much for me. I not only ride on your back, I also waste your time.'

Who could have told him, 'Master, the time spent with you is the brightest moment of my life; the effort made for you is the very purpose of my being. You say, I am doomed to carry you, but I feel as if some divinity has cast his shadow upon me.'

The day I recited the entire *Sikandarnamah* from memory for him, he was so delighted that it seemed as if I had placed before him all the joys of the world. He showered prayers and blessings upon me. Caressed my head, took a rupee coin out of his pocket and gave it to me as a reward. I took it with reverence, kissed it, touched my eyes with it, and folded it in my turban as if it had been a gift from Sikander himself. He held his arm up in prayer and said, 'You have achieved that which I could never achieve myself. You are blessed. God has been kind to you. Chintaram, you may have been born a shepherd but you are like Moses. God will shower you with greater favours.'" After telling me that story, Dauji put his head on his knees and fell silent.

9

As my examinations drew nearer, Dauji became a stern task master. He saw to it that every minute of my day was filled with work. If I finished work on one subject, he would descend on me with books about another subject. If I got up to get a glass of water, he would follow me and ask me to recite important historical dates.

He made it a point to meet me at the school gate in the evenings. One day, I slipped out of the back gate. From the next day onward, he began to wait for me outside my class room. Sometimes I got so irritated that I would shout at him and even call him a dog. That would annoy him, but he would merely say, "Look Domini, is this the way to talk? When you get married, the first thing I'll tell your wife is that my dearest son used to call this old man a dog." He wouldn't say anything more.

He never called me by my real name. He called me Domini but only when he was annoyed. Whereas he referred to my elder brother as Beta Aftab or Barkhurdar Aftab, he called me by a different name everyday. Golu, however, remained his favourite name for me. It was followed by Tamboori and Mister Havanak. There were times when I really gave him a lot of trouble. If I got fed up of solving yet another algebraic equation, I would kick the pile of books in front of me and begin to sing:

"I will sit in front of you and weep
But I'll not tell you the cause of my sorrow."

Dauji would look towards me with surprise, but I would merely clap my hands and, then begin to sing a qawali.

"No, I'll not tell you why I cry
Why I cry, why I cry.
No, no, no, I will not, I will not
Tell you the cause of my sorrow.
My sorrow, my sorrow."

He would merely smile, pick up my notebook, open a new page and hold my hands.

"Listen, son," he would say kindly, "This is not a difficult equation."

But the moment he released my hands and tried to explain the equation to me, I would begin to clap and sing once again.

"Look, son, am I not your Dauji?" he would ask gently.

"No," I would retort bluntly.

"Then who is your Dauji?" he would ask sadly.

"He is the real Master," I would point my finger up towards the sky and say mischievously, "He is the real Master, He is our true Father." Then I would mockingly ask him "Come, tell me goat, who is our real Father?"

Annoyed, he would get up and I would put my arms around him and say, "Is Dauji angry?"

He would smile and say, "Let me go, Tambooray. Let me go, son. I want to get a glass of water. Let me drink some water."

I would pretend to be hurt and say, "When he has to explain something to me, Dauji says he is thirsty."

At that, he would sit down and say, "When you saw that number, why didn't you use the third formula, and even if..." He would not drink water for days afterwards.

10

It was the second week of February. My examinations were a month and a half away and had begun to haunt me like a nightmare. I myself had decided to work hard, but I couldn't get the hang of geometry. Dauji tried his best to explain the subject to me, but without much success. At last he said, "There are only fifty-two theorems. Memorize them. There is no other solution." I began repeating them over and over again so as to memorize them. But the theorem I committed to memory at night, I forgot by the next morning. I almost gave up in despair. One night, after Dauji had made me draw different geometrical shapes and repeat all the theorems, he seemed worried. I often got stuck, much to his disappointment. He urged me to go to sleep and went to his own room. I sat down with my pencil and notebook and continued to revise the theorems till half-past-one at night. The problem was that as soon as I shut my book and tried to write, I would get stuck after a few sentences. The look of disappointment on Dauji's face rose before me, and I redoubled my effort, but without much avail. I was nearly in tears. I went out into the courtyard and sat down on the stairs to cry. I sat there for sometime with my head on my knees and wept. It was a cold night and I began to shiver. I sat like that for more than an hour. It occurred to me that, for the sake of Dauji's reputation, I should quietly leave the house and never come back. The moment, however, I made up my mind to leave and stood up, I saw Dauji, wrapped up in his blanket, standing next to me. He hugged me affectionately. The entire verandah began to echo with my sobs. Dauji kissed my forehead and said, "There you go, Tambooray. I didn't think you were so cowardly." Then he wrapped his blanket around me and walked me back to my room. He made me lie down in my bed, covered me with a quilt, and sat down on a chair with his legs tucked under him.

He said, "Euclid is difficult. It seems to have defeated you for now. It had caused me no end of trouble also. Hazrat Maulana had numerous books on arithmetic and geometry which I copied down carefully into my notebooks. Soon there was no problem which could stump me. I thought that I had become an expert in the subject. But one night, as I lay in bed thinking about a problem, I got confused. I lit my lamp, drew the diagram and began to ponder over it. I could solve the problem mathematically, but I couldn't work it out geometrically. I wasted pages after pages throughout the night but, unlike you, I didn't break down and cry. Early next morning, I took the problem to Hazrat Maulana. He drew the diagram on a piece of paper and began to explain the solution to me. But, soon, he too got stuck at the very point where I had got confused. He said, 'Chintaram, I can't teach you anymore. When a teacher and his student can't solve the same problem, it is time for the student to find another teacher.' I picked up courage, and replied, 'If someone else had said that, I wouldn't have believed him. Every word of yours, every sentence you utter, is like the command of God for me, that is why I am silent. How can a slave contradict his master? But I am deeply hurt.'

He said, 'Don't be sentimental and let me finish what I have to say.'

I bowed my head and said, 'Sorry.'

He said, 'In Delhi, Hakim Nasir Ali Seestani is an expert mathematician. If you really want to learn mathematics, you should go to him. I'll write him a letter.'

When I expressed my willingness to follow his advice, he said, 'Get permission from your mother. If she agrees, come back to me.'

But it was difficult for me to ask my mother to give me her consent. I, therefore, delayed talking about it to her. Whenever Huzoor asked me, I told him that I was busy painting the house; that I would talk to my mother as soon as I was free.

The next few days were full of anxiety. I tried day and night to solve the dilemma I was in. Unable to find a solution, I became more tense. I wanted to go to Delhi, but I could neither get permission to do so from Huzoor, nor a letter of introduction till I had talked to my mother. How did I finally discover a way out? Well, one night, when the whole village was asleep and I was as despondent as you are now, I opened my mother's box and stole two rupees out of her life's savings, leaving behind just enough for her to live on. Then I slipped out of the village — May God have mercy upon me and may the souls of those two elders forgive me. I know I have sinned and that my head shall remain bowed in shame before those two noble souls till the end of time — Before I left the village, I went to the garden near the haveli where Huzoor used to sit and teach. I knelt before his seat, kissed the ground, and said, 'I am an unfortunate man and I have to leave without your permission. But I shall never forget your blessings. If you don't forgive me, I shall lay myself down at your feet and die.' After that I put my lathi on my shoulder and left the village — Are you listening?" Dauji asked me as he looked at me intently.

"Yes," I whispered, as I lay quietly wrapped in my quilt.

Dauji once again resumed his story, "God really helped me. In those days the railway line between Jakhal, Jind, Birsa and Hissar was being laid. That was also the shortest route to Delhi. I got a job as a labourer on the railway line. I worked for one day and walked for two. Supporting myself like that, I reached Delhi in sixteen days.

I had finally arrived at my destination, but I still had to achieve the real object of my quest. No one could tell me where Hakim Nasir Ali Seestani lived. I searched for two days without success. Luck, however, was still on my side and I was in good health. New houses were being built for the British. I found work as a labourer once more. Every evening after work, I went in search of Hakim Sahib's house, and at night slept soundly on a mat spread out on the floor of a dharmshala.

There is a saying — seek and you shall find. At last, one day, I found Hakim Sahib's house. The next evening, I presented myself to him. He was sitting on the floor of a small room with his head bowed, gossiping with a few friends. His back was towards me.

He asked, 'Who's there?'

I folded my hands and said, 'I have come from Punjab, and...' Before I could complete the sentence, he said, 'Oh, so you are Chintaram?'

I stood without uttering a word.

He said, 'I got a letter from Ismail. He wrote to say — Chintaram may come to see you. He ran away from home without my permission. Help him.'

As I continued to stand without uttering a word, he said, in a voice which was soft as silk, 'Come in, Miyan. Have you taken a vow of silence?'

I stepped forward, but he continued to sit with his head bowed like a new bride. Then he said in a tone of great courtesy, 'Barkhurdar, sit down.' After I sat down, he said to his friends, 'Stay for a while, let me exchange a few words with this young man.' Then he said to me, 'Tell me what are the aspects of mathematics that you don't understand?'

With great hesitation I told him. He put his hands to his shoulders, slowly pulled up his kurta to reveal his back and said, 'Draw that puzzling diagram on my back with your fingers.'

I was stunned. I did not have the courage either to do what he had ordered or to escape. When I didn't make a move, he said, 'Miyan, hurry up. I am blind. I have no use for paper and pencil.'

Still afraid, and with trembling fingers, I drew the diagram on his broad and smooth back. After I had finished drawing the shape, he said, 'Now draw a line from B to C.'

I was bewildered. I didn't understand anything. When I tried to draw a line arbitrarily, he said sharply, 'What are you doing? Is that the point?' Then he said himself, 'You'll get used to me slowly. The point C is about six fingers below my left shoulder. Draw the line from there...'

Allah-ho-Akbar, Allah-ho-Akbar, how very learned he was! What a voice he had! And how brightly he spoke! He continued to talk for a while and I sat listening to him entranced. It seemed as if the lines I had drawn on his back would soon begin to burn with light."

Dauji seemed lost in the recollections of his days in Delhi. His eyes were open. He was looking towards me, but without seeing me.

I asked him anxiously, "What happened then, Dauji?"

He got up from his chair and said, "It's late into the night. Go to sleep, I'll tell you about it later."

When I insisted like a spoilt child, he said, "First, promise that you'll never again despair and that you will consider these simple problems of mathematics to be as sweet as small cubes of sugar."

"I'll regard them as halwa. Don't worry," I said. Still standing, he wrapped his blanket around him and said, "Well, the result was that I stayed with Hakim Sahib for a year. He was a deep ocean of learning and he helped me to wash some of the dirt of ignorance out of my eyes. When I returned to the village, I went straight to see Hazrat Maulana and placed my head at his feet.

He said, 'Chintaram, if I had the strength, I would pull these feet away from you.'

I burst into tears. He placed his gracious hands on my head and said, 'I am not angry with you. But a year is a long time. If you decide to run away again, take me with you.'"

Dauji's eyes were filled with tears. Before I could say anything, he had turned around and left the room.

11

The very thought of the approaching examinations made me tremble with fear, but I also put on weight. Dauji was afraid that I would grow fat. Indeed, he was so concerned that he would take my hand in his and say, "Come on, live like a horse of noble breeding, and not like a donkey in a stable!" I hated that saying and told him so. My protests, however, had no effect on him. His concern about my weight crossed all limits. One morning, before going out for his walk, he woke me and shook me, despite my protests, pleas, curses and abuses, till I got up and put on my coat. He pulled my arm and dragged me out of the house. It was winter, and at four in the morning there was no other living soul out in the lanes. We could hardly see anything in the darkness, yet he insisted that we take a walk. While I muttered angrily, he said, "You aren't still fully awake. Look at how this Tamboora protests." After sometime he said, "Sing something, Tamboorey, think about something, instead of walking like a zombie." After we had crossed the boundary of the village and the cold air of the morning had forced me to open my eyes, Dauji let go of my arm. We walked past the area of the Sikhs, left the river behind and didn't pause at the graveyard. When we reached the hillock, I panicked. People didn't go across it even in the afternoon, because the ruin of a city was buried under it. Ghosts used to haunt it and were in the habit of eating the hearts of those who walked there. I started trembling with fear. Dauji wrapped my muffler around my neck a little more snugly, and said, "Run around those keekar trees ten times, then take a deep breath and come back. I will wait for you here."

In order to escape from him, I ran straight towards the keekar trees. But instead of running around them, I sat down on a rock nearby. I calculated as to how much time it would have taken me to run six rounds. Then I got up and ran four times around the trees. I returned to the same rock and did some deep breathing exercises. A strange animal began to howl near the keekar trees and I got a cramp in my muscles. I thought it best to go back to Dauji. I was seething with anger as I walked towards him. When I reached him, however, I was surprised to see that he was kneeling on the stony ground, holding his head in his hands, and reciting his favourite couplets loudly like a lunatic —

> "Don't be so cruel my love,
> for tomorrow is the day
> of reckoning,
> and you will feel ashamed
> when you stand before your God."

Soon after that he began to beat the ground with both his hands and then shake his finger as if he was scolding someone standing before him, "Look carefully, think again, I am...I am telling you...listen..." He then seemed to threaten someone. After a while he fell to the ground, and began to repeat over and over again, "Don't be so cruel, don't be so cruel." Later he began to cry. I watched him in amazement for sometime. Then I let out a scream and, instead of running towards the village, ran back to the keekar trees. I was sure that Dauji knew magic and was grappling with a jinn. I was also certain that I had seen a jinn standing before him. The jinn looked exactly like the one I had seen in the illustrations of *Alif Laila.* The jinn, I knew, had thrown Dauji to the ground because Dauji's magic had failed. That is why he was screaming, "Don't be so cruel, don't be so cruel," over and over again. I sat down on a rock and began to cry. After a while Dauji came upto me. He looked as if nothing had happened and said, "Let's go Tambooray." Still trembling with fear, I began to follow him. On the way back, he took both the ends of his loose turban in his hands and began to sing lustily, "O Farid, with long hair, keep on walking, keep on walking."

I knew I was walking behind a magician. I had seen him change his shape before my own eyes. He had grown long hair which lay scattered over his shoulders. After that day I was determined never to go out for a walk with him, even if he were to cut me into pieces.

A few days after that incident large clods of earth and stones began to fall into our courtyard. Bebe began to howl like a bitch with pups and clung to Dauji. Then she pushed him so violently that he fell to the ground. Soon she began to scream at him hysterically, "You old sorcerer, you have cast a spell on the house. This is the result of all your Persian recitations. Your black magic has rebounded on us. The jinns you have let loose are now throwing rocks at us. They want to ruin us, destroy us...Oh, help, he is going to burn me, he is going to kill me. Listen people, this old man is trying to murder me and my son, Aminchand. He has cast a spell upon us. He wants to break every bone in my body..."

Dauji loved Aminchand even more than he loved his own life. Why should he have become his enemy? I was puzzled, but I was sure that Dauji had let loose the jinns who were now troubling us. This time I took Bebe's side and, for the first time since I had known him, Dauji shook me angrily and said, "You are an idiot and Bebe is the mother of fools. Is this the result of all my teaching? Now you believe in ghosts! I am sorry, but you have disappointed me, really disappointed me. Instead of thinking rationally, you support a hysterical woman. I am sorry. Really sorry." When I left them and went upstairs, Bebe was still shouting.

That very evening, as I was on my way back to Dauji's house, I ran into Rano. He winked at me and asked caustically,

"I believe stones have been raining down on your Pundit's house? I hope you didn't get hurt?"

I didn't want to exchange words with that scoundrel, so I walked on without saying anything in reply.

Late that night, in the middle of an explanation of a geometrical problem, Dauji asked me, "Do you really believe in jinns, ghosts and demons?" When I said that I did, he laughed and said, "You are a simpleton. I shouldn't have got angry at you. Why didn't you tell me earlier that jinns exist and that they can throw stones? Instead of paying Vali and Fatey to build a barsati for us we could have requested your jinns to help us build it. But tell me, do jinns only know how to throw stones or can they also cement bricks together to build a wall?"

"You can make fun of me if you like, Dauji, but don't complain when one of the bricks lands on your head!" I retorted angrily.

Dauji said, "No brick thrown by one of your jinns can injure me, because there are no jinns. No jinn can lift a brick and throw it on your head, or on your Bebe's head, or on my head." Then he added, "Listen. The law of physics states that something cannot be created from nothing — Do you understand?"

"I understand," I said, petulantly.

12

While our village had a High School, it had no examination centre. We had to go to the district headquarters to take our Matriculation Examinations.

At last the day when we had to leave the village to take our exams arrived. All the students of my class and their parents gathered around the lorry that was to take us to the examination centre. Of course, Dauji was there too. How could he have stayed away? The parents of other children gave them their blessings, but Dauji, who had prepared a detailed summary of all that we had studied through the year, showered me with questions and provided me with answers. He jumped from questions about the reforms of Akbar to questions about the weather and the causes of why seasons change. As soon as he finished with one set, he would ask, "There was another king who dressed and behaved like a Hindu. He was always drunk and was under the spell of a woman who made him dance to her tune. Who was he?" "Jehangir," I answered, and "Noorjahan," both of us intoned together. "What is the difference between the active and passive voice?" I defined both of them. "Give examples." I gave examples. By this time all the other boys had boarded the lorry. In order to escape from Dauji's clutches, I quickly got into the lorry. But he cornered me once more and said, "Use the word 'breath' in two different sentences." I did that. By that time the lorry started to move. Dauji ran beside it and shouted, "Tambooray, remember 'marayan ghordi' and 'makayan murgi...marayan ghordi...makayan murgi'..." The voice was soon left far behind. I thanked God that after a year of living in bondage, I could breathe freely again.

I did well in History on the first day, I did even better in Geography on the second day. The third day was Sunday. The Mathematics paper was on Monday. On Sunday morning I received a twenty page long letter from Dauji which was full of formulas and equations.

After the Maths paper, when I compared my answers with my friends, I discovered that I had got eighty percent of my answers correct. I was overwhelmed with joy. I was so happy that I seemed to walk on air. As soon as I stepped out of the verandah still chuckling with delight, I saw Dauji standing with a sheet wrapped around him reading the question paper which he had borrowed from another student. I hugged him tightly and shouted, "I'll get eighty percent marks, eighty percent."

He asked me sharply, "Which questions did you get wrong?" Still swaggering, I replied, "The one about the four walls."

He snapped at me, "You must have forgotten to subtract the doors and the windows."

I put my arm around his waist and swaying like a tree, said, "Yes, yes — let the windows be damned."

Dauji said, in the voice of a man who had suddenly aged, "You have ruined me, Tambooray. For three hundred and sixty five days, I cried myself hoarse — be careful when you answer such a question. Didn't I tell you that repeatedly? But you didn't pay any attention. You have thrown away twenty marks...a full twenty marks."

When I looked at Dauji's face, I felt as if the eighty marks I had attained had no meaning compared to the twenty marks I had lost. All the way back home, he kept muttering to himself, "If the examiner is kind, he'll give you two marks. At least your method was correct."

After that, Dauji stayed with me till the last day of the examinations. He sat with me everyday till twelve at night in the sarai where I was staying along with my other class-mates, and spent the rest of the night at the house of a friend of his. He would be back at eight in the morning and walk with me to the examination hall.

As soon as the examinations were over, I avoided meeting Dauji as much as I could. I pretended that I had never known him. I would spend my days wandering with my friends and my evenings reading novels. Once in a while I would go to his place to greet him, but only if I found the time. He wanted me to spend at least one hour a day with him so that he could prepare me for college. But I was determined never to fall into his trap again. I was ready to fail a hundred times in college, but I was not willing to be taught by him. In fact, I didn't even want to talk to him. If, by mistake, I asked him a question, he would say, "Translate it into Persian." If I did that, he would ask me to break it up into its grammatical parts. One day, after I had chased the havaldar's cows out of our courtyard, he asked me if the word 'cow' was a noun or a verb. Even the most ignorant child in the fifth standard could have told him that 'cow' was a noun, but he insisted on telling me that it could be used both as a noun and a verb. "'To cow down' means to threaten." This happened well after the examinations and while I was waiting for the results. Soon, I was terrified of meeting him anywhere.

One day, when I was going out hunting with a few of my friends, I pleaded with them not to take the road in front of the Munsif's office, because I was sure that if Dauji saw me he would ask me to use the words 'hunt', 'gun' and 'bullet' idiomatically. If I saw him in the market, I would turn into another lane to hide from him. Whenever I went to his house, I would spend most of my time there talking to Bebe. He often scolded me and said, "Like Aftab, you have also begun to ignore me." I would laugh mischievously and say, "I play a lot."

The day my results were announced my father and I went with a small basket of laddus to Dauji's house. Dauji was sitting, with his head bowed, on his prayer mat. When he saw my father, he stood up. He went inside, fetched a chair and placing it next to his mat, said, "Doctor Sahib, I am ashamed, but even his results are an example of the strange ways of God. I was sure that he would pass in the first division, but I was wrong. His foundations were weak."

"I missed it by only one mark," I said, interrupting him sharply.

He looked at me and said, "You don't know how depressed I am about that one mark. Anyway, I still thank God."

Then he and my father got absorbed in talking to each other and I began gossiping with Bebe.

After I went away to college, I replied to Dauji's letters regularly in the beginning. But soon our correspondence became irregular and then ceased altogether. Whenever I went back home during the vacations, I would make a formal visit to all my teachers. I would also go and pay my respects to Dauji. By then he had stopped asking me questions. He was, however, always happy to see me, and he was particularly pleased with my coat and tie. He would refuse to let me sit on a cot and insist that I fetch a chair for myself. The books I brought back from the college library always interested him, and despite my promise that I would bring them over to his house, he always came to my house to examine them.

Aminchand had by then dropped out of college and joined a bank in Delhi. Bebe still stitched clothes to support the family. Dauji continued to go to the courts, but rarely earned anything. Bibi wrote letters regularly. She was happy in her new home. However, after spending one year in college, I discovered that Dauji and I had drifted far apart.

The girls I used to play with when I was a little boy suddenly became shy of meeting me. In my second year in college, I was a little more successful in spending my holidays away from home. Travelling to Abbotabad was, after all, more attractive than travelling to my village.

It was during this period that I bought a pink-coloured writing pad and a packet of envelopes of the same colour. I couldn't, of course, use them to send letters either to my father or to Dauji. That year I didn't meet Dauji during the Dussera vacations, nor during the Christmas celebrations, nor during the Easter break. Soon, I lost all sense of time...

As the day of the country's Independence approached, people began to fight each other, and soon there were violent riots all around us. We began to receive news of disturbances throughout the country. My mother insisted that all of us should return home. Our village, she thought, was the safest place for us. Soon refugees began to pour in from everywhere and they brought with them the news that the country had finally gained its freedom.

One day a few houses in our village were set on fire and there was a fierce fight in the streets. The army imposed a curfew and, immediately after it was lifted, all the Hindus and the Sikhs living in the area fled.

When my mother sent me that afternoon to inquire after Dauji, I saw that the lane in which he lived was crowded with unfamiliar faces. A bull was chained in the middle of the courtyard of Dauji's house and the door behind it was covered with a jute curtain. I ran back home to tell my mother that Dauji and Bebe had abandoned their house. My voice choked as I told her that I felt as if Dauji had left us forever and that we would never see him again; that Dauji had abandoned us.

Three days later, as I was returning from the mosque at sunset, after collecting the names of the refugees who had taken shelter there so that I could send them blankets, I saw a crowd of about two hundred people in the open ground next to Dauji's house. Young refugee boys, armed with lathis, were shouting slogans and curses. I tried to force my way through them, but refrained from doing so when I saw that their eyes were burning with rage and hatred.

I overheard one of the boys tell an old man next to him, "It seems that he had gone to a neighbouring village. When he returned, he barged into a house which he claims is his."

"Which house?" the old man asked.

"The house of the refugees from Rohtak...When they caught him, they discovered that he was a Hindu!"

Just then someone from the crowd shouted, "O Rano, come here quickly...We have caught a relative of yours...the Pundit...your relative..."

At that moment, Rano was busy herding his goats into their enclosure. He stopped, ordered one of the boys with a lathi to look after them, and plunged into the crowd.

My heart sank with fear. I knew that they had caught Dauji.

Without seeing the victim, I began to plead with the people who stood near me, "Please don't hurt him. He is a good man...a pious man...Please...he is...he..."

The people in the crowd looked at me menacingly. A young man brandished a chopper in front of my face and said, "Maybe, I should teach you a lesson...Keep your damned kindness to yourself..."

Someone else said, "You didn't suffer, did you?" Others began to curse me.

Scared, I ran to the other side of the crowd. There I saw that Rano and his friends had surrounded Dauji. Rano had taken Dauji by his chin and was shaking his head violently and mocking him, "Come on, son, speak." When Dauji stood silently, one of the boys knocked off his turban and said, "First, let's chop off his bodi."

Rano cut off Dauji's bodi with the sickle which he carried with him to cut branches of trees.

The same boy then asked, "Should we kill him now?"

Rano, however, said, "No, he's too old for that. He can help me look after my goats."

Then he put his fist under Dauji's chin, lifted his head and said, "Recite the Kalma, Pundit."

Dauji asked quietly, "Which one?"

Rano slapped Dauji's head so hard that he staggered and nearly fell to the ground, "Bastard, do you think there are five or seven Kalmas?"

When Dauji had finished reciting the Kalma, Rano gave him a lathi and said, "Come, the goats are waiting for you."

Bareheaded, Dauji begun to walk behind the goats as if he was an angel with long and flowing hair.

Original in Urdu.
Translated by Vishwamitter Adil and Alok Bhalla.

NARENDRANATH MITRA

THE FOUR-POSTER BED

1

It was Maqbool who brought the letter from the post-office. In his little boat he ferried across the canal everyday to deliver milk at the Chaudhury mansion. One portion of the building housed the village post-office. Maqbool was on his way out when the post-master himself stepped out, called him back and gave him a letter for Rajmohan Roy.

The spacious courtyard had a bamboo lattice frame stretched diagonally across it. Rajmohan was spreading the wet jute over the frame with great care. The servants were at hand to help. But the work required patience and care. But even he lost his patience on seeing the condition of the letter!

"Haramzade, what have you done?" he screamed at Maqbool.

Maqbool was surprised, "Why, what is wrong, Karta?"

Rajmohan scolded him, "Look, just look, at the state of this letter. I say, did you have to soak the letter in the canal too? You rascal, your habit of adding water to milk will not keep you from adding water to everything, will it?"

Maqbool looked grave. "Don't say that, Karta. There is no water in the milk I sell. My boat doesn't have a platform. You refused to help me get one. What can I do? I kept the letter near the bow, it must have got a little wet."

Rajmohan flared up. "A little wet! Ah, do you think I don't see through your trick of getting that wooden plank out of me? Really, Maqbool, I declare there is no one who is a greater cheat than you in this entire neighbourhood! Hey, come now, you're not leaving already, are you? Rest a while. Have a smoke."

On the verandah outside the northern room, there was always a complete arrangement for a leisurely smoke — an earthen bowl with glowing cinders, tobacco and even a separate hookah against the wall for the Muslims. Maqbool sat down grumpily to smoke his tobacco.

Rajmohan laid the jute aside and looked at the letter. Ever since his cataract operation a few months earlier, he needed his spectacles for reading and writing. "Kalu, bring me my glasses, will you?" he called out to his servant. "You'll find them by the almanac on the table. Bring them to me quickly." The nickel-framed spectacles had thick lenses. He wiped the glasses with care and put them on cautiously. A glance at the envelope made him happy. He looked around with a proud smile. "My daughter-in-law's letter. Asima has written the address too. Obviously, the Babu has no time. She writes better than he does anyway. Who'd say that this is a woman's hand? Look, Kalu, look at the style of the letters — so well formed — just like a man's hand. Look."

Kalu was perhaps thirteen or fourteen. He had never learnt to read or write. But now he was called upon to express an opinion on the calligraphy. He peered at the English letters on the envelope and murmured with appreciation, "You are right, Dhala Karta, she writes so beautifully. She is herself so beautiful. Her manners are as charming as her speech is sweet. On her last visit she gave me two rupees. I was reluctant to accept them of course, but would she listen? But such is the manner of the ladies of your caste, Karta, so different from us."

Kalu far outweighed his lack of years and education by his tact and diplomacy. Rajmohan was pleased. He smiled indulgently. "Caste is not all there is to it, you silly boy," he said. "Consider her family, her background. She is the granddaughter of the famous Ambika Bose of Chandipur. What a great man he was! In learning and wisdom he had no equal. A girl from such a family — would I pick a nobody for a daughter-in-law?" He tore open the envelope. "You saw the handwriting, Kalu, now mark the language," he said. "Do you think a lawyer can write better than this? Come here, Maqbool, listen to this," he called. Rajmohan began to read aloud.

"Respected Father,

It has been a long time since we heard from you. We are worried when your letters don't reach us regularly. The thought of your living there alone with only a few servants makes us sad. That we are not near you, and are unable to look after you in your old age makes us even more unhappy. But what is to be done? You did not listen to us; you refused to leave East Pakistan. All your neighbours sold their houses and property and came away. The Banerjees, the Mukherjees, the Rahas, the Sahas, the Kundas, the Nandis are all here. Most people seem to have emigrated. The village must be practically deserted! You still refuse to come and prefer to live there alone. Nor do you think of the future. Your friends and neighbours, people of your age, are more practical. They have made good money and have settled down well here. They are now men of substance. But you have done nothing for yourself!

In fact, we hear that you have told people that the house is yours, the property is yours and that you'll not sell a twig, an inch from what is yours. You'd rather the Muslims grabbed everything but you will not sell! Truly, it's your house, your property. You must do what you please. What right have we to comment?

But today I write this letter for a favour. You have seen the rooms we have rented at Beleghata. The walls are damp and the floor is cold. The children sleep on the floor. This has affected their health and your beloved grandchildren — Kanu, Tenu, Rina, Meena — never seem to be free of fever. The medical bills go up every month. If I mention cots and bedding to your son, he scolds me. Where is the money, he asks?

Please do us a favour. My grandfather had given me a four-poster bed as a wedding gift. I shall be grateful if you could sell it and send me the money so that I can buy some cots for your grandchildren. I can't bear to see them suffer any more.

You cannot possibly object to this. Please keep in mind that the four-poster does not really belong to your family. It is a part of my dowry. Its sale would not hurt your prestige. You can say that you sold it at my insistence. This is the jute season. The Muslims will have money in hand. This will be the right time to make a sale. Moreover, what is the point in keeping it? Of what use will it be to anyone? It might just get termite-infested and rot. It will be wiser to sell it. Let the money from the sale at least be of some use to your grandchildren.

We are all well here. The pressure of office work leaves your son little time. He will write to you separately. Please arrange to sell the bed immediately.

Do write to us regularly. Accept our respectful obeisance.

Yours affectionately, Asima."

Suren had not written separately. He had just added a line of persuasion at the end of his wife's letter — "I am sure you'll have no objection to Asima's request."

"No, no, why should I object? I dare not object to anything. Do just what you wish — just what you please!" Rajmohan threw the letter away in disgust and gave loud instructions to his servant. "Kalu, go get that four-poster bed from the East room," he raged. "I will not keep it in my house any more. I'll throw it in the junk-yard. Whatever she brought from her father's house, she has carefully collected and taken away. Only the bed remained. If that is what she wants now, let her have it. I will not keep it any longer. And her sheep of a husband, her slave, adds — you should not have any objection!"

Rajmohan's anger increased.

"No, no, I have no objection at all. I will not touch food or water, till I throw that bed out of my house. Go get that bed out, Kalu. No, no, I will listen to no one." Rajmohan brushed Kalu's interjections aside. "My word is final, what I have said must be done. I piss on the bed, do you hear? Till I'm rid of it, there'll be no peace for me, Kalu. The fire will not burn out; the pain in my heart and mind will not cease."

Rajmohan rushed towards the room himself, pushed the doors open and stepped insid e. Suren and Asima had used that room whenever they had come home on holidays. Even last year. A framed photograph of the couple hung on the wall. The huge four-poster bed was placed close to the southern wall near the two wide windows. Rajmohan had covered the mattress well with thick burlap. He never failed to check it daily for rodents and termites. He himself dusted it with the towel he carried over his shoulder.

In the opposite corner of the room, dry white jute fibre and paddy lay in separate heaps on the floor.

Rajmohan called out to Maqbool, who had also followed him up to the door, "Come into the room, Maqbool, dismantle the bed and take it away."

"Do you really wish to sell this bed, Dhala Karta?" asked Maqbool hesitantly.

Rajmohan was adamant. "Yes, if I can get the money, I'll sell it today and send a money-order to Calcutta."

Maqbool stepped into the room. That room had no icons or puja vessels. There wasn't even any drinking water. So even farmers and labourers could enter the room freely.

Maqbool looked covetously at the beautifully carved four-poster bed. It was a fine piece of craftsmanship. Made entirely of good teak, its four legs were shaped like tiger's paws. The wide headboard had elegantly carved designs decorating it. On the panel, there was a line of creepers at the top and at the bottom, and a row of tiny elephants was chiselled in between them in elaborate detail.

"Will you really sell this bed, Karta?" Maqbool asked again. "Of course, after the manner in which your daughter-in-law has written the letter, with the subtle taunt, a man of your self-esteem can't possibly still keep it," he added. "Well, Dhala Karta, you can do something for me. You can give it to me."

Rajmohan looked at Maqbool in surprise. "To you?" he exclaimed.

"Why not, Karta?" Maqbool continued. "Of course, I don't want it for free, I'll pay a good price for it. You wanted to throw it away anyway into the dump-heap. To give it to me would mean the same thing, wouldn't it? Kindly let me have it, Karta."

Rajmohan's rage still smouldered. Why not, he thought to himself. Maqbool was right, the bed deserved to be in his lowly hut. Mean as his son's wife was, that would serve her right. The home of the common labourer was the proper place for the gift from her father's house!

Rajmohan looked at Maqbool. "But can you manage it?" he asked. "Can you pay me cash for it immediately and clear my house of this junk today, this moment?"

Maqbool answered confidently, "I can, Master. I'll go home now to bring the money while you dismantle the bed."

2

Maqbool Sheikh's house was close-by. On the southern side of Rajmohan's house was an abandoned and dilapidated building overgrown with weeds. Beyond that was a narrow ditch, which remained dry through the summer, but was now filled with rain water. Maqbool's house was on the other side of that ditch.

Tied to the mango tree near the abandoned house on one side, and to the trunk of the tamarind tree near Maqbool's hut on the other side, was a flimsy bamboo bridge. Actually, it comprised of only two poles, one to walk on and another narrower one to hold onto.

In his excitement, Maqbool ran across the unstable bamboo bridge.

Under the tamarind tree was a small hut. Its roof was made of a rusty and corrugated iron sheet. Its mud walls were framed partly with bamboo and partly with reeds. Its earthen floor was damp. Along the sides, a few earthworms tried to burrow into the inviting softness. There was a small courtyard in the front, slippery with water. The water from the ditch lapped against the hut and threatened to flow into it.

In the courtyard sat a young woman, fair skinned, twenty-one or twenty-two years of age. She wore a bright sari and was chopping watercress. Two emaciated children, about four and five years old, played with water weeds. A coin, with a black thread through it, was tied around their waists. Otherwise they were naked. Along the eastern side of the courtyard, jute sticks were hung up to dry on a bamboo fence. They would later be used either as fuel or to repair the walls of the hut. Behind the drying jute sticks, partly hidden from view, stood a famished cow munching straw and occasionally swishing its tail to brush aside the flies. Almost breathless with haste, Maqbool ran into the courtyard and called his wife eagerly, "Get up, Fati, get up. Give me some money quickly."

Fatima pulled the end of her sari over her head, and turned to look at her husband. Her large eyes were full of amazement. "Whom are you talking to? Where do I get the money from?" she asked.

Maqbool smiled mysteriously and then proceeded to tell her about his secret savings. Carefully hidden in the hollow of the dried bamboo were a few notes saved painstakingly over the years by selling jute, selling milk and occasionally a couple of trees. Maqbool directed Fatima to bring the money to him.

But Fatima hesitated, reluctant to part with their savings. "With this money you said that you'll buy a cow, repair the hut, buy me some ornaments," she reminded Maqbool. "I'll not give you this money even if you kill me," she added stubbornly.

Maqbool smiled at her. "Believe me, I'm buying an ornament not only for you but for both of us. We'll wear it together," he said. "What a beautiful bed it is, Fati, you've never seen anything like it and neither have I." Maqbool proceeded to give her a detailed description of the beautiful four-poster and of the events of the day. The Karta was angry and was selling the bed cheap, he explained. Such an opportunity should not be missed. If there was any delay, perhaps the Karta's anger would cool, perhaps someone else would take it. Then there would be nothing for Maqbool but regret. Earlier, when the Hindus had left, they had sold away all their belongings, their furniture and utensils practically for a song. The Munshis, the Kazis and the Sikdars had bought them all. Maqbool had not been able to touch anything. He had no money then. Now a chance had come and it should not be missed. Let there be at least one precious possession in Maqbool's home.

Fatima softened a little but she was still skeptical. "But where will you keep such a princely possession in this shabby hut?" she asked.

Maqbool lifted her chin and turned her face towards him. He said softly, "If my hut is good enough for my Begum, for the light of my heart, it is surely good enough for the bed too."

Maqbool entered the room and took the money out of the hollowed bamboo. There were fifty-two rupees in notes and also some coins. He counted out fifty rupees and returned the change to his wife. He rushed back again across the bridge with the money.

Around the old house, Yakub, the chowkidar, was looking for creepers to make fishing rods. He saw Maqbool hurrying by. "Where are you rushing off to like a race horse, Miyan?" he called.

Maqbool paused. "Why, is that you, brother chowkidar? Come now, come with me, I need your help. I'll explain later. I'll also make you a fishing rod." Maqbool caught Yakub's hand and pulled him along. "You come with me now," he said.

Rajmohan had already dismantled the bed, and had brought it out into the courtyard. Maqbool placed the money near his feet. "Here is the money, Dhala Karta," he said.

"What is the money for?" said Rajmohan. "You take away this bed and throw it into the canal. I will not keep it in my house any more."

Maqbool said, "I would have taken it, Karta, indeed even asked you for it, had it been yours to give. But it belongs to the young mistress. It is a gift from her father's family. So please accept the money on her behalf and send it to her."

Maqbool's words pierced Rajmohan's heart like a poisoned arrow. Maqbool was right. The bed did not belong to him. He had no right over it. Asima had made that quite clear in her letter, every line of which was written with a pen dipped in the inky venom of her heart.

"Alright, alright," Rajmohan yelled. "If money is what that haramzadi wants, I'll send her the money. This is not a bed but my funeral pyre. Take this object out of my sight, Maqbool."

With the help of Yakub, the chowkidar, Maqbool whisked away the bed immediately and rowed it across the canal in his little broken boat, instead of carrying it across the bridge.

Placing the heavy wooden posts on the mud bank, Yakub remarked, "You have made a good bargain, brother. This bed will not cost less than two hundred rupees, I can assure you."

Maqbool evaded the matter of the price. He said, "That stubborn old man is such a miser, brother. He is like a demon guarding his possessions. So many Hindus have left, but that old man refuses to stir. Because of him there is no chance of plucking fruit or picking some firewood from his orchard. Who will live in that house once he closes his eyes, tell me? Will that funk, Suren, return?"

"Suren has gone for good. He will not dare to return to Pakistan," agreed Yakub.

Maqbool continued in the same vein, "You just wait and see. Let the old man close his eyes and I'll make his house a real Pakistan! My children, my relatives will walk over those cement floors. You say I've made a bargain, brother, but I think this is a dead loss. I could have got it for free — I could have grabbed it from the old man."

Maqbool paused a little and thought to himself. "No brother," he said, "I do not really mean that. It is better to pay for something, than to take it by force. The thing then belongs to you, and no one can accuse you. What do you say, brother, am I not correct?"

Yakub nodded his head. "You are right," he said.

3

Within a few hours, the news had spread through the entire neighbourhood that Rajmohan had sold the expensive four-poster for almost nothing. The same Rajmohan who never sold a tree, a bamboo stick, or even a sheaf of straw because that would have hurt his prestige, had given away that elegant and expensive four-poster for the meagre sum of fifty rupees!

Sharat Shil, Muraru Mandel, Gedu Munshi, Chadan Mridha and others could not contain their curiosity any longer. All the neighbours assembled in Rajmohan's courtyard.

"Have you lost your mind, Karta?" asked Sharat. "Why did you give away that beautiful object for fifty rupees? I would have given you one hundred and fifty for it."

"Arrey, a hundred-and-fifty is nothing," said Gedu Munshi scornfully. "I would have given you two hundred and fifty, Karta. Why didn't you tell me?"

Rajmohan became angry, and said, "Go away, all of you, don't irritate me. I haven't sold anything. I gave it away, I threw it away. Do you understand? Now go."

Before leaving, however, Chadan Mridha hesitated and said entreatingly, "Cupboards, chairs, tables, trunks — if you decide to sell anything at all, Karta, please let me know first. I'll pay you immediate cash and the right price. I will not cheat you."

Chadan Mridha was the most prosperous farmer in the neighbourhood. He had made good money from his jute business. He also owned about a hundred acres of cultivable land. He was well-respected in the Muslim community.

Rajmohan almost ran after him crying, "You leave my house at once, Mridha, get out. You can take away and enjoy whatever you want after I die. I haven't sold anything yet and while I live, I will not sell a single thing from my house."

Thoroughly intimidated by Rajmohan's anger, the neighbours slunk away. The old Master had become eccentric, they whispered among themselves. And why not? Living all by himself, alone in that big empty house, far from his son and daughter-in-law and his grandchildren, it was no wonder that he had gone mad.

After they had all departed, Rajmohan brooded over the matter. Cheated, he had been cheated, there was no doubt. Impulsively and in a rage, he had acted foolishly. It was like eating food off the mud floor to spite the thief! And he had eaten mud! He sat thinking pensively. Then he called his servant, "Kalu, get the boat ready. I'll go to Kumarpur."

Kumarpur was about a mile and a half away from Sonarpur. Rajmohan worked in the Registry Office there, writing out documents. Lately he had begun to find work difficult. His hands trembled. The letters became smudged, sometimes almost illegible. People were reluctant to give him documents any more. But he could not manage without the work. He went to the Registry Office daily and waited hopefully on the office verandah.

"Why should you bother, Dhala Karta?" everyone asked him. "You are now old. Why should you take so much trouble? Now leave all this."

"I can't eat properly, Harabilas," replied Rajmohan. "I have tried keeping away but I can't eat properly. I lose my sleep and feel restless."

Before rowing him across in his small boat, Kalu enquired, "Won't you have your lunch, Karta?"

"No, I don't want any lunch today," Rajmohan replied. "You have some cold rice with you, haven't you? That'll do." Then in an emotion-choked voice, he burst out, "O Kalu, what have I done? I have eaten mud with my own hands, haven't I, Kalu?"

"I tried to prevent you, Karta. But you..." Kalu stopped in confusion and stared at his Master helplessly. Then softly he murmured, "Come, Karta." Karta, Dhala Karta, indeed! In his youth, Rajmohan was the fairest and the handsomest man in the neighbourhood and in the entire village. Tall and fair, with a bright complexion, a broad forehead, a straight and aristocratic nose and dark eyes, he had the looks of a prince. At sixty-five, his face no longer had the same glow, nor did his body have the same arrow-like stature. He stooped a little. His skin was wrinkled and his complexion had darkened. He had lost all but two of his beautiful and firm teeth. But Rajmohan had truly become the Dhala Karta in other ways. In the last few years all his hair had turned white. His eyebrows were white, his moustache was white, the tufts of hair on his chest were white — white like the fibers of the ripe jute.

"Come, Karta, get up," urged Kalu.

"Yes, I'm coming," replied Rajmohan. Throwing a none-too-clean kurta over his shoulders, carrying his torn slippers in hand and clutching an old, patched umbrella, Rajmohan stepped into the little boat with a heavy heart.

The boat left the canal and sailed into the Kumar river.

4

Returning late in the evening, Rajmohan took a lantern and went straight into the eastern room. Half of that room was empty. He couldn't bear to remain in the room any longer and hurried out. But the emptiness of the room haunted him. It seemed to pursue him and settle in his heart. His heart ached with the emptiness.

Rajmohan went into the north room, his bedroom. He changed his clothes, washed and then sat down for his evening prayers. But he continued to feel restless and anxious. The empty space of the east room rose before his eyes. Instead of his mantra, he kept recalling the four-poster that had filled that empty space.

Suddenly, Rajmohan was overwhelmed with a feeling of utter loneliness. He had no one he could call his own, no one at all. He remembered the face of his wife, Sarala, who had died ten years ago. He remembered the pain of separation from his beloved son and daughter-in-law and the grandchildren. They were all his, yet totally lost to him. Everyone seemed to have moved or gone forever.

Rajmohan alone kept a solitary vigil in that empty shell of a house. There was no one in the whole world who could share his loneliness.

Next morning, he sent Kalu to call Maqbool. Maqbool did not come. He told Kalu that he was very busy. Later when he had some time, he would meet the Master.

Rajmohan gnashed his few remaining teeth in anger. "The impudence of that rascal! I call him and he says he is busy. I'll see how busy he is!"

Kalu said consolingly, "What can you do, Karta? These are their days, their rule — so the saplings are more belligerent than the big old bamboos!"

Rajmohan said, "Hmmn."

Soon he got up and walked slowly towards Maqbool's house. Walking was painful for Rajmohan. Arthritis had almost crippled him. He limped painfully, dragging his left foot. Passing by the wild shrubs and puddles, Rajmohan, crossed the bamboo bridge carefully, entered Maqbool's courtyard and called, "What are you doing, Maqbool?"

Maqbool had just returned after delivering milk. He sat on the verandah with his wife, braiding some twine. Fatima went into the room quickly on hearing Rajmohan's voice. Maqbool called out, "Come in, Karta, come in." There was no hint of a welcome in his voice, though he did offer his wooden seat to Rajmohan.

"Please sit down, Karta. What is the matter? I would have come myself. Why did you trouble yourself?"

"I've just come to see you, to see how you are doing," Rajmohan said. "You've built your hut well, I see. It is big enough to accommodate your growing family. But why have you put these old tin sheets on the roof? Replace them with new ones." As he spoke, Rajmohan turned a rapid glance towards the room.

Maqbool had already reassembled the four-poster in his hut. It filled the entire room. Pushed under the bed were some boxes and utensils — Fatima's household stuff. The bed did not have a mattress. Rajmohan had not given the mattress to Maqbool. Fatima had spread out a reed mat on the bed and had covered it with a soiled and torn sheet. A couple of dirty pillows were placed on one side.

What had they done to his beautiful four-poster, thought Rajmohan in disgust. He couldn't bear to look at its pitiful state. He looked at Maqbool, and said, "Yes, change the tin sheets. If the roof leaks, the water will spoil the room."

Maqbool replied, "I wish I could, Dhala Karta, but where is the money? I hope to buy many things — a cow, a good boat — but where is the money?"

Rajmohan lowered his voice, "I have brought your money back."

Maqbool stared at him. "What did you say?" he asked.

"Come," said Rajmohan, "I have to talk to you. I'll explain." He left his seat and stepped into the courtyard.

But Maqbool did not move. "Talk to me here. Tell me whatever you wish to say. There is no one here."

But Rajmohan would not listen. He pulled Maqbool by the hand and took him outside the hut.

The place was surrounded by water and covered with wild shrubs. The canals flowed on three sides and the river on the other. Scattered over a small area were a few more huts belonging to the Muslims. Some were already immersed in water, a few others remained above water like isolated islands. Rajmohan walked towards the bamboo grove that lay to the south-east of Maqbool's hut.

"What is the matter, Karta?" asked Maqbool. "Tell me what you wish to say."

Rajmohan took out some money kept folded at his belt. They were the same notes that Maqbool had given him the day before. There was a new five rupee note with them. Rajmohan offered them to Maqbool. "Count them," he said. "There are fifty-five rupees in all. I have added five rupees for you to buy some sweets for the children."

Maqbool had already guessed Rajmohan's intentions. He looked hard at him. Rajmohan did not like the look in his eyes. They appeared bloodshot.

Rajmohan stepped back a little. Maqbool was a dark-skinned young man of thirty or thirty-two, taller than Rajmohan and sturdily built like a coconut tree. He had strong, muscular limbs and a head full of dark curly hair. He had also started to grow his beard which now covered his face and made him look like a wild animal.

Maqbool smiled to see Rajmohan take a few cautious steps back. "Are you afraid, Karta? Don't worry, after all you are an old and a well respected man in these parts. Can I insult you? But take back that money. My children don't eat sweets. They'll get worms and stomach-aches if they do. You go home, Karta. I will not return the four-poster."

Rajmohan felt his face redden at the insult. He burned to the tips of his ears with shame and humiliation. He tucked the money into his belt and said menacingly, "Alright. But remember this, Maqbool Sheikh, winter is not over with one December. You may have got your Pakistan but that doesn't make all of you governors!"

After Rajmohan left, Fatima came out of the house and asked in fear, "What has happened? Why is Karta so angry?"

"What else? After selling his bed, he wants it back now. He brought the money to tempt me," said Maqbool.

"What a mess!" exclaimed Fatima. "So what did you say?"

Maqbool smiled shyly, "I caught his feet and begged him to take away my wife if he so wishes, instead of the bed."

Fatima exclaimed bashfully, "You said all these things to an old man? Have you no shame?"

Maqbool did not answer. He was enjoying his own joke. Fatima realized that Maqbool was just teasing her. He had not said those things to the Master at all.

"Well, if you love your wife so much, Miyan, and don't care for anything else," said Fatima more firmly, "then why are you so obsessed with this bed? Why don't you return Karta's bed to him? You know he is not such a straight-forward man. He won't do you any good, but if he tries to harm you, who'll stop him? Whatever you say, we live humbly with our children. My heart trembles when I think of these things."

Maqbool looked at his wife, "Let it tremble, Bibi. You look best when your heart trembles."

Fatima pulled the end of her sari, which had slipped down, shyly over her bosom and moved away quickly. "It is impossible to talk to you," she complained, "and you have the eyes of..." she couldn't think of an apt comparison.

Maqbool laughed. He said, "These are the eyes of a young man, Bibi, the eyes of a passionate young man. They are not like the shadowed eyes of the old Karta. These eyes are different. Inequality and injustice of the world make them red with anger; beautiful objects of the world make them burn with desire!"

A few days later, Maqbool was summoned to Rajmohan's house. Two carpets were spread out on the wide northern verandah, one for the Muslims and one for the Hindus. Between the carpets were placed the tobacco tin, the earthen bowl of cinders and three hookahs of different sizes — two for the Hindus, one for the Muslims.

There were no more high caste Hindus in the neighbourhood. Those who remained were of the lower castes, dark-skinned. Sharat Shil, Murari Mandal, Phatik Karmakar, Nibaran Rajak — all of them were obliged to Rajmohan. They had received his help in some form or another. Among the Muslims were Chadan Mridha, Badan Sikdar, Gedu Munshi.

As soon as Maqbool arrived, Gedu Munshi began to talk to him in an authoritarian tone. "You haven't behaved well with Karta. All the Hindu gentlemen have gone away but Karta has not left us. He has not severed the bonds of our relationship and holds us close to his bosom. We till his land, visit his house, come to him in need. You must return the Karta's possession to him; restore what belongs to him."

"Please don't make such unfair demands, Munshi Sahib," said Maqbool. "Karta gave me the bed with his own hands, he spoke of selling the bed himself. He has taken money from me. Yakub chowkidar is a witness. How can he now ask me to return it?"

Rajmohan sat glumly on a wooden seat. There was a lantern placed to his right. He turned up the wick and also raised his voice, "Have I taken your money? Is fifty rupees the right price for that four-poster, just because you say it is?"

"But you agreed to that price, Karta. Besides, the price depends on one's ability to pay. I cannot pay more than fifty rupees so I bought it for that price," said Maqbool.

"You are not being reasonable, Maqbool," said Sharat Shil. "You may not have the ability to pay, but perhaps someone else has. Either you pay Karta another hundred rupees or bring the bed back."

The Hindus nodded their assent to the judgment and the Muslims raised no objections. The hookahs passed from hand to hand but the matter was not yet resolved.

"If this is your notion of justice, I cannot accept it," declared Maqbool in a firm voice. "I have paid a price for the bed. I will not return it. You may go to the civil court, the criminal court or wherever you wish, I don't care."

"Keep quiet, you mean fellow. A small man with a big mouth!" scolded Gedu Munshi. "Go home and think it over.

Discuss it with your wife, through the whole night if necessary. Then come and tell us tomorrow."

After Maqbool had left, Gedu Munshi and Chadan Mridha turned to pacify Rajmohan.

"Don't mind him, Dhala Karta," they said. "We all know that he is a headstrong and an obstinate fellow. Does he listen to anyone? But let us see, we shall try to persuade him. After all where can he go with the bed? How long will he be able to hold onto your property? But you have also acted rashly in your anger, Master. You haven't left us with much to say."

They left one by one. Before leaving, Sharat Shil said, trying to console Rajmohan, "You see, Karta, all the Muslims are together in this. They have all given him their secret support or how can Maqbool have the impudence to defy you and say that he will not obey you. You have to bear this quietly, Karta, in keeping with the times. You have lost just one bed. Haven't so many given away their houses and lands practically for nothing? How does it really matter? Have they all died? One must learn to live with these things. You will also not die for the loss of this bed. Don't we know that you can stack your room with five such beds if you so wish! Now go to bed, Karta, it is late already."

Sharat smoked for a while and then he took his leave. The lamp hurt Rajmohan's eyes. He put out the light and sat in the darkness. Kalu had spread his mat on the east verandah and was already asleep. The house and the neighbourhood had become quiet. There was no sound anywhere.

Rajmohan felt alone and very helpless. He had to bear the brunt of the humiliation alone. If that haramzada had been at home at such a time and had stood by his side, he would not have felt so vulnerable. But he would not come nor would Rajmohan ask him to come. Let him live happily wherever he was.

Rajmohan had often heard of quarrels and misunderstandings between father and son. Such things had not happened between him and his son, yet his son had gone away. His temperament, upbringing and education did not correlate with Rajmohan's views. He cared nothing for all that his father valued more than life — the ancestral home, the land, the paddy and jute fields, the plants, trees and rivers of their birth place. He did not wish to know his country or her people. He only valued his job and a pile of dry books. He had shut his eyes to the real people and searched his books for the meaning of humanity. No, there was no sharing of minds between father and son. His son had left the village and settled elsewhere even before the formation of Pakistan. Now Rajmohan and his son were the citizens of two different nations and belonged to two different eras.

A cold and damp wind stirred the leaves of the deodar tree that stood at the southern boundary wall. How tall it had grown. Rajmohan had planted that tree with his own hands. It had grown in front of Rajmohan, like Suren had, but it was still here. It had not deserted him and disappeared from sight!

"You are closer to me, dear tree, than that enemy of mine," Rajmohan whispered. "For you there is no Hindustan-Pakistan. You have not become distant after a few years of education. You too cling to the soil of your birth like I do. There is none closer to me than you are, deodar."

He had received offers for that tree also, even upto the sum of twenty-one rupees. Rajmohan had always been adamant about not selling his property. "I buy, I don't sell," he often declared with pride.

He had never sold anything in his life save once. Rajmohan's heart ached at that thought. Why had he done it? What madness had suddenly seized him? Would he ever be able to get it back? He had helped so many people recover their property, would he not be able to recover his own? He had to get it back, somehow.

5

Rajmohan couldn't find an easy way to get his four-poster bed back. He could not find any occasion to trap Maqbool. Maqbool did not farm Rajmohan's land nor had he borrowed any money. Getting him embroiled in a fabricated lawsuit would not be a wise move. It might not be easy to find witnesses to give evidence against Maqbool, now that the land was Pakistan. It would serve no purpose except perhaps to provoke the leaders of the Muslim community.

Unable to punish Maqbool in a dramatic way, Rajmohan devised ways of harming him by other tactics. He used to buy half a seer of milk from Maqbool daily. He started getting the daily supply from Wahen instead. When he hired farm labour,

Maqbool was always the first to be called, the practice was stopped.

Maqbool was not a farmer in the proper sense of the word. He worked in the fields as a temporary labourer. During the jute season he cut and washed jute fibre, during the paddy harvest he was among the extra workers. When there was no field-work, he did various odd jobs like clearing the undergrowth, collecting and chopping firewood and so on. For all such jobs, Maqbool was always employed at Rajmohan's house. Now he was being avoided, in fact, totally boycotted. After most of the Hindus left, Maqbool was already short of work. With Rajmohan's animosity, chances of getting work became negligible. There was less demand for hired hands among the Muslims because even the prosperous Muslim farmers did the manual work themselves. With such scarcity of work, Maqbool was in serious trouble.

Kalu relayed all the news to Rajmohan. Rowing him to Kumarpur in the little boat one day, Kalu remarked, "That son of a Sheikh is in a proper fix. You are clever, Karta. Not killing him outright, you are starving him to death. How dare he defy you? Does he have as much wit as you have in a single tooth?"

Rajmohan's hollow cheeks spread in a smug smile, "And I've lost nearly all my teeth, Kalu!"

"What you have is enough, Karta," Kalu assured him. "Even your gums are strong enough to crush him."

Maqbool was becoming desperate. He swore to his wife viciously, "I'll wait a few more days. Then I'm going to kill that damned old man. I'll grab his possessions in front of his eyes."

Fatima was full of trepidation. "Please don't say such things," she begged. "Don't even allow such thoughts to enter your mind."

"Why not?" asked Maqbool defiantly. "I'll be jailed and hanged. I don't care. I'll die after I've killed him too."

"But what will happen to us?" wailed his wife. "You mustn't think of such things. Don't let anger rule your actions. You have your children to think of, do you realize? Feed them and clothe them to prove your worth. Behave like a real man."

Maqbool made an indistinct grunt.

"What do you mean by that?" Fatima continued. "Anyone can jump around and show off with threats like that. Is that something so great? The real test is in caring for the family, keeping the children well and healthy. Have you looked at my little darlings properly, my Sabdul and Majnu? See how thin they have become?" She pulled her two emaciated little children into her arms and caressed them gently, as if trying to compensate for their lack of nourishment with her love. She turned her reproachful eyes on her husband.

"Just look at them," she urged.

Maqbool kept his angry red eyes fixed on his wife's face and cried in a rough voice, "Don't drive me mad, Fati. My blood is boiling, don't drive me to murder."

Fatima grasped his hands. "No, there is no need for murder. Please listen to me," she pleaded. "Return the Karta's four-poster to him. What need have we for such luxuries? With two square meals a day, our mats will be comfortable enough. We will sleep in peace."

Maqbool snatched his hands away. His eyes were bloodshot. "Beware, Fati. If you say such things, I'll break your jaw. And don't keep saying Karta's bed, the Karta's bed. It is no longer his. I bought it with my own money. I didn't steal it or rob it. I bought it with my hard-earned money. It is mine, do you understand?" Maqbool went into the room and clutched one of the posts of the bed as if it was being taken away from him.

A little later, he sharpened his axe and went in search of work. The situation was no different. The poor Muslim farmers of the village could not afford hired help. Who else was there to employ him? He walked around aimlessly with repressed anger, planning vengeance. But he did not really kill Rajmohan or rob him. He stole some small things instead — not from Rajmohan's house, but from the orchard — a bunch of betel-nuts, a couple of coconuts, some fruit.

When Rajmohan learnt about the theft, he shouted curses and threatened to inform the police. He arranged for a local lad to watch over the orchard by promising him some money.

But nuts and coconuts do not appease hunger. Maqbool faced severe hardship. There was hardly any rice at home. The rainy season was always distressing even otherwise. On one hand there was scarcity of work and on the other the prices of rice, pulses and oil rose steeply. The jute harvest was over and the paddy season had not yet begun. Fallow time meant general inactivity. This season the suffering had become unbearable. It rained heavily and the huts became water-logged. If the season was difficult for everybody, it was even more so for Maqbool. The few rupees he had saved had been spent on the four-poster. His hands were as empty as his stomach. The children were unmanageable. The constant quarrels with his wife made life in the hut intolerable. Fatima foraged for food for the children and sometimes managed to cook a handful of rice with bits of watercress or tapioca. Sometimes, she caught a few shrimps and minnows with the end of her sari from the canal.

One day the Master's servant came to inquire, "Hello, Maqbool Miyan, how are you?"

Maqbool frowned at him, "I am well. How about you, the rich servant of a rich man?"

After exchanging general pleasantries, Kalu disclosed the real purpose of his visit. "Karta is willing to add ten rupees to the fifty rupees, Maqbool," he said. "Please return the four-poster to him. Don't be stubborn, understand?"

Maqbool was so angry that he almost attacked him. "I have understood. Now I'll make you understand for all time," he cried. "Get out of my house. If you dare to come again with such a foul suggestion, I'll break your legs. I'm warning you."

Kalu ran away in fear, but others came with similar proposals. Chadan Mridha and Gedu Munshi took Maqbool aside and reasoned with him. He must, they told him, sell the four-poster. The Master need not know and even if he did, what did it matter? Maqbool had paid fifty rupees for it, Chadan Mridha was ready to pay sixty-five. Gedu Munshi raised his offer to seventy-five. But Maqbool shook his head. He had not bought the four-poster to sell it again, but for his own use. Gradually, the price for the four-poster bed touched the round figure of one hundred rupees. But Maqbool did not budge. He would not sell the four-poster bed to anyone. He would use it for himself, sleep on it with his wife and children. Gedu Munshi and Chadan Mridha gnashed their teeth and heaped abuses on him, "Die, fool, die of starvation. Take your bed with you to your grave!"

Even Fatima showed her irritation that day. "Well, what kind of a man are you?" she asked. "I would have understood had this been an acre of land which would give us crops through the year; had it been a cow which would have given us milk through the year, had it been a tree which would have given us fruit through the year. But why do you insist on keeping this piece of dead wood in your hut and starving for it?"

Maqbool looked long at his wife, but instead of losing his temper, he spoke with patience and affection. "Why do I keep it? You will not understand, woman. You are born a woman, it is impossible for you to understand such matters. That is not dead wood to me, Fati. It has life and that life sustains my self-respect as a man."

Fatima replied with scorn, "If you are so concerned about your self-respect, why don't you go out of the house in search of some work? I have heard that our village is now in Pakistan and has a Muslim government. Why must we then starve to death?"

Maqbool had already made enquiries. Who would give a job to an illiterate like him? His wife's remark made him smile sadly. "The poor like us have no Hindustan or Pakistan, Fati; there is only gorestan — the graveyard."

6

After a couple of days, Maqbool sold the cow. It had calved thrice and was not yielding much milk anyway. It had become a skeleton for want of fodder. It was better to sell it to the man from the next village than to send it to the slaughter-house.

Maqbool sold his little boat next. He gave Fatima some money to buy provisions. With the rest, he bought an old ferry boat. Every morning he rowed to Kumarpur and waited hopefully for passengers. If luck favoured him he earned a rupee or two. But there were gloomy days when no passengers came. He returned empty-handed late at night. On the days he ferried passengers to distant villages, he couldn't return home at all but slept in the boat anchored to the bank.

The times were very hard for Maqbool.

It was during one of those days when Maqbool was away and Fatima sat lighting some jute sticks to start her cooking that Rajmohan came to their hut.

"O Maqbool, are you home, Maqbool?" he called. Fatima stepped behind the reed fence and pushed her son forward. "Go tell Karta, that he is not at home. He has taken the boat out. Ask Karta what he wants," she prompted her son.

Though he was five years old, Maqbool's son was not very articulate. He spoke a few words with his parents but in front of strangers he wouldn't open his mouth. Fatima had to continue the conversation from behind the fence.

"I am suffering from a bad cough," explained Rajmohan. "You have a vasaka tree in your yard. Will you give me a few leaves, daughter-in-law?"

Fatima smiled and said, "Why, certainly, Karta. Please wait in the verandah. I'll get a few leaves for you."

"No, no. Don't bother. I'll pluck them myself." He slowly stepped onto the verandah and glanced into the room. A sudden pain stabbed his heart. His bed, his four-poster. But what a terrible condition it was in. The elegantly carved legs of the bed were stained with grease and lime. Then there were the dirty sheets and the pillows. It was disgusting. How could such a lowly hut be worthy of such a treasure? What did they know about looking after such expensive furniture?

After conversing a while in a general way, Rajmohan brought up the main reason for his visit. "If you don't mind, daughter-in-law, I'll tell you something," he said. "Please persuade Maqbool to return the four-poster to me. I'll pay him whatever price he wants."

Fatima was stunned. She stood quite still behind the fence. Then she said slowly but firmly, "No, Karta, I can't tell him that. You came for some vasaka leaves. Please collect the leaves. Do not discuss these matters with me." Fatima moved away.

Fatima's answer was like a slap on his face. Rajmohan stood stiffly for a while, staring at the four-poster, before walking away. He had lost all desire to collect the vasaka leaves. He plucked a few leaves absent mindedly on his way out.

There was a small temple in the compound. The idols of Radha and Govinda were installed there. Peacock feathers on his crown, a flute in his hands, his eternal companion to the left, Brajamohan Rasaraj Srigovinda had a serene gaze and a smile on his lips. Rajmohan finished his bath and sat quietly on the temple platform meditating on his mantra. He touched his head to the floor and prayed, "Merciful Lord, please remove the bonds of my worldly desires. Guide me towards the path to your

Vrindavan. Let my greed and passion, my pain and humiliation mingle in the red dust of Vraja, the playground of your love."

Rajmohan felt cleansed of all pettiness. But not for long. The next day he required vasaka leaves again. He coughed loudly in front of the servant. He needed the vasaka leaves urgently.

Even though she heard him coming that day, Fatima did not rush to hide behind the fence. Nor did she ask any questions. She stood silently in the corner farthest of the hut, alarmed that the Master might raise the issue of the four-poster again. Rajmohan guessed the meaning of Fatima's behaviour. He plucked a few leaves from the vasaka tree but did not go away immediately. He sat on the verandah and started chatting with Maqbool's son, Sabdul. He could not control his eyes however, they moved of their own volition to peer into the room.

The vasaka tree lost almost all its leaves, but Rajmohan's cough did not ameliorate nor did he stop visiting Maqbool's hut.

Maqbool spoke to his wife one night, "I hear that Karta comes here every day? He comes and waits in the verandah."

Fatima said, "Yes, he comes to pluck some vasaka leaves."

Maqbool laughed and said, "That's nonsense. He comes for you. The old man has taken a fancy to your beautiful face."

Fatima was indignant. "Don't talk nonsense," she said.

"Then tell me the real reason," said Maqbool.

Fatima replied, "What is there to say. You know it as well as I do."

"Yes, I know," said Maqbool. "But, beware, Fati. If you are tempted by money and agree to sell it, I will not let you live."

"Are you mad?" exclaimed Fatima. "Because I know he'll mention the four-poster, I avoid speaking with him. But the old man has evil eyes. All the while he is here, he keeps looking into the room. I don't like it at all. Whatever, you say, my heart trembles. We live with our children. Anything might happen. People have evil eyes."

Maqbool laughed scornfully. "What nonsense. Those old eyes have no evil left in them. His venom is that of the water-snake. People don't die if it bites them. You can sleep in peace. I'll also warn the old man not to come near my home again or I'll break his legs..."

7

As it happened, there was no need for Maqbool to threaten Rajmohan. Rajmohan was ill with high fever and blood-dysentery. He was unable to leave his bed. The village doctor was summoned. He said, "Roy Sahib, you must inform your son and daughter-in-law. The disease is especially debilitating for a man of your age."

Rajmohan shook his head. "No, doctor, not now," he said. "I'll tell you when to inform them. It seems there is some talk of promotions in the office. If my son takes leave now, he'll miss his chance. This will pass." Rajmohan had withdrawn two hundred rupees from his account and had sent the money to Asima. Would she have believed that the four-poster had been sold for only fifty rupees? She would have thought that her father-in-law had kept the rest of the money.

The doctor called everyday. But the disease only got exacerbated.

In the meanwhile, Maqbool's misfortune had also increased. On the market-day at Naopara, Maqbool had tied his boat to a tree with a chain before going off to make his purchases. When he returned, the boat was missing. Somebody had broken the lock to steal the boat. The village was notorious for thieves. Gedu Munshi's father-in-law lived in that village and he was known to have contacts with the thieves. Maqbool did not fail to understand the conspiracy, but there was nothing he could do. He managed to catch a boat home.

From the very next day, he was in dire straits. His condition was worse than before. Now there was no cow or boat to sell. There remained only the hut and the huge four-poster.

Rajmohan heard all the news even as he lay on his bed. Sharat Shil came in jubilantly. "This was bound to happen," he said. "He dared to defy you. Won't he be punished for that?"

After a few days, Kalu whispered softly. "Have you heard, Karta? It seems Maqbool will sell the four-poster to Atajaddi Sikdar of Talakanda. Atajaddi is building a new house. He'll furnish his new house with the four-poster."

Rajmohan responded dispiritedly, "Let him."

Kalu said, "It seems the price is a hundred and fifty rupees."

Rajmohan said, "Let it be so."

"Atajaddi will come himself this evening with a bag of money," Kalu added.

Rajmohan turned on his side. "Let him come," he said. That evening Kalu took leave for a few hours to see a play in the next village. The stage was set in the Mullah's house for the play *Mir Kasim*. People would flock from all the neighbouring villages to see it. Kalu left early to ensure a good seat.

Boobi, the maid, brought in a bowl of soup. Rajmohan did not touch it. The night grew dark and quiet. Rajmohan stirred restlessly in the bed. He couldn't sleep. He got up suddenly. His legs trembled with weakness. He groped in the darkness for his cane. The bunch of keys hung at his waist. He locked the room and stepped outside. The sky was overcast with dark clouds and it had already started to drizzle lightly. But Rajmohan did not turn back for a lantern or an umbrella. Leaning heavily on the cane, he walked out slowly.

Soon he reached Maqbool's hut and stood in the courtyard. He cried out in a thin shrill voice, "Maqbool, haramzade, come out immediately."

Maqbool opened the door of the hut. "Who is it?" he asked. "It is Karta's voice. Is it you, Karta?"

In a weak and quivering voice, Rajmohan said, "Yes, it is me. You finally sold the four-poster, you rascal. You sold it without letting me know."

Maqbool stood speechless for a few moments. "Who told you that?" he asked softly.

"Never mind that," said Rajmohan. "Can you conceal such matters? Even the flies carry news."

"But you are ill. How did you come in this darkness and rain? How did you cross the canal?" asked Maqbool with concern.

"I walked along the mud-bank," replied Rajmohan.

"How terrible," exclaimed Maqbool. "Come, please come in, Karta."

"What shall I do in your hut now? You have already done the worst thing possible," said Rajmohan.

"No, Master, I haven't done anything. You come in and see for yourself," said Maqbool. He caught Rajmohan's hands and pulled him inside. Rajmohan's body was burning with fever. He wore no shirt nor did he have any shoes on. The dhoti around his waist was wet. For one who could not take a step without his spectacles, he had forgotten to wear them. Maqbool called his wife urgently, "Get up, Fati, and light a lamp quickly. I need to reassure Karta..."

Weak with hunger, Fatima was lying on the bed. She got up hurriedly and pulled the end of her sari over her head with her left hand. But the torn sari did not cover her face. Two children, who looked like skeletons, lay on the other side of the bed.

"Then you have not sold it? You still have it?" Rajmohan asked, as he sighed with relief.

"I still have it, Karta," Maqbool said reassuringly.

"Didn't Atajaddi come?" asked Rajmohan.

"He did come," said Maqbool. "He offered an additional sum of ten rupees over the earlier one of a hundred and fifty rupees. I refused him, Karta. We have been starving for the last two days. But I had the strength yet to turn him away. I have been able to stave off the pangs of hunger. My wife was crying. Do you know what I told her, Karta? I said, woman, give me this one night. Clutch your hungry stomach and sleep. Let me keep my pride for one more night. Let me keep the four-poster bed for a few more hours!"

"Maqbool!" exclaimed Rajmohan.

"Karta!" answered Maqbool.

No one could speak for a while.

Fatima held the kerosene lamp over their heads. In the faint light of the smoky lamp, for a few precious moments, the two lovers of the four-poster bed — two men of different creeds, two men of different complexions, one fair and the other dark — two lovers of the four-poster bed stared at each other speechlessly.

Maqbool then turned to his wife and said, "Fati, lift the children and let them lie on the floor. Let me dismantle the four-poster and return it to Karta."

"What are you saying Maqbool!" exclaimed Rajmohan.

"Yes, Karta. You take the four-poster back," said Maqbool. "I could keep it today, but what if I can't keep it tomorrow?"

Maqbool stretched his arms to pull the children away. Rajmohan caught his arms. "Stop," he ordered.

Then he spoke softly, almost to himself. "All these days when I came to your hut, Maqbool, to look at the four-poster stealthily, I always saw it empty. Today my four-poster is no longer empty. Today my pedestal is no longer empty. Today I see them, I see my beloved Radha-Govinda on the pedestal. The pedestal is no longer empty." Rajmohan paused. "Now take me home, Maqbool," he said.

Maqbool took the lamp from Fatima's hands.

"Come, Dhala Karta," he said.

Original in Bengali.
Translated by Tutun Mukherjee.

SAADAT HASAN MANTO

OPEN IT

The special train left Amritsar at two in the afternoon and reached Mughalpura eight hours later. Many of the passengers were killed on the way, many were injured and a few were missing.

When Sirajuddin opened his eyes the next morning, he found himself lying on the cold ground of a refugee camp. There was a seething crowd of men, women and children all around him. Bewildered by it all, he lay staring at the dusty sky for a long time. There was a lot of noise in the camp, but old Sirajuddin was deaf to it. He didn't hear anything. Anyone who saw him, would have assumed that he was in deep and agonized thought about something. His mind, however, was blank.

Sirajuddin lay gazing absent-mindedly at the dusty sky, till he suddenly caught sight of the sun. The warmth of the sun's rays penetrated every nerve of his body. He woke up with a start. A nightmarish vision rose before his eyes — flames, loot...people running...a station...firing...darkness and Sakina.

Overcome by fear and anxiety, he began searching for Sakina in the crowd like a demented person.

For three long hours he called out "Sakina...Sakina." He looked for her in every corner of the camp, but found no trace of his young and only daughter. There was an uproar all round — some of the refugees were searching for their children, others for their mothers; some for their wives and others for their daughters.

Dejected and tired, Sirajuddin sat down, and tried to recall exactly where and how he had lost Sakina. Suddenly, the nightmarish vision of his wife's body flashed before his eyes — he saw her lying on the ground with her entrails hanging out. After that his mind went blank.

Sakina's mother was dead. She had been killed before his very eyes — but where was Sakina? Before closing her eyes for ever, Sakina's mother had urged him, "Don't worry about me — run, take Sakina away at once..."

Sakina was with him — both of them had run barefoot. Sakina's dupatta had slipped to the ground. She had screamed at him when he had tried to pick it up, "Let it be, Abba!" But he had picked it up. As soon as he remembered that, he put his hand in his coat pocket and pulled it out. He still had Sakina's dupatta...but where was Sakina?

Sirajuddin tried to think, but he couldn't. Had Sakina managed to reach the station with him? Had she boarded the train with him? Had he fainted when the rioters had attacked the train? Had they abducted her?

He could find no answers to any of his questions. Sirajuddin needed help and sympathy, but then everyone around him needed help and sympathy. He wanted to cry, but he could shed no tears. He had lost the capacity to moan.

A few days later, Sirajuddin pulled himself together and talked to some people who were willing to help him. They were eight young men who owned a truck and were armed with guns.

He showered them with his blessings, and described what Sakina looked like. "She is fair and very beautiful — takes after her mother, not me — She has large eyes, black hair and a big mole on her right cheek. She is my only daughter. If you bring her back, god will bless you."

Those self-appointed social workers reassured Sirajuddin, with a great deal of confidence and sincerity, that if his daughter was alive they would find her and bring her back in a few days.

The young men tried their best to find her. At the risk of their lives, they went to Amritsar. They managed to rescue many men, women and children and helped them locate their families. But even after ten days of searching, they couldn't find Sakina.

One day, as they were returning to Amritsar to help a few more refugees, they saw a girl standing at the roadside. The moment she heard the truck, she began to run.

The social workers stopped the truck and ran after her.

They caught her in a field — she was beautiful and had a large mole on her right cheek.

One of the young men said to her, "Don't be frightened. Is your name, Sakina?"

Her face became even paler. She didn't reply. The other young men reassured her, only then did she admit that she was indeed Sirajuddin's daughter.

The eight young men were very kind to Sakina. They fed her, offered her milk, helped her into the truck — she didn't have a dupatta and felt rather awkward. She tried to cover her breasts again and again with her hands.

Many days passed — Sirajuddin received no news about Sakina.

Each morning, he visited different camps and offices looking for Sakina. He failed to get any information about her. Each night, he prayed for the success of those young social workers, who had promised him that if his daughter was alive, they would bring her back to him in a few days.

One day, he saw the social workers in the camp. They were sitting in their truck.

The truck was about to leave. He ran upto them and asked one of them, "Son...Have you found my Sakina?"

"We'll find her, we'll find her," they said simultaneously, and drove off.

Sirajuddin again prayed for the success of the young men, and felt a little relieved.

That evening there was some commotion in the camp very near the place where Sirajuddin was sitting. Four people, walked past him, carrying someone.

When he inquired, he learnt that they had found a girl lying unconscious near the railway tracks and had brought her to the camp.

He followed them.

They handed the girl over to the hospital.

Sirajuddin stood leaning against a pole outside the hospital for sometime. Then he slowly walked into the hospital.

There was no one in the room. Only the body of a girl lay on the stretcher.

He walked up closer to the girl.

Someone suddenly switched on the lights.

He saw a big mole on the girl's face and screamed, "Sakina!"

The doctor, who had switched on the lights, asked, "What's the matter?"

He could barely whisper, "I am...I am her father."

The doctor turned towards the girl and took her pulse. Then he said, "Open the window."

The girl on the stretcher stirred a little.

She moved her hand painfully towards the cord holding up her salwar.

Slowly, she pulled her salwar down.

Her old father shouted with joy, "She is alive. My daughter is alive."

The doctor broke into a cold sweat.

Original in Urdu.
Translated by Alok Bhalla.

S.H. VATSAYAN 'AJNEYA'

THE REFUGE

"No, Devenderlalji, you cannot do that!" Lawyer Rafiquddin pleaded, but he also seemed worried and dejected. Once more, he said, "No, Devenderlalji, you cannot do that!"

Devenderlal acknowledged Rafiquddin's plea, but expressed his utter helplessness in the matter, "Everyone has left. I am not afraid of you, indeed you are my only support. But as you know, once fear grips people and they begin to run away, then the entire scenario changes completely. Each one begins to suspect the other; begins to regard the other, for no reason at all, as his enemy. You are respected in this mohalla, but how can one trust outsiders? Besides, you yourself have witnessed the kinds of incidents that are taking place..."

Rafiquddin interrupted him and said, "No, we'll lose face! How can you leave your own home and become a refugee in your own city? We will not let you go — we will force you to stay. It is the duty of the majority to protect the minority, and to make sure that they don't abandon their homes and run away. If we can't protect our neighbours, how can we possibly protect our country? I am sure that the Hindus in Punjab, where they are in the majority, must be thinking and acting in the same way. Please don't leave, don't! I'll take the responsibility of protecting you, I promise."

Devenderlal's Hindu neighbours had disappeared one by one. Whenever he had met some of them in the afternoon or evening, he had asked them, "So Lalaji (or Babuji or Punditji), what have you decided?" They had replied, "What is there to decide? We are still here, we'll see..." But by the evening or the next morning, Devenderlal would notice that they had taken a few of their belongings and had disappeared. Some had left Lahore, while the others had moved to Hindu localities in the city itself. Now the situation was such that the four houses to the right of his house were vacant, while the fifth, which was owned by a Muslim gujar, had buffaloes tied in one part while the other was occupied by ordinary Muslim craftsmen and workers. On the left, all the houses between Devender's and Rafiquddin's houses were unoccupied. Mozhung lay beyond Rafiquddin's house, and beyond it was a locality occupied only by the Muslims.

Devenderlal and Rafiquddin were very old friends and they discussed the departure of every family. Finally, when Devenderlal told him that he too was thinking of leaving, Rafiquddin was shocked and cried out in distress, "Devenderlalji, you too!"

Rafiquddin's assurances persuaded Devenderlal to stay on. It was decided that should, God forbid, Devenderlal be in any danger, Rafiquddin would not only warn him in advance but would also make the necessary arrangements for his safety. Devenderlal's wife had left a few days ago for her mother's house in Jullunder. He had written to her and had asked her not to return, but to stay on there. Only Devender and his pahari servant, Santu, were now left in Lahore.

But this arrangement did not last long. On the fourth day, Devenderlal discovered that Santu had fled. Devenderlal made himself some tea, and was going to wash the vessels when Rafiquddin came to inform him that there had been a massacre in the city, and that soon groups of killers would start out from Mozhung too. And that since there was no time to flee to any other place in the city, Devenderlal should pack some essential and valuable belongings and move to his house. He could return once the present troubles were over.

Devenderlal had nothing valuable in the house. His wife had taken all the jewellery with her and, besides the money in the bank, he didn't own much. Although to a householder everything in the house seems valuable, Devenderlal reached Rafiquddin's house with his baggage in an hour's time.

The mob reached Mozhung at around three in the afternoon. In the evening, Devenderlal watched his house being broken into and everything in it being looted. By nightfall the city was in flames, and the smoke made the humid night even more suffocating.

Rafiquddin watched everything in silence and with a sense of utter defeat. Only once did he mutter, "I was fated to see this day too — and that too in the name of freedom! Ya Allah!"

But when God throws one out of one's own house, then he doesn't even give one shelter in one's own lane.

Devenderlal, of course, couldn't leave the house, only Rafiquddin ventured into the city during that time. Since there was no possibility of doing any work, he merely wandered around, bought a few things and brought back the latest news for Devenderlal. Both of them would sit together for a long time and discuss the future of the country. Devenderlal didn't notice it at first, but he slowly began to realize that, in addition to a note of anxiety in Rafiquddin's voice, there was also a kind of pain which he couldn't precisely identify — Exhaustion? Sorrow? Detachment? Defeat? He wasn't sure...

The city was deserted. Dead bodies lay rotting here and there; the houses that had been looted, were now burning. Some respectable people of the city had requested a well-known doctor to visit the various mohallas; since everybody respected him, his word would surely carry weight and he would be allowed to visit the patients. He started out with two Muslim leaders. He visited two or three mohallas, before he reached a Muslim locality. He had barely taken out his stethoscope and bent over to examine a patient, when a relative of the patient stabbed him in the back...

A railway employee had given shelter to many people who had been rendered homeless and had lost everything. He had informed the police that he had given refuge to these homeless people, and had requested the police to protect their lives and property. The police arrested not only him and the refugees, but also the women of the house. In his absence, his house was looted and set on fire. His family and he were released after three days, and two armed guards were provided for their security. Fifty steps away from the police station, the armed guards suddenly opened fire on the family. The man and three women were killed. His mother and wife lay wounded on the street...

The atmosphere was vicious, horses of rage were whipped into murderous frenzy by hatred and envy, religious groups spread poison everywhere, and the flames of communal frenzy were fanned by the police and the bureaucracy! There were times when Devenderlal felt that Rafiquddin and he were the only ones who were still sane and normal, while everything around them was burning with rage, smouldering, crumbling and turning to ash...That strange note in Rafiquddin's voice which had puzzled him till now, slowly became clearer — it was a note which was at once rough and full of shame...

Nearer the proposed border of Hindustan and Pakistan, hundreds of Muslim refugees had found shelter in a Sikh village. But when the villagers in the neighbourhood and the people of Amritsar threatened them, the people of that Sikh village decided to escort their guests upto the Amritsar railway station, so that they could reach the safety of a Muslim locality. About two hundred and fifty villagers, armed with swords, formed a defensive cordon around them and escorted them to the station — no one was injured...

After narrating that episode, Rafiquddin said, "Each one of us is helpless. It's difficult to stand alone, eventually one has to give in. In this case even an entire village had to admit defeat. But they kept their word, till the end, one has to give them credit for that. They escorted the refugees to safety..."

Devenderlal looked questioningly at Rafiquddin, but didn't say anything.

Six or seven people came to see Rafiquddin one evening. He took them to the sitting room and shut all the doors. Their conversation lasted for about two hours. They spoke to each other in whispers, but once in a while a loud exclamation would escape them and would reach Devenderlal's ears — "stupidity," "betrayal," "Islam"...Devenderlal did not even try to figure out what they were saying. After two hours, when Rafiquddin came out of the sitting room, Devenderlal suppressed the natural urge to ask him questions. But when Rafiquddin tried to walk past him without saying a word and with his head lowered, he couldn't contain himself anymore, and asked in a plaintive voice, "What's the matter, Rafiq Sahib? Is everything all right?"

Rafiquddin looked up at him, but did not say anything. Then he lowered his eyes again.

Devenderlal said, "I understand. You have to put up with humiliation because of me. Apart from the risk. You should let me go now. Don't risk your life for me. I am grateful for all that you have done. I am indebted..."

Rafiquddin placed both his hands on Devenderlal's shoulders and said, "Devenderlalji!" He was nearly in tears. Suddenly, he turned away and went inside.

At dinner, Devenderlal once again asked him, "If you don't willingly give me permission to leave, I shall have to quietly slip away. Tell me the truth, what did they say to you?"

"They threatened me, what else?"

"Even then, what threat did..."

"What threat? Are there different kinds of threats? They want a victim — by shouting slogans if they can. Otherwise by setting fire."

"Really! Now I insist. I will leave. At present I am alone, I'll find my way. You have a family — and those people are determined to destroy everything."

"They are goondas!"

"I shall leave today..."

"How is that possible? After all, it was I who had insisted that you stay here; I have a responsibility towards you."

"You did so with the best of intentions — now you have no further obligations..."

"Where will you go..."

"I'll see..."

"No. This is impossible."

After an argument, it was decided that Devenderlal should leave. Rafiquddin would arrange for him to hide in the house of a Muslim friend in the neighbourhood — it would not be comfortable there, but it would be less dangerous. His life would be saved and they would have time to think about how to get him out.

Devenderlal reached the garage of Sheikh Ataullah which was behind his house and hidden from the main road by trees. There was a narrow and dark room next to the garage. It had a verandah which was surrounded by a wall. It must have been used by a driver once upon a time. The room had no other opening except the door into the garage and the front door which opened into the verandah. There was a cot on one side and a pot in one corner. The floor was made of clay. A small pit had been dug next to the gate. The purpose of that pit was obvious from the clay pot and the mixture of lime-powder and clay which lay in a heap next to it.

Devenderlal stood still like a statue for a while once his trunk and bedding had been put in a corner of the room and the front gate had been locked. Freedom! If earlier a foreign government had put our people behind bars because they wanted to be free, now, after independence, our own brothers imprison us because they want to save us from being killed! Soon, however, the human instinct for survival urged him to look around the garage, the room and the verandah and make himself comfortable.

The garage, he thought, was fine. It smelled a bit, but he could shut the door. There was no question of taking a bath — but there was enough water to wash his hands and face.

The room, he thought, was fine too. It was dark and there was no question of reading anything in it. But there was enough light that filtered in from the verandah for his ordinary tasks because there was a lamp at the corner of the Sheikh's house. In fact, if he stood on tiptoe in one particular corner of the verandah, he could perhaps manage to read something. But he had forgotten to bring a book with him to read!

Devenderlal took a step into the room and then hesitated. Another thought occurred to him and he stood still once more. One could sing and shout in a government prison, here one would have to be silent!

He remembered having read somewhere that prisoners sought to alleviate their loneliness by making friends with sparrows, pigeons, squirrels or cats; or by studying the behaviour of ants and spiders in their cells...He looked all around him once more. But he couldn't accept that one could make friends with mosquitoes!

He stood in the verandah and looked up at the sky. At the sky of an independent country! And rising from below, like a prayer — smoke from houses in flames! An offering of incense! A red chandan, a chandan of blood!

Suddenly he saw a shadow on the wall — a cat. He called to it, "Come, come," but it continued to stare at him with fixed eyes.

Where there is a cat, there can be no loneliness. Devenderlal went inside, spread out his bed and slept soundly for a while.

Food was sent to him only once in the evening. It was, however, enough for two meals. The pots in the garage and the room were filled with water at the same time. A young man used to bring the food. He was not a servant; Devenderlal's guess was that he was Sheikh Sahib's son. The young man never uttered a word. When Devenderlal had asked him on the first day about the conditions in the city, the young man had looked at him strangely. When Devenderlal had asked him again if the city was peaceful, he had merely shaken his head to indicate that it wasn't. "Is everything all right at home?" The youth had nodded.

Devenderlal would have put enough food by for a second meal, but he decided that, since food came only once a day, he would also eat only once. He ate a heavy meal at one sitting and gave the remaining food to the cat. The cat had become very friendly. It would sit in his lap and eat the food. Then it would take a bone or two into the corner of the courtyard and chew it. Sometimes, it would sit next to him and purr.

That is how he spent the evenings, till it grew dark. He would, then, go to sleep. In the morning, he would do some exercises in the courtyard in order to remain physically fit and spend the rest of the day either playing with small pebbles, or watching the sparrows sitting on the wall or listening to the pigeons cooing somewhere far away. At times, he could hear bits of conversation from Sheikhji's house. He had begun to identify the different voices and, within the first few days, was acquainted with the life of the members of the household. The woman with the loud voice, was probably Sheikh Sahib's wife; the woman with a voice which had a shrillness and a roughness which comes with age, was some old woman who lived in the house; the woman with a youthful and modest voice, who always replied when the first voice called, "Zaibu! Ni Zaibu," could only be Sheikh Sahib's daughter. He often heard two male voices also — one was that of Abid Miyan, who was Sheikh Sahib's son and brought him food; the other voice, which was heavy and slimy like lard, was that of Sheikh Sahib himself. Devenderlal could hear Sheikh Sahib's voice, but could never decipher the words — only a shrill voice can be clearly heard from a distance.

Devenderlal liked and trusted Zaibu's voice. Not because it was the voice of a young girl, but because it was modest and gentle. Sometimes, he rebuked himself for being a hopeless romantic, who found the youthful voice of a woman attractive, and wondered if Zaibunissa's voice too spread the poison of hatred amongst the people. Was that possible, he wondered?

Sheikh Sahib was, perhaps, the head clerk in a police department. When Rafiquddin had brought him here he had said that a policeman's house would be safest; there was some truth in that, but precisely because it was the safest, it was also the cause of a lot of problems. He wasn't surprised that people in such a household also spouted venom.

When he ate his food, he wondered who had cooked it, which hand had served it. From the conversations he had overheard, he had gathered that most of the cooking was done by that old woman with a shrill and rough voice, but that it was served by Zaibunissa. That thought always made him eat more than he should have...

One day, the monotonous routine of Devenderlal's life was suddenly broken when, instead of the usual large Muslim rotis, he was served small Hindu phulkas. In addition to meat, there was also rabbadi, instead of shahi-tukra which he had been served sometimes, or phirni which had been sent to him once. Devenderlal stared at the food for a while after Abid had served it and left. His fingers toyed with the phulkas — he picked up one and then put it back. For a fleeting instant, the vision of his own house flashed before his eyes. Once again, he picked up a phulka, and dropped it back on the plate.

Suddenly he was startled!

There was a piece of crumpled paper hidden in the folds of one of the phulkas.

Devenderlal opened it.

There was nothing on it.

He was about to roll it up once again and throw it away, when he stopped. He went out into the courtyard, stood tiptoe to see more clearly in the faint light and looked at the paper. There was a sentence scribbled on it: "Feed the dog, before eating the food yourself."

Devenderlal tore the paper into small bits and crumpled them in his hand. Went back into the garage and buried them in a hole. Then he returned to the courtyard and began pacing up and down.

He didn't know how to react. He was much too disturbed to think. Only one name kept running through his mind, Zaibu...Zaibu...Zaibu...

After sometime he went and stood next to the plate of food.

That food was meant for him — for Devenderlal. It had not come from his friend's house, but it had come from the house of his friend's friend. From the house of his host, of his protector.

From Zaibu's house.

From Zaibu's father's house.

Is there a dog here?

Devenderlal began to pace up and down again.

A shadow moved across the wall of the courtyard. The cat sat on the wall.

Devenderlal called out to it. The cat jumped down onto his shoulder. Devenderlal took it onto his lap and began to caress it. The cat started purring. Devenderlal went into his room. He caressed the cat for some more time and, then said, "Listen son, you are my guest, just as I am Sheikh Sahib's guest, isn't that so? What he wants to do to me, I want to do to you. I don't want to, but I am going to do it. Whether he too wants to do it to me or no, is what I want to know. That is why I am going to do to you what he wants to...No, all this is confusing. All right, you eat the leftovers everyday, today I'll eat what you leave. Yes, that is right. Here, eat this..."

The cat ate the meat. It wanted to grab the bone, but Devenderlal took it in his lap and fed it the rabbadi. The cat lapped it up. Devenderlal kept stroking it as it lay in his lap.

Animals instinctively know what they should or should not eat. How would they survive otherwise? All animals have this instinctive sense, and the cat has it more than most animals, that is why, unlike a dog, it cannot be tamed. What the cat eats can be eaten by everyone — though it's another matter that the cat eats rotten fish, while human beings do not.

Suddenly the cat snarled furiously and leapt out of his lap. It screamed, as if in pain, and jumped on to the wall and then climbed upto the terrace of the garage. He heard it snarling and spitting at its own shadow for sometime. After a while it writhed in pain, whimpered pathetically, shrieked without much energy, groaned, let out a long sigh, and finally, gasped for breath and died.

Devenderlal stared at the food again. He couldn't see anything clearly, but he stood motionlessly with his eyes fixed on the plate.

Azadi! Brotherhood! Country! Nation...

One had told him that he would force him to stay back, but had turned him out of his house. The other had not only offered him shelter, but had also given him poison.

And a warning as well, that he was being poisoned!

Devenderlal couldn't help but reproach himself. This shocking incident couldn't be understood in terms of the shifting sands of politics, but could only be endured philosophically.

Devenderlal realized that the real danger in the world lay not in the strength of evil, but in the weakness of good. The lack of courage of those who are good, is the greatest evil. Dark clouds are not responsible for the night. Night falls when the sun declines.

He picked up the food and left it out in the verandah. Took two sips of water and started pacing up and down again.

After a few moments, he went inside and opened his trunk. Glancing at everything in it, he picked up a few papers, two photographs, a bank pass-book and a large envelope. He slipped them into the pocket of his black sherwani. He went out into the verandah again and stood listening for some sound.

Then, he jumped over the wall, and down onto the road outside — he didn't quite know how he managed to do that.

What happened after that doesn't need to be recounted. There were other incidents that happened to him, but like everything else in life they were inconclusive. Only stories have conclusions. A story is crafted by human logic, or commonsense, or skill, or a sense of beauty, that is why human beings recognize it as fiction and take pleasure in it. But incidents in real life depend on some power other than that of human reason — perhaps, on fate, or nature, or coincidence, or the supernatural or God. Perhaps, that is why human beings cannot comprehend them at once. That is also why it is not necessary to describe what happened to Devenderlal after his escape. It should suffice to say that about a month and a half later, when Devenderlal made an appeal to his family over the radio from Delhi and announced his address, he received a brief letter from Lahore.

"I cannot but praise God a thousand fold for having helped you to escape. I hope that you are once again united with the people to whom you appealed over the radio. I want to ask your forgiveness for what my father did or tried to do. It was I who foiled his plans. You don't owe me a favour — my only request is that, if you come across someone in your country who is in a similar situation, don't forget this incident. I make this request, not because that person may be a Muslim, but because you are a human being! Khuda hafiz!"

Sheikh Ataullah's heavy and slimy voice echoed in Devenderlal's mind. Zaibu! Zaibu and then the cat on the roof of the garage, who had writhed in pain and had let out a long moan before it had died.

He crumpled the letter into a small ball and flicked it aside.

Original in Hindi.
Translated by Rachna Sharma and Alok Bhalla.

INTIZAR HUSAIN

THE CITY OF SORROW

When he heard that, the First Man said, "I have nothing to say. I am dead."

Startled, the Third Man turned to look at the First Man in surprise and fear.

The Second Man, however, didn't react at all. In a disinterested voice, he asked, "How did you die?"

The First Man replied, in a matter of fact way, "She was a dark girl. Her hair was long and reached down to her waist. She had a red bindi on her forehead. There was a dark, young man with her. I asked the young man — Is she related to you? He replied — She is my sister. I said — Strip her naked. When the girl heard that, she turned pale and began to tremble like a willow tree. The young man pleaded with me — Please don't ask me to do that. I was insistent. I pulled my sword out of the scabbard and yelled — Strip her naked. When the young man saw the naked sword in my hand, he shuddered with fear. Slowly, with great effort and with shaking hands, he reached for his sister's saree. The girl screamed and covered her face with her hands. And, before my very eyes, those trembling hands..."

"Before your eyes? Really?" asked the Third Man with surprise.

The Second Man continued to sit unmoved by what he had heard. In an emotionless voice, he asked, "Was it then that you died?"

"No, I remained alive," the First Man replied blandly.

"You remained alive! Really!" the Third Man exclaimed in astonishment.

"Yes, that's what I said. I saw all that and remained alive. I lived to see that young man repeat what I had done. He caught a woman in a burqa who was running away in fear. The old man with her pleaded — O young man, have pity on us. Do not ruin our reputation. The young man's eyes burned red with rage as he shouted — Is she related to you? The old man replied — Son, she is my wife. Grinding his teeth together, the young man ordered — Old man, strip her naked. When the old man heard that, he went pale with fear and stared with wide eyes at the young man. Intoxicated with rage, the young man grabbed the old man by his neck and screamed — Old man, strip your wife naked. He said that and I..."

"Died," the Third Man completed the sentence in anticipation.

"No. I remained alive."

"You remained alive! Really!"

"Yes, I remained alive. I heard all that, I saw all that and I remained alive. Afraid that the young man would recognize me, I hid my face and ran away. But I was finally trapped by a crowd. I was about to pull out my sword and throw it away, when a man forced his way through the crowd and stood before me. He looked into my eyes and said — Don't throw down your sword. That's against the laws of valour. I hesitated and looked back at the man. He continued to stare at me. I lowered my eyes. Feeling utterly defeated, I said — There is no other solution. I must live. As soon as I said that, the man's eyes began to smoulder with rage. He spat on my face with contempt and turned away. Suddenly, a sword flashed above his head. He spun around and fell on the ground. His body lay drenched in blood. I washed my face in his hot blood and..."

"Died," the Third Man said, anxious to complete his sentence once again.

"No. I remained alive. I put my sword away, and I remained alive. Suddenly, that young man reappeared from nowhere. When he saw me, he stopped. He walked upto me and glared at me. Then he growled — Aren't you the same man? After some hesitation, I said — Yes, I am the same man. As soon as I said that, the young man turned around and disappeared into the crowd. I stood where I was. A few moments later, the young man came back. He was dragging a young girl with him. He pushed her before me. When I finally recognized her face, which was covered with grime and dust, and was hidden behind her wild hair, I was stunned. The girl looked at me and wept bitterly. I was utterly shattered. The young man asked me venomously — Is she related to you? I hesitated and then replied — She is my daughter. The young man said quietly — Strip her naked. That innocent and helpless girl began to tremble with fear. I fainted and..."

"Died," the Third Man added with anxiety in his voice.

"No," the First Man said and paused. After a while, he said in a whisper, "I remained alive."

"Remained alive! Even after that? Really!" the Third Man asked in amazement.

"Yes, even after that. I said all that, I heard all that, I saw all that and committed all those acts and remained alive...Ashamed of myself, I slunk away from there. I hid in the shadows of houses, ran across streets in fear and finally reached the neighbourhood where I lived. Terror had gripped the street. There was still some light, though darkness had begun to creep over everything. The street, which was normally full of hustle and bustle in the evening, was silent and empty. The street dog, who was watching over it, growled when he saw me. That was strange. In the past, he had always wagged his tail and greeted me affectionately when he saw me coming. That day there was hostility and fear in his eyes, and his hair stood on end. He snarled at me and backed away as if I were an alien creature. A wave of fear swept over my body. Carefully, I edged past the dog and managed to reach the door of my house. The door was bolted from the inside. I knocked at it softly. No one answered. It seemed as if there was no one on the other side. I was surprised. I knocked again a bit more loudly. There was still no sound from within. A cat, which was walking across the low wall of the house next door, stopped when it saw me. It looked at me strangely, as if I were an enemy, and then quickly slunk away.

I knocked at the door again and called out — Open the door. A woman's voice asked cautiously from inside — Who is it? That was my wife's voice. I was surprised that she hadn't recognized my voice that day. Confidently, I replied — It's me. Slowly and carefully, she opened the door, watched me nervously and said — You? I was crushed. I replied — Yes, it's really me. I walked in. There was an eerie silence in the house. It was dark inside and outside. Only a small, dim lamp was burning in the verandah. A prayer mat was spread on the floor. My father was sitting on it and silently telling his beads. My wife whispered anxiously — I thought my daughter had returned. I was shocked. I looked at her to see if she had already received the news about our daughter. She stared at me. It seemed as if her eyes were glued on my face. Trying to get away from those eyes, I walked into the verandah and knelt beside the prayer mat. My father picked up the lamp and gazed at my face for a long time — You? he asked. I replied — Yes, it's me. My father continued to study my face in the dim light of that lamp. Then, with disbelief in his voice, he muttered — No. I said — It's really me, father. I am alive. My father didn't say anything for a while. He shut his eyes and said — If you are alive, I must be dead. The old man took a deep breath and died.

My wife walked upto me and said viciously — You...your father is dead, your daughter has been raped and dishonoured...you are dead. At that moment, I realized I had died."

The First Man fell silent. The Second Man stared at his blank face and vacant eyes for a long time. Then he declared dryly, "What he says is true. He is dead."

By then the Third Man was even more bewildered than before. He, too, looked at the First Man and, then, unexpectedly asked, "Where is your father's corpse?"

"My father's corpse?" the First Man was taken aback by the question. He paused, and then replied, "I left it behind."

"Why didn't you bring it with you?"

"How could I have carried two corpses? You don't know how difficult it was for me to carry my own corpse."

The Second Man, who had till then listened to everything and spoken in a detached and dispassionate manner, suddenly sat up with a start and said, "O, I had almost forgotten. My corpse was left behind."

"Your corpse!" exclaimed the Third Man, who had been curiously inspecting the face of the First Man. Then he turned to look at the Second Man in disbelief.

"Yes, my corpse," the Second Man replied and began to mumble, "I should have brought my corpse with me. Who knows how they will treat it."

"Are you dead too?" the Third Man asked.

"Really!" the Third Man looked at him in wonder. "How did you die?"

"How can a dead man tell you how or why he died? I simply died," said the Second Man and fell silent. After sometime, he began talking once more in his toneless voice, "The doom which had been hanging over others, finally reached the ruined city too. I walked about stealthily. I knew that our fate would not be different from theirs.

Passing through a bazaar, I suddenly caught sight of a dark girl, and stopped. Her saree, which was in tatters, couldn't cover her nakedness. The bindi on her forehead was smudged. Her hair was wild and her face was covered with dust. She was a very slim woman, but her stomach was big. There was terror in her eyes. I watched her apprehensively. When she saw me, she stopped. She was the same girl whom I had...She too recognized me. She covered her face and screamed — No, no! She fled in terror. My blood froze. I was sure she would have me arrested. Hiding my face, I ran. I ran for a long time. Sometimes I hid in one neighbourhood, sometimes in another. Each street I ran through was a blind alley, every neighbourhood I took shelter in was a trap. I couldn't find a way out of the city of ruins.

After a long time, I came to a strange town. Dead bodies lay scattered everywhere. There wasn't a single living human being in sight. Surprised and bewildered, I went from one neighbourhood to another, from one lane to another. The bazaars were shut, the roads were desolate, the houses seemed empty. Occasionally, some window on the upper floor of a house would open cautiously to reveal two frightened eyes, and then would shut at once.

I didn't know what to think of that strange town. It was inhabited, but the people who lived in it seemed to be imprisoned in their own houses.

Finally, I came to an open field. A large crowd was gathered there. The children were crying with hunger, the lips of the adults were chapped, the breasts of the mothers were dry; fresh faces had withered, fair women were covered with dust.

When I reached the crowd, I asked — Tell me, O people, what city is this? What calamity has befallen it? Why have the houses become prisons? Why does dust blow through the streets?

They answered — O unfortunate man, this is the city of sorrow. We are the doomed ones whose life has been destroyed. Now we sit here waiting for death.

When I heard that, I looked into their faces. Each forehead was marked with woe. Each face was under the shadow of death. Still curious, I asked them — Tell me truthfully, O people, are you not the ones who came here from far off places to build your homes in the city of peace?

They answered — Yes, you have recognized us. Now our homes lie in ruins.

I said — O people, your homes lie in ruins now, but tell me, what was the city of peace like before?

They replied — We swear by God, we had to endure the injustices of our own people.

I laughed when I heard them say that. They were shocked when they saw me laugh. I laughed louder. They were even more shocked. I laughed still louder. They were horrified. I continued to laugh uproariously. They were utterly bewildered.

Soon, the news spread through the town, that a strange man had arrived in the city of sorrow and that he was laughing.

— Even on a day like this?

— Yes, even on a day like this.

People were amazed and terrified. They gathered around me. At first they were afraid and watched me laugh from a distance. Then they gathered courage, and came and stood close to me. Soon they began to talk to each other in whispers.

— This man is really laughing.

— Who is this mad man?

— Where has he come from?

— God knows.

— He is not their spy, is he?

— Maybe.

They looked at each other apprehensively.

Then I said — Listen people, I am not one of them.

— Then where are you from?

— Where am I from? I stood lost in thought for a while.

At that moment, an old man stepped out of the crowd and addressed me — If you are not one of them, you should weep.

— For whom? I asked.

— For the descendents of Israel.

— Why?

— Because what happened to them in the past, is happening again. What happened once, will happen again.

When I heard that, I stopped laughing. Concerned, I said — Old man, have you noticed that the earth never accepts those who leave their homeland?

— I have learnt that from experience, I have seen that with my own eyes. The earth does not forgive.

— Even the land where one was born?

— Yes, even the land where one was born. Even the land which promises peace and shelter. I was born in a place called Gaya. The mendicant of Gaya learnt that there is only suffering in this world, that nirvana is not possible here, and that the earth cannot be trusted.

— And the sky.

— Everything under the sky is an illusion.

Unconvinced, I replied — I must think about that.

— Even thinking is an illusion.

— But thought is man's real wealth.

The old man retorted — Even man is an illusion.

— What, then, is the truth? I asked wearily.

— Truth? What is that?

— Truth, I said confidently, is the Truth!

With great simplicity, he replied — What you call Truth is also an illusion.

When I heard that, I said to myself — This old man is under the shadow of death and this city is on its way towards extinction.

I left those people to their fate and escaped. I wanted to live.

Soon I reached another strange place. There the crowd was continuously swelling. People were playing drums of victory.

I asked — O people, what place is this? What age am I in?

Someone whispered in my ear — This is the age of decadence, and in this place everyone is taught a lesson.

— And who is that man on whose face someone has just spat?

That man looked at me bitterly and asked — Don't you recognize him?

— No.

— O disfigured one, you are that man.

— Me? I was shocked into silence.

— Yes, you.

When I looked at the face of that man carefully, my eyes opened wide with surprise. I was really that man. I recognized myself and died."

The Third Man said, "After recognizing one's real self, it is difficult to live."

The First Man turned towards the Second Man and said, "O, so you were the man on whose face someone spat?"

"Yes, I was that man."

"I thought, I was the one who was spat upon," the First Man said.

"You?"

"Yes, I was under that impression. Anyway, I now know that I was under some delusion. It wasn't I who was spat upon, but you," the First Man said with a sense of relief in his voice. Soon, however, he began to feel uncomfortable once more. The thought that someone may have spat upon his face made him wince with pain. When he spoke again, his voice was no longer as casual as it had been earlier. He turned to the Second Man and said, "You are mistaken. I am sure, I was the one who was spat upon."

The Second Man said, in his usual expressionless voice, "I looked very carefully at the face of the man who had been spat upon. His face was exactly like mine."

The First Man studied the Second Man carefully from head to toe. Suddenly, an idea occurred to him and he said, "Is it...is it possible...that you are me?"

"I am you! No, that is not possible. I know myself. I am not under any delusion."

"How can you say that you know yourself?" the First Man asked.

The Second Man answered, "I know myself because someone spat on my face."

"But that is how I know myself too," the First Man said. "That is why I suspect that you are me."

"How is it possible that every face which has been spat upon is your face?"

"True. It is, however, possible that your face is not your face, but mine," the First Man said.

Now the Second Man was really confused. He looked suspiciously at the First Man. Both looked at each other apprehensively and asked each other a variety of questions. Finally, the Second Man admitted defeat and said, "We are dead. How can we possibly recognize each other?"

The First Man answered, "Did we recognize each other when we were alive?"

The Second Man didn't know how to respond. At that moment, the Third Man came up with an unusual proposition. He asked, "Which of you has brought his corpse with him?"

The First Man replied, "I have brought it with me."

The Third Man then suggested, "Why do you argue in the abstract? There is no point in firing salvos in the air. Go and look at the corpse. That should help you distinguish truth from falsehood."

Both the contestants accepted the proposal. The three of them went to look at the corpse. When the Third Man, however, saw the corpse, he was shocked. He exclaimed, "Its face is disfigured. It is beyond recognition now."

The Second Man said, "If the face of the corpse is disfigured, then it is certainly mine."

"But my face too was disfigured," the First Man said.

"When was your face disfigured?"

"My face was disfigured when I forced the young man to strip his sister naked," the First Man replied.

The other two stared at him. Simultaneously, they asked, "And you continued to live even though your face had been disfigured?"

"Yes, I continued to live even though my face had been disfigured. I did so till the moment my father saw me and closed his eyes. Then I died."

That reminded the Second Man of his own father. "My father too died after seeing me. I went to him for comfort. I appealed to him and said — O father, your son died today. My father looked at my disfigured face and said — It is good that you died before you came to see me. If you had come to me when you were still alive, I would have cursed you to suffer life till doomsday. Those were the last words he uttered. Immediately afterwards, he died."

The First Man said, "Our fathers were more worthy of respect than their sons. And how did we treat them? I brought my corpse with my disfigured face here, and left my father's corpse behind."

Startled, the Second Man said, "I didn't think of it in that way either. I, too, left my father's corpse behind."

The Third Man laughed bitterly and said, "During the first migration, we left the graves of our ancestors behind. This time we left their corpses behind." He stopped laughing and grew sorrowful. Memories of the first migration rose before him. In the dim light of the past, he saw a number of faces. A stream of bright faces. He saw the stream swell in his imagination. Faces, which he would never see again, flowed before his eyes. Then he thought of the second migration, and the same...

In disbelief, he said to himself, "I don't know whether I migrated or not, but a vast number of bright faces have once again vanished from my sight. How many bright faces had vanished from my sight in the past. How many bright faces have vanished from my sight again." Then he thought of the sadness which had cast its shadow over those bright faces in the past; he recognized the same sadness that had cast its shadow over the faces this time.

Sadly, he turned to the First Man and the Second Man, and said, "What I had said earlier was not true. The same thing happened during both the migrations — each time we left with our faces disfigured, and each time we left bright faces behind."

The Second Man continued to stare into blank space for sometime and then suddenly stood up. As he was about to leave, the other two asked him, "Where are you going?"

He replied, "I should at least bring my father's corpse here."

"You can no longer bring corpses from there."

"Why not?"

"Because all the roads are closed."

"Really? Does that mean that my father's corpse will remain there?"

"What will you do with your father's corpse here?" the First Man asked. "Look at me. I brought my own corpse here. Now I carry it around with me on my shoulder."

"Why don't you bury it?" the Third Man asked.

"Where can I bury it? Is there any place left here for me to bury it?"

"You mean, there isn't any place left for burial?" the Second Man asked.

"No. There is a lot of burial ground. But far too many graves have been dug already. There is no place left for more graves."

When he heard that, the Third Man wept. The other two looked at him in disbelief, and asked, "Why are you crying?"

"I am crying because I have yet to die and there is no place left here for new graves. Where will I be buried?"

"Aren't you dead already?" the other two asked, as they looked at him carefully.

"No, I am still alive."

The other two stared at him in surprise. "Do you want to continue to live? Are you sure you are still alive?"

"Yes, I am alive, but..."

"But?" the other two asked him.

"But I have disappeared."

"Disappeared?"

"Yes, disappeared. Do you know that in this calamity many people have disappeared?"

"Do you also know," the First Man added, "that many of those who have disappeared, have been killed?"

"I know, but I am not amongst those who have been butchered."

"Many died the way we died."

"I am also not amongst those who died like you."

"How do you know that you are one of those who disappeared?"

"The truth is that in the city of ruins it is impossible to find those who are still alive. But the corpses of those who have been slaughtered are found everyday. If I had been killed, my corpse would have been found by now."

"If you are not dead, you should be amongst those who were captured. And if you are amongst the captured, you have completed the circle."

The Third Man was puzzled. He asked, "Completed the circle? What do you mean?"

"I mean that after wandering from one place to another, you have returned to the city you once left. A similar thing happened to a companion of mine. He was captured and taken to the place where he had been born. While he was contemplating escape from there, his friend asked him — Why do you want to run away from here? What does this soil say to you?

That man wept and said — When I look out of this prison window, I see fields of mustard sway in the wind before me. They are now in bloom because basant is near. The conjunction of my captivity and my place of birth have created a crisis. It will be calamitous if basant too arrives.

Basant, the place of birth and captivity...No, the three of them should never come together at the same time. They are painful. That man escaped from captivity and disappeared."

"Disappeared?" the Third Man asked with a start. "Are you sure that I wasn't that man? It is possible. When mustard fields bloom in my place they create a crisis in me too."

"No, you are not that man."

"Basant, the place of birth and captivity..." The Third Man mumbled and fell into deep thought. After a long time, he said, "No, that man couldn't have been me. I wasn't ever captured."

The First Man said, "Isn't it strange to go back to the place of one's birth as a captive?"

The Third Man frowned and said, "Yes, it is strange indeed. My grandmother used to narrate stories about the Mutiny. She used to tell me how many people had been killed during that uprising. They left their homes and never went back. There was a woman who fought the British valiantly. When her home was ruined, she left her fragrant city and disappeared into the forests of Nepal. For years she wandered from forest to forest like the vagabond breeze, and then she vanished." He paused, took a deep breath and continued, "Instead of getting lost in the cities of torment, it is better for a man to disappear into some dark and dense forest."

He stopped talking. Something reminded him of the first migration. Lost in thought, he sat quietly for a long time. Then he sighed, and said in a voice full of regret, "Alas, if only my hijrat had been in the forests of Nepal."

The First Man, Second Man and Third Man were now silent. Silent and still. It seemed as if they had lost all interest in talking or moving. Time passed. They continued to sit silently and without moving. At last, after a very long time, the Third Man felt a little uncomfortable. He looked at the First Man and then at the Second Man. They were sitting like stones and staring blankly into the empty space. He wondered if he too had turned into stone. To convince himself that he hadn't turned into stone, he deliberately raised his arms and yawned loudly. Reassured, he said to himself, "I am alive." Then he turned towards the other two and asked, "Should we leave?" He wanted to announce to them that he was really alive.

The other two didn't respond for sometime. Then they slowly turned their eyes away from the empty space ahead and looked at the Third Man. Disinterestedly they asked, "Where should we go? There is no place for us to go to now. We are dead."

Terrified, the Third Man looked at their disfigured faces and at their eyes which had neither light nor life. He said to himself, "I should leave before I too turn into stone." He sat lost in thought for a long time. Then he took courage and stood up. The other two watched him make an effort to leave, and asked in a voice which had neither curiosity nor emotion, "Where will you go?"

He replied, "I'll go and find out where I am." He paused, and after some thought, asked, "I am not amongst the captives, am I? Have I been taken back there?"

"Where?" the First Man asked.

It appeared, however, that he hadn't heard the First Man. Staring at the Second Man, he asked, "Are you sure that he had escaped from prison?"

"Yes, he saw the mustard fields in bloom and escaped from the prison of his city."

"Are you sure, I wasn't that man?"

"No, I am not," the Second Man said, and looked at the Third Man carefully. That was the first time that the Second Man had gazed at the Third Man with such attentiveness. With a start, he asked, "Were you not in the city of sorrow."

"Yes, you do recognize me. I was in the city of sorrow."

"It took me some time to recognize you, because your face has been disfigured. But when you were in the city of sorrow, and were sitting with those who were waiting for death, your face wasn't mutilated. When and how did it get disfigured?"

Ashamed, the Third Man replied after some hesitation, "My face was disfigured when I turned my back on those people."

"It is strange that you managed to escape. All the roads to the city of sorrow were closed. Weren't you caught?"

"How could I have been caught? Who could have recognized me? My face had been so disfigured that it was unrecognizable."

"That means, your disfigured face was your salvation."

The Second Man interrupted him and said, "Don't delude yourself. If he is still hiding there, he'll be caught either today or tomorrow."

"I am worried about that too. That is why I want to go and find out where I am."

"Even if you find out where you are, what difference will it make?" the Second Man asked.

"I'll try to find a way of escape."

"Escape?" the Second Man looked at him with astonishment. "You have disappeared. Don't you know that all the escape routes are closed?"

"That is true. But how long can I remain amongst those who have disappeared. I must find out where I am. Besides, who knows, I may be able to find a way out."

"You are a simpleton. Where will you go?"

"Where? I'll come here. After all, those who had escaped earlier had come here too."

The First Man looked at him and said, "Here? There is no place here. Didn't I tell you that my corpse is lying without a grave?"

The Second Man looked at the other two and said, "Listen, you men with disfigured faces, didn't I tell you about the man from Gaya? The earth is a place of suffering. Everything under the sky is an illusion. Those who have been uprooted, can never find a place where they can flourish again."

The Third Man was overcome with despair. The Second Man continued to stare at the Third Man for such a long time that he felt he had turned into stone.

After sometime, he said, "Listen, you who have disappeared. Sit down. Don't ask where you are. Realize that you are dead."

Original in Urdu.
Translated by Vishwamitter Adil
and Alok Bhalla.

ATTIA HOSAIN

AFTER THE STORM

The flowers were awkwardly crowded into the small-necked bottle. Its paper label had not been successfully washed away and had triumphantly survived in its scratched mutilation.

On and around the bottle there was dust. There was a film of dust on everything. It crept up with the hot wind that found its way into the room inspite of shut doors and windows. Green paper on glass panes shut out the glare that burned away colour from earth and sky and the sensual delight of vision from the eyes.

The heavy sweet scent of the flowers reached out into the skin-drying air with a cooling touch. The flowers were white and wax-petaled among thick deep green leaves. Their buds were tightly wrapped in slender pale green sepals. They were allies in the battle against the cruel summer — lying cool on hot pillows — around earthenware water pots — strung in garlands sold in scented streets by singing men — adorning women when gold and silver grew heavy with heat and sweat.

This summer the battle was lost before it began. The desolation it brought was the visible expression of desolate hearts. The tainted wind blew hot from blazing homes, and carried the dust of devastated fields, and the dead...

She tore me out of the shroud of my thoughts, a child small and thin, with serious anxious eyes and a smile on her face, a garland in her hand. She looked at the bottle and the flowers.

"Do you like them? I put them there. This is for you too." I bent my head and she slipped the garland over with a faint smile and stepped back.

"I knew you were coming today and I cleaned your room."

"Who are you?"

"Your servant. I've been put in charge of this part of the house," she said with proud responsibility.

"What is your name?"

"Bibi."

"How long have you been here?"

"A long time. Just before I left home there was the fair at Shahji's tomb." She sounded uninterested, then said brightly: "Do you need anything? The others are all sleeping. You rest and then I shall bring you some tea. I have put cold water for your bath in the buckets."

"Weren't the buckets heavy?"

"Oh no — I always brought water from the well."

I could not tell her age. Her assured manner made me feel younger than herself. Her eyes had no memories of a childhood. Her body was of a child of nine or ten, but its undernourished thinness was deceptive; she could have been eleven or twelve. There was no telling how many years of childhood, life had robbed her of.

She came every morning with flowers no one else cared to pick, and every evening with garlands no one else cared to thread.

"Aren't they pretty? In my home we had two big bushes near the well. I made garlands for my mother and aunt."

The nails of her peasant hands were worn with work. By now I knew her story, but knew she had to tell it herself how and when she willed.

"Had you any brothers and sisters?"

"After my sister was married, she went to live far away; a whole day's journey by bullock cart. My brother was older than me. He could read and write. He was clever. You will teach me, won't you?"

She kept her clothes very clean — old discarded clothes which were cut down for her and hung loosely on her. She wore tight pyjamas that were easier to clean than loose ones, and she kept her head covered like the older women, with a 'dupatta' that was made from a torn cotton sari. She used to dye them herself and was fond of bright colours. Her hair was combed back smoothly from a centre part, oiled and plaited with a rag. The pigtail was short and stood out stiffly. She was not a pretty child, and one would not have noticed her. But she was now a symbol and around her hovered the ghosts of all one feared.

Sometimes she threaded buds into the pierced lobes of her ears.

"I had gold earrings," she said proudly, but with no reproach. "My mother said after the next harvest she would buy me gold bangles."

"When we had feasts, I was sorry I had no bangles."

I had bought her glass ones.

When she brought me tea she said, "Do you like these English cakes? My mother made such lovely halwa — you would have loved it."

"Do you remember your father?"

"He died long ago. We lived with my uncle and aunt. He kept labourers to help in the fields."

One day she suddenly put her head on my lap — "I like you. Will you always keep me with you?"

Then I asked her, "Bibi — how did you come here?"

I wanted to lay my ghosts of imagined horror, and hear her tell me what actually happened.

"The police brought me. I was at the railway station. Then they took me to a place where there were lots of women and children. I ran away from them."

"Why?"

"I don't know. I got up at night and ran away. Then I came here."

"Who brought you?"

"The police."

Her mind refused to fill the gap between the refugee camp and her adoption.

"What happened to your mother?"

Her voice was self-detached — a child telling a fairy story. "I don't know. I was with Chand Bibi. I had gone to visit her."

"Who was she?"

"Oh, she was brave. She had a big house where I played. She fought and fought and killed so many of them — then her arm was cut off."

"Where was your mother?"

"At home. They said the house was full of blood. They said Chand Bibi kept on fighting until her arm was cut off."

"Who said?"

"Some people — I ran into the fields and a man said 'Come this way,' and he carried me, we hid in the sugar-cane — then he put me on a train, and I came here. See how long this garland is. You can put it twice round your neck."

In the bottle she had put fresh flowers.

IBNE INSHA

OUR COUNTRY

"Who lives in Iran?"

"The Iranians live in Iran."

"Who lives in England?"

"The English live in England."

"Who lives in France?"

"The French live in France."

"What country is this?"

"This is Pakistan."

"The Pakistanis live here, don't they?"

"No, the Pakistanis don't live here. The Sindhis live here. The Punjabis live here. The Bengalis live here. This community lives here. That community lives here."

"But the Punjabis also live in Hindustan. The Sindhis also live in Hindustan. Why was another country created?"

"Sorry, it was a mistake. We shall never repeat it again."

Original in Urdu.
Translated by Alok Bhalla.

IBNE INSHA

PAKISTAN

Geographical Map : CEATO lies to the east of Pakistan, CENTO to the west; Tashkand lies to the north, and the sea to the south. Does that mean one can't run away from the country?

Pakistan is divided into two parts — East and West Pakistan. They are separated from each other by a great distance. How great that distance is, we have begun to realize only today. Both have their own boundaries.

Punjab lies to the north of West Pakistan, Sindh lies to the south, India to the east and Baluchistan to the west. Miyan, what about Pakistan itself? Is it located anywhere? — These days, research is being done on that very question.

East Pakistan is surrounded on all sides by East Pakistan!

Original in Urdu.
Translated by Alok Bhalla.

SURAIYA QASIM

WHERE DID SHE BELONG?

Munni Bai was her name. Was it the name given to her at her birth? She did not know. Indeed, she did not know if she had a name given to her when she was born. She only hoped that she had one. After all, her parents could not have carried her about all the time without a name.

But her parents! Who were they? She did not know. All that she did know was that she must have had them. How else could she have come into this world? But who on earth were her parents? She did not remember either of them.

What could her mother have been like? Was she a beautiful or a repulsive creature? To go by her own looks, her mother, whoever she was, must have been at least attractive. Beauty rarely, if ever, emerges out of an ugly womb.

But what about her father? What did he look like? What did he do for a living? And, come to think of it, to which community did he belong?

These were the questions Munni Bai never tired of asking herself. Not that she wanted to be ready with an answer, lest someone asked her these questions. In the world in which she lived, parentage did not matter; looks and youth alone did. And Munni Bai was a ravishing beauty at seventeen!

With her Venus-like face, round breasts, slim waist, she was acknowledged, not only in Hira Mandi, but throughout the city of Lahore, as a girl to be possessed. And possessing her was not difficult — anyone could possess her. She lived to be possessed — of course, at a price. Her body was for sale.

This acknowledged princess of Hira Mandi did not like what she did. But there was nothing else she could do. Besides, what would "Ma" have said if she had refused to do what she was bidden?

Ma was a matronly figure who ran the brothel whose chief attraction was Munni Bai. Ma was alternately brutal and kind towards her. There were six of them, including Munni Bai — the youngest and the loveliest of them all.

Ma treated Munni Bai with greater affection — real or simulated, for she was the chief source of her income — than she did anyone else. The cane rod was so sparingly used on Munni Bai that it seemed as though it was reserved for the others.

Munni Bai could recall only one occasion when she had been thrashed by Ma. That was when she had the audacity to ask forbidden questions. Finding Ma in a genial mood one day, Munni Bai had asked, "Ma, who were my parents? How did I come to be where I am? Why do I have to do what I do?"

Ma's face had suddenly turned red. In a flash she had picked up the cane rod which had lain hidden behind her and had used it mercilessly on her "darling daughter" — as she used to call Munni Bai.

As the victim writhed in pain, Ma went on, "The answer to your first question, you bitch, is that I don't know who your parents were. You're a foundling. I found you crying and lying unattended on the road, the main road, mind you, equidistant from a mosque and a temple. Vehicles moved past you, but no one had the heart to stop and attend to you, let alone pick you up, feed and fondle you.

Fortunately for you, and unfortunately for me, I happened to be passing that way at that time. I took pity on you that winter evening. I picked you up, wrapped you in my shawl and brought you home, where you still find yourself.

Since your parents — pox be upon them, whoever they were — had left you halfway between a mosque and a temple, I could not decide whether you were a Hindu or a Muslim, whether I should give you a Hindu name or a Muslim name. Therefore, I gave you a name used by both Hindus and Muslims in our world.

That, anyway, has always been immaterial in our house. On Diwali, as you know, we burn diyas and worship Goddess Lakshmi with greater piety and gusto than most Hindus. And throughout the month of Ramzan, all the inmates of this house observe the fast. So what difference does it make whether you are a Hindu or a Muslim? You are, in fact, better than both because you combine both in you."

Despite her bulk and stern exterior, Ma knew that age had begun to take its toll on her. No, she was not exactly old. Middle aged, yes; but not old. She had just crossed fifty, but considering the sort of life she had led, was forced to lead, she looked old and, what was worse felt old.

Ma paused for breath before she could atone for her heartlessness by answering the other questions. "I have also answered, you bitch, your second question in the process of answering your first. The question of how you came to be where you are. Your third question, why you have to do what you do, is more easily answered. You eat during the day what you earn at night, and you've got to have something to eat if you want to stay alive."

Having thus explained everything, Ma strode back to her room and shut herself in. When one of the girls took food to her room, Ma refused to open the door from within, saying that she was not hungry.

That night Munni Bai could not sleep. She tossed in her bed. She could not lie on her back which still ached. Now suppose some customer called! What was she doing? What could she do?

She was the first choice of every customer, and her refusal to oblige him might turn him away forever if he was a regular. After all, there were other kothas in Hira Mandi! The competition was stiff.

And Munni Bai could not afford to lose customers. No woman in this profession could. Plainly, it was a question of making hay while the sun shone; and youth somehow did not seem to last even as long as the sunshine did. If the sun went down in the evening, it arose the next morning. But once youth sank into old age, it never rose again.

Munni Bai hated to even think about it. Hadn't Ma said that she had to eat during the day what she earned at night? Munni Bai knew that a time was bound to come when the night would yield nothing to see her through the day.

Contemplating such bleak prospects between the spasms of pain resulting from the caning she had received, Munni Bai switched off the light and lay in darkness. Suddenly she became aware that the door of her room was being opened stealthily as though by a burglar.

Now she could distinctly hear advancing footsteps as someone entered her room. Who could it be? A burglar? What was there in the room for a burglar? Indeed, she herself had nothing which could be stolen. The elite of the society had already robbed her of the only precious thing she had ever possessed.

The soft tread sounded familiar. Yet Munni Bai did not move in her bed and kept her eyes closed. Someone approached her cot and sat down beside her. A hand, which was muscular enough to be masculine, touched and then slowly lifted her unbuttoned blouse, unstrapped the loosely hanging bodice and, with the utmost care gently touched the lacerated back. An instant later Munni Bai, with her eyes still shut, felt the sensation of some ointment being applied softly to her bruised back. The ointment smelled of sandalwood.

Munni Bai felt so relieved and so touched that she sat up, embraced Ma and cried like a child.

Days passed, and with each day Ma's establishment attracted more clients than any other in the whole of Hira Mandi. Everybody wanted Munni Bai and only Munni Bai. She on her part made herself available to as many of her customers as she could.

However, Munni Bai's heart was not in her profession. But she had to keep herself alive, and the only way to do so was by overcoming the feeling of disgust and revulsion that often suffused her heart.

In the privacy of a closed room, she was totally at the mercy of the master of the moment. Some dealt with her brutally and she suffered in silence. With the passage of time her body became inured to every kind of treatment. But her soul still squirmed.

As she was kept busy through the best part of every night, Munni Bai had more hours to herself during the day than anyone else in the establishment. With nothing to do in those idle hours, she would lose herself in thought.

She would particularly think about two of her customers who also called themselves her lovers. They came to her at different times, but they spoke the same language. They made love and talked hate. As she lay in bed totally spent, Munni Bai would suddenly start hating them — hating them for the innate hatred they divulged so soon after making love to her.

Raj Kamal was about twenty-five and extremely virile. But since he had a wife at home, and a rich one at that, without whose benefactions he would be out on the streets begging, he had to divide his passions between Munni Bai and his wife. Thus he could not inject full ardour into his love-making with Munni Bai. So he made up vocally for what he lacked sexually.

He would often tell Munni Bai, in the gentle flow of amiability induced by satiated lust, "These good-for-nothing fellows, the Muslims, who cannot live for a day without loans from us, have already started living in a fool's paradise. They are already dreaming of a country of their own from which non-Muslims like you and me would be expelled."

Munni Bai would invariably interrupt him, "What do you mean by saying — non-Muslims like you and me? How do you know that I am not a Muslim? And what if I am?"

"But that's impossible! A beauty like you can only be a Hindu," Raj Kamal would assure her with considerable vehemence.

His outbursts would amuse Munni Bai. She would tease him. "Still, what if I turn out to have been the child of Muslim parents? Would you have desisted from making love to me?"

"Don't talk rot," he would shout at her. "I have been making love to you because you are such a ravishing beauty, and a ravishing beauty can never be anything but a Hindu. I am convinced of it." But it was clear everytime that he was a bit nettled.

"Raj, tell me one thing honestly. Suppose, for the sake of argument, that a Muslim country comes into being. Suppose also that I am then adjudged a Hindu and expelled from it, as you too would be. Would you abide by me in whatever country we both happen to be?" Munni Bai could not keep count of the number of times she had asked this question, but everytime the answer was the same.

"What a silly question, Munni Bai!" Raj Kamal would scoff. "No force on earth can drive us from our homes and hearths. Lahore — Hira Mandi particularly — belongs as much to us as it does to the Muslims. Nobody can dislodge us from our city." And he would pause a little before adding, "If, God forbid, that comes to pass, I shall be with you, although we are not married, till death do us part."

Munni Bai was not one to let it go at that. "What will you do with your rich wife? You can't commit bigamy, much less murder!"

Raj Kamal would leave her room at that point, saying, "We'll cross the bridge when we come to it."

Munni Bai's other lover was Jafar Khan, who claimed to be a thoroughbred Pathan. "Today you are not exclusively mine because rich kafirs are as attracted to you as I am and they can outbid me. But when Pakistan is formed, and after we have driven out all the kafirs, Munni Bai, you will belong only to Jafar Khan." This was his most frequent boast.

Munni Bai would ask him the same questions she asked Raj Kamal, and his reaction would be the same as that of his unknown rival. "I have been making love to you, Munni Bai, because you are a fairy, a hourie from behisht and a hourie can only be a Muslim. I am sure of that," he would say.

Both Raj Kamal and Jafar Khan showed conviction without either of them revealing the source. Munni Bai would tell the latter, "Suppose your dream of a nation of and for the Muslims is fulfilled and you discover that I am not a Muslim, what will you do?"

Jafar Khan would stare banefully at Munni Bai for a second or so and then say, "If, Allah forbid, it is discovered that you are a Hindu, I shall convert you to Islam and marry you."

Munni Bai treated his bravado with just as much contempt as she did Raj Kamal's boasting. If Raj Kamal was totally dependent on his rich wife, even for his meals, not to speak of his extravagances, Jafar Khan and his wife were both more or less equally poor. Munni Bai had it on good authority that every time Jafar Khan spent a night with her, smothering her with money at night, he was afraid of being arrested the next morning for theft or burglary. There was more fear than passion in his love-making.

Munni Bai would persist, "Tell me, honestly, Jafar Khan, would you find me less desirable if you discovered just now that I wasn't a Muslim? I really don't know whether I am a Muslim or a Hindu. I was found on a road halfway between a temple and a mosque. Maybe that is symbolic of the fact that I am part Hindu and part Muslim."

"How can anyone be part Hindu and part Muslim? I feel it in my bones that you cannot but be a Muslim," he would say decisively and also a bit testily.

Munni Bai had known too many men even in so short a life not to be able to read Jafar Khan's thoughts. She knew that what he really felt in his bones was not that she was a Muslim, but that he was finding it difficult to maintain one wife and would not be able to assume the responsibility of taking care of another being.

Then began those memorable months of disgrace by the end of which the Hindus had won, the Muslims had won, but humanity had lost. As an area frequented by members of all communities, it had initially been presumed, that Hira Mandi would be immune to destruction. But the hope proved false.

Professional jealousy which had festered for years found an outlet in communal frenzy. The rioters and arsonists were made to believe by frustrated denizens that Ma, like every other inmate of her establishment, was a Hindu. Consequently, the establishment had to be wound up before it could be burned down.

With her wards in tow, Ma fled Lahore before it was too late. Only Munni Bai seemed to wish to tarry a little. She kept looking for Raj Kamal and Jafar Khan, amongst the frenzied crowds with flaming torches but there was no trace of either. Maybe Raj Kamal had managed to cross the border and was waiting for her on the other side, but whatever could have happened to Jafar Khan? And to think that both had promised to abide by her through thick and thin!

Finally, Ma and her wards reached the refugee camp in Delhi, tired but without injury and in one piece. True, here they lacked the comforts which they had been accustomed to in Hira Mandi, but at least there was no danger to their lives.

They were grieved to see countless refugees mourning the loss of their kinsmen. But Ma and her group had no kinsmen, only clients. Therefore, there was no sense of loss. They could not have cared less if all their clients had been done to death. They had rendered services for what they had been paid for, and so they were quits. Human bonds are not forged in commercial transactions.

With the passage of time popular frenzy abated; murderers and arsonists had either tired of what they had been doing or had run out of objects of hate. It was not yet back to business, but the business of destruction was nearly over.

The authorities announced one day that the refugees who wanted to leave the camp and start life anew would be given all assistance. Munni Bai kept hoping that some day, somewhere, she would run into Raj Kamal and remind him of his promise to take care of her. Why, she would even remind him of his promise to marry her!

Munni Bai had seen brides and envied them. She had herself had the experience of a new bride without ever having been married. She wished to get married.

One day, Ma returned from a tour of the city of Delhi and announced to her flock that she had fixed up a house for them to live in. It sent a wave of jubilation through her companions. With their meagre belongings held close to their chests, they trooped out of the camp, engaged a tonga and got into it.

Ma gave an address to the tongawalla and after what looked like eternity the vehicle stopped in front of a partly damaged house.

The tongawalla addressed Ma, "Bibiji, this is the house where Salma used to stay with...her...companions. What a beauty she was! Nawabs and rajas used to visit her frequently. She has now gone with her group to Hira Mandi in Lahore."

In no time at all, women who were giggling and joking with each other appeared on the balconies of the surrounding houses. One look at them made it clear to Ma and her group that they were kindred spirits. Meanwhile the tongawalla said, "Bibiji, this is known as G.B. Road."

It was then that the ugly reality of the situation dawned on Munni Bai. She turned to Ma and asked in a voice without emotion. "Ma, the Muslims asked for Pakistan and they got it. The Hindus wanted to see the backs of the Muslims and they got Hindustan and are happy. We asked for nothing. Why, then, have we had to suffer so much?"

Ma did not answer the question. Instead, she led her party into the room.

Within days the newcomers were accepted as part of the 'community'. Despite all her harrowing experiences, Munni Bai had managed to retain her charm. Word soon spread that an exceptional beauty from Hira Mandi, where her name had been on everybody's lips, had arrived . But Ma, who knew all the tricks of the trade, also knew how to handle the publicity. She quickly spread the word that the beauty from Hira Mandi would be accessible only to the very rich.

Munni Bai's neighbour told her, "I am afraid Ma is going about it in the wrong way. Where are the very rich now? So many Hindus and Muslims have perished in the holocaust and so much property has been destroyed that I doubt if there is any rich man around, whether Hindu or Muslim. Even the poor belonging to both communities have perished."

The same night two limousines stopped in front of the house within an hour of each other. The first disgorged a raja, who sent in his compliments, accompanied with a bundle of notes, and expressed his desire to spend some time with the fabled beauty from Hira Mandi. He was obliged. But no sooner had he left when another limousine arrived, disgorging a nawab who desired the same satisfaction, paid generously for the service rendered and departed.

Before retiring for the night Munni Bai asked Ma, "Ma, Pakistan has been formed, but the nawabs in India are as rich as they ever were. The Hindu rajas have been shouting from the housetops that the nawabs, who have not been butchered, have been pauperised. And yet they have enough money to spend lavishly for one night's pleasure. Who lost and who died in the Partition?"

Original in Urdu.[•]
Translated by Mohammed Vazeeruddin.

MOHAN RAKESH

GOD'S DOG

There were lots of people sitting everywhere with their heads hanging down, as if they had come to mourn someone's death. Some of them had opened their bundles of food and were eating. Two or three of the men had even placed their turbans under their heads, and were sleeping on the ground, beside the road which ran past the compound wall. The chole-bhaturewalla was doing good business as usual, and a small queue had formed in front of the municipal water-tap. Sitting on a chair near the water-tap was a petition-writer, who was frantically typing application forms. He was so busy that he didn't even have the time to wipe the streams of perspiration which flowed from his forehead down to his lips. A few tall and hefty Jats, with white beards, leaned on their lathis, while they waited for him to finish. A curtain, made of jute cloth, which the petition-writer had strung up to protect himself from the sun, fluttered wildly in the breeze, His son, sat on a mat next to him, memorizing his lesson from an English primer — C-A-T, cat — cat means billi; B-A-T, bat — bat means balla; F-A-T, fat — fat means mota. Joking with each other, a few babus, with their shirts half-unbuttoned and their files under their arms, were slowly making their way from the registration branch to the records branch. A chaprasi with a red belt, depressed by the crowds around him, was sitting on a stool and making some mental calculations. He often muttered to himself and shook his head. It was September and the entire compound was bathed in bright sunlight. A few baby sparrows, who were learning how to fly, had hopped down from the branch of a tree and were trying to reach it again. A few large crows were strolling up and down the porch. An old woman, seventy or seventy-five years old, whose head shook and whose face was nothing but a web of wrinkles, was asking everyone she met, if she could legally inherit the land allotted to her son after his death...

In the hall inside, the files moved slowly. A few babus gathered around the central table to drink tea. One of them recited a couplet for his friends from the latest ghazal, which he had written on an official paper. His friends listened to him as if they were convinced that he had lifted the ghazal from an old issue of *Shama* or *Beeswin Sadi*.

"Aziz Sahib, did you write those couplets today, or are they old ones which you suddenly happened to recall?" asked one of the babus with a dark complexion and a thick moustache, as he winked at his friends. Everyone standing around smirked.

"It's a new ghazal!" Aziz Sahib declaimed as if he was standing in a court and defending himself. "I don't remember if I recited something on the same subject earlier." Then he examined the faces of everyone, laughed and said, "Let some mad researcher find out..."

The appreciative laughter of his admirers was interrupted by a number of voices saying "Shh...shh." That meant that the Commissioner Sahib had finally arrived in his office. In the brief pause that followed, the file of Surjit Singh, son of Gurmeet Singh, moved from one table to the next table for appropriate action. Surjit Singh, son of Gurmeet Singh, walked out with a smile on his face, and the babu who had passed his file left, with a crisp five rupee note in his hand, to have tea with his colleagues outside. Aziz Sahib lowered his voice and began reciting the next few couplets of his ghazal.

A bell rang in the Sahib's office. The chaprasi jumped up and went inside, and immediately afterwards came back and sat down on his stool again.

After getting the chaprasi to adjust the curtain on his window, the Commissioner Sahib signed the papers on his desk without looking at them, lit his pipe and pulled out the latest issue of *Reader's Digest* from his attaché case. He had already gone through Laetitia Baldridge's essay on why she loved Italian men. He decided that he wanted to read J.D. Radcliffe's essay on open heart surgery next. He turned to page one hundred and eleven and began reading about the new heart operation.

At that very moment, he heard some noise outside.

Four new people had joined those who were sitting under the tree in the compound. One of them was a middle aged man. He took off his turban, spread it on the ground and sat down on it. He leaned back on his hands and stretched his legs out in front. A woman, who looked slightly older than the man, and a young girl sat down on one end of the turban; a thin young man stood beside them, staring at everything around him with surprise. After having stretched out his legs fully, the middle-aged man began to speak so loudly that he even attracted the attention of people outside the compound wall. As he spoke, he smacked his thighs with his hands, "The government takes time! In five to ten years the government will decide whether my petition should be accepted or not. Bastards! Even Yamraj keeps count of our days. When the days allotted by him are over, I'll find out that the government has accepted my petition."

The chaprasi planted his feet firmly down on the ground and stood up. The people who had been either sitting or sleeping in the compound, turned to look at him. A few people gathered around the tree.

"I appealed to these bastards two years ago, to allot me some land, instead of giving me a pit. But in two years my application hasn't moved out of those two rooms!" The man, it seemed, was now giving a speech to the crowd. "It takes time for the application to travel from one room to the next! It even takes time for it to move from one desk to the next! The government takes its own time! Look, today I have arrived here with my entire family. Now you can take as much time as you want. After starving me for seven years, the bastards allotted me a pit three acres wide, so that I could bury the bones of my ancestors in it! I made an application asking them to allot me half the area — but land, not a pit! No action has been taken for two years on my application. I am starving, but the application is still being considered."

The chaprasi arrived on the scene with his lathi. His forehead was wrinkled, his eyes were blazing with anger. He pushed his way through the crowd and stood next to the man.

"Hey Mister, get out of here!" he shouted, as he banged his lathi on the ground. "Get up...out...!"

"Mister will not get up from here today!" the man said, as he spread out his legs a little more. "Mister is now the King of this place. Earlier, Mister used to bow before the uncrowned Kings of this country. But from today he will bow before no one. Now he is the King here — an uncrowned King. He is shameless and fearless. No one can order him about. Understand that, King Chaprasi!"

"You'll soon find out who gives orders here!" King Chaprasi screamed angrily, "I'll hand you over to the police and they'll beat all your royalty out of you."

"Ha, ha!" the uncrowned King laughed. "Your police will beat all my royalty out of me! Call the police! I'll stand here naked before the police and say, come beat the royalty out of me! How many of us Kings will they beat? There are three other Kings with me. My brother's widow — his body was ripped apart in Pakistan. My brother's son who already suffers from tuberculosis. And my brother's daughter who is now of marriageable age — her unmarried elder sister is still in Pakistan. Today I have bestowed Kingship on each of them. Go call the police and ask them to beat the royalty out of us — go, you son of a bitch!..."

Many babus came out of the office. On being called a son of a bitch, the chaprasi lost control over himself. He grabbed the man by his arm and started dragging him away. "You'll soon find out who is a son of a bitch. I'll beat you till..." he kicked the man with his worn boot. The woman and her daughter moved away in fear. The boy stood aside and started crying.

The babus pushed their way through the crowd and pulled the chaprasi away from the man. The chaprasi continued to curse and mutter, "Bastard, he comes to my office and abuses me. I'll show him..."

"You are not the only son of a bitch here. All of you here are dogs," the man continued. "All of you are dogs, and I am also a dog! The only difference is that you are the dogs of the government — you tear people to bits and bark at the orders of the government! I am God's dog. I live by his grace and bark at his command. There is justice in his house. I am the guardian of that house. You are thieves who want to ruin his house of justice. It is my duty to bark at you, that is my master's command. I hate you. All dogs hate each other. You are my enemy and I am your enemy. I am alone. You can gang up and beat me. Chase me out. But I shall continue to bark. You'll never force me to stop barking. My Lord's fire burns within me, Waheguru's strength pulses through me. You can lock me up wherever you like, but I shall continue to bark till your ear drums burst. Bastards. Pet dogs of man, go and chew on the bones thrown away by him; go wag your tails and beg..."

"Please Babaji, enough," one of the babus pleaded with folded hands. "Have mercy and do not curse us. Tell me your name and your case number."

"My name is 1226/7. The name given to me by my father and mother has been devoured by those dogs! Now the only name I have is the one given to me by your office. It is 1226/7. I have no other name. Remember my name. Write it down in your diary. Waheguru's dog 1226/7!"

"Babaji, please go now. Come back in a day or two. The work on your application has almost been completed."

"Has almost been completed! My life too has almost been completed! Now, let's see if the work on my application ends first, or my life ends first; who is more efficient, the government or God? Your work will end in your office, my life will end in my coffin. After all their education, the bastards have only learnt two words — 'perhaps' and 'almost'. 'Perhaps' your papers have been forwarded — work on your application has 'almost been completed'. Take the file out of 'perhaps' and shove it into 'almost completed'! Take it out of 'almost completed' and dump it into 'perhaps'! The investigation has almost been completed. Perhaps there will be a report in three or four months. Today I have left both the words, 'perhaps' and 'almost', back at my house. I am sitting here and I will continue to sit here. I want a decision on my application today and now. Talk about 'perhaps' and 'almost' to your clients standing around me. Continue to make a fool of them." Disappointed by the results of their good-will, the babus went back inside one by one.

"Let him sit."

"Let him shout and scream."

"The bastard wants to cheat the government."

"Let him bark himself to death."

Still grumbling, the chaprasi also went back and sat on his stool. "I should have kicked the bastard's teeth in. The fellow doesn't understand that the babus are the real bosses, and one must do as they say, otherwise..."

"Arrey Baba, try to be patient. Here you have to beg. Give a bribe. Threats will get you nowhere," advised someone from the crowd.

The man stood up.

"But God's command has to be obeyed by everyone," the man said, taking off his shirt. "God has commanded this uncrowned King to go naked into the Commissioner's office today. The Sahib will lash his bare back. Kick him to death. But the King shall not crawl. He shall not give a bribe. He shall not kneel in prayer. He only prays to God. So with the blessings of his God..."

But before he could carry out his threat, two people grabbed his hands and restrained him from opening the knot of his tehmad. The uncrowned King struggled to free his hands. "Let me go and find out, if Mahatama Gandhi struggled for freedom so that these people could misuse the freedom he won for us? Corrupt it? Give it a bad name? Tie it up in their petty files and let it rot? Make people curse it in their hearts? They will notice you only if you stand naked before them. Only a man feels ashamed. I declare that I am not a man, I am a dog..."

Suddenly there was panic in the crowd. The Commissioner Sahib had come out of his office. He was frowning, and his face was tense as he walked upto the crowd.

"What's the matter? What do you want?"

"I want to see you, Sahib," the man replied, glaring at the Sahib. "I was allotted a pit three acres wide. I have come to return the pit to you, so that the government can convert it into a lake where its officers can go fishing in the evenings. Or, build a dungeon there and lock up all the other dogs like me."

"Stop this rubbish and bring me your file."

"My file is with you, Sahib. It's been with the government for two years — with you. I have nothing except this body and these two rags which cover it. They will also be snatched away from me in two days. That is why I want to take them off today, so that I am nothing more than 1226/7. Soon 1226/7 will be beaten and sent to meet his Maker!..."

"Stop talking nonsense, and come to my office."

Saying that, the Commissioner went back to his room. The man picked up his shirt, and said, as he followed the Commissioner, "I have been making the rounds of this place for two years. No one paid me any attention. I pleaded, but no one listened to me. I begged, but no one heard me!..."

The chaprasi pushed the chick curtain aside for him, and he walked into the Commissioner's office. The bell rang, the files moved, the babus were summoned, and half an hour later, the King emerged with a smile on his face. He addressed the people who had been waiting for him anxiously, "You'll get nothing if you whimper like mice. Bark, all of you bark together! Bark, till the ear-drums of those bastards burst! Bark, go on, bark you dogs!..."

His sister-in-law was waiting for him near the gate with her two children. He put his hands on the shoulders of the two children, and walked out like a real King.

"If you are timid, you hang your head and wait for years. You get your petitions typed and drink water from that tap. The government takes its own time. Become shameless. Only the shameless are blessed a thousand fold!"

He suddenly stopped and burst out laughing.

"Friends, the shameless are blessed a thousand fold!"

After he left, gloom descended once again over the entire compound. The crowd began to dissolve. People slowly walked back to their places. The chaprasi once again sat down on his stool, and dangled his legs. The boy from the canteen nearby took a kettle full of tea into the office for the babus. The petition-writer began filling in the forms once more, and in tune with the clatter of the typewriter, his son began repeating his lesson over and over again, "P-E-N, pen — pen means kalam; H-E-N, hen — hen means murgi, D-E-N, den — den means andheri gufa...

Original in Hindi.
Translated by Alok Bhalla.

RAMESH CHANDRA SEN

THE WHITE HORSE

This is an event from the chronicle of riots.

A period of relative calm has set in after several successive days of bloodbath in Calcutta. Both Hindus and Muslims have ventured out of their homes in their respective localities with a degree of freedom. But there is tension in the air.

One afternoon, a white horse appeared in the empty cab stand. Its skin was spotlessly white, the tuft in its tail shone in the sun.

The creature looks like a lost wayfarer. No one has seen it before in the locality. It must have lost its shelter and its master, and wandered around till it fetched up in this place. Hunger makes it sniff at the road surface, the dust swirling up from its breathing. Of course it can find nothing to eat. It sniffs at the smelly rubbish and turns its face away.

Sheila's mother noticed the horse from her window. She said, "The poor thing seems starved. Both the groom and the coachman must have fled."

Sheila, her newly married daughter, was standing close by. She said, "They may have been killed."

"Oh!" — her mother's face fell.

Though she had not seen any actual killing, she had seen one or two horrible things happening. And many stories had been told, both of murder and of things crueller than murder. She had felt physically ill afterwards, and could not eat or sleep. But she still could not bring herself to believe that man could be so ruthless. "They may still be alive," she said.

The white animal brings a fresh whiff of life into the riot-torn locality. The boys are totally absorbed in the horse. The small ones are delighted at its sight. The bigger ones come close and caress its body. It neighs with pleasure when they rub its neck.

Speculation is rife. Almost everybody decides that it must belong to a raja or a landlord. They talk about its feed: what a rich man's horse eats and how much. Someone says, "Do you know that these horses are given drinks, and foreign stuff too?" Nontey comments, "Of course, it's drinks that give them so much spunk."

One boy is cussed enough to differ. He says, "I think it's a cab-horse." There is an immediate roll of laughter. Nontey says, "Oh yes, you must have seen helluva lot of them! You come from England, don't you, and ride around in carriages."

While everyone is discussing the horse, Jamuna Prasad manages to push a piece of rope into the horse's mouth for a bridle, and gets on its back. He has a small stick in his hand.

He is about twenty-two or twenty-three, dark and slim, and wears a vest. For a living, he buys up film-show tickets and sells them at a premium right in front of the booking window. Then he gambles away his earnings in the pavement den in half an hour's time; if a little is left, he manages to get a drink or two and shouts at everybody.

But he has become quite popular in these days of rioting. Whenever a temple is under attack nearby, his shouts are the loudest. He leads the mob in its rush to the spot.

He has become very friendly with the white soldiers posted in the locality by offering cigarettes and cups of tea to them. The boys call him the Military Tea Canteen.

But these last few days, he hasn't had any time for his usual round of activities. He is almost always on horseback. He keeps saying, "I've become a sergeant now." He doesn't listen to anyone and is completely uncaring. The only sound you hear from him is the tchk- tchk his tongue gives out as it strikes the palate.

Habul says to him, "Well, you are doing all the riding, aren't you? Do we only watch? This won't do, you know."

Jamuna tells him, "All right, go and fetch me paan and cigarettes from the corner-shop. I'll let you have a ride then."

"What about money!"

"Mention my name. Tell him, it's Jamuna Prasad who wants it." Habul comes back in a few minutes' time. He says, "No go. He wants money."

"Bastard! Son of a sheep! I'd saved the bastard's shop; and he made heaps of money from gambling. Now the bastard wants money for a two-paisa paan!" He rides away towards the shop. Habul does not get his ride.

This time of the year usually brings a crowd of boys to the temporary stall erected for community worship of the goddess. The clay artist fashions the straw figure, kneads the clay, daubs it on the straw. The boys stand around in a crowd and watch; they are delighted when they have a chance to help out the sculptor with fetching and carrying.

This year the stall has not yet been erected, and the boys are still busy with the horse. They have named it Chand, that is, the moon.

But the gloss of its coat and its beauty wane day by day. Chand drags a foot and, behind the left hind leg, a small sore festers. Sheila's father, Hrishikesh Babu, is an influential old man, a patron of the young people. He asks Habul, "Do you feed the horse at all?"

Habul says, "Nontey has perhaps fed him." Nontey, on being asked, says, "I don't really know. Jamuna may be able to tell."

When Sheila's mother hears of it, she buys some chaff from the shop downstairs and asks her son, Santu, to take it to the horse. It picks up a little of the chaff, but does not eat any more. Santu's friend, Khokon, suggests, "The fodder has got stuck in Chand's throat. Come, let's fetch water for him."

They both fetch water, but one has brought it in an earthen pot which has too narrow a mouth, and the other's mug has sprung a leak. So the horse does not have a drink.

There is no other container, so the boys go to the tea-shop nearby and bring some tea in a broken saucer. "Go on, Chand, drink up," they say. "Gokul's tea is nice, try it."

But the fame of Gokul's tea does not attract Chand at all. He sniffs at the saucer once or twice and turns his face away.

The horse has grown even thinner and has a sick look. The sore is worse. But Jamuna continues to ride it. Hrishikesh tells him, "Spare the horse a little, Jamuna, or it will die."

Jamuna has drunk himself into a stupor. He speaks in his mixture of Hindi and Bangla; the gist is — why fuss over a mere animal, when thousands of human beings are getting killed? He smiles a crooked sharp smile. It flashes like the honed blade of a dagger.

Towards evening Hrishikesh mobilized the boys to lead the horse into an empty garage nearby; a bucket of water and a bundle of hay were provided too. When they came out after tending to the horse, a truck full of vigilantes rushed by, and there were shouts of, "Get indoors, all of you, get in."

Next morning, they saw that somebody had locked the garage. Hrishikesh's bucket was at the door, and the horse was standing by motionless. Its eyes lacked lustre, it did not have strength enough to flick its tail at the flies. It looked in imminent danger of toppling down.

Santu hurried over to fetch a handful of chick-peas. Chand did not touch it. Nontey said, "Give it to me, Santu. I may be able to feed it. You know we had a carriage once, and I used to feed the horses."

But the dumb animal did not bear out Nontey's self-confident assertion. Nontey said, in his own brand of English, "There's a great deal of seriosity in its ailment."

Sheila's mother was in despair. "Oh look, the poor thing doesn't have the strength to stand on its legs. But if it once lies down, it won't be able to get up again."

Sheila asked, "Is it true that horses sleep standing up?"

Hrishikesh said, "Who told you such nonsense? They lie down to sleep once a week or so."

It was ten in the morning. The hot sun lashed your skin. Chand fidgeted in the heat, and the boys walked him down to the portico of Tebu's house to find him shelter. Nontey reassured them, "It's just that white-skinned animals can't stand direct sunlight. There's nothing to worry about."

Just at that moment, a short stocky old man appeared at the crossing. He looked around in all directions and entered the street. The man had a full white beard and whiskers, the body was bare above his dirty lungi, and he had a fez on his head; a tin mug in his hand glistened in the sun.

He would have attracted notice in any case. But just at that moment, he stands out so much in a Hindu locality that people just stare at each other. Hrishikesh Babu exclaims, "Oh no! Why did he have to come here now?"

But the old man appears to be unconcerned. He seems to be looking for something or somebody. His eyes scan the entire length of the street twice.

He misses the white horse at first, but the next time his eyes brighten as he catches sight of it. The old man runs to the horse and caresses it as he mutters endearments in his dialect, "Ah! Sohrab, what's happened to you, my boy!"

The animal shivers at the familiar touch. He looks up, and his gaze expresses much that human language cannot quite reach.

Budo walks up to the old man and asks in broken Hindi, "His name is Sohrab, is it? We call him Chand."

The old coachman says, "It's the same really."

Nontey asks, "Is this horse yours?"

"No, sir, it's a cab-horse. I am the groom, and also the coachman."

Nontey says, "That means the horse is yours."

The old man smiles, "As you say, sir."

He fetches water in his mug from the street tap and holds it to the horse's mouth. When the horse finishes the water, the boys cry, "Joi Hind!"

The groom had brought a paperbag of chick-peas in the folds of his lungi. He fed the horse from his palm. When the chick-peas were finished, he turned to the boys and said, "Can you get some more, sirs?"

"Of course," Nontey said, and ran. Habul, Goba and others ran off too. Four paper-bags full of chick-peas arrived together.

When the animal was a little better, the old man said, "Sohrab will eat only off my hands when he is ill."

He started reminiscing — how much was paid for the horse, how old he was, how many teeth he had cut, and so on.

People would look at Sohrab's gait and speed and would ask him why he had yoked this race-horse to a hackney cab. He would touch his own forehead and answer, "It's just our fate, sir. Animals have to obey fate, just like human beings."

He asked Hrishikesh, "Will everything cool down, sir? Will hackney cabs run again? There won't be any fear on the street?"

The man was thinking of the peaceful old days. Hrishikesh could not find anything to say in answer.

Just at that moment the sleeping ogre awakes again. It rises up and stretches its limbs at the crossing nearby. Rumour spreads like wildfire — killing has started in Lalpatty. From the main road, a section of the mob rushes into the street, like a tide swiftly moving from a river into a creek. There are aimless movements and shouts and calls to arms.

The old groom looks around, tries to find reassurance from the boys. Sohrab has a piteous look too; perhaps he realizes the danger to his master.

Nontey tells the groom, "You have nothing to fear."

But the old man does not seem to find reassurance in the hundreds of pairs of cruel eyes turned in his direction.

A number of people advance from the crowd. Jamuna, Nontey, Habul and other boys make a cordon round the old man. Hrishikesh tries to quieten the crowd. He says, "This man is innocent. Don't beat him up."

Voices speak in different tongues, Hindi, Bengali, English — "He is not a man, he's the devil."

"So you've already forgotten Metiabruz!"

"A tooth for a tooth."

Hrishikesh says, "Don't you know they saved us in many places?"

"So what? We've done it too. Don't listen to such rubbish!"

It was futile to argue or explain, and dangerous too. Jamuna and Nontey said, "You keep quiet, uncle," and stood straight in front of the mob. Jamuna said, "Come on, the lot of you, let's see who can beat us up, come on."

A boy cried, "No one can touch the groom, our white horse's groom."

The mob stood undecided for a moment. Then the shouting started again. Brickbats were thrown at the boys.

Just at that moment, someone cries from the top of the four storey house in the corner, "The army's here!"

There is a rush to get away. Everybody hides, creeping into open doorways and narrow lanes. Jamuna Prasad drags the old groom with him and runs into Hrishikesh's house.

Rat-tat-tat, speaks the gun.

The soldiers get off their trucks and start marching. The only sound you hear in the entire area is made by their boots.

A weird silence reigns. All doors and windows are closed. No one has courage enough to even open the blinds to satisfy their curiosity. Fear of the unknown marks each anxious face.

About an hour later, Nontey and Jamuna Prasad venture out. The old groom follows. The door opens into the empty, sun-parched street, looking like a burning ghat. They turn their gaze to the left and start.

The horse lies sprawling on the street, the head on the pavement, the body on the roadway. His white body stands out against the dark asphalt. There is a small round hole on the right temple.

The old groom calls, "My Sohrab!"

Sohrab does not respond. This is the very first time the horse fails to respond.

Sohrab is looking into a sky as clear as diamonds, with eyes which match its transparency. There is no pain or grievance in his gaze. Hrishikesh is there too now. He looks into the eyes of the white horse and suppresses a sigh.

Original in Bengali.
Translated by Mihir Bhattacharya.

KRISHNA SOBTI

WHERE IS MY MOTHER?

When Bahadur Yunus Khan of the Baluch Regiment looked at the sky, the moon had completed half of its nightly journey. He had seen the moon and the stars after four days. Where had he been during that time? Down, deep down, in the realm of nightmares...where all the ditches were filled with human blood. Where he had, like a subtle magician, sprayed the land with bullets. But...but that wasn't a nightmare. He was fighting for the creation of a new country. And the call for the freedom of one's country must be obeyed; the self must be sacrificed!...So, where had he been over the last four days? Everywhere! Gujranwala, Wazirabad, Lahore! In his truck. Tearing across the land. How far had he travelled? For whom, for what? For his country, his people, and...? And for himself! No, he didn't love himself that much! Standing on a road which stretched far into the horizon, Yunus Khan watched the flames as they leapt up from the villages burning all around. He had heard those screams before. People always scream when their houses are set on fire. He had witnessed other fires before. He had seen children thrown into fires...and women and men. He had seen neighbourhoods burn all night and had seen charred bodies in every street. Was he disturbed by what he had seen? Why should he have been? Freedom can't be won without bloodshed, revolutionary wars can't be fought without bloodshed and...and his small and lovely country had been born out of such a revolutionary struggle! That's right. He had fought day and night for it. His eyes were full of sleep now, but he had to reach Lahore. Get there on time. To make sure that no kafir was left alive.

Even on that cold night, the very thought of a kafir made Yunus Khan's blood boil with anger. He felt as if all his wounds had reopened again. He started the truck again. And drove it fast.

Death had passed through the villages on both sides of the road. Charred and mutilated bodies lay in piles near fields of wheat. Cries of "Allah-ho-Akbar" and "Har Har Mahadev" could be heard at a distance. "Catch him, catch him"..."Kill him, kill him"..."No, no, please no"...Yunus Khan heard all of them. He was witnessing the birth of a new Mughal Empire — Marvellous, far greater than the first one.

The moon was disappearing below the horizon. The misty light of the moon had a tinge of blue. Perhaps, the blood spilt on the earth had turned into poison and spread in the sky.

"Stop, stop the truck," Yunus Khan shouted, as his hand reached for the brake. What was that? A faint, small shadow! A shadow? No — a little girl lay unconscious by the roadside. Her salwar was soaked in blood.

Yunus Khan stepped down from the truck. She had been wounded. But why did he stop? Had he ever stopped for the dead before? But she was a wounded child...So what? He had seen countless bodies of dead women...No, he had to pick her up. If he could save her then...then...But why did he want to do that? Yunus Khan couldn't understand it himself...But he couldn't leave her there...Even if she was a kafir.

Yunus Khan picked her up in his strong arms. Laid her down on the seat of the truck. The child's eyes were shut. Her thick hair was wet. With blood, perhaps. And, on her face...? Her pale face...was splattered with blood.

Yunus Khan ran his fingers through her hair. His fingers got covered with blood...Was he trying to comfort her? No, Yunus Khan had never been so sentimental before. Why did he feel pity now — why did his hands touch her with so much compassion? He didn't understand it himself. Little did the child, who lay unconscious, know that the hands which had killed her brothers were now caressing her so lovingly.

The girl lay in Yunus Khan's arms...A vision rose before his eyes...not the eyes of a murderer, but the eyes of a man full of veneration...the vision of a very cold night in Quetta — He saw himself standing, with his arms around his pretty sister, Nooran. She was twelve years old. They watched their mother, who was a widow, close her eyes and die...

The wind was loud and strong. He stood in the graveyard after he had buried his sister, his beautiful sister, tender as a flower. She had left the world forever and ever...Yunus Khan began to cry as he recalled that day.

He held the little girl in his arms just as he had once held his sister...But where was that other Yunus Khan, who had butchered people with such ease for four days...had killed them for his religious faith...had played holi with blood? Where was he? Where?

Yunus Khan felt shaken, disturbed. He had stopped too long to question himself. He had to hurry, the girl was wounded! He patted her gently once more, looked at her kindly, almost with reverence, and then quickly started the truck. Suddenly conscious of his duty, he realized that he should have left much earlier. Perhaps, the girl could still be saved — her wounds could be treated and bandaged. He drove the truck fast, very fast. It sped through the night. He thought to himself, "Why am I doing all this? For her alone? Thousands have been massacred. She may be a lot of trouble. Besides, I am fighting for the freedom of my country!"

Lahore was approaching. Railway tracks ran parallel to the road. Shahadra — and then the truck sped towards Lahore. Where should he take her? To Mayo Hospital or to Sir Gangaram?...Why to Gangaram? Yunus Khan was startled. Was he going to return her to her people? No, no, he would look after her himself. The truck stopped in front of Mayo Hospital.

Soon after, Yunus Khan was heard pleading with the doctor, "Save her, do what you can to save her...Doctor, doctor, please..."

"Yes, yes, we shall do our best to help her."

The child lay in the hospital. Yunus Khan went back to his duty. But he also looked after her, and did everything that was required. But he was anxious.

The streets of Lahore were burning. They were full of smoke. Groups of panic-stricken, frightened people passed through them under the protection of the army. But there were also soldiers who joined large gatherings of hooligans and laughed with them. Dead men lay piled everywhere like garbage. Bodies of naked women lay scattered in the deserted streets. The silence of the city was broken by slogans — slogans which were screamed loudly.

But Yunus Khan, who had killed tirelessly till yesterday, was very calm. He had walked very briskly that evening. It seemed as if he wasn't going to a hospital, but was going home.

Why was he so concerned about an unknown child? She wasn't even a Muslim — she was a Hindu, a Hindu!

Her bed seemed to him to be far from the door, very far. He had to take long strides to reach it.

The girl lay on a metal bed. Her head was wrapped with white bandages. Her eyes were still shut as if she was afraid of looking at a dreadful scene. Her pretty and innocent face was marked with fear.

What could he say to her — How should he address her? "Nooran," he almost called out to her, but stopped. He stretched out his hand to touch her. His fingers gently caressed her head and his voice choked.

Suddenly the girl stirred. Still unconscious, she began to shout with fear, "Camp, camp...we have reached the camp. Run...run...faster..."

"No, don't be afraid — open your eyes and look."

"Fire, fire...they are shooting...the soldiers ..."

When she saw him leaning over her, she screamed.

"Doctor, doctor...doctor, please save her."

The doctor, who had seen all this before, said, "She is afraid of you. That's because she is a kafir."

"Kafir..." The word echoed in his ears, "Kafir...kafir...why save her then? Kafir?...No, — I'll look after her."

That is how they passed those nights of carnage. Yunus Khan continued to do his duty in the army, while the child lay in the hospital.

Then came a day when the child recovered. Yunus Khan went to the hospital to take her away.

The girl stared at him with her large, dark eyes. There was fear, hatred and suspicion in them.

When Yunus Khan touched her head, she trembled with fear. She thought those hands would strangle her. She shut her eyes in terror. She couldn't understand anything. "Where are they? Who is this Baluch?...Oh what a dreadful night that was!

Where was her brother?" With an awful start she remembered that her brother's head had been chopped off with a scythe!

Yunus Khan watched her for a while and then said softly, "You are well now. Shall we go home?"

The girl began to shake with fear and shouted, "No, no...where is my home? You will kill me."

Yunus Khan wanted to believe that she was Nooran...But that girl wasn't Nooran. She was a stranger, who was mortally afraid of him.

The girl pleaded with him, "Don't take me to your house. Send me to the camp. They will kill me here — they will kill me..."

Yunus Khan was forced to lower his eyes. He no longer felt like a brave, powerful and ruthless soldier. He felt miserable, helpless...weak.

He looked at her compassionately and wondered, "Did any relative of hers survive? I will look after her." He was overcome with a strange sense of pity.

He smiled and then touched her gently, "Come, don't be afraid — you are like my own..."

Sitting next to Yunus Khan, the girl thought to herself that he would take her to a lonely spot and kill her...shoot her or stab her! She held his hand and pleaded, "Khan, don't kill me, please don't kill me...please!" Her face was pale with terror.

Yunus Khan said to her in a voice full of kindness, "Be patient, don't cry. I will look after you like my own sister. You will live with me."

"No!" the girl shouted with hatred in her voice and began to strike him with her fists. "You are a Muslim...You'll kill me."

Suddenly she started screaming, "Where is my brother? Where is my sister? Where is my mother...?"

Original in Hindi.
Translated by Alok Bhalla.

IBRAHIM JALEES

A GRAVE TURNED INSIDE-OUT

Ayesha desperately longed for the earth to open and to be buried in it forever, but the aeroplane carried her far above the ground.

This was the first time that Ayesha was travelling by air. That is why, the moment the plane took off from Kathmandu airport, she started screaming loudly with terror. Two air-hostesses rushed towards her and tried to calm her down, but Nurul Amin, the young man accompanying Ayesha, told them in Urdu, which he spoke with a typical Bengali accent, "Don't worry, Bibi log — I have successfully brought her all the way from Dhaka to Kathmandu and have saved her on numerous occasions from committing suicide. She is hysterical. Go away and leave her to me, I will shut her up with a single sentence!"

Then Nurul Amin said something in Bengali and Ayesha fell silent at once. Her eyes wide with fear and surprise, she turned to look at the earth below. She stared at the vast green fields spread out like a carpet, at the rivers which threaded them like white pearl necklaces, and at the roads and highways with toy-like trucks and cars. Perhaps she thought — Man is a strange creature! He may be fed up with life and long for death — yet the moment he faces death, he becomes speechless; he trembles with fear before death and tries to hide behind the ample and protective body of life.

Poor Ayesha! — She was one of those millions and millions of lost, helpless, oppressed people of this earth, who, from the moment they are born till their last day, neither want to live nor wish to die.

— Disgusted with life!

— And afraid of death!

From Karachi to Delhi, Delhi to Dhaka, Dhaka to Tokyo, Tokyo to Washington and from Washington to Sydney, there are millions of people in this world who neither want to live nor wish to die. Though they live on the surface of the earth, they actually seem to spend their lives in graves. The four walls of their small houses are but graves turned inside-out. When these people actually die, their grave-like houses sink into the ground, resum their original purpose and remain proper graves forever.

Ayesha was not a Bengali, but a Bihari. She was the daughter of Mehmud-ur-Rehman, a motor mechanic in Patna, and the wife of Abdul Waheed, a taxi-driver. She hadn't gone to Dhaka because she had been lured there by a political vision or had been enchanted by the idea of Pakistan. She had merely followed her husband to Dhaka because, in this male-dominated world, a wife's nationality is determined by her husband's. That is why in the files of the Census Bureau, she was listed as a Pakistani citizen, though all her Bengali neighbours in Taanti Bazaar called her, even after twenty-four years, Ayesha Bihari. She had left her salwar and kameez hanging on a hook in Patna in her parent's house, and now wore only a saree like the other Bengali women. Indeed, she tied it so well that whenever she went out shopping to the main street in her locality, her long hair swinging down to her waist and her saree wrapped tightly around her body, the Punjabi owner of Crescent Store, Choudhary Kushi Mohammad, used to get so excited that he would start drooling, and in order to attract attention to himself, start shouting vulgar comments:

> O Balay Balay! There is magic in this Bengalen!
> Hai re! May your boat sink,
> May you be cursed for revealing such beauty!
> One who hasn't seen this beauty of Bengal
> cannot claim to live in Pakistan!

Apart from her large black eyes, her loosely tied hair and her typically wrapped saree, Ayesha had also learnt to speak Bengali. She had learnt to speak it so fluently over the last twenty-four years that the neighbouring women often whispered to each other: "...Come, I bet you twenty to ten that Ayesha is not a Bihari, but has sprung from the seed of a Bengali...!"

Yet after having lived so comfortably and cheerfully like a Bengali for twenty four years, suddenly one day Ayesha was reminded of the fact that she was not really a Bengali — that she was a Bihari — that she was not the daughter of the soil — that, even after twenty-four years, she didn't belong there — that she was stateless.

Powerful voices, zealous and angry voices of fiery young orators, blared out hate-filled speeches from loudspeakers at Paltan Maidan, Race Course, Moti Jheel and Bait-ul-Mukarram; they said such things that it seemed as if Islam had been pushed back by some thirteen hundred years, just as Pakistan had been pushed away by some thirteen hundred miles. But when Bengali and Bihari goondas began to kill each other indiscriminately with knives and sticks, and hooligans hired by politicians began to loot houses and violate the sacred bodies of the women of their opponents, Ayesha's life and honour were saved by her ability to speak Bengali in Taanti Bazaar and Urdu in Mohammadpura.

And now, once again in the aeroplane, it was a single Bengali sentence which persuaded Ayesha to give life one more chance.

One of the air-hostesses asked the other in Urdu, "Rabab Darling, you know Bengali well. What was that magical sentence in Bengali which made her stop bellowing like a buffalo...?"

Rabab Darling, translating that sentence into Urdu, said, "The young man only said, "Shut up, you bitch, down there on earth you used to beg for death, and now that you have a chance of embracing death, you have lost your nerve...!"

The first air-hostess, suspicious of Ayesha's true identity, said to Rabab Darling, "I am sure she isn't that Bengali's wife. He has abducted her. That's why she was protesting so loudly about going with him."

Nurul had not abducted Ayesha, nor had he forced her to go with him from Dhaka to Kathmandu, nor was he coercing her now to go from Kathmandu to Karachi. He had merely lied to her, lied cruelly, about her daughter when he had told her that she would be able to find her and hold her in her arms once again.

Ayesha had trusted Nurul like a brother, because they had been neighbours at Taanti Bazaar, and only a common wall had separated their houses. His wife, Ameena, and Ayesha had been great friends, and had shared all their secrets with each other. Apart from being neighbours, their husbands had also shared the same profession; both of them were taxi-drivers.

Long before Ameena had got married to Nurul, a local goonda, Hassan Ullah, had fallen desperately in love with her and had wanted to marry her, but her father had thrown him out of the house. Since then, Ameena's marriage to Nurul had rankled Hassan like a thorn and he had always been on the look-out for a chance to possess her luscious and youthful body. That is why whenever Nurul and Hassan Ullah quarrelled in public, Ayesha's husband, Abdul Waheed, always supported Nurul, and on one occasion even thrashed Hassan Ullah.

When the language riots suddenly erupted between the Bengali and the Urdu speakers, Hassan Ullah got his chance to take revenge on Ameena. He put on the uniform of a Mukti Bahini soldier, which he had snatched from one of them, seized the jeep of a Bihari businessman and, accompanied by his henchmen, raided Ameena's house. She was alone at home. Hassan Ullah stripped her naked, dragged her out and threw her into the jeep. Maulana Shamsul Haq, the Pesh Imam of the mosque across the road, who had been watching the entire incident hidden behind a minaret, covered his eyes with his hands, muttered "lahaul villa quuvat" and then began to mumble his prayers rapidly:

> Ya Allah! Be compassionate to us Muslims!
> Ya Allah! Show the path of virtue to the Pakistanis!
> Ya Allah! If this is what you wanted us to witness
> why did you create Pakistan?

That night when Nurul Momin and Abdul Waheed heard the news of Ameena's abduction, both of them pulled out their old knives. Ayesha, fearful of being left behind a widow, screamed like any other fanatic and said, "Why must you get involved in this fight, Razia's father?...Don't forget that you are a Bihari — Hassan Ullah is a Bengali — So is Nurul...Let him go and rescue his wife from the clutches of that goonda...Why should you interfere?..."

But at that moment, Abdul Waheed didn't regard himself as a Bihari — or Nurul as a Bengali — Nurul was his dear friend and friendship, he thought, had no nationality, love knew no geographical boundary...Annoyed by Ayesha, he ran after Abdul to offer him his support.

Ayesha also ran after her husband and Nurul...What she had feared happened...She reached Hassan Ullah's house too late. A bullet fired from Hassan Ullah's pistol had pierced her husband's heart, and Hassan Ullah, in a drunken rage was pulling Nurul's hair and screaming, "...Sala — Pakistani jasoos...Your Ameena — no, my Ameena — no, the lower part of your Ameena's body speaks such beautiful Bengali — that I feel as if I am in Heaven..."

Ayesha couldn't stand it any more. She fainted and fell across Abdul's lifeless body.

After she regained consciousness, she saw an injured Nurul sitting by her side and learnt from him that her thirteen year old daughter, Razia, had also been abducted. When she failed to find Razia, the poor woman banged her head in despair against a wall and tried to kill herself. But Nurul stopped her and comforted her. "Sister", he said, "Aysho — you must live for Razia. She is alive and safe in Qazi Kabiruddin's house. Come, I'll take you to him."

Qazi Kabiruddin was a Bihari. Apart from being a big factory owner, he was also an intimate friend of Sheikh Mujib and Tajuddin and had donated huge sums of money to the Awami League. That proved that he was not a spy for the Pakistani army. Only a taxi-driver like Abdul Waheed could have been accused of being in the pay of Pakistan.

Ayesha, for the sake of her daughter, pulled herself together and went with Nurul to Qazi Kabiruddin's house. In fact Nurul had felt guilty because it was in order to save his wife that Ayesha's husband had lost his life; it was because of him that she had become a widow and had lost her daughter. Nurul could neither bring her husband back nor did he know who had abducted her young and beautiful daughter. Ayesha suspected that Nurul had lied to her and she wanted to nail him down. That is why she had pretended to be gullible and had followed him to Qazi Kabiruddin's house. As they approached the Qazi's house, Nurul lost his nerve and tried to prevent her from going any further. Instead of stopping, however, Ayesha ran towards the Qazi's house wailing, "Razia...Razia...my daughter...my Rajoo..." Nurul ran after her.

On the one side was the feeble, tender cry of a widowed, daughterless, hungry and sick woman and on the other side were the full-throated, frenzied slogans of millions and millions of men:

Joy Bangla...Joy Bang Bandhu...
Amar Desh...Tumar Desh...

Amar Neta...Tumar Neta...
Sheikh Mujib...Sheikh Mujib...

At that very moment, when Ayesha was running towards the Qazi's house, the first flag of Bangladesh was being unfurled on the lawns of the Race Course. Everyone in Dhaka was running towards the Race Course where the last General of the Pakistani army was about to lay down his arms before the first Commander of the army of the Bangladesh...The voice of a spirited young man was booming from the loudspeaker, "Today, everyone who lives here, whether he is a Bengali or a Bihari, a Hindu or a Christian, is free. From today, everyone will lead a good life..."

At that moment, Ayesha didn't want a good life, she only wanted to find Razia...

When she reached the gate of Qazi Kabiruddin's bungalow, she was stopped by his watchman who had been alerted by Nurul. Nurul quietened her down by raising false hopes and went into the Qazi's house himself. Later he came out accompanied by Qazi Kabiruddin's aged aunt. He had somehow persuaded her to tell a comforting lie instead of revealing the awful truth about Razia. She placed her hand on Ayesha's head and consoled her. Then she told her, "Your daughter, Razia, has been sent for her safety to Karachi with Qazi Basheeruddin's wife and children." And when Nurul too raised his hands in prayer towards the holy mosque in the holy city of God and vowed in the name of the martyrs of Islam that the old woman had spoken the truth, Ayesha, the daughter of the Sayyeda, believed them and allowed herself to be persuaded to go to Karachi.

Who knows the secrets of the heart...! Who knows whether Nurul had agreed to help Ayesha, because he thought of her as his sister, or whether he had decided to take Ayesha to Pakistan, because he was afraid Hassan Ullah would neither let him live in peace in Dhaka nor leave Ayesha alone...Or whether he had thought that if he couldn't drive a taxi in Pakistan, then he could at least use Ayesha as his taxi —! Who knows, because when a man doesn't get his three meals a day and has to suffer, then he thinks that even a pig is halal — and a pig is an animal which has neither modesty nor sexual shame.

Who knows the secrets of the heart...! Only Nurul knew what lay hidden in the depths of his soul...He took possession of all the gold and money that Ayesha still had left with her, and using Razia's name as a magnet, dragged her from Dhaka to

Calcutta, and from Calcutta to Kathmandu. And now, he had persuaded her to take a P.I.A. flight from Kathmandu to Karachi. Ayesha was migrating for the second time, not because she had been lured by a political vision, or had been enchanted by the idea of Pakistan. She was merely doing what Nurul had asked her to do for he was the only one who seemed to sympathize with her and was the new man in her life. Nurul was taking her to Pakistan and had promised her a new life there.

When Ayesha had first migrated from Bihar to East Pakistan, someone had asked her, "Why are you going to East Pakistan?"

At that time Ayesha, like millions of Ayeshas, had replied, "Ask Rajjo's father!"

Twenty four years later, she was migrating once again. This time someone asked her, "Why are you going to West Pakistan?"

Ayesha replied, "Ask Nurul!"

Poor Ayesha, she was only conscious of the fact that she was sitting in an aeroplane and nothing more...that she was going to West Pakistan.

Ayesha had travelled only once by train. That was when she had migrated from Bihar.

During the riots of 1947, rich Muslims of Patna, their relatives, dependents and mistresses, had fled in aeroplanes for safety to Pakistan. Poor Muslims like Abdul Waheed and Ayesha, taxi-drivers, small traders, iron-smiths, cobblers, barbers, washermen, masons and others, had slowly crawled towards Pakistan in over-crowded trains. Some had been killed on the way, others robbed; they had been pushed, shoved and jolted towards East and West Pakistan. It was on one such train, in which Abdul Waheed and Ayesha had been packed like sardines, that Abdul Waheed had assured his pregnant wife, "Wait till we reach Dhaka, Aysho!...We shall begin a new life there. Quad-i-Azam has said that Pakistan has been created for poor Muslims like us. In Pakistan no Muslim will be poor or destitute again. We shall have our own house in Dhaka. No cruel and hard-hearted landlord, like our Patna money-lender, Ghanshyam Das, will dare to throw us out."

And now Ayesha was migrating once again...perhaps for the last time.

In this world, a poor man can never speak about his last migration, his last migration can only be towards heaven.

During their first migration, her husband, sitting next to her in a crowded railway compartment, had woven before her sleepless eyes, beautiful patterns of a new and comfortable life in Dhaka in East Pakistan.

And now, during her second migration, Ayesha was sitting in an aeroplane next to another man, who was neither her husband nor her brother, but who was also weaving before her eyes, beautiful patterns of a new and comfortable life in Karachi in West Pakistan.

"One of the cooks who had migrated to Pakistan, told me that everyone is rich and well-off there. It's only in Bangladesh that, sala, all the poor people of the world live. Don't worry Ayesha, as soon as you reach Karachi, you will meet Razia and begin a new life. Quad-i-Azam had said that in Pakistan there will be no poor Muslims. In Karachi we will have our own house and no goonda will be able to throw us out..."

Ayesha mumbled, as if in a dream, "Razia's father had said the same thing, Nurul!"

Then, after a thoughtful pause, she asked, "Nurul — if Qazi Basheeruddin took my Razia with him, why didn't he also take his brother, Qazi Kabiruddin, with him?"

At first, Nurul had been surprised by the question, but he quickly regained his wits and said, "Idiot!...How could Qazi Kabiruddin leave his house, his land, his jute mills, cinema houses, petrol pumps and import business behind and go to Karachi?...A man with so much wealth cannot leave Dhaka. Besides, he is a great friend of our Sheikh Mujib and Tajuddin. He has donated a lot of money to the Awami League. That is why he asked Sheikh Mujib for permission to send his brother to Pakistan. The other day Qazi Basheer's driver was telling me that in Pakistan, Qazi Basheer is as well settled as his brother is in Bangladesh. He has a big bungalow in Karachi — may be a factory — a petrol pump. I will only agree to work as Qazi Basheer's driver."

Ayesha remained unconvinced, and asked him, "Nurul, if we don't find Qazi Basheer's bungalow in Karachi, where will we stay?"

Nurul didn't have a ready answer. In order to divert her attention, he looked out of the window of the aeroplane and pointing to the earth down below, said, "Look Aysho...Allah Miyan has given us so much land and yet, sala, poor people like us can't even get a small plot of land where we can raise a hut. All we get is a few yards of land for our graves. Rich people like Qazi Kabiruddin in Bangladesh and Qazi Basheeruddin in Pakistan have large bungalows — The government says it has no land, but look below...so much land down there is still empty."

If one looks down at the earth from an aeroplane, one can see vast areas of unoccupied land on which millions and millions of poor people can be settled. The poor, however, do not realize that the rich people of the world have divided the earth amongst themselves, and that they defend the boundaries they have made; indeed, the entire earth has been divided into five continents and hundreds of countries:

There ends the land of Bangladesh,
And there ends the land of India,
Now begins the land of Pakistan,
Beyond it is the land of the Arabs,
The land of the English.
The land of the French,
The land of the Germans,
The land of the Italians,
The land of the Americans.

This perhaps is the land of Daulat Khan,
And that the land of Kirori Mal,
The Municipal Corporation's land,
The land of the Town Planning Authority.
This is neither Allah Miyan's land
Nor the people's land,
Neither Nurul's land,
Nor Ayesha's land,
This is the Land Department's land...!

Ayesha's young daughter, Razia, was like a bearer cheque. How could the goondas not have cashed it? — They must have encashed it back there in Bangladesh. How could Ayesha even expect to find her in Pakistan? And how could Qazi Basheeruddin's bull-terriers let Nurul and Ayesha enter the gate of their master's bungalow? When the dogs barked and Abdul Hashim, who was Qazi Basheeruddin's old and faithful Bengali servant, came out, he immediately recognized Nurul and embraced him. After listening to Nurul's story, he advised him not to meet Qazi Basheer. It would be better, he said if Nurul sought the help of poor Bengalis like himself. They would give him shelter. He told them to go to a particular address, "Jaffer Mohammad Husain, Nurul Islam, Syed Ahmed, Abdul Hasnat and others live in their huts, which they have put up on Fazloo Dada's enclosure on the left side of the Country Club's graveyard. You can also build a hut there. I will talk to my Sahib about employing you as his driver — he needs one — after all, you are a trustworthy man. I go to Fazloo Dada's basti every Sunday — by then, Insha Allah, I may be able to bring you good news...Tell me, do you need any money now?"

Nurul replied gratefully, "Abdul Hashim bhai — I still have a couple of hundred rupees left. They should be enough for me to build a hut and buy a few kitchen utensils, a cot etc. But you must get me that job. After all, how long can we survive on a few hundred rupees without a job?"

Abdul Hashim looked meaningfully towards Ayesha and said, "Yes, yes...I understand...Two persons together...you and your —?"

Nurul stopped him quickly, "My sister — our Waheed's widow —"

Abdul Hashim sighed, patted her head affectionately and said, "Poor Waheed!"

When Nurul and Ayesha turned and walked towards the Country Club's graveyard, Ayesha's eyes fell on a slogan scrawled in charcoal on a wall. She read it silently : "Biharis...go back."

On their way, they passed the tomb of Qaid-i-Azam. They stood in front of the beautiful tomb built of marble and admired it for a long time. When they walked away from it, they felt as if the tomb of Qaid-i-Azam was following them and did not want to let them out of its sight.

Ayesha asked hesitatingly, "Nurul — Qaid-i-Azam had said something..."

Nurul cut in sharply and said, "Ayesho — Don't you see that Qaid-i-Azam has been imprisoned in his tomb? — So keep quiet..."

Did Ayesha understand what Nurul meant? Is that why she kept quiet?

Next to the wall of the Country Club, was Fazloo Dada's enclosure, in which the huts of the poor Bengali refugees had sprouted out of the graveyard. The huts were so close to the graveyard that the dead didn't have to be carried from their huts to their graves — they were merely toppled out of one grave into another.

In the graveyard — properly constructed graves!

In the Bengali settlement — graves turned inside-out!

Fazloo Dada and the other residents of the Bengali settlement warmly welcomed Nurul and Ayesha...There was still some space left for a grave or a grave turned inside-out.

Nurul went to the Lallo Khet Market with Sahmat Ullah to buy some bamboos for his hut, a mattress, one basket, two cots, a few aluminium utensils, a lantern, a tin stove, some flour and rice, etc. By evening, Nurul had built a hut and was very happy that he was starting a new life again.

But just before sunset, two tall, muscular men arrived. They pretended to be officials from the Government's Land Department. One of them accused Nurul of illegally grabbing Government land and dragged him to the police station, hitting and kicking him all the way. Meanwhile, the other man, who was drunk, entered the hut and, in order to punish Ayesha for illegally grabbing Government land, made a grab for the land of her body.

The women of the settlement, who heard Ayesha's cries for help, felt so ashamed that they covered their ears with their hands. And when a few of their own men, troubled by their conscience and unable to bear the screams any longer, decided to intervene, their wives begged them with folded hands not to, "Ayesha is already a widow...why do you want us also to become widows...?"

The men forgot their self-respect and their show of bravery.

The next morning, when Fazloo Dada and the inhabitants of the slum peeped into Ayesha's hut, they saw her naked body on the floor. In order to save Ayesha's honour after her death, they started moaning loudly, "Hai, hai! Poor Ayesha has been bitten by a snake...!"

Yes, Ayesha had been bitten by a snake who had left his underwear behind...He was a funny snake...! He wore an underwear...!

"Overturn Ayesha's hut!" Fazloo Dada ordered his henchmen.

Everyone helped to overturn her hut in such a way that it sank into the earth and became her grave.

They covered it with dust. Fazloo Dada also picked up a handful of dust, and throwing it on her grave said bitterly :

"Not Patna...not Dhaka...not Kathmandu...not Karachi...the truth is...it was her own dust which lured her to this place..."

Fazloo Dada was right...Poor people like Ayesha are buried under dust alone...not under marble!

Original in Urdu.
Translated by Viswamitter Adil
and Alok Bhalla.

SAADAT HASAN MANTO

MOZEL

Tirlochen was looking at the sky for the first time, for the first time in four years, and that too because he was upset and had gone up to the terrace at Adwani Chambers so that he could think rationally in the open air.

The sky, clear and cloudless, stretched tautly like a grey tent over all of Bombay. Scattered lights extended to the horizon. It seemed that the stars had fallen from the sky, alighted on the tops of buildings, which in the darkness of the night looked like large tree trunks, and now glimmered on them like glow worms.

Being under the open sky was a totally new experience for Tirlochen, a new feeling. He realized that in the four years he had spent in his flat, he had been deprived of one of nature's great blessings. It was nearly three o'clock. The air was light and buoyant. Tirlochen was used to the mechanical breeze of the fan which weighed him down. When he awoke in the mornings, he felt as if he had been beaten all night. But now, in the fresh morning air, every pore of his body seemed to be joyously absorbing the freshness. When he came up to the terrace, his mind was heavily burdened with disturbing thoughts, but in half an hour the fever in his brain had abated and he found himself thinking rationally.

Kirpal Kaur and her entire family were in a neighbourhood dominated by staunch Muslims. Several houses had already been burnt down and a great many lives had been lost. Tirlochen might have brought Kirpal Kaur and her family out of there, but a twenty-four hour curfew had been imposed, there were Muslims everywhere, and surrounded by these dangerous Muslims, Tirlochen felt helpless. In addition to that, there was news pouring in from Punjab of the widespread killing of Muslims by Sikhs. Any hand, any Muslim hand, could reach out at any time, seize Kirpal Kaur's delicate wrist and push her towards the well of death.

Kirpal's mother was blind, her father was a cripple, and her only brother was in Devlali overseeing a new contract.

Tirlochen was vexed with Kirpal's brother, Niranjan. Since he read the newspaper every day, he had warned Niranjan a week ago about the rapidly spreading disturbances. "Forget about these contracts for the time being," he had told him, adding quite openly, "We're going through a very delicate phase and although you must stay with your family, it would be even better if you brought them over to my house. It's true there isn't much space, but in times of trouble one can manage." Niranjan ignored his warning. And when Tirlochen finished lecturing him, he smiled under his thick moustache and said, "Yar, you worry needlessly. I've seen many such disturbances here; this is not Amritsar or Lahore, this is Bombay...Bombay. You've been here for four years, I've lived here for twelve years...twelve years."

What did Niranjan think Bombay was? He probably figured this was a city where disturbances, if they did develop, would disappear of their own accord, as if by magic. Or he might have thought this was a storybook castle which was impervious to catastrophe. But Tirlochen could see very clearly that the mohalla was not safe at all. As a matter of fact, he would not be surprised if he read in the next morning's paper that Kirpal and her parents had been murdered.

He was not concerned about Kirpal's blind mother or her handicapped father. It would be fine, as far as he was concerned, if they died and Kirpal was spared. Better too if her brother also got killed, because then the way would be cleared for him. Niranjan was not just a stone in Tirlochen's path, he was more like a khangar. And so, when Tirlochen talked to him, he called him 'Khangar Singh' instead of Niranjan Singh.

The morning air blew lazily. Tirlochen's head, without a turban, felt pleasantly cooled. But inside his head innumerable thoughts ran about haphazardly...Kirpal Kaur was a new comer in his life. Although she was the sister of Khangar Singh, who was a strong, well-built man, she herself was small and delicate. She had been raised in the village but she did not have any of the hardness, the coarseness and masculinity that characterize most rural Sikh women who engage in a great deal of physical labour.

Her features were minute, as if still in an early stage of development; her breasts were small and needed many more layers of fat. She was fairer than most Sikh women, her complexion was like raw cotton, and her skin had the texture of mercerized fabric. She was an extremely shy person.

Tirlochen and she were from the same village. But he had not lived in the village long. After completing his primary education there, he had moved to the city to continue his schooling and became, thereafter, a city person. He visited his village often, but he had never had the occasion to hear of someone called Kirpal Kaur in all that time. Perhaps that was because he was always in a hurry to get back to the city.

College days were in the past now. There was a distance of ten years between the college building and the terrace of Adwani Chambers, and this distance was filled with unusual happenings that constituted Tirlochen's life. Burma, Singapore, Hong Kong...and then Bombay again, where he had been living for the last four years.

In these four years, this was the first time he had examined the sky at night, a vision which was not altogether displeasing...a thousand lights glimmered on the roof of the taut, grey tent and the air was light and buoyant.

As he thought about Kirpal, he suddenly remembered Mozel, the Jewish girl who lived in Adwani Chambers. Tirlochen had fallen deeply in love with her; he was in love upto his knees, as they say, and it was the kind of love that he had never experienced before in all of his thirty-five years.

He saw Mozel for the first time when he moved into a flat at Adwani Chambers which he had rented with the help of a Christian friend. At first glance, Mozel looked like someone dangerously mad. Short brown hair covered her head; her querulous lips were covered with red lipstick which was badly chapped and caky and reminded him of dried blood. She was wearing a long, loose white dress with a low neckline, the better part of her large, bluish breasts clearly visible. Her arms, which were bare, revealed a fine layer of down — it seemed she had just walked out of a hair salon after getting a hair cut, tiny hairs forming a covering on her bare skin.

Her lips were not really full but the manner in which the dark lipstick had been applied gave them the appearance of being thick and fleshy.

Her flat was directly across from his. Between the two was a narrow passage, a very narrow passage. Just as Tirlochen approached the door of his flat, Mozel came out of hers. The sound of the wooden clogs she was wearing caught his attention and he paused to look at her. Mozel stared at him through her unruly hair that hung over her eyes, and laughed; Tirlochen was flustered. Quickly he got out his key and turned towards the door. At about the same time Mozel's wooden clogs slipped on the cemented floor and she fell over him.

When Tirlochen attempted to pull himself together, he realized that Mozel was sprawled over him in such a way that her dress was pulled up all the way, and her bare legs were spread on either side of his body. As he made an effort to extricate himself, he became entangled with her; he was all over her, like soap suds.

Mozel patted her dress in place with a smile when Tirlochen, quite out of breath, offered an apology.

"These clogs are no good," she said, and slipping her feet into her shoes again, she walked off, taking wide strides.

Tirlochen had thought it would be difficult befriending Mozel. But they became good friends soon. However, Mozel was extremely stubborn and caused Tirlochen much heartache. She ate with him, drank with him, went with him to the cinema, spent whole days with him on the beach at Juhu, but when he tried to go beyond kissing and hugging, she spurned him. She did it in a way that caused his fervor and his passion to become entangled in his moustache and beard.

Tirlochen had never been in love before. In Lahore, Burma and Singapore, he had occasionally bought women for a price for a few hours. He had not, even in his wildest thoughts, imagined that in Bombay he would fall deeply, inextricably, in love with a wild Jewish girl. Her thoughtlessness and lack of consideration were strange. At his request she immediately got ready to go to the cinema with him. But when they were seated in the theater, she would begin to look around, and as soon as she saw an old acquaintance she would wave frantically and then go off to sit with him without asking Tirlochen first.

They are sitting in a hotel, Tirlochen has ordered special food for Mozel, but she suddenly spots an old friend, and dropping everything goes over to sit by his side. Tirlochen burns with anger.

Tirlochen lost his patience with her often, because she left him frequently to be with other friends and sometimes he did not see her for weeks. She might affect a headache or complain of indigestion, which Tirlochen knew was an impossibility since her stomach was hard like steel and could never be thrown out of gear.

"You're a Sikh," she would say, when they finally got together. "You're not going to understand these delicate matters."

"What delicate matters? Those concerning your old lovers?" Tirlochen would ask, angered and bitter.

With her hands on her broad hips, her strapping legs placed apart, she would retort, "Why are you always taunting me about my lovers — yes, they're my lovers and I like them. I don't care if you're jealous."

"How will we ever get along if this continues?" Tirlochen then questioned her argumentatively.

This made Mozel roar with laughter.

"You're a Sikh after all, you idiot!" she exclaimed. "Who asked you to try and get along with me? If you want to get along with someone, go get yourself a Sikhni from your village and marry her — with me, this is how it will always be."

Tirlochen immediately softened. Actually Mozel was his greatest weakness; he wanted to hold on to her at all cost. It was true, he often suffered humiliation at her hands — he was belittled in the presence of ordinary Christian boys who were nothing. But he had decided to withstand all for love.

Normally humiliation and degradation result in feelings of vengeance. But that was not so in Tirlochen's case. He had stuffed cotton in his ears and shut his eyes to keep out a great many things. He liked Mozel — he not only liked her, but he often told his friends, he was in love with her upto his knees. He felt there was nothing else to do except submerge the rest of his body into the mire, and be done with the matter altogether.

For two years, he continued in this wretched manner. But he was always loyal to her. And one day, when he found Mozel in a good mood, he drew her into his arms and asked, "Mozel, don't you love me at all?"

Mozel extricated herself from his arms, sat down on a chair and stared absently at the hem of her dress. Then she raised her heavy-lidded Jewish eyes, batted her thick eyelashes and said, "I cannot love a Sikh."

Tirlochen felt as if someone had placed live coals on his kesh under his turban. His whole body was on fire.

"Mozel!" he shouted. "You are always making fun of me — you know that you're not just making fun of me, you're attacking my love."

Mozel rose and shook her short brown hair in an attractive gesture. "If you shave off your beard and let your hair down, you'll have young boys running after you, I promise; you're beautiful."

More live coals seemed to have descended on Tirlochen's kesh. He moved forward, pulled Mozel towards himself and fastened his thickly moustached lips on her dark, pink mouth.

Mozel detached herself from his embrace. "I brushed my teeth this morning, you don't have to bother," she said calmly.

"Mozel!" Tirlochen was shouting again.

Mozel withdrew a small mirror from her vanity bag and proceeded to examine her mouth on which the thick layer of lipstick had become cracked.

"By God, you don't make proper use of your moustache — I could clean my navy-blue skirt with it; with some petrol we'll be all set."

His anger, after having reached a climax, was now deflated. He quietly sat down on the sofa. Mozel came and sat beside him and began unravelling his beard, taking out the pins one by one and holding them between her teeth.

Tirlochen was beautiful. When he was younger, before the hair on his face appeared, he had often been mistaken for a girl when he was seen with his kesh down. But now the heavy bulk of hair concealed his features. He was well aware of this fact. But he was a dutiful young man, there was in his heart a reverence for religion, and he did not want to separate himself from the things that were part of religious observance.

When his hair was completely unravelled and hung loose over his chest, he asked Mozel, "What are you doing?"

The pins still held between her teeth, she smiled. "Your hair is so soft — I was wrong to say you could clean my navy-blue skirt with it — Tirlochen, give it to me. I'll braid it and have a first-class handbag made for myself."

Sparks flew in Tirlochen's beard.

He addressed Mozel seriously, "I've never made fun of your religion — why do you ridicule mine — look, it's not nice to make fun of anybody's religious beliefs. I would never have tolerated this and the only reason I do is because I love you very much — don't you know that?"

Mozel let go of Tirlochen's beard. "I know that," she said.

"Well then?" Tirlochen began entwining the hair on his beard and retrieved the pins from Mozel's mouth. "You know very well that my love is not nonsense — I want to marry you."

"I know," she said, shaking her head in a characteristic gesture, and got up to examine a picture on the wall. "I too have made up my mind to marry you."

"Really!" Tirlochen jumped up excitedly.

Mozel's pink lips opened in a broad smile and her healthy white teeth shone for a moment. "Yes."

His beard half-done, Tirlochen clasped her to his breast. "When? when?" he asked her.

Mozel moved away from him. "When you have this hair cut short."

Tirlochen, who could have agreed to do anything at this moment, said, "I'll have it cut tomorrow," without really giving much thought to what he was saying.

Mozel tapped her feet on the floor.

"You're talking nonsense, Tirloch — you don't have the courage!"

She succeeded in casting out from Tirlochen's mind and heart any ideas about religion that might have remained. "You'll see," he declared.

"I'll see." She ran to him quickly, kissed him on his moustache and saying, "Phoo...phoo," she left.

It is useless to mention what troubled thoughts raided Tirlochen's mind that night and what agony he underwent, because the next morning he went to the Fort and had his kesh cut and his beard shaved, keeping his eyes shut through it all. Clean finally, he opened his eyes and studied his face in the mirror for a long time; it was a face that the prettiest girls in Bombay would be compelled to look at appreciatively.

Tirlochen began to feel the same chill that had engulfed him the moment he came out of the salon. He hastened his step on the terrace which was overlaid by a network of pipes and water tanks. He did not want to remember the rest of the story, but escape seemed impossible.

He had stayed home for a whole day after he had his hair cut. The following day he sent his servant with a note to Mozel, saying he was sick and wanted to see her. Mozel came. When she saw him without his hair, she froze for a second. Then, with a loud, "My darling!" she ran to him and plastered his face with kisses.

She stroked his soft cheeks with her hand and ran her fingers through his hair which had been trimmed to an English-cut, and muttered loud exclamations in Arabic. She shouted so much that her nose began to run and when she realized what was happening she lifted the hem of her dress and wiped her nose with it. Tirlochen blushed. He lowered her skirt hastily and admonished her. "You should wear something under this," he told her.

Mozel appeared not to care. "I feel comfortable — this is just fine," she stated, a smile appearing on her lips on which the lipstick had cracked in several places.

Suddenly Tirlochen remembered the first time he had met her, when he had bumped into her in the hall and they had become entangled in a strange manner. He hugged Mozel.

"We'll be married tomorrow."

"Sure." Mozel rubbed the back of her hand against the softness of his chin.

They decided the wedding would take place in Poona. Because it was to be a civil marriage, a ten-day notice was required and since it would be a court proceeding, Poona was the most logical choice. It was not far and many of Tirlochen's friends lived there. The plan was to leave for Poona the following day.

Mozel worked as a sales-girl in one of the shops at the Fort. Not far from there was a taxi-stand where Mozel had instructed Tirlochen to wait for her. He arrived at the appointed time and waited two-and-a-half hours. But she did not show up. A day later, Tirlochen found out that she had left for Devlali with an old friend who had just bought a car, and that she would be away for an indeterminate period of time.

What agony did Tirlochen suffer? That is a long story. To put it briefly, he hardened himself and forgot Mozel. Not too long afterwards he met and fell in love with Kirpal Kaur and came to the conclusion that Mozel was a contemptible woman on whose heart hung heavy stones and who, like a bird, flitted from one place to another.

However, once in a while, the memory of Mozel returned, gripping his heart fiercely, then flying off, disappearing. She was shameless, she was callous, she was inconsiderate, yet he liked her. And for this reason he was forced to think of her sometimes, forced to speculate about her whereabouts and wonder what she was doing in Devlali, whether she was still with the man who had bought a car, or with someone else. Although he was well acquainted with her character, he was deeply hurt by the thought that she was with someone other than himself.

He had spent not only hundreds but thousands of rupees, but he had done so voluntarily. Mozel was not expensive. She was attracted to things that were really cheap. Once when Tirlochen wanted to buy her a pair of gold earrings he liked very much, she saw a pair of gaudy and inexpensive earrings, fell in love with them instantly and begged Tirlochen to buy those for her.

To this day, Tirlochen could not figure out what kind of a girl she really was, or what the fabric of her being was. She lay by his side for hours and allowed him to kiss her; like soap he blanketed her entire body, but she never permitted him to go a step further than that, saying in a teasing tone, "You're a Sikh — I hate you."

Tirlochen was certain, she did not hate him. If she hated him, she would not associate with him at all. She lacked self-control and would never have spent two years with him. She would have told him what she felt frankly and openly. She disliked underwear. It made her feel uncomfortable and although Tirlochen had, on several occasions warned her of the necessity of wearing one, and had attempted to arouse her sense of modesty and propriety, she had refused to wear it.

She became irritated when he talked of modesty.

"This is modesty — what nonsense is this? If you're so conscious of it, why don't you close your eyes? Is there any kind of dress in which one may not become immodest, or through which your gaze can't travel? Don't talk nonsense with me. You're a Sikh, I know you wear a silly underwear resembling shorts, under your pants; this too is part of your religion, like your beard and your hair. You should be ashamed — you're an adult and you still believe that your religion is concealed in your underwear!"

In the beginning, Tirlochen was greatly angered by what she said. But later, after some serious thought, he often gave in and began to see a fragment of truth in her arguments. When he had his beard shaved and got a hair-cut, he felt, with absolute certainty, that he had been carrying an unnecessary burden of hair which really had no meaning.

Tirlochen came to a halt when he reached the water-tank. He cursed Mozel vehemently and put her out of his mind. Kirpal Kaur, a chaste girl with whom he was in love, was in danger. She was in a neighbourhood populated by staunch Muslim families and several incidents had already occurred there. Who cared about the curfew, though? If the Muslims in the chawl so desired, they could very easily get rid of Kirpal Kaur and her parents.

Lost in thought, Tirlochen walked over to the water-pipe and sat down on it. His hair had grown considerably. He was sure that within a year he would have his kesh back again. His beard had grown too, but he did not plan to wear it long. There was a barber at the Fort who trimmed it so well, it was hard to tell it had been trimmed at all.

He brushed his fingers through his long, soft hair, sighed, and was about to rise from the water-pipe when he suddenly heard the harsh sound of clogs. Who could it be? There were several Jewish women in the building and they all wore wooden clogs when they were at home — the sound was closer now. Then he saw Mozel standing beside the other tank, wearing her usual, long, loose dress worn typically by Jewish women; she was stretching lazily and lustily, so lustily that Tirlochen thought the air around them might burst open.

Tirlochen got up from the water-pipe. He wondered where she had suddenly come from. And what was she doing on the terrace at night?

Mozel stretched again. This time Tirlochen felt his bones rattle.

Her robust breasts heaved within the confines of her loose shirt. Flat and circular bruises floated before Tirlochen's eyes. He coughed. Mozel turned around and saw him. Her reaction was mild. Dragging her feet noisily, she walked up to him and stared at his diminutive beard.

"You've become a Sikh again, Tirloch?"

The hair on his face began to prick him.

Mozel came nearer and rubbed the back of her hand on his chin. "This brush is now ready to clean my navy-blue skirt," she commented with a smile. "But I left the skirt in Devlali."

Tirlochen remained silent.

Mozel pinched his arm. "Why don't you speak, Sardar Sahib?"

Tirlochen did not wish to repeat his past mistakes. But he looked closely at Mozel's face in the foggy, early morning light — there was no particular change in her, except that she seemed to have lost some weight.

"Have you been sick?" Tirlochen asked her.

"No," Mozel answered, bouncing her hair about.

"You look thinner."

"I'm dieting." Mozel sat on the water-pipe and tapped her clogs on the ground. "So you — that is, you're becoming a Sikh again?"

"Yes," Tirlochen retorted boldly.

"Congratulations!" Mozel took off one of her clogs and began tapping it on the pipe. "Have you fallen in love with another girl?"

"Yes," Tirlochen admitted quietly.

"Congratulations! Is she someone from this building?"

"No."

"That isn't very nice." Mozel was now twirling her shoe around her finger. "One should always think of one's neighbours."

Tirlochen said nothing. Mozel stood up and coming closer, touched his beard with her fingers.

"Did the girl ask you to grow your hair?"

Tirlochen was uncomfortable; he felt as if the hair of his beard had become entangled as it does when being combed.

"No," he said rigidly.

The lipstick on Mozel's mouth reminded him of stale meat. When she smiled Tirlochen had a vision of the butcher's shop where jhatka meat was sold, and in his mind he saw the butcher slice a massive artery in two with his knife.

She smiled again, then laughed. "If you shave this beard now, I swear by anyone you ask me to, I'll marry you."

Tirlochen wanted to say he loved a decent, chaste and pure-hearted virgin and he was going to marry her; that compared to her, Mozel was a harlot, an ugly, stupid, inconsiderate woman. But he was not a mean or petty man. All he said to Mozel was, "Mozel, I've made up my mind to marry this simple, religious girl from my village. For her, I decided to grow my hair again."

Mozel was not accustomed to prolonged thought. But she did reflect for a few moments, then turned towards Tirlochen and said, "If she's religious, how will she accept you? Doesn't she know you cut your hair once?"

"She doesn't know yet — I started growing my beard soon after you left for Devlali, merely to get even — but then I met Kirpal Kaur, and now I tie my turban in such a way that only one person in a hundred can tell that my kesh has been cut; I'll grow it back soon." Tirlochen began running his fingers through his long, soft hair.

Mozel raised her long, loose dress up to her thighs and scratched a fair, fleshy thigh. "That's great...these bloody mosquitoes, they're here too — just look how they bite!"

Tirlochen looked away. Mozel wet a finger with saliva and rubbed it over the spot where she had been bitten. Then she lowered her dress and stood up.

"When are you getting married?"

"Nothing is certain yet," Tirlochen replied and became pensive.

They were both silent for the next few minutes. Then, sensing his anxiety, Mozel started laughing.

Tirlochen needed a sympathetic ear even if it were Mozel's. He told her the whole story. Mozel started laughing.

"You're an idiot of the first order! Go and get her — what is the problem?"

"Problem? Mozel, you'll never understand the intricacies of this matter, of any matter — you're a careless sort of girl — that is why you and I haven't been able to keep our relationship going, and for this I'll be sorry for the rest of my life."

Mozel struck the pipe angrily with her foot.

"Sorry be damned...you silly idiot — you have to think about how you are going to save your, what's her name, from being killed...you're sitting here shedding tears of regret about relationships...We could never have had a permanent relationship because you're a silly man, a coward. I want someone courageous...but let's not talk about that now. Come, let's go and get that Kaur of yours."

She grasped Tirlochen's arm.

"Get her from where?" Tirlochen asked her confusedly.

"From where she lives; I know the neighborhood well, come with me."

"But wait, there is a curfew there."

"Not for Mozel — come."

She dragged him by the arm to the door which opened onto the stairs leading down. She was about to open the door when she suddenly paused and looked at Tirlochen's beard.

"What is it?" Tirlochen asked.

"Your beard," Mozel said. "Well...it's okay, it's not too big...if you walk bare-headed no one will know you're a Sikh."

"Bare-headed? I'm not going there bare-headed," Tirlochen declared in bewilderment.

"Why?" Mozel queried.

Tirlochen pushed back a lock of hair from his forehead. "You don't understand — she has never seen me without a turban before...she thinks I have a kesh and I don't want to reveal my secret."

Mozel stamped her feet angrily on the threshold. "You really are an idiot! You stupid ass, it's a question of her life, what's her name, that Kaur of yours with whom you're in love."

Tirlochen tried to explain, "Mozel, she's a very religious girl, if she sees me without a turban, she'll begin to hate me."

Mozel became infuriated.

"Oh, your love be dammed! I ask you, are all Sikhs stupid like you? It's a question of her life and you insist on wearing your turban — perhaps that underwear too which looks like a pair of shorts."

"That I wear all the time," Tirlochen confessed.

"That's just great! But think, the problem now is that the mohalla is full of Miyan bhais who are mean and ruthless — if you go there wearing your turban you will be slaughtered."

"I don't care," Tirlochen declared. "If I go there with you, I'll go with my turban on; I don't want to jeopardize my love."

Mozel was exasperated and, as she seethed with anger, her breasts lurched against each other. "You ass, where will your love be when you're not there — your, what's the name of that fool — when she's not there, her family is not there? You're a Sikh, by God, you're a Sikh and an idiot at that!"

"Shut up!" Tirlochen lost his temper.

Mozel burst out laughing. Then she raised her arms, which were covered with a fine layer of down, and circled them around Tirlochen's neck. Swinging a little, she said, "Darling, let's go — whatever you say — go and put on your turban, I'll wait for you downstairs." She turned to go.

"But wait a minute," Tirlochen said, stopping her. "Aren't you going to change your clothes?"

"This is all right," she replied, her hair bobbing vigorously. And with the "khat, khat, khat" of her shoes, she left. Tirlochen could hear the sound even when she was down on the first floor. He swept back his hair with his hand, and went to his flat. He changed quickly, set on his head the turban which was already furled, then locked the door of his flat and left the building.

Standing on the footpath, her sturdy legs wide apart, was Mozel, smoking a cigarette as she stood there like a man. When Tirlochen approached her, she blew a whiff of smoke in his face teasingly.

"You're disgusting!" Tirlochen said irritatedly.

Mozel smiled. "This is not new. Other people have called me disgusting before this." Then she glanced at Tirlochen's turban. "You've done a good job with the turban — it does appear that you have a kesh."

The bazaar was completely isolated. A mild breeze blew timidly as if fearful of the curfew. Street lamps cast a feeble light. About this time the trams usually started running and people began to appear in the streets; there was quite a bit of hustle and bustle at this hour of the morning. But right now it seemed no man had ever come this way and no one was likely to.

Mozel walked ahead of him. Her clogs rang resoundingly on the flagstones. The sound broke the stillness abruptly and Tirlochen cursed her silently for not having changed into something else before she left. He was tempted to tell her to take off the clogs and walk barefoot. But he was sure that she would refuse to do his bidding, so he remained silent.

Tirlochen was terrified. The stirring of a single leaf made his heart beat violently. But Mozel walked on unafraid, exhaling cigarette smoke casually as if she were out on a leisurely stroll.

At the crossing a policeman roared, "Ai, where are you going?"

Tirlochen recoiled in fear. Mozel approached the policeman boldly, shook her hair and said, "Oh, you didn't recognize me — Mozel," adding, with a finger pointing towards a gully, "there, my sister lives there — she's sick — I'm taking the doctor to her."

While the policeman examined her face searchingly, she took out a packet of cigarettes from somewhere and offered one to him. "Here, smoke," she said.

The policeman took the cigarette. Mozel removed from her mouth the cigarette she had been smoking and handed it to the policeman. "Here, light it."

The policeman drew on the cigarette. Mozel winked her left eye at him and her right eye at Tirlochen, and dragging her clogs noisily, she walked off towards the gully through which they had to pass in order to get to Kirpal's mohalla.

Tirlochen was quiet. But he could sense that Mozel was deriving some strange pleasure from her defiance of the curfew — she liked playing with danger. She became a problem for him when she went with him to Juhu. Fighting the gigantic waves of the ocean, she would go far in the water while he watched her anxiously, afraid that she might drown. When she returned, her body would be blue and bruised, but she did not seem to care.

Mozel was ahead of him. He walked behind her. He looked about him fearfully, half-expecting someone with a dagger to appear from somewhere. Mozel came to a halt. When Tirlochen came up to her, she made an attempt to reason with him.

"Listen, Tirloch dear — it's not wise to be so scared; if you're afraid, something is bound to happen. Believe me, I know what I'm talking about."

Tirlochen remained silent.

When they had crossed one gully, and were at the gully beyond which Kirpal Kaur's mohalla lay, Mozel came to a standstill. Not far from them, a Marwari's shop was being systematically looted. She studied the situation for a moment. Then she said, "It's all right," and they resumed walking.

A man, carrying a large tray over his head, bumped into Tirlochen. It was apparent to him that Tirlochen was a Sikh. He reached inside his salwar belt swiftly, but Mozel came forward, swaying on her feet as if drunk, and pushed the man away.

"Ai, what are you doing?" she mumbled in a drunken tone. "Killing your own brother? I want to marry him." Then she turned to Tirlochen, "Karim, pick up the tray and put it back on his head."

The man withdrew his hand from his belt and gave Mozel a lewd stare. He then leaned forward and poked her in her breasts with his elbow.

"Have fun, sali, have fun," he said, picked up his tray and was gone.

Mozel touched her breasts, "Not disgusting — everything goes — come on."

She started walking again, faster this time. Tirlochen followed, increasing his pace.

They crossed the gully and came to Kirpal Kaur's mohalla. "Which way now?" Mozel inquired.

"The third gully, it's the corner building," Tirlochen answered nervously.

Mozel turned in that direction. It was very quiet. Although this was a well-populated area, not a sound could be heard, not even that of a child crying.

When they came to the gully, they witnessed a riot in progress. A man ran out of one corner building and disappeared into the other building. Several moments later, three more men emerged from the same building, looked about them briefly, then dashed into the other building. Mozel stood still. She motioned Tirlochen to withdraw into the darkness. "Tirlochen dear," she whispered to him cautiously, "take off your turban."

"I can't take it off, no matter what happens," he replied quietly.

"As you wish, but don't you see what's going on out there?" she was annoyed with him.

Both of them could see very clearly what was happening out there. There was trouble, trouble of a very mysterious nature. When two men came out of the building on the left with sacks on their backs, Mozel shuddered, shaken to the core of her being. A dark, red liquid dripped from the sacks. Mozel nervously chewed her lips; she was probably thinking what to do next. After the two men had disappeared beyond the farther end of the gully, she turned to Tirlochen.

"Look, this is what you have to do — I'll run towards the corner building, you come running after me, fast, as if you're pursuing me — understand? But we must be quick."

As soon as Tirlochen had indicated that he understood the plan, Mozel darted off in the direction of the corner building, her clogs echoing noisily on the flagstones. Tirlochen ran after her. In a few minutes they were both inside the building, at the foot of the stairs. Tirlochen was out of breath, but Mozel seemed fine.

"Which floor?"

"Second," Tirlochen answered, anxiously wetting his lips. Tirlochen was behind her. There were large spots of dried blood on the stairs; Tirlochen grew faint when he saw them.

When they arrived at the second floor, Tirlochen went down the corridor and knocked gently on a door. Mozel stayed by the stairs.

Tirlochen knocked again and with his mouth close to the door whispered urgently, "Mehnga Singh Ji, Mehnga Singh Ji."

"Who is it?" a small, thin voice was heard from the other side of the door.

"Tirlochen."

The door opened slowly, Tirlochen beckoned Mozel to come, she ran up to him and they both went in quickly. Standing by her side, Mozel saw a slim girl who looked terrified. Mozel looked at her closely for a moment; she had fine features and a beautiful nose which was now reddened from a cold. Mozel hugged her, and taking the hem of her own dress she wiped the girl's nose with it.

Tirlochen blushed.

"Don't be afraid, Tirlochen has come to take you away from here," she told Kirpal Kaur lovingly.

"Tell Sardar Sahib to get ready quickly," Tirlochen said, "and Mataji too — but hurry up."

Suddenly, they heard shouts from the floor above — shouts of triumph and screams of fear.

A small, stifled scream escaped from Kirpal Kaur's throat, "They have got them."

"Who?" Tirlochen asked.

"Never mind that now," Mozel grabbed Kirpal Kaur's arm before she could speak. "It's just as well. Now take off your clothes."

Then, before Kirpal Kaur had a chance to react to Mozel's order, Mozel came up and took off Kirpal's shirt in one quick move and set it aside. Dazed and shaken, Kirpal Kaur hugged her naked body with her arms. Tirlochen turned his face away. Next, Mozel removed her own dress and slipped it over Kirpal Kaur's head. She herself was now completely naked. Then she loosened Kirpal Kaur's salwar belt and pulled the salwar down.

"Go, take her now," she ordered Tirlochen, adding, "But wait." With that she proceeded to undo Kirpal Kaur's plait. "Go, get out of here quickly."

"Come," Tirlochen said hastily. He was about to leave when he stopped suddenly and looked at Mozel who stood naked before him, like a clean, white eyeball. The soft down on her arms stood on end due to the cold.

"Why don't you go?" Mozel asked him in exasperation.

"What about her parents?" Tirlochen ventured hesitatingly.

"To hell with them! Just take her and go."

"What about you?"

"I'm coming."

Just then they heard men's voices on the stairs, the sounds were soon followed by a loud banging on their door, it seemed they were intent on breaking it down.

Kirpal Kaur's crippled father and blind mother were in the other room, moaning.

Mozel, reflected for a moment, bounced her hair and said, "I can think of only one thing now — I'll open the door..."

Kirpal Kaur suppressed a scream in her dry throat. "The door..." she gasped.

"I'll open the door," continued Mozel. "You run after me, I'll go up the stairs...you follow me...these men at the door will forget everything and come after us..."

"And what then?" Tirlochen queried uneasily.

"Your, what's her name, will use the diversion to get away and no one will bother her in that dress."

Tirlochen explained the whole situation to Kirpal Kaur as fast as he could. Mozel screamed loudly, opened the door and fell over the men outside. Taken by surprise, they quickly moved aside and she ran up the stairs. Tirlochen went after her.

Mozel was climbing the stairs blindly, the clogs still on her feet, and the men, who seconds ago were attempting to break down the door, turned and pursued them. Suddenly Mozel's foot slipped; she came stumbling down the stairs, her body hitting every stone stair and the steel banister as she fell, landing finally on the cement floor.

Tirlochen descended the stairs in a hurry. Bending over her he saw that her nose was bleeding and there was blood trickling from her mouth and ears. The people who had tried to break the door earlier, were now gathered around them. Everyone was watching Mozel's naked and fair body which was covered with bruises.

"Mozel, Mozel!" Tirlochen exclaimed, shaking her arm.

Mozel opened her large, Jewish eyes which were now reddened and swollen, and smiled.

Tirlochen removed his turban from his head, unfurled it and covered Mozel's body with it. Mozel smiled again, winked at him and said, as blood bubbled from her mouth, "Go and see...if my underwear is still there or not — I mean ..."

Tirlochen left her and walked over to Kirpal's flat. Mozel tried to look at the men standing around her.

"He is a Miyan bhai...but a really mean and ruthless one...I call him Sikh ..."

Tirlochen returned. He indicated by a look that Kirpal Kaur was safe. Mozel breathed a sigh of relief. With that, blood gushed out of her mouth.

"Oh, damn it ..." she whispered and wiped her lips with her down-covered wrist, and then addressed Tirlochen.

"All right darling, bye-bye."

Tirlochen wanted to speak but the words were caught in his throat.

Mozel pushed away Tirlochen's turban from her body. "Take away...this religion of yours." And her arm fell lifelessly over her robust breasts.

Original in Urdu.
Translated by Tahira Naqvi.

KAMLESHWAR

HOW MANY PAKISTANS?

What a long journey! I don't understand why I keep thinking about Pakistan again and again — why it troubles me so much?

Salima, have I ever been unkind to you, hurt you? Why are you then so unfair to me and so unjust towards yourself? You laugh. I am sure that your laughter is full of poisoned arrows. It is certainly not touched with the fragrance of the mehndi flowers which suffuse the night as the wind blows over them. The wind! The very thought of it amuses me. You used to tell me that I was "touched" by the winds that had swept across our days! Do you remember, Salima?

I am sure that you remember those days. Women never forget anything. They only pretend to forget. Otherwise it would be difficult for them to go on living. It is strange to think of you either as Salima or as merely another woman. I would like to think of you only as Bano. The same Bano who used to bring me mehndi flowers. Your breath seemed to mingle with their fragrance. You would blow on the flowers as if to say, "Only when the wind blows over them do you know how fragrant they are!" To tell you the truth, Bano, I was "touched" by that wind — intoxicated by it. But now I hesitate to call you Bano. I wonder if you would ever again care to be reminded of that name. Besides, what does that name mean to you now?

That night I really did want to climb those stairs to your room once again and ask you a question, remind you of something. But then I said to myself — How could you have forgotten it; it was impossible for you to have forgotten anything.

O God! You don't know how many Pakistans were created along with the creation of that one Pakistan. In how many hearts, in how many places! The creation of that one Pakistan solved nothing. It merely confused everything. Now nothing is what it seems to be.

That night, too, everything was confused. I don't know if it was the voice of the peepal tree in the backyard or of Badru Miyan which had cried out, "Kadir Miyan!...Sala Pakistan has been created...O sister, Pakistan has been created...!"

How terrifying was that moonlit night! You were lying naked in the courtyard downstairs, Bano. Bathed in moonlight! The leaves of the peepal tree in the backyard were rustling in the wind, when Badru Miyan's voice seemed to rise from the very depths of hell, "Kadir Miyan!...Sala Pakistan has been created...O sister, Pakistan has been created...!"

Let me tell you about the three stages of my life's journey. During the first stage I was intoxicated by the fragrance of Bano's mehndi flowers. The second stage was completed when I saw Bano lying naked in the moonlight. The third stage began when she stood before me at the door, holding the frame with both her hands and asked, "Is there someone else...?"

Yes, Bano, there was someone else...

Bano, after that single, terrifying moment of bewildering silence, why did you laugh? What had I done to you? Were you seeking revenge? On me? On Muneer? Or was it on Pakistan? Whom were you trying to humiliate? Me? Yourself? Muneer? Or...?

Oh, why does Pakistan come between us again and again? How does that nation concern us? Alas, Pakistan is the name of that reality which separates the two of us. It's that truth which falls between us like an abysmal silence. It's that blank void between our families, our friends and our communities which makes us insensitive to each other. Pakistan is a dark blind space; a space without feeling; a space where the sufferings of others are no longer sufferings, and the joys of others are not joys. Perhaps, Pakistan is that barren and still place where there is no wind or breath to stir the fragrance of mehndi flowers. It must be so. Otherwise, why should I have been forced to leave Chinar and wander like a dervish?

Do you remember Chinar where the mehndi flowers used to bloom along the wall of the Mission School? We used to take the path which led from the school to the peepal tree at the bank of the Ganga and, sitting on the broken walls of Raja Bhartrhari fort, eat imli.

How can I forget the evening when Zamin Ali, the compounder, told my father, "I know it's not true, but how will you convince people? Send Mangal away for a few days. If he stays here everyone will gossip about his affair with Bano. Marriage is out of the question. It may lead to communal riots."

You can't imagine how shocked I was when I heard that. Must I leave Chinar? I was, however, compelled to leave it...Oh, how beautiful were the nights at Chinar! The waters of the Ganga; the boats going to Kashi; the ruined walls of Brathari's fort!...And the courtyard of the check-post at the banks of the river where I used to wait for you — wait for you to come — wait and wonder if you would escape from those narrow lanes at last, from those alleys of mud and drain-water, and reach the banks of the Ganga. You never did escape!...I waited...and waited...

When did we suddenly cease to be children? We didn't realize that our innocent meetings had become the subject of gossip. We had grown up and our friendship was regarded with suspicion.

We didn't suspect that our love would create communal tensions in the village. How did that happen Bano? Why did that happen? But, of course, you wouldn't have an answer either.

We never met again after those days.

Slowly, the three stages of my life's journey passed. At none of the stages did we have the chance to stop and talk to each other. Neither when the fragrance of the mehndi flowers had intoxicated us, nor when I saw you lying naked in the moonlight, nor when you stood at the door holding the frame with both your hands and asked, "Is there someone else?"

Mehndi flowers, Chinar, my house, our love...

The red-brick road used to meander past my house to the main bazaar, run along the bank of the Ganga and go right upto the gate of Bhartrhari's fort. It used to make a sharp right turn at the check-post. There was another path which was unpaved. Dirty water used to flow across it in small rivulets and disappear into the sands of the Ganga. That path led to the house in which you lived, Bano.

Beyond Bano's house was land full of mud and drain water. The Mission School lay on the other side of that land. It was once a British bungalow. It was surrounded by a hedge of mehndi flowers and a field of wild dhatura plants. Those dhatura plants used to cause me anxiety. When there was communal tension in the town because of us, Bano had somehow managed to meet me at the check-post and had said, "If the maulvi and his followers continue to harass me, I'll eat dhatura leaves and commit suicide. Don't you dare to leave the town without me. If you do, remember that Gangaji flows near by. So, think before you..."

We didn't talk much that day. She left. I couldn't tell her about the turmoil in my house. Everyday someone or the other threatened my father in the streets of the village. Everyone was afraid that I would be killed or that the Muslims would suddenly attack our house.

Pakistan had already been created in those days, Bano! Your father, however, continued to write his *Bhartrhari Namaha*:

"Long ago I became a wanderer, mother,
From a wanderer, I became a fakir.
The last days of this faithless one
Will be unhappy.
I leave my people behind
Take good care of them.
Having become a fakir
I have ruined my Kingdom
I have left it desolate."

People used to say that your father, the drill-master, had lost his senses, that was why he was writing his *Bhartrhari Namaha*, the life of a Hindu saint-poet. "He isn't a turk — he is a local labourer — a damned low-caste convert!" It was then that we learnt that a true Muslim had to be a descendent of some Irani-Turani! That the Muslims of Chinar were not real Muslims! People used to keep their distance from the drill-master. But when they heard of my affair with you, they all took arms as if they were the real defenders of Bano!

I know, but you don't Bano, that the drill-master had no objection to our affair. But he was helpless and had to say, "I'll do whatever the Maulvi Sahib asks me to do." He had even visited my father secretly once, and had wept bitterly. Even after that day, however, he continued to write his *Bhartrhari Namaha,* though he didn't have the courage to read it out to anyone. I learnt that he hadn't abandoned his work on *Bhartrhari Namaha* the day I was forced to leave the town. The clerk of the check-post had slipped a piece of paper into my sweaty hand when I had gone to take leave of him.

It was a terrifying night. Murder was in the air. Everyone was apprehensive. Nobody knew when the village would begin to resound with the cry "Ya Ali, Ya Ali," and when people would begin to slaughter each other. Even the Ganga was flooded. The peepal tree on its banks trembled. The wind was fierce. The ruined fort was full of strange whispers. My father, and half a dozen Hindu youths — yes, I must admit that, Bano — had escorted me to the station so that I could leave the village alive.

At first, everyone had advised me to go to Jaunpur and stay with my uncle. But then, I don't know who decided that I should go to Bombay and try to get a job in the railway workshop at Kurla where another uncle of mine was employed.

What a dreadful night it was, Bano! How humiliated I felt as I made my escape. Conflicting thoughts pounded in my brain. At times I thought that I should go back to my house, pick up a hatchet and kill all those Muslims of yours — paint the streets red with blood and win you. And if I failed, kill you and drown myself in the Ganga.

But, I was also ashamed and scared. I knew that though the drill-master had no objection to our affair, he had kept quiet. I also knew that he hadn't abandoned his work on his *Bhartrhari Namaha*. Perhaps, if he hadn't continued to write it there wouldn't have been so much opposition.

The air in the village had been poisoned — it was as if a snake had bitten each of its members. Father had been warned that I shouldn't show my face in the village the next morning. There were discussions well into the middle of the night. By the time they ended there was only one train left — the goods train to Mughal Sarai.

Yes, I was escorted to the station by half a dozen Hindu youths. We avoided the main bazaar and took the path which ran past the ruined fort. The road was dark. The clerk of the check-post lit our way with a lantern and managed to slip a piece of paper into my hand. It was then that I realized your father was still working on his *Bhartrhari Namaha*.

Why have you become a mendicant
And given up friends, soldiers and courtiers?
Why have you adopted a life of poverty
And left behind both narcissus and poppy?
Why have you worn robes of saffron
And taken off expensive shawls of silk?
Why do you wander from door to door,
Singing God's name,

And have gone far from Kamroop, Dhaka and
Bengal?
Why have you left us in your madness
And abandoned your Kingship?

It was madness, perhaps — silks, shawls, narcissus and poppy — they were all real. But peepal, akh, mehndi and dhatura were no less real than the narcissus flowers, Bano!...So was Pakistan real... What could we have done with Pakistan!

There were lots of people at the platform with us. The goods train left at two thirty in the morning. My father was very upset and despondent. Everyone was scared and felt humiliated. Perhaps, that was why they were all very angry. It seemed as if there would be communal riots even after I had left the village. God help us, I said to myself, if these Hindus start a riot on their way back from the station! Pounce upon the Muslims as they sleep and cut them to pieces!...How difficult it is for a Hindu to be a Hindu, Bano! As soon as a man becomes a Hindu, he loses something precious.

How painful was that parting! There was a slight chill in the air and the stone floor of the platform was very cold. The Vindhya Hills in the distance and the palm trees across the railway tracks watched us silently.

What can I say now? I had never imagined that I would be driven out of my own house like this. No one who has ever been humiliated and driven out of his own village, can ever be at peace again. I can still recall those lanes where Bano lived. I used to wait for her at the check-post for what seemed like eternity. And then walk through those lanes looking for mehndi flowers scattered on the ground. They would mark the spot where Bano had reached, and beyond which she had been prevented from going by someone who had either called her back, or questioned her, or forcibly stopped her.

The truth is that Pakistan had pierced through my heart like a sword that day. I know that people had been forced to convert; had changed their names; had been killed...shame, fear, anger, tears, blood, madness, love — all these had been burnt into my soul that day. To tell the truth, even if I had been able to possess Bano after that day, it would have been worthless. I would never have been able to recover the past again...Bano had been locked up in her house... The wind had ceased to blow over the mehndi flowers...

The train left and I began to wander from place to place like a dervish. I knew I could never return home again.

I was sure that Bano's father couldn't have continued to live in Chinar without feeling suffocated. But I learnt nothing about Bano's fate, except that she hadn't drowned herself in the Ganga. That she was alive somewhere — happy, unhappy, anxious. Perhaps in someone else's bed. In love. Praying for her husband's health like any honest wife. Colouring her hands with mehndi. Looking after her children. Joyous, perhaps; full of regrets for the past, perhaps... But I was certain that she would never forget that moment when time had suddenly stood still for both of us — that moment when a nation called Pakistan had been created — that moment of torment which will never cease...

Well, Bano, what happened was fated. I reached Mughal Sarai. I then went to Allahabad and from there to Bombay. My uncle found me a job in the Kurla railway workshop, but after a few weeks, I moved to Pune. I got a job in the workshop of a hospital where artificial limbs were manufactured. I was convinced that neither your family nor mine would be able to continue to live in Chinar. But I never imagined that my father would send me news of the migration of such a large number of other families also.

The fact of the matter is that Chinar as we knew it had been destroyed. When something like Pakistan comes into existence, a vital part of one's being dies. The crops no longer grow. The sky is torn into bits. The clouds no longer bring rain. The winds cease to blow.

A few years later my father wrote to me that he had left Chinar along with the families of eight Muslim weavers and two Hindu carpenters in search of the fields, the rain, the wind and the sky. They had moved to Bhiwandi. I didn't know that Bano's family, too, had migrated with him. What job could a drill-master have found there? I did wonder about that. That my father had moved to Bhiwandi, did make sense — he was a cotton merchant. They must have suffered a lot in the beginning.

My father's letters were deliberately vague. In none of them did he mention that he lived with your family in the same house in Baja Mohalla; that your people had occupied the ground floor and he lived in the rooms upstairs. Did the drill-master agree to that arrangement out of a sense of guilt? The others who had migrated with them lived either in Bengal Pura or Nayee Basti.

I really did want to come and see you, Bano. But to tell you the truth, I was still very angry. And, when I heard that you were in Bhiwandi and had got married, I was very upset. Besides, my father had subtly hinted to me that I should stay away from Bhiwandi for sometime. He said that he had a lot of regard for the drill-master and didn't want him to feel embarassed or humiliated by my presence. The drill-master, he insisted, was blameless in the whole affair.

What an awkward situation it was! How could I have lived in the same house with you?

I was torn by conflicting thoughts and feelings. Supposing I had been unable to contain the anger which I had suppressed for so long?

What would have happened if Pakistan, which had been smouldering inside me, had burst into flames?

Or, if I had tried to prevent you from sleeping with your husband?

Or, if I had driven him out of Bhiwandi, just as I had been pushed out of my house?

Or, if I had lost control over myself one night and broken into your room...?

Of course, my father and the drill-master had convinced themselves that they were blameless. But what about me? They had lost nothing. I was the only one who had suffered. Since the day I was forced to leave Chinar, I have been wandering from place to place with a mask over my face, gloves on my hands, and a dagger in my belt...

But, Bano, there were communal riots even in Bhiwandi. Not because you and I loved each other, but because the two communities had no love for each other. I was shocked when I heard about the riots. I didn't know what would happen afterwards. Five years earlier, I had been accused of causing trouble. But this time, I wasn't around...I had stayed away from Bhiwandi deliberately. I was afraid, I would cause a riot if I saw you again...

But when, at last, I saw you...

Moonlit Night and Bano.

I reached Bhiwandi about ten days after the riots. As I entered the city, I saw the charred remains of houses, like gaping black holes, between tall buildings. There was nothing but ash, rubble and dust everywhere. The air smelt of smoke, of recently extinguished fires. It was sharp, acrid and pungent, and it scratched and clawed its way deep into one's body. Bano, you must have smelt it too.

When I got down at the bus station late in the evening, everything was quiet. There were a few policemen standing idly beneath a large cinema poster. Most of the buses were empty. There were no passengers going to Sange Minar, Ali Bagh, Bhorwarda or Sinnar — not even to Shirdi.

Under the shed of the local bus stop, I saw a few more policemen. They were huddled under it like gypsies. Were it not for their guns, which were stacked together like sugar-cane, I wouldn't have guessed that they were policemen.

The roads were deserted. I saw only a few people walking aimlessly in the grounds outside the dak-bungalow where the Collector had set up his office. There were no taxis to Thane or Kalyan.

Perhaps, you knew what it was to walk through riot-torn cities. I didn't. Desolate streets. A strange, eerie silence. A blankness. One either sees nothing or notices everything with an uncanny attentiveness — Why does one become either wild or acutely sensitive? Especially when one isn't personally involved.

Even in a small town like Pune, it is difficult to find out how to get to Baja Mohalla. Well, I somehow found my way to it and even located the house. But it seemed to be empty. Can human beings endure such silence and stillness?

To tell you the truth, Bano, for a moment I thought that if I hadn't left Chinar it, too, would have become silent and still. Then I thought about you, Bano. How could I face you? I lost my nerve. For a moment I felt as if I hadn't left Chinar and you hadn't aged at all.

The door of the house was open. I walked in without making a noise and found myself in a courtyard. There were two pots of water in a corner. Near them there were two shadows. One woman was naked from her waist upwards. The other was sitting in front of her, and was massaging her breasts. Startled, I stepped back into the street again.

As soon as I came out, I saw the drill-master. He recognized me at once, but didn't know how to greet me. He stood for a while puzzled and uncertain. What could he have said to me or asked me? I went to his rescue, and asked him, as if he was a stranger, about my father.

"He left for Chinar two days ago," he replied.

"Two days ago?" I couldn't think of anything else to say.

"Yes, he didn't want to stay back. A few other families went back with him," he said.

I, immediately, understood why my father had gone back to Chinar and why the drill-master had refused to. After all, the reasons why my father had left Chinar were different from those of the drill-master — or from mine. The drill-master had been exiled by history, and those whom history exiles, can never return...I had been forced to leave only by a few people.

Since my father was no longer in that house, I didn't know what to do. There were riots in the city. Where could I have stayed? It was impossible for the drill-master to invite me to stay with him. After all, you were in the house. Yet, how could the drill-master have left me standing in the street like a stranger? He still had a sense of decency.

"Did my father take all his things with him?" I asked.

"No, most of them are still here," he replied.

"Did he lock his house?"

"Yes," he replied and then after some hesitation, added, "I have a duplicate key."

"I would like to stay in his room for the night. I have to go back tomorrow," I said. I had no choice. Where could I have gone in that strange city?

He left me standing alone in the street and went inside. A moment later he returned with the key and a candle. He led me upstairs, opened the lock, gave me the key and said, "Have you had something to eat?"

"Yes," I replied and went inside.

"Let me know if you need something," he said, as he walked downstairs. The biographer of Bhartrhari was shrewd enough to say, "Let me know," instead of, "Come to the door and ask."

Everything was very quiet.

I pulled my cot upto the terrace so that I could escape the oppressive heat of the room. Or was it in the hope of seeing you, Bano!...It was a moonlit night. The air was still. I decided to sleep on the open terrace.

What a strange night it was, Bano! You didn't know I was upstairs. I wonder what the drill-master had told you? If the police hadn't come the next morning, you wouldn't have ever known...

I waited for a long time for the sound of footsteps. I did hope that you would come upstairs. But after a while the excitement died down. After all, I thought to myself, a wife's place is beside her husband.

The peepal tree in the backyard was bathed in moonlight. I had placed my cot at a place from where I could look down into the courtyard. But what I saw was dreadful.

Bano was lying on a cot bathed in moonlight. Her blouse was open and her saree was pulled upto her waist. Her breasts were full like balloons. She was convulsing with pain and thrashing about like a fish out of water. Once in a while a fountain of milk squirted out of her breasts. Milk streaked down her stomach and glittered like mercury in the moonlight. A big drop of milk lay in the depression of her navel like a pearl.

"Hai Allah!" Bano moaned.

"Try to sleep, Bano," I heard her mother plead.

"They are bursting," she wailed and squeezed her breasts hard with both her hands.

"Let me help," her mother said, and started massaging Bano's breasts gently. Streams of milk squirted from them. Bano continued to moan and weep. Her naked body was soon bathed in milk and it glittered in the moonlight.

Bano's mother frequently wiped her breasts with the hem of her saree and then squeezed the milk out of it into the drain nearby. A small stream of milk slithered through the drain like a white snake.

Oh Bano! What I saw shocked me.

Agitated, I paced up and down the terrace late into the night. I lay down only after I saw that Bano had finally covered her breasts with her saree and had gone to sleep. What a nightmare that was! I saw breasts full of milk hanging from the sky...!

I had just gone to sleep when I was woken up by knocking on the door in the backyard. I thought I heard someone wailing, "Qadir Miyan!...Sala, Pakistan has been created!...O sister, Pakistan has been created...!" After a moments silence, I thought that I heard the same voice cry out, "Qadir Miyan, now we'll tie ehram here itself and perform talbiya. This is where we'll perform Haj... Alright, Qadir Miyan?"

Had I not seen the peepal tree in the backyard, I would have said that the voice had risen from the depths of Hell and I would have run away...But what a strange nightmare it was — Blood rained from the sky, corpses walked in the streets, fountains of blood spurted out of chopped heads, naked bodies danced in the flames...

Then the leaves of the peepal tree crackled in the wind. They sounded like clerks typing in a hospital. Their sound was familiar. Everything else was horrifying.

The next morning my head felt heavy. My eyes were red. My hands and feet were numb. I had to get up early because the police wanted to ask me some questions. The drill-master had woken me up. He was trembling with fear.

"It's the police," he said. "They are asking about you."

"Why?"

"They make inquiries about every outsider."

I was furious. Tell me, Bano, when I was forced to leave my house, why didn't they come to ask me why I was leaving?

Pakistan, Bano, is the fragmentation of man...It is the refusal to consider the whole man...

I understood that when the police took me away for questioning early in the morning.

You and I, Bano, had become victims of Pakistan. We had been entrapped by it...

At the police station, they asked me all sorts of questions. Why had I come to this area...? What could I have told them? Why does a man wander from place to place? The police would have really harassed me had the drill-master not come to my rescue. He told them everything about me. The fact that Master

Sahib was a Muslim was of great help. The testimony of a Muslim was the best proof of innocence that a Hindu could have had. But I did wonder if Master Sahib hadn't committed the same mistake as he had committed in the past by continuing to write his *Bhartrhari Namaha*.

After the police released me, your father and I sat down on a log of wood lying nearby. Neither of us knew what to say to each other. The silence became oppressive.

The drill-master was the first one to speak. "Badru has gone crazy," he said. "He has been sitting under the peepal tree since the riots broke out. All his looms were burnt. Did you hear him call out to Qadir Miyan last night?"

There were three or four other people sitting at the Teenbati cross-roads. Perhaps, they had gone to the police-station to stand bail for someone or to give information. They looked depressed and afraid. The maulvi was telling those who were sitting around him, "The Prophet has said that the trumpet shall sound thrice. At the first sound of the trumpet, people will begin to tremble with fear. Terror will grip their souls. At the sound of the second trumpet, everyone will die. And when the trumpet sounds the third time, everyone will stand before the Lord to be judged. That is how it shall be. The first trumpet has sounded..."

"Are you still writing your *Bhartrhari Namaha*?" I asked Master Sahib.

"Yes," he said, and recited the following lines :

"I am only a wanderer,
Staying here for a night!
Talk, let the night pass quickly,
and the sun rise again!"

After he finished reciting those verses, he looked around. There were wild yellow flowers growing in the cracks of the wall nearby; birds were hopping in the tall and thick grass which was growing on the ground all around. The flutter of wings, yellow flowers...The Master Sahib watched them in silence for a while.

I broke the silence and asked, "Last night..."

"Yes, that was Badru. He has gone mad. All his looms were burnt. Since then he has been sitting under the peepal tree and screaming curses," Master Sahib said.

"In the house..." I asked, gathering courage.

Master Sahib then told me the entire story — he told me about what happened to you, Bano. You had given birth to a child in Dr. Sarang's Nursing Home, three days before the riots erupted. The rioters had set the Nursing Home on fire. Pregnant women had jumped out of the second storey to save themselves. Some women had even thrown their new born babies out of the windows. Two women had died. Five children had been burnt to death. Bano's baby, too, had died when she had thrown him out into the street below. There was a massacre. Bano had somehow managed to escape and reach home safely. Now her breasts were full of milk and she was in agony.

"It's time I went back to Pune," I said, trying to find an excuse to get away.

"Go to Chinar if you can, to see your father," the drill-master said.

"Why, is he not well?"

"No. He lost an arm during the riots. Our house was attacked. We would all have been slaughtered were it not for him. He ran out into the streets and confronted the goondas. Someone struck his arm with a sword and severed it. Blood spurted out from his amputated limb. Your father picked up the arm which had been cut off and fought the attackers with it till he fell down unconscious. The goondas threw fire-bombs into our house and ran away. Your father lay in the street with his severed arm clutched in his other hand...We took him to the Military Hospital. He was released eight days later. The day after his release, he left for Chinar."

We sat in silence for sometime.

The birds were still hopping in the grass.

"He said that he would get himself bandaged in the Chinar Hospital...O God, have mercy upon us!" The drill-master covered his eyes as he said that.

Where was I? In what kind of world? Who were these people? Was I amongst human beings? Was I living through a nightmare?

The drill-master and I walked back home. I went upstairs. Later I heard Bano, her husband, Muneer, Master Sahib and his wife arguing with each other.

"I don't understand why you insist on staying here?" Muneer said.

"You won't understand," Bano shouted in reply. "I must give birth to a child in this country on this very earth. Only then will I leave."

When I leaned over the balcony and looked down into the courtyard, I saw Muneer trembling with rage and screaming, "Do what you like. Sleep with anyone you want to. Find someone to give you a child."

"You can't anyway," Bano screamed back at him.

I was shocked. Were they talking about me?

I was wrong. A moment later, Bano added, "You are impotent because you sell blood to get money for your drink."

Muneer slapped her. There was a lot of shouting and screaming.

"Don't I know?" Bano said, and continued to shower curses at Muneer. "Every time you go to Bombay, you sell your blood. Then you lie in bed and shiver all night."

It was terrible to hear you curse and weep, Bano! Each one of us was in agony, each one of us had made our own Pakistan. We had all been disfigured. Mutilated. Crippled. We were only half-alive!

What a dreadful moonlit night it was. I stole out of Bhiwandi in the same way as I had left Chinar. I took a taxi to Thane.

The air was full of the bitter smell of ash; breasts full of milk hung from the sky; fountains of blood spurted out of bodies standing at the cross-roads...

Thane! From Thane, I went to Bombay in a bus and, from there, took a train to Pune. There I lay in bed with a fever for several days.

What an awful age we live in...And what a strange creature man is! Disfigured, crippled, bloodied, he continues to live.

Bano, can you imagine what passes through a man's being, when in his loneliness and agony, he hears the voice of a woman ask, "Is there anyone else?" Can you guess, Bano?

Is There Someone Else?

About five months later, I received a letter from my father. He had returned to Bhiwandi. His cloth business wasn't doing well, because of the Sindhis and the Marwaris. The market was dull. Nor were all the looms working. Because he had lost one arm, and had begun to walk a little crookedly, the people in the market place had begun to call him tonta. He was rather amused by that. He had also written that Muneer had left for Bombay with Bano. No one knew whether they were still in Bombay or had gone to Pakistan. The drill-master had gone mad. He had now begun to do his drill exercises at home and write the story of Brathari at school.

...If I had not gone to Bombay that day, Bano, I would never have met you. What a painful meeting it was! I was so ashamed of myself.

You must have thought that I visited prostitutes often. To tell you the truth, Bano, I do visit prostitutes. I do so because of you.

I was in Bombay for a few days. I had broken my journey there on my way to Bhiwandi. After I reached Bombay, I lost heart and wondered what I would do in Bhiwandi.

At the station I met Kedar, a friend of mine who lived in Bombay. He had stayed with me in Pune. Kedar suggested that we spend the evening together.

You had nothing to do with that evening, Bano.

Kedar and I had a few drinks at a pub in Colaba. Then we walked till we reached the Handloom House. We turned into the lane that runs by its side.

If I go back there now I'll recognize the lane, but at the moment I can't recall the details of the locality. We walked down that lane for a while and then took a right turn. Perhaps, there was a cigarette shop at the corner. A few cars were parked in the lane. It was, I think, a locality where the Bohra Muslims live. It was very clean. The building had a lift. The staircase was also very clean. Kedar and I climbed up the stairs. After walking up five floors both of us were out of breath. We could smell food being cooked in one of the apartments. Kedar stopped in front of a door and rang the bell. The flat didn't seem to be very well maintained.

The door opened. We were confronted by a Sindhi. He was wheezing. He took us into a room and made us sit down on an ordinary sofa. The Sindhi was gasping for breath so badly that it seemed as if he would collapse and never regain consciousness.

Kedar and the Sindhi disappeared into another room. A few minutes later I heard Kedar's laughter.

I was restless and uncomfortable. I went and stood near the window to catch some fresh air. I could see dirty roof-tops everywhere.

The Sindhi returned. He was still wheezing. "Beer," he rasped, "Will you have some beer?"

"Yes," I replied.

He sent a boy to get a bottle of beer. He didn't drink any himself.

"You," he asked, asthmatically, "Bombay..."

He wanted to know if I lived in Bombay.

"No, I live in Pune."

"Visit?" he asked, panting heavily.

"No, I had some work here."

"Are you a businessman?"

"No, I had some personal work. I am on my way to Bhiwandi."

He continued to sit next to me and breathe heavily. I was getting impatient. But Kedar soon reappeared. When the Sindhi saw Kedar standing before him, he got up with a start. I too got up. All three of us stood silently in the middle of the room. Kedar paid for my beer.

Suddenly, the door of a room opened and a woman handed Kedar a bunch of keys. Seeing me standing next to Kedar and the asthmatic Sindhi, she asked, "Is there someone else?"

I turned around to look. It was you, Bano. You were standing there in a blouse and a petticoat, holding the door-frame with your hands, and asking, "Is there someone else?"

Yes! There was...There was someone else...

There was a moment of agonizing silence. You, too, had recognized me. There was a contemptuous, a venomous smile on your lips...or did I imagine it?

Were you taking revenge? Against me, Muneer, or Pakistan? Or were you taking revenge against yourself?

I went downstairs. Kedar followed me.

I wanted to climb the stairs again and ask, "Bano, was this fated to happen?"

Where should I go now? Where should I hide? There are Pakistans everywhere. Where can I find the kind of life I desire? How can I live an undivided life?

Bano! Pakistan is everywhere. It inflicts wounds on you and me. It humiliates us. It defeats us everytime...

Original in Hindi.
Translated by Vishwamitter Adil and Alok Bhalla.

SYED WALIULLAH

THE STORY OF THE TULSI PLANT

The house stood about a hundred yards from the wide brick-and-mortar bridge that curved like a bow. Two storeyed and large, it rose steeply from the road. There was no practice of leaving space for pavements along the road in this country. The house had also not shown the courtesy of leaving any land in the front. But there was a lot of land behind the house. Stretching beyond the inner courtyard that was ringed by the bathroom, the toilet and the kitchen was an extensive area covered by a dense, almost impenetrable, grove of fruit trees. The tough, long grass had woven a thick canopy with the leafy mango, jamun and jackfruit trees, imparting to the place the dusky gloom of sunset even under the bright mid-day sun, and making the earth exude a damp and musty smell.

When there was so much land, why couldn't some space have been left in front of the house for a garden, they wondered? Even if there was no garden, had there just been some open ground, they could have made a little garden themselves, thought Mateen. Planted with care some lovely seasonal flowers, fragrant gandharaj, bakul, hasnahana and a few roses. And rested there in the cool evenings after an exhausting day at office. They could have bought a few comfortable cane chairs or canvas armchairs and sprawled around in relaxed abandon, making pleasant conversation. Amjad was fond of his hookah. In keeping with the ambience of the little garden, he could have bought himself a gargara, an elegant ornamental one, with a long pipe, ideal for the leisure of the long tranquil evenings. Kader could tell an interesting story. In the cool, light breeze of the evening, fragrant with the smell of flowers, his story would have been touched by the magic aura of fantasy and become spell-binding. Or, on a moonlit night, there would have been no need for a story at all. Wouldn't it have been enough to sit in quiet solitude, gazing at the moon as it climbed the horizon slowly and come face to face with it? — such thoughts grew more insistent after an exhausting day at the office. He longed to climb those steps that rose almost straight from the main road onto the second storey of the house.

They had seized the house. It was not as if they had to fight for occupation, nor had anyone readily surrendered it out of fear of their physical prowess. Having come into the city in the aftermath of the Partition, they had been searching frantically for shelter and had come upon that house quite by chance one day. The huge house stood empty, totally deserted. They had initially hesitated, in surprise. Then they had surged forward wild with excitement. They had broken the lock and entered the house, driven by such thoughtless frenzy — like children collecting raw mangoes scattered by the rough winds of baisakhi — that their actions did not seem like daylight robbery at all. Had a sense of guilt tried to creep into their minds, it would have been swept away by the shrieks of derisive laughter.

In the afternoon when the news reached the city, unwanted visitors had started arriving in hordes — all in search of a roof over their heads. But they had resisted them defiantly and were belligerent. What was this, a free-for-all? Later, calmly and cool headedly, they had explained, "Look sahib, there is no more place — all the rooms are full. Even that small dark room has four cots, each three-feet by two-feet. If a few chairs and a couple of tables are added to it, there wouldn't be any space to move." They had also expressed sympathy. "We understand your difficulties; why, haven't we undergone such travails ourselves? But brother, you are unfortunate. Had you come but four hours earlier...why four, barely two hours ago, that fat gentleman from the accounts office took that small room in the corner downstairs. The room is adjacent to the road but that is not a problem. It has the advantage of having a government lamp just outside the window. There will be no problem if the current goes off."

The entire country was in a turmoil, experiencing great upheaval and change. But it wasn't as though law did not prevail in these parts. So the police duly arrived to investigate the matter.

The erstwhile owner of the house had not appealed to the government for reclamation. Under the existing circumstances, it was improbable that he would have, even if he had known. It was indeed too much to expect of a man who, in great fear, had managed to disappear with his large family without a trace, from the country within a couple of days. The informants were those who hadn't been able to reach the house in time, four hours, even two hours earlier, because they had been too busy planning a raid elsewhere in the city.

But talking of sheer luck, who knew when misfortune would befall them? They had to be vigilant. Desperation forced even the meek to take up arms. A physical confrontation might really not be necessary, but they were prepared to face the worst.

The circumstances were explained to the police in such a tactful way that the sub-inspector did not raise further objections and returned with his team. He submitted his report in which he, of course, described all the complexities of the case. His complex report was best shelved thought his superior officer, to avoid having to simplify it. Besides, what was the hurry? To waste sympathy on those who had run away was foolish and when the absentee owner had not pressed his claim, then why take on unnecessary trouble? Besides, those clerks were decent, harmless fellows, not the unscrupulous kind to sell the door and window panels or the beams of the roof in the Chorbazaar.

The house grew animated overnight. In Calcutta, many of them had lived in the dingy and filthy areas around Blockman Lane, Khalasipatti, Kamru Khansama Lane or in the musty and noisy surroundings amongst the book-keepers in Baithak-khana or the tobacco-sellers in Syed Saleh Lane. The spacious rooms of the house, wide windows opening onto long verandahs reminiscent of the bungalows of the indigo overlords, the open courtyard backed by the wooded orchard, exhilarated them and filled them with inexpressible delight. Though they couldn't occupy separate rooms like lords, the airy rooms, full of light, gave them immense pleasure and the chance, perhaps, to live again. They felt that the breath of freshness would fill their blood with new vigour and vitality, give their faces the healthy lustre of the hazaar-do-hazaar-walas, free their bodies of the debilitating germs of malaria and kala azar.

Yunus, for example, had lived in Macleod Street. Inspite of the anglicised name, the street was veritably a dustbin overflowing with the morning garbage. He had lived in a tottering and dilapidated double storeyed building with some leather merchants from Kutch. He had once heard somewhere that the smell of leather was beneficial, it killed tuberculosis germs. At least the noxious and rank smell of leather overcame the stench of the open drains. Why, it was overpowering enough to conceal the stench of a dead rat or a cat lying in the corner of the room decomposing for days. So Yunus had found living with leather expedient. Moreover, that point about the germs being destroyed was advantageous. Physically, he was rather frail and weak; he was not in good health either. Now, lying in a pool of golden sunlight pouring in through the wide windows of the large, south facing, second storey room of the house, Yunus shuddered at the memory of the nightmarish days in Macleod Street. He wondered how much harm had been done already. Had he some money, he would use it to get his lungs examined. It was better to be careful than sorry.

By the side of the kitchen, in the left corner of the courtyard was a foot-high brick platform bearing a small tulsi plant. One morning, Modabber was strolling around the courtyard, chewing a neem twig for mechchowak. Suddenly his glance fell upon the tulsi plant. It was strange that he had not noticed it earlier. He was rather an excitable sort, often creating a furore over the slightest matter. All of them came down to see what the present cause of his agitation was.

Modabber pointed at the tulsi plant. That plant had to be uprooted immediately. As the current occupants of the house, they could not tolerate any signs of Hinduism.

They looked at the little tulsi plant. The spreading tint of brown had made the dark green leaves dull and lifeless. Grass and weeds had grown around the base within a few days of its neglect. But it was strange how it had remained hidden from view for so long, now catching them unawares. They stood around in stupefaction.

The house had seemed so empty. Except for a few names scratched in an immature hand on the wall along the stairs, the house had seemed unpossessed, abandoned. That assumption underwent a subtle change and stirred deeper levels of awareness. By revealing itself, the tulsi plant had suddenly disclosed another story.

Seeing their hesitation, Modabber roared again. What was there to think about? The plant had to be uprooted.

They did not know much about Hindu rituals, vaguely recollecting that at dusk, the mistress of the Hindu household, the grihakartri, lit the lamp at the base of the tulsi. She pulled the end of her sari around her covered head, touched her forehead to the platform and prayed for the well-being of her family. Surely, someone had also placed an evening lamp at the base of that neglected tulsi plant. Surely, when the lone evening star dazzled in solitary splendour in the sky, then in the deepening shadows, the lambent flames of that lamp had grown brighter at the devout touch of somebody's blood-red sindoor. Had it been so lit, year after year? The winds of adversity could have swept through the house, the lamp of someone's life could have been extinguished, but the ritual of lighting the lamp every evening had never stopped, even for a day.

Where was the mistress of the house now, the grihakartri, who had placed the lamp at the base of the tulsi plant year after year? Why had she left? Where had she gone? Mateen had worked in the railways once. He wondered if she was in Calcutta or Asansol or Baidyabati or Howrah — or perhaps Lilna — where she could be living with relatives. Beside the vast railway yard, a soft red-bordered sari hung on the clothesline. Perhaps it had belonged to the mistress of the house that they now occupied. But wherever she was, when the shadows deepened every evening, her eyes would be brimming with tears at the memory of the deserted tulsi plant in the house far away.

Yunus had not been feeling well since the previous day. He said, why not let the plant remain? What difference would it make anyhow, they were not going to offer any puja. In fact, a tulsi plant was good to have at home. The extract of its leaves was useful for the treatment of colds and coughs.

Modabber looked around. Everyone seemed to agree with Yunus. Bearded Enayat had the temperament of the maulvi among them. Not only did he read the namaaz religiously five times a day, but also spent the morning reading the *Koran*. Even he was silent. Was he also thinking of the tears that must fill the eyes of the grihakartri every evening when she remembered the abandoned tulsi plant?

So the tulsi remained unhurt.

The atmosphere of the house was stimulating. The listlessness and apathy that had overcome them in Calcutta had almost disappeared. Time passed in great camaraderie — in spirited discussions and heated arguments about varied issues of social, political and economic interest. Communalism was often debated.

Modabber accused the Hindus of being the offenders. The Partition was the result of their orthodoxy and insularity. He cited innumerable instances of their prejudice and persecution. His fulminations made the others furious. Maqsood Miyan, who had leftist inclinations, tried to neutralize the charges. No, the Hindus were not entirely to blame, besides how were the Muslims any better, he argued. Modabber snarled at him. The so-called leftist's needle of allegiance wavered. After all, nobody could be certain about such things. If they swore that the others were responsible, couldn't the others also do the same? The matter was quite complex and could not be so easily resolved. Perhaps what Modabber said was right. How could all of them be wrong — did they not understand their own people? The needle oscillated before settling finally to the right. Its impulsive and illogical tendency was responsible for often discrediting it and branding it leftist.

On the way to the washroom by the side of kitchen, the eye automatically fell upon the tulsi plant. Somebody had cleared the weeds. The leaves which had been turning a dry brown, looked revived and had regained their rich colour. Somebody had watered it and was caring for it — not openly of course. The outward appearances had to be kept up in society, after all.

Yunus had thought that he would never have to return to the filthy lodgings of the leather merchants in Macleod Street, and that he had at last found a shelter full of freshness and light, and the chance to live again. But he was wrong. Not only Yunus, but all of them who had believed that, even though good food was scarce in that house, they would enjoy that precious commodity of life — comfort — each of them was wrong. But they had been saved from making another error. Had there been some open space in front of the house, they would have made a little garden there and then the marigolds would have grown tall and blossomed. That would certainly have been a big mistake.

Modabber came in anxiously and announced that the police had arrived. But why? They rationalised that the police might be pursuing some wily thief who had slipped into the house. That would be like the story of the rabbit. Unable to escape from the hunter, the rabbit sat cowering; it closed its eyes and thought that nobody could see it. The real thieves were those who did not merely hide, but also kept their eyes closed.

The sub-inspector held his old-fashioned hat under his arm and wiped his brow. He looked rather helpless. Two armed constables stood behind him. Both sported flowing moustaches but looked even more helpless. They were looking up and seemed to be counting the beams in the ceiling. Or, they were perhaps watching the pair of pigeons, one white and the other grey, which was busy building their nest in one of the ventilators. The constables had their guns handy.

Mateen enquired politely, "Whom do you want?" "All of you," came the answer. "You have occupied the house illegally and must vacate it within the next twenty-four hours." The sub-inspector showed them the order.

They imagined that the owner of the house had returned. He must have come to the house directly from the station, and having taken note of the situation, rushed to the police station. Afzal craned his neck to see if the owner had also come along. But there was no one else other than the two constables.

Why, had the owner complained, they wanted to know.

No, the government has requisitioned the house, came the answer.

They stood silent in shock. Finally, Mateen protested, "but we are also the government's people!"

How stupid people can be sometimes! Even the constables lowered their eyes from the ceiling and stared in surprise. Their amazed eyes spoke volumes.

A shadow of gloom descended upon the house. There was no end to anxious speculations. Where could they go, they wondered. Some of them declared furiously that they wouldn't go anywhere. Whosoever tried to forcibly remove them and dared to cross the threshold would first have to step over their dead bodies! They recalled that somewhere, some students had occupied a house by force and had exasperated all attempts of the big bosses of the government to oust them. The angry talk made their blood warm. They decided that they would not leave. Those who came would have to step across their dead bodies to take possession of the house.

Their blood boiled for several days. They could not eat, could not sleep. There was just talk, bitter and fiery talk. Eventually, the talk petered out. And when the talking stopped, it didn't take long for the blood to cool.

They were not students. They had proudly announced to the police the other day who they were. They had been upset to hear that the government had requisitioned the house, and then they had claimed loudly that they too were the government's people.

One day they all left. They went like a storm, leaving behind parts of old newspaper, frayed pieces of a clothes-line, bits of bidis and cigarettes, a tattered shoe. The doors and windows of the house made in the style of the indigo overlord's bungalow, stood wide open. But they would not remain so for long, colourful curtains would hang there very soon.

By the side of the kitchen in the courtyard, the little tulsi plant was drying up again. Its leaves were turning brown. Nobody had watered it from the day the police had ordered the house to be vacated. They did not remember the tulsi plant. Did they not remember the tearful eyes of the grihakartri either?

Why they had not remembered, only the tulsi plant could tell. It could be nurtured if they so wished; it could be destroyed in a moment if they wanted to destroy it. In other words, the life and well-being of the tulsi plant could not be insured by its own powers of self-protection. It was vulnerable.

Original in Bengali.
Translated by Tutun Mukherjee.

LALITHAMBIKA ANTHARJANAM

THE MOTHER OF DHIRENDU MUZUMDAR

Do you know who I am? My name is Shanti Muzumdar. I am ninety years old. Born and brought up in a small hamlet in East Bengal. Gave birth to nine children — seven boys and two girls. Five I sacrificed for India, four for Pakistan. Adopted all the children of the new generation as my children and grandchildren. I wanted to die on that soil. All my ancestors were born on that soil and became part of it. If the soldiers of the Mukti-fauj had not carried me on their shoulders and forcibly brought me here, Shanti Mutassi too, would have fallen with honour in the battlefield and attained salvation.

Is it a question of fear? Why should one be afraid? None of Shanti's children were, after all, ever afraid, were they? The bones of five of my children turned to dust in this soil. But, my children, what Shanti Mutassi does not like a bit is this coming back as a refugee, an outsider. You may not know this. But Bharat was never just a handful of earth for us.

The divine mother as *Suphala, Sujala, Sasyashyamala* — we brought up our children as we meditated on the thousands of dazzling swords that adorn her many hands. We sacrificed them for her liberation...The first soldiers of India's freedom struggle, the brave and selfless martyrs — have you heard their stories...Are they a part of your history?

Memories surface. Thrilling memories. Neither of one person, nor of one family. The pitiful story of a whole region. The story of Shanti Muzumdar would make it all clear to you. Listen...our home is in the centre of the region you now call East Pakistan. A zamindari holding towards the left of where the river Padma flows eastwards into the sea.

Floods occur frequently there. At times like this, the villagers used to take refuge in the hall next to the Durga temple.

The brides of the Muzumdar family alone used to sit on the terrace of the huge mansion, and watch the dance of destruction of the waters of the Padma. They never used to come out of the antah-pur. Never saw other men. When Cheriya Chittapan, Abani Muzumdar's wife, was in labour, he insisted on sending for a doctor from the city. But the elder Muzumdar, who held the title Raja Sahib, did not give him permission. According to tradition, even if one of the women in the Muzumdar family fell ill, none but Yama could enter the antah-pur.

Dressed in red silk, with sindoor on my forehead, I first came as a bride to this house in a closed palanquin, when I was just nine. I did not venture out of the house till I was fifty. When my eldest son Dhiren, was in college, he once begged me to come at least upto the door of the parlour to meet a friend of his. When the Governor Sahib and his wife visited us, even *he* wanted me to go out and receive them. Yet, I didn't yield to any of these requests. It was just not possible for women, born in the second half of the nineteenth century, to step out. We were afraid of breaking the law. But then, when our children themselves became the breakers of everything...?

Husbands on one side — children on the other, when such an agonizing battle takes place, which side should a mother take? Whom should she support? Such an intense conflict of duties, my children, you will never comprehend...never.

The Muzumdars were intensely patriotic. We were feudal lords, zamindars, village chieftains in several places; zamindars and village-chiefs. Besides, my husband was a Rao Bahadur, honorary judge and member of the advisory committee of the honourable British government. The Governor and the Viceroy had often been our guests. The family had also decided to send the eldest son, Dhirendu into the ICS as soon as he passed the B.A. He used to say, "Rao Bahadur is just a title. But the ICS will bring with it both money and power."

Unaware of all these plans, Dhiren used to commute between home and Calcutta. He was brilliant in his studies. Handsome. Soft-spoken. Above everything else, people used to praise his sympathy for the poor. He always used to have a group of the under-privileged with him. Some of whom were put up in the ante-room, some in the dark attic of the barn. Food from the kitchen was sent to them. How much money he used to take from me for people like these! But I was always delighted to hear Dhirenbabu being praised for his kindness.

One night, he brought to the antah-pur a woman in purdah. "Mother, she is an ascetic and belongs to the Bhairava community. She doesn't meet or talk to people. Could you accommodate her in the small room next to the prayer hall? And you yourself should take food to her."

I felt happy. For in times, when other young men normally ran after whores, my son looked after the needs of sanyasins.

The sanyasin was always reading or writing something in the dark room. When the written pages piled up, Dhiren took them away. Their conversations sounded as if they were chanting mantras. But whenever I went there with food, the old woman would quickly cover her face and stand facing a corner. Perhaps, because I was not one of her disciples.

One amavasya night, when it was raining hard and the river was in flood, Dhiren summoned me to the dark room and said "Mother, the sanyasin wants to take leave of us tonight. Before leaving she wants to meet and bless you. Come..." Saying this he tugged at the saffron cloth that covered the sanyasin's face. I was shocked. A man! A young man! He could have passed off as Dhiren's elder brother. With folded hands he said, "Forgive me mother, I am Surya Sen. Also known as Master-da. We worship our motherland in the form of Maha Kali. Swords in a hundred hands! Chakras in a hundred hands! The blood smeared head of the enemy! Intestines for garlands...But now for the first time I have seen the goddess as Annapurna; I have seen her as the compassionate one. I want this image to remain in my heart for ever. Bless me."

As Master-da bent down and touched my feet, his eyes filled with tears. Neither could I hold back my tears. Was this the well-known Surya Sen?...The terrorist! The traitor! Whom the police were frantically looking for. As I stood with my hands placed on his bent head, my heart cried out, "Surya Sen...no...Master-da. Is the mother who gave birth to you, my elder sister?"

Time was running out. A boat waited in the river Padma. Dhiren and he got into it. I stood startled, watching their boat being rowed through the turbulent waters of the Padma, till it disappeared. Shanti Muzumdar, the woman who had never stepped out of the antah-pur, died that day. In her place was born another woman called Banglamata. Yet I pretended to know nothing. Aware of everything, I lived two lives at the same time.

Several days later when Surya was captured and sent to the gallows by the police, Dhiren's father said, "Look, this will be the fate of the traitors like him. What problems these people create. Only yesterday the Governor told me — Muzumdar Sahib, your elder son is so brave. We have decided to enlist him in the police force." When I heard that I broke down and couldn't hold back my tears. Was it because of the news of Surya Sen's death? Or, was I thinking of my son as a future police commissioner? I don't know...let us leave it at that. Even after Master-da's death, Dhiren continued to bring home different types of people. I had to grant asylum to many. But suddenly one day, someone threw a bomb. When *he* learnt from a police officer that his son also was among the suspects, Niharendu Muzumdar, his father stormed into the antah-pur and screamed, "No, no , I have no such son. My eldest son is dead." He turned towards me and commanded, "If that traitor comes here, don't even give him water. Hand him over to the police."

Even after this incident, and inspite of being a faithful and an obedient wife, this mother gave shelter to her son several times, gave him all that he wanted. With tears, I used to beg, "My son, please promise me that you won't go anywhere."

A few days before he was arrested in connection with the Chittagong conspiracy, he told me, "Mother, do you know that in olden times, the mothers in Greece used to sacrifice their eldest sons to the Goddess of war. Dying for one's motherland is salvation. Isn't my mother a goddess? Dedicate your eldest son to the motherland. You still have eight more children."

I broke down, "My son, a mother is more important than one's motherland. A mother has a heart which can be broken. A country is mere rock and earth."

Dhiren kissed my forehead, "No, my mother. This country is composed of the hearts of crores and crores of mothers like you. All of them feel pain; all of them are anxious and in tears. If I am to die for the liberation of this grief-stricken motherland, my mother should smile and sing *Vande Mataram*. Promise me mother, that you will smile."

Saying this he touched my feet and went away. Later when I heard of his death in a dynamite explosion during an attack on an arsenal, I sang *Vande Mataram* right in front of his father who was stricken by sorrow and rage. Crying, laughing, screaming like a mad woman, I sang at the top of my voice:

"Oh, ye mighty swords that dazzle in her thousand hands..."

Oh...I am thirsty, my children. My throat is parched...Give me a little water...cold water...yes? Recalled all this. After all, I am now just an outsider, who has come here as a refugee begging for your mercy. Dhirendu Muzumdar faded from people's memories a long time ago. So how can they be now expected to remember his mother?

Dhiren's ghost haunted his younger brothers too. Sharadindu, who had gone to England to study law, shot a white man in front of the Indian Office and later committed suicide. Nityendu and Satyendu didn't even go to college. Their father had a paralytic stroke. Our properties were confiscated. But the Muzumdar household continued to be well-known. It became the home of all the freedom fighters in the country. It was in the cellar of our house that Tarakeshwar was arrested. Ganesh Ghosh, Savitri, Kalpana...and many others like them, came there regularly. Have you heard of Priti Vardhar? The best friend of my daughter, Minati. Poor girl, she was not cut out to be a revolutionary. The sight of blood used to make her feel giddy. Can you believe it...it was this girl who later threw a bomb at the European Club in Chahartali and swallowed potassium cyanide before the police could catch her. The freedom that you now enjoy, sprouted in the blood of these people. Nityendu, Satyendu and Minati are not alive to see it...Later the Congress came, Gandhiji came. When Gandhiji argued that Gopinath should not be forgiven, I told him: It is you whom history is not going to forgive. Bapuji, courage is not a crime. By killing and dying for their motherland, these Bengali youth have become immortal.

When they divided the country finally in the name of religion and caste, I asked the great emperor Nehru: With whose consent did you cut off Bengal's head? With whose permission did you separate us? Here no one is a Hindu, no one is a Muslim. We are all Bengalis. We are one. If the head and the body are separated, then like rahu and ketu they will play a very destructive game. Both the sun and the moon will come under total eclipse. Mark my words!

Yes, that eclipse has occurred. This time it has captured everything in its shadow. During the time of the Partition, we too thought of running away to India. But later we decided: Come what may; here or there, it is all the same. Wherever you are, if you serve your country and live in unity, there will be prosperity. Thus, once again, we engaged ourselves in the service of the new nation. Below the damaged roof of the Muzumdar mansion people once again gathered to meet the Mataji. Walked along with Gandhiji in Noakhali. Opened a sevashram in Chittagong. Organised a solidarity meet in Dhaka. Didn't transgress the law anywhere. Yet the authorities suspected us. They dismissed Subhendu who was a professor in Dhaka. Samarendu was not even given the license to practice as a doctor. Jogendu died while engaged in relief work during a flood. My children, this has always been the fate of the Bengalis. Even nature is hostile to us. The sea will continue to invade the shore. Storms will rage. The Padma will be flooded once again. Cholera and starvation will spread. Can we confront all this with caste and religion? My youngest daughter married a Muslim. We used to live together. Those were the days of listening to my three year old grand-daughter, Nazeema, sing the Tagore song, "Sonar Bangla..." Oh, the soldiers snatched that child, and killed her by throwing her onto the road.

That was the end, my children. That was the end! For me there was only one thing left — the land...which was my mother and daughter...the land in which I was born...my Bengal...and its ever angry rivers, lakes and people. Even that is now no longer mine.

Mujibur Sahib used to say, "Shantidevi, you are the symbol of Bengal! You are our mother! You are our grandmother! May Bengal be liberated with your blessings!"

There was only very little blood left in my veins. Yet I cut my forefinger and marked his forehead with my blood.

"Go forth and be victorious, my son! Go forth and be victorious! May you have the good fortune to liberate Bengal!"

Shanti Mutassi was lifted up and carried by her grandchildren, the soldiers of the Mukti fauj and finally brought to India. And here she is supposedly a refugee! Supposedly a beggar woman! Supposedly an outsider!

Is that true, Indira, tell me! Has Shanti Muzumdar come here as a refugee?

Is the mother of Dhiren, Samaren, Satyen and Nityen an outsider here?

I pose this question from the land of Tagore, Sarat Chandra, C.R. Das and Netaji. Is Shanti Muzumdar an outsider or does she belong here? If you tell me that this is not my country, I won't let myself die on this soil. Oh...once again I am unable to hold back my tears. I feel giddy...No, I won't cry. The mother of Dhirendu Muzumdar won't cry. Come. Let us sing that song together as we used to:

Oh, ye mighty swords that dazzle in her thousand hands...
Suphalam, Sujalam...Sasyashyamalam Mataram...Vande Mataram...

Original in Malayalam.
Translated by T. Muralidharan.

VISHNU PRABHAKAR

I SHALL LIVE

The party had ended a long time ago, the guests had departed and the moon had risen in the sky. Laughing happily, Pran turned towards Raj. He always tried to make her feel happy. It was to please her that he had come to Mussourie. Raj's eyes were fixed on a road winding down a distant mountain. In the hazy light of the moon, the road, which twisted and turned down the mountain, was barely visible and it made the outline of the horizon appear to be even more distant.

The truth was that Raj was deep in thought and was trying to untangle her past from the future. She was startled by Pran's laughter. She looked up. The look in her eyes made Pran apprehensive. He asked, "Are you feeling well?"

Pretending not to have heard the question, Raj asked in a soft whisper, "How well do you know that young man who was sitting on your right?"

"The one in the blue coat?"

"Yes."

"He is staying with Kishen these days. I had asked Kishen over because his wife has gone down to the plains. Do you know him?"

"No, I just wanted to know."

"Oh, I understand now. He played a lot with Dilip. Some people really love children."

"Yes, but his love was a little excessive."

"What do you mean?"

"Didn't you notice that Dilip refused to get down from his lap?"

Pran laughed and said, "Children respond to the one who loves them the most. They are as gentle as the autumn moon."

Both of them looked at Dilip. Covered with a satin quilt, he was sleeping peacefully. A lock of golden hair lay on his forehead. He looked angelic in the moonlight. A smile played on his lips. Raj whispered, "How beautiful he is!"

Pran said, "Sometimes it seems that someone must have thought of inventing the moonlight after seeing a child."

Their eyes met. They understood that there was a storm brewing beneath the innocent banter but neither of them said anything more. Raj gently picked up Dilip in her arms and carried him to the room inside. As she hugged him, he stirred a bit, but calmed down the moment she put him down on the bed. She stood gazing at him for a while. It seemed as if she was looking at him for the first time, but her trance was quickly broken. Pran came in and asked, "Why are you staring at him, Raj?"

"For no reason at all."

He laughed and said, "It seems that even love discriminates."

As Raj moved away, she said, "Listen, please don't ask that friend of your friend over again."

But that was not a request, there was fear in her voice. Pran was confused. Worried, he asked, "Why not?"

Raj didn't reply. She quietly left the room, sat down in her chair in the verandah again and began staring at the winding road in the distance. The distant shouts of the coolies had died down. The clouds had covered the sky. Suffused with moonlight, they looked mysterious. Raj felt as if the mysterious light in the clouds had also become a part of her inner being and had destroyed her peace. Her eyes filled with tears and she suddenly flung herself on the back of her chair and began to weep. Pran was neither startled nor annoyed. He stood and watched her weep for sometime. After Raj's crying had finally subsided and she had wiped her tears, he said, "Are you feeling better now? Come, let's go for a walk."

Raj turned her tear-stained face towards him and said, "Pran, I want to go away."

"Where?"

"Anywhere."

Pran said, "You have lived long enough, you should know how uncertain life is. A moment ago everything was bright and clear, now everything is lost in the mist."

"I don't want to lose myself in the mist."

Pran made a gesture with his hands and said seriously, "As you wish. You are always free to leave. I haven't kept you here by force."

Raj didn't move. She continued to sit deep in thought. She sat like that throughout the night. The next day she seemed even more lost in thought. She didn't let Dilip out of her sight even for a single moment. She took him to the swings on the Mall herself. Took him for a walk, fed him. Sang lullabies to him, hugged him and rocked him to sleep. After he had gone to sleep, she sat down in her chair and began to cry again.

It was a misty and moonlit night again. The sky was cloudy and calm. Like the world outside, Raj seemed calm, although her soul was in turmoil. Pran had vowed not to say anything to her that day. He didn't try to stop her from doing anything. Even now, as she stared at the winding road, trying to find a way out, he stood quietly behind her with his hands on her chair.

At that very moment they heard someone walking up the stairs. Raj suddenly exclaimed, "He has come!"

"Who?"

"That friend of your friend."

She hadn't even completed her sentence, when they saw him walk into the verandah. Pran noticed that he hadn't come alone. He was accompanied by a man and a woman. They seemed related. The woman was exceedingly beautiful, but at that moment she seemed very tense. There was a look of apprehension in her eyes. A shiver ran through Pran's body, but he went forward to greet them. He smiled and said, "Please come in...Namaste. Didn't Kishen come with you?"

"No, he couldn't come."

"Please sit down."

After they were all seated, Pran looked at the strangers and said, "We haven't been introduced."

"She is my sister. And he's my brother-in-law."

"Oh," Pran smiled, folded his hands and looked at them. He felt strangely disturbed. He regained control over himself and asked, "Where do you live?"

The friend of his friend replied, "Where do we live? God has so uprooted us, that we can't find a place to settle down again."

Pran said, "Yes, everyone knows what has happened, but whom can we turn to for help?"

Then he turned to Raj, who was still like a statue, and said, "Maybe they'd like some tea."

The friend quickly replied, "No, no, please don't make tea for us. We have come on a very important matter."

Pran said, "Tell me."

The friend hesitated. Pran continued, "Perhaps, you would like to talk to me in private."

"Yes."

"Let's go and sit there."

They pulled up their chairs and sat in a corner. After a pause, the friend said, "Pardon me, but I want to ask you a few questions. I hope you won't consider me impertinent."

"No, go ahead and ask," said Pran smiling. "Questions are never impertinent."

The friend hesitated, and then asked shyly, "Is Dilip your son?"

Pran's heart beat loudly. He maintained his poise, however, and replied calmly. "Yes! He is now my son."

"Now?"

"Yes, he wasn't always mine."

"Really?"

"Yes. Raj had found him while she was fleeing with a group from Lahore."

"What!" the friend exclaimed. "Where did she find him?"

"In a train near Lahore."

"Pran babu, Pran babu! You don't know, but he's my sister's child. I recognized him the moment I saw him. O Pran babu, you don't know how much they have suffered." He jumped up and called out, "Bhai Sahib, Bhai Sahib. We have found Ramesh!"

He turned to Pran and said, "Do you want proof? I have his photographs here."

He pulled photograph after photograph out of his pocket in order to convince Pran. The entire scene had changed.

The woman cried, "Where is he? Where is my Ramesh?"

Raj didn't say anything. She ran into the bedroom and clutched Dilip to her bosom. The next moment, all the others stood around her. They were all very excited, but Pran was still calm. He said to Raj, gently, "Dilip's mother has come, Raj."

"His mother!" Raj screamed, "Go away all of you. Why have you come here? Dilip is mine. I am his mother."

Dilip's mother said to Raj, "You really are his mother. You gave him a new lease of life."

When Raj heard that she began to tremble. The moment she looked up and saw Dilip's mother, she couldn't take her eyes off her. By then Dilip had woken up and was scared by what he saw. He refused to get down from Raj's lap. The very presence of strangers made him angry.

A few months ago when Raj had found him, he was not yet a year old. During those days everyone was scared. People were running away from their homes to save their lives. There was a lot of killing. Bodies were piled up everywhere. All sense of humanity had been drowned in a river of blood.

Raj had found herself on a refugee train. When it was attacked, people fled in all directions. She too collected whatever she could of her belongings and ran. It was only later that she had realized that she had also picked up Dilip. That was strange. She had lost everything that was hers, but had found a child who had slept peacefully through those bloody hours. When she reached the refugee camp and discovered the child, she exclaimed, "O God, you snatched everything from me and gave me this child as a gift in return." She didn't have much time to think about it then. She picked up the child and fled towards India. On the way, whenever she had to choose between her own safety and the child's life, she had risked her own life to save the child's. And now that child, whom even death had not succeeded in snatching away from her, was to be taken away from her because she wasn't his mother.

"No, no...Dilip is mine," she wailed loudly.

Pran came up to her and said calmly, "Raj! There is something even more precious than being a mother, and that is protecting the motherhood of someone else."

"No, no," she screamed hysterically. "I don't want anything that precious. I don't want to be that fortunate."

"Fortune can't be turned away by you, but you can make something fortunate happen out of misfortune."

Raj suddenly turned to Pran and said, "Are you asking me to give them the child?"

"I am not asking you to do anything. He's their child. You can do a good deed by returning it to them. By performing your duty, you'll find the kind of peace that you will never find by doing anything else. You are amongst the fortunate ones. Don't ruin your good luck, by giving in to momentary cowardice."

Raj looked at Pran once more, and then slowly put the child in his mother's lap. Her hands were shaking, her lips were trembling. As soon as Dilip's mother hugged him, Raj screamed, "Go away, go away all of you, at this very moment."

Pran didn't oppose her. He walked Dilip's parents upto the staircase. They wanted to say something to him, but before they could speak, he said, "I am convinced that the child is yours. You have now found him. May everyone be as fortunate as you, but I have one request."

"Tell us, we'll do anything for you."

Pran continued as if he had not heard them, "Never come here again."

They were surprised, "Why?"

"I shall be grateful."

"But..."

Pran refused to listen. The next day Raj and he bid goodbye to Mussourie. Raj was like someone who had no life left in her. She had turned very pale. Her eyes were swollen. Since that day, Pran never said anything which could remind her of Dilip. But do memories return only because someone provokes them? They often erupt from within like a fountain. They continued to surge up within Raj also. In order to contain them, Pran took her to Lucknow. Then to Calcutta and Madras, and finally to Delhi. Days passed, months went by. Slowly, time helped Raj to forget Dilip. Pran began to concentrate on his business once more. But he also continued to hope for something. He wanted to see Raj lose herself in the innocent play of a child again. He often went to an orphanage in the hope of adopting a child, but never succeeded in taking one home. As soon as he decided to do so, a voice within him would whisper, "You don't know when its parents will return to claim the child for their own." And he would walk away.

Raj was always pained whenever Pran mentioned a child. Sometimes she would even faint. She had begun to love solitude. She was despondent about the past and skeptical about the future. Pran understood that, like everything else in the world, her present state was only temporary. The moment the circumstances changed, she too would change. Who knew what would happen if he were to bring another child home.

He was still caught in this dilemma when he noticed a man sitting in his hotel and staring at him. Pran didn't pay him any attention. After all people did stare at others. Indeed, that seemed to be the latest fashion of the times. His neighbour, for instance, climbed upto the terrace of his house to stare at Raj whenever he could. Raj had even complained about him.

But the man in the hotel continued to follow him the next day, and then the day after that. He followed Pran everyday. Pran was rather upset. Pran found the man's behaviour rather strange. He was never around when Raj was with him. Raj never got a chance to see him either.

One day, Pran decided to confront the man. When he saw the man sitting at his usual place in the hotel, he walked upto him and put his hand on the man's shoulder. The man stood up with a start and said, "What, what do you want?"

"That's what I want to know," Pran replied.

Surprisingly, the man who had been trembling a moment ago, asked calmly, "So you have understood. Pardon me, I wanted to talk to you myself."

"Why didn't you?"

"Because I wasn't confident. As you well know, these days one invites death by talking about such matters."

Pran was convinced of his sincerity. He became anxious. "What you say is right, but you can say what you want to without fear."

The man replied, "What I have to tell you is difficult. I hope you won't be hurt."

"No, tell me."

The man hesitated for a moment, and then quickly asked, "Who is the woman who lives with you?"

"What do you mean?"

Pran continued in a deliberately slow voice, "She is everything and nothing to me."

"I want to know if she is your wife?"

"My wife?"

"Yes."

"No."

"No?"

"No."

"Are you telling me the truth?" There was a strange mixture of joy and elation in the man's voice.

"Yes. I have told you the truth. I have never walked around the sacred fire with her."

"Then?"

"As I was fleeing from Lahore, I found her in a difficult situation with a small baby in her arms."

"You brought her here with you."

"Yes."

"What happened after that?"

"What happened? She started living with me."

"Do people believe that she is your wife?"

"Yes, that's obvious. What else can people assume? But why do you want to know?. Do you know her?"

"Yes, she is my wife," the man answered nervously.

"Your wife!" Pran exclaimed.

"Yes."

"And you have been following her around stealthily like a thief?"

The man turned pale, his lips became dry. But he suddenly looked up and said, "There is a reason for that. I won't hide it from you. During those troubled days, I couldn't protect her."

Pran didn't know why he held the man's hand. He said, "Did you run away and leave her alone? That does happen sometimes."

"No, I didn't run away, but I didn't risk my life to save her."

"Does she know?"

"I don't know."

"But you are afraid that she knows."

"I am not afraid, but I am certainly ashamed."

Pran felt as if someone had slowly cut through his inner being with a knife. He maintained his external poise, however, and asked, "Is it true that Raj is your wife?"

The man replied in a tearful voice, "What can I say? I tried to find her. I made a report about her at every camp, radio station and police station."

Pran asked, "Are you willing to take her back?"

Without a moment's hesitation the man replied, "Yes, that's why I am here."

"You have no doubt about it at all."

"Doubt?" The man exclaimed. "Why should I add to the burden of my sins by doubting her? Mahatmaji..."

"Then come with me," Pran said, interrupting him, "Come along."

"Now?"

"At this very moment. Where do you live?"

"Jullunder."

"Are you employed?"

"Yes, I have a job at a school."

"Weren't both your children killed?"

"No, only one was."

"Really?"

"Yes, the other lives with me."

Pran suddenly felt elated. He said quickly, "Then listen, Raj is at home. Take her away with you. I'll give you a note for her."

"Won't you come with me?"

"No, I have to go out of town. I have some urgent work to attend to at Lucknow. She'll be unhappy if she sees me. You understand."

"I understand."

"You are fortunate. I congratulate you and am impressed by your courage."

Before the man could tell him how grateful and touched he was, Pran had placed a note in his hand and disappeared.

The note read :

"Raj!

Brave people can make mistakes, but it is against their nature to deceive someone. Even then, all you need to do is to write a few words to me and I shall come to you. I hope, however, that you'll never have to. You know me. You know I shall live bravely till my last breath.

Pran."

That man stood still for a long time. He felt as if someone had dropped a diamond into the outstretched hands of a pauper. But he hadn't been a pauper by birth. That is why his courage didn't betray him as he began to walk down the road Pran had pointed out to him.

Pran returned after fifteen days. Till he saw the door of his house, he was mortally afraid. But when he saw the lock on the door, his entire body trembled. He opened the door and walked in blindly. He collided against the crib and fell. He hit the side of the bed. Involuntarily, a groan escaped from his lips. He had hurt his head and was bleeding. It was only when he rubbed his head, that he noticed the blood, the crib, the bed and the house. Silence lay over everything in the house. Things were in their usual place. Pran almost called out, "Raj!"

Suddenly he was afraid, "Where is Raj? Oh, she has left. Her husband came back. Her son is alive. How cruelly does happiness deceive one! It vanishes unexpectedly and then returns. Raj has found her husband and her son. Dilip found his parents. And I...what did I find?"

There was a noise on the terrace. The neighbour who used to stare at Raj looked in. When he saw Pran, he asked him sternly, "So you have finally returned?"

"Yes."

"Where had you gone?"

"Lucknow."

"Was your work urgent? I am afraid that during your absence..."

"What happened, tell me?"

"Your wife..."

"My wife?"

"I am afraid, she ran away with someone."

"Ran away? Really? Did you see her?"

"Pran babu, I knew it all along. She seemed to be that kind of person. About fifteen days ago someone came to see her. At first, she scolded him as soon as she saw him."

"Did you hear what she said?"

"Yes, I was present. I heard her scream — Go away. Who asked you to come here? Why have you come? I will call him!"

"Really, is that what she said?"

"Yes."

"Then what happened?"

"Then what happened? Pran babu, that man turned out to be shameless. He didn't leave. He gave your wife a letter, and then stood before her with folded hands. He fell at her feet."

"You saw all that?"

"Yes, clearly."

"Then?"

"He fell at your wife's feet, and she began to weep. After that, I don't know what he said to her, but she fainted. And then — how can I tell you, I feel ashamed. I stopped myself from jumping over the wall and strangling him. I said to myself, why should I get involved in the affairs of someone else. You'll soon be back. I kept a look out for you late into the night. When I woke up the next morning, I noticed that both of them had fled."

"Did they leave that very night?"

"Yes."

Pran took a deep breath, and said, "That means he told me the truth."

The neighbour was startled, "What?"

"Yes. He did what he should have done."

Then he looked at his neighbour who was standing like a statue and said, "Bhai, he was Raj's husband."

"Raj's husband!" the neighbour exclaimed in bewilderment.

"Yes. You know what we had to endure when we escaped from Punjab. I had rescued Raj from a pile of corpses. At that time she thought that her husband had been killed. That is why she agreed to live with me."

The neighbour, who till then had been unable to speak a word, said, "He agreed to take her back, even though she had lived with you?"

Pran replied, "That's what you saw."

The neighbour didn't know what more to say. After sometime he asked, "Where is your own family?"

"While we were trying to escape, my wife and her parents were swept away by a river. My children died one by one on the way."

"Bhai Sahib..." the neighbour screamed. But he couldn't say anything more. He merely continued to stare at Pran.

Original in Hindi.
Translated by Alok Bhalla.

NARAIN BHARATI

THE CLAIM

"Bhai, who is responsible for giving out the money claimed here?" Joharmal asked the men standing in the verandah of the Camp No. 2 office.

"Uncle, no one here gives out the money claimed; here one merely puts in an application stating the claim," said a man standing nearby, smiling at Joharmal's innocence.

"Uncle, come here," said one of the persons sitting with the typist, "I am also putting in a claim. This officer is typing it."

"Bhai, we don't even know how a claim is to be made. Of course, my son studies in an English school. But here the officers have their own requirements. Later on they will tell me — you haven't done this and you haven't done that. That is why I told my son, when there are so many other expenses to be borne, a rupee or two charged by this officer for filling our forms will not make us poorer."

"Come and sit here," said one of the persons, as he moved up to make place for Joharmal.

"Oh God!" said Joharmal, as he sat down on the bench. "Yesterday, Manikmal was saying that the government will give us compensation for the property left behind, that is why the government is asking people to write applications — what and how much was left behind. I thought that since we have lost so much property, we should also give it in writing," Joharmal said, as he took a bidi out of his pocket.

"Bhai, do you think the government will simply count the money and give out cash! These are all only estimates; but every one is in a fix — if we don't make a written application, and if by some good luck the government decides to honour its word and pay out the money, then everyone will shout and curse. So let us remove this anxiety, for whatever is written in one's horoscope will happen. Even if we don't get anything, we shall not be worse off than we are now," said one of the old men to Joharmal.

The typist continued typing and simultaneously kept on muttering, "The public road to the west, Khan Mohammad's building towards the east, the caravan sarai of Seth Phagunmal in the north — the area three thousand square feet, two storyed..." Then he turned to look at the people sitting there. One by one, he typed the forms for all of them. Then, turning to Joharmal, he asked, "Yes, what can I do for you?"

"Bhai, I shall write whatever you ask me to. We have left our world, our honour, our friendships; everything that was ours has been left behind there. When will God have mercy on us and allow us to inhabit our homes again?"

"What is your name?"

"Name? Sir, my name is Joharmal."

The typist hit the keyboard and repeated, "Joharmal...Yes... Joharmal...son of?"

"Joharmal, son of Bhai Wasiomal."

The typist began typing again and asked, "What is your surname?"

"Nangdev."

The typist typed it. "Okay. Where did you stay in Pakistan? Which taluka and district?"

"All right. Village Halla, Taluka Kamber, District Larkana."

The typist kept on typing. "Have you brought the details of your property?"

"What details?"

"Details, such as, how many acres of land, how many houses and their whereabouts, total area and the estimated value? Whether the land was leased or purchased outright? If it was purchased, for how much? Have you got any documents as proof or receipts from the Revenue Officer for the payment of taxes? What was the total value of the land? All these details are required."

Joharmal was stupefied. All these things were new to him. He thought, "I have not brought anything. Manikmal had told me that the officer will record whatever you tell him, but here...! But I am after all a Sindhi. Is that not sufficient proof?"

Seeing Joharmal immersed in thought, the typist again asked. "How much property have you left behind in Pakistan? How many houses, how much other property?"

Reacting as if he had suddenly woken up from a dream, Joharmal said, "Bhai, let me put it like this...My dear friend, you confused me. Okay, write. Joharmal, son of Wasiomol, surname Nangdev. I have left the whole of Sind in Pakistan. I am now putting in the claim for the whole of Sind, it should be given back to me. The proof of the claim is that Joharmal is a Sindhi, his language is Sindhi and his culture is Sindhi."

"How can I write that? How much of it belongs to you?"

"What have I left behind in Sind? What have I left in Sind? I have left my Sind. If it is not my own, then whose is it? We Sindhis left all our comforts and came here and you still think that I don't remember Sind or that I have forgotten it? If you think that then, my dear Sir, you are mistaken. Never believe that. Every part of my body is replete with memories of Sind. I am a Sindhi and Sind is mine. I have the right to put in a claim for it. We hear that the Punjabis got Punjab, the Bengalis got Bengal. What crime have we committed that we are denied our Sind!" Joharmal became emotional.

All those who were sitting there started laughing and even the officer smiled.

"Let me ask all of you to be the judges," Joharmal said, turning to those who were sitting there, "You...all of us left our Sind. Did the officer ask you the same difficult questions or, considering that I am an old man, is he making fun of me?"

"No. I am not making fun of you. I am telling you honestly that it is a rule of the Government that any one who has left his personal property behind, can put in a claim for it, but not for anything else. See, every one has put in a claim for his own house and land. Topanmal, son of Godumal Premchandani, from the village Sajawal, taluka Mirokhan, district Larkana, two houses — one-storyed, area two thousand square feet, facing west; and land, fifty acres — total property worth about fifteen thousand rupees. He has put in a claim for fifteen thousand rupees."

Joharmal's face became pale. He had never even thought or dreamt that Sindhis would forget their Sind so easily and that each one would go his own way. Turning to the officer he said, "Are you not a Sindhi? Were your forefathers not Sindhis? Did you not drink water from the river of Sakkur? Did you not bathe in the river Sindhu? And you still say, that I cannot put in a claim for Sind? Our ancestral Sind, where our forefathers lived their lives; where we grew up. Have we no right over it? I shall never again meet my brothers Rajab, Ramzan and Mehboob, the barber. Can I get back their friendship?"

Joharmal once again became emotional, tears filled his eyes.

"But, Sir..." the typist tried to explain once again.

Interrupting the typist, Joharmal said, "Let it go, Sir, let it go. I have no claim to make. Let it go to hell! What else can I claim? What other details can I give you? My friends, their friendship was dearer to me than my fields. Sind was my native place. I immigrated because my son-in-law forced me to and my daughters cried bitterly...Otherwise I would never have left Sind!"

The typist realized that what Joharmal had said was a hundred percent correct. "The only true claim we can make is for our Sind. We must get it back," he said to himself. He too had many friends in Sind — Anwar, Hussain Ahmad and Ali, with whom he used to go to the Ramzan Gardens for a stroll. He had been in love with Nooran, the niece of the Haji of the village — Haji Urs. When he had gone to see her for the last time before leaving for India, Nooran had told him, "Don't forget me. Allah willing, you will be back soon and inherit these fields and buildings." All that flashed through his mind. The whole map of Sind rose before his eyes — fields, friends and the entire community. He thought, "Korea was also partitioned like this and even today the people are fighting for a united Korea."

Suddenly the typist said, "Yes, Sir, we shall surely go back to Sind. Sind is ours, yours and every Sindhi's. Your claim is right, it is the true claim. It may be wrong in the eyes and books of the government, but it is the real and original claim. It is not just your claim, but mine too and that of every Sindhi. Don't be disappointed, Sir. The time is not far off when the Sindhis will wake up from their slumber and put in their claim for Sind — the claim for Sind — the claim for Sindhiyat! When there is true democracy in India and Pakistan, this artificial wall will be demolished and you — all of us, shall certainly get our claim."

Original in Sindhi.
Translated by Sree Israney.

KHWAJA AHMED ABBAS

THE DEATH OF SHEIKH BURHANUDDIN

My name is Sheikh Burhanuddin.

When violence and murder became the order of the day in Delhi, and the blood of Muslims flowed in the streets, I cursed my fate for having a Sikh for a neighbour.. Far from expecting him to come to my rescue in times of trouble as a good neighbour should, I could not tell when he would thrust his kirpan into my belly. The truth is that till then, I used to find the Sikhs somewhat laughable. But I also disliked them and was somewhat scared of them.

My hatred for the Sikhs began on the day when I first set my eyes on one. I could not have been more than six years old when I saw a Sikh sitting out in the sun combing his long hair. "Look!" I yelled with revulsion, "A woman with a long beard!" As I got older, this dislike developed into hatred for the entire race.

It was a custom amongst the old women of our household to heap all afflictions on our enemies. Thus, for example, if a child got pneumonia or broke its leg, they would say, "A long time ago a Sikh, (or an Englishman), got pneumonia: or, a long time ago a Sikh, (or an Englishman) broke his leg." When I was older I discovered that this referred to the year 1857 when the Sikh princes helped the firangi to defeat the Hindus and Muslims in the war of independence. I do not wish to propound a historical thesis but to explain the obsession, the suspicion and hatred which I bore towards the English and the Sikhs. I was more frightened of the English than of the Sikhs.

When I was ten years old, I happened to be travelling from Delhi to Aligarh. I used to travel third class, or at the most in the intermediate class. That day I said to myself, "Let me, for once, travel second class and see what it feels like." I bought my ticket and I found an empty second class compartment. I jumped on the well-sprung seats; I went into the bathroom and leapt up to see my face in the mirror; I switched on all the fans. I played with the light switches. There were only a couple of minutes for the train to leave, when four red-faced 'tommies' burst into the compartment, mouthing obscenities — everything was either "bloody" or "damn." I had one look at them, and my desire to travel second class vanished.

I picked up my suitcase and ran out. I only stopped for breath when I got into a third class compartment, crammed with natives. But as luck would have it, it was full of Sikhs — their beards hanging down to their navels and dressed in nothing more than their underpants. I could not escape from them; but I kept my distance.

Although, I feared the white man more than the Sikhs, I felt that he was more civilised — he wore the same kind of clothes as I. I also wanted to be able to say "damn" and "bloody fool" — the way he did, and like him, I wanted to belong to the ruling class. The Englishman ate his food with forks and knives, I also wanted to learn to eat with forks and knives, so that natives would look upon me as being as advanced, and as civilised as the white man.

My Sikh-phobia was of a different kind. I had contempt for the Sikh. I was amazed at the stupidity of men who imitated women and grew their hair long. I must confess I did not like my hair cut too short; despite my father's instructions to the contrary, I did not allow the barber to clip off more than a little when I went to him on Fridays. I grew a mop of hair so that when I played hockey or football it would blow about in the breeze like that of English sportsmen. My father often asked me "Why do you let your hair grow like a woman's?" My father had primitive ideas and I took no notice of his views. If he had his way, he would have had all heads shaved bald, and stuck artificial beards on people's chins...That reminds me, that the second reason for hating the Sikhs was, that their beards made them look like savages.

There are beards and beards. There was my father's beard, neatly trimmed in the French style; or my uncle's which went into a sharp point under his chin. But what could you do with a beard to which no scissor was ever applied, and which was allowed to grow like a wild bush, fed with a compost of oil, curd and goodness knows what else! And, after it had grown a few feet, combed like hair on a woman's head! My grandfather also had a very long beard which he combed...but then my grandfather was my grandfather, and a Sikh is just a Sikh.

After I had passed my matriculation examination, I was sent to the Muslim University at Aligarh. We boys who came from Delhi, or the United Provinces, looked down upon the boys from Punjab; they were crude rustics who did not know how to converse, how to behave at table, or how to deport themselves in polite company. All they could do was drink large tumblers of buttermilk. Delicacies, such as sewain with essence of kewra sprinkled on it, or the aroma of Lipton's tea, were alien to them. Their language was unsophisticated to the extreme, whenever they spoke to each other it seemed as if they were quarrelling. It was full of "ussi, tussi, saadey, twhaadey — Heaven forbid!" I kept my distance from the Punjabis.

But the warden of our hostel (God forgive him), gave me a Punjabi as a room mate. When I realized that there was no escape, I decided to make the best of a bad bargain and be civil to the chap. After a few days we became quite friendly. This man was called Ghulam Rasul and he was from Rawalpindi. He was full of amusing anecdotes and was a good companion.

You might well ask how Mr. Ghulam Rasul gate-crashed into a story about the Sikhs. The fact of the matter is that Ghulam Rasul's anecdotes were usually about the Sikhs. It is through these anecdotes that I got to know the racial characteristics, the habits and customs of this strange community. According to Ghulam Rasul the chief characteristics of the Sikhs were the following:

All Sikhs were stupid and idiotic. At noon-time they lost their senses altogether. There were many instances to prove this. For example, one day at 12 o'clock noon, a Sikh was cycling along Hall Bazaar in Amritsar when a constable, also a Sikh, stopped him and demanded, "Where is your light?" The cyclist replied nervously "Jemadar Sahib, I lit it when I left my home; it must have gone out just now." The constable threatened to run him in. A passer-by, yet another Sikh with a long white beard, intervened, "Brothers, there is no point in quarrelling over little things. If the light has gone out it can be lit again."

Ghulam Rasul knew hundreds of anecdotes of this kind. When he told them in his Punjabi accent, his audience was left helpless with laughter. One really enjoyed them best in Punjabi because the strange and incomprehensible behaviour of the uncouth Sikh was best told in his rustic lingo.

The Sikhs were not only stupid, but incredibly filthy as well. Ghulam Rasul, who had known hundreds of them, told us how they never shaved their heads. And whereas we Muslims washed our hair thoroughly at least every Friday, the Sikhs who made a public exhibition of bathing in their under-pants, poured all kinds of filth, like curds, into their hair. I rub lime-juice and glycerine in my scalp. Although the glycerine is white and thick like curd, it is an altogether different thing — made by a well-known firm of perfumers of Europe. My glycerine came in a lovely bottle, whereas the Sikhs' curd came from the shop of a dirty sweetmeat seller.

I would not have concerned myself with the manner of living of these people, except that, they were so haughty and ill-bred as to consider themselves to be as good warriors as the Muslims. It is known over the world that one Muslim can get the better of ten Hindus or Sikhs. But these Sikhs would not accept the superiority of the Muslim, and would strut about like bantam cocks twirling their moustaches and stroking their beards. Ghulam Rasul used to say that one day we Muslims would teach the Sikhs a lesson that they would never forget.

Years went by.

I left college. I ceased to be a student and became a clerk; then a head clerk. I left Aligarh and came to live in New Delhi. I was allotted government quarters. I got married. I had children.

The quarters next to mine were occupied by a Sikh who had been displaced from Rawalpindi! Despite the passage of years, I remembered what Ghulam Rasul had told me. As Ghulam Rasul had prophesied, the Sikhs had been taught a bitter lesson, in humility at least, in the district of Rawalpindi. The Muslims had virtually wiped them out. The Sikhs boasted that they were great heroes; they flaunted their long kirpans. But they could not withstand the brave Muslims. The Sikhs' beards were forcibly shaved. They were circumcised. They were converted to Islam. The Hindu press, as was its custom, vilified the Muslims. It reported that the Muslims had murdered Sikh women and children. This was wholly contrary to Islamic tradition. No Muslim warrior was ever known to raise his hand against women and children. The accounts published in Hindu newspapers were obviously fake. I wouldn't have put it beyond the Sikhs to murder their own women and children in order to vilify the Muslims.

The Muslims were also accused of abducting Hindu and Sikh women. The truth of the matter is that, such was the impact of the heroism of the Muslims on the minds of the Hindus and the Sikh girls, that they fell in love with young Muslims, and insisted on going with them. These noble-minded young men had no option, but to give them shelter, and thus bring them to the true path of Islam. The bubble of Sikh bravery was burst. It did not matter how their leaders threatened the Muslims with their kirpans, the sight of the Sikhs who had fled from Rawalpindi, filled my heart with pride in the greatness of Islam.

The Sikh who was my neighbour, was about sixty years old. His beard had gone completely grey. Although he had barely escaped from the jaws of death, he was always laughing, displaying his teeth in the most vulgar fashion. It was evident that he was quite stupid. In the beginning he tried to draw me into his net by professions of friendship. Whenever I passed him, he insisted on talking to me. I do not remember what kind of Sikh festival it was, when he sent me some sweet butter. My wife promptly gave it away to the sweepers. I did my best to have as little to do with him as I could. I snubbed him whenever I could. I knew that if I spoke a few words to him, he would be hard to shake off. Civil talk would encourage him to become familiar. It was known to me that Sikhs drew their sustenance from foul language. Why should I soil my lips by associating with such people!

One Sunday afternoon I was telling my wife of some anecdotes about the stupidity of the Sikhs. To prove my point, exactly at 12 o'clock, I sent my servant across to my Sikh neighbour to ask him the time. He sent back the reply, "Two minutes after 12." I remarked to my wife "You see, they are scared of even mentioning 12 o'clock!" We both had a hearty laugh. After this, many a time when I wanted to make an ass of my Sikh neighbour, I would ask him, "Well, Sardarji, has it struck twelve?" The shameless creature would grin, baring all his teeth and answer, "Sir, for us it is always striking twelve." He would roar with laughter, as if it were a great joke.

I was concerned about the safety of my children. One could never trust a Sikh. And this man had fled from Rawalpindi. He was sure to have a grudge against Muslims and to be on the look-out for an opportunity to avenge himself. I had told my wife never to allow the children to go near the Sikh's quarters. But children are children. After a few days I saw my children playing with the Sikh's little girl, Mohini, and his other grand-children. This child, who was barely ten years old, was really as beautiful as her name indicated; she was fair and beautifully formed. These wretches have beautiful women. I recall Ghulam Rasul telling me that if all the Sikh men were to leave their women behind and clear out of the Punjab, there would be no need for Muslims to go to paradise in search of houris.

The truth about the Sikhs was soon evident. After the thrashing in Rawalpindi, they fled like cowards to East Punjab. Here they found the Muslims weak and unprepared. So they began to kill them. Hundreds of thousands of Muslims were martyred; the blood of the faithful ran in streams. Thousands of women were stripped naked and made to parade through the streets. When Sikhs, fleeing from Western Punjab, came in large numbers to Delhi, it was evident that there would be trouble in the capital. I could not leave for Pakistan immediately. Consequently, I sent away my wife and children by air, with my elder brother, and entrusted my own fate to God. I could not send much luggage by air. I booked an entire railway wagon, to take my furniture and belongings. But on the day I was to load the wagon I got information that trains bound for Pakistan were being attacked by Sikh bands. Consequently my luggage stayed in my quarters in Delhi.

On the 15th of August, India celebrated its Independence. What interest could I have in the Independence of India! I spent the day lying in bed reading *Dawn* and *The Pakistan Times*. Both the papers had strong words to say about the manner in which India had gained its freedom, and proved conclusively how the Hindus and the British had conspired to destroy the Muslims. It was only our leader, the great Mohammad Ali Jinnah, who was able to thwart their evil designs and win Pakistan for the Muslims. The English had knuckled under because of Hindu and Sikh pressure and handed over Amritsar to India. Amritsar, as the world knows, is a purely Muslim city. Its famous Golden Mosque — or am I mixing it up with the Golden Temple! — Yes, of course, the Golden Mosque is in Delhi. And in Delhi, besides the Golden Mosque, there are the Jamma Masjid, the Red Fort, the mausoleum of Nizamuddin and Emperor Humayun, the tomb and school of Safdar Jang — just everything worthwhile bears imprints of Islamic rule. Even so this Delhi (which should really be called Shahjahanabad after its Muslim builder Shahjahan) was to suffer the indignity of having the flag of Hindu imperialism unfurled on its ramparts.

My heart seemed rent asunder. I could have shed tears of blood. My cup of sorrow was full to the brim when I realized that Delhi, which was once the footstool of the Muslim Empire, the centre of Islamic culture and civilisation, had been snatched out of our hands. Instead, we were to have the desert wastes of Western Punjab, Sindh and Baluchistan inhabited by an uncouth and uncultured people. We were to go to a land where people do not know how to talk in civilised Urdu; where men wear baggy salwars like their women folk; where they eat thick bread, four pounds in weight, instead of the delicate wafers we eat at home!

I steeled myself. I would have to make this sacrifice for my great leader, Jinnah, and for my new country, Pakistan. Nevertheless the thought of having to leave Delhi was most depressing.

When I emerged from my room in the evening, my Sikh neighbour bared his fangs and asked, "Brother, did you not go out to see the celebrations?" I felt like setting fire to his beard.

One morning, the news spread of a general massacre in old Delhi. Muslim homes were burnt in Karol Bagh. Muslim shops in Chandni Chowk were looted. This then was a sample of Hindu rule! I said to myself, "New Delhi is really an English city; Lord Mountbatten lives here, as well as the Commander-in-Chief. At least in New Delhi no hand will be raised against Muslims." With this self-assurance I started towards my office. I had to settle the business of my provident fund; I had delayed going to Pakistan in order to do so. I had only got as far as Gole Market, when I ran into a Hindu colleague in the office. He said, "What on earth are you up to? Go back at once and do not come out of your house. The rioters are killing Muslims in Connaught Circus." I hurried back home.

I had barely got to my quarters, when I ran into my Sikh neighbour. He began to reassure me, "Sheikhji, do not worry! As long as I am alive no one will raise a hand against you."

I said to myself, "How much fraud is hidden behind this man's beard! He is obviously pleased that the Muslims are being massacred, but expresses sympathy to win my confidence; or is he trying to taunt me?" I was the only Muslim living in that block, perhaps I was the only one on that road.

I did not want these people's kindness or sympathy. I went inside my quarter and said to myself, "If I have to die, I will kill at least ten or twenty men before they get me." I went to my room where, beneath my bed, I kept my double-barrelled gun. I had also collected quite a hoard of cartridges.

I searched the house, but could not find the gun.

"What is huzoor looking for?" asked my faithful servant, Mohammad.

"What happened to my gun?"

He did not answer. But I could tell from the way he looked that he had either hidden it or stolen it.

"Why don't you answer?" I asked him angrily.

Then he came out with the truth. He had stolen my gun, and given it to some of his friends who were collecting arms to defend the Muslims in Daryaganj.

"We have hundreds of guns, several machine guns, ten revolvers and a cannon. We will slaughter these infidels; we will roast them alive."

"No doubt with my gun you will roast the infidels in Daryaganj, but who will defend me here? I am the only Muslim amongst these savages. If I am murdered, who will answer for it?"

I persuaded him to steal his way to Daryaganj, to bring back my gun and a couple of hundred cartridges. When he left, I was convinced that I would never see him again.

I was all alone. On the mantelpiece was a family photograph. My wife and children stared silently at me. My eyes filled with tears at the thought that I would never see them again. I was comforted by the thought that they were safe in Pakistan. Why had I been tempted by my paltry provident fund and not gone with them? I heard the crowds yelling.

"Sat Sri Akal..."

"Har Har Mahadev..."

The yelling came closer and closer. They were rioters — the bearers of my death warrant. I was like a wounded deer, running hither and thither, with the hunters' hounds in full pursuit.

There was no escape. The door was made of very thin wood and glass panes. The rioters would smash their way in.

"Sat Sri Akal..."

"Har Har Mahadev..."

They were coming closer; death was coming closer and closer. Suddenly, there was a knock at the door. My Sikh neighbour walked in — "Sheikhji, come into my quarters at once."

Without a second thought, I ran into the Sikh's verandah and hid behind the columns. A shot hit the wall above my head. A truck drew up and about a dozen young men climbed down. Their leader had a list in his hand — "Quarter No. 8 — Sheikh Burhanuddin."

He read my name and ordered his gang to go ahead. They invaded my quarter and under my very eyes proceeded to destroy my home. My furniture, boxes, pictures, books and carpets, even the dirty linen was carried into the truck. Robbers! Thugs! Cut-throats!

As for the Sikh, who had pretended to sympathise with me, he was no less a robber than they! He was pleading with the rioters: "Gentlemen, stop! We have prior claim over our neighbour's property. We must get our share of the loot."

He beckoned to his sons and daughters. All of them gathered, to pick up whatever they could lay their hands on. One took my trousers; another a suitcase. They even grabbed the family photograph. They took the loot to their quarters.

You bloody Sikh! If God grants me life I will settle my score with you. At this moment I cannot even protest. The rioters are armed and only a few yards away from me. If they get to know of my presence...

"Please come in."

My eyes fell on the unsheathed kirpan in the hands of the Sikh. He was inviting me to come in. The bearded monster looked more frightful after he had soiled his hands with my property. There was the glittering blade of his kirpan inviting me to my doom. There was no time to argue. The only choice was between the guns of the rioters and the sabre of the Sikh. I decided, rather the kirpan of the old man than ten armed gangsters. I went into the room hesitantly, silently.

"Not here, come in further." I went into the inner room like a goat following a butcher. The glint of the blade of the kirpan was almost blinding.

"Here you are, take your things," said the Sikh.

He and his children put all the stuff they had pretended to loot, in front of me. His old woman said "Son, I am sorry we were not able to save more."

I was dumb-founded.

The gangsters had dragged out my steel almirah and were trying to smash it open. "It would be simpler if we could find the keys," said someone.

"The keys can only be found in Pakistan. That cowardly son of a filthy Muslim has decamped," replied another.

Little Mohini answered back, "Sheikhji is not a coward. He has not run off to Pakistan."

"Where is he blackening his face?"

"Why should he be blackening his face? He is in..."

Mohini realized her mistake and stopped in mid-sentence. Blood mounted in her father's face. He locked me in the inside room, gave his kirpan to his son and went out to face the mob.

I do not know what exactly took place outside. I heard the sound of blows; then Mohini crying; then the Sikh yelling full-blooded abuses in Punjabi. And then a shot and the Sikh's cry of pain "Hai."

I heard a truck engine starting up; and then there was a petrified silence.

When I was taken out of my prison, my Sikh neighbour was lying on a charpoy. Beside him lay a torn and blood-stained shirt. His new shirt also was oozing with blood. His son had gone to telephone for the doctor.

"Sardarji, why did you do this?" I asked him again.

"Son, I had a debt to pay."

"What kind of a debt?"

"In Rawalpindi there was a Muslim like you, who sacrificed his life to save mine and the honour of my family."

"What was his name, Sardarji?"

"Ghulam Rasul."

Fate had played a cruel trick on me. The clock on the wall started to strike...1...2...3...4...5...The Sikh turned towards the clock and smiled. He reminded me of my grandfather with his twelve-inch beard. How closely the two resembled each other!

...6...7...8...9...we counted in silence.

He smiled again. His white beard and long white hair were like a halo, effulgent with a divine light...10...11...12...The clock stopped striking.

I could almost hear him say, "For us Sikhs, it is always 12 o'clock!"

But the bearded lips, still smiling, were silent. And I knew he was already in some distant world, where the striking of clocks counted for nothing, where violence and mockery were powerless to hurt him.

Original in Urdu.
Translated by Khushwant Singh.

MASOOD ASHAR

A VERY OLD STORY

After coming out of the railway station, he looked back again, and felt ashamed of what he had done.

"What nonsense! How far back can one look anyway? Besides, it isn't certain that he will return."

By then his shadow was under his feet. There was no chance of it being trampled under the feet of others.

The road stretched before him into the distance. He was reassured. He put his things down on the steps leading out of the station and leaned against a pillar. He stood facing the station and his shadow lay in the direction of the city.

His companions shook hands with him one by one and ran to catch the bus going towards the city. He watched each of them leave, but remained silent. He continued to stand quietly. Later he saw his own friend leave him and move towards the bus going to the city. Even then he kept quiet and continued to watch.

Then he laughed, "How will that boy come now? Why should he come? In fact, we had abandoned him. The truth is that we had got rid of him. No one wanted to take him along. How could we have accompanied him everywhere?"

However, he also suspected something else. That boy had played tricks on him throughout the journey. "Maybe he will come back. It is possible that he has hidden himself somewhere, just to tease me, and will suddenly appear before me when I am thoroughly upset."

The boy had been mischievous all through the trip. He would suddenly disappear at some station, and would not be seen for hours on end. And after a lot of time and many stations had passed and they had given up hope of his return, he would come back quietly and sit behind one of them, pretending that he had never gone anywhere, that he had been sitting there from the very beginning of the journey.

When they glared at him, he would smile at them in such a way that they would look at each other and laugh.

"Where did you go?"

"Why did you go?"

The boy never answered them and they always felt ashamed at having asked him so many questions. After all, he hadn't even told them where he had come from or who he was.

"Yes. Who is this boy?" He hadn't thought about that. Neither of them had asked the boy. At that time they hadn't felt that it was necessary to find out.

...I always forget how a story ends. That is why I am criticised. At least some people criticise me. All I know is that I can never remember how a story — any story — ends. It has just occurred to me that I also rarely remember the beginning of most stories. All I can ever recall are a few details, a few incidents that happen in the middle. I try to remember the beginning and the end, but my mind, my memory refuse to help me. The beginning of a story doesn't even interest me, and the meaning of a story can't be discovered unless one recalls its end. The incidents in the middle are described in order to find a meaning...

They looked at that innocent and simple child who had a smile on his lips and was gazing at them with his clear eyes. The boy had no bedding of his own. In fact, he possessed nothing. He was empty handed.

"Why is he alone?"

"Who is he travelling with?"

"With you," the boy's eyes seemed to say in reply. All their questions dissolved in the intense heat of the railway carriage.

They only knew where they were going. They didn't know where each of them had come from or who the others were. None of them had thought it necessary to find out. Those questions were meaningless for them, and they had no time to worry about meaningless questions.

They had all met in a railway carriage. What had brought them together, however, was that innocent and simple looking boy. He had become the centre of their interest and attention, the object of their conversation, their purpose.

They didn't know when he had come and sat next to them.

When I turned around and looked, I saw him sitting near me. He was watching me with helpless and piteous eyes. I asked people sitting around who he was and what troubled him. But they were as ignorant as I was. When the ticket-collector, after checking our tickets, turned towards the boy each of us realized at the same time why he seemed so troubled.

"Who is he with?"

"He is with me."

"He is with me."

After that they were all convinced that the boy was travelling with them, and that it was their responsibility to look after him. They felt that they were all travelling together.

Space and time do not change in dreams. Even if centuries pass in dreams and thousands of events occur, the space and time in which the dreams occur always remain as they had been. They have a reality which is other than the reality of the daily world and are, therefore, more real. Come to think of it, love too becomes real only when the loved one is no longer around. Even childhood and youth, have a reality which is more real.

He looked carefully at the faces of those leaving the station and laughed. He laughed at his memory. No face was familiar. They were all the faces of strangers; each was different from the other.

"When I look at faces in a crowd, I begin to wonder why no one looks like the other."

"No, bhai, one can discover resemblances."

"Yes, perhaps, resemblances, but only upto a point. The features are always different. Try to study the faces in a crowd."

"The best thing to do is never to look at people's faces."

"How is that possible? We are forced to look at people's faces."

"Forced to?"

"Yes, we are forced to. One sees strange things in a crowd. People resemble each other, and yet are different. That is startling. But it also makes one laugh. The truth is that when I see different faces in a crowd, I laugh till I begin to ache."

"But...have you never seen identical faces?"

"Identical faces?"

"Yes, identical."

"Well...maybe one in a million..."

"Maybe one in a million, but identical nevertheless."

He shuddered. He felt a strange shiver run down his back, as if someone had drawn a sharp line down his spine.

"That must be terrifying."

"What must be terrifying?"

"Looking at identical faces."

They began to laugh loudly.

"Look, God never makes identical faces. Only man does that. He makes a mould and continues to cast identical things."

They suddenly became serious.

"Have you ever thought about another matter?"

"What?"

"New faces are more terrifying."

"New faces?"

"Yes, new faces, like new ideas, are terrifying."

It was his turn to laugh, and he laughed loud and long.

"In fact, people like faces which are familiar and remind them of someone."

When they opened their bundles of food to appease their hunger, all their questions vanished. That boy also joined them.

They should have thought about who they were travelling with and what kinds of people they were. But they were all in such a hurry that they had no time to think. Had they delayed even a little they would have missed the train. And the border would have been closed. They were terrified of the border being closed. If the border had been sealed, how could they have reached the place they were fated to reach?

Had the boy been with them from the beginning? That boy with an innocent face and a smile in his eyes? Had they begun their journey together?

It was a deserted, forlorn station. The train had stopped there because the tickets of the passengers had to be checked. Only those who had to cross the border stayed on the train. The station had no platform. There was only a tin roofed shelter standing in the middle of a sea of sand. In one corner there was a small room for the station master. Next to the tin-roofed shelter were two babool trees.

A tent had been pitched on the burning sand in front of them. The names and addresses of each of the passengers were recorded there. The passengers stood in a line before the tent.

"What about the boy? Who will be his guardian?" They asked each other and then fell silent. But after they emerged from the tent they were all happy that each one of them had declared that the boy was travelling with them.

An earth-worm crept forward slowly. It pulled its soft, slimy, jelly-like body as far as it could, but left its tail behind glued to the ground. Its body turned brick-red and then pale-pink. It seemed that if it tried to crawl any further, its body would snap in two. But suddenly, its tail also crept forward and it regained its size.

The man who showed them that began to laugh afterwards. "It is only the earth-worm which can travel like that!"

"Ah, you haven't seen the worm which arches its back so far up in the air that its tail touches its head? It then rolls forward, with its head and tail joined together."

They had seen that man in a crowd where everyone was trying to get himself identified separately. Now he was trying to teach them a new philosophy.

They had crossed the border and were resting on the sandy platform under the shade of the empty carriages of a goods train. At some distance, food and other items were being distributed.

"There is only one solution," one of them said.

"What?" He looked around. The boy had gone away somewhere.

"We should make use of the boy."

"Make use of the boy?"

"Look here, even if we reach that city, who knows how long we will be without work? We should have something with us."

"But what has the boy got to do with that?"

"We will get our rations only once, won't we?"

"Is that so?"

"And the boy can get a share of the rations many times."

"What are you trying to say?"

"If we go a second time, we'd be recognized. But if that boy is with each of us and..."

"Won't he be recongnized?"

"No."

We gathered lots of things from the ration shop, lifted them onto our shoulders and got into the empty carriages. The boy sat behind him and leaned against his back.

"Where will you go?" He was surprised by his own question. He had asked that question for the first time, and had asked it after crossing the border. They looked at the man as if he had asked something they all wanted to ask.

"Yes, where will you go? Why don't you tell us?"

"You haven't yet told us where you will go."

"And please, find out from him who he is travelling with."

"This is difficult. Whom will he go with?"

"With you."

"No, with you."

"Alright, he will go with you. He is so attached to you."

"With me?" He said. He was worried. "How can he go with me?"

He quickly moved away from him as if the boy was about to cling to him. The the man looked at the boy as if he was someone who was standing somewhere far, far away.

He stood staring at the platform. Dark clouds covered the sky and his shadow was lost in the darkness. The travellers had left for the city one by one. Soon all those who wanted to go to the city would leave and he would be left there, standing alone. Anxious and afraid, he stood on tiptoe and looked towards the platform. He thought that he might still be released from his feelings of shame and regret. But he saw no one far and wide.

"After all, how far back can one turn and see?"

He turned around and placed his foot where he imagined his shadow could have been. From the top of his head to the tip of his toe, he felt numb.

Even if the boy returned now, would he be able to recognize him?

Original in Urdu.
Translated by Vishwamitter Adil and Alok Bhalla.

NOTES ON THE AUTHORS

Khwaja Ahmed Abbas: Born in 1914, in Panipat, Haryana, he worked as a journalist in Bombay for most of his life. A well-known Urdu writer, he was a leading member of the progressive writers group. He was a prolific writer of novels, short stories and film-scripts. *Char Dil Char Rahen* and *Diya Jale Sari Raat* are amongst his better known works.

Ashfaq Ahmed: An Urdu writer of considerable merit and reputation, he was born in 1925 in Ferozepur district, India. He studied at Government College, Lahore. He was the editor of the journal *Dastan Go* and *Lailo Nahar*. He has, thus far, published a few collections of short stories (*Tota Kahani* is well-known), a short novel (*Mahmann-e-Bahar*) and a book of Punjabi plays.

Lalithambika Antharjanam: Born in 1909, she was amongst the first women to begin writing in Malayalam. Her novel *Agnisakshi* won the Sahitya Akademi Award in 1963. She wrote a number of novels, collections of short stories and essays. She died a few years ago.

Masud Ashar: Born in 1931 in Rampur, India, he migrated to Pakistan in 1952 and became a career journalist. In 1954, he joined the daily *Imroz*. He has published two collections of short stories and has co-authored a book on political parties in Pakistan and an anthology of Urdu literature.

Narain Bharati: A prominent Sindhi writer, he was born in Larkana district, Pakistan, in 1932. He has, thus far, published more than fifteen volumes of short stories and numerous collections of folk songs.

Attia Hosain: Born in 1913, in Lucknow, she was the first woman to graduate from her family. At present, she lives in England. She has, thus far, published one novel (*Sunlight on a Broken Column*) and one collection of short stories.

Intizar Husain: Born in the 1920's, in U.P., India. He migrated to Pakistan after the Partition. Considered to be one of the most important writers in Urdu, he has, thus far, published six collections of short stories, three novels (*Basti* is considered to be a classic), and a volume of essays. Recently, he was given the first Yatra Literary Award.

Ibne Insha: Born in 1927, in Ludhiana, India, he migrated to Pakistan in 1947. He ived in Karachi till his death in 1978. A fine poet in Urdu, he was also a satirist and a writer of short stories. He also wrote books for children. *Urdu Ki Akhri Kitab* and *Es Basti Ke Es Kuche Men* are amongst his best known works.

Ibrahim Jalees: Born in 1923, in Gulbarga, Karnataka, he worked as journalist in Hyderabad (Deccan). During his life-time he published a series of novels, short stories, plays and satirical essays in Urdu. His best remembered novel is *Chalees Crore Bhikari*. He supported the razakars in Hyderabad, and after the police action, migrated to Pakistan. He died in 1977.

Kamleshwar: Born in Mainpuri, Uttar Pradesh in 1932, he was amongst the founding editors of *Nayi Kahaniyan*. He is one of the most highly respected Hindi writers and has published a large number of novels, short stories and plays. *Lautey Huvay Musafir* is one of the best novels about Partition.

Saadat Hasan Manto: Born in 1912 in Ludhiana, he migrated to Pakistan in 1947. Considered to be one of the greatest Urdu short story writers, his writings have been recently collected in five volumes. Apart from writing short stories, he also wrote film-scripts, radio plays and essays. He died in 1955 in Lahore.

Narendranath Mitra: Born in 1916, he worked as a journalist for the *Anand Bazaar Patrika* in Calcutta. He published more than forty-seven novels and several collections of short stories in Bengali. He died in 1975.

Vishnu Prabhakar: Born in 1912, in Muzaffarnagar district, Uttar Pradesh. He worked for some time in the All India Radio. He has, thus far, published more than 80 novels, 59 plays and numerous collections of short stories in Hindi. A few years ago, he was given the Jnanpith Award.

Suraiya Qasim: Born in 1945. She lives in Chandigarh and works as a journalist. She has, thus far, written a few short stories and poems in Urdu.

Mohan Rakesh: Born in Amritsar in 1925. He studied at the Oriental College, Lahore, and taught at Elphinstone College, Bombay, and D.A.V. College, Jullunder. Associated with the "Nayi Kahani" in Hindi, he published two highly acclaimed novels (*Adhe Adhure* is regarded as a classic), plays (*Ashard Ka Ek*

Din has been performed repeatedly) and a few collections of short stories. He received the Nehru Fellowship and the Sangeet Natak Akademi Award. He died in 1972.

Ramesh Chandra Sen: Born in 1894, in Calcutta. He worked as an Ayurvedic physician all his life. He wrote novels and short stories in Bengali. Perhaps, his best known work is *Kajal*.

Sant Singh Sikhon: A well-known Punjabi writer, he was born in 1908 in Lyallpur district, Pakistan. His novel, *Lahu Mitti* (which was first written in English) is regarded as a classic of Punjabi literature. He has also written plays and short stories. In 1972, he was given the Sahitya Akademi Award.

Krishna Sobti: Lives in Delhi. She was born in 1925 in Gujarat, Pakistan. She was educated in Lahore and Delhi. In 1980, she received the Sahitya Akademi Award. Her novels *Dar Se Bicchudi, Mitro Marjani* and *Zindagi Namaha* are highly acclaimed.

S.H. Vatsayan 'Ajneya': A celebrated Hindi writer, he was born in 1911, in Kusinagar, Uttar Pradesh. He published four novels (of which *Shekhar: Ek Jeevani* is the most famous), collections of short stories and more than twelve volumes of poems. He won the Jnanpith Award in 1978. He died in 1989.

Syed Waliullah: Considered to be one of the first Bengali writers in Bangladesh, he was born in Noakhali. He wrote highly successful novels, short stories and poems, many of which have been translated into English. He died in 1971.

GLOSSARY

Abba	Father
Abbajan	Father
Ajwain	Oregano
Al-Hamdu-lillah	Praise be to God
Ameen	Amen
Amma	Mother
Ammi	Mother
Angeethi	Stove
Azadi	Freedom
Azan	Call for prayers
Babu	Respectful term of address for men
Bade Abba	Grandfather
Badi Amma	Grandmother
Bade Bhaiya	Elder brother
Bahen	Sister
Bahu	Daughter-in-law
Baisakhi	Harvest season
Basant	Spring
Basti	Town
Behist	Paradise
Bhai; Bhaiya	Brother
Bhog	Food offered to a diety
Bigha	A measure of land
Bismillah	In the name of Allah
Chacha	Father's brother
Chachi	Father's brother's wife
Chandan	Sandal-wood powder or paste
Chaprasi	Peon
Chillum	Earthen pot of a hookah in which tobacco is burnt
Chorbazaar	Thief's market
Chunni	Cloth draped by women over their heads and shoulders
Diya	Earthen lamp

Dharmshala	Public inn for pilgrims
Firangi	Foreigner
Gali	Lane
Goonda	Hooligan
Granthi	Priest in a gurudwara
Hazar	Thousand
Hijrat	Exile; wandering
Houri	Celestial nymph
Huzoor	Sir
Jagir	Inheritance
Jasoos	Spy
Ji	Yes
Kafir	Infidel
Khalsa	Sikh
Khangar	Big rock
Khichdi	Dish of rice and lentils; also means, hotchpotch
Khuda	God
Kirpan	Small dagger
Lathi	Stick
Mama	Mother's brother
Mandi	Market
Mantra	Ritual chant
Maulvi	Mulsim religious teacher
Mehndi	Henna
Miyan	Respectful way of addressing a Muslim man
Mussalla; Mussalli	Abusive way of referring to Muslims
Nirvan	Release from the cycle of life and death
Paan	Betel-leaf
Paandan	Box for keeping betel-leaves
Phuphi	Father's sister
Poush	Festival months of December and January
Prashad	Offering in a temple
Puja	Prayer
Purdah	Veil
Qul huwallah-ho-ahad	Say God is one

Rasool	Messenger of God
Sadhu	Ascetic; mendicant
Sala	Bastard (used colloquially)
Salaam	Greetings
Sali	Bitch (used colloquially)
Salwar	Loose pyjama
Seth	Rich businessman
Sherwani	Long coat
Tahsildar	Officer of a district
Tehmad	Lungi
Thana	Police station
Thanedar	Policeman
Tonga	Horse-driven carriage
Tongawallah	Driver of a horse-driven carriage
Vaid	Doctor
Waheguru	God of the Sikhs
Yamraj	God of death
Yar	Friend
Zalim	Evil man
Zamindar	Landlord
Zindabad	Long live

VOLUME III

CONTENTS

Saadat Hasan Manto
Toba Tek Singh 1

Ismat Chughtai
Roots 9

Samaresh Basu
Adab 21

Upendranath Ashk
The Fodder-Cutting Machine 29

Mohan Rakesh
The Claim 35

Asif Aslam Farrukhi
The Land of Memories 43

Intizar Husain
An Unwritten Epic 59

Maheep Singh
The River and the Bridge 79

Mulk Raj Anand
The Parrot in the Cage 85

Kartar Singh Duggal
Kulsum 91

Dipendranath Bandyopadhayay
Jatayu 95

S.H. Vatsayan 'Ajneya'
Post-Box 105

Amrit Rai
Filth 111

Bhisham Sahni
Pali 119

Sultan Jamil Nasim
I am Game 143

Aga Sohail
Outside the Haveli 150

CONTENTS

Gurmukh Singh Musafir
The Abandoned Child 181

Gulam Abbas
Avtar: A Hindu Myth 191

Krishan Chander
Peshawar Express 207

N.G. Gore
A Mouthful of Water, A Mouthful of Blood 217

Ved Rahi
Death 229

Qurratulain Hyder
When the Prisoners Were Released, the Times Had Changed 239

Notes on the Authors 255

Glossary 259

SAADAT HASAN MANTO

TOBA TEK SINGH

Two or three years after the Partition, it occurred to the governments of India and Pakistan that along with the transfer of the civilian prisoners, a transfer of the inmates of the lunatic asylums should also be made. In other words, Muslim lunatics from Indian institutions should be sent over to Pakistan, and Hindu and Sikh lunatics from Pakistani asylums should be allowed to go to India.

It is debatable whether this was a judicious step. Nonetheless, several high-level conferences took place and the day of the transfer was fixed. Following a great deal of initial investigation, those inmates who had relatives in India were retained there, while the rest were transported to the border. Since there were no Hindus or Sikhs in Pakistan, the question of retaining anyone there did not arise. All the Hindus and Sikhs in the asylums were taken to the border in the custody of the police.

What happened in India is not known. But here, in the Lahore asylum, the news of the transfer resulted in interesting speculation among the inmates. One man, who had been reading *Zamindar* regularly for nearly twelve years, was approached by a friend.

"What is Pakistan?"

"A place in India where they manufacture razors," he answered after much deliberation.

His friend appeared to be satisfied by the answer.

A Sikh lunatic asked another Sikh, "Sardarji, why are we being sent to Hindustan? We can't even speak their language."

"But I know the language of the Hindustanis," the first one interjected with a smile, adding, "Hindustanis are devilish, they strut about haughtily..."

During the course of a bath one morning, an inmate shouted, "Pakistan Zindabad!" so loudly that he slipped on the floor and fainted.

Some of the inmates were not deranged at all. Many of them were murderers whose relatives had bribed the asylum authorities to keep them there so that they would be safe from the hangman's noose. These men had some idea of what was going on and knew something about Pakistan. But they did not have all the facts. Not much could be ascertained from newspapers alone, and since the guards on duty were illiterate for the most part, little information could be gained by talking to them. All they knew was that there was a man, Mohammed Ali Jinnah, who was known as Quaid-e-Azam, and that he had founded, for the Muslims, a separate country called Pakistan. Where was Pakistan? What were its boundaries? They did not know. For this very reason all the inmates who were altogether mad, found themselves in a quandary; they could not figure out whether they were in Pakistan or India, and if they were in Pakistan, then how was it possible that only a short while ago they had been in India when they had not moved from the asylum at all?

For one lunatic, the entire issue of Hindustan-Pakistan and Pakistan-Hindustan resulted in further disorientation. One day, while he was sweeping the floor, he suddenly suspended his activity and climbed onto a tree where he remained for nearly two hours. During that time, he lectured extensively and non-stop on the matter of Pakistan versus Hindustan. When ordered by the guards to come down, he climbed higher up; when threatened with force, he said, "I want to live neither in Pakistan nor in Hindustan — I will live on this tree."

He descended from the tree when his fever cooled somewhat and embracing his Hindu and Sikh friends, he cried bitterly. He was saddened by the thought of their impending departure to India.

One morning, a Muslim engineer who used to spend most of his time walking, back and forth, in one particular spot of the garden, suddenly took off his clothes and begun running about naked.

A fat Muslim from Chiniot, who had once been an active member of the Muslim League, and who bathed at least fifteen times during the day, suddenly gave up bathing altogether. His name was Mohammad Ali. One day he announced that he was Quaid-e-Azam, Mohammad Ali Jinnah. Following his example, a Sikh in his enclosure announced that he was Master Tara Singh. Blood would have been spilled, but luckily both men were declared to be dangerous and confined to separate quarters.

There was a lawyer in the asylum, a young man from Lahore who had lost his sanity over a tragic love affair. He was deeply grieved when he discovered that Amritsar had become part of India, because the girl he had been in love with was from there. She had rejected this young lawyer, but despite his mental state he still cared for her. And he cursed all the leaders, both Muslim and Hindu, who were responsible for splitting Hindustan in two — his beloved had become a Hindustani while he was now a Pakistani.

Some of the other inmates tried to comfort the lawyer. They told him he would be sent to Hindustan where his beloved lived. But he did not wish to leave Lahore for he felt that his practice would not thrive in Amritsar.

In the European Ward were two Anglo-Indians. When they heard that the English had given Hindustan freedom and left, they were devastated. In the course of several secret meetings, they discussed the future of their status in the asylum. Will the European Ward be retained? Will they continue to get breakfast? Will they be forced to eat the bloody Indian chappati instead of bread?

A Sikh who had been in the asylum for fifteen years used to mutter constantly to himself. "Oper di gur gur di annexe di bay dhania di mung di daal di of laltain," he kept saying, over and over again. He slept neither at night nor during the day. According to the guards, he had not slept at all in fifteen years. He did not lie down either. Sometimes he leaned against a wall.

His feet and ankles were swollen from standing too much, but inspite of the bodily discomfort he experienced, he refused to rest. With great seriousness he listened to all the talk about the matter, he assumed a solemn air and replied, "Oper di gur gur di annexe di bay dhania di mung daal di of di Pakistan government," his usual gibberish.

Later on "of di Pakistan government" was replaced by "of di Toba Tek Singh government." Now he began asking people where Toba Tek Singh was, for that was his hometown. But no one could answer that question for him. And if someone did make an attempt to figure out the present status of Toba Tek Singh, more confusion would follow. It had been rumoured that Sialkot, which was once Hindustan, was now in Pakistan; who could say where Lahore, which was in Pakistan today, would be tomorrow, and was there anyone who could guarantee that both Pakistan and Hindustan would not disappear someday?

This man's kesh had become thin and straggly and since he seldom bathed, his kesh and his beard had become glued together, giving him a ghoulish appearance. But he was a harmless man. In fifteen years, he had not once been involved in a brawl with the other inmates. The guards only knew that he was from Toba Tek Singh, where he owned land. He had been a well-to-do landowner. Then, without warning, he had become insane. His relatives had bound him with iron chains, brought him to the asylum and admitted him there.

They came to visit him once every month, inquired after his well-being and then left. Their visits continued until the disturbances began which was when they stopped coming.

His name was Bishan Singh but people now called him Toba Tek Singh. It was apparent that he was impervious to the passage of time. But he waited for the visit from his relatives and was ready for them when they came. Before their arrival he would tell the guard his "visit" was coming; he bathed, scrubbed his body with soap, oiled his hair and combed it, put on his best clothes which he had reserved for this occasion, and then went to see his visitors. He remained silent when they addressed him. Sometimes, however, he muttered, "Oper di gur gur di annexe di bay dhania di mung daal di of laltain."

He had a daughter who was grown up now. As a child, she cried whenever she saw her father, and she continued to cry for him when she was a young woman.

When the disturbances began, Bishan Singh started asking the people at the asylum where Toba Tek Singh was, and since he was unable to receive a satisfactory answer, his curiosity increased. His "visit" had also stopped coming. He had been able to sense the impending visits of his relatives. But now it seemed that the little voice in his heart, which told him they were coming, had been stilled.

He longed for his visitors, who had been sympathetic and had brought him gifts of fruit, sweets and clothing. He was convinced they would be able to tell him if Toba Tek Singh was in Pakistan or in India, his conviction stemming from his belief that his family came from Toba Tek Singh.

In the lunatic asylum there was a man who believed that he was God. Bishan Singh asked him about Toba Tek Singh. The man laughed raucously. "It is neither in Pakistan nor in Hindustan," he said, "because I haven't given any orders yet."

Bishan Singh pleaded with this "God" to give the orders, so that the question of Toba Tek Singh could be settled once and for all. The man said that he was too busy; that there were too many other orders to be taken care of.

Finally Bishan Singh lost his temper. "Oper di gur gur di bay dhania di mung di daal di of wahay guruji, the khalsa and wahay guruji the fathey!" He probably wanted to say that if the man had been a Sikh God instead of a Muslim God, he might have helped him.

A few days prior to the transfer, Bishan Singh was visited by an old Muslim friend. Seeing him, Bishan Singh turned to leave. The guard restrained him. "He's come to see you," he said. "This is your friend, Fazal Din." Bishan Singh glanced at his friend briefly, then began muttering his customary nonsense. Fazal Din came forward and placed a hand on his shoulder.

"I wanted to come and see you earlier, I've just been so busy. Your family has left for Hindustan, everyone is fine...I helped them in whatever way I could. Your daughter Roop Kaur...?" he paused in mid-sentence.

"Roop Kaur?" Bishan Singh looked thoughtful.

"Yes...she...she's fine too," Fazal Din said haltingly. "She also left with the others."

Bishan Singh remained silent.

"They requested me to check on you every once in a while," Fazal Din continued. "Now I hear you're being taken to Hindustan. Give my regards to Bhai Baleer Singh and Bhai Vadhwa Singh...and sister Amrit Kaur. Tell Bhai Baleer, I am all right. One of the two cows he left behind has calved, had two calves...one died six days after the birth...and if there's anything more I can do, tell them I am ready any time. And here, I brought you some sweets."

Taking the bag of sweets from him, Bishan Singh handed it to the guard who was standing nearby.

"Where is Toba Tek Singh?" he then asked Fazal Din.

"Where is Toba Tek Singh?" Fazal Din repeated in amazement, adding, "Where it was before?"

"Is it in Pakistan or in Hindustan?" Bishan Singh asked.

"In Hindustan...well, no, no, in Pakistan, I think." Fazal Din became flustered.

Bishan Singh was muttering again. "Oper di gur gur di annexe di bay dhania di mung di daal di of Pakistan and Hindustan of di dur fitay moonh!" And with that he walked away.

All preparations for the transfer had been completed. Lists of patients had been exchanged and the day of the transfer had been set.

On an extremely cold day, lorries filled with Hindu and Sikh lunatics left the asylum in Lahore, accompanied by the police and some higher officials. At Wagah, the superintendents from both sides met and, after the initial formalities were out of the way, the actual transfer began and continued all night.

Getting the lunatics out of the lorries and handing them over to the Indian officials proved to be an arduous task. Many of them refused to leave the lorries and those who did, ran about wildly, making it increasingly difficult for the guards and other officials to keep them under control; those who were naked tore off any clothing that was forced on them, many swore and cursed, one or two sang, some fought with each other, others cried or wailed. Confusion was rampant. The women were also a problem, and the cold weather made everyone's teeth chatter.

The majority of the lunatics were not in favour of the transfer because these people could not comprehend the reasons for being uprooted from one place to be thrown into another. One or two, not completely mad, shouted, "Pakistan zindabad!" and "Pakistan murdabad!" This infuriated both the Muslims and Sikhs, and altercations between them were avoided with great difficulty.

When Bishan Singh's turn came to cross the border, he asked the official who was entering his name in a register, "Where is Toba Tek Singh? In Pakistan or in India?"

The official laughed and said, "In Pakistan."

On hearing this, Bishan Singh leaped back and ran towards the remaining group of men who awaited their turn. The Pakistani soldiers caught him and tired to force him back to the check-point. He resisted strongly.

"Toba Tek Singh is here!" he yelled. "Oper di gur gur di annexe di bay dhania di mung daal di of Toba Tek Singh and Pakistan!"

The authorities attempted to reason with him. "Look, Toba Tek Singh is in Hindustan now — and if he's not there yet, we'll send him there immediately." But he was adamant and would not budge from the spot where he stood. When the guards threatened to use force, he installed himself in a place between the borders and stood there as if no power in the world could move him.

Because he was a harmless man, he was not coerced and was allowed to remain in that place while the transfer continued.

Before the sun rose, a piercing cry arose from Bishan Singh who had been quiet and unmoving all this time. Several officers, and the guards ran towards him; they saw that the man who, for fifteen years, had stood on his legs day and night, now lay on the ground, prostrate. Beyond a wired fence on one side of him was Hindustan and beyond a wired fence on the other side was Pakistan. In the middle, on a stretch of land which had no name, lay Toba Tek Singh.

Original in Urdu.
Translated by Tahira Naqvi.

ISMAT CHUGHTAI

ROOTS

The colour had drained from our faces. Food hadn't been cooked at home for the last six days. The children had not gone to school, and had made life miserable for themselves and for everyone else. They hit each other, ran around, were noisy and performed somersaults as they had always done, as if nothing had happened on 15th August. The wretched children were not even concerned about the fact that the British had left, and that before leaving, they had wounded us so deeply that it would take years for our wounds to heal. The operation on India had been performed by such incompetent hands and with such blunt instruments that generations had been destroyed. Rivers of blood flowed everywhere. And no one had the courage to even stitch the open wounds.

If it had been an ordinary day, one could have told those wretched children to go outside and raise as much dust and noise as they pleased, but for the last few days the atmosphere in the city had become so foul that all the Muslims had gone into hiding. There were locks on their doors and policemen stood on guard outside. The Muslims felt as if salt was being rubbed into their wounds. The Civil Lines area was, as usual, peaceful. After all, filth spreads the most where there are cesspools, and hatred inflicts its deepest wounds where there is ignorance and extreme poverty. It was in such places and amongst such people that the worst passions had been aroused in the name of religion. The entire atmosphere had been polluted. On top of it, the growing number of refugees who were coming down from Punjab everyday, had added to the fear in the hearts of the members of the minority community.

There had been two riots already, but in the Mewar Hindus and Muslims had become so intermingled that it was difficult to tell them apart from their names, features or clothes. Those who could have easily been distinguished from the rest of the population had left for Pakistan the moment they had got a whiff of what was going to happen on 15th August. As regards those who had been living in these regions for generations, they had neither the sense nor the ability to understand what the real problem between Pakistan and India was. There was no one who could have explained it to them either. There were some who had been tempted to leave for Pakistan by stories that wheat was available there for four rupees a seer, and that nans, which were as long as the palm of one's hand, were being sold there for four annas. They had begun to return. Because once they had reached Pakistan, they had realized that in order to buy wheat at four rupees a seer they needed money, and that nans which were as long as the palms of their hands and cost only four annas still had to be paid for. And money neither grew in the fields nor was it sold in the shops. It was as difficult to come by money as it was to fulfill their desire to live.

When there was an open call to throw the Muslims out of our region, it created a lot of difficulties. The Thakurs refused. They insisted that the community was much too intermingled and that it would be necessary to employ a large staff to identify the Muslims. To do so, they said, would be a waste of money. They could, however, help people to buy forest land for the refugees. After all only animals lived in forests and they could be driven out whenever necessary.

There were still a few well-established Muslims families left. They were either the employees or the favourites of the Maharaja. The question of their leaving didn't arise. There were some other Muslim families who were determined not to leave. Our family was one such. We were in no hurry to leave.

Things changed, however, the moment my elder brother arrived from Ajmer. He incited everyone, aroused their anger, made them lose their sense of reason. Even then no one really took the question of migration seriously. No one would have paid him much attention had Chabba Miyan — may Allah have mercy upon him — not instigated trouble.

My eldest brother had made up his mind to leave. He had, however, stopped arguing and had admitted defeat as far as the rest of us were concerned. Chabba Miyan, unfortunately, one day decided to scrawl 'Pakistan Zindabad' on the school wall. Roopchandji's children opposed him. They, at once, rubbed out the slogan and wrote 'Akhand Hindustan' on the wall instead. The result was a fight and both sides proclaimed loudly to everyone their decision to erase the very presence of one another from the face of the earth. The matter got out of hand. The police had to be called and the few Muslim children who were involved, were rounded up and sent back to their homes.

As soon as the children returned home, the mothers of Haiza town rushed out as usual to hug their darlings. In the past, whenever Chabba returned after fighting with Roopchandji's children, his mother would thrash him with a shoe and send him back to Roopchandji's house with the instruction that he should be given a dose of castor oil and quinine. Roopchandji was not only our family doctor, he was also my father's friend, his sons were the friends of the sons of our family, and the women of his family were the friends of the women of our family, and even the children of the two families were close friends. The two families had shared their lives for a long time. So closely related were the three generations in each family, that no one could have ever suspected that after the Partition there would be a quarrel between them.

There were, of course, supporters of the Muslim League, the Congress and the Hindu Mahasabha in both the families. They argued fierceiy with each other on matters of religion and politics, but only as if they were playing a football or a cricket match. For example, my father was a Congressi, while Doctor Sahib and my eldest brother supported the League. Gyanchand was a Mahasabha man, my younger brother was a communist, Gulabchand was a socialist. The wives and the children belonged to the parties supported by their husbands or their fathers. Generally when there was an argument the majority would support the Congress. The communists and the socialists would abuse everyone loudly, but would end up supporting the Congress. That would leave the enthusiasts of the League and the Mahasabha to fight it out. They were, of course, bitter enemies of each other, but they would always support each other against the Congress.

Over the last few years, however, the support for the League, as well as for the Mahasabha, had increased. The Congress had been completely eliminated. Under the leadership of my eldest brother the entire new crop of the house, with the exception of a few Congress supporters, had formed a wing of the National Guard.

In the other family, a small group of the Sevak Sangh had been set up under the guidance of Gyanchand. There was, however, no decline in the love and friendship between the two families.

"My son, Lalu, will marry only Munni," the Mahasabha supporter, Gyanchand, would tell her father, the League supporter. "I will present her with golden anklets."

"Yar, I only hope they won't be gold-plated," Bade Bhai would retort.

The National Guard would write "Pakistan Zindabad," on the walls of the town, and the followers of the Sevak Sangh would rub the slogan off and write "Akhand Hindustan" instead. All this happened when the question of the formation of Pakistan was still a subject of jokes and laughter.

Abba and Roopchand would listen to all this and dream of a united Asia.

Ammi and Chachi would stay clear of politics, and talk about haldi, dhania and the dowry for their daughters; the daughters of the families would concern themselves with the designs of the clothes each of them was wearing. Along with salt and spices, medicine was also sent from Doctor Sahib's house. If someone even sneezed, he'd run to consult Doctor Sahib. Whenever one of us fell ill, Ammi would make rotis stuffed with dal and dahi-vadas, and invite Doctor Sahib to join us for dinner. Doctor Sahib would arrive, holding the hand of one of his grandsons. His wife would invariably instruct him, before he left the house, "Don't eat there. Did you hear what I said?"

"Alright, but how else will I collect my fees? Listen, send Lalu and Chunni also."

It was always great fun when Ammi was ill. Ammi was terrified of Doctor Sahib. She would say, "No, I will not be treated by him. He'll tease me." But no one would agree to go to town to fetch another doctor. The moment Doctor Sahib heard that Ammi was unwell, he'd come to examine her.

"If you eat all the pullav by yourself, you'll fall ill," he would say to tease her.

"Everybody isn't like you," Ammi would retort from behind the purdah.

"You only pretend to be ill. You merely have to send for me, I'll come running. Why go through this ritual?" he would say, with a mischievous twinkle in his eyes and a smile on his face. Ammi would jerk her wrist away. Abba would watch all this and quietly smile.

If Doctor Sahib came to see one patient, everyone would line up to be examined. One would be worried about a pimple. One would have an ear-ache and another a nose-bleed.

"How they torment me, Deputy Sahib! I should give poison to one or two of them! Do you think I am a veterinary surgeon that you pounce on me like animals?" he would say, irritated by the number of patients.

And if he heard that a new child was expected, he would begin to curse the entire human race.

"Yes, medicine is free! Let more children be born, they can always be dumped on me."

But the moment he heard that the pains had started, he would anxiously pace the open space between our houses. He would scream and shout at everyone. Neighbours and friends would gather. He would curse the father of the child, slap him, scold him!

The moment, however, he heard the cry of the new-born child, he'd rush up the steps of our verandah, open the door and walk into the room, dragging Abba with him. Abba, too, would be tense and anxious. The women in the room would curse them and cover themselves with a purdah. He would check the baby's pulse, thump its back and say, "Good show, my lion." Then he would cut the umbilical cord and bathe the child. Abba would nervously perform the duties of a nurse, while Ammi would scream, "O God, is that child a human being or a pup in a kennel!" Only then would the two of them run out of the room like two mischievous boys.

When Abba had a paralytic stroke, Roopchandji had retired from the hospital and his entire practice was restricted to our family and his. Other doctors treated Abba, but Doctor Sahib always accompanied Ammi and the nurse to the hospital. After Abba's death, Doctor Sahib not only continued to love the family, but also became aware of his responsibilities towards it. He got the school fees of the children waived, prevented Gyanchand from demanding a dowry for his daughters. No important decision was made in the house without consulting him. Even when it was decided that two more rooms should be added to the western wing of the house, Doctor Sahib was consulted.

"Why don't you build two rooms on the second floor instead?" he had advised. His suggestion was debated. When Mazzan decided that he didn't want to study science for his F.A. examination, Doctor Sahib had thrashed him with his shoe. Mazzan changed his mind. Farida fought with her husband and returned home. Her husband went to seek Doctor Sahib's help, followed by his second wife. When Shiela married into his family, our problems of finding a midwife were solved. The poor woman would give up her hospital duties in order to help the midwife. Not only did she not charge her fees, she always presented the new born child a kurta and a cap on the sixth day.

But now, when Chabba came home after a fight, he was greeted as if Mahmud Ghazni had returned house victorious. Everyone asked him about his deeds of bravery. In that babel of tongues, only Ammi remained silent. She had in fact refused to speak, since the day the tricolour had been unfurled over Doctor Sahib's house and the League's flag over ours. It seemed as if a chasm, which was miles long and deep, had opened up between our houses. She had watched the unfathomable distance with tears in her eyes and shame. Later, trouble about the refugees started; the parents of the eldest daughter-in-law barely managed to escape with their lives and Nirmala's in-laws arrived from Rawalpindi after having lost everything. The distance between the two houses seemed to crawl with venomous snakes.

When Choti Bhabhi sent word that her son had a stomach ache, Shiela Bhabhi sent the servant away. No one argued about the incident. Everyone in the house stopped paying attention to his own ailments. Badi Bhabhi forgot to throw hysterical fits and began packing her belongings.

"Don't you dare to touch my trunk!" When Ammi finally opened her mouth, everyone was stunned.

"Won't you come with us?" Bade Bhaiya asked sharply.

"No. Do you think I'll die amongst the Sindhis! Among those shameless people who wander about in kurtas and pyjamas!"

"Why don't you go to your younger son's house?"

"Aye, why should she go to Dhaka? Those Bengalis slurp rice as they shove it into their mouths with their hands!" Mumani Bi, the mother-in-law of the younger brother, taunted.

"Then go to Farida's place in Rawalpindi," Khala said.

"Tobah, may Allah save me from falling into the hands of the Punjabis. They talk like the fiends of hell." That day my quiet and gentle mother spoke without regard for those she insulted.

"Aye Bua, you are like the woman who is in the claws of a wolf, but refuses to go to her daughter's house. Aye bi, stop behaving as if the emperor has invited you...Look at her, nothing is good enough for her, no one is elegant enough for her; she is like..."

The atmosphere was as such tense, but that remark caused a commotion. My mother became even more angry.

"Why are all of you talking like children?" the leader of the National Guard asked. "Don't talk nonsense. Ammi, do you want us to stay here and be killed?"

"You may go, but where can I go in my last days?"

"Do you want the kafirs to kill you?"

Khala counted the pieces of her baggage. Along with the gold and silver, she had also packed dry methi, packets of bone-powder, and even Multani matti. She was so concerned about her things that it seemed as if without them the Sterling reserves in the banks of Pakistan would fall dangerously low. She was forced to use the cotton from the mattresses, which had been thoroughly soaked by the urine of her children, to make her bundles. Utensils were stuffed into gunny bags; beds were dismantled and their legs were tied together with ropes. Within a few days, a well-established household was transformed into piles of misshapen and crooked bundles.

Indeed, the luggage seemed to have sprouted feet and seemed to dance and skip through the house. It would rest for a while and then begin to hop and jump again.

Ammi's trunk, however, stood where it was.

"If you have decided to die here, no one can stop you," Bhai Sahib finally told her.

My simple and innocent Amma continued to stare at the dusty sky with her restless eyes, as if she too was wondering — Who will kill me? When?

"Amma has become senile with age," whispered my younger brother.

"She doesn't know what torture the kafirs have inflicted upon innocent people. If we have our own country, at least our lives and property will be safe."

If my agonized mother had a sharper tongue, she would have retorted, "What is this strange bird called, our country? Tell me, where is that country? This is the land where you were born, which gave birth to you; this is the earth on which you grew up; if this is not your country, how can some distant land where you merely go and settle for a few days become your country? Besides, who knows if you won't be driven, pushed out of there too? Who knows if you won't be told to go and settle in some other place? I sit here like a flickering lamp. A small gust of wind will extinguish me, and put an end to all this turmoil about choosing one's country. This game of destroying an old country and founding a new nation is not very interesting. There was a time when the Mughals left their own country to establish a new empire here; now we plan to go elsewhere to find a land of our own. A nation seems to be no better than a shoe! If it becomes a little tight, discard it for a new one!"

But she remained silent. She seemed even more tired than before. It was as if she had been searching for her country for centuries, and had lost her own soul in that search. She was exhausted, she couldn't move anymore.

People came and went. But Amma sat rooted in her place like a banyan tree which survives even as the storms rage around it.

But when the caravan of her sons and daughters, daughters-in-law and sons-in-law, grandsons and grand-daughters passed through the outer gate and, under the protection of the police, climbed into the waiting trucks, she was heart-broken. Anxiously, expectantly, she gazed across the chasm which now separated our house from Roopchandji's house. The house on the other side seemed as far away as a distant cloud. Roopchandji's verandah was empty. Children peeped out once or twice, but a hand dragged them back inside.

Amma's tear-filled eyes caught a glimpse of people in the other house peering at us through the cracks in closed windows and from behind the chick curtains.

After the trucks left, raising a cloud of dust, the door of the house across opened slowly, and Roopchandji came out stealthily like a thief. He stood on the verandah and looked through the dusty haze towards the empty house across the road, searching for a glimpse of a familiar face. Having failed to see anyone in the desolate house, he lowered his eyes like a guilty man.

Amma left everything, all the good-will she had earned, all the wealth she had accumulated throughout her life, in the hands of the merciful God, and stepped out into the verandah of her house. Her old heart had shrivelled. She was apprehensive like a little child. She felt as if ghosts would pounce on her from all sides and strangle her. She felt giddy and clung to a pillar. When she looked up, her heart leapt into her mouth. She saw the room in which her husband had first embraced her; where the veil had been lifted for the first time from the face of an innocent and trembling bride, where she had become a part of the life of the house forever. And in that room on the other side, her first daughter had been born...the memory of her eldest daughter flashed through her mind like lightning. Her daughter's umbilical cord had been buried in one corner of that room. In fact, the umbilical cords of all her ten children were buried there; ten souls had come into this world in that room. Ten living and breathing creatures, ten human beings who had been born from her womb, had abandoned her that day. She felt as if she was a splinter which they had pulled out and thrown away into the thorny bushes on the road side and had made their escape. In search of honour and peace, in search of wheat sold at four rupees a seer. The room was still glowing with their innocent eyes. She ran into the room with her arms outstretched, but found that there was no one there. That day her lap, which newly wedded brides used to long to lay their heads upon so that their own wombs would not remain barren, was empty. Bewildered, she fell on the floor. She could do nothing to recover the past, to recall those who had left.

She staggered into the next room. It was there that the man with whom she had spent fifty years of her life, had turned his face towards the wall and died. It was in front of that door that his body had been lowered into a coffin. The entire family had stood around it. He had been fortunate because he had passed away surrounded by the love of his children, but he had left his companion behind. She felt like a corpse which had been abandoned without a coffin. Her feet refused to move any further. She sat down at the spot where she had lit the lamp with trembling hands beside her new born children ten times. But there was no oil left in the lamp that day and the wick had burnt itself out.

Roopchandji paced up and down his verandah. He cursed and shouted at everyone — his wife and children, the servants, the government, the silent street that stretched before him, the bricks and the stones, the knives and the swords; indeed, the entire universe seemed to cringe before his volley of curses. He was particularly angry at the empty house across the road which seemed to mock him. It was as if he had, with his own hands, demolished it brick by brick. He wanted to brush something out of his mind. Wanted to peck it out with all his strength. But he was irritated by his inability to get rid of it. He couldn't uproot it from his soul because it had gripped him like the roots of an ancient tree. He felt as if someone was slowly scraping the skin off his body. He groaned loudly and then suddenly fell silent. He stopped cursing, stopped pacing up and down. After a while he got into his car and left.

That night, after everything was quiet in the street, Roopchandji's daughter-in-law entered our house, through the back door, like a thief, with two plates full of food in her hands. She and my mother sat across from each other without saying anything. They didn't speak, but they looked at each other with sympathy and understanding. When women gossip maliciously their tongues run like scissors, but the moment their emotional life is attacked they seal their lips.

Finding herself alone, doubts and anxieties assailed my mother throughout that night. "I hope no one has attacked them in the dark and killed them. These days trains are being stopped and passengers are being slaughtered. We had all fought for this land for fifty years, had shed our blood for it, and today we are being asked to leave it and establish a new nation somewhere. Who knows if they will prosper there? Will the new land suffuse the new crop being sown in it with sap? Will the transplanted saplings wilt? May Allah protect Choti Bahu, her child is due at any time now, who knows in which forest she will give birth to it. They left everything behind — home, comforts, jobs, business.

Will the predatory birds have left anything for them in the new land? Or will they be forced to return shamefaced? If they return, will they be granted another chance to establish their roots in this soil? Who knows if this old skeleton of mine will still be around when the seasons change?"

Who knows what that old woman muttered to herself for hours on end as she clung to the walls and the doors of the house? After sometime she became calm. Did she sleep? No. All night long that old woman imagined, as in a nightmare, that her young and beautiful daughters were being paraded naked in the streets, that their bodies were being cut into pieces, that her sons and grandsons were being skinned alive. Who knows when horror invaded the house and she felt as if the final crisis was upon her? One may not love life, but even the flame of a lamp trembles before it goes out. Besides, while natural death is terrifying enough, it is worse when it comes in the shape of demonic men. We had heard that even old women were being dragged by their hair through city streets till their skin had been ripped off and their white bones revealed. Human beings still hesitate to leave such a world.

The knocking on the door outside increased. Death, it seemed, was in a hurry. Suddenly the doors flew open. Lights came on. Someone called as if from the bottom of a well. Was it the voice of her eldest son...? No, perhaps it was the voice of one of her other sons. It sounded as if it was coming from the other shore.

So, everyone had at least reached the new country. But so soon? The second son! Followed by her youngest son! She could see them clearly enough. They were accompanied by their wives and children. All of a sudden the entire house came alive; all the ghosts of the house, it seemed to that unhappy woman, had decided to gather around her. But the young and the old touched her lovingly. A smile began to play on her lips. She was overwhelmed with happiness. All her sorrows scattered; they swirled into the surrounding darkness and vanished.

When she opened her eyes again, she at once recognized the touch of the fingers which were checking her pulse. Standing behind the purdah, Roopchandji said, "Arrey Bhabhi, if you had sent for me, I would have come. Why did you have to enact this elaborate ritual?

But today, Bhabhi, you will have to pay me my fees for bringing your good-for-nothing children back from Loni Junction. These scoundrels were running away. They didn't trust even the Superintendent of Police."

The old woman's face glowed with a smile. She sat up. She was silent for a long time. Slowly two teardrops rolled down her face and fell on Roopchandji's wrinkled hands.

Original in Urdu.
Translated by Vishwamitter Adil and Alok Bhalla.

SAMARESH BASU

ADAB

The stillness of the night was shattered by the military jeep which drove past the Victoria Park, in one quick turn.

Section 144 and curfew were in force in the city. The Hindus and Muslims were at each other's throats. With choppers, spears, daggers and wooden rods. Assassins had fanned out on every side. It was the night of the long knives.

The marauders were out on the streets, looting. The dark night, torrid with death, lent a strange intensity to their joy. Basti after basti was aflame. The dying screams of women and children merged with the tension in the air. The noisy army trucks leapt into the fray with gunfire spraying in all directions — to preserve of all things, law and order.

Two lanes merged at a single point. A dustbin lay overturned at the crossing. Using that as a cover, a man crawled out from one of the lanes — on all fours.

He did not dare raise his head and lay inert for a while.

But his ears were keenly glued to the faint sounds coming from the distance. Nothing could be deciphered. It could as well have been Allah-ho-Akbar or Bande Mataram.

Suddenly the dustbin moved a bit! His every nerve tautened in anticipation. Clenching his teeth, straining his sinews, the man waited; expecting something terrible to happen. A few moments passed.

It was still and quiet all around.

Perhaps it was a dog.

To chase it away, he pushed the dustbin gently. There was silence for a while. Then the bin rattled again. Curiosity coupled with fear now. The man raised his head slowly. From the other side, emerged another head. A man! Two men on two sides of the dustbin, both terrified, absolutely still. Their hearts beat wildly; the look in those two pairs of eyes — scared, suspicious, anxious — slowly grew intense. Neither could trust the other. Each thought the other man was a killer. Their eyeballs locked, both waited for the other to strike. But neither did.

Now an identical question took shape in both their minds. Was the other person a Hindu or a Muslim? The answer to this question would have perhaps brought about the final denouement. That is why neither could flee. Out of fear that the other might strike!

Dwelling in doubt and discomfort for a while, both became impatient. Finally, one broke the ice, "Are you a Hindu or a Muslim?" "You answer that question first," the other replied.

But both refused to reveal their identity, suspicious of the other. The first question soon got buried. Another cropped up. "Where do you come from?"

"From that side of the river. And you?"

"From Chasara — near Narayanganj. And what do you do?"

"I have a boat. I ply it. And you?"

"I work in a mill in Narayanganj."

There was silence once again. In that darkness where nothing can be seen, both tried to guess what the other looked like. They tried to see each other's attire.

But darkness and the dustbin made this impossible. Suddenly, some trouble erupted nearby. There was an uproar. A medley of different chants broke the stillness of the night.

Terrified, the mill worker and the boatman cringed.

"They are coming close," the terrified worker whispered.

"Yes, come, let's get away from here," the boatman replied, equally scared.

The worker stopped him. "No, don't get up. Do you want to die?"

The boatman became suspicious again. What were the other man's intentions? He looked straight into the mill worker's eyes.

He was also staring at him and, as soon as their eyes met, he said, "Sit. Don't do anything now."

The boatman became tense instantly. Was the other man threatening him? Suspicion clouded his mind all over again. He asked, "Why?"

"Why!" the mill worker spoke in a harsh whisper. "What do you mean, why? Do you want to die?"

The boatman did not like the way he said this. He tossed around in his mind all the possibilities, and then steadied himself. "No, I'll stay here, in this dark, dingy lane for you!" he exclaimed, sarcastically.

Sensing his stubbornness, the other man also became suspicious. "Your intentions don't seem good to me!" he muttered. "You haven't yet told me which community you belong to. What if you get all your chaps to come and kill me?"

"What are you saying!" forgetting where they were, the boatman almost screamed out aloud in hurt and anger.

"I've said the right thing! You don't understand how people behave at times!"

There was something in his voice that made the boatman relax.

"If you go, will I stay on here alone?"

The tumult in the distance dies down. Silence returns like death once again. The moments pass in brutal terror. The terror of waiting for death. In the dark lane, on either side of a dustbin, two people think about the danger they are trapped by, their homes, their mothers, wives and children. Will they ever be able to return to them alive? Would they be there even if they did?

Suddenly, without any warning, the riots had struck. Like thunder! Amidst all the laughter, the chatter in the market-place, suddenly death swooped down on everyone: killing, looting, blood flowing like water down the river! How can people turn so heartless, so cruel — so easily? What a cursed race! The mill worker sighed. Seeing him, the boatman did likewise.

"Care for a smoke?" Extracting a bidi from his pocket, the worker held it out to the boatman. By sheer habit, the boatman caressed the bidi, twirled it around his ear a few times and then, gripped it tightly between his lips. The worker, in the meantime, tried to light a match. He hadn't noticed earlier that his kurta was wet. The matches, too, were damp. After several strikes, a faltering blue flash could be seen.

Disgusted, he threw the stick away.

"This bloody matchbox has turned soggy!" he mumbled and took out another stick.

Somewhat impatiently, the boatman got up and came to sit beside the worker.

"It will light, don't worry, give it to me." He almost grabbed the matchbox from the worker's hand. Striking it a few times, he actually managed to light a match.

"Allah be blessed! Come on, light your bidi quickly!"

The worker was shocked! He paled as if he had seen a ghost. The bidi fell from his lips.

"You...?"

A light breeze snuffed out the matchstick. A pair of eyes widened again, out of mistrust and anxiety in the dark. A few silent moments passed.

The boatman stood up suddenly, he said, "Yes, I am a Muslim. So what?"

The weaver replied fearfully, "Nothing, but..." Pointing to the bundle under the boatman's arm, the weaver asked, "What's inside that?"

"A couple of frocks for my daughter and a sari for my wife. Don't you know it's Id tomorrow?"

"I hope there's nothing else there!" the worker's fears persisted.

"Are you implying I'm lying? If you don't believe me, check it yourself." He held out the bundle for the worker to rummage through.

"No, no, what is there to see, my brother! But you know what the days are like? You tell me, can you trust anybody?"

"That's it. Brother, I hope you haven't got something on you?"

"I can swear on God I don't even have a needle on me. I shall be glad to return home with my life intact." The mill worker offered a body search.

The two sat down again, side by side. Lighting their bidis, they smoked intently together, in silence.

"Okay!" the boatman spoke in a manner as if he was addressing a relative or a friend.

"Okay, you've not been able to tell me what all this killing is about."

The worker read newspapers. He knew a little about what was going on. So he answered testily, "The fault lies with your people! They have started all this."

The boatman objected, "I don't understand all this. I'm only asking as to what will come about from so much killing. Some men from your side will die and some from mine. How will the country gain?"

"That's exactly what I'm saying. What can happen? Nothing except this!" he sticks up his thumb in a familiar gesture. "You might die or I, and our wives and kids will have to beg. In the last riots, they hacked my brother-in-law into four pieces. My sister was widowed and her children landed on my shoulders!"

"We are not human beings. We are like vicious dogs!" the boatman complained, in impotent rage.

"True."

"Who thinks of us? Amidst all this rioting how will I earn? Who will give me food? Will I ever get my boat back? They may have sunk her by now. Every month, the nayab from the zamindar's house would take my boat across the river, to attend court. The zamindar would tip me five rupees and the nayab would pay another five as fare. That would make ten rupees. It paid for my monthly expenses. Will the Hindu babu come near my boat again, after all this?"

The worker, about to say something, checked himself. The sound of heavy boots came near. There was no doubt that the sound was nearing from the main road.

Alarmed, they looked into each other's eyes.

"What shall we do?" the boatman quickly placed the bundle under his arm.

"Let's run. But which way shall we go? I don't know the roads very well out here."

The boatman suggested, "Let's go any place. We won't take police beating just like that. You can't trust the bastards!"

"Yes. You're right. Tell me which way to go — they're almost here! This way!"

The boatman indicated the southward end of the lane. He said, "Let's go. If only we can reach the ghats of Badamatali, we needn't be frightened any more."

Ducking their heads, they ran along breathlessly after crossing the head of the lane, landing on Patuatuli Road. The deserted road sparkled in the electric lights. Both stood frozen for a while — hopefully, no one was watching them! But, there was no way they could have delayed. Scanning both ends of the road once again, they ran westward. They had covered some ground when, suddenly, they heard the sound of hooves. They saw a rider some distance away coming towards them. There was no time to think. They hid in a narrow lane, normally used by sweepers.

A little later, an Englishman brandishing a revolver rode past them with great speed, raising the sound of the clattering hooves in their hearts. When the sound faded in the distance, they peeped around and came out of their hiding place.

"Walk along the curb," the mill worker suggested.

Keeping out the shadows, they quickly walked on.

"Stop!" the boatman said in a low voice. The worker stopped in his tracks, surprised.

"What's happened?"

"Come here!" Holding the worker's hand, the boatman led him behind a paan shop.

"Look here!"

The worker followed the boatman's gaze and saw a house with the lights on. In the adjoining balcony stood about 10 to 12 armed policemen. Before them stood an English officer, saying something and gesticulating through a haze of smoke from his pipe. Below the balcony, holding on to the reins of a horse, was another policeman. The restless and fidgety horse was continuously tattooing the ground with his hooves.

The boatman said, "That's the Islampur outpost. If we go a little further, we can get through the lane to the left of the outpost — to reach Badamtali ghat."

The worker's entire face clouded over with fear, "Then where?"

"That's why I'm suggesting you stay here. You'll gain nothing by going to the ghat," the boatman said. "This is a Hindu area and Islampur belongs to the Muslims. Go home when you wake up in the morning tomorrow."

"And you?"

"I am going ahead," the boatman's voice turned hoarse with anxiety and fear, "I won't be able to stay on any more. Today is the eighth day since I last got news of my people. Only Allah knows what's happened to them! If only I can enter the lane somehow! If I don't find a boat, I'll swim across."

"What are you saying!" Anxiously, the worker held on to the boatman's kurta. "How can you go like that!"

"Don't hold me back please. Let me go. You don't understand that tomorrow's Id. The children must have sighted the moon today. They must be waiting to wear new clothes and sit on their father's lap. My wife must be crying. I can't, brother, I can't. I don't feel happy," the boatman's voice faltered. The mill worker's heart also tautened. The fingers holding the boatman's kurta slackened

"What if they catch you?" his voice became heavy with fear and concern.

"They won't be able to catch me, don't worry! Stay here, don't get up. I'm going. I'll never forget this night. If fate wills, we'll meet again. Goodbye."

The boatman left, walking carefully.

With a heart full of suspense, the other man stood still. His galloping heartbeat refused to become normal. He remained alert.

"God," he prayed, "let not danger strike again."

The moments passed in bated breath. It was a long time. The boatman must have gone by now. How hopeful his children must have been to wear their new clothes. After all, the heart was the heart of a father. He sighed. The wife would break down and cry upon his chest, having got her husband back.

"You've returned from the jaws of earth?" she'd say. A smile lit up a corner of the mill worker's mouth. And what would the boatman do then? The boatman would... "Halt!"

The worker's heart missed a beat. Some men in boots were running around. They were screaming and saying something.

"The dacoit is running away!"

Stretching out, the mill worker saw a police officer with a revolver in his hand jump onto the road. Shattering the silence of the entire locality, he fired his revolver twice.

Bang! Bang! Two blue sparks of fire! In suspense, the worker almost bit off his finger. Leaping onto his horse, the officer raced into the lane. He had heard the death cries of the dacoit.

Before the bewildered eyes of the worker emerged a picture of the boatman, with his small bundle of clothes now slowly turning crimson with his blood. The boatman was saying, "I couldn't make it, brother. My children and wife will weep on a festival day. The enemy stopped me..."

Original in Bengali.
Translated by Rina Nandy.

UPENDRANATH ASHK

THE FODDER-CUTTING MACHINE

When the Muslims of Islamabad, who lived across the railway line, fled for their lives, leaving all their possessions behind, the wife of our neighbour, Lehna Singh, became aware of new opportunities.

"How long will you sit here like an impotent man?" she taunted Lehna Singh. "Others will seize the best houses before you."

Sardar Lehna Singh could take a lot from his wife, but he could never tolerate being called 'impotent'. Therefore, he tightened his turban, tucked in his tehmad, tested the sharpness of his kirpan and set out to capture one of the best houses in Islamabad.

He had only reached the courtyard, when his wife came running after him and gave him a big lock. "How will you establish your right over it, if you don't lock it?"

With a lock in one hand and a kirpan in the other, Lehna Singh marched in the direction of Islamabad.

We lived on Khalsa College Road, near Putli Ghar in Amritsar. There was an open courtyard next to our house. Sardar Lehna Singh used to sell fodder-cutting machines there. In one corner of the courtyard, there were a few dark rooms. Because there was a shortage of houses in Amritsar, Sardar Sahib used to live in those rooms. Initially, he had invested about two thousand rupees in the machines but the war (and the economic prosperity of the farmers) had helped his business to thrive. Money had brought with it household goods and rising expectations. In the beginning, both husband and wife were ecstatic about the courtyard and the dingy rooms. But after sometime, Lehna Singh's wife, who was now called 'Sardarni' by everyone, became intensely dissatisfied with the place.

The efficiency of the fodder-cutting machines was demonstrated for prospective customers in the courtyard. The machines were lined-up in the courtyard, and throughout the day they mechanically cut grass with their sharp knives. Lehna Singh's wife could no longer bear the continuous noise of the machines, nor could she tolerate the sight of the bundles of grass which lay scattered everywhere.

Lehna Singh, on the other hand, though he now wore a silk turban, a silk tehmad, and a boski shirt which came down to his knees, instead of a striped cotton shirt, had not changed. He was neither bothered by the dingy rooms, nor by the noise of the machines, nor by the bundles of grass. Indeed, he was quite delighted by his surroundings. He was one of those Sikhs about whom another Sikh writer had said, "No matter what the circumstances, a Sikh is always a Sikh."

It wasn't as if Lehna Singh was thin and weak. He was a strong and a well-built man, and the proof of his manhood were his five children who clung to Sardarni like leeches. Sardarni had called him impotent because that was her way of provoking him into action. If she wanted Lehna Singh to do something which required thought, she used to call him 'stupid', and if she wanted him to do something which required physical effort, she used to say that he was 'impotent'. She was, of course, a rather coarse woman. Money and good clothes, after all, don't make a person cultured. Though Sardarni may have been proud of her wealth, she had no ambitions of being called cultured.

When Lehna Singh reached Islamabad, he found himself in the middle of a violent riot. People of one religion were busy slaughtering people of another religion, with the same mechanical efficiency with which his machines chopped grass. Sardar Lehna Singh also pulled out his kirpan and was determined to prove that he was a man by killing the first Muslim who came his way. He didn't have to kill anyone, because he didn't come across a single Muslim. The roads, however, were blood stained, and there was a lot of screaming and shouting nearby.

As he prowled around the area, he saw his friend, Gurdial Singh, break into a house.

Curious, Lehna Singh stopped to watch him.

"I am taking possession of this house," Sardar Gurdial Singh said casually and continued to break the lock.

Lehna Singh tucked the end of his turban into the folds and looked carefully at the house his friend has taken over. He then remembered that he too must hunt for a house. A little further down the lane, he saw a house which was bigger and better built than the one his friend had broken into. There was a big lock on its door. Without a moment's hesitation, he picked up a big stone from the road and smashed the lock open with a few sturdy blows.

The house wasn't really as big as it looked, but compared to Lehna Singh's dingy rooms it was heavenly. It may have belonged to a clerk with some taste. It had a small radio and a gramophone. The trunks were open, but there were no clothes or jewels in them. Perhaps, the owner of the house had fled to a refugee camp or to Pakistan before the violence and the killing had started. Even then, he had left behind a number of useful things. Lehna Singh was so happy that he put his wrist to his mouth and bleated like a goat. Then he tightened his tehmad and began taking stock of the things in the house.

He sorted out the things in the house. The useful ones he kept to one side and the other things he threw out. Then he fixed the big lock he had brought with him on the door outside, requested Gurdial Singh to keep an eye on the house and went back home to fetch his luggage.

When he reached home, he realized that he had no means of carting his luggage across. How could he have found a tonga during the riots? He took his bicycle and rode up to see Ramdhan, the milk-man. In the past, he had often rented Ramdhan's bullock-cart to carry his machines. He begged and cajoled Ramdhan, and finally persuaded him to let him have the cart for twice the normal rent.

When he had loaded all his luggage on it and was ready to leave, his wife demanded that he take her with him. He tried to reason with his good wife and tell her that she should go there only after all the other Sardarnis had moved there. "There are lakhs of Sihani", Lehna Singh explained. "But they are still only women and in riots, it's the women who suffer the most." He also explained to her that she was needed to protect the courtyard. "Refugees are pouring in all the time. If they find the courtyard unoccupied, they will take possession of it."

The Sardarni agreed, but just when Sardar Lehna Singh was about to leave, she suggested that he should take one of the fodder-cutting machines with him to the new house so that there would be no doubt left in anyone's mind that the house belonged to Sardar Lehna Singh, the seller of fodder-cutting machines.

The Sardarji liked the Sardarni's suggestion very much.

Although there was practically no space left on the cart, one fodder-cutting machine was loaded on the top of the luggage. It was secured with a rope so that it wouldn't fall. Soon Sardar Lehna Singh reached his new house. As he passed by Sardar Gurdial Singh's house, he noticed that Gurdial's wife and her children had already moved in. He felt that he had made a big mistake. He, too should have brought his wife with him. "If that weakling, Gurdial Singh, can bring his wife, why can't I?"

The moment that thought occurred to him, he unloaded his luggage in front of the locked door of his new house and said to Gurdial Singh, "Bhai, keep a watch on my luggage, I'll go back and fetch my wife. She'll keep your wife company."

Lehna Singh turned his bullock-cart around and drove back over the road he had just taken. When he reached his house, he urged his wife and children to get ready to leave with him at once.

But, by the time Lehna Singh reached Islamabad with his wife and children, an hour and a half later, he noticed that someone had broken the lock on the door of his new house. His luggage had vanished. Only the fodder-cutting machine stood outside like an alert watchman. Worried, Lehna Singh went to call Gurdial Singh, but some other Sardar emerged from his house. He learnt from him that Gurdial Singh had found a better house in another lane and moved. Sardar Lehna Singh pulled his kirpan out of its scabbard and went towards his new house to find out who had stolen his things.

The moment, he stepped onto the verandah, two well-built Sikhs blocked his way, pointed towards his wife and children sitting on the bullock-cart and told him that the house was not meant for refugees. "It belongs to Sardar Balwant Singh." The moment Lehna Singh heard the name of the thanedar, his kirpan slipped back into its scabbard and his turban became a little loose.

"Huzoor, I had put my own lock on that door sometime ago."

"Get out of here. Go to court and file a case. Are you trying to claim someone else's property?"

They pushed Sardar Lehna Singh out of the verandah. At that moment, his eyes fell on the fodder-cutting machine and he exclaimed, "See, that is my fodder-cutting machine. Ask anyone here. They all know me."

But Lehna Singh didn't recognize any of the Sikhs or the Lalas, who came out of the houses they had occupied.

"Why don't you say that you need the fodder-cutting machine?" said one of the Sikhs, who had pushed him aside. Then he turned to his friend and said, "Kartar Singh, throw that machine out. They are poor refugees. What will we do with that damn machine?"

Both of them picked up the machine and threw it out.

When Lehna Singh decided to finally go back to his courtyard, after wandering aimlessly for a few hours in search of his belongings, his wife and children were on foot and the fodder-cutting machine had been loaded onto the bullock-cart.

Original in Hindi.
Translated by Alok Bhalla.

MOHAN RAKESH

THE CLAIM

There were just three passengers in the tonga, when it left the stand. If the bus had not appeared in the distance, Sadhu Singh would have waited a bit longer for a fourth. For as soon as the bus pulled up, his passengers would invariably climb out of the tonga and board it. Thus the necessity of departing just before the bus arrived. Until then, though, he would not leave the stand without a fourth passenger, however impatient his other passengers were. The bus cost five paise for a ride from Kachari to Model Town, so the tonga also travelled that route for five paise apiece. If there were four passengers he could make five annas. Otherwise, by driving his horse one-and-a-quarter miles he would gain just ten to fifteen paise. He had made three trips since morning to Model Town, but had collected barely seventeen annas. His horse panted so heavily in the scorching June sun, that it was hardly prudent to work him so hard for a mere ten paise. But without it he could not even buy feed. Very few people travelled in summer and he was, moreover, in competition with the bus which took barely five minutes to go from Kachari to Model Town.

"Go, Afsar, go! Make a sacrifice! Go!" Standing up, he turned the reins and began to employ his whip. Till he had crossed the washermen's sector, he hoped he might meet some passenger on the road. But the whole sector was empty, with the exception of a few washerwomen dozing in the doorways. Emerging from the area, he loosened up on the reins and moved out a bit on the pole in order to distribute the weight better.

As the bus came up from behind, the woman seated at the back began to yell, "You coaxed us into your tonga and now you're clopping along as if you've come out to do a tour of the streets! If it was to take this long, you might have said so and we could have taken the bus. If we didn't have something important to do, do you think we would have come out in such heat?"

Leaping up, Sadhu Singh moved farther out onto the pole and started cracking his whip. "Go! Test your mettle, sacrifice your youth! Run with the speed of a bullet! Memsahib is getting angry. May your speed be blessed, Afsar! Strike up a gallop!"

But even under the crack of the whip, Afsar did not increase his speed. He shook his head back and forth a few times and continued on at his own pace. The bus came up from behind blowing its horn and passed on ahead, leaving the tonga in a cloud of dust.

"Look at that! The bus has gone on ahead! And you claimed we'd get there first!" the woman said again.

Without bothering to reply, Sadhu Singh kept on cracking his whip. And Afsar, disregarding the whip completely, continued to trot on.

The road was no more than a mile and a quarter long. After the sun went down, it could be crossed in a snap. But in the full heat of the afternoon there was no shade and the whole vicinity seemed shrivelled and desolate. In certain spots, the coal tar of the street had melted. And the neighbouring ponds, usually of a depth of nine feet, had completely dried up. Sadhu Singh began to wonder how hot it would get if this was just the beginning of summer.

"Go, Raja! Go, boy! May your life be blessed. Be generous and go like a bullet! May your mother's milk be blessed!"

The tonga's three passengers were headed for the Claims Office. The Sikh, sitting towards the front, was saying that his claim for 60,000 Rupees had been accepted — half of which he was getting in cash and the other half in some form of property. The woman sitting at the back was cursing those officials who were processing her claim of just 18,000 Rupees. In Gujaranwala, they had four houses and an orchard of three-and-a-half acres. If it had been four acres, they would have got more money. Had they known that beforehand, they would have filed a claim for four acres. They had perished due to their own honesty! She had two young girls at home whom she had to leave alone, while making the daily rounds from Batala to Jullunder. Her husband had died making such trips and she herself was constantly ill.

"I don't know whether I'll get to see the money from these butchers during my lifetime or not! I guess I'll die like this in torment and leave my children behind lamenting." Her tone was more that of someone who was lodging a complaint than of someone conversing with others. From the expression on her face it appeared as if she had just that moment suffered a terrible shock.

The man beside her was sitting silently, his forehead wrinkled in deep thought.

"Madam, have you got anything from your claim?" the Sikh sitting opposite asked sympathetically.

"As of now I've got 6,000 in all," she said. "But I have children at home. What can I do with 6,000? My children are used to eating and wearing the best. I could spend that much on them in a month! And they say, I got that money so quickly only because I'm a widow. They did me a favour giving me so much!" And she began to wipe her eyes with the hem of her sari.

The man, who had been sitting silently, turned towards the other and said somewhat scornfully in his guttural voice, "It's true when they say the intellect of woman is enchained!"

"How have I angered you, that you should insult me?" The woman, wiping her tears, suddenly flared up. "I didn't ask for your property. I'm lamenting all that I have left behind."

"You're not alone there. We've all come here leaving our ancestral homes behind. Thank God, you've got 6,000! There are some among us who've not got even a paisa. Our problem is that both husband and wife are alive and well. If I were to perish, my children might get a few pieces of bread! I'm going blind, my joints ache — by living, am I any better than the dead? But there's such blindness in the government office that they don't see man's necessities — they just keep their accounts of the living and the dying. If I were to be given a thousand rupees today, I could open a little shop. My children don't even have a torn shirt to wear!"

"That's really a question of one's personal fortune! Can someone's sorrow in any way console another?" the Sikh asked, interrupting. "Both you and I have experienced sorrow, as has this lady here — which one of us here is not unhappy? Some are less, some are more so."

"You're getting 60,000 Rupees! What do you have to be unhappy about?" the man became even more fretful.

"And that I am getting it is also a matter of luck," the Sikh replied. "I used my head when I filed the claim, and look at the result! If I hadn't, we would have been sent away with 10,000 or 20,000."

"You filed a claim for more than you were worth?"

"Our property was worth 150,000 Rupees. But we found out that if we filed a correct claim, we wouldn't get nearly that much. So, praying to Waheguru, we filled out a claim that might realize for us, more or less, the true worth of our property. But those crooks nonetheless accepted a claim for only 60,000. There are six of us brothers — so we'll have to be satisfied with 10,000 apiece."

"I said as much to him but he just wouldn't listen!" the woman began to rub her hands despondently.

Both men looked towards her inquiringly.

"I kept telling him that no matter how much we left behind, we should file a claim for double. But he was such a fool that he insisted on claiming only what we were worth. Why should we be dishonest now, no matter what sufferings we have had to undergo! If he were here now, I'd ask him who was happier — us or all the crooks in this business. Some people have collected two or three times what they left behind. And I sit here with 6,000! God, these people are slowly starving my children to death!"

The man sitting next to her turned his face away and put his hand on his forehead. The Sikh again expressed his sympathy. "Nothing comes out of crying, madam. Whatever is fated is precisely one's lot. The Creator has already determined all of this. Be satisfied with what you get."

"Am I the only one who should remain content? The whole world might enjoy itself and I ought to rest content with my lot!" And she went on crying.

"Get there as fast as you can, driver! Why are you going so slowly?" the man beside her said, becoming impatient.

Irritated, Sadhu Singh cracked his whip time and again but there was no change in the horse's trot. Then he began to crack the whip across the horse's back. "To hell with you, Afsar! May a wasp sting your tail! Go quickly, boy!" But despite the fear of the wasp, Afsar did not quicken his speed..

Having deposited them outside the Claims Office, Sadhu Singh did not meet a single passenger on his return. He stopped for a while by the turning towards the market but no pedestrian appeared on any of the three roads that converged there. A few rickshaw pullers were sleeping in the shade of Shop 13. Sadhu Singh felt like having the shopkeeper make him a glass of lime juice and then perhaps lying in the shade for a while. But there was no shady place to tie the tonga nor any drain pipe from which to water the horse, which was alternately neighing and hanging its tongue out, almost prostrate with heat. Even the seventeen annas in his pocket were not really his own. To buy feed for the horse, he needed at least two rupees. So he wetted his lips with his tongue and turned the horse's face in the direction of the city.

He drove the tonga along the straight, desolate road where even the trees stood with their branches drooping, oppressed by the heat. Nearby, birds were chirping in some bushes.

Sadhu Singh slackened the reins, half reclining on the back-seat and letting his mind hover among the branches of that mango tree which he had planted with such pleasure in the courtyard of his home in Pattoki. Through nine years of familiarity that nine-rupee-a-month house had come to seem like his own. How many times had Hiran said that if you plant and tend a tree in another's house, one day you'll only leave it for others to enjoy! But who would have thought then that he would leave the house, never to be lucky enough to even pass by it again!

These days, the mango tree should be producing good fruit. And Hiran?

Fruit had appeared on the tree for the first time that year. And in his happiness, who knows how many unripe mangoes he had eaten!

"Why are you intentionally ruining your teeth?" Hiran would ask, irritated.

"It's the fruit of my own tree, darling! My teeth wouldn't spoil eating it." And he enfolded Hiran's half-bloomed youth in his wide embrace.

The mangoes had turned from green to yellow and from yellow to red when the riots began. Blood flowed in every street of Pattoki. At midnight, the rioters entered their sector of the town. When their door was broken down, he was lying close to Hiran on the charpoy. Quickly, he decided to spring towards the backyard and did so. But Hiran, standing a few times on tiptoe, was unable to make the jump. And before she could summon the courage to try again, a hand from behind yanked her back.

Darkness, fields and railway tracks — lifeless hands and feet and hunger — ticket, coupon, card and number —

Name : Sadhu Singh

Father's name : Milkha Singh

Caste : Khatri

Property : None

Money : None

Claim : ?

What claim could he make —?

That mango tree of his, for whose maturity he had waited impatiently — eating whose green fruit, he had been spoiling his teeth — the years of the future to be spent in the shade of that tree?

The house's own special smell, which, emanating from a bundle of clothes, enveloped everything right up to the walls of the courtyard. That smell —?

And the evenings which were spent lying in the courtyard, staring at the sky?

And all the plans of the coming life which rose up in the mind, while going in and out of his house?

"Tell me, Hiran, will your first child be a boy or a girl?"

"Shame on you, what are you saying?"

"Okay, shall I tell you? Your first will be a girl. Then two boys. Then another girl."

"Be quiet! Why are you jabbering so?"

"The second girl will be more beautiful than the first. She'll have hair as soft as yours, the same huge eyes and right here by the chin a mole —"

"What are you doing?"

"I'll give her a pinch like this and she'll screech like this —"

That feeling —? That thrill —? That imagination —? That future —? Name: Sadhu Singh; Father's name: Milkha Singh; Caste: Khatri; Number —? Claim —?

The mango tree would have grown big by now. The smell of the walls of the house must have changed. And Hiran —? Who knows whose children are in her lap today?

Sadhu Singh straightened and sat up, as the tonga again reached the washermen's sector. Everyone seemed to be dozing by now. He jerked continuously at the reins. The horse's neck lifted a bit then bent again as usual.

Reaching the stand, Sadhu Singh watered the horse at the drain pipe and taking the feed from under the seat, put it before him. The horse thrust his mouth into the feed as he stroked his back. "If God keeps you well, Afsar, the old days will return again. Eat! Fill your belly!. Your claims must be filled. May your life be blessed —!"

And Afsar, stretching long his neck, silently continued to eat.

Original in Hindi.
Translated by Richard Williams.

ASIF ASLAM FARRUKHI

THE LAND OF MEMORIES

I went out to find what I had lost,
In the enemy cities...

Pablo Neruda,
"A Man in Search of Things" (1969).

As the train approached the station, Abbajan became agitated like a thirsty man about to reach a well. And as soon as the train stopped at the station, he jumped down, knelt on the ground, picked up a bit of dust and applied it to his forehead like a tilak. Tears flowed down his face, but a smile played on his lips. Tariq looked at me as if to say, "I knew this would happen."

Throughout the journey, Abbajan had been uncontrollably excited. He had paced the compartment restlessly, recited couplets, opened the window to look out, lit cigarettes, and after a few puffs, tossed them far away. His face seemed as if it had been covered by dark clouds which, unable to contain themselves much longer, would pour down rain without restraint.

Tariq and I sat very quietly throughout the journey as if the gravity of the situation had overwhelmed us. At one stage, Tariq pretended to keep beat on a tabla and sing "Country roads take me home." But no one laughed.

Had we anticipated such a situation, we wouldn't have left home. But having once set out on the journey, it was impossible to retrace our steps. The train was already at the station. Besides, Abbajan was obsessed with a desire to walk on the soil of this land again.

While Tariq helped to unload the luggage, I placed my foot on Indian soil for the first time, as if I was participating in a sacred ritual. As soon as I stepped onto the platform, I felt uncertain and confused. The loud clatter of the wheels of the train was still resounding in my ears. I hadn't yet fully realized that, instead of standing on a moving and violently swaying floor of the train compartment, I was standing on firm, dry and soft earth.

As the train began to slowly pull out of the station, I said to myself, "The string which tied us to the land we have come from is about to snap. We are now in a new country which has its own customs, its own centre of gravity."

I looked all around. The sun was about to set behind the station which had been built in the old colonial style. Relics of the colonial days, the hustle and bustle of the station, the rush of passengers, the screaming and the scuffling of the coolies, the fakirs, the vendors, and the spectators, the children, the dogs...we were familiar with them. Were we really in a different country? How different was it from ours? The name of the railway station was written in English and, below it, in Devnagri. Did those letters, which resembled long-legged spiders, announce the name of the place we had heard about since our childhood — Fatehgarh? What about the signs above the water taps — Hindu Pani...Muslim Pani? What did they mean?

I wanted to ask Abbajan, but he was looking at everything with tears in his eyes. It seemed as if each object there contained dim recollections of a world which had been once familiar.

Abbajan was lost in tracing images of his past. We hailed a yakka and loaded all our luggage into it. When we looked at the pale- face of the yakkawala, we couldn't believe that the man who was wearing a torn tehmad with square-checks, and was puffing at a bidi, was a stranger; that he didn't ply his yakka on the lane past our house in Karachi.

"Where do you want to go?" he asked politely.

"Fatehgarh...to Manjhlay Miyan's Kothi," Abbajan replied. He smiled as if, instead of directions, he was giving the yakkawala a magical key to some hidden treasure. Then he turned to us and said, "Our ancestral home was so famous that it was used as a landmark by everyone."

The yakkawala turned around and stared at us, but didn't say anything. When the yakka started moving forward slowly, he turned around to look at us again out of curiosity, as if we weren't passengers, but ghosts from some forgotten cave and were offering century old coins to the shopkeepers.

"Have you come from Pakistan?" he asked.

"Yes, Bhai," Abbajan replied. "I thought I should show my children where we had once lived. You see, I belong to this place. My umbilical cord is buried here. Now that I am returning after thirty years, I feel as if..." He stopped abruptly in mid-sentence when he saw the look on our faces. But it was impossible for him to keep quiet for long. He said, "Tell me, Miyan yakkaywalay, since when have you been living here? In the past, I used to know yakka drivers — Kallu, Putwa, Hafeez, Mithwa, Gauri Shanker..."

"Some died. Others migrated to Pakistan. A few of them are still here," the yakkawala replied indifferently.

"I feel strange returning to my native land after so many years," Abbajan said softly. His face was flushed with excitement.

We had agreed to come to India only to please him. Tariq and I had actually planned to spend our holidays this year in Canada with our uncle. That trip would have been exciting. We would have talked about having been to a foreign country. The journey to India didn't interest us — the same dark people, familiar features, similar crowds, deafening noise, corruption, chaos, poverty, filth — we were familiar with them. Instead of being in a foreign country, I felt as if we were loitering through Lalukhet and Gharibabad. I looked at everything with a critical eye. Everything around me seemed dismal and bleak.

When Abbajan had first declared his intention of travelling to India, Tariq had asked, "Why do you want to go there? Aren't you forgetting that you had burnt all your boats...I mean, set fire to your trains...before coming to Pakistan?"

I, too, had opposed the idea of the journey. "The India which you wish to see, can't be reached by train...you'll have to travel in a time machine."

But our protests were of no avail. Even after having migrated to Pakistan, memories of India were buried deep in Abbajan's soul, just as dreams of old college romances lie in the hearts of married men.

His condition was such that if by chance he heard the name of Fatehgarh or Farrukhabad on the "Listener's Choice

Programme of Film Songs" on the All India Radio, his heart would begin to beat with excitement. "I wonder who could have requested that song? In my days, there were two Gopals there. God knows which Gopal this is...? The song is nice and it was sung by Lata. The miracle is that the song we are hearing in Karachi is being heard, at this very moment, in the town we left long ago."

Whenever he heard about Hindu-Muslim riots in India, he would stop eating. And, during the India-Pakistan test matches, his heart would be torn in two.

Abbajan's longing to visit India was so intense that even Ammi's opposition didn't make any difference. The merest mention of the journey to India would infuriate Ammi. She had firmly refused to go to India, and had decided to move to Choti Khala's house during our absence. When we left her at Khala's house, she had wept bitterly.

Ammi was only five years old, when communal riots in Delhi had destroyed her home in Khari Bawli. She had, with her own eyes, seen her pleasant home being looted and set on fire. Her brothers and sisters had saved themselves by hiding in a cellar for days. Her grandfather had kept his loaded rifle by his side, and her grandmother, a packet of poison.

They had somehow managed to reach the Old Fort, where they had to live without shelter for many more days. With great difficulty they had got a place on the train to Lahore. The train had been attacked by Sikh mobs on the way. Half the passengers had been slaughtered.

Even after years of a peaceful and calm life, Ammi had not been able to forget those nightmarish days. She still refused to travel by train. When she came to the station to see us off, and saw Tariq and me in the train, she went pale.

Choti Khala whispered in her ears, "Shame on you, Baji. Are you going to let Dulha Bhai go alone to India? What about all those girls he used to write ghazals for during his college days? They must still be there!"

Suddenly, I felt Abbajan's hand on my shoulder. He shook me and said, "You'll see the Kothi in a few minutes." He leaned forward so that he would be the first to catch a glimpse of the house.

The yakka creaked along the road slowly. There was a long row of yellow flats on both sides of the road. We looked around, but instead of the Kothi we only saw birds in the crimson sky — noisy and shrieking birds returning to their nest. And crows, lots and lots of crows. It seemed as if they had gathered there for the funeral procession of a king and were waiting to devour the corpse.

"Where is it? Which one is it?" Tariq asked impatiently.

We could see nothing, even in the distance, which even faintly resembled the Kothi we had heard about all our lives.

"You probably can't see it from here," Abbajan replied, disappointedly. "Things change. So much time has passed. When we were your age, we could see the Kothi from here. From a distance it seemed as if its balconies were like camels slowly crossing a desert."

Abbajan was lost in memories once again. The same longing, which had embraced him like an old friend when he had stepped onto the Indian soil, cast its shadow over his face again.

"Look," he said, "The yakka used to take a turn at that corner. Lawyers used to live there. Shabban Lal Vakil had a house there. So did Ayub Vakil. Ayub Vakil sold his house and migrated to Pakistan. His house, it seems has been converted into an Income Tax Office now...Look, there is Sheesham Bagh, Diggi Taal, Paththarwali masjid...A moulsari tree used to grow at that bend in the road...Hakimji's house used to stand there...And then our Kothi...Beyond our Kothi lay Kali Bari and Gola, where grain was stored. Kali Mai used to be worshipped at Kali Bari. There was a temple there. In the mornings one could hear bhajans and the sound of temple bells...There is one image I remember still. Roopwati, the daughter of the Brahmin of the temple, used to ring the temple bells in the morning...She used to weave champa flowers in her long and loose hair; she wore a skirt and a blouse and, standing with bare-feet, would ring the temple bells. When she rang the big bell, it seemed as if her entire body was swaying in unison with it...That image still hovers before my eyes..."

"But where will we stay? In the Kothi?" Tariq asked, interrupting him.

"There is no problem about finding a place to stay Everyone knows me here. We'll stay somewhere. Only Ausaf Bhai perhaps lives in the Kothi now. He will be delighted to see you. When I used to live there, we used to fight all the time. Munnay and he also fought continuously. After meals, Munnay would deliberately belch loudly and recite the following nonsense jingle:

Dam bakra hazam, dam bakra hazam,
Sath mein lambokari Ausafchi bhasam.

That always annoyed Ausaf Bhai, and he would chase us to give us a thrashing. Now that he knows that we have migrated to Pakistan and there is no one left to demand his share of the family's wealth, he writes warm and affectionate letters to us...But why can't we see the Kothi yet?"

The yakkaywala, who had been listening to Abbajan, could restrain himself no longer. He said, "Are you related to Ausaf Bhaiya? Have you come from Pakistan?"

He stopped the yakka, got down and looked at Abbajan intently, as if he was trying to remember his face. Then he exclaimed, "You are Aslam Bhaiya, aren't you? Aslam Bhaiya, the son of Manjhlay Miyan! Don't you recognize me? I am Allamu! Allamu!"

Abbajan jumped down from the yakka and asked enthusiastically, "Allamu? Is it really you? You have changed so much. When did you start driving a yakka?"

"What can I do, Bhaiya? One has to fill one's belly somehow. I gave up my barber shop a long time ago. My clients stopped calling me to marriages. They want their hair cut like Englishmen. Instead of dying of hunger, I turned to this profession. Tell me about yourself, Bhaiya. How have you been?"

"Thanks be to Allah, I am well. Do you remember, Allamu, how I used to hide from Bhaijan and smoke cigarettes secretly? Once, when I was strolling in the Company Bagh and smoking, you caught me and pulled my ears. I begged you not to betray me at home. You agreed, but on the condition that I would never smoke in future. Do you remember, Allamu?"

"Those days were different, Bhaiya. Even a family barber could stop a child from doing something wrong."

Tariq and I were dismayed to see Abbajan, whose subordinates trembled before him, embrace the yakkawala in the middle of the road.

"Who lives in the Kothi now? Does Ausaf Bhaiya still live there?" Abbajan asked.

"Ausaf Bhaiya left for Farrukhabad a long time ago. It is now a Kothi only in name. The old citizens of the place still refer to this locality as Kothi Manjhlay Miyan out of habit."

"And what happened to the Kothi?" Abbajan asked slowly, for the words stuck in his throat.

"What can I tell you? See it for yourself," Allamu said and stopped the yakka.

Tariq and I looked around curiously. A small two room house stood before us. A sign board, which had — Mahila Vidyalaya — written on it in English, hung on the wall outside.

"When did this happen?" Abbajan asked dejectedly.

"The Kothi was pulled down seven years ago. They covered the drain which ran a little further ahead, and built an officer's colony over the entire area. This school is a part of it."

"And what happened to the banyan tree which used to stand in front of it?" Abbajan asked in a trembling voice, as if he was the banyan tree facing the axe.

"It was cut down."

"*Inna lil lahay wa inna alaihay rajay uoon,*" Abbajan intoned, and sat down dejectedly on the side of the road.

I wondered what links I had with that house? I had never seen my ancestral home, but had heard so much about it from Abbajan. He had often described to us in detail, each of its rooms and verandahs. Now it had vanished without a trace. It was only a house. It wasn't the Taj Mahal whose destruction would be an insult to the traditions of the Indian Muslims. It was strange, however, that a house and a few trees which lay buried in an era which has long passed, had still not been forgotten; they hadn't been erased from memory.

I wondered where we would stay now. The yakkawala had put our luggage down and left. He had refused to accept the fare, and before leaving he had insisted on giving Tariq and me four annas each, because he had seen Abbajan's 'children' for the first time!

As we sat with our luggage by the roadside, I was reminded of the elegies from the Bible about the exile of the Jews. Where could we go now? What difference did it make that our ancestors had lived here for centuries?

The people who walked past us, looked at us suspiciously. There was, in particular, a fat Hindu, dressed in a dhoti, and with a large turban on his head, who had been staring at us for a long time. When we saw him, we were reminded of the stories about the Hindu-Muslim riots we had heard so often. As soon as he started walking in our direction, Tariq pointed in his direction and exclaimed in fear, "Look...Abbu...!"

That man walked straight upto Abbajan, put his arms around him and hugged him tightly. We saw that he was sobbing!

"This is Bhupendar Chacha, children! Say adab to him," Abbajan said.

We said, "Salaam." Then we suddenly remembered that salaam was out of place here. We didn't know how to do namaskar, therefore, we said, "Good evening." We felt happy that we had settled the matter with dignity.

We were familiar with his name. He had been Abba's dearest friend in his childhood. It was with him that Abba used to run away from school and steal fruit from various gardens.

"Why are you sitting here? I have a house and it is at your disposal. Come, let's go home."

Bhupendar Chacha took us to his house. It had an old courtyard with an old-fashioned wooden door. After we had bathed and changed our clothes, thalis full of hot kachauris and tarkari were placed before us. Tired and sleepy, we could hardly keep our eyes open, but Abbajan and Bhupendar Chacha talked late into the evening. It seemed as if they were still two small boys playing truant from school, and were roaming through the gardens and lanes holding hands.

"Do you remember the thrashing Master Bachan Lal gave us?"

"He never thrashed us. It was Munnay who got the beating."

"Where is Munnay these days? In Karachi?"

"And where are the other boys we knew?"

"Do children still play hockey in the parade ground?"

"A new bridge has been constructed at Langar Ghat...Now even the Kanpur Express stops here!"

Both swapped stories about the past with each other as if they were sharing guavas stolen from some garden. They were happy like the children playing by the roadside.

What really surprised me was to see Bhupendar Chacha mix with us freely even though he was a Hindu. We had heard different stories about the Hindus.

The next morning, I picked up courage, and asked him about it. He began to laugh, and said, "Wah Miyan Bhateejay! Thank you for certifying that your Chacha is not a bigot. The relations between the Hindus and the Muslims of this town were so harmonious that even your certificate would not have sufficed. Each community, whether in their day to day interactions with each other or during their festivals, respected the customs of the other. Every year during Id, when your father, grandfather and uncles returned from the Idgah after namaz, Hindus stood at the doors of their houses and sprinkled itar on their clothes. Your grandfather used to come to our house every year on Id, embrace my father, eat sewayin and give me a silver coin as eidi. Similarly, your grandmother sent us halwa during Shab-e-Barat. She used to hire a Hindu cook to make halwa and send it in a platter carried by a Hindu, especially employed for that purpose. Nobody thought that the Hindus were being unduly concerned about pollution taboos. Each one respected the individuality, the feeling and the faith of others. During Diwali, the house which was lit the brightest was Manjhlay Miyan Ki Kothi. And during the forty days of Moharrum, sabeel was made at our house, and sharbet was mixed with milk...But, I must stop this long lecture. If you get ready, I'll take you around the town."

Bhupendar Chacha took us to the new section of the town. It had well-kept and clean houses. There were flowering bushes before each house. Clothes were hung outside to dry in the sun. The roads were properly tarred and children rode up and down on their bicycles. The smell of food being cooked rose from somewhere, and film-songs being played on a transistor floated in the air. Life seemed to flow along its normal, daily and peaceful routine.

"Look, how our region has prospered," Bhupendar Chacha said, pointing towards a row of newly built houses. "How modern it has become!"

"You call this modern," Tariq interrupted him. "Come to Karachi where we live, and..."

"I am talking from my perspective, son," Bhupendar Chacha said. "Now we have a power house, new housing colonies and two new colleges. A large hospital has been built. And factories too."

Father nodded his head without showing much interest. His thoughts were elsewhere.

"Haven't you noticed these changes, Aslam?" Chachaji turned to him and asked.

"I have noticed them. It's a matter of pride that this region has progressed so much. But, personally, I feel sad and lost. While we were talking about our past last night, it occurred to me that this place is, in reality, a graveyard of memories. Here the golden days of my childhood and youth are buried. Looking back at them, and thinking about the future, I feel as if my past has no relation to my present life. It has a separate life of its own in which we have no role to play; it is independent of us, unconnected to us. It makes no difference to this place that we, who were born and brought up here, no longer live here, do not belong to it. Here life continues, absorbed in its own rhythms, oblivious of our presence. When I realize all that, I feel sad and lost; I feel hurt."

Bhupendar Chacha was touched by these words, "It had never occurred to me that you would feel like a stranger in your own country. Anyway, let's go to our old haunts, to areas you were familiar with."

Abbajan said, "I was apprehensive of the fact that the land where I was born, the earth on which I grew up, would refuse to recognize me. That even if it did recognize me, how I would be able to walk through those old lanes and say, O lanes of my native city, look at me! See what I was and what I have become!"

I thought to myself, "What about us? What relation do we have with all this?" I closed my eyes. I had always visualized this place with closed eyes. And now that I saw it with my eyes open, I didn't find anything which was different. I had a strange feeling that I had passed through these lanes and neighbourhoods before. I didn't recall the details, but I had a dim memory of them. It was as if I was recalling a dream of some previous life. These lanes which we were passing through were not as strange to us as we were to them. Tariq and I had heard about them often in the past.

Whenever our aunts and uncles got together, memories of these places arrived with them like uninvited guests. They spent hours talking about their past — Akram, do you remember when Ashfaq afimi came crying to us and told us that his father was dead...Anwar, do you recall that place, that incident, that story? We had inherited those memories; they had been passed to us in our blood; they were a part of our genetic make-up; a chromosomic map which determined our character. I had heard so much about our ancestral home at Fatehgarh that I could have repeated its history without a pause. I was sure that if I was left blind-folded at the crossroads, at the centre of town, I would be able to go, straight like an arrow, to the house of my ancestors, even though I had never actually seen it.

Why had our bonds with that past not snapped? What was its nature? Our generation had not been a part of that culture, it had never experienced that society. We had not seen its glory vanish like the setting sun. As far as we were concerned, it was as fascinating as the life of man in prehistoric times. It was mythical. Why should we feel nostalgic for something which was invisible? But I was also aware of our heritage, and was also conscious of the sad fact that we had lost it. I suddenly understood that time has a design and we are part of its texture. I also realized why our parents talked about the past as if it was a legendary era. The past which had once seemed absurd and a bore, began to acquire meaning.

My father looked youthful and fresh; his eyes glowed with joy; his face was marked with excitement. He shook me, and said, "Look, Maqsudan Lal Vakil used to live in that house. Do you know what his real name was? Madhusudan. But we used to call him Maqsudan. The next house used to belong to Farooq Sahib. You remember his Begum, don't you?"

Yes, I did. She had died three months before our trip to India. During her last days, she had become delirious and used to scream, "No, no, no. I won't die in a strange house." She would jump out of bed and rush out of her house in a frenzy. And when people brought her back she would shriek, "I don't want to die in a foreign land. I want to go back home to

Fatehgarh." Throughout the night she would shout the names of people she had once known, but who were dead and forgotten, "Shannu Shah dakiya, Allah Rakho, Teen Thonk, Jafer Dapali, Cauwa Dho, Kharinjaray Wale Jhaboo, Kundan, Bijan, Mauan, Matoll, Nani Pathani, Nassan..." Pus used to ooze out of her breasts. Doctors had said that she had breast cancer. But was that her real problem? Were it not her memories that had become cancerous? After all, even memories, like diseases, can have a relapse. Otherwise, why should my father have laughed and cried at the same time?

Every inch of the ground made my father see his past clearly. Here he had spent his childhood playing "idi idi arrey arrey," there he had spent his boyhood flying kites; here he had recited ghazals as a young man, there he had gossiped with his friend. There were faces associated with every house, every street and every corner, faces which had been lost forever except in dreams. His eyes glowed, his voice was tearful. It seemed as if he couldn't decide whether he should dance with joy or lean his head against a wall and weep. He embraced everyone who passed by, much to our embarrassment. Bhupendar Chacha, who was holding Abbajan's hand, was repeatedly wiping the corner of his eyes with his little finger.

People watched us with surprise as we went by. Tariq and I blushed with shame. We couldn't hide the fact that we were with the gentleman who was pointing at everything like a tourist guide and recounting its history, and at such speed that he seemed like an over-wound toy. We couldn't make them realize that we were exiles in search of our roots.

Before the situation became really absurd, Abbajan spotted a tea shop and shouted with delight, "Arrey, Wali's Hotel!" Before Bhupendar Chacha could stop him, he had dragged us into it. It was smaller and much dirtier than our Irani hotels. While Tariq and I covered our noses with our handkerchiefs, he went straight upto the fat Sikh sitting at the counter and asked, "What happened to Wali who owned this hotel?"

The Sikh shrugged his shoulder and replied, "I don't know. He must be around somewhere."

"I have countless memories associated with this place. I was born here, Sardarji. I have come from Pakistan," Abbajan's voice became sentimental.

"From Pakistan?" that Sikh, who had been sitting like a statue of stone, suddenly came to life. His eyes opened wide and he asked quickly, "Have you ever lived in Pindi, ji? That is my native town."

Father didn't say anything in reply. He was lost in his own thoughts.

"In Rawalpindi, there is a locality named Mohalla Banni. Have you seen it? We are from there. We had a house there."

"Wali's son, Najjan was my friend."

"I had bought this place before the Partition. But never mind, consider this as your place. Please sit down and have some tea." Saying this the Sikh got up from his chair and shook Abba's hand.

"Do you know we used to come here every evening to drink tea, smoke cigarettes and argue about the Muslim League and politics. Alim, Mirza Naimullah Baig, Rabbani Sahib, Zameer and myself. We heard Mountbatten's speech about the Partition on the radio sitting here."

"Our house was on the third street from..."

"We used to recite poems and argue fiercely..."

It was obvious that neither of them was paying attention to what the other one was saying. Each was interested in his own past.

Tariq pulled Abbajan's sleeve and said, "Come, let's go, Abbu."

"Yes, yes," Abbajan's reminiscences had to make a forced landing. "Everything has changed," he said and shook hands with the Sardarji.

The Sikh shook his hand and tittered, "If you go to Rawalpindi, do visit Mohalla Banni..."

Tariq was completely bored by now. We came out and looked around. A heap of onion peels lay in front of us. A cow was busy feeding on them. Monkeys were swinging from the branches overhead. Was there any relation between those monkeys and us? They were also relics from a distant past to which we could not return.

Abba and Bhupendar Chacha also came out. Father was still continuing with his roll-call of old associates. "Where is so and so? What happened to such and such?" When he asked about Shafaat he suddenly stopped "Where is he? Where is Shafaat?"

I was familiar with that name. I remembered a face in round glasses, in a faded photograph, in Abba's album. Was he Abba's cousin?

"Shafaat is dead," Bhupendar Chacha replied.

"Dead? Oh my God!" Abbajan was stunned. Neither of them said anything for a long time. At last, Bhupendar Chacha broke the silence, "Shafaat's wife and children still live here. Why don't you meet them?"

So we went to a small two-room house. It burst into pandemonium the moment we entered. A battalion of children threw down their bats and balls and surrounded us. Old women, in fluttering ghararas, came rushing to greet us. Some embraced us affectionately, while others wanted to know the price of onions in Pakistan. Mothers paraded their children before us for inspection. "Aye Chattan, say chaam to Aslam." "Taya...Taya Abba, maam...Taya Abba, chaam!" Tariq and I stood in a corner and enjoyed watching the parade.

Suddenly, Abbajan said to us, "Why don't you go in and meet your cousins?"

We went into a room where several young men of our age were having a heated argument about whether Khurshid or Juniad had recited naat better at Id-e-Milad that year.

We sat quietly for we didn't know what to say. Tariq offered them chewing gum. One of them accepted it politely and put it in his pocket. Another swallowed it whole without chewing it!

"Backward!" Tariq whispered in my ear.

Meanwhile, our relatives in the "old country" too were amused by our appearance. We seemed like strange tourists to them, with jeans and T-shirts, cameras around our necks and chewing gum in our mouths. Were we really their cousins?

In the courtyard, several old woman were sitting with their large paandans open. They turned their attention to us when we came out of the room. Chewing paan, they interrogated us. They frowned, looked down their noses, peered through their glasses and scrutinized us from head to toe. One of them asked us, "So, you are Aslam Miyan's son! In which class do you study?

Shabash! How many sons does your Bawa have? Don't you have any sisters?"

I got irritated. I wanted to get away from from those goat-legged creatures in crushed cotton ghararas, those faded sherwanis, the paan-stained teeth, walls stained with spit, rough charpoys, hanging flower-pots, lotas and empty matkas. Those people reminded me of our poor relatives who lived in thickly populated areas of Karachi like Khokhrapar, Malir, Lalukhet and Golimar, where their large families were stuffed into small houses. If we ever came across them on occasions other than marriages and funerals, we felt ashamed and embarrassed. We were more familiar with our cousins who had settled in Europe and Canada, even though we met them only once in three or four years.

After a while, we went back to Abbajan.

"Let's go, Abbu," Tariq said abruptly.

"Why? So soon?" Abba asked.

"Yes. We've had enough."

"Don't you like it here?"

"Is this the place you had praised so much?" Tariq asked. "Is this what you brought us to see? This qasba, this small town?"

Shocked and puzzled, Abbajan looked at Tariq in disbelief. The trees in the luxuriant and green garden which once grew between father and son, began to wither and the heap of dry leaves began to increase steadily...

Original in Urdu.
Translated by Vishwamitter Adil
and Alok Bhalla.

INTIZAR HUSAIN

AN UNWRITTEN EPIC

1

In Qadirpur, too, such a fierce battle broke out that people put their hands over their ears in denial when they heard it. Confusion was rampant. Human lives everywhere went for a penny a pound, give or take a few ounces. One person was killed taking two steps back, another taking four steps forward. One was hit in the back, another in the chest. How could Qadirpur, insignificant as it was, have stemmed the tide that had shaken even the roots of mountains? Thanks to Pichwa's presence, Qadirpur became the scene of a memorable feat. Knowing they were facing death, friends put on their shrouds, asked for their mothers' blessings, committed their wives to God, and marched into the battlefield with such valour and majesty that they revived the memory of wars fought in ancient times. A fierce battle broke out, with incredible bloodshed — heaps of corpses lay everywhere. Nor were the Jats wanting in character and ceremony. They came out mounted on caparisoned elephants, lighting up the night with their torches. Qadirpur's entire fame rested on Pichwa, so the bravest of the Jats had gathered there from far and near. The elephants were lined up, the cannon, gunpowder, arrows and swords were arranged, and the Jat army, weighed down with equipment, set off to conquer Qadirpur. In the branches of the banyan tree near the idgah, Majid sat on guard. Seeing a light beyond the trees further away, he pricked up his ears and very carefully studied the situation. Listening attentively to all the noises and peering into the distance, he tried to analyze the light. Finally, certain that the expected moment had at last arrived, he banged out the news on his drum. As soon as the drum was struck, chaos broke out in the houses of Qadirpur. Asleep on the roof, Naim Miyan's two sons, Owais and Azhar, lost their senses when they heard the slogans and drumbeats. Owais was speechless. Azhar, unable to do anything else, got up and leapt over the roofs coming at last to the roof of the Weavers' Mosque. There was a gap between the roofs here and Azhar had to stop in his tracks. He had no idea what he should do next. Keeping guard below, Rahmat thumped his club and challenged him, "Who's there?" Azhar pulled himself together with great difficulty and somehow or other managed to identify himself. Rahmat laughed and said, "Miyan, you have disgraced the name of Aligarh College." Despite Rahman's opinion, both Azhar and Owais were alumni of Aligarh, and in pre-Partition days, whenever they had participated in political rallies and enthusiastically shouted the slogan, "India will be divided, Pakistan will be created," their voices had resounded with an unusual note of determination. After the Partition of India, however, they had begun to talk senselessly and extravagantly.

When Naim Miyan woke up, Azhar's cot was empty and Owais was standing speechless. Confused, he grabbed his rifle and cartridge case, but the people at the meeting-place suddenly raised the cry, "Allah-o-Akbar!" with such gusto that the cartridge case fell from his hand. There had been a vigil at the meeting-place. People were now coming out, each one holding up his weapons.

Straightening his turban, Jafar put his javelin in position and started to draw on the hookah as he went out. Behind him, Pichwa straightened his waist-cloth and called out, "This is no time for the hookah, my friend." Jafar put down the hookah and went out thumping his javelin. Pichwa tightened and knotted his waist-cloth with great satisfaction and arranged the silver-covered amulet on his neck. Then he rolled up his shirt-sleeves, spat on his palms and weighed the club in his hand. On his way out, he called out to Mammad. Annoyed at getting no answer, he called out again, "Hey Mammad, you son of a bitch, where the hell are you?"

Throwing his vest around his neck, Mammad leapt out of a corner. "Here I am, ustad."

"Hey, you son of an ustad, are you coming out or not?" When he reached him, Pichwa's tone softened, "Now look, you hang on in the Weavers' Mosque trench, and I'll take care of everything here."

After he had given Mammad these instructions, he left the meeting place followed by a few of his young wrestlers. As he came out, he glanced at the haveli. Kalwa was to lead the unit posted there. As soon as he saw Pichwa, he snapped to attention and shouted, "Don't worry, ustad, I'll break anyone who comes here in half."

Pichwa was most worried about the haveli entrenchment. And he had reason to be. All the women of the Qadirpur settlement were collected inside it. Although there was a dark well inside the haveli, and each woman had been clearly told what her duty required her to do in an eventuality, a few nooses had also been set up for good measure. Pichwa had stationed several of his brave young men at the haveli and had told them, "I'll roast each of you bastards alive if you show the slightest weakness." Confident of Kalwa's bravery and satisfied with what he had said, he went on, weighing his club. A feeling of urgency had now become noticeable in the drumbeats, and in the distance the conch shells had begun to sound as well. Pichwa quickened his steps. People were beginning to pour out of the other houses. Qurban Ali came out of his house brandishing the leg of a cot. When he heard the noise, he hurriedly searched everywhere in the house but could not find even an ordinary piece of wood, let alone a regular weapon. First anger, then the pressure exerted by man's instinctive inventiveness, made him fall upon a cot and tear it apart in a flash. Although Saiyid Hamid Hasan had several beautiful walking sticks brought from Nainital and Dehra Dun as gifts, he had nothing resembling a club. Hurriedly scrambling around, however, he and his wife finally managed to unearth a rotten, old sword. Munshi Sanaullah did not have to face this problem at all. In the front courtyard lay a piece of bamboo used to clear out cobwebs from the rooms; he picked it up as he rushed out. Nor did the Subedar Sahib have to worry about a club. He had a match-lock gun which he always kept clean. In the crowd of clubs, the raised barrels of a few other rifles were also visible. His vest pocket loaded with pellets, Hamid held in his hand a shiny black pellet bow of sheesham wood. A few steps behind Pichwa, stood Rasula and Bhallan carrying on their shoulders an entire arsenal, including fireworks shaped like pomegranates, horns, and swords. Allah Razi's party came behind them, dragging an odd-looking cannon. Now this cannon had been fired only once before, but unfortunately in the direction of Allah Razi's companions. Allah Razi had not had the foggiest idea how the damned thing worked. So, several men had been badly wounded and a few others arrested by the police in connection with the incident. Now, however, Allah Razi was sure that it would not be his companions but his enemies, he would blow up into bits.

Normally armed with clubs, Pichwa's companions, responding to the demands of time, had made a small modification in their weapons. No longer plain clubs, they now had short spears attached to them. Pichwa's, however, was the same as it had always been, except that, having soaked in oil for three days, it was a little more slippery than usual. So what? The slipperiness that comes from oil makes a club shimmer; it does not, however, affect its 'clubness'. It is the spear that destroys the 'clubness' of a club. With a spear attached to it, a club is no longer a club but a spear. Mammad's, Kalwa's, Rahmat's and Jafar's clubs had thus been reborn as spears. Pichwa's, however, was still just a plain old club — to modify it would have meant a change in his entire mode of thinking. This club had become an inextricable part of his being. In a way, it had given up its separate existence and become an indissoluble part of his personality. Pichwa's club, consequently, was not merely a club; it was Pichwa's club. Nor was it like the staff of Moses, for that staff had a power of its own apart from Moses; while Moses needed the staff, the staff did not need him. Pichwa's club was, at any rate, Pichwa's club. And although it too had performed many miracles, the miraculous power lay in Pichwa's arms, not in the club itself. The best proof of this is the time that Pichwa was accidentally forced to fight without his club. Seeing him unarmed, the companions of Tidda, the wrestler, thought they could at last finish him off. Without hesitating a minute, Pichwa immediately took off his head cloth, tied a coin up in it and started showing his skill. Within five minutes, he had three of them lay their clubs down in sheer helplessness — in addition, the many wrists he broke were a bonus. And then he let them have it, banging their heads with their own clubs. Tidda's companions were not so brave that they could face a determined opponent: a few cracked heads and off they went.

Tidda's poor young men were, of course, merely small fry. Pichwa was always ready to take on an entire village. It so happened that Pichwa was present when the people of Lachmanpura had angrily surrounded the Subedar Sahib. No doubt the Subedar had enraged them by firing at peacocks when he could not find any ducks. Anyway, commotion broke out everywhere. Lachmanpura was nearby and country bumpkins rushed up carrying cudgels. Hardly one to stand around at such a time, Naim Miyan was off like a shot as soon as he heard all that noise. Hamida, at the end of his wits, darted off into a nearby corn field. Only Allah Razi apparently escaped unharmed, but as luck would have it, he landed in a field where a farmer was ploughing. The peasant slapped him first and asked questions later. Saiyid Hamid Hasan's lack of speed proved his undoing. Lacking any other alternative, he tried to sweet-talk them into letting him go, but his peasant captors knew better than that. The Subedar Sahib just stood there — utterly befuddled, unable to think or do anything. Pichwa was incensed. With a "Ya Ali," he took up his club and beat them mercilessly, killing several peasants, smashing countless wrists, and spraining as many wrist-joints. And when the Subedar Sahib and Pichwa returned to Qadirpur, they brought along, in addition to the slaughtered peacocks, a whole pile of very fine, heavy clubs.

It was only a coincidence that Pichwa and Tidda were at odds at that time over the hill-woman Billo. Although Pichwa was not averse to female company once in a while, he was not particularly one for running after women, as his real interests lay elsewhere. Tidda and he had already fought over the affair with Nasira. Nasira had been legitimately accepted as a member of Tidda's wrestling group, although other people were not willing to accord her that status. Pichwa was never one to hold his tongue, and whenever he sat at Allah Razi's pan shop, put pan in his mouth and took a puff of his bidi, he became even more boastful.

As he sat there one day, seeing Nasira he lost control of himself and shouted out, "Pay attention to me, not to others." Nasira was very embarrassed. When Tidda found out about it, his blood began to boil. He would have crucified anyone else, but here it was a case of a camel against a mountain. Still he was so incensed that he took this affront of Pichwa's as an act of aggression. The quarrel festered for several months; several skirmishes took place, but Tidda ended up being humiliated each time. It was not just this quarrel alone; Tidda and Pichwa had never got along with each other.

Although Tidda was proud of his expertise, Pichwa refused to admit he had any. Whenever anyone mentioned Tidda, Pichwa would blow up. "Bah, that son of a barber, that bastard, what expertise does he have? Miyan, his party always puts up the poorest show in the wrestling matches at the taziyas."

"But, Khalifa," replied Allah Razi mischievously, for the sake of continuing the argument, "he's training very hard these days."

Pichwa grew even more heated, "Oh, to hell with his training; what'll it get him anyway? It's razors he's worked with. What does he know about wielding a club?"

Mammad was now warmed up. "Ustad, this son of a barber must really want to get beaten up again. He thinks he's the great wrestler, Gama, but one slap and all the stuffing will come out of him."

"Miyan, I've already beaten that jerk's brains in, but that stupid fool still comes back for more."

Mammad was not the kind to be content with the great deeds of the past. He immediately retorted, "Ustad, that was a long time ago, and soon it'll be forgotten. I swear to you, ustad, I'll beat those jerks till they can't stand up."

"Now wait a minute, boy. I'm itching for a fight with Tidda myself. I'd clip his wings, but he keeps avoiding me."

Pichwa's excuse was partially correct. Although Tidda's group was not all that weak nor were they short of words when it came to talking big, the fact is that whenever the chance to confront Pichwa presented itself, Tidda somehow always managed to avoid a showdown.

People with common sense in Qadirpur knew that Pichwa was a master of the art of banaut, but the superstitious kind circulated all sorts of stories about him. They said that Pichwa knew magic. And Bhallan suspected this more than most. He had openly expressed his feelings several times, "Miyan, I don't know what it is, but Pichwa certainly has extraordinary powers."

Rasula not only vehemently confirmed this, but also provided the proof, "By God, the thing that baffles me is that Pichwa once threw a jinn down to the ground. Now, I've seen a lot of banaut in my time. I don't care what you know about fighting with sticks, but no one can win against a jinn. You take it from me, he knows some spell!"

While Allah Razi's suspicions about Pichwa's magical powers were aroused by the amulet Pichwa wore around his neck, Hamida often swore, "I saw it with my own eyes. Behind the idgah, in a broken-down grave, Pichwa was standing on one foot reciting something. There's no question that some fakir has given him a charm, and that charm is where his power comes from."

Jafar's story, however, was different. He would say,

"Miyan, the thing is that Pichwa showed such great courage when those bloody Hindus wanted to tear down the Weavers' Mosque. Miyan, you should've seen the way he moved his stick; he made those fools lose their wits. Well, that night what did Pichwa see in a dream, but that Maula Ali was patting his back. So you see, this is all a result of Maula Ali's blessings; otherwise poor Pichwa and his banaut would not amount to much."

But these were all differences of opinion about cause and effect. That Pichwa was brave, had been eminently proved. Pichwa never gave people sufficient time to doubt his courage. Every now and then, he would up pick a fight with some group on one pretext or another, and thus show off his prowess. Never concerned about how things would turn out, Pichwa fought without any fear or thoughts of loss or gain. Moreover, possessiveness had never tainted his art. Rather, it was the fight itself that mattered to him, and his club-weilding was free of any selfish motive. Consequently, when the storm of communal riots began, Pichwa put all other considerations out of his mind, and concentrated on the fact that he would now have a chance to display his skill with the club publicly. With both authority and excitement, he ordered his band, "Tighten your belts, lads. After a long time, dear Almighty God has finally heard us. We're going to have the time of our lives — God be praised!"

When the members of the group heard this, they could not contain their happiness. Mammad burst out with, "I swear by the Master, if Qadirpur doesn't win, Mammad is not his father's son."

Kalwa boasted, "It's true, my club is moth-eaten from lying around. But now I'll dye it red again and bring out its true colour."

Pichwa's companions made the same kind of elegant and showy preparations for the coming fight and bloodshed that people normally make for Id. But all the elegance was wasted, for the tide of the fight turned before their very eyes. And after that it was not a question of Qadirpur conquering, but of Qadirpur remaining undefeated. It took Pichwa a long time to sense the change in the wind. Offensive campaigns were all he had ever known, but what defensive action meant he came to learn the hard way. When he heard about the creation of Pakistan, he received the news with a feeling of immense chill. He wrung his hands in disappointment and said with deep regret, "Miyan, while we sat here rotting, they won the battle over there."

Then, he got angry, and roundly cursed himself and all the people of Qadirpur for having been caught unawares. Certainly, Pichwa was glad that the battle had been won, but he was also grieved that it was not his blood that had helped build this empire. After he had lamented enough, he said, "Miyan, what was to be has happened. Come on, let's go to the peepal tree by the idgah and at least put up a Pakistani flag." The other people of Qadirpur fainted when they heard about Pichwa's idea. They tried hard to reason with him and explained to him where Pakistan actually was. Pichwa was flabbergasted. He could not understand how Qadirpur, where he lived, could be outside Pakistan. After listening to what they said, he gave up the idea of hoisting the Pakistani flag, but then, with Mammad and Kalwa goading him on, he decided that, since Pakistan had excluded them from its brotherhood, they would create their own separate Pakistan. Consequently, they decided to fly an Islamic flag on the banyan tree by the idgah representing Pichwa's group, and not the flag of Pakistan. People were even more upset when they heard that. Already in bad shape, poor Naim Miyan lost his senses altogether when he heard about Pichwa's intention. He talked to Pichwa at great length and tried in every way to dissuade him from taking that step. All Pichwa said was, "Now you listen to me, Miyan, no Congress flag is going to fly in Qadirpur; we're going to put up the flag of Pichwa's wrestling group." Naim Miyan was extremely worried and upset, but what could he have done? Pichwa was no longer under his control. He had been very obedient and respectful earlier, but for several days now Pichwa had begun to openly complain about him, making public his rebellion. Actually, even Naim Miyan was no longer what he had been before. Although he was still called the leader of the Muslim League, he no longer had anything to do with it. He had been very proud before and would get very irritated if anyone so much as mentioned the Congress. He felt it beneath his dignity to talk to a Hindu.

As soon as the Partition was announced, however, there was a change in his behaviour. With the sudden creation of Pakistan, poor Naim Miyan was terribly confused and started to avoid even the mention of the Muslim League and Pakistan. But, in any case, what he did in the end saved him. Before the end of August, he had flown off to Pakistan. As he left Qadirpur with his family, he said, "We're just going to Delhi," but about a fortnight later, the Subedar Sahib received a letter from him from Lahore. He had written, "Brother, all the higher-ups I met in Delhi told me that the lives and fortunes of Muslims are no longer safe in India, and that we must go to Pakistan. We had a very hard time getting here but, thanks be to God, we reached our country safe and sound. Azhar Miyan has got a job in the Rehabilitation Department. God willing, Owais Miyan will also find a job soon. There's nothing left there now in Qadirpur. You should try to come too. By God's grace, I have some influence here, and we can work something out."

When Pichwa heard about the contents of the letter, at Allah Razi's store, he roundly cursed Naim Miyan. But what good was it to beat the trail when the snake had already slunk away? Perhaps Naim Miyan may have stayed on for a few more days, but in fact it had been Pichwa himself who had forced him to leave. Although Naim Miyan had explained the situation over and over to him, once Pichwa had got it into his head, he had to go and put his flag on the peepal tree. Although the battle would eventually have taken place anyway, the Jats had initially hesitated because of Pichwa. But this action of his was especially provoking and, as the Jats acted on the principle of not putting off till tomorrow what can be done today, they attacked Qadirpur. Now it is true that Pichwa's companions had beaten the hell out of the Jats in the fight, but Naim Miyan was not so stupid that he could not see what was brewing. He knew that the calamity had been averted — but only for a while longer.

Panic broke out in Qadirpur as a result of Naim Miyan's letter. Three days later, Munshi Sanaullah packed up and left for good. On market day that week people found good bargains in household goods at the second-hand dealer's shop. Especially noticeable were Saiyid Ali Husain's Nainital walking sticks, Qurban Ali's sheesham wood cots, and Munshi Sanaullah's china.

2

3 April 1950

How could I have known several months ago when I started writing this story that it would be ruined? If I had, I would have finished it on the spot. As I wrote the story, I realized that the character of Pichwa could not be contained in a short story. Justice could only be done to him in a full-length novel. Moreover, I thought, no epic poem has yet been written on the riots. Now, I am no poet — so let me try writing a prose epic. And then, this is not the time for writing great poetry. Now, when we have no great epic heroes, I am surely very fortunate to have a character like Pichwa fall right into my lap. But how could I have known then that after the first riot was over, another would break out and Pichwa would come to Pakistan? How could that same Pichwa, who confronted the riot himself, have staggered and been pushed out? What terrible things had happened at Qadirpur? Where did Kalwa and Mammad drift off to? I have no idea. How could I have had the nerve to ask Pichwa about all this? I'm just sorry that the design of my novel is ruined. Both Pichwa and I are unlucky. He was not fortunate enough to become the hero of an epic, and I am fated to treat the lives of insignificant people in worthless two-penny stories. People may look down their noses at this. It's true that Pichwa wasn't a great general or a splendid and glorious king; nevertheless, he had a certain dignity and greatness. And I never said my novel had to be called a Shahnama. An epic can also be called Jumhurnama. Anyway, there's no use arguing about it; it's all just a matter of conjecture now.

7 April 1950

I can't figure out how to write about living things. I write about dead things. How can one possibly write about living things? There's a certain amount of definiteness about them. They don't have hidden corners and evocative shadows. You can write reportage or political poetry about living things, but not short stories or lyric poetry. I feel very nervous when I see living things. The critic who said that a writer should always keep a window open while writing is a fool. Who said you should keep a window open during a storm? I'm just amazed at how people can write with their eyes open. I have to write with my eyes closed. I take up the pen only after the subject comes to permeate my mind totally. The trouble, though, is that as long as I can still see the subject, it doesn't settle down in my mind. As long as I lived in Qadirpur, it never occurred to me that Pichwa had it in him to become the subject of a story. When I came to Pakistan, my ties with Qadirpur were broken, and its life and people became a story for me. I didn't care whether Pichwa was alive or dead. As far as I was concerned, he was dead. Out of sight, out of mind. I started to write thinking him dead, but here he is, a living, breathing picture moving around in front of me, and consequently, the character that had settled down in my mind has vanished like the horns off a donkey's head. Down with real life; it's stolen from me the hero of my novel.

12 April 1950

Day and night, I've been haunted by the question of whether or not I should write my novel. Sometimes I decide to start writing. After all, people do write about living subjects. Everyone is naked in his bath, but if I take off my clothes, will I start a a riot? Still, I just go on thinking, My head is with me, but my heart is on strike. To hell with writing — the character I had constructed with so much care and difficulty is no longer intact, to say nothing of the living personality. In Qadirpur, Pichwa's living personality looked more like a character in a short story, but now that he's come to Pakistan, new traits are emerging in him. I always thought of Pichwa as experiencing unrequited love, and this is the way I imagined the hero of my novel. But now I see more than unrequited love, he's experiencing an unrequited desire for employment. When I met Pichwa this morning, he said, "Miyan, get me some kind of work. I have no damned place even to rest my feet on. Babu, if I can't find a job, at least get a house allotted to me."

I was astonished to hear Pichwa say that. He had never been worried about daily necessities in Qadirpur. Here he begs for food and wants a roof to cover his head. Where and how can I get him a house and a job? All I can do is make him the hero of my novel. Originally, I thought I would cast him as a twentieth-century Tipu Sultan, but now that he's come to Pakistan and wants a place to put up his feet and rest, and something to fill his belly, all the height and grandeur of his character has been destroyed.

Pichwa is wandering around looking for work. Today he went to see Naim Miyan about this problem, but he is scarcely the Naim Miyan he was — he doesn't talk to outcasts now. He scolded Pichwa, "Everyone just marches into Pakistan expecting to get something, as if his father had buried a treasure here. They just don't realize that there isn't that much room in Pakistan."

Pichwa complains that Naim Miyan has put on airs ever

since he moved to Pakistan. What's he complaining about? Naim Miyan is at the top of the heap — if he can't boast, who can? Obviously, in Qadirpur, Pichwa would never have stood for such harsh words, nor would Naim Miyan have had the nerve to look askance at Pichwa. He was always tongue-tied in front of Pichwa. In its own home, however, even the ant becomes a tiger. Clearly Pakistan is Naim Miyan's home and not Pichwa's.

20 April 1950

You can't teach an old dog new tricks. Pichwa may have lost everything he had but he still has a poetic temperament. Even in his unrequited desire for work, he looks like he has experienced unrequited love. His eyes burst out of his head when he saw the farmlands of Pakistan. He told me, "Miyan, if I could just get a bigha of land, what a change you'd see in Pichwa. Now, I'd put in a mango grove and I'd have a wrestling arena dug on one side where we'd have tests of strength. If you came here in the rainy season, Miyan, I'd give you such mangoes that you'd forget Malihabad."

I answered, "Look, you day-dreaming fool, who's going to give you a bigha of land. This land doesn't belong to you or me — it belongs to the zamindars."

But when Pichwa is caught up in what he's saying, his feet don't stay on the ground. He answered, "The zamindars, too, are Muslim brothers. You just watch. Whoever I beseech in the name of Allah and the Prophet Muhammad will not hesitate to give me a small bit of land."

You see Pichwa's strange logic — that zamindars too are either Hindus and Muslims.

22 April 1950

I feel as if the desire to create is decreasing in me. Sometimes I blame myself for this and sometimes external events. Everytime I take up my pen, the slogan, "Long live Pakistan," goes up with such force that I drop the pen. The cry goes up everywhere for "constructive literature." I can't hear anything else in this babble. What is this animal called "constructive literature?" Things are recognized by their opposites. I've never yet seen anything destructive in literature.

If literature isn't destructive, how can it be constructive? Literature is neither constructive nor destructive; it is just literature.

After one of my friends had gone on and on and talked his head off about constructive literature, I was just boiling, and I said in no uncertain terms that I wanted to write about homosexual love. He was incensed and said, "That's a very sick love."

"Alright, you suggest a healthy subject," I replied angrily.

"Write about Pakistan," he said.

I can neither figure out what I should write about Pakistan nor how I should write it. Pakistan is a living reality, a fact -- and I don't have the power to turn a fact into fiction. Pakistan is a reality, while Qadirpur has become a story, a story I can tell. I don't have the power to paint the land of Pakistan, but Qadirpur doesn't need to be painted; it's a story in itself. Its earth is reddened with the blood of its devoted sons. The reddened earth there, the air full of cries for help, the charred houses, the demolished mosque, the ruined wrestling arena — all these things tell a story eight hundred years old. I can tell this story with all the pain and sorrow that's in it, and I can describe with full feeling the deeds of the vanquished Arjuna of this *Mahabharata*, but this Arjuna — he's the real problem now. How can I write the Mahabharata of Qadirpur? The Arjuna of this *Mahabharata* is now the picture of failure and he wanders around the streets and lanes of Pakistan looking for a house and a job. He doesn't get these two things and he continues to fall from his true place.

2 May 1950

"Miyan, what kind of order is this?" Pichwa was so ferocious that I felt as if he was ready to bite me. I shuddered. Then it entered my head that this wasn't Qadirpur but Pakistan, and that Pichwa didn't have the same power here.

Surprised, I asked, "What order?"

Pichwa spat out the words, "The order that refugees who have come here can damn well go back to India."

I didn't know what to tell him. I calmed him down with difficulty, explaining, "Brother, don't lose your temper. It's just that Pakistan is full to the rafters now. Where can these new refugees be housed? Moreover, some higher-ups went to Delhi and they say all the Muslims in India are doing fine."

At this, Pichwa was even more incensed, "Miyan, would I lie to you, I, who've come from Qadirpur?"

I know Pichwa is not a liar. He may have a thousand faults, but lying isn't one of them. But even if I know that, the world believes only what the big-shots say.

3 May 1950

How the land shrinks, how food becomes scarce — the reason is simple enough, but I can't help it if Pichwa is too thick-brained to understand it. They say there was once a King. He traversed a great distance while hunting. He began to pant, and his lips became dry and crusted. Then he saw an orchard. He stopped in the garden to catch his breath and asked the gardener for water. The gardener's daughter plucked a pomegranate and brought it to him. She squeezed half of it into a glass, and the glass was full to the brim. The King drank the pomegranate juice and was refreshed. Then he set off to hunt again. On the way he thought, "Not only do many pomegranates grow in this orchard, only half a pomegranate is sufficient to fill a glass. Why not tax them?"

By and by, the King came back to this orchard and asked the gardener for water. The gardener's daughter squeezed a whole pomegranate into a glass, and then another, but still the glass didn't fill to the brim. She involuntarily cried out, "Father, our King intends evil!"

Surprised, the King asked, "Just how do you know the King intends evil?"

The gardener replied, "Maharaj, when the King intends evil the crops begin to fail."

You don't need great intelligence to understand a simple thing like that. Both the ignorant gardener and his daughter understood it, but Pichwa — his head is full of cow-dung.

Pichwa said, "Miyan, make me the King of Pakistan for just one day and then I'll show you how I'll make those fiends who own lots of land, big houses and several factories jump up and down. I'd beat them black and blue and give a share to each of the refugees." Snapping his fingers, he said, "Look Miyan, I'd take care of everything, just like that."

But I don't believe him — he's always boasting. What he doesn't seem to understand is that if he really were made the King of Pakistan, he too would change. The only people with a sense of responsibility are those without it. It is too many responsibilities that produce what is called irresponsibility. What's irresponsible is not a person, but a chair.

5 May 1950

The farther I run from politics, the more it pursues me. Until Pichwa came to Pakistan, he was a genuine fictional character. But now that he's here, he's become an important political issue. Now, whenever I think about him, I end up in a political morass. Why isn't he allotted a house? Why can't he get a job? Why is he being sent back to India? In short, I get caught in the maze of politics whenever I think about him. It's not that I can't talk about politics. I can say quite a lot about things like refugee rehabilitation, minority agreements, and abandoned property arrangements. Nor have I kept my mouth shut out of politeness. But why should I poke my nose into politics? Although I feel strongly that my creative talents are being ruined, that doesn't mean I should hold my nose and dive into the cesspool of politics. A frustrated singer should stay a frustrated singer; he has no business becoming a reciter of elegies. I wouldn't interfere even if someone sprinkled this whole terrestrial ball with kerosene and set it on fire.

I'm afraid of external life, the most disgusting aspect of which is politics. Politics makes me tremble just as the butcher makes the cow tremble, and in fact, politics brings the same doomsday for the writer as the butcher does for the cow. The joke is that politics not only slaughters both literature and the writer, it's the one that eventually gets all the plaudits as well.

6 May 1950

My creative desire continues to cool, and whatever magic there was in the fictional potential of Pichwa's personality ebbs away. He no longer seems like a person at all; he seems more like a chess piece. First he's in this square, then he goes to that one, then he's shoved back again to the first one. The characters of a novel are supposed to be human beings — how can I make someone like him the hero of my novel? If I really sweated and churned out a novel with chess pieces for characters, would anyone respect it? Could a novel about chess pieces be called anything but a game of chess?

7 May 1950

I thought it was just so much bravado, but he did really go back for good. What men call conscience is really a shameless thing. It never dies completely but remains half-dead or pretends to be dead, and can come to life any time at all. He asked me heatedly, "Will the leaders go with us too?"

I laughed and answered, "If they went, who would govern Pakistan?"

This made him angrier and he cursed Naim Miyan left and right.

I had told Pichwa to take it easy if he really had to leave and not to be in a hurry, that the government itself would take care of all the arrangements for the trip. This made him furious. "Should I take money for a shroud here and make my grave in India? I don't want a charity shroud."

8 May 1950

Pichwa's departure has revived the plan for my novel. But who knows, he might suddenly come back and mess up the plan. Is it inconceivable that death might take him? After all, people don't live forever. A person can die in a split second. It is entirely conceivable that the heat of Sind might finish off this man from the Doab, or that someone might throw him out of the train, or that the train he's travelling in might be attacked. In short, death just needs an excuse. What couldn't happen if God willed it; slaughtering people is certainly an amusing sport, but...but why would He ride a horse at the bidding of others?

20 May 1950

It's been nearly a fortnight since Pichwa left. I don't know who else is left behind in Qadirpur now, but I've heard that the Subedar Sahib is still hanging on there. I fired off a letter to him but there has been no answer yet. I have no idea where that person ended up after galloping down the sands of Sind. I'd hesitate to say he even got across the border. I wouldn't be surprised if he took a liking to the dust of Sind. Or perhaps the land of Pakistan was offended and hugged the departing guest to her bosom. Doesn't the earthly heart of a country throb for its people even if the hearts of fellow-countrymen do not? Both this new country and its uninvited hosts are fantastic: the uninvited guests complain that the hosts lack foresight and have no feeling for the difficulties of their guests. Regardless of whether there's room in the country, Pichwa left because there's no longer any room in the hearts of the people here. And Pichwa left defiantly. He said it was dishonourable to stay here any longer. Where has the truthful watchman of all the false notions of honour wandered off to? I have no idea. How concerned he was about his own individuality! How concerned he was about guarding his personal honour! I don't know if he was able to guard his personal honour or not. All I can say is this — when the whole nation is being disgraced, does the honour of an individual count for anything? What difference does it make?

21 May 1950

I wait for the postman every day. I keep looking at the door. When the mailman comes, he brings several letters at a time but not the one I'm waiting for. What's happened to the Subedar Sahib that he doesn't answer? Has he also passed away? A person's life is uncertain to start with, and the Subedar Sahib was even then sitting with one foot in his grave. And what happened to that daring fellow Pichwa? Did the earth swallow him, or the sky devour him? Did the winds carry him off, or a snake bite him? Man is no more than a bubble, but proud Pichwa went to fight the wind with a lamp.

23 May 1950

> This bowl of the cup, this sorrowful world,
> this night where people light the lamp, O
> Cup-bearer?

So that person has gone for good and not only that, he has ended up miles away from Pakistan. He has crossed the borders of both Pakistan and India and has entered the country which isn't marked by any borders, where countless refugees arrive every day and are settled in no time at all. The Subedar Sahib's letter — should I call it a letter or an elegy — has come. I didn't think the Subedar Sahib, in between hunting geese and deer, would start writing elegies. He writes:

"Your letter took a long time to reach me, but I'm thankful it came. It was late in coming for two reasons. First because the address was written in a language that everyone else here except me denies knowing, and second, because Qadirpur is no longer Qadirpur. Now its new residents call it Jatunagar.

You have fired off questions one after another. Which ones should I answer and how? The times you talk about, brother! Where is Qadirpur now? As the poet says, 'The sunlight has vanished with the sun.'

Here there is no longer a Tidda, nor an Allah Razi, nor people flying their own flags on the peepal tree by the idgah. When Qadirpur became too small for its people, some sank into it, and the rest were driven off. You ask what condition the wrestling arena behind the Weavers' Mosque is in, and I doubt if there is even a mosque here any more. The mosques would gladly mourn the loss of their worshippers and the wrestling arenas the loss of their young men — but where is there a mosque or an arena today? Allah Razi's store? Your question reminded me — Hindu butchers don't sell halal meat there now.

Your country had no room for Pichwa, but the earth of his former country clasped him to her bosom. I was not able to meet this fortunate person, but one day the whole village got very excited, and I saw hanging on the same branch of the peepal tree by the idgah, where Kalwa and Mammad had flown the flag of their party, their master's head.

I felt very strange reading your letter. Whatever the reason, you remembered us. Now and then, continue to remember us with scraps of letters. We are not strangers:

Why do you think of us as strangers?
We are from the same place you are.

I am getting old and pretty soon the lamp of my life will be snuffed out. Whom will you write to then in Qadirpur? Do remember the two things I said about the address."

What a strange letter the Subedar Sahib has written! Is it a letter or the concluding sentences of some epic tale? I think I'll end the novel I'm writing, that is my Qadirpur *Mahabharata*, with this letter. And what a death indeed this crazy Pichwa found! His life was a drama, and so was his death. The one undramatic event in his life was his flight to Pakistan. If only he hadn't come to Pakistan. Pichwa disgraced himself by coming to Pakistan and threw a monkey wrench into the work of my novel.

25 May 1950

Pichwa is dead, but my novel is still not coming together. My hands start to shake whenever I take up my pen. Sometimes I feel as if I have murdered Pichwa. What devil got into my head that wanted him dead? If novels and stories got written this way, writers would be tried for murder every day.

27 May 1950

Every day I resolve to start writing my novel, but I haven't done so yet. I pick up my pen and put it down again. I wonder why I'm writing this novel. People don't care about human emotions here — the mention of human emotions is still an afterthought. The appreciation of literature stems from a concern for humanity. My nation doesn't value human beings; how can it care about literature? Why should I debase my creative talent and disgrace my pen?

I have definitely decided not to write my novel. But how long can I just sit at home and do nothing? I thought that I ought to start moving around. I'm so disinclined to shock people that I wouldn't want to do anything spectacular. I would even be content to go into the despicable slave trade, but it's not permitted privately now — the governments have taken it over. Naim Miyan says, if it hadn't taken me such a long time to come to my senses, he would have had some big factory allotted to me.

Now he has promised to have a flour mill allotted. I have to work somehow — if not a factory, then a flour mill.

29 May 1950

Naim Miyan has turned out to be a useful person to have around. Somehow, he had a flour mill allotted to me. As the owner of a flour mill, I see a strange kind of change in myself. As long as I was stuck in the web of literature, I felt cut off from my nation. Remaining wedded to literature would have meant being neither here nor there; I would neither have written the novel, nor would I have done any other kind of work. Now, however, I consider myself a responsible citizen — a dutiful member of a rising nation.

1 June 1950

I'm writing in my diary for the last time today. From tomorrow onwards, I won't have enough time for it. Keeping a diary gives one something to do when one is unemployed. The arrangements for the mill have been taken care of. God willing, it will start tomorrow. Since the going price in the city for grinding flour is five paise for five seers, I thought that at my place I would charge only four paise for five seers so that people would begin to patronize the new mill right away.

Original in Urdu.
Translated by Leslie A. Flemming
and Muhammad Umar Memon.

MAHEEP SINGH

THE RIVER AND THE BRIDGE

When the train left Lahore station, my heart sank. We were going towards that place, where fourteen years ago, there had been a conflagration. Lakhs of people had died in that fire, lakhs still carried memories of their wounds. I felt as if the train was entering a long, dark and deep tunnel. And that we were about to offer everything we had to the surrounding darkness.

We were about three hundred pilgrims. There were many women and children with us. We had made a pilgrimage to every gurudwara in Lahore. After the welcome we had received there, we were not afraid of the reception we would receive at Panja Sahib. Yet who could be sure when the beast in man would wake up and destroy everything?

I was thinking about all this, when I looked at my mother. She was staring fixedly at the land outside. Her chin was resting on her hand and her elbow was on the window. The crop had been harvested. The land all around was flat and bare. I felt as if the flat and bare plains were a reflection of her soul. I looked towards the other passengers in the compartment. They, too, seemed to be profoundly sad. I couldn't understand why everyone had suddenly become so despondent.

"I am sure you remember this area well," I said to mother, in order to distract her. "You must have travelled on this route thousands of times?"

My mother looked at me and smiled. It was the smile of someone who had lost everything. She said, "I remember each and every station on this route. But, today, this region seems to be so alien. I am travelling over this route after fourteen years. I always took this route in the past. As soon as I crossed Lahore, a strange sense of joy used to surge through me. And as I approached Sarai, my village, the face of each and every person would appear before me as in a vision. So many people would come to the station to receive me..."

Old memories came flooding back. My father had set up his business in Uttar Pradesh. All my brothers and sisters had been born outside Punjab. I remember that while my father used to visit Punjab once a year, my mother went there at least twice or thrice a year. The youngest of her children always accompanied her.

I remember the days when Punjab had been partitioned, and the five rivers of Punjab had turned red with blood. Mother still insisted on going there. Everyone opposed her, as if she had decided to jump into fire. And, indeed, to go to Punjab at that time was like jumping into fire. But all of us knew that it would not be easy to persuade Mother to change her mind. She merely laughed at our objections. She returned after about twenty days. She even managed to send by train some of our belongings from our village. With her, however, she only brought back her spinning wheel and her curd-churner.

Later, the flames spread throughout Punjab. Houses, villages and cities were reduced to ash. When the fires subsided, it seemed as if a wide and deep chasm had appeared between Amritsar and Lahore. The land on the other side seemed to have moved somewhere far away. We forgot that our village lay on the other side of the chasm, that a metalled road ran along the bank of a canal, and that the river Jhelum wound its sinuous and joyous way over the land like a happy and youthful maiden.

That day, I was travelling with my mother, across the chasm and over a bridge which had been constructed for the sake of political diplomacy, towards the land which had once been a part of our lives and was now so utterly alien to us.

I was turning the pages of a book, when Ma turned to me and asked, "Will the train stop at the Sarai station?"

I thought for a while, and said, "Yes, it should stop. But it'll get there around two at night. All of us will be asleep. We won't even know when we go past it. Besides, there is nothing at Sarai which belongs to us anymore."

My mother seemed irritated. She said, "You had no relation with it anyway."

I had obviously hurt my mother. Without saying anything more, I looked down and started reading my book.

Slowly, it became dark. Ma opened her bundle and took out something to eat. One of my distant uncles was also with us. After eating a little, the three of us began to make preparations for sleep. Within a few minutes, Mamaji began to snore. I too lay down on one of the berths. Ma, however, continued to sit as before.

After sometime, I woke up with a start and saw Ma still staring into the darkness outside. I looked at my watch, it was half-past ten. I said, "Ma, why don't you also rest for a while?"

"Alright," she said, and reclined on her berth. In that state of half-wakefulness, I had a frightening dream. I don't remember the details, but it made me very anxious. I felt as if red water was swirling around me and I was splashing through it. I suddenly woke up and looked around me nervously. Ma was shaking me. She was tense and excited, and she was trembling.

"What is it?"

"Find out why there is so much noise outside."

I leaned out of the window to look. The train had stopped at a small station. The platform was lit by the dim light of a lamp hanging from a lamp post and there was a strange hum in the air. My hair stood on end. Stories about what had happened fourteen years ago flashed through my mind like lightning. I remembered how rioters had stopped trains and massacred the passengers. Mamaji stood beside me shaking me by my shoulder.

"What is the matter?"

At that moment I heard someone from the crowd yell, "Arrey, is there anyone from Sarai on the train?"

"What station is this?" I asked my mother.

Ma said, "Sarai...my village."

A voice from the crowd outside called out loudly once again, "Arrey, is there anyone from Sarai on the train?"

I looked at Ma. Her face was glowing with pride.

"Ask him what the matter is."

I leaned out of the window. There were people walking up and down the platform and shouting, "Arrey, is there anyone from Sarai on the train?"

I asked a man who was passing by, "What is the matter?"

"Is there anyone from Sarai travelling with you?"

"Yes, I am from that village," Ma said, as she stepped forward.

"Are you really from Sarai?" the man asked, as if he couldn't believe it.

"Yes."

As soon as Ma said that, there was a commotion on the platform. People gathered in front of our compartment at once. There was a chorus of voices.

"Are you really from Sarai...?"

Ma replied emphatically, "Yes, from this very village."

There was an uproar in the crowd. Someone asked, "Which family did you belong to?"

Ma looked at me. I replied, "My father's name was Sardar Moola Singh. She is my mother."

"Are you Moola Singh's son?" Many voices exclaimed simultaneously, "Are you Moola Singh's wife?...Ravel Singh's sister-in-law? Are they all well...?" As they inquired after our family, many people thrust small bundles into our hands. They were full of almonds, walnuts, raisins. Overcome with emotion, we couldn't utter a word. We quietly accepted the gifts and placed them on our seat. Soon there was a small heap of bundles on the berth.

I was astonished. Ma covered her head with her dupatta and greeted everyone with folded hands. Her lips were quivering with uncontainable delight. No word escaped her lips, but her eyes welled over with tears.

The guard standing nearby, raised a green lantern and drew a whistle from his coat pocket. Three or four people surrounded him and pleaded, "Arrey babu, let the train stop for a few more minutes. She is from our village." One of them forced the guard, who was holding the green lantern, to lower his arm.

"Bharjaiji, how is Sardarji? Why didn't he come with you for a darshan of Panja Sahib?" an elderly Muslim asked.

My mother pulled her dupatta a little lower and said in a barely audible whisper, "Sardarji is no more."

"What...? Moola Singhji has passed away? Was he ill?"

Ma remained silent. I replied, "He had an ulcer in his stomach. One day, it suddenly burst and the following day he died."

"He was a very good man. May God give him a place in his dargah," one of them prayed. There was silence for a few moments.

"Bharjaiji, are your children well?"

"Thanks to Waheguruji, they are well," Ma said softly.

Lots of voices rose simultaneously and said, "May Allah give them a long life."

"Bharjaiji, why don't you come back here with your children?" someone said. Lots of voices spoke at the same time, "Yes, Bharjaiji, come back here...come back."

There was a chorus of voices from the platform, "Come back here...come back."

I heard Mamaji, who was standing behind me, mutter angrily, "Scoundrels! First they beat us and drive us out of here, now they want us to come back. Thugs!"

But the people standing on the platform had not heard him. They continued to repeat, "Bharjaiji, come back here with your children. When will you return? You couldn't have forgotten your village? Bharjaiji, do come back..."

My mother was unable to say anything. She continued to adjust her dupatta and bow to everyone with folded hands.

The guard, who had moved away from the crowd, raised the green lantern once more and blew his whistle. The engine hooted. The train started. The crowd walked alongside our compartment.

"Alright, Bharjaiji, salaam...Alright, son, salaam...give Ravel Singh my salaam...give everyone our salaam!..."

My mother stood with her hands folded and said something which couldn't be heard over the noise. The train slowly gathered speed. We leaned out of the window and folded our hands. The crowd stood on the platform and continued to wave to us.

After the train left the station, I pushed the gifts aside and turned to say something to my mother.

She was crying uncontrollably. Tears were flowing down her face as if a dam had burst. She wiped her eyes again and again with her dupatta.

The train reached the bridge over the Jhelum. It roared and clattered over it. I leaned out of the window to look at the Jhelum bridge. I had heard that it was very strong. I watched the bridge, made of iron and stone, rush past me in the night. I looked down. It was pitch dark down below, but I knew that the river, with its clear and cool water, flowed quietly under that bridge of iron and stone.

Original in Hindi.
Translated by Alok Bhalla.

MULK RAJ ANAND

THE PARROT IN THE CAGE

"Rukmaniai ni Rukmaniai," the parrot in the cage called in the way Rukmani's friends used to call her when they entered the alleyway of Kucha Chabuk Swaran in Lahore. And he repeated the call even before she could answer him as she was wont to do when she wanted to humour the bird. She did not answer but sat crouching on the fringe of the road about half a furlong away from the Amritsar court.

"Rukmaniai ni Rukmaniai!" the parrot called again.

She was peering through the little clouds of dust raised by the passing motors and tongas and yakkas in the direction from which, she had been told, by the roasted gram-stall keeper, the 'Dipty Collator' was to come and she remained heedless to the parrot's cry.

"Rukmaniai ni Rukmaniai!" the parrot called shrilly and went on repeating the cry with the sure mocking bird's instinct that if he kept on calling her she would answer.

"Han, my son, han..." the old woman said after all, wearily. There had been a dull ache behind the small knot of hair on the back of her head and, now, with the mounting heat of the September morning, it seemed to her like the rumblings of the dreadful night when murder and fire had raged in her lane.

Little rivulets of sweat trickled through the deep fissures of old age which lined her face and she shaded her eyes, with the inverted palm of her hand, to probe the sunlight more surely for the vision of the Deputy Commissioner. Her contracted, toothless mouth was open and a couple of flies came from the direction in which she looked and settled on the corners of her lips.

She waved her left hand gingerly to scatter the flies. But they persisted and set up an irritation in her soul through which she felt a panic seize her belly.

"*Ni tun Kithe hain*?" the parrot cried another cry which he had learnt from the old woman's friends who invariably asked on entering the lane, "Where are you?" For she used to be away earning her living as a maid of all work, cleaning utensils for the people in the bigger houses in the lane, or was mostly hidden from view in the inner sanctums of the dark ground floor room by the wall in the gully.

"Son, I don't know where I am..." she said listlessly, in the effort to keep the parrot quiet by assuring him she was taking notice of him. "I only know that if Fato had not given me her burqah to escape with, I should not be here..."

"*Ni tun ki karni hain*?" the parrot persisted with the third call which Rukmani's friends used to utter.

"Nothing, son, I am doing nothing...only waiting..." the old woman said tiredly, as though now she was holding a metaphorical conversation with her pet to keep her mind occupied. For, from her entrails arose a confusion which was like the panic she had felt at the mad mob bursting with shouts of "Allah ho Akbar! Har har Mahadev! Sat Sri Akal!" on the night of terror when she had fled from the lane.

There had been flashes of blazing light; cracking of burning housebeams; smoke, smoke, choking smoke...And she had thought that her last days had come, that the earth itself was troubled through the misdeeds of the Kaliyug and that soon the dharti would open up and swallow everything. And then Fato had come and told her she would be murdered if she did not leave.

"*Ni tun ki karni hain*?" the parrot repeated. "*Ni tun Kithe hain...?*"

"Nothing son, nothing," Rukmani answered, "And I don't know where I am..." And as she looked steadily towards the junction of the Mall Road and Kutchery Road and saw no sign of the Deputy Commissioner, her last phrase seemed to get meaning.

"Rukmaniai ni Rukmaniai!" the parrot called again.

Her answers to his metallic shrill nasal cries did not irritate her anymore, but relieved the heavy pressure of the demons of the dreadful night on her head and her chest and her bowels.

"*Ni tun ki karni hain*?" the parrot persisted.

"Son, I am waiting for the Sahib, so that he can give me some money to buy bread with...They say that the Congress Sarkar will give back what we have lost, son, they say — I heard at the station, son, at the station!...Are you hungry my son — you must be hungry...I shall buy you some gram from that stall keeper when the Sahib gives me money..."

"Mai, you are dreaming! You have gone mad!" the gram-stall keeper said. "Go your way to the town, you may get some food at the Durbar Sahib temple. You won't get anything from the Dipty Collator..."

"*Vay jaja*, eater of your masters!" she shouted bitterly. Such common sense as that of the complacent gram-seller seemed to break the pitcher of her hopes. And she mooed like a cow in defiance at the end of her speech.

"Acha, don't abuse me. I only said this for your own good," the stall keeper answered as he whisked the flies off his stall with the end of a dirty apron.

"Oh, why did I leave home to wander like this from door to door!" old Rukmani whined almost under her breath. "Oh why did you have to turn me out of my room in my old age, God...Oh why...Why didn't I tie the rupees I had earned in a knot on my dupatta!...Hai Rabba!..."

She moaned to herself, and tremors of tenderness went swirling through her flesh. And tears filled her eyes. And in the hazy dust before her the violent rhythms of the terrors of falling houses and dying, groaning men and heavy, shouting men, danced in macabre trembling, waves of sunlight, dim and unsubstantial like the ghosts on a cremation ground before whom she had always cowered every time she had attended a funeral.

"Rukmaniai ni Rukmaniai!" the parrot called and brought her to herself.

Crackling flames of heat now assailed her. And she sweated more profusely. And yet she crouched where she was, only shuffling like a hen sitting over her eggs.

"At least go and sit under the shade of the tree," the gram-seller said.

The pupils of her eyes were blistering with the glare. She wiped her face with the end of her dupatta and heaved as though she was lifting the weight of a century's miseries up with her. Then she took the handle of the iron cage in which her pet parrot sat, and bent-backed but staring ahead, ambled up to a spot where the precarious shadow of a kikar tree lay on the rutted earth.

"*Ni tun Kithe hain? ni...*" the parrot's monologue continued. So did her self-communings, aroused by the anonymous, meaningless, repetitive calls: "Nowhere, son, nothing, nothing..."

She had hardly settled down when suddenly a motor whirred past, with a motor cyclist ahead and some policemen in a jeep behind, scattering much dust on the fringe of the roadside.

"There goes your Dipty Collator" said the gram-stall keeper.

"Hai hai! Come my son!" she screamed as she shot up with great alacrity and picked up the cage in her hand. "Come, I will join my hands to the Sahib and fall at his feet."

"Mad woman!" the gram-seller said cynically.

She heeded him not, but penetrated the clouds of dust.

Behind her, and on all sides, she could hear the sound of rushing feet storming towards the gloomy gates of the kutchery. And their cries whirled in the air, "Hujoor, Mai Bap, hear us! Sarkar! Dipty Sahab!...We have come on foot all the way from Lahore...You..." She nearly fell as the more powerful men among the crowd brushed past her and their own women.

"Rukmaniai! *Tun kithe hain?*" the parrot in the cage cried even as he fluttered his wings in a panic at the voices and the hurtling feet.

The old woman did not answer but sped grimly on. Only, in a moment, the dust storm which was proceeding towards the court was turned back by a furious whirlwind from the opposite direction. A posse of policemen charged the refugees with lathis and angry shouts which drowned the chorus of voices of which Rukmani's sighs and her parrot's cries had been a part.

In the delirium of motion which was set afoot by the lathi charge of the police, all valour was held at bay and turned back.

Rukmani was brushed aside by some desperate arm until she reeled and fell not far from where she had sat waiting for the Sahib. But she clung to the handle of the cage in which her parrot sat as she lay moaning in suppressed, helpless whispers.

The parrot fluttering furiously as though he was being strangled called out shrilly: "Rukmaniai! Ni Rukmaniai! *Ni tun Kithe hain!... Ni tun ki karni hain!*"

But the old woman, though concerned for him, had turned in upon herself with a sudden dimness that seemed to be creeping upon her.

After the crowd had been cleared, and the dust settled, the gram-seller was irritated by the parrot's constant cries from his perch. He was afraid that the old woman had expired. But as he came near her, the parrot called her more shrilly and she answered faintly, "Han, han son, han," and the man knew that she was still alive. He lifted her up and found that her hands and arms were slightly grazed.

"Come and sit in the shade, mother"! he said.

"Acha, son, acha!" she moaned.

And she lifted the cage and proceeded towards the shade.

The parrot was a little reassured as he saw the gram-seller helping his mistress and he shrieked less shrilly.

"Come, my little winged one, I shall give you some gram to eat," the gram-seller said to him.

"May you live long, son!" the old woman blessed the gram-seller in a feeble, strained, moanful voice.

"Rukmaniai ni Rukmaniai! *Tun kithe hain? Tun ki karni hain?...*" the parrot called now in a slow measured voice.

"Han han, son, han my son...I don't know where I am! I don't know..."

Original in English.

KARTAR SINGH DUGGAL

KULSUM

"What strange gift has the old man brought me today?" he wondered.

The rapid and loud footsteps of the young schoolmaster disappeared into the silence of the dark house. There was a kitchen on the right. It was empty. A prayer mat lay outside the kitchen door. The old man used to sit on it and recite his prayers. A rosary, carelessly thrown aside, lay on the mat. The rest of the house was in darkness even though the sun had not yet set. The young schoolmaster stared into the darkness searching for something. "What gift has the old man brought me? It is something you can neither eat nor drink, he had said."

When his eyes got adjusted to the darkness, the schoolmaster saw a young girl standing against a pillar. She was tall, well-built and fair, her long hair fell over her shoulders like a jasmine creeper full of sweet-smelling flowers. The schoolmaster stood before her enchanted.

"It is something you can neither eat nor drink!"

There was a bed near the wall. It was covered with a bed-spread with colourful designs.

"My name is Kulsum." Then there was silence for a long time. The schoolmaster sometimes looked at the bed and sometimes at the woman who seemed to have stepped out of a fairy-tale. He stood there as if he had been bewitched.

"My name is Kulsum. What's your name?" her lips opened like rosebuds.

The young schoolmaster felt as if the blood had drained out of his body and, unable to stand any longer, sat down on the bed. He felt as if he had been walking ceaselessly for the last twenty-five years of his life.

Now he understood why the old man had been so impatient. Why he had sent him so many messages —"Tell the schoolmaster there is a gift waiting for him." But how could he have come before the school had shut for the day? It was only in the evening, after all the children had gone home, that he had found the time to visit the old man. When he asked him about the gift, the old man had replied cryptically, "It is something you can neither eat nor drink."

The gift was really something that one could neither eat nor drink!

Oh, but he could have devoured her! He could have become drunk on her beauty. He could have kissed her and possessed her, absorbed her into his being. The young schoolmaster trembled with passion, and his eyes glittered with strange intoxication. A frenzy of delight ran through his body.

"Perhaps, this is what they mean by freedom," the schoolmaster said to himself. "We got our Independence only yesterday. Yes — *Sare jahan se acha Hindustan hamara* — A day after Independence there is a houri standing before me."

Kulsum! A touch would soil her!

"My name is Kulsum."

The young schoolmaster remembered that the Hindu and the Sikh-girls had not been able to step out of their homes even in the daytime. Muslim goondas used to tease them and no one ever dared to question those ruffians. Punjab was ruled either by the British or by the Muslims. The Muslims living in Punjab had never objected when the Hindus and the Sikhs were insulted, their houses were looted, or their wives and daughters were abducted in broad daylight.

But that day, a woman who had been snatched from some fairy-tale stood before him. She seemed like a vision revealed to him after seven veils had been lifted. Every limb in his body ached with desire. His eyes burnt with lust. He smiled lasciviously and lunged at the girl. He grabbed her arm and pulled her towards the bed. But the woman resisted him. Struggled to stay where she was. The schoolmaster pulled her towards him again. But the girl held onto the pillar as if she had been glued to it.

"Please talk to me first," she pleaded.

The young schoolmaster was obsessed. Like an insane man he tried to pull her towards himself again and again.

"Marry me. Marry me first. How can I sit on a bed next to a stranger?" the girl begged.

The young schoolmaster's face darkened with mad, bestial passion. There was rage in his eyes. He wanted to rape her. Without uttering a word, he continued to pull her towards the bed.

"Please don't hurt me. I beg you, don't do it. Marry me first. I was engaged to a man of your age. Tall and well-built like you. His forehead was as broad as yours; his teeth were like your teeth —white like pearls. My father and mother, my brothers and all my relations were hacked to death with swords by the rioters. I don't know how I escaped. I was running aimlessly like someone who has lost her wits when that old man caught me and brought me here. On the way here, he promised that he would find me someone to live with. Marry me, please."

The schoolmaster, it appeared, had heard nothing. Every part of his being seemed to be drunk with desire. Once again, he tried to drag her to the bed with all his strength. But the girl did not let go of the pillar. She refused to move an inch.

"Marry me. I beg you on my bended knees. First marry me. Has any young woman ever prayed thus for marriage? Has an unmarried girl ever spoken like this? Marry me! Please! I shall repay you for your kindness."

The young schoolmaster heard nothing, saw nothing. Enraged with desire, he tried to force her towards the bed. Suddenly that helpless woman turned on him like a lioness and pushed him with all her strength. The schoolmaster tripped and fell backwards on the bed.

"Let me, with folded hands, beg you to marry me." As she said that, she began to weep bitterly. The schoolmaster got up in a rage and ran out of the house. The old man was sitting under a neem tree spinning cotton. When he heard the school master's tale, he threw aside the spindle he was spinning and cursed the girl, "The bitch wants to be married first, does she?" He rushed into the house and locked the door behind him.

Three minutes later, the old man came out knotting his tehmad. "Go in now, Masterji, go in now without fear." Then he picked up the jug of water that stood near the door and walked to the neem tree and began washing his hands. Slowly, hesitantly, the schoolmaster re-entered the house. In the darkness of the room, he saw the girl sitting at the edge of the bed. Her back was towards him. Her silk salwar was crumpled. Her chunni no longer covered her head. One wet strand of hair lay on her cheek. Streams of sweat flowed down her neck. The young schoolmaster went and sat down next to her on the bed. This time, the girl didn't get up and walk away from him. The schoolmaster placed one hand on her shoulder. She didn't move.

"Kulsum," the young schoolmaster called out to her softly. The girl, who had begged and pleaded with him three minutes ago, was now silent.

The room was now completely dark. Perhaps it was night outside.

Original in Punjabi.
Translated by Alok Bhalla.

DIPENDRANATH BANDYOPADHAYAY

JATAYU

The sound of the train faded away till it merged into the drone of crickets. Then it was dark again. A few trees of various shapes, swathed in inky cobwebs drawn from the sky, earth and emptiness, stood scattered around in incredible postures.

There were no fireflies that day either. Even they don't glow on the night of the new moon. The darkness lay as thick as mud. No deepening, no lightening, no light and shade, there was nothing. The month of poush. The cold dew fell, like drops of darkness. And set in this fantastic atmosphere, the little gathering lit by lanterns looks even more unreal. Only the figure of the goddess is under a jute canopy. Dasharathi has modelled the image this time too. A dark blue body. Simmering. A bright red tongue. Elongated eyes. Some heads round her neck, in her hands. As if fresh from the slaughter.

Preparations have been made for Sandhi Puja. The old priest, squatting on the reed mat and staring bemused at the goddess, is murmuring mantras in a story-telling tone. Occasionally, he sighs and cries out in a broken voice, "Maa, Maa." The call, like a bat's wing, churns up the darkness and fades away. Four drummers have come. The little boy keeps time on the gong. They are sitting around smoking pot. They will have to play soon when Nityacharan dances. The sacrifice after that, and the puja.

The arena has been laid out in front of the goddess. The area, about eight or ten spans in length and breadth, has been dug up and made slippery by pouring water. It is even difficult to walk here. On this Nityacharan will fly like a bird. Bell-metal braziers on his head and in his teeth. Fire in the braziers. And with twisting body and on perfectly balanced feet, Nityacharan will weave his strange dance. He will dance within the flames. He will dance bearing flames. Nityacharan will become a flame.

Self-important young men rush about on small errands. The last minute anxious, disorganized bustle seems irrelevant in the unearthly atmosphere and amidst fantastic preparations. Someone needlessly piles some more jackfruit leaves before the sacrificial goat. People shift back a little, feeling the heat from the flames even before the fire is lit. Women sit apart. The puja is set against the cremation ground. So there are no children about to make a din. But all the village dogs have come along. They wander about, sniffing the ground.

Durga pulled slightly at the sari on her head. She was sitting at the very end of the women's row, squeezed into a corner. The night was a shade darker here. In the past, her place had been right in front on this night. Where the faint heat of the fire would play touch and go with her. Where she could see every pose, every glance of Nityacharan's clearly. Durga stared distractedly at the slippery, muddy arena and tried to think, "Before this, long ago, I was somehow... somewhat...I was..." She suddenly realized that now she couldn't think at all.

She noticed with indifference that the other women were paying her special attention today. Acknowledging her importance as Nitya's wife. Surprised, Durga understood that the respect due to her association with Nityacharan had not dried up yet. At once her thighs began to burn. With bated breath, and eyes screwed shut Durga sat inert. That fear, oh, that fear again, now. Her heart beat hard. The nerve-ends in her fingers and toes seemed to drone out an unintelligible cricket song.

She had seen the man in the crowd at the station on her way back from work. Looking at her, he winked with his left eye and smiled. Durga walked quickly away and managed to board a women's compartment. All the way back, she trembled like a dry bamboo leaf. Who was that man? Why did he look at me like that? Why did he smile? Did he have glasses? No, a thin moustache. Was he wearing a dhoti, or trousers? I can't remember, I can't identify him, I don't recognize him. Why did he smile? Does he know me? Which station was he going to? Or was he just following me?

At every station, she tried to look for him, disguising her keen search with an absent glance. Just before alighting, she noticed a young man near the railings, lighting a match and forgetting to light his bidi in turn, while staring at her face. Without another glance, Durga took the path through the fields. Is it the same man? But he doesn't have a moustache, and is in pyjamas. Then why did he look at me? Is it that man, or another one?

She tries to recall the faces one after the other. But no the image emerges clearly. She can't remember anything distinctly. A featureless form hovers vaguely before her eyes. Her breath comes short in her effort to identify the face. A hairy hand, just a hand, pinches her breast violently. Then clamps down on her throat.

The path through the fields was crowded that day. Everyone was going to see the puja, the dance. Durga could hear Nitya's name in many voices, snatches of stories, sometimes half-mythical. Those who knew her, smiled and talked to her. And those who didn't, stared at her in wonder, starting a whispered conversation among themselves. Pursued by an indefinable dread, Durga skulked past like an animal, her ears alert, full of suppressed anxiety and suspicion.

Can't stand crowds. I don't like them. I am afraid. When people smile and talk to one another my heart sinks. When someone looks at me, I feel like running away. When I suddenly come across someone I don't know, I become suspicious. I tremble when I see an acquaintance talking to a stranger. Can't stand crowds — I hate them. I can't trust anything. I feel a plot thickening round me. I know the net will slowly spread upto here. It will spread slowly. I will be caught. Then a hand will point its finger at me and say, "Here it is, here." That hand will not tickle my belly or claw at my throat. But I will die. I will go. I don't know where. There was peace in the house. I spent days lying low in my own house like a thief. My confident man, also hid like a thief with me. Everyone was sorry for us. We were almost wiped out, yet we somehow survived. But today he has come out of his shelter. He has dragged me out. I don't like crowds. I can't stand the eyes. I am afraid something will happen. Maybe even today. I shall spend every moment in restless watching. But my anxiety must not show. What will I do then? Oh, what will I do? Then I...that man...that hand...will dance. I shall watch the dance.

He looked like a hero then.

He had on a tight-fitting pair of shorts. His naked body had a slippery sheen. The dirty rag clinging to his loins seemed to float like oil on water.

Nitya had preened himself today. Had fluffed up his hair with soap. Had put a vermilion mark on his forehead. Round his neck and arms were luscious beads like bright, ripe berries. His chest glistened with the pride of smooth, slender leaves. Manly hair covered his thighs, also his legs. The whole body was a tumult of muscles and veins, all distended, intertwined. Nitya's eyes were glazed. His lips perpetually held the careless, absent-minded smile of the very obstinate.

Then the fire caught with a whoosh. It spread rapidly. A net fencing of fire. Nitya within the fence. Nitya has no hands. The net will wind round once, twice, three times, and shrink to a tiny fence. Nitya is dancing with flaming braziers on his head and in his teeth. He steps gently, lovingly, on the slippery mud.

And the sticks beat on the drums. The skin has been heated and tied taut. The kingfisher feathers adorning the drums seem to form a hero's canopy for a dark, dancing, sculpture in stone. Gleaming liquidly in the firelight. Clear and sharp are the notes of the gong. "Maa, Maa," calls the old priest in his cracked voice. The sacrificial goat cries out once in terror and falls to chewing the jackfruit leaves. And the dogs howl in unison and begin scratching the ground.

Durga was staring in silence at the fire. Fire in the heart of the earth. Fire in the heart of darkness. The flames, a vortex of a hundred hues. And smoke. The darkness shimmers, the flames shimmer, the smoke shimmers. Even the drumbeats have become one rapid shimmering sound.

I have not seen such fire for a long time. There is dance in Nityacharan's blood. No one thought he would dance this time. The one who spends the whole year hanging his head in shame and stupefaction, lives off his wife's earnings, is now standing tall as in bygone days. Everyone is gazing in admiration. And I find it horrible. It's revolting. In the firelight, I can see every stitch on his severed elbows. Has he no shame! He must have thought up some plot. I don't trust anything. What more is wanted? Ah, what do you want? Why has he made me sit like a joke in front of everybody, and gone off to dance? Is he suspicious? Suspicion! Is there? That day I...that day...I...that day...fire...much bigger, the whole house burnt down. They pushed my father in. Father was running from room to room. His hair, his beard caught fire. He pulled his dhoti off. All his life, my father went from village to village reciting tales from the *Puranas*. But no Puranic hero came speeding like the wind to save him. They didn't let my father out. And when the sky split open with the demonic scream from my father's sweet Purana versed throat, with the sound of bursting bamboos, with the sound of the Muslim call to prayer, they laid me in the open field lit by the burning house. My mother beside me. A hand began pinching my breast. Cinders from the house came flying into my eyes. I was feeling very hot, yet I shivered with cold.

"Maa, Maa," shouted the old priest again.

Startled, Durga looked at him. I have not called anybody mother for such a long time. Vaguely, she recalled where she was. Here, next to this cremation ground, this side of the river. My mother's gone, my father's gone, my country's gone. My mother did not receive her last fire. I have not called anyone mother for such a long time. What is the old priest shouting? Who will answer him? Does anyone? Does anyone ever? Then why did this happen to me? Why did this happen to me? Running away and living in the station, and then marriage to Nityacharan. They cleared the forests and settled the village by force. Houses came up. Capricious, forceful, the man strides about with his head held high, with a reckless air; even on this side of the river, he is not afraid of anything, or of anyone. Yet when living with him, I am half-dead with fear. I am terrified of that hand. I can see the hand clearly. A palm rough with cracked skin, blackened nails, swollen veins like sewer worms. Wants to destroy my new shelter. Wants to place me like a criminal before a pair of unclouded, trusting eyes. Fondles me and pinches my breast. So many nights I have clawed at Nityacharan's arm and screamed in my sleep. He has caressed me and calmed me down. Stubbornly, he would say, "Everything will be alright, here on this side, you will have everything again." He would console me like a mother. I haven't called anyone mother for such a long time.

"Maa, Maa," it was the old priest again. And suddenly the sound of drums faded a little. Then somebody threw in a bunch of jute-sticks. With superhuman dexterity, Nitya ignited the second fence. The fire caught and spread. Two fences burnt in concentric circles. Nitya is dancing at the centre. The sound of drums is gradually rising to a crescendo. Beating faster. The gong clanging loudly. And the sacrificial goat, suddenly frightened, has begun to call out. Shadows of the flames tremble in its eyes. And the monotonous cry of the goat enveloping Nityacharan's ghostly dance in that darkness, the image of Kali, the sound of drums, some human silhouettes and the sorcery of fire, have together created a brutal trap.

Who weeps softly in my ear? The man had a habit of striking his chest in times of passion. Who weeps softly in whispers? Wife, I can't go into the open street like this, armless, crippled. Nityacharan could not beat his chest that day. Wife, I'm stuck at home, and you go out to work! Could not beat his chest. Wife, what do you do till so late? Wife, why are you chewing paan? Wife, how come you get new saris? Wife, I know only you. Someone weeps softly, in whispers.

The sound became clearer. It has thundered across the far bridge. A goods train. Some lights in front, a fire in the engine room, a few people. Craning to look this way.

The dancing Nityacharan seemed to stare at the train in uncomprehending amazement. His feet speeded up, unknowingly. Unknowingly too, the drumbeat grew faster. Unconsciously every one was screaming "Maa, Maa," in chorus with the old priest. Thunderstruck, Durga watched the brazier fall from Nityacharan's head, as if he would shake off all superfluities in deep disdain. The roaring of the dogs drowns the goat's cries and rises with the wind. The train can be heard distinctly, as though Durga can just reach out and touch it. Little black stone-chips, planks of worn-out wood, shining rails. The wheels roll on. The nuts and bolts pound a metallic beat. The two rails shiver and shake. The train runs on. Two or three bundles of betel nuts were tied around his stomach, on his chest and back. They heard near the bridge that the train was going to be stopped midway for a search. All the stuff had to be carefully suspended under the bogeys of the moving train. The lines were shivering and shaking. The banks were shaking. The wheels, nuts and bolts pounded incessantly. And suddenly, abruptly, Nityacharan slipped. He fell between the lines, so he did not die. He tried to stop the train by pulling at it with his two bare hands. In fear, perhaps, or in defiance. The iron wheels bit off a wrist and a forearm. And now again that whisper, weeping in the ears. Why did this happen, wife, why did it happen? Who weeps? I've done no wrong. Who weeps, wife, wife, oh my wife! Then the sound of the train merged into the drumbeats like a sigh. Inexplicably, everyone moaned "Maa, Maa" again, fierce, yet somehow scared.

Then Nityacharan was dancing within two circles of fire. Sometimes the flames and smoke would screen him from view.

He treads on thick, slippery mud. Sweat pours from his body. The man who looked like a hero a while ago, now turns the heart cold. For his eyes are red and his mouth holds that defiant, ruthless smile. Looking at that naked, powerful body without arms, it suddenly seems as if a being from the *Puranas* has descended on this earth. Before him is a chariot of fire. The figure of Kali has pushed out her tongue in shame.

Somebody had thrown in more jute-sticks. Nityacharan lit the third fence. This time the flames sprang up in the mud. There are only about two or three spans left to dance in. The fire seems to come from Nityacharan's body. Some people groaned in fear. Some have risen in excitement. The old priest shouts, "Maa, Maa." But no one joins him this time. The scapegoat is straining desperately at the tethering rope. Its dry tongue lolls out. And the dogs are whining. Even the dogs are scared. Weeping.

Someone grips her neck hard. Raising dazed eyes, Durga saw it was the young daughter-in-law of a neighbouring house. She is unaware that she is holding Durga. Someone says in Durga's ear, "Witch." Durga looked slowly round as if waking from sleep. No one. Someone says, "For your sins." Someone says, "I die." Durga tries to reach out with both hands and seize the feet. Her hands lie inert on her lap like two dry leaves.

Even the drummers are dancing in frenzy. Sweat pours off marble bodies. The old priest starts dancing before the goddess. It looks as though the stranger in the men's row, who had been staring at her for a long time, is swaying his hips slowly and taking dancing steps in her direction. Durga saw that now all the men and women had begun to dance. And the flames are dancing in three circles. Red, yellow, purple. The smoke is dancing. Ash, brown, black. The smoke smothers the fire. It swells and grows. Becomes grey. The curtain in the hotel swells and grows. Becomes grey. A couple of chairs block the exits of the cubicle from the inside. The fan is spinning overhead. Yet she is feeling very hot. But shivering with cold. She sees the house burn in front of her eyes — her father running from room to room, unable to escape, hears the Muslim call to prayer, feels the cinders in her eyes. Then the sound of the train, the wheels rolling on the rails, the metallic pounding of the nuts and bolts, Nitya trying to stop the train with two hands, the cinders in her eyes. A radio is playing on the hotel counter. Then the hairy hand, without tenderness, tickled her throat, a ring on the finger. Durga tried desperately to squeeze her own throat with both hands and scream.

No one heard. On the tracks behind them, a train sped shrieking by, casting on the way an eerie pattern of light and darkness. Vulcan on the run. And the fire leaping in three fences. Nityacharan dances, the whole gathering dances. Even the drumbeats dance.

A shout comes from within the fences of fire:

"Wife?"

"What is it?"

"Come, let's die."

"Oh, no. Death scares me."

"So, what will we do?"

"Tell me."

"Live like this?"

"Yes, please. At least you will live."

"Will you live like this?"

"I don't know."

"Live like this?"

"Yes, please. At least we will live."

"O wife, will you live like this?"

"I can't go on."

"Then, what do you say?"

"I can't go on."

"Then what do you say?"

"I can't go on."

"Come let's die."

"I can't go on."

Durga went on murmuring brokenly, "I can't, I can't, I can't, I can't." Again somebody said in her ear, "Witch." Someone said, "For your sins." "Maa, Maa," cried the old priest. Many trembling voices joined him in fear, devotion, excitement. Nityacharan's eyes were like Kali's tongue. His body was bursting in sweat. His steps now fell at random on the mud. He would collapse any moment. He threw off the brazier in his mouth. Close to him burns the innermost fence. Fire in the mud, fire on the earth. Burning high. Leaping in a dance. Random steps in a dance of fire. He can collapse any moment now. The elbow stumps look strange. A weary, superhuman spirit, exhaustedly flapping its wings. And the mongrels have joined the scapegoat in a whining choric lament.

Durga saw the fire advancing like a twisting serpent. The three fences became one. The three worlds became one. And churning the flood of fire, someone arose and thundered, "I have come. I know. You cannot escape me." Durga knelt, mesmerized. Nityacharan could not be seen any more. Their settlement is burning. Then the chariot of fire speeds towards Calcutta. The curtain of the hotel-cabin where she works is burnt up. Like a cruel tyrant the fire began to burn up everything. A little boy fled crying, holding a doll in his hands. The fire spread. People ran panting towards the river. The river was as dry as a desert. The Padma was a dry desert. The fire pursues me. Where will I run? Cinders fly into my eyes. Durga feels very hot. Yet she shivers violently with cold. Inarticulately she says, "Who gave me such a heavy burden?" She says, "I did not want you to die, I never wanted that. Oh, how I long for life!"

Then Durga saw vividly, her destiny standing in the circle of fire. The foe she never could quite identify, but who had poisoned her every moment with fear, had invaded Nityacharan's body, and was beckoning Durga with his broken wing lifted high, "This way, this way, here is the place."

Original in Bengali.
Translated by Bhaswati Chakravorty.

S.H.VATSAYAN 'AJNEYA'

POST-BOX

There was no member of my own family with me in the refugee camp, but I did meet people who knew the whereabouts of each of them and could give me news about their safety. A man can endure the greatest of calamities if he can say, "No one dear to me suffered." I wrote many letters while I was in the camp — some to my own relatives and some to others who were anxious to learn about my fate. I addressed the envelopes, took stamps out of the pocket-diary and pasted them on the envelopes, and then left the camp to post them. It was a holiday, but I didn't have to buy anything at the post-office. I had noticed a post-box on my way to the camp and merely wanted to post my letters. I knew that the letters wouldn't be delivered immediately. The refugee camp was in a small town, and people in such towns are never in a hurry. It's only in large cities that people are anxious about getting things done quickly, with speed and with efficiency, because everyone there is busy, has work to do, and is convinced that his work is urgent and must be attended to at once.

When I reached the post-box, I discovered that the metal flap covering its slit had been so twisted that it was impossible to slide a letter through it with ease. Letters got caught in the slit. I succeeded in pushing my letters through it after folding and crumpling each one separately. As I was struggling to get them in one by one, I noticed that a small boy was watching me from a distance. I didn't pay him any particular attention, though I vaguely smiled at him. He reminded me of my own childhood, when I used to find post-boxes no less important than the Taj Mahal or the pyramids. A post-box, I thought, could perform magic — it could send a letter, which was dropped into it, to any destination, without moving from its place. And that particular post-box, which I was struggling with at that moment, must have seemed even stranger to the boy — it was so twisted that it was a freak amongst post-boxes. The boy must find, I thought, my struggle to put a letter through its slit, rather amusing.

After dropping the last letter into the box, I turned towards the boy and smiled at him once more. This time, I noticed that the expression on his face had changed — instead of looking curious and anxious, he seemed hopeful.

As I turned to leave, the boy took courage and asked me, "Where do the letters from that box go?"

I replied, "Everywhere. Where do you want to send your letter?"

"To my father."

"Yes, but where? Where does your father live?"

As I questioned him, I noticed that he was holding a crumpled post-card in his hand. I held out my hand and said, "Let me see..."

He hesitated for a moment and then gave me the post-card. I straightened out its creases and saw that, while there was something written on it in a large hand, it had no address. I laughed and said, "Come, you have to write the address on it also. What's the address?"

"I don't know — only my father could tell you," he said. I noticed that his lips had begun to tremble and that his eyes were filled with tears.

I asked him gently, "Where do you live?"

"Shekhupura..."

I understood the situation in a flash. I looked at him carefully. He was almost five years old. His face was bright and fair, though it was at that moment streaked with dirt; he wore an old shirt and a torn coat, but had nothing on below his waist; there were dry wounds on his bare legs and his feet were swollen. He was bare headed, his hair was brown and his eyes, which still had the innocence of childhood, seemed to be full of suffering.

"Veeranwali."

"Does your father live there?"

"No, he is no longer there..."

"With whom did you come here?"

"With a man."

"What's his name?"

"I don't know. I met him on the way."

I sat down in the verandah of the post-office, leaned against the railings and started talking to him. The boy's name was Roshan. He had left his home with his mother and his Chacha for Lahore. His father had accompanied them upto Shekhupura, but then had left them to go to another village to fetch Roshan's Bua and Phupha. Both of them were old and had no children of their own who were still alive — their two sons had been killed in the Eastern front during the war with the Japanese. His father had promised to meet them in Lahore.

On the way to Lahore, they had met up with other people who were also going there. As they were travelling, some people had opened fire on their group and killed a number of them. Roshan's Chacha had been amongst those who were killed. Others, who had survived that attack, hurried forward as fast as they could.

Though Roshan's father had agreed to join them at Lahore, the group the boy was with had decided not to head in that direction, for they had been told that the situation there was bad. On the second day, they were fired upon again and more of them had been killed. Later, they were attacked by a large group of men armed with lathis and axes. The men in Roshan's group had put up a stiff resistance and the fight had been fierce. But the attackers were greater in number and many people in Roshan's group had been killed. The men who had attacked them had abducted the women in the group. One of them had also tried to drag Roshan's mother away. His mother had screamed, but her abductor had tried to gag her by pressing her face hard against his shoulder. She had dug her teeth into his shoulder and had refused to let go, even though her assailant had tried to shake her off. After a struggle, he had finally managed to push her away from him, had thrown her down on the ground, and then smashed her face in with the blunt end of his axe. She had screamed. Roshan had shut his eyes, and when he opened them he had seen that her eyes, nose, jaws had been reduced to a bloody pulp. There was nothing left of her face. Yet the man, who had planted one foot on her chest, continued to hit her with his axe.

Some of the survivors in Roshan's group had grabbed his arm and dragged him away with them. They had run as fast as they could and had finally managed to shake off their attackers. The women who had fallen behind had been abducted. Eight or ten days later, Roshan had managed to reach Jullunder. Roshan was the only member of the group which had first set out from his village to reach safety. All the others were strangers to him. The one who had helped Roshan was in the same refugee camp as I was in. Roshan was unhappy in the camp and wanted to return to his father.

The boy wept as he had told me his story. I could have asked him a few more questions but did not feel the need to probe further. What he had told me was sufficient.

I said, "Roshan, I would advise you to go back to the camp and stay there. I'll broadcast your name and address over the radio. If your father hears it, he will write you a letter and then come to fetch you. Do you understand?" As I said that, I patted him on his back.

"And my letter. I want to send it to him."

I was startled.

"Yes, your letter..." What more could I have said? It would have been a sin to deceive a small child, so I added, "Why don't you send this card to your village in Shekhupura?"

"But my father isn't there..."

"He went to your Bua's place. Do you know the name of her village?"

"He went there to fetch her, not to stay with her."

"Yes, you are right," I said. The boy's logic was absolutely correct. What could I have told him? What address could I have asked him to write on the card? I thought a bit and said, "The post-office in your Bua's village will forward it to him."

"The post-office? How would the people there know my father's address? You don't know anything. Give back my letter..."

I wanted to say, "Yes, you are right, son. I don't know anything." But at that moment, I only mumbled, "Here..."

He took the card from my hand. I had carefully flattened it out, but he clutched it so hard in his hand that it got crumpled again. I got up and slowly walked away. As I was leaving, I noticed that his tears had dried and that confidence and infinite patience had returned to his face. It seemed as if he was certain that someone more knowledgeable would come to the post-office and tell him how to send his letter to his father.

Original in Hindi.
Translated by Alok Bhalla.

AMRIT RAI

FILTH

Everyone introduced himself quickly and efficiently — .

"I am Roopkishore Saxena. I practice law in Kanpur. Your conversation was so sweet and enticing that I couldn't resist joining you." (As if anyone needed an explanation or had asked for one!)

The second gentleman said, "My name is Harbans Singh (No, he didn't have a beard). I am the General Manager of Dayaram Batra's firm. At the moment, I am on my way to Calcutta to start a new business with a capital of one lakh."

The third gentleman said, "Oh, they call me Purushottam Das Khatri. I own a small shop in Delhi, in Connaught Place — a jewellery shop."

The fourth gentleman said, "I am Raman, S.S. Raman (No, he wasn't related to C.V. Raman — Roopkishore Sahib had already asked him about it...That doesn't mean that Roopkishore Sahib always says and does the wrong thing or that some things are wrong merely because Roopkishore Sahib does them!). I neither live in Delhi nor in Calcutta, rather I live in both Delhi and in Calcutta. In Delhi, I spend my life in a hotel...Sahib, Hotel Nirula is lousy and uncomfortable. Now you tell me, Harbans Bhai, why do they cook brinjal everyday? This is the season for peas and tomatoes."

Harbans, supporting him, said, "Whenever I ask them to buy tomatoes, they inform me that there are none available in the market."

Raman Sahib turned red with anger and said, "The bastards. Which market do they go to? I see nothing but tomatoes in Delhi these days...And then they charge you three hundred rupees a month...Swines!...My wife and children live in Calcutta. I told my boss clearly, I need fifteen days a month with my wife and children and if he can't give me leave then he can have my resignation."

Wheatish brown in colour, his face looked strangely unhealthy and tired; it was a cruel face like that of a constable's. On it there wasn't a trace of intelligence or freshness, it was hard and lifeless like a plank of wood. It was a clean-shaven face, pitted with marks of chicken-pox and small-pox (It is strange that small-pox marks can be seen more clearly on brown or fair skin, than on dark skin). His nose was like a blob. His thick lips were coloured red with betel-leaf juice — lips which were truly extra-ordinary. His chest was soft, loose and flaccid — it seemed to cling to his body like a big black worm. His mouth smelled of anise seeds. He had eaten a lot of anise seeds so that its pungent and aromatic smell could disguise the smell of cheap liquor (No, no, there's no mistake in the story. Don't make the mistake of believing that someone who travels by first-class only drinks Johnny Walker or White Horse!). But the result was quite disgusting, for his mouth now stank of liquor and anise together.

"Roopkishore Saxena. I practice law in Kanpur." I don't know if this information is sufficient for you to draw a clear picture of the man in your mind. For me, however, it was enough to identify the man named Roopkishore Saxena out of the lakhs who live in Kanpur. This wasn't because I met him the day I travelled by Toofan Mail from Tundla to Kanpur. I would have recognized him even if I hadn't seen him earlier. That is why when he introduced himself, I didn't feel as if I was meeting a stranger, but as if I had known a man named Roopkishore Saxena, the lawyer, for decades; as if he couldn't have had any other name than Roopkishore Saxena; as if the man who sat before me had to be Roopkishore Saxena and couldn't have been any other person!

Roopkishore Saxena, the lawyer from Kanpur, wore a woollen Gandhi cap on his head. The top half of his body was covered by a coat with four pockets and the lower half by a loose pair of trousers with stripes which were about as thick as an earthworm. It seemed as if a lizard had decided to put on trousers, stand up on two legs and start walking!

There is nothing much to say about the other two, except that their faces were fair, clean and polished like marble.

One can't say anything bad about these people. In fact, they are the cultured and the civilized people of society. They wear good clothes (some people don't have the decency to do even that much!) and are never seen in public without a well-cut suit; like to smoke cigars and cigarettes (now look at Mr. Raman, he even keeps a box of Burma cheroots with him); pay their respects to all the big and small officers; serve vegetarian and non-vegetarian food at home; travel only by first-class; give expensive silk and cotton clothes to their wives, present them with gorgeous (if artificial) pearls and diamonds, and take them for a stroll down Connaught Place or Hazrat Ganj or Chowrangi or Colaba; and speak at great length on all matters of State and society. Indeed, they are in every way, respectable citizens of society. You can't point a finger at them about anything. They say that when they hear news of violent riots or killings they are genuinely upset (some even faint!). They never do a single thing (good or bad) which goes against the existing values and customs of society.

Its another matter that in the privacy of their homes, they torment their wives, stare lustfully at the wives of other people, tell each other such filthy jokes that even a horse-cart driver would stop his ears with his hands in embarrassment, and that when they are with people of their own kind, they don't mind vomiting out all the dirt that is inside them. Of course, when it suits them they keep their lips sealed, don't utter a word more than is required for the occasion, and grimace when someone else uses dirty words in public as if to say that they have never been touched by the breath of such words. When these great souls open their hearts, however, they infect everything around them with all that is foul and stinking.

When the curtain was first raised on the scene to be described here, Babu Roopkishore Saxena (the lawyer from Kanpur) was sitting apart from everyone. The conversation between Raman, Harbans Singh and Purushottam Das Khatri, however, was so alluring, that Babu Roopkishore had to take part in it. Like a drunkard who passes a bar and can't resist entering it, Babu Roopkishore could never resist joining a good conversation.

They weren't really talking about anything in particular. The three of them already knew each other. They lived in the same hotel and were talking about old and familiar things — complaining about the food and describing a friend who was loyal and decent, who knew how to fulfill the obligations of friendship, who never hesitated to offer help, but who had one failing — he couldn't resist women. As Harbans put it, "Women were his weakness." Since he wasn't greedy for money, he couldn't be bribed. But if he saw a woman, he couldn't help running after her, just as a bird-trapper follows a beautiful bird from tree to tree with his basket or a hunter tracks a deer through the forest with his gun. It was as if the sight of a woman kindled the same passion in Harban's friend as the sight of a deer did in a hunter...He had to stalk every beautiful woman he saw for she was the only true inhabitant of the forest of his soul.

Harbans was narrating tales of his friend's adventures with great enthusiasm to his companions — telling them how he had once, despite the watchman's attempts, barged into his friend's office and found him with his anglo-Indian stenographer...

Everyone cackled with delight: each of them saw in those stories reflections of his own naked desires. Now they could participate in the pleasures of a sinful life and yet take conscious and legitimate pride in leading lives which were spotlessly clean. At that moment, they thought that both were possible. Sometimes Raman or Khatri would dig for more scandalous information from Harbans, at other times, Harbans would not only provide them with juicy details himself but would also regale them with more stories about his friend.

The delectable gossip session went on for a long time. At first Babu Roopkishore, who had joined them, was slightly reserved because he wanted to appear to be respectable, but there finally came a moment when he couldn't stop himself from taking part in the playful and mischievous conversation!

The story about Harban's friend and the anglo-Indian steno reminded Babu Roopkishore of a young mill-owner who refused to employ male stenographers, and who always fired his female stenos every month so that he could invite women for interviews to his office.

Each of the wise and decent listeners sighed at the same time with longing and envy: Alas, if only we too could do that!

Khatri said, "I am sure they got a lot of typing done!"

Roopkishore at once caught Khatri's meaning and said, "Yes, in a day at least one letter got typed. The entire day was spent in discussing whether one should say 'We beg to acknowledge receipt of your letter dated...'or 'Your letter dated — was duly received...'!"

And then, following in the footsteps of Harbans, Babu Roopkishore told them, with all the savouriness of detail and the delicacy of gesture, the story of the time when he went to visit the young mill-owner at his office (no one dared to stop him because he was one of the consultants of the company!) and saw him sitting close to his steno and "dictating" a very important letter to her!

This anecdote was received with great enthusiasm by everyone. They all cackled again with pleasure and surprise, asked for more details and challenged him to take them further and further into the private life of the mill-owner.

They liked Babu Roopkishore's story so much, that they unleashed a flood of their own stories...

Somehow, without anyone becoming aware of it, the conversation drifted towards the riots in Punjab. They started telling stories about women who had been abducted and the atrocities that had been committed. These stories are always so scandalous that, even if listeners have never been affected by riots, they always listen to them with pleasurable attention. The riots merely added to the fascination of the stories a thousand fold. Whereas earlier, only a few girls used to be kidnapped, and there were only a few incidents of brutalities, now more than a lakh of women had been abducted and the incidents of barbarities were so many, that it was difficult to keep count of them. Also, whereas in the past, only Muslim goondas had been courageous enough to do such deeds, now even the Hindus and the Sikhs had a hand in them, and had proved to the Muslims that they were not only as brave as they were, but were even greater goondas!

Lakhs of men had died, lakhs of children had been orphaned, lakhs of women had lost their homes and honour. Now all that remained were their stories, stories which were told and heard by people as they smacked their lips with an epicurean's delight.

Suddenly, Babu Roopkishore asked a question which so stunned everybody, that it seemed as if they had been struck by a brick. "Do you trust the Muslims?" he asked.

Harbans said, "These days they seem to be devout followers of Gandhiji and Pundit Nehru. Almost everyday someone makes a statement of loyalty."

Roopkishore mocked him and said, "One can't believe those statements. A dying man will say anything."

Harbans tried to defend himself, but without much conviction, "Even then..."

Roopkishore laughed knowingly and said, "No, Bhai, I can't swallow any of those statements."

Then he said a bit loudly, as if he wanted to underscore the importance of each word, "I am convinced, beyond a shadow of a doubt, that a Muslim can never be a true supporter of Hindustan..."

Purushottam Khatri, who had been quietly following the drift of the conversation, said, "Then the swine will get killed!...Do you know what we did in Delhi?"

Everyone waited with baited breath for Khatri to inform them. After being silent for about thirty seconds so that the gravity of his words could properly sink in, Khatri proclaimed loudly, as if he was the voice of prophecy from the skies, "No Muslim will ever dare to show his face in Delhi again — You can now see a Muslim only around Jama Masjid where he sits hiding in his small cell, pale and wizened with fear..."

Then, like a clever story-teller, Khatri paused for another thirty seconds, and when he was convinced that he had cast his spell over his listeners, especially on Babu Roopkishore, he added, "Now when a Muslim comes across a Sikh even his bones begin to tremble."

Harbans Singh took this as a commendation of his entire race and, feeling puffed up with pride, said, "The truth is that what we did in western Punjab was equally wonderful. We didn't allow the newspapers to publish the entire story. But people are convinced that the ratio was three is to two —."

Babu Roopkishore, who didn't understand the meaning of mathematical language, asked, "What does that mean?"

By now Khatri was convinced that Roopkishore was really a naive man who wasn't even aware of the progress society had made. Roopkishore was old fashioned enough, he thought, to believe that a Muslim still thought of himself as some kind of Maar Khan and believed that the Hindu was a hopeless coward. The times have changed, he wanted to say. Now the Muslim gets tit for tat.

But, at that moment, Harbans cut in and said, "Three Muslims for two Hindus."

Astonished, Roopkishore exclaimed, "Really?" He stared with wide-eyed wonder at the messenger of the Gods who had brought such exciting news! He felt a strange sense of peace and happiness race through his body! He was so ecstatic that it is surprising he didn't swoon in a fit. But he controlled himself and asked, with a touch of suspicion still in his voice, "It is too good to be true. Can I really believe that in Punjab more Mussalleys have been killed than Hindus!"

Because he wasn't sure if the news was correct, his voice had dropped to a whisper and trembled with emotion.

Khatri said, "Why are you so surprised? The Hindus are surely no longer inferior to anyone in anything, indeed they are superior. I can only tell you about Delhi. In Delhi, where their ancestors had ruled for eight hundred years, the Muslims were roundly thrashed. When you come to Delhi, I'll show you around."

Those stories robbed Babu Roopkishore of his voice. They warmed the cockles of his heart. He was besides himself with joy.

After sometime, Babu Roopkishore asked, as if he was seriously considering the twists and turns history could have taken, "That means if Gandhiji hadn't stopped the riots, then..."

Harbans cut in and said, "Not one bloody Muslim would have escaped alive, each one would have been sent to his grave here." Then, he smiled.

Khatri said, as if trying to plead, "But the Congress and Gandhiji have to worry about world opinion also. Gandhiji and Pundit Jawaharlal Nehru are more intelligent than either of us. We are only concerned about our religion, they have to make sure that Hindustan doesn't get a bad name in the world — . "

At this, Roopkishore said dramatically, "If only they were as concerned about what the malichas did to our wives and daughters as they were concerned about world opinion..."

Khatri intervened and said, "You can be sure that they are concerned...If you consider the matter carefully, you'll realize that the Indian Union isn't less aware of all this than Pakistan. The only difference is that here everything is done in a diplomatic manner, so that when the snake is killed the stick does not break!"

As Khatri said this, he winked at all those who were watching him.

At once, everyone understood what he had said. These people, equipped with prophetic vision, now understood the secret meaning of all those appeals for peace which Gandhiji and Pundit Nehru had made!

Roopkishore was now puzzled only by the fact that it had taken him such a long time to understand something so simple.

Harbans felt that he had been insulted and was still smouldering with anger. He had been deeply hurt by Roopkishore's words. He was sure that the talk about how the Muslims had dishonoured the wives and daughters of the Hindus and the Sikhs, had been aimed at him, Harbans Singh, to humiliate him — .

"Chee, shame on your manhood! And you call yourself a Sikh. Look at what the Muslims did to our wives and daughters and you couldn't do a thing! Chee, chee, you call yourself a man!"

At last Harbans said, as if he needed to defend himself against unjust accusations, "It's not that we didn't do our share of things, Mr. Roopkishore. It's a different matter that what we did wasn't publicized!"

Then Harbans told them softly, in whispers, passionate stories about Muslim women who had been abducted in west Punjab...He told them about how they had been kidnapped, how they had been kept, fifteen or twenty together, in a house, how many had been sent to brothels; he told them about the beauty and grace of these women, about how they had been set upon by groups of Hindus and Sikhs; he told them how the heads of those women who had protested had been separated from their bodies, and how even those who had quietly submitted their youthful bodies had finally been sent to Hell...

The eyes of the story-teller and his listeners glowed with infernal light!

It's being rumoured, that there will be a new animal in the Calcutta Zoo next year. The newspapers haven't yet published the details about its shape or colour, but I have a feeling that I have seen it somewhere.

Original in Hindi.
Translated by Alok Bhalla.

BHISHAM SAHNI

PALI

1

Life goes on and on. Its ends never meet. Neither in the mundane world of realities nor in fiction. We drag on drearily in the hope that some day these ends would meet. And sometimes we have the illusion that the ends have really met.

Manohar Lal and his wife had also lived under a similar illusion once. They believed that a great calamity had at last passed over their heads. That the knots that had formed in their lives had been disentangled. But knots of life never get fully unravelled even in stories, much less in one's life. No sooner is one knot removed than another knot forms in its place. The story thus never comes to an end. It is a great thing that life still goes on. It maintains its continuity though it assumes a new shape at every turn and confronts us with a new question mark at every step.

One end of Manohar Lal's and his family's life was left behind in a small town distantly situated across the border of Pakistan, a country newly carved out at the time of the Partition of the country. With their meagre belongings, the little that they could carry, Manohar Lal and his family had also joined the caravan of the countless uprooted people heading for India. The dust raised by their feet hung like a haze in the atmosphere. Like a big river forming into many channels on its onward sweep towards the sea, this vast concourse of unfortunate humanity also proceeded towards the boundary line demarcating the two countries.

Manohar Lal, his wife and two children — a little girl in her mother's arms and Pali, a boy of four, holding his father's finger — trudged along, carrying their bundles over their heads, their weary eyes searching their way through the haze, their ears perked for any stray remark that might guide them onto the correct path. They were anxious to know the lay of the land and, more than that, what was in store for them.

On the last day, the refugee camp had started emptying out. Carrying their belongings on their heads the refugees left the camp and proceeded towards the convoy of lorries, ranged one after the other along the road, which would carry them to the border. Holding his son's finger and carrying a heavy bundle over his head, Manohar Lal went towards the lorries, his wife, Kaushalya following him close at his heels, her baby daughter nestled in her arms. Like her husband, she also carried a big bundle over her head. The refugees were frantically throwing their things into the lorries and storming their way into the vehicles, some of them wriggling in through the windows. Manohar Lal was struggling to push his way towards the entrance when he suddenly realised that his son, Pali, was not holding his finger. Kaushalya had already managed to enter the lorry. Manohar Lal showed no alarm, thinking that the child must be somewhere around. The sensation of the child's grip still lingered on his hand. Everybody was pushing forward madly from behind. There was a babble of sounds and the crowd got more and more frantic with the passing of every moment. The camp managers shouted at the top of their voices, urging the passengers to hurry up and get into the lorries. They must cross the border before nightfall.

When Manohar Lal failed to find Pali around, he really got anxious. He rushed back crying, "Pali! Pali!" but failed to get any response. Getting alarmed, he raised his voice. His son's name "Pali" rang in the air above the pervading din. Then he started running aimlessly alongside the lorries. The lorries had started leaving one by one. The lorry in which his wife was standing with her suckling child was jam-packed and its horn was blowing insistently, warning the people that it was ready to start. Manohar Lal's throat had gone dry shouting "Pali! Pali!" His legs shook and his head reeled. Such was the irony of the situation for this homeless man — he was shouting for his son on a road crowded with people, and yet it appeared as if he were shouting in a desert.

He was still searching for Pali when the lorry started moving. His wife's anxious eyes were fixed on her husband in the crowd and, to her horror, he suddenly disappeared from her view. Alarmed, she started wailing. Locks of hair tumbled over her face, blinding her for a moment, and her child nearly slipped from her arms. She breathed heavily, her chest working like bellows.

"Stop! Stop! Hai, stop the lorry!"

But nobody listened to her. All of them had their own worries to contend with. They were all shouting and crying. Hers was not the only family being driven from its home. There were many who had managed to load only half of their luggage onto the lorry, and had to leave the the other half scattered on the road. An old woman, apparently a grandmother, was having difficulty in climbing into the moving lorry. She was being pushed from all sides, and struggled to keep her foot on the footboard. As the lorry moved forward, Kaushalya's eyes went wide with horror. In a daze, she searched for only one image in the crowd — her husband. Then she burst out crying, her plight was like that of a bird whose nest was being destroyed before its very eyes.

She heard someone shouting, "Stop the lorry! Stop the lorry!" Other voices joined the cry. The lorry slowed down.

Who can say whether it is the situation that decides or it is man himself who is the deciding factor? It could even be Fate taking a hand. Events take place and life's problems peep through them and mock at us. Kaushalya had even thrown out one of her bundles and was going to hand down her wailing child to a man standing on the road when she saw Manohar Lal running up. But their son was not with him. God only knew which whirlpool had sucked in poor Pali.

Manohar Lal heard some voices being directed towards his wife: "The child must be somewhere here." The people gestured to Manohar Lal to come nearer. "Get in, get in!" they advised him. "He must have got onto some other lorry." There were other voices, loaded with venom and irritation, "Will the lorry keep waiting for your child? If you want to search for your child, you'd better get down from the lorry." The people had suddenly become callous. If they had not seen Manohar Lal running up, perhaps Kaushalya would have got down from the lorry, wailing and they would have thrown her luggage out after her. They were right. They must get across the border before nightfall. So many lives were at stake. Surely, the lorry could not keep waiting for one child.

The hearts of the refugees had dried of all sentiments. The same Pali had once got lost and the whole mohalla had gone out in search of him. And here someone kept crying repeatedly, "Get down, you! If you want to search for your child, get down and let us proceed!"

2

The husband and wife could not decide whether to get down from the lorry or proceed in it. Having failed to find any trace of Pali, Manohar Lal and Kaushalya kept looking out onto the road. Slowly the town was left behind and the noise abated. Only Kaushalya kept wailing. The trees, the fields full of greenery, swept past their gaze. Pali, lost somewhere in the crowded small town, receded from his parents. Kaushalya's wailing slowly changed into a whimper. The mental anguish of the passengers expressed itself in the moans of the insane and then changed into heart-rending cries before petering out in anguished silence. The lorries moved on lurching from side to side. Slowly the morning haze cleared up. Looking up at the vast expanse of the impassive sky where one or two stars were still winking at him, Manohar Lal tried to console his wife. "We may yet find him," he said. "He can't get lost like this. Some kindly soul must have taken charge of him and pushed him into some other lorry." He looked at Kaushalya's abstracted gaze and, seeing the grief on her face, he said in utter desperation, "What can we do if we don't find him? God has been benign enough to spare a child for us. We must be thankful to him for that. You know Lekhraj's three children were killed before his very eyes. It's God's will. We must resign ourselves to it."

Kaushalya's empty eyes were still glued to the road. There was nothing strange about losing a child under these circumstances. There was no sense in creating such a hubbub over it. As time passed the uprooted passengers fell to talking with one another. The women also followed their men's example. Here and there they could also hear the sound of laughter.

The evening shadows lengthened as they neared the border. The convoy stopped for a short while at one point. Manohar Lal got down promptly from his lorry and ran past the lined-up lorries, shouting, "Pali! Pali!" He peeped into all the lorries through the windows but he got no response from any lorry. His voice seemed to be echoing back from the wilderness. He could not find Pali anywhere.

On reaching the border the refugees were transferred to other lorries which were parked there to receive them. The lorries raced through the darkness towards Amritsar. The sky, studded with myriads of stars, looked mysterious. Overwhelmed by the immensity of the situation, the refugees had become very quiet and some of them had started dozing to the rhythmic jolts of the lorries. There were others who just sat there staring at nothing. Manohar Lal's wife had again started crying; her incoherent weeping made people think that she was going mad. Then her crying changed into moans and the onlookers felt reassured that she was not yet mad. She must indeed be missing her child very much. At last she rested her head against Manohar Lal's shoulder and fell asleep. Manohar Lal silently resolved that if he failed to find Pali, he would go back to his old town in Pakistan and, following up certain clues, try to locate him and bring him back home.

The convoy tore through the darkness on its way to Amritsar. Everyone was too absorbed in himself to think of what lay in store for him. Perhaps their minds had stopped thinking. Fate had thrown a black curtain across their eyes so that they could not even discern a ray of hope through it. There was only the jolting of the lorries and weariness. Their eyes had become glazed and their throats were parched and above them were myriads of twinkling stars which seemed to mock at them.

That night, after crying for hours when Pali fell asleep at last, his head resting against Zenab's bosom, his sobs slowly dissolved in a sea of affection. A woman's bosom is the greatest shield against man's afflictions and the greatest source of love and affection. Zenab had, it seemed, made a citadel of love for the child. For the first time in her life, Zenab was overwhelmed by a sense of joy which only a woman bereft of a child can experience. A tiny delicate body was clinging to her, as if the child was specially made to fit into the contours of her body.

Her heart swelled up with maternal feeling. "Why don't you speak?" she asked the child.

Shakur, who had been lying in the courtyard on a cot adjacent to Zenab's, kept gazing at the sky sprinkled with millions of stars. It reminded him of Zenab's deep blue chunri in which she had first come to his house as a bride. Her chunri had glittered like stars. As he looked at her face glowing from behind her chunri, Shakur had felt as if the sun had descended into his courtyard.

Shakur made a living by selling chinaware. Carrying a big basket loaded with cups, saucers, plates and pots over his head, he would go from lane to lane and from street to street hawking his wares, waving a thin cane stick over his basket. He had been doing it for years together. Late that afternoon, as the evening came down upon the small town, he had chanced upon a small boy who had been thrown to his side by the ebb and tide of the crowd. He was standing at the corner of the lane crying, "Pitaji! Pitaji!"

Shakur had stopped on seeing the small boy. Then he had sat down by the boy's side and uttered soothing words to him. He had wiped the child's tears with the end of his kurta and the child stopped crying. "Come, I'll take you to your father," Shakur had said. "But where's your father?" Holding the child's hand, Shakur had taken him to the place from where the convoy of lorries carrying the refugees had departed. The lorries had left long ago and even the dust raised by them had long since settled down. The refugee camp was lying deserted. In the darkness of the night, when Shakur climbed the steps to his house, Pali was fast asleep, his head resting against Shakur's shoulder.

3

Shakur was a god-fearing man. When the rioting started in the town, he kept himself aloof from the trouble-makers. When the grain market was set on fire and there were stray cases of stabbing in the streets, Shakur had remarked, "It is God's anger visiting us." He would repeat this remark every time there was a violent occurrence.

"Why are you silent?" Shakur asked his wife.

"What's there to say?" Zenab said in a lazy voice, which trailed into silence. She was enjoying the feel of the child's small body. She felt for a moment as if all the obstructions in her path had disappeared and her body was getting lighter. But she did not want to tell her husband that she had come upon a precious boon. Even the touch of that small unknown child as he clung to her had sent a thrill through her body.

"All the Hindus and Sikhs have left their houses," Shakur said. "They have gone for good. The camp is empty. Now nobody will venture this way."

Zenab gave no reply. The child mumbled in his sleep, heaved a deep sigh and, resting his head upon Zenab's bosom, again fell asleep.

Zenab looked up at the sky. It was looking resplendent as if auguring her good fortune. As if echoing Shakur's thoughts, she said, "Leave him where you have picked him up from, lest some unfortunate curse falls upon us."

"Why should any curse fall upon us? We are giving the child shelter," Shakur mumbled. "Even if we deliver him to the police station, they can't restore him to his parents."

They were trying to read each other's minds.

"What's his name?" Zenab asked rubbing her cheek against the child's cheek.

"How do I know? When I asked him he said 'Pali, Pali'."

"These Hindus have such queer names. What a funny name! Pali! If I had a son I would have named him Altaf."

They lay silent for a long time lost in their own thoughts. If nobody came to claim the child, he would become hers. A child prancing about in her courtyard. She hoped nobody would turn up to enquire. The tailor, Mahmud, had kept a Hindu woman in his house and no one had bothered to investigate. Mir Zaman had ransacked the Hindu tailoring shop next to his and had kept the stolen things in his shop for all to see. Nobody had taken him to task for it. And as for her, she was only giving refuge to a child — a lost child whom her husband had picked up, on finding him crying in the street. What was wrong with it? But Shakur's mind was sometimes filled with fear.

On waking up the next morning, when the child found himself among strangers he again started crying and repeating "Pitaji, Pitaji!" Zenab put a bowl of milk against his lips and kept fondling his head and caressing his back. But little Pali would not stop crying and broke into hiccups. Zenab's eyes went to the door lest someone should hear the child crying and force his way into her house. Yes, the child was there all right, but all said and done it was a stolen child. What if someone got wind of it? She must keep the child hidden from prying eyes for some days.

Pali stopped crying at last. Now he sat in a corner, maintaining a grim silence and emptily staring this way and that. He kept sighing and Zenab sometimes felt that with the coming of the child, she had herself become rootless.

Shakur had thought that within a day or two, after becoming familiar with his environment, the child would start feeling at home. But he still had his misgivings. One never knew. His parents may be knocking about in search of their child and may track him down to this house. There were still a large number of refugees who had yet to migrate. He feared that the police may come to know about the lost child and that they may create serious trouble for him.

4

The first two days were nothing short of an ordeal. On the third day, the child became a little communicative. He saw a white cat sitting on the wall of the courtyard and beamed at it. The cat jumped down and sat down on the floor. The child ran towards it crying, "A cat! A cat!" Zenab felt so happy.

There was a knock on the door. It sounded loud and ominous. Zenab and Shakur looked towards the door in alarm, their hearts pounding hard.

"They have come!" Zenab said apprehensively. "The people to whom the child belongs!" Fear streaked across her eyes.

"Could be the people from the police station!" Shakur said, his fear mounting moment by moment.

Another powerful blow. It was like a heavy lathi crashing against the door. "Open the door!" A voice invaded the house from across the door.

As Shakur proceeded to open the door, Zenab hurriedly moved into the inner room with the child.

It was neither the police havaldar on the other side of the door nor the child's parents. It was the bearded maulvi of the neighbouring mosque standing there, holding a thick lathi. There were two men standing behind him, both armed with lathis.

"Is there a kafir's child in here?" The maulvi barked, stepping into the courtyard. "Who has brought him here?" The two men wielding lathis had also followed the maulvi into the courtyard.

"Are you hiding some other kafir also in your house?"

Shakur ran in and hurriedly returned carrying a murba.

"I swear by the *Holy Koran* we are not hiding any kafir in our house," Shakur said. "We have only given shelter to an orphan boy."

"Where's that orphan?"

"Ji, he's sleeping inside."

The maulvi cast a suspicious look at Shakur and then tapped the floor sharply with his lathi.

"Produce him before me! I want to see him."

Zenab came out carrying Pali in her arms.

"So you are giving refuge to a kafir's child?"

"I've adopted the child, Maulvi Sahib. It's no sin to adopt a child," Zenab said in a firm steady voice.

"Have you had him circumcised? Has he read the kalma?"

New life surged back into Zenab. The maulvi had not come to snatch away the child from her. He had come only to make him a Musallman. Zenab stood silent before the maulvi.

"Why don't you speak? You give a kafir's polluted child a place in your lap. You give him your breast to suckle. Do you want to nurture a snake?"

The maulvi's argument had driven Zenab against the wall. No, she couldn't refute his argument. Why hadn't she thought of it before? But she had found nothing polluted about the boy nor did he look like the young one of a serpent. She was going to speak when the maulvi banged his lathi on the ground and said, "Bring this kafir's son to the holy mosque. Early tomorrow morning. Or you must be prepared to face serious consequences!"

The maulvi dramatically took a full turn and walked off towards the door. As soon as the maulvi had gone Zenab tossed her head happily and smiled. All that the maulvi wanted was that the boy should say the kalma and be circumcised. Why wait till tomorrow? She was prepared to do it right now. What was there to fear? He had not threatened to take away the child from her. He had not even hinted at it.

The circumcision was performed the very next morning. Little Pali was terrified at the sight of the razor and clung to Zenab's legs.

The circumcision done, the maulvi petted and consoled little Pali ignoring the fact that all the time the child had kept uttering "Pitaji! Pitaji!" in great agony. The maulvi did not mind it at all. He just smiled indulgently. The neighbours came and felicitated Shakur and Zenab.

The maulvi gave the boy the gift of a red rumi cap with a black tassel and himself placed it on the boy's head. Zenab gave him a brand new white muslin kurta to wear and helped him to put it on then and there. The maulvi then lifted the boy and placed him in Zenab's arms.

"Take him!" the maulvi said happily, "He's your own child, not a kafir's. He belongs to the whole community."

The child was renamed Altaf — from Pali to Altaf. Carrying Altaf in her arms, Zenab went around distributing sweets in the mohalla.

Gradually the child took to his new ways. Within a year little Pali, now crockery-seller Shakur Ahmed's son, Altaf Husain, became a familiar figure in the area. Now he played in his courtyard hawking chinaware, aping his father's drawn-out lusty cry. He would collect all the utensils from the kitchen and put them in a basket which he carried on his head and trot round the courtyard announcing like his father, the articles he had to offer for sale.

When the month of Ramzan came, he would plant himself in the middle of his courtyard and proclaim to the beat of an empty tin canister, "Get up, you pious Muslims! Wake up from your sleep! Keep your holy fast!"

Shakur and Zenab lost no time in putting Altaf in the school attached to the local mosque where, sitting on the brick platform outside the mosque, he memorized the *Koran* along with the other boys, swaying his back rhythmically in consonance with the lines from the holy book. Zenab and Shakur's lives started revolving around a new orbit with Altaf as its focal point. They wove their dreams around Altaf. One day Shakur would stop going around, hawking his wares from door to door. Instead he would set up a regular shop where father and son would sit together conducting sales. They would not be at the mercy of others. They would be their own masters and sleep peacefully with not a care in the world. Zenab eagerly looked forward to the day when Altaf's bride would set foot in her house, wearing ceremonial ankle bells.

Two years passed happily in this manner. One day the chinaware seller was not at home and little Altaf was at school. Only Zenab was at home. Sitting behind the tarpaulin curtain, she was grinding wheat.

There was a knock at the door. "My man is not at home," she replied from where she was sitting. "Come in the evening."

After a pause a voice said, "There's a court summons in Shakur Ahmed's name. He has been asked to report at the police station."

Zenab stopped grinding the wheat. Adjusting her pallu over her head she came and stood behind the tarpaulin curtain. A tremor of fear ran through her spine. "What's the matter, ji?" she asked.

"Send him to the police-station tomorrow morning. It's urgent."

"What for, ji?" Zenab asked in a tremulous voice.

"They have come from Hindustan to claim the child. There is a letter to that effect."

Zenab again trembled from head to foot.

"Send him to the police station tomorrow morning," the man repeated. "Don't forget."

She heard the man's retreating steps from behind the curtain.

5

There are some wounds which heal with the passage of time, leaving a mark on the mind. But there are certain griefs which slowly eat into the heart like termites, completely ravaging the body. There is nothing a man can do about it. When Kaushalya reached India with her husband, her lap was bereft of a child.

That day if the convoy of lorries had safely reached the border and Manohar Lal had gone across it with his wife and child, they would have forgotten about Pali's separation from them as time passed. But, unfortunately, it did not happen like that. They had just crossed the city limits when something untoward happened. The convoy was passing along the road when a mob suddenly emerged from the fields flanking the road, raising war cries. Rushing up, they blocked the road. They wore masks and brandished swords and spears and shouted filthy abuse. Most of the lorries had already passed but the last three could not escape the attention of the marauders. Those in the lorries heard the same heart-chilling sounds of the brandishing of swords and spears, which Manohar Lal and Kaushalya had heard back in the town from where they were escaping. Kaushalya did not even know when she felt a heavy jolt and fell down. She only heard Manohar Lal's voice, "Here, give me the child." Then that sound also faded as she got another powerful push from behind, which sent her crashing to the floor of the lorry. When she regained her senses she heard whistles blowing all around her in the darkness, to the accompaniment of groans behind her. She felt something clammy on the floor under her hand. It could have been water, it could as well have been blood. The lorry suddenly started and, as she looked out, she felt as if the stars were also moving with the lorry. Her throat was parched and she felt desperately in need of water. Then the stars started revolving and she passed out.

6

Even on reaching Delhi, Manohar Lal could not get over the feeling that he was still lying crushed under a heap of dead bodies. He feared that if he could not extricate himself from under this heap, he would die under the weight of these dead bodies. While foot-slogging on the roads of Delhi along with his wife, bemoaning the loss of his children, he realised that if he did not turn his face against the calamities of the past he would perish on these very roads of Delhi. He hired a push-cart and set up shop on it in one of the bazaars of Delhi. When he returned home, late at night, tired and weary, and found his wife moaning as if she was on the verge of insanity, his courage would desert him. What if she really went mad? How would he take care of her with so many other problems on hand? The small spark of life that was still left in him would also be extinguished.

Taking her hand in his own, Manohar Lal assured Kaushalya that it was not too late for them to have another child. But at the mention of children her condition would worsen; she would start trembling and sometimes she wailed in such a heart-rending manner that even Manohar Lal got jittery.

The government had set up big establishments to trace abducted women and lost children and retrieve stolen goods. Government officials made frequent trips to Pakistan in this connection. Manohar Lal took time off from his work to visit these government offices and meet influential people in order to seek their help in tracing his child. But he was just a nobody and no one took much notice of him. Month after month passed but he found no lead. It was not easy to trace a lost child in a town swarming with people. When he had begun the job, he had hoped that he had only to visit the town and identify the particular spot where Pali had got separated from him. He would find Pali at the beginning of some lane looking eagerly out for his father. He would immediately pick up the child in his arms and on returning to Delhi, put him in Kaushalya's lap.

What vain hopes! Things were just the reverse of what he had thought. Much less pick up a thread out of a tangled mass and go where it led him, he didn't even know where the thread was and where to start. For two full years, Manohar Lal's case kept hanging in the air. Then he was allowed to accompany rescue parties consisting of government officials and social workers that visited Pakistan from time to time. Manohar Lal would pick up his metal tin trunk and join them. But every time he returned pulling his hair in despair.

Two years later, he at last got a definite clue to his son's whereabouts. He learnt that the boy was living in his erstwhile hometown with one Shakur Ahmed who owned a chinaware shop. This time Manohar Lal was quite sanguine that his trip would not prove abortive.

The first time the havaldar came with the summons for Shakur, Zenab felt greatly upset, her condition being like that of a fish that had been thrown out of water. Her dreams were crumbling before her very eyes.

When Shakur came in the evening, his face turned pale on hearing the news. The news soon went round the mohalla and many sympathizers dropped in to console Shakur. The maulvi also came tapping his lathi on the ground.

"You need have no fears," the maulvi said. "How dare they touch the child? Now he has accepted Islam. We won't let him fall in the hands of kafirs."

Maulvi Sahib's words revived Zenab's drooping spirits. He was right. Now he was not the same child who had slept in

Zenab's arms on the first night of his arrival in her house. If someone had come to claim him at that time, she wouldn't have stood in his way. But now things were different.

The elders of the town went into a huddle and it was decided that Maulvi Sahib would himself deal with the police. Maulvi Sahib had an ingenious device up his sleeve. The police havaldar would be tutored to report that he had not found Shakur at home and hence the summons could not be served on him. If the havaldar persisted in making the calls, Shakur and his wife would go away from the town for a few months and stay somewhere else with the child.

"The havaldar be damned!" Maulvi Sahib said, "I know how to cut him down to size!" He went away tapping his lathi and feeling very important.

A strange game of hide-and-seek started thereafter. The high-ups in the governments make agreements but it is the petty government functionaries who execute these agreements. The orders would come from above to produce the boy before the authorities. A police constable from the police station would come to the right house. He would bang on the door, make threatening noises, pocket a rupee and write on the summons papers that he had found the house locked. He added that on enquiry he had learnt that the inmates had gone away and there was no knowing when they would return.

It was not a question of a small bribe nor one of returning an adopted child. The matter was taking on a religious slant. By not sending away the child they were doing a service to religion — something which was considered to be a pious act.

Months passed and merged into years.

On one occasion, the entire rescue party descended upon Shakur Ahmed's house but found it locked. They had got news in advance and the family had disappeared before the arrival of the party. Shakur Ahmed, it transpired, had gone to Shekhupura to meet his brother and they had no information as to when he would return. As the party reached Shekhupura, it learnt that Shakur Ahmed had left the place only a day earlier with his wife and child for Lyallpur. "Yes, there was a child with them. But we do not know the man's address. He didn't leave any address behind before going away."

In this game of hide-and-seek, three more years passed. Manohar Lal's face had started turning dark. His cheeks became deeply lined and his hair showed streaks of gray. He was full of despair. He had even lost the ability to discern truth from falsehood. Life was mauling Manohar Lal with the same ferocity with which a hawk tears a bird apart with its beak.

Whether it was the result of Manohar Lal's determination or the effect of Kaushalya's sighs, after seven long years Manohar Lal found himself sitting in Shakur Ahmed's courtyard. He had gone there with a government rescue party and a woman representative of a social service organisation. From the Pakistan side, there were two police officers and a magistrate to conduct the proceedings. The meeting had become possible due to the intervention of a high Government of India official who had moved his counterpart in Pakistan.

At the meeting, Manohar Lal was required to prove that the child was really his. There was a legal angle to it and he had to conform to a set procedure and convince the officials as to his right to the child.

There was tension in the courtyard. The Maulvi Sahib was sitting a little apart from the officials. A lot of people had gathered outside Shakur Ahmed's house. Zenab was sitting in the verandah behind a tarpaulin curtain. Her face looked pale but her eyes were sharp and watchful like the eyes of an eagle guarding its nest. Altaf Hussain sat leaning against her, looking tense and bewildered. Zenab squeezed his shoulder again and again.

Before the proceedings started Maulvi Sahib came out with all sorts of threats perhaps to intimidate Manohar Lal.

"Nobody can take away the child. No kafir can touch him," he kept muttering.

The man heading the Indian party requested the magistrate several times to ask the maulvi to keep quiet. He reminded the magistrate that if the maulvi did not stop interfering, it would increase the tension.

After the Partition of the country the blood on the roads and streets had long since dried but its stains were still faintly visible here and there. The fire that had engulfed the houses had died out long since but the charred frames were still standing. The mad frenzy of the Partition had abated but its effects still lingered in the minds of the people.

"Call the child!" the magistrate said, starting the proceedings.

"We have not stolen anybody's child," Zenab's agitated voice came from behind the curtain. "Why should I send him out?"

"Produce the child before me," the magistrate repeated his orders. Shakur Ahmed went behind the curtain to fetch the child.

Manohar Lal's heart was pounding hard. The most decisive moment of his life had come. He was eager to have a look at his long lost child. At the same time, his mind was assailed by doubts and fears.

The boy was made to stand before the magistrate. Seeing the crowd in the courtyard, he became nervous and clung to Shakur's legs. Putting his finger in his mouth, he looked around at the people as if stupefied.

"Son, come here," the magistrate said. "Look, who is here. Do you know any of them?"

"Nobody should prompt the boy," the police officer said in a warning tone. "Let the child decide for himself."

Manohar Lal himself failed to recognize his own son. An eight-year old boy, a Rumi cap perched on his head, dressed in a muslin kurta and salwar. Manohar Lal's eyes were beginning to deceive him. He stared at the boy for a long time. Then the image of his own child flashed through his mind and his throat choked with emotion, "Pali!" he cried. "Pali, my son!" But the voice died in his throat. Even otherwise, he was not supposed to draw the boy's attention to himself.

The boy surveyed the people sitting in the courtyard. His expression recorded no change at the sight of Manohar Lal. He was looking scared as before — only a little more so. Manohar Lal watched him intently. He had grown quite tall and fair and handsome and healthy. Manohar Lal felt that the time of decision had come and gone. The dice seemed to be loaded against him. Shorn of all joys, his life would remain bare and empty like a sandy waste.

Breaking the silence the maulvi said, "So you have seen it. The child has failed to recognise him. Had he been this man's child he would have dashed forward to him. And look at this man's audacity — he has come to demand another's child!"

The lady social worker was greatly annoyed. "Come here, son," she said. "Look, who's the man sitting in front of you?"

"No prompting please!" the police officer warned the social worker. "Leave the child alone. Let him find out for himself."

Zenab was sitting inside, holding her breath. She was feeling uncertain.

Addressing Shakur the social worker said, "You've yourself admitted that he is not your child — that you've adopted him."

Before Shakur Ahmed could reply the maulvi banged his lathi on the floor and said, "We don't deny that he is an adopted child. But how can one accept this man's contention that the boy is a Hindu child and belongs to him?"

The magistrate nodded his head as if he was in agreement with what the maulvi had said. He looked now at the child, now at Manohar Lal. Manohar Lal felt more and more depressed. His own child was standing before him and all he could do was to watch him listlessly. The opportunity had really slipped through his fingers.

"The child has become nervous," the lady social worker said.

"Please keep quiet!"

"What more do you want now?" the maulvi said. "Its already decided. You people may go."

The social worker turned to Manohar Lal, "Yes, now I remember," she said. "Where's the photograph you had shown me the other day?"

By way of proof Manohar Lal had not been able to bring anything except a small photograph. At Kaushalya's request he had got himself photographed along with her at the Baisakhi fair. Little Pali was sitting in his lap. But the photograph could serve no useful purpose. Pali had not grown quite big and bore no resemblance to the little Pali of the photograph. Manohar Lal took the photograph out of his pocket and passed it on to the magistrate.

"My son is there in this photograph. It's the same child. You can see for yourself."

Shakur Ahmed flared up. "Janab, this photograph proves nothing," he said to the magistrate. "I too have a photograph."

He went in and came back with a framed photograph. Wiping it with his sleeve he handed it to the magistrate.

"It's the same child whom you see standing in front of you," he said indicating towards the boy in the photograph. "You can verify for yourself."

"Come here, child." The magistrate placed Manohar Lal's photograph in front of the boy without making any comment, convinced that he would not be able to recognise anybody in the photograph.

The boy looked intently at the photograph for sometime. Then, lifting his hand, he placed his forefinger on Manohar Lal's image in the photograph and cried, "Pitaji!" Then his finger slowly moved towards the woman in the photograph. "Mataji!" he exclaimed.

The child's eyes remained fixed on the photograph. A strange restlessness seemed to have seized him.

Manohar Lal burst out crying. He thrust the end of his turban into his mouth to suppress his sobs.

The magistrate placed the other photograph in front of the child. The child beamed. "Abbaji! Ammi!" he exclaimed.

A wave of joy surged through Shakur Ahmed's mind. Zenab peeped out from behind the curtain. Her eyes were brimming with tears.

The maulvi's face had remained taut all this time. But now his expression suddenly mellowed.

"Now he is a Musallman's son, not a Hindu's. He has read the kalma," the maulvi said with an air of finality.

"Please be quiet!" the social worker cried.

"Why should I remain quiet? This man had thrown him away and disappeared. We brought him up!" The maulvi's voice rose.

Hearing the maulvi's loud and threatening voice the boy ran and clung to Shakur's legs. Then he ran towards the verandah and hid behind the curtain.

They must have heard what was going on in the courtyard for suddenly slogans resounded outside Shakur's house, "Allah-ho-Akbar!"

The lady social worker and the two Indian officials put forward the plea stoutly that since the child had recognized his father, he should forthwith be restored to him without further ado. But things seemed to be taking an ugly turn. The tension was mounting. While the child was sitting in Zenab's lap with his arms around her neck, the complexion of the problem was undergoing a change. It had become a Hindu-Muslim question. Questions like "Whose child is he? Who had brought him up?" seemed to have become extraneous to the situation.

Finding himself at the end of his tether, Manohar Lal had a brain-wave. Getting up, he went and stood near the curtain. Folding his hands he said, "Bahen, I'm not begging you for my child. I'm begging you for my wife's life. She has lost both her children. She misses Pali very much. His absence is driving her insane. Day and night she keeps thinking of him. Please have pity on her."

The space behind the tarpaulin curtain remained steeped in silence. The officials of both the countries watched the curtain intently. The maulvi rose to his feet. He had no doubt in his mind that Zenab would hurl the choicest abuse at Manohar Lal from behind the curtain. Instead, they heard the sound of sobbing behind the curtain. "Take away the child. I do not want an unfortunate woman's curse to fall upon me. How could I have known that you had lost both your children?"

Manohar Lal felt like going behind the curtain and falling at the woman's feet.

An hour later the child was given a send-off. Amidst tears, Zenab and Shakur helped the child to put on new clothes which had been specially made for the forthcoming Id. They put a new rumi cap on his head. Then Zenab said, "I will part with the child on one condition. You must send him to us every year on the occasion of Id to stay with us for a month. Do you agree? Then give me your word."

Manohar Lal's body tingled. His hands still folded in supplication, he said, "He is your wealth, Bahen. I give you my word. I'll remain indebted to you all my life."

The cart of life started moving again. The same meandering paths, the same turnings, the same ups and downs. If things had ended there the narration would have assumed the form of a story, holding something of interest for everybody. But nothing ever ends, nothing ever comes to its finality. The powers that be scored out one more name from the long list of the 'Abducted' and transferred that name to the list of the 'Found'.

The government jeep was travelling at great speed. By the side of the driver sat an armed guard and next to him the police officer. At the back of the jeep sat father and son, tightly set against each other, and opposite them the lady social worker. The child looked lost and forlorn. In contact with the boy's warm body, Manohar Lal's body had again started tingling warmly. The cords of affection which had snapped were again slowly joining together.

They crossed the border in the afternoon. Getting down from the Pakistani jeep they submitted their papers to the scrutiny of the Indian authorities stationed at the other side of the boundary line. Manohar Lal, his son and others then drove off in another jeep towards Amritsar.

The jeep had not gone far when the lady social worker, as if acting on a sudden impulse, stretched out her right hand, whisked off the rumi cap from the boy's head and flung it outside the jeep. The red, black tasselled cap, flying in the air, landed in the dust at the edge of the road.

"My cap!" the boy's hand went to his head. "Hai, my cap!"

The lady social worker leaned towards the boy, "You are a Hindu boy. Why should you wear a Muslim cap?"

Manohar Lal did not appreciate the brusque manner in which the cap had been removed from the boy's head and thrown away. "That must have hurt the boy's feelings. He doesn't know that it is a Muslim cap," Manohar Lal said to the social worker. "Why did you throw it away? Stop the jeep. I must retrieve the cap."

The boy had pulled a long face and was on the verge of tears. His hand on his head, he kept moaning over the loss of his cap. "Oh, my cap!" he cried again and again.

"He is still a child, ignorant of these things," Manohar Lal explained patiently. "See, he's still crying."

"Let him cry," the woman said. "Crying is not going to do him any harm. You're not going to give him a rumi cap to wear, are you? He'll stop crying in a short while."

The jeep raced on, raising clouds of dust behind it.

Far away from the border, in a small town, where a lot of refugees had settled down, news spread with the speed of lightning that Manohar Lal and Kaushalya's son had returned. The impossible had happened. God's mill, they said, grinds slowly but it grinds fine. The boy was returning after seven years. A lucky child indeed. The women kissed the child's head and lowered their heads in gratitude to God. "See, Bahen, the child you were holding against your bosom was snatched away by death right from your arms and the one who had strayed away from you and was knocking about alone and forlorn has come back hale and hearty. Nobody can harm a person who has God's benign protection."

Back home the child kept whimpering as he had done many years ago on the first two or three days of his arrival in Shakur's house. On the first day of his arrival he watched his mother, Kaushalya, from a distance. He saw nothing of those traits in her which he hazily remembered to have marked in her as a mother. The loss of her children seemed to have wrought havoc with her youth. Dim memories of the past were slowly reviving in the child's mind — hazy, nebulous, incoherent. He vaguely remembered his small sister lying in his mother's lap. And the buffalo that stood tethered outside their door and on whose back he used to have a joy ride. Also the wooden bed that was a permanent fixture outside their house. He could hear a babble of sounds rising higher and higher every moment. The identity of his mother had gradually started returning to his mind. But sometimes, he still wondered whether the boy who was standing before her, finger in mouth, and brazenly staring at her, was he really Pali? He felt more and more confused.

Three or four days passed in this manner.

Then came Sunday. The dholak began beating in Manohar Lal's courtyard from early morning. The women of the mohalla gathered in the courtyard and sang in tune to the rhythmic beat of the drum. Two small cotton carpets had been spread in the courtyard and a few cane seats were lined against the walls. There were also a few cots in case there was an overflow of guests. Kaushalya was looking her normal self; she was not as silent or withdrawn as before. Now she even laughed sometimes. That morning she wore a red chunri bordered with threads of gold — a red chunri, a traditional Hindu symbol of matrimonial bliss and good fortune.

Manohar Lal was all attention to the guests. He was not tired of telling his friends that those people back in Pakistan had taken great care of his son. He could not match the attention and affection they had showered on him. He would indeed remain indebted to them all his life.

The narrow courtyard filled with guests. Holding a big platter of laddoos, Manohar Lal was about to go round to distribute the sweets when Pali did something very strange. He had been sitting by the side of his mother, listening to the women playing the dholak and singing, when he got up abruptly and fetched a mat from inside. He spread it on the floor, knelt down on it, and started saying his namaz. The people sitting in the courtyard watched Pali with curiosity. But their curiosity soon changed into dismay.

"What's going on, Kaushalya?" a woman asked. "What's your son doing?"

Manohar Lal felt embarrassed at his son's strange antics in front of his guests. He should have anticipated this and done something to prevent it from happening. He apologetically said to the man standing by his side, "Every afternoon right at this hour he sits down to say his namaz. He instinctively comes to know that it's time for namaz."

"Don't you stop him?" a voice asked.

"He's still a child. He'll learn soon enough."

A man who was regarded as a big shot in the mohalla said in a loud voice for all to hear. "He must at once get rid of this nasty habit. We don't want to have a Muslim among us."

The boy continued with his namaz while the people around him watched with feelings of disgust.

Manohar Lal said as if in self defence, "You know those people didn't have a child of their own. And..."

"Manohar Lal!" the big shot, who was regarded as the Chaudhri of the mohalla, cut Manohar Lal short, "You know that those people have foisted a Muslim convert on you and yet you have nothing but praise for them."

The boy was still kneeling on the mat. With his hands raised upwards, he was repeating his namaz prayers. The Chaudhri went and stood by the boy's side.

As soon as he finished his namaz and began wiping his face with both his hands, the Chaudhri caught him by the wrist and dragged him into the middle of the courtyard.

"What were you doing?" he asked the boy.

Pali was unnerved. "I was saying my namaz," he said in a faint voice.

"We won't allow you to do such silly things in this house," the Chaudhri barked at Pali. "No namaz hereafter. Do you understand?" Turning to the people standing around him, he remarked, "Those Musallas have planted the poison of fanaticism in his mind. And at such a tender age!"

He stood thinking for a while. "Better call a pundit," he said in a decisive tone to a friend. "And also a barber. We must perform the boy's mundan. And let him keep a proper tuft. Those rascals! They have planted a Musalla on us."

Pali stood there looking utterly confused.

"What's your name, boy?"

Pali looked timidly at the massively built Chaudhri and mumbled in a subdued voice, "Altaf. Altaf Husain, son of Shakur Ahmed."

The Chaudhri glared at the boy. With great difficulty, he restrained himself from slapping the boy. The boy felt that the pressure of the man's grip on his wrist had increased. He gave the man a terrified look.

"No, your name is Pali — Yashpal!"

The boy stood silent and then mumbled, "Altaf."

"Repeat that name again and see what happens. I'll pull out your tongue!"

"Have you seen these Musalla's doings?" the Chaudhri said turning to the people standing around him. "They call it conversion — religious conversion. Reform!"

The barber arrived, followed by the pundit. There was also a man accompanying the pundit carrying ghee and other ingredients for performing a havan.

The boy was again made to sit on a mat. The barber sharpened a razor on his palm and according to the directions given by the pundit, started shaving the boy's head. As long as the ceremony lasted, the boy sat with his head bowed and sobbed. Once he got up in fright, cried, "Ammi, Ammi, Abbaji!" and ran towards the wall, of the courtyard. Standing with his back against the wall he looked at the Chaudhri like a deer at bay watching a hunter. At the suggestion of the Chaudhri, Manohar Lal went to fetch the boy. He held the boy's hand and gently brought him back to the mat.

A tuft of hair was left in the middle of his cropped head. Pali was bathed, given a brand new dhoti and kurta to wear. To the chanting of mantras, he was given a sacred thread.

"Child, what's your name? Say five times. Pali, Pali, Pali..."

Some time later, looking every inch a brahmachari, Yashpal stood at the door with folded hands, seeing off the guests. The relatives and guests caressed his head and blessed him as they departed. Manohar Lal distributed laddoos.

At that time, sitting in their lonely courtyard hundreds of miles away, Zenab and Shakur were making all sorts of conjectures. Zenab said, "He is gone and with him has gone all the gaiety of this house. At this time I used to go out into the street in search of him. He would try to hide from me — running into all nooks and corners. I could never know where to find him. Oh, it was such fun! Well, what do you think? Will he come to visit us on Id? Will those people send him here? I think they will. "

"Oh, yes, you once told me you had a cousin living in Bareilly. We shall go and stay with him and meet our son. What do you think of that?"

She wiped her eyes again and again.

Original in Hindi.
Translated by Jai Ratan.

SULTAN JAMIL NASIM

I AM GAME

A volcanic eruption. The lava gushing out of the volcano and flowing down.

Such was her life — marked by explosions powerful enough to shake its very foundation, as happens in the case of a building. And then another explosion, coming soon after, equally powerful, reducing the four walls of life to rubble.

She felt entombed in the sprawling rubble of her own existence. What else is there in a tomb except darkness and utter loneliness? She had not experienced such darkness in her life ever before. She felt as if she was eternally groping in the dark to find a way out. And her loneliness was so intense that she could not even hear her own voice.

When Afroze's mother woke up in the morning she saw that the sunlight had climbed over the roof. Her daughter's bed was empty. She looked up at the sun. It must be past eight, she guessed. Afroze must have left for school by now.

She cursed herself for having overslept. The foolish girl! So she had gone to school on an empty stomach. Even without drinking a cup of tea! Her gaze travelled towards the kitchen. The chulha was burning and the water was boiling in the tea kettle, steam hissing out of it like a thin wreath of smoke. Poor girl! She must have thought of preparing some tea for herself and then realized that there was no time for it. Specially for a girl like her who was in the habit of leaving her bed late. Well, now she would make the best of a bad situation and prepare a cup of tea for herself.

She removed the kettle from the chulha and throwing away the boiled water proceeded towards the bathroom to get fresh water from the tap there, that being the only tap in the house. The bathroom door was shut. As she pushed the bathroom door open, something like lightning blinded her eyes. After taking her bath, Afroze was wiping her body with a towel. As if electrified,

Afroze gave her mother an alarmed look. "Oh, mother...!" she exclaimed and quickly sat down on the ground, ineffectually trying to hide her nakedness with her small towel.

As if coming out of a daze, Afroze's mother moved away from the bathroom door and sat down on her cot. Emerging from the bathroom, properly dressed for school, Afroze gave her mother a shy look as she walked past her and proceeded to dry her hair with her towel, tossing her head every now and then.

Afroze's face glowed like bright daylight. As her mother looked at her face, many questions invaded her mind like the darkness of the night — questions for which she should have found answers a long time back. But having remained bent over her sewing machine, day and night, she had become oblivious to everything except the clothes she was sewing on the machine. Today, as never before, she realized she had wasted her life in measuring her customer's bodies without caring to size up her own daughter's growing body. In the meanwhile, her daughter's youth had stolen a march over her in stealthy steps. She had even failed to hear the sound of those footsteps for they were drowned in the noise of the sewing machine. Today, she felt as if she was seeing her daughter for the first time — as if she had relegated her to the limbo of time soon after her birth. The girl had already crossed the fourteenth year of her life. She recalled that she herself was fourteen when her husband, Nayáz Sahib had come into her life, having accepted her hand in marriage. And then this girl had arrived to bring joy into their lives.

One thought leading to another, Afroze's mother recalled her days of youth, her marriage with Nayaz Sahib, Afroze's birth and her husband's death in an accident. His death had occurred four years ago, but during this period her life had been marked by cataclysmic changes. East Pakistan had become Bangladesh and those whom she regarded as her own had become aliens. So much so that due to quirks of fate, people had become aliens in their own country. With all props of help gone, Afroze's mother had to shift to a refugee camp where she found herself face to race with starvation and where women were not above trading their bodies to come by some money. She was in dire circumstances when Majid, her aunt's son, had come to her as a godsend. A wayward youth of shady character and reckless ways, he had turned a new leaf and had seemingly redeemed himself by doing humanitarian work in those troubled times. Shuttling between Dhaka and Karachi, he had pulled many hapless girls out of chaos and found asylum for them in Pakistan. All along, Afroze's mother had kept Majid at arm's length on account of his vagabondage and erring ways. But now his vagabondage had stood him in good stead. Along with fifteen other girls, he had escorted Afroze and her mother from Dhaka to Kathmandu and from there taken the party to Karachi. Perhaps even Nayaz Sahib could not have played such a heroic role.

Reaching Karachi, Majid did all that he could to help Afroze's mother to find her bearings. He bought for her a small house in the downtown area of Karachi. As for those fifteen uprooted girls, he vaguely hinted that he had entrusted them to the care of a humanitarian agency.

As Afroze's mother saw it, Majid's old ways had again asserted themselves in Karachi. He would suddenly disappear and not show up for two or three months at a stretch. It was a period of revolutionary changes in which the people like Afroze's mother had to endure a lot of suffering. In Majid's absence when it became difficult for Afroze's mother to procure even two meals a day, she took in sewing work at home to keep her going. One problem that was causing her still greater anxiety was that her daughter was growing up fast, uninhibited by the adverse conditions perpetrated by the revolutionary upheavals. She knew of no device by which she could arrest her daughter's growth. And here she was basking in the sunshine of her own youth, unmindful of her mother's anxiety.

One good thing about Majid was that he was taking special care of Afroze. At his instance, her mother had put her in school and he had bought books for her. Though he was often missing for long periods, yet he went out of his way to provide mother and daughter with the essentials of life so that Afroze's mother should not have to stretch her hand before others. For that matter her income from private tailoring was unpredictable like the out-of-season rains. Being obliged to Majid, she was prone to turn a blind eye to his misdemeanours and the kind of reckless behaviour, he was heir to. However, it went to his credit that during this period his behaviour towards them had remained exemplary; he never gave them a chance to complain, so much so that Afroze's mother had started addressing him as Bhai Majid.

In the ashes of her mind, Afroze's mother kept raking up embers of the past events of her life, some gay, some sad, but none of these had been able to dim Afroze's fair image. That morning, when she returned to her room after attending to her chores, she found Afroze's overnight clothes lying in a heap on her bed. Afroze had hurriedly removed her clothes to put on her school dress before leaving for school. Holding her shirt from its shoulders as she held it before her to examine it, she felt as if she was holding her own shirt. The sight of the shirt shackled her mind. Afroze was indeed growing up fast and it was time that she seriously went about finding a match for her. Her own financial condition being what it was, not to talk of two or three years, she would not be able to amass sufficient money even in ten years, to arrange Afroze's marriage. She thought she would talk about it to Majid. If he agreed to give her a helping hand, it would surely make things easier for her and she would be able to marry off the girl within the next two or three years.

She gathered Afroze's clothes and hung them on the clothes-line. She put away her comb in the alcove and had just picked up her mirror to put it away when some thought led her into the courtyard. She stood there a long time looking at her face in the mirror. There was not a line of age on her face — only a faint brooding shadow like the falling evening dusk. She scrutinized her hair for streaks of grey in it and could find none. How foolhardy of her to indulge in such fanciful thoughts. Only four years ago when her husband was alive, he used to go raving mad praising her beauty. No doubt, she had suffered much and undergone great hardships during four years since her husband's death. But neither these hardships nor the passing years had taken toll of her beauty; she was as beautiful as before. But by the same reckoning, Time had worked the other way in her daughter's case. While it had stood still in her case, it had taken wings in her daughter's case and she was fast maturing into womanhood.

Majid happened to walk in just then. She thought it opportune to share her thoughts with him.

"Majid Bhai, Afroze has been asking for a burqa for the past few days," she said.

"Well, I'll have one made for her," Majid replied nonchalantly.

"She has also grown out of her shirts."

"I'll get new ones made to her size."

"Majid Bhai, burqa or no burqa, I think it's time that we thought of her marriage."

"Marriage? Whose marriage? Afroze's? But I had other ideas for her in my mind — some big plans."

Afroze's mother looked at Majid expectantly, hoping that he would be more explicit about his plans. But instead of coming out with his plans, he changed the subject.

"Apa, how much do you manage to earn every month?" he asked her.

Afroze's mother gave him a surprised look. "You know well that I don't have a steady income," she said. "It ranges between a hundred and hundred and fifteen, and some months not even that."

"I wonder how the two of you manage to live on such a meagre income."

"Yes, you're right, Majid Bhai," she said in a gloomy voice, finding that Majid had touched a raw nerve. "Times are hard and living has become so costly. We can hardly fill our bellies with the money I rake in from these tailoring jobs. But for your help, I would have been nowhere. Whatever little I have — these utensils, pieces of furniture and all that — is the result of your benevolence."

"And if I withdraw my hand of benevolence?" Majid said in a mock serious tone.

"Then we shall starve. I'll be forced to remove Afroze from her school. But, Majid Bhai, why are you asking such questions?"

"To tell you the truth, Apa, I'm tired of the hectic life that I have been leading. I left Dhaka many years ago and since then I have been working hard day and night without a moment's rest. In the beginning, I was alone and had to fend only for myself. I managed with what little I earned. But now that you have come into my life my worries have mounted. I want someone to share my worries. If I am taking you into my confidence it is with a specific purpose. If you take my advice, we can easily come by some money and lead a comfortable life. You must think of the poor girl, Afroze. At her age, she would also like to have a good time like any other girl. We have also to do something about her dowry. Well, I think I can take the responsibility of marrying her off in a good family. There are such filthy rich people living in Karachi."

Afroze's mother was listening to Majid with rapt attention.

After a lapse of such a long time was Majid's mind still working along the same lines in which her mind worked soon after coming to Pakistan? The horror of it! But she had inured herself against such an eventuality. Majid's upright behaviour towards her had inspired confidence in him. Her fears and all those ugly thoughts, she believed, were nothing more than a figment of her imagination. Ultimately, she had come to regard him as a brother.

But there is no knowing a man. Was it that after such a long time, Majid was now going to reveal himself in his true colours? Within the narrow four walls of her house, she saw Majid's shadow assuming new dimensions.

Her past and her present. And Afroze's future — what did it all add up to?

"Majid Bhai," she said in a tired voice," today, more than ever before, Afroze is weighing on my mind like an unbearable burden. I'm prepared to do anything for you. You have only to tell me."

"I can remove this burden from your mind just in a day. You have only to tell me and it shall be done."

"I'm listening."

"As luck would have it, this morning I ran into a rich man of Karachi. Perhaps, he saw Afroze on her way to school. Today he spilled the beans. I have given him word."

"What do you mean?"

"I've agreed to his proposal."

"What proposal? I haven't even seen the man. I know nothing about him and you say that you have given him your word."

"What's there to see? He is prepared to shell out any amount of money."

"What for?"

"Only for a night," Majid said with alacrity. "It's now up to you to bring Afroze round."

For an instant, Afroze's mother failed to comprehend what Majid was driving at. Was he uttering words, blazing forth red hot lava? When its implications dawned upon her, her heart sank and the world seemed to have crashed around her. More than on any other day, she realized with greater intensity how her daughter was blossoming in the first flush of her youth. And, today, a price was being tagged on to her youth. She felt darkness creeping upon her. It was Majid's doing.

"What are you thinking of?" Majid said. "Wealth does not knock on one's door a second time."

Afroze's mother flew into a rage. Had she not been under so many constraints, she would have scratched Majid's face.

"I...I...never expected this from you of all persons," she said, in a voice full of hatred. "You have been like a snake in the grass. I don't want your help. I don't want your money. You evil-minded man, get out of my sight!"

She did not know when Majid left her house and what his parting words were. Her whole body seemed to be afire. It had never occurred to her that things could take such a turn.

No, she could not contemplate such a situation even if the world turned upside down.

She had spent a night in a refugee camp in Dhaka. The night had come dancing out of nowhere and was devoured by the outstretched tentacles of a blazing fire. It was a night in which hunger had raged like fire in her stomach. She had seen Afroze's chapped lips and life expiring in her eyes. Nearby, she had seen outstretched feminine hands greedily grabbing crumpled notes. Was she now seeing the dawn of the same prolonged night of long ago? Was it ushering in the morning? But what kind of morning? Oh, God, one is punished for one's crimes. But why punish one for one's helplessness?

A month passed. And then more months. Afroze often asked her mother why uncle Majid had stopped visiting them and why she was not being sent to school. Her mother's income from tailoring had also decreased considerably. Why didn't she tell uncle Majid about their state of affairs? Afroze did not want a burqa and did not mind if there was no money to pay her school fees. But how could she do without food? She must eat to survive.

That day, Afroze's mother put on her burqa and set out in search of Majid.

When he came, she said with downcast eyes, "If it concerned me alone, I would have certainly committed suicide without a moment's thought. But I have also to take my daughter into account. She is dependent on me and I have perforce to think of her. The other day you opened the door of hell for me. I am ready to enter it. Go and fix up with anyone you can find. For fifty or a hundred or any amount you can pin him down for."

Majid looked at her as if he had started doubting her sanity. Then he said in a crackling voice, "Apa, you are asking for fifty or a hundred. That's nothing. With Afroze's grace, they would shower fifties and hundreds on her every day!"

Afroze's mother gave Majid a hard look. "Now go," she said in a brittle voice. "I don't want a customer for Afroze..."

"Oh!"

"I want one for myself. I'm game!"

Original in Urdu.
Translated by Jai Ratan.

AGA SOHAIL

OUTSIDE THE HAVELI

1

In winter the sun rises leisurely and then, with elaborate grace and style, looks around and casts its gaze on the surface of the earth. It was early in the morning, the earth was still shrouded in darkness, the buildings and the trees stood silently wrapped in white sheets of mist, only a single ray of light sparkled on the highest tower of Nawab Yousuf Ali Khan's haveli.

Nanusakka picked up his empty leather-bag in which he carried water on his shoulder, pressed both his hands under his armpits for warmth and still shivering in the cold, left for work in the municipal office. Dirty, unwashed and shivering children emerged from their small houses outside the main gate of the haveli, and gathered around the fire which had been lit by Rehman Kahar. Rehman Kahar's son-in-law, Latif Husain, got onto his bicycle, promised to bring back some peanuts for the children, and rode off to the railway station, where he worked. Even before the sharp and squeaking sound of his bicycle had died down, Baban Dhobi came into sight walking beside his sleek and cleanly scrubbed bull which was loaded with a large bundle of dirty clothes. The sound of bells around the bull's neck finally dispelled the magic of sleep. When Allahrakha, who had just walked out of the stable after brushing the horses and giving them fodder, and was now busy trying to light his hookah, saw Baban Dhobi, he called out, "Salaam-alekum."

"Malekum-salaam, Bhai Allahrakha how is mizad sarith?"

And Allahrakha, looked at him with contempt and mockingly said," 'Mizad sarith' has 'phalue'!"

Mir Sahib, who was on his way back from the masjid, kissed his prayer beads and said, "Baban Dhobi, will you always remain a brainless idiot and never learn to talk like a decent human being? You have been made in God's own image, why do you torture his language so sinfully? It's not 'mizad sarith,' but 'mizaj sharif, mizaj sharif.'

When no one paid any attention to Mir Sahib, he walked into the courtyard of the haveli still mumbling his prayers. He sat down on a bed which didn't have any sheet covering it and began to mutter something to himself. The moment his son, Ali Husain, saw his father, he began to write something furiously in a notebook.

Baban Dhobi took two puffs from Allahrakha's hookah and continued on his way. The jingle of the bells around his bull's neck could be heard for a long time.

Gulam Husain, who was Nawab Sahib's driver, pulled the carriage upto the front door of the haveli. All the neighbours and their children crowded near the southern gate of the haveli to wait for the Sarkar to emerge from the front gate. As soon as the Sarkar appeared in the courtyard wearing a mashroo pyjama, an Iraqi higloo achakan, a woollen jacket, bright red shoes and a cane, Mir Sahib was the first to greet him with respect and courtesy. When the Sarkar emerged from the front gate, all his servants bowed to him with great deference. The Sarkar, however, merely glanced at them, acknowledged their salaams with a stiff nod of his head, and sat down in the carriage. For a brief moment, he gently felt his fair and healthy cheeks with his hands and then raised one finger towards the driver to indicate that he was ready to depart. The driver bowed low in acknowledgment and Allahrakha went and stood on the low step at the rear of the carriage. The driver handed over the reins of the horse to his master and stood besides Allahrakha. Then the carriage drove off. The sound of its clatter could be heard for a long time. The moment its sound faded into the distance, however, women and children swarmed out of their houses like chicken who had been let out of their coops. The children shouted and screamed as if they had been suddenly given a holiday from school.

Through a small opening in the window in the upper part of the haveli, Alia Begum looked down onto the lane below and saw Ali Husain going to his college with a bundle of books under his arm.

Anna came upto her and said, "Badi Sarkar has asked me to convey her greetings to you. She wants to know if you have escaped the evil eye of people and are well. She is longing to see you."

Alia Begum replied sharply, "Why didn't you give Ammijan an answer on my behalf?"

"What should I have told her?"

"Whatever you wanted to."

"O may the Lord punish me for my sins," Anna sounded as if she was really being punished.

"Don't bother me. I want to be left alone." As Alia Begum said that she noticed that her mother, wrapped in a shawl, was standing quietly behind her. She bowed to Ammijan respectfully. Anna bowed to her thrice and disappeared.

Begum Sahiba stared angrily at Alia Begum for a while. Alia Begum lowered her eyes and quietly withdrew.

Later that afternoon, when Abbajan came back from the durbar and sat down in the dining room, Alia Begum waited nervously for him to scold her. Abbajan, however, looked at her and Sameena Begum, who was sitting beside her, with love and kindness. After sometime he asked all the servants to leave them alone. Only Anna stayed behind. Abbajan gave Begum Sahiba information about the district, talked to her about the countless legal battles the family was involved in, battles which had been bequeathed to him by his forefathers and on which he had already wasted a lot of the wealth of the district under his control. There seemed to be no end in sight for the court cases.

As soon as the sun set, the Sarkar went out in his carriage for some fresh air and later, after dinner, settled down for the night to listen to music and watch his favourite dancing girls. Only then did Alia Begum breathe a sigh of relief and feel relaxed.

Soft sounds of music crept through the closed windows of the women's room in the haveli. Ammijan, who was sitting reading her namaz, shut her ears with her hands. Anna spread out her dupatta, turned towards Madina and began to mutter something under her breath. Alia Begum had become used to that scene for she had watched it everyday.

As soon as the sun set, the verandah was covered with a curtain and an angeethi was lit. Anna sat down on her bed. Begum Sahiba reclined against her long pillow on her couch to chop betel-nuts and make paan. She sent boxes full of paan into the music room.

Sameena Begum sat wrapped in a quilt on Alia Begum's bed and said, "Baji, tell me what happened to the Princess after the Red Prince fell in love with the Blue Fairy and threw her into a dark well?"

"What could have happened to that poor Princess?" Alia Begum asked with a sigh as she lay under her quilt:

"What other nourishment, Laila
Can your lovers hope for —
Eat a piece of their own hearts
And drink their own blood in sorrow?"

"O poor woman, poor woman! She must have died in sorrow. Isn't that what happened?"

"No, Bibi. If only she had died, she would have been rid of a life of torment. But she was doomed to live so that she could slowly be tortured to death."

"O Allah, that is horrible. Baji, don't tell me such awful stories again. I get frightened. I feel as if I am the Princess and the Red Prince has thrown me into a dark well. I feel suffocated." Actually, Alia Begum really did feel as if she was being suffocated inside the haveli. The night became colder. Everyone went to sleep. Alia Begum, however, lay awake feeling miserable about her life. The haveli, Abba and Ammijan seemed to be a part of some magical romance. She recalled the story of a Princess who was trapped in a haveli. A black giant cut off her head and hung it on the wall outside. Later, with the help of magic, he joined her head backward. The Princess, when she regained consciousness, said, "Allah." The giant asked her once again if she would marry him. When she contemptuously rejected his proposal, the angry giant cut off her head once more. Then, accompanied by a furious storm and a lot of thunder and lightening, he vanished. Alia Begum thought that she was that dead Princess and that her corpse was lying in the haveli. The black giant would soon return, read some magical incantations over her and the entire haveli would burn and crumble into ash in an instant, and...Her heart began to beat fast with tension and fear. The snores of people sleeping in the haveli terrified her. She lifted a corner of her quilt to look towards her mother's bed. What she saw stunned her. "Oh Allah, what magic is that!" she exclaimed softly.

Music could still be heard creeping out of Abbajan's rooms. Cautiously, she moved the curtain of the verandah aside and looked into the courtyard. She saw Ammijan standing on one leg, with her hair scattered wildly over her shoulders and a copy of the *Koran* on her head, performing some magical ritual. She at once buried her head in her quilt. All sorts of strange thoughts raced through her mind.

Whenever Anna's daughter, Buta, came to the haveli, Alia Begum felt that there was another world beyond the haveli where human beings lived. Buta massaged Alia Begum's feet and told her countless stories about people who lived in that other world. Alia Begum's thirsty soul listened to them with strange delight and was comforted by them.

"Do you know that the white masjid on the banks of the Gomati is haunted by jinns?" Buta said. She was an extremely superstitious woman. "The Jama Masjid, which stands at the corner of Tahseenganj and is on the road which goes towards Husainabad, is haunted by jinns even in the daytime. I swear by God, there are jinns...They are as tall as the palm trees...One night, exactly at twelve, when Gulam Bi's son, Sardar, was walking back from the Jama Masjid, he saw a corpse lying across the street. It was as wide as the street itself. When he removed the sheet covering it, he found another sheet under it. When he removed the second sheet, he found another and then another sheet under it. As he was about to lift the seventh sheet, he heard a voice thunder, 'Don't do that or you will repent it all your life. Go your way!'"

"Hai Allah, why did Sardar uncover the corpse? Is he so fearless?"

"Arrey Bibi, these men are all hopeless. They are not afraid of anything. I wouldn't go near that place, even if someone were to offer me a lakh of rupees. Once I went with my mother to Jama Masjid to pray for Badi Sarkar's health. What did I see there? The masjid was empty. There was a single candle flickering in a corner. Bibi, the gates of the masjid are so tall, that even if ten elephants were to stand on each other, they would not be able to reach the top. In that large masjid, there was an old man reading the namaz. When I turned around, after I had said my prayers you know what I saw...? The old man had vanished! I began to tremble. I told Amma, she too began to shiver with fear. No, Bibi, I shall never go there again. May Allah forgive me," as she said that, she held her ears with her hands and repeated, "I'll never go there again."

"He must have been a jinn."

"Of course, what else could he have been? After all jinns live there."

2

Ali Husain, who was the son of Nawab Yousuf Ali Khan's gatekeeper, knew that he deserved a better life. He was well aware of his actual worth. His real quarrel was with his fate. He thought that he was doomed to lead a life of defeat and sorrow. That is why he didn't want the pundit to read his palm. But Mir Sahib, who was keen that the astrologer should predict his son's future, shouted at him in anger and said, "Don't be a fool. After every twelve years even the luck of the worm which eats garbage changes. We, at least, are human beings. Go and show your palm to the pundit. Who knows when you'll come under the influence of a lucky star."

Ali Husain continued to read his book in silence.

The women, who lived in the small houses outside, had surrounded the pundit and were asking him all sorts of questions. The noise was so great that nothing could be heard clearly. Each one wanted the pundit to read the lines on the palms of her hand and predict her future, as if the pundit wasn't a human being but an angel who had the Book of Fate open before him.

"Brahmanji, when will my daughter's hands be painted yellow with mehndi?"

"Brahmanji, will my daughter's father get well soon?"

"O Punditji, tell me that I'll win my case."

Punditji, who had a turban on his head and a tilak on his forehead, and wore a white dhoti and a jacket, opened his book, chanted the name of Rama a few times, uttered a few ritual verses, shut his eyes, calculated something on his finger tips, and said, "Your daughter will certainly get married before Dussera."

"May you be blessed Punditji, may you live long."

The brahmin again calculated something and said, "You will win your case, but you will have to pay a heavy price."

"O Brahmanji, have mercy upon me, please."

"Don't be afraid. The danger can be averted if you feed ten brahmins."

"How much will it cost me to feed ten brahmins?"

The Pundit again made some calculations, and said, "Twenty annas."

"O no! Twenty annas. Please, Punditji, can't you reduce that?"

"The ceremony could cost you less, but it may not be effective."

"How much less?"

"Ten annas."

"Not a paise less than that?"

"No."

"O Punditji, we live in hard times. Before the rains such a feast used to cost only five annas."

"These days you can't even buy chana for five annas. You must feed ten brahmins, ten. A brahmin doesn't eat everyday. But when he does eat, he eats well, so that he doesn't feel hungry for two or three days at least!"

Ali Husain buried his face in his book.

Mir Sahib, who was getting more and more impressed by the brahmin's learning, was about to say something, when Allahrakha, who was taking the horse from the stable to the lake, saw the crowd of women surrounding the brahmin and started singing lustily:

"I have lost my days, longing for my love,
longing for my love.
Read the lines of my fate, Brahmin.
I have lost my days, longing for my love,
longing for my love.
When will I meet her, Brahmin...
May you, by the grace of God,
May you, by the grace of God tell me —
You'll meet her in this season

You'll meet her in this month...
O, yes, yes, yes, in this season, in this month...
I have lost my days..."

The brahmin made his escape through the open gate of the haveli and walked into the courtyard. When he looked around the narrow courtyard, he saw two cots, a low stool covered with a cloth, a broken wooden box and two rusty tin cans. On the wall there was a shelf made out of a plank of wood placed on two large nails. A few books lay on the shelf. A lamp stood on an upturned tin can. Another tin can had been converted into a table on which there were some sheets of paper, pens and ink.

Ali Husain continued to sit on his bed without paying attention to the pundit. Mir Sahib took Punditji by his hand, persuaded him to sit down beside him on his cot and said, "He's my son. He has passed the Entrance Exam and is preparing to do his B.A."

"May he be happy and well! May he live long!"

"Why don't you acknowledge Punditji's blessings, Ali Husain?"

Ali Husain carelessly waved his hand in Punditji's direction.

Punditji was delighted and said, "May you live long, son."

Then Punditji looked at Ali Husain's forehead curiously and said, "Mir Sahib, your son is very fortunate. I swear by God that he will be successful in life, very successful. Indeed, only those who are blessed by the moon are as lucky as he is. Come here, son, let me look at your hand."

Mir Sahib couldn't contain his excitement, and said "Show him your hand, son. How much longer will we have to live this life of poverty, Punditji?"

Ali Husain extended his hand, but without much interest.

"Amazing! One can only wonder at God's lila," Punditji exclaimed, as he studied the lines on Ali Husain's hand. "Mir Sahib, this young man will be blessed by the Goddess Lakshmi and by the Goddess of power. He will acquire learning and will be happily married. To tell you the truth, Mir Sahib, even princes and kings rarely have lines like this."

Mir Sahib's eyes began to glow with excitement. But then he suddenly became sad and said, "His mother passed away before he was even two years old." He wiped his eyes with a cloth and added in a tearful voice, "I have looked after him with great affection since then. Had his mother lived for a few years longer, she would have showered him with love."

Punditji, who had heard Mir Sahib with sympathy said, "Didn't you get married again?"

"How could I? Another woman would have been concerned about her own happiness, about her own home. Why would she have looked after him? Soon she would have had a child of her own and abandoned him to his own fate. I said to myself, pray to God and cast aside all thoughts of a second marriage. So, Bhaiya, with Allah's grace, I am still here. Let's see how much longer I am fated to stand on guard at someone else's gate."

There was only a dim light on the wooden staircase. The atmosphere, from the bottom to the top of the staircase, was suffocating. With pounding hearts, Mir Sahib and Punditji climbed up the steps. They were afraid that the wooden stairs, which creaked badly, would break.

This was the first time that Mir Sahib, who had lived for years in the courtyard below, had been given the permission to climb up the stairs. He was ecstatic, for he felt that he had been summoned to Paradise.

The stairs led into a round room with lots of doors with round arches. The world outside the haveli could be seen only through one of the arched doors. Chandeliers hung from the ceiling. The plaster on the walls had cracked and the paint had faded. Next to each door, there were lotus shaped lamps which hung down from chains nailed to the wall. They must have, once upon a time, illuminated the room. Now they were covered with cobwebs. In one corner, there was a kerosene lamp. Its smoke had left a column of soot on the wall right upto the ceiling. A few broken chairs lay scattered here and there.

Mir Sahib at once realized that Nawab Sahib's style of living was nothing but a show; a disguise to cover up the fact that his coffers were empty.

After requesting Punditji to sit down on one of the chairs, Mir Sahib walked upto a door with a curtain and said, "Salaam, Badi Sarkar. I have come as you had ordered."

Anna's voice from behind the curtain said, "Badi Sarkar wishes me to acknowledge your greetings on her behalf."

Mir Sahib said, "Punditji has also come with me. He too offers you his homage.

After a slight pause, Anna said, "Sarkar wants Punditji to consult her horoscope and tell her when these difficult days will end and when Nawab Sahib will regain his lands."

Mir Sahib turned to Punditji and said, "Did you hear that request?"

Punditji knelt on the floor and drew some diagrams. Shut his eyes in concentration for a while, made some calculations on his finger tips and then sat down on the floor with his head held in both his hands.

"What's the matter, Punditji?" Mir Sahib asked.

Punditji merely recited a couplet in reply:

> "If I don't utter a word my heart will be singed.
> If I do say something my mouth will be burned."

There was a slight movement behind the curtain and someone sobbed. Everyone became numb with fear. Mir Sahib stood spellbound, as if he had seen a snake.

3

Ali Husain was trying to read by the dim light of a lamp.

Mir Sahib finished his evening namaz, raised both his hands and begged God for mercy. He rolled up his prayer mat, looked towards Imam Husain's mausoleum, wept for a while over the fate of Imam Husain, and read the following prayer:

> As Salaamalaieká ya abab Abdullah
> As Salaamalaieka ya ibne Rasool Allah
> As Salaam alekum o Rehmatullah Barkat ho...

Then he sat down comfortably on his bed, picked up his paan box, chopped a few betel-nuts, cleared his throat loudly and recited the following verse:

> "Anees saw the glory of the sun
> Only when it had begun to decline."

When Ali Husain still didn't say anything, Mir Sahib said, "The lesson I learnt today is that life is transitory."

"What's the matter, Abbajan?"

"What everyone had suspected is true."

"Meaning?"

Mir Sahib stood up, looked around him carefully and then whispered conspiratorially in Ali Husain's ear, "It's all a show, a facade. There is nothing left, the coffers are empty.'

"Really!"

"Yes. There is nothing left. What you see is merely a charade."

"What'll they do now?"

"Allah alone knows."

4

Buta fainted while she was massaging Alia Begum's feet. When she opened her eyes, she found herself lying on a bed. She at once became aware of her status as the daughter of a servant, and got up with a start. There was, after all, a difference between herself and the elder daughter of the house. How could she lie on the same bed as her mistress? She was afraid that if Badi Sarkar saw her, she would flay her alive and stuff her body with straw.

Still not fully conscious, she stumbled back to the courtyard where her mother was asleep. She thought she heard someone in the darkness walk away from the courtyard with a heavy step. She thought it was a jinn, and was so terrified, that she trembled and clung to her mother.

Her mother asked her angrily, "What's the matter, Buta?"

"I am afraid, Amma."

"Go to sleep. There is nothing to be afraid of."

"I swear by Allah, Amma, I just heard someone walk away."
"There are no jinns, you idiot. Go to sleep."

As soon as Buta heard the word jinn she lost her nerve and began to tremble even more. She thought that, at any moment, a hand would emerge from the dark and clutch her throat. She began to tremble like a leaf in the wind. Blood drained from her face and she stood spellbound.

5

Mir Sahib snored so loudly that Ali Husain woke up with a start. He was even more astonished when he heard sounds of singing coming from somewhere inside the haveli at that time of the night. Once in a while, he heard Nawab Sahib laugh so loudly that the walls and the doors of the haveli shook. He lifted his quilt and looked at the flame of the earthen lamp still burning in a corner. It spread a yellow light over everything. Ali Husain thought that the whole world had been infected by jaundice.

Sometimes, at night, he could catch a glimpse of the moon through the wide cracks in the doors of the haveli. But that night when he opened his eyes there was no sign of the moon in the sky. The night was cold and dark. Mir Sahib's loud snores were really terrifying. He had, however, been startled from his sleep by another thought which had pierced through his entire body like the sharp pain one feels when a boil bursts. It had suddenly occurred to him that he was not the only one awake in the haveli. Somewhere behind those walls, Alia Begum and Sameena Begum too were awake...

He had, of course, met Alia Begum and Salima Begum in his childhood. He remembered the day when he had, holding his father's finger, walked into the haveli for the first time. Anna had taken him into the presence of Badi Sarkar. She was reclining, with dignity and elegance, in a throne-like chair, against two large round pillows. Her maids, serving girls and servants stood respectfully around her with their arms held in front of them.

Anna had said, "Boy, say salaam to Badi Sarkar."

He had raised his small trembling hand, bowed his head and in a thin voice said, "Adavarz."

Badi Sarkar had nodded her head in acknowledgment and said, "It is sad that Allah called his mother away when he was still an infant."

Someone asked, "What happened?"

"Arrey Bibi, this child's mother and I had played with each other when we were children. That unfortunate woman died even before this child was forty days old. Someone had cast an evil spell on her. She fell ill, took to her bed and passed away soon afterwards."

Many of the women surrounding Badi Sarkar had intoned simultaneously, "Oh no, oh no...May God have mercy..."

Sitting next to Badi Sarkar were two small girls. They had round faces, glowing cheeks, brown hair, wide eyes and skin which was as fair as silver. He had thought that they looked like fairies and the entire scene had pleased his heart. The two girls had looked at him with curiosity and surprise.

Badi Sarkar had caressed his head, wiped the tears in her eyes with a handkerchief and put two silver coins in the small pocket of his chikan shirt. After that Anna had walked him out of the room, and when they reached the top of the staircase, she had called out, "Mir Sahib, your son is coming down. Check his pocket."

He had never been summoned to the ladies' quarters again. Nawab Sahib had given strict instructions that no male above the age of five should be allowed in. But Ali Husain had often hung around in the verandah downstairs, in the hope that one day he would be sent for again, and that he would be able to play with Alia Begum and Sameena Begum. He carried that hope with him when he went to the madarssa and then to school. He turned from a baby into a young boy and from a young boy into an adult. But he was never again admitted into the ladies' quarters. The purdah upstairs was so strict that even a bird couldn't have flapped its wings in those rooms without permission. Indeed, the names Alia Begum and Sameena Begum were never uttered before him. They were always referred to as Badi Bittiya and Choti Bittiya, even when the stories were about them. Neither of them were sent either to a madarssa or to a school. Women used to go to their rooms to teach them. An English woman was hired at five hundred rupees a month to teach them English. Ali Husain was aware of all that. But he never again caught sight of Badi Bittiya and Choti Bittiya.

6

Preparations for Moharram always began many days before the festival. The walls were replastered and white-washed. White sheets were spread on the couches in the sitting-rooms. Golden filigree was stitched around the borders of black satin flags. Taziyas were placed at the front doors. The ganga-jamuni alams, which looked like five-fingered claws, shimmered so brightly that it was difficult to look at them for long. Rose-water bottles were placed in trays of silver. Together they created an atmosphere which was strangely grand and royal.

Lotus shaped chandeliers were lit in the evenings. Candles were placed in candelabras with five, four and two branches. Incense was burnt and rose-water was sprinkled on everything. The mingled perfume of incense and rose added to the mysterious charm of the haveli. At night, women from the neighbourhood came to recite the noha. Their loud lamentations were at once melancholic and heart-warming.

In the mornings all the male adults held a majlis. The rich and the respectable men of the city gathered at the haveli. Dressed in black, they mourned the death of Imam Husain. During those days Nawab Sahib always sat in the diwankhana wearing a black sherwani, a black churidar pyjama and a dopali cap. His black dress made his fair complexion even more attractive. No one could resist admiring the extraordinary elegance of his dress.

At the time of the majlis, Nawab Sahib would push the black satin curtains, tied with golden strings, aside, to reveal the pulpit with taziyas embroidered with gold and silver threads, alam tabut and Shab-e-Zuljinah. People would stand respectfully before it and made their supplications. Mir Sahib would light the incense sticks. The man who told the story of Imam Husain, would first kiss the pulpit and then recite from the Rubaiyat of Meer Anees:

> "The world is a strange last sarai of life,
> Where wayfarers stop, then depart forever.
> When old age arrives, it stays forever,
> When youth departs, it departs forever."

Standing in the crowd, Mir Sahib would shout, "Hey, hey," and then add, "It's the truth, it's the truth."

After that the story-teller would begin to narrate, in great detail, the story of the conflict between good and evil at Karbala. His voice had so much passion and power that he never failed to touch our hearts. Yazid and Husain seemed to appear before us with the clarity of a vision. All those gathered there could never refrain from crying uninhibitedly at the fate of Imam Husain. Mir Sahib would beat his breast and weep. Tears, like two streams of Ganga and Jamuna, would even flow down Nawab Sahib's face. Ali Husain always found it astonishing that Nawab Sahib, who laughed loudly till late at night with singing girls, could now weep so uncontrollably, and look as if he had just returned after burying his entire family.

Mir Sahib was obsessed by the imambara of Husainabad. He didn't, however, go there with his son to listen to the majlis. He went there with Ali Husain out of greed so that he could get, along with the rest of the crowds, at least two servings of roti and salan, pulao and sweets.

Two soldiers, with their guns on their shoulders, always stood on guard at the gate of the imambara. Beyond the gate was a canal, and across the canal was a bridge, and on the other side of the canal were the vast and open courtyards of the imambara. Those broad and spacious courtyards, with chandeliers and candelabras, flags with gold and silver embroidery, twenty-foot tall candle-stands wound with silver threads, colourful taziyas and multi-coloured mirrors were impressive. On either side of the imambara stood two tombs with white turrets and domes. In one corner was a small and pretty masjid. The white imambara, surrounded by a vast and green garden seemed to shimmer like a drop of dew on a new leaf in sunlight.

During the majlis of Moharram, the imambara was always so crowded that it seemed as if there wasn't place even for a sesame seed. Shoulder would rub against shoulder. Food would be distributed at all the four gates between eight in the morning and one in the afternoon. There would be so much pushing and shoving that one felt suffocated.

There was many a majlis in the city. Mir Sahib, however, always took Ali Husain to Kaban Sahib's majlis. When Kaban Sahib sat on the twelve foot high pulpit in his family's imambara and began the sermon, the space between the imambara and the far corner of the neighbouring market would be packed with men, women and children dressed in green and black clothes. Ali Husain would watch the children pretending to be the mendicants of the imambara and reciting the hymns prescribed by traditions. He would be fascinated by the book-sellers, the water-carriers, the professional mourners, and the lovers of Husain who would beat themselves with chains and small knives. As soon as Kaban Sahib began to read the sermon, a profound silence would descend on the crowd, and when the slogans in praise of God were raised it would seem as if the voice of the crowd would pierce the sky and shake the very foundations of paradise.

At night, when the imambaras of Asafi, Shahnajaj and Husainabad were lit, it would seem as if the sun had risen again. Ali Husain would sit by the banks of the canal and watch the lights twinkle like fire-flies in the water. Mir Sahib would have to drag him back home. Then he would dress Ali Husain in a green shirt and a green cap, hand him a bottle full of sharbat and take him inside the haveli. When they approached the ladies' quarters, curtains would be drawn, and the women would withdraw behind them. Mir Sahib would go to the alam of Hazrat Abbas and Ali Husain would offer sharbat to the children from his bottle. As soon as they left, the women would recite the noha. Some women, who had been specially invited from Saadatganj to read the noha, had such sorrowful voices that they never failed to touch the heart.

"Loot leyo Banjara banwah
Loot leyo Banjara..."

When they read the noha, Ali Husain always felt as if the arteries of his heart would burst and blood would drain from his body. Amongst those voices, however, he would also strain to hear the voices of Alia Begum and Sameena Begum, and would silently pray to God to grant him the bliss of listening to them at least once more. His longing was never fulfilled. He was doomed never to hear their voices again. Perhaps, there was a strict guard even over their voices...

Ali Husain turned over in his bed, shut his eyes and tried to go back to sleep. At that very moment the silence of the morning was pierced by the muezzin's cry, "Allah-ho-Akbar, Allah-ho-Akbar..."

Mir Sahib got up to recite the kalma. He said his prayers with devotion and feeling, and asked God for blessings.

Then he read a hymn of supplication:

"Give me peace of mind
Oh God who gave me birth..."

7

It was an oppressive afternoon. Hot winds were blowing across the open fields and the city streets. The sky was covered with dust. The sun was overhead and the heat was intense. The tar on the road had melted. The city seemed completely deserted.

Suddenly a tonga, pulled by a starved and half-dead horse, appeared at the far end of the road which ran past the haveli. The clip-clop sound of the tonga and the loud, encouraging noises made by the tongawalla were blown away by the dusty winds. The tonga stopped in front of the southern gate of the haveli.

Mir Sahib got down from the tonga. Then he turned back to help a thin, old man descend from it. The old man had a white sheet wrapped around his shoulders. He had long white hair, a white beard and white eye-brows. A necklace of beads hung around his neck. It glowed in contrast to his sallow face and made him look even more mysterious. He wore wooden sandals on his feet.

As soon as the two of them got down, the tongawalla parked his tonga under the shadow of a neem tree and ran to the pond nearby to get water for his horse in a bucket. The horse was panting badly.

Mir Sahib led the strange old man upto the door of the sitting room of the haveli and knocked. The door opened. Mir Sahib and the old man walked in. The door closed behind them. The sound of their footsteps could be heard on the bare floor for sometime. Then it faded and there was silence once more.

The sitting room was gracefully kept. A white sheet covered the couch. A few round cushions lay on it. A fan, pulled by a servant, hung from the ceiling.

Nawab Sahib sat reclining against a cushion. He wore a wine-coloured kurta, embroidered with chikan work, and a narrow pyjama. His hair had turned grey and his face was tense and shrivelled. His physical appearance was not only a sign of ill-health, but also of the sorrow of his heart. The room in which he sat seemed sad and forlorn like a widow whose world lay shattered around her. Once upon a time, that room had been filled with music and dance. God knows how many women, beautiful like fairies and glowing with passion, had made it shimmer with excitement and gaiety. There was no warmth in it now, no fervour. The hot fires of desire had cooled. Maybe there was still an ember or two left in the ash, but Nawab Sahib looked like an illustration for the following lines from a Persian poem: "Look at the face, but ask not about his health." There was only a dim and dying flame that still burned in his eyes. It seemed as if his soul felt that it was trapped in a desolate body and was desperately flapping its wings and trying to get out.

Mir Sahib had also grown old and weak.

Shah Sahib, the mysterious old man, sat down besides Nawab Sahib and stared for a while into nothingness. A few sticks of incense burned in front of him. After sometime he looked up and, with his red eyes, gazed steadily on Nawab Sahib's face. Nawab Sahib lowered his eyes, sighed and mumbled, "Alhamd-ulf-Alhaudulf."

It seemed as if his lonely soul was beating its wings against his desolate body.

"There is a basement in this haveli," Shah Sahib said.

"Yes, that's true," Nawab Sahib affirmed.

That was a revelation for Mir Sahib. It made him very apprehensive.

"No one has ever entered it. My late grandfather had forbidden it. He had said that it was haunted by a ghost."

"Forty pots full of gold coins hang from its ceiling," Shah Sahib said. "How can you say you are poor and have no money, when there is treasure buried in your basement?"

Mir Sahib trembled with fear when he heard Shah Sahib describe the wealth as if he had seen it clearly with his own eyes.

Shah Sahib said, in a thundering voice, "If the pots of gold are not taken within forty days, they shall be contaminated by sin. My spirits have informed me that the gold coins will turn into snakes and scorpions."

Nawab Sahib's eyes began to glow with the vision of wealth. He got up from his couch, fell at Shah Sahib's feet and exclaimed,

"Shah Sahib, if what you say true, I shall become your bonded slave for the rest of my life. I shall give you whatever you ask for, as much money as you need. But tell me, how can I lay my hands on that wealth?"

"O friend," Shah Sahib said, "I don't need money."

"Money is a curse for the peace of the soul," Nawab Sahib said.

Shah Sahib raised a finger in the air and said, "I shall pray for you in the mosque by the river for the next forty days. On the fortieth day, at midnight, I shall come back here to help you."

Mir Sahib was stunned. He was shocked to realize that the harmless old man, with whom he had ridden in a tonga for three miles, was a sorcerer who could decipher mysteries and knew the secrets of the underworld. How quickly had he unveiled the hidden wealth of Nawab Sahib's family! He couldn't contain his anger against Ali Husain, who had been touched by the new spirit of the times, and didn't believe in magic and ritual. Now that Ali Husain was in a university, he had begun to think too much of himself. In fact his feet hardly seemed to touch the earth anymore. If only he realized that, even in the present, there were fakirs whose hearts were blessed and whose souls burned with divine fire. That it was in the footsteps of such souls alone one could find blessings, be illuminated. Mir Sahib was so overcome with gratitude that he began to weep.

Shah Sahib turned to him and said, "Old man, dedicate yourself to the service of Allah. He is hidden within you. Don't try to find him anywhere else. He burns in your heart. To learn about God, know thyself."

When Mir Sahib heard Shah Sahib's exhortation, tears began to flow down his face. He fell on Shah Sahib's shoulders and began to weep uncontrollably.

It was strange to see both Nawab Sahib and Mir Sahib lying at Shah Sahib's feet. The servant, who had been pulling the fan, was astonished. Even though he was dying of hunger, he wanted to run at once to Allahrakha and tell him, "There is a treasure hidden in the basement of the haveli. You'll die of envy if I tell you how much."

At that moment a maid servant came running into the room. She stopped suddenly when she saw that strange sight. But after a brief pause she began to scream loudly, "Sarkar, Nawab Sahib, something awful has happened!"

Nawab Sahib and Mir Sahib stood up at once, and asked, "What's happened?"

"Alia Begum has fainted."

"How?"

"I don't know. She was up on the terrace. She had just taken a bath. Her hair was still loose. Maybe a ghost..."

Nawab Sahib shot past her and ran towards the ladies' quarters of the haveli. The entire place was in an uproar. Some women were lamenting, "O God, O protector of the earth, help us, save our daughter." Others were fanning Alia Begum with a copy of the *Koran*, while some others were sprinkling water on her face from a steel cup. Begum Sahiba was sitting with Alia Begum's head in her lap and crying. Anna was massaging her fet and praying:

"O Ali, O god who removes all troubles.
O God who leads us by our hands.
Come to our aid, Mir
Save our daughter, O God."

Sameena Begum and Anna's daughter, Buta, were standing out in the courtyard and crying uncontrollably. Alia Begum stirred a little and began to mutter something through her clenched teeth. Then she began to moan and groan as if she was in pain. Her body lay listlessly on the floor. Her hands and feet were cold and numb. Her eyes were shut.

Nawab Sahib said, "Please move away from her. Let her breathe some fresh air." He caressed her head and softly called out, "Bibi, my daughter."

Alia Begum lifted both her arms and put them around her father's neck, and started weeping, like a young bride who was about to depart from her parents' home with her husband. There were tears in her father's eyes and Badi Sarkar began to weep inconsolably. Anna too started crying loudly. Sameena Begum buried her face in a pillow and wept.

Buta, who had recently been married, collapsed on the floor, without concerning herself with the fact that the mehndi on her palms had yet not faded, and that she was still wearing her bridal dress. She was weeping for Alia Begum, who was innocent and beautiful, and whose large eyes had always filled her with unknown dread. She had, in fact, once told her mother, "Amma, there is something strange about Alia Begum's eyes."

Amma had scolded her and said, "What's so strange about them, you stupid girl?"

"She has an evil eye. A jinn has cast a shadow over her. That's why her eyes are slightly red and seem as if they are intoxicated."

"Shut up you silly girl. Control your tongue. You'll get into trouble if someone overhears you."

"It's the truth, Amma."

Later, when she had got married to Allahrakha, and had repeated the same thing to him, he had laughed loudly and said, "My love, when a girl grows up, she should get married. That's all, otherwise..."

"Otherwise? What happens if she doesn't?"

"If she doesn't, she does evil things if she has a bad temper. If she is good natured, she burns like wet wood and deliberately falls ill."

"Allah. I hope Alia Begum hasn't fallen ill."

That day, when Alia Begum was lying unconscious, Buta wanted to tell everyone what Allahrakha had said, but she didn't have the courage. After all the entire incident was a bit shameful.

Alia Begum still had her arms around her father's neck and was sobbing.

When the people who lived outside the haveli, heard the commotion inside, they gathered at the gate to find out what had happened, whispered the news to each other, and expressed a variety of opinions. The women of the neighbourhood entered the haveli.

The noise outside woke up Ali Husain. He stretched himself, covered his mouth to suppress a yawn and wondered what had happened. At that moment the door of the courtyard opened and Nanusakka and Rehman Kahar walked in.

"What's happening Nanu Chacha? Why is there so much of noise?"

While Nanusakka raised both his arms, as if to invoke the blessings of God, Rehman Kahar said, "I have heard that a ghost has possessed the eldest daughter of the house, and she has fainted. Beyond that I don't know anything."

8

Exactly at midnight, when everything was quiet and still, and the haveli was shrouded in darkness, Shah Sahib got up from the couch. Nawab Sahib and Mir Sahib, who had been watching his ritual performance with awe, also stood up. Shah Sahib was wrapped in a white sheet and had a long necklace of prayer beads in his hand. The room was filled with the smoke of incense and the smell of camphor. The flickering candle light made it seem even more mysterious.

With trembling hands, Mir Sahib placed a pair of wooden sandals in front of Nawab Sahib, and then picked up a lamp and led the way towards the steps which went down into the cellar. The clatter of Shah Sahib's wooden sandals was so loud, that it seemed as if he wasn't walking on the floor, but was walking over loudly beating hearts. Nawab Sahib had a large key in his hand. No one uttered a word. Slowly they climbed down the steps and stood in front of the large door of the cellar which had been lost in darkness for years. Nawab Sahib put the key into the lock, as Mir Sahib brought the lamp close upto it. The lock turned. Shah Sahib pushed the door open, said, "Bismillah" and stepped inside. For a few minutes there was no sound. Then the silence was broken by the sound of Shah Sahib's steps as he returned. When he came back to the door, he indicated with a gesture that Nawab Sahib should follow him. When Mir Sahib too stepped forward, Shah Sahib glared at him and waved him aside. Nawab Sahib and he then disappeared into the cellar.

Mir Sahib waited outside the door all night. He didn't hear any sound from inside. Slowly the night faded into morning and he heard the azan. He said his prayers and then, suspecting that something had gone wrong, opened the cellar door. He stood at the top of the steps, but couldn't see anything in the darkness. It was so hot and oppressive inside that he felt faint. He immediately came out of the cellar. He was puzzled, and didn't know how to explain the mysterious disappearance of Nawab Sahib and Shah Sahib.

The next day, there was an uproar in the town. The police was informed. In the presence of a few important and respectable people of the town, the police broke down the cellar door and recovered the bodies of Nawab Sahib and Shah Sahib. The post-mortem report indicated that both had suffocated to death. But Mir Sahib, along with a large number of other people, believed that they had died because something had gone wrong with the magic, and that evil spirits had killed them. It is difficult to describe the scandal the event caused.

A few days after the calamity, Mir Sahib went upto the curtained verandah in the ladies' quarters and said, "Sarkar, I don't believe the police. Shah Sahib was a well-known sorcerer. I am convinced that there are pots of gold in the cellar."

Begum Sahiba gave him permission to secretly investigate the cellar. Mir Sahib, however, didn't have the courage to go there alone. He had, after all, witnessed two unnatural deaths. Therefore, he summoned a few trusted labourers, and had them open the ventilators of the cellar for fresh air and light. The following morning, he entered the cellar. It was a very large place, but there was no sign of pots of gold in it. When he informed Begum Sahiba, she herself went down to confirm his report. She too returned empty handed.

After his death, Yousuf Ali Khan's household scattered like autumn leaves. Mir Sahib and his son, Ali Husain, left for Pakistan. They settled in Karachi. Ali Husain got a job as a lecturer in a college. Soon, however, he noticed that the conditions of life there were quite different, and that even if one worked oneself to death in a job, one would have no money left to do anything with.

Mir Sahib had nothing to do. He lived near the sea at Manorrah. Everyday he went out for a walk on the beach and watched the ships dock at the port and then depart. One day, he met a Memon Seth, and somehow so impressed him, that the Seth began to sing songs praising him.

Mir Sahib was still an honest and a decent man. At first, in order to test him, the Seth entrusted him with business worth a few hundred rupees. Later he gave him work worth thousands, and when he discovered that Mir Sahib hadn't cheated him even by one single paisa, he placed his entire business, worth lakhs and crores, in his hands, and left for Europe.

Ali Husain soon realized that the Seth was like a hen which laid golden eggs. He began to take an interest in Mir Sahib's business affairs. Within a few years, Allah showered so much grace on them, that Mir Sahib first bought a piece of land from a society, then built a house worth lakhs on it. Then he set up a large office, and Ali Husain installed air-conditioners in it. They hired smartly dressed servants, bought cars and expanded their fish-trade with lots of nations.

Whenever Mir Sahib drove out in one of his cars to catch a breath of fresh air, he thought of Nawab Sahib's horse carriage and said to himself, "In Pakistan, Allah has blessed me with so much wealth that I can buy the likes of Nawab Sahib many times over." When Mir Sahib stood at the sea shore and watched his goods being loaded and unloaded, he said to himself, "Compared with this, the world of Nawab Sahib was no larger than a well. How ignorant we all were to regard it as an ocean. How stupid and vulgar were those stories of magic and ghost haunted cellars. The reality is that the sea is spread across three-fourths of the face of the earth. There is nothing but water as far as the eye can see." The waves of the sea leapt, danced and fell on the shore, and then receded.

Now, when Mir Sahib went to a majlis during Moharram, he made sure that his dress, his car, his house and his wealth made a fine impression on people. He made a special effort to find those people who had once seen him sitting at the gate of Nawab Sahib's haveli. When those who had known him in the past, saw his wealth, they were really astonished and perturbed. Stories about his wealth began to be passed on from one person to the next. And Mir Sahib, who used to donate money for the majlis, and weep with genuine sorrow at the fate of Imam Husain, now cried only because he was required to do so by custom.

Ali Husain began to move in the upper circles of society. He spent his time gossiping with charming foreigners, drinking the best of wines, and declaiming about politics and money. When he got tired of staying in the country, he went to Europe on business. He returned to his country only after he had his fill of the night-clubs, bars and ballrooms there. In order to impress his father with his efficiency and accomplishments, he pretended that his trip had been a business success. His father, of course, saw through the deception, but chose to ignore it. In this manner, father and son spent their lives in comfort and luxury.

One day, Mir Sahib, on some strange impulse, suddenly decided that he wanted to visit Lucknow again, and that his son should accompany him. Ali Husain had no interest in going back to Lucknow. Mir Sahib was, however, insistent. He still nursed the secret hope that he would be able to get Ali Husain married, either to Alia Begum or to Sameena Begum. After all, Mir Sahib was not merely rich, he was a millionaire, and what greater favour could he bestow upon the impoverished family of the late Nawab Sahib, than to offer his son as a husband for one of the daughters of that household. So Mir Sahib secretly arranged to have thousands of rupees transferred to India through traders who were known to him, and took a P.I.A. flight from Karachi to Bombay. He collected his money from the traders in Bombay and took a flight to Lucknow. He checked into Carlton Hotel and, that very evening, accompanied by Ali Husain, went to Nawab Sahib's haveli.

It was the beginning of winter. The sun was slowly setting and a mist was quietly settling over everything. The tall palm trees looked lovely in the fading light. The red glow of the setting sun had caught the highest point of Nawab Sahib's four-storyed haveli. Allahrakha had just yoked his horse to the tonga and had set out. When Mir Sahib saw him, he ordered the driver to stop the taxi, and shouted, "Allahrakha! Arrey Miyan, listen. O Allahrakha!"

Allahrakha was puzzled and startled when he saw two strange men sitting in the taxi. He wondered how they knew him. He got down from the tonga and walked upto the taxi, but failed to recognize Mir Sahib and Ali Husain.

Mir Sahib said, "Arrey Miyan, it's me — Mir Ali Hassan. And this is my son, Ali Husain."

"Arrey, Mir Sahib!" Allahrakha exclaimed.

"Mizad sarith. Salaam alekum, Ali Husain Bhaiya. Welcome back."

Excited, he hugged both of them, and then shouted out to the neighbours, "Mir Sahib has come."

He turned to Mir Sahib and said, "It's sad that after Nawab Sahib's death, everything was ruined. Everyone left. You too went away."

Ali Husain, who had been silent till then, asked, "Do you still ply your tonga, Allahrakha?"

Allahrakha laughed and said, "What else can I do, Bhaiya? If I don't ply this tonga, how will I eat? I have a large family." There was a slight hint of sarcasm in his voice, as if he was asking whether he should be flying an airplane, instead of plying a tonga.

Ali Husain looked at the courtyard of the haveli where he had spent many years of his life. He felt pained and disgusted, and thought to himself, "Allah, Allah, how many years did we spend here living like animals!" His eyes turned towards the staircase. They were still as decrepit, dark and damp, as they had always been.

Suddenly, they heard Anna's voice from the rooms upstairs, "It's time for purdah."

"Oh, no," Ali Husain said to himself, "We seem to have leapt back into the past. Compared to the beautiful, modern and industrial towns of Europe, with their streets, buildings and, healthy and liberated women, Lucknow is backward, defeated, old and decrepit."

He was so disturbed that he turned to his father and said, "Baba, let's leave, I feel suffocated."

Instead of saying anything in reply, Mir Sahib glared at him.

At that very moment, they heard a beggar coming towards them, singing in a voice which was sad and touching. The beggar sang:

"If I don't utter a word my heart will be singed
If I do say something my mouth will be burned."

Then he tuned his single-stringed instrument and sang:

"The lila of this world is strange, O Lord,
I lost the wager of love, I thought I had won..."

Mir Sahib said, "His voice is full of pain."

Allahrakha laughed and said, "He's the bahman you once knew, Mir Sahib. The poor man is now blind and has to beg."

"Really!" Ali Husain said, "The same one who used to..."

"Yes, yes, Bhaiya, the same one who used to come here."

Extremely agitated, Mir Sahib called out, "Punditji, arrey, Punditji...O Bhai, Bahman."

The blind beggar stopped singing and asked, "Did someone call me?"

"Yes, yes, I called you. Mir Ali Hassan."

"Mir Sahib!" the brahmin exclaimed. He blinked his sightless eyes and rapidly walked towards him tapping his stick. "You!"

Mir Sahib went upto him, placed his hands on the brahmin's shoulders. The brahmin also extended his hands and touched him. But when his fingers felt Mir Sahib's expensive suit, he stopped and let his arms drop to his sides. Then he asked, "Is that really you, Mir Sahib?"

Trying hard to control his excitement, Mir Sahib said, "Yes, yes, it's me." Then he took the brahmin's hands, placed them on Ali Husain's shoulders and said, "This is my son, Ali Husain. Bahmanji, as you had predicted, we are millionaires."

The brahmin sat down on the ground and said, "I am glad that you acknowledge my learning. Didn't I tell you that your son's forehead had the light and glow of emperors and kings."

Mir Sahib said, "You were hundred percent right, Bhaiya."

Mir Sahib took a hundred rupee note from his pocket, placed it in the hands of the brahmin and said, "Here, Punditji, keep this."

The brahmin felt it with his fingers and asked, "What is it?"

Mir Sahib said, "Money."

Allahrakha who had been staring at the note with wide eyes, said, "It's a hundred rupee note. Go, Punditji, enjoy yourself. You'll never forget that you met a rich man."

The brahmin kissed the hundred rupee note, touched his forehead with it reverentially and started putting it in his pocket. Suddenly, he thought of something, stopped and said, "Where do you live these days, Mir Sahib? I heard that you had gone away to Pakistan."

"Yes, I live in Karachi."

The brahmin took a step forward, extended the hundred rupee note towards him, and said, "I can't accept this."

"Why not?" Ali Husain asked sharply.

"Because a hundred rupees is a lot of money. What will I do with it? Give me one rupee."

"Arrey, Punditji, consider it to be no more than one rupee," Mir Sahib said.

"No. No, I can't take it."

Allahrakha asked angrily, "Why, Bahmanji? What's the matter?"

The brahmin said, "It's like this. I come this way everyday. People give me alms and I get to hear familiar voices." Then he banged his stick hard on the ground and added, "That way I keep in touch with this earth. You know what will happen if I accept a hundred rupees? I'll not be able to come back to this place. Mir Sahib, if you give me one rupee, I'll accept it."

Ali Husain clenched his teeth and muttered something under his breath. Mir Sahib took the hundred rupee note back and gave the brahmin a one rupee note in exchange. The brahmin blessed him a hundred times and left. They heard Anna's old voice call, "It's time for the purdah."

Mir Sahib and Ali Husain walked upto the ladies' section of the haveli. Two chairs had been placed for them in front of the curtain.

Allahrakha said, "Mir Sahib is here."

Mir Sahib bowed and said, "I have come to pay you my respects."

Ali Husain didn't want to follow his father's example, but he too bowed and said, "Adab."

Mir Sahib had been so deeply affected by what the brahmin had said that he seemed a bit distracted.

Anna said, "Badi Sarkar accepts your greetings. Her complaint is that you deserted this house. She didn't expect you to do that."

Ali Husain was hoping that he would, at last, after having waited for so very long, be able to catch one glimpse of Alia Begum and Sameena Begum, and that one of them would be, perhaps...

Mir Sahib said, "What can I say, Badi Sarkar? I had to think of the future of my son. Allah has been merciful and has granted us lots of favours. If you would agree to come to Karachi, I shall lay down everything I have at your feet and serve you faithfully till the end of my life."

After sometime, Anna said, "Badi Sarkar says, Allah be praised. If she goes to Karbala she will certainly visit Karachi. But she has no plans to go out in the near future."

Ali Husain found these traditional formalities painful. He longed to rush upto the curtain, push it aside and walk in boldly. But he couldn't bring himself to do that.

Mir Sahib put a bundle of ten thousand rupees tied in a handkerchief, sent it into the Begum Sahiba and said, "Sarkar, I couldn't get you anything from Karachi. Please buy a few gifts for Badi Bittiya and Choti Bittiya."

Badi Sarkar accepted the gift and Mir Sahib thought that he had finally won. He was confident that she would agree to marry one of her daughters to his son.

The following afternoon, Mir Sahib and Ali Husain were invited for lunch at the haveli. From Ali Husain's face, it appeared as if he was already in possession of his beloved. Mir Sahib looked elated.

After an elegant meal, Anna placed an old, but expensive shawl in a tray before Mir Sahib and said, "Badi Sarkar has sent you this as a gift."

Mir Sahib bowed and accepted the gift.

Then Anna placed a handkerchief and a colourful cloth in another tray before Mir Sahib and said, "Badi Sarkar requests you to present this to your son's wife."

Mir Sahib saw that the bundle of ten thousand rupees, which he had offered Begum Sahiba yesterday, had been returned to him, and that one golden guinea had been placed on top. Mir Sahib lost heart and admitted defeat. He realized that the haveli was a proud fortress and that it would take something more than money to conquer it. In that haveli, he was still no better than what he had always been. Both father and son took their leave and came out of the haveli.

When Ali Husain looked up at the old window of the haveli with longing, he thought that he saw someone quickly draw a curtain across it.

Mir Sahib and Ali Husain got into their taxi. They heard Allahrakha sing :

"I have lost my days, longing for my love,
longing for my love.
I have lost my days..."

The taxi started moving. When Ali Husain looked back, he caught a glimpse of something white flash past a window and then vanish.

Mir Sahib felt that the haveli had raised its proud head once more.

Original in Urdu.
Translated by Vishwamitter Adil and Alok Bhalla.

GURMUKH SINGH MUSAFIR

THE ABANDONED CHILD

A husband and wife stole out of the back door of their house and ran into the wheat field.

The sun was setting. Its rays fell on their faces. They looked anxious and pale with fear.

The man was tall and well built. The woman was slender and pretty. Every now and then they stopped to hear the shouts of people from the other side of the village. They continued to run towards the berry tree growing on the embankment, separating one field from the other.

The husband's name was Qasim. He was the son of Hashim Ali, the Zaildar of the village. The wife's name was Zeenat. Hashim Ali had left the village with a caravan of the villagers a few hours ago. Till that day, Hashim Ali had been confident that his village was safe. There had been rumours that the neighbouring village had been attacked and that a group of attackers were heading towards the village. A man, riding a horse, had come to tell them that a group of iron-smiths had been wiped out. But Hashim Ali had assured everyone, "Be calm, don't panic. The richest Sardar in the neighbouring town is my friend. He is even thinking of sending his children here for safekeeping." But that morning when Hashim Ali had gone to see the the Sardar and seek reassurance, he had seemed a bit worried. Some of the Sikhs who were with him, had taken him to one side and said, "Don't be deceived. The people who have recently come from Bhasin, have formed an armed band and they are not willing to listen to reason."

As soon as Hashim Ali had reached his village, he had called a meeting of everyone. It had been decided that they would leave the village. There was a lot of screaming and moaning. People wept as they gathered their luggage together in bundles. Sikh children who had played with Muslim children embraced each other. Karan held Siraj in his arms and said, "No, Tai, I'll not let him go." Siraj's mother pulled her son away and said, "We no longer have a place here." People picked up this, threw down that in a hurry. They gave things to their friends for safekeeping. Then they picked up their luggage, loaded it on their backs and gathered together in the lanes outside. The soul of the village was ready to leave its body. Old men wept when they saw the walls of their houses. Even Hashim Ali had tears in his eyes. He urged Qasim not to stay behind.

"Don't worry," Qasim said, "Zeenat is too weak to walk with Mubina in her arms. Don't worry. We'll follow on the horse and catch up with you on the other side of the border."

Some other young men also stayed behind. They thought they would help those who had to stay back.

The people who left in the caravan left their country behind; their homes and wells behind; their soil behind; their berry trees, which had the sweetest berries imaginable, behind. As they walked past the well, Ibrahim's wife couldn't help exclaiming, "I just spent twenty rupees on that pulley." Many other eyes paused on once favourite spots, beloved spots. Suddenly, all that was familiar vanished from their sight. Their eyes were now fixed on all that shimmered on the other side of the border.

Someone came running from the town with the news that armed men, riding on horses, had reached the brick kiln. Qasim ran towards the stable. But it was empty. He ran back home, shouting, "Zeenat, Zeenat, pick up Mubina. Someone has let the horse loose. Now we'll have to hide in the fields behind the house."

They had just reached the wheat fields, when the armed gang entered the village and walked towards its central square.

They heard others running past them. "They are our own people," Qasim said.

There was such a lot of commotion in the village that it seemed as if the sky had fallen down.

Mubina had not yet woken up, but she had begun to stir. It was a difficult situation.

"She will start crying at any moment. The gang will soon reach our house."

Two men on horses rode past the embankment. It seemed as if they were chasing someone who was trying to get away.

"Zeenat, give Mubina to me. I'll leave her under that lasuda tree before she wakes up. She'll sleep there. The moment the gang leaves the village, I'll come back for her."

"I don't think we should do that."

"Come on, hurry up. That's the only solution. Her safety, and ours, depends upon it. If she wakes up, all of us will be killed."

They heard the sound of firing in the village.

"Give her to me. Quickly."

Zeenat kissed Mubina. Qasim took Mubina from her hands and placed her down under the lasuda tree. He suddenly caught a glimpse of a gold chain around her neck. It had been given to her by his mother. At first, he thought he'd take it with him. Then it occurred to him that it might tempt someone to pick up the child and look after her well.

"May God protect you," he said, and joined Zeenat.

At that very moment, they heard a lot of noise coming from their house.

"Follow me quickly. Be careful. Come on, come on."

Frightened by the noise, they ran further into the fields.

"Hai, Mubina must be crying," Zeenat said, and stopped running.

"Leave Mubina to Allah. Come on. There is no time to stop." Pushing their way through the crops, they reached the other side of the field. Zeenat was terrified.

"You wait here for a minute. I'll go to that embankment and see what's happening."

The night was dark and frightening. The birds were screaming. The cry of the birds, which had once accompanied Qasim to the madarssa, now seemed to be the call of death. The well, beside which Zeenat's bridal party had rested a few years ago, seemed to be like the mouth of Hell.

The clouds thundered. A gentle shower of rain caressed Zeenat's cheeks. She suddenly remembered that Mubina had not drunk anything. But it was impossible to go back and fetch her.

When it became a little less dark, Qasim and Zeenat walked towards the river. When they reached the river, they discovered that there were lots of people already there. There was only one boat with two boatmen to take them across. Even though the boatmen were Muslims, they were demanding twenty rupees each to row people across. Many women had taken off their jewels and had offered them to the boatmen. Two women, who had failed to persuade the boatmen to take them across, were sitting dejectedly on one side.

Zeenat took off two of her gold bangles and handed them to Qasim. He also asked her to give him the other two bangles, and he put them in his pocket.

Then he walked upto the boatmen and spoke to them in an authoritative voice, "O Miyan, aren't you afraid of God? Would it please you, if these young girls fell into the hands of your enemies. Besides, these bangles are made of gold and are not less than a hundred rupees a piece."

The boatmen were intimidated by Qasim. They agreed to take a boat full of refugees across the river. The border was no more than a quarter of a mile from the other shore, and the land in between was not inhabited.

Rain fell throughout the night. Water would collect on the broad leaves of the lasuda tree and then roll down when they shook in the breeze. Drops of water fell on Mubina's face. She cried helplessly. She cried through a part of the night and slept through the rest. Somehow, she survived the night.

The next morning when she opened her eyes, golden sunlight fell on her face. She kicked her legs and arms. The gold chain around her neck glittered.

The raiders had carried away all the heavy things from the village at night. They hadn't stayed for long. Even goondas are frightened by the silence of a deserted village. The next morning, however, after they had eaten well, they returned once more. The village presented a strange sight. Trunks were smashed open, people ran in every direction, women wept.

Someone inside pushed the window of Zeenat's house open. The man who had opened it looked out and saw the wheat-fields rippling in the sunlight. Then his eyes fell on the lasuda tree whose leaves were still wet with rain.

"What is that!" he exclaimed. "A small child under the tree!"

He ran out of the house, crossed the field and reached the lasuda tree. As soon as Mubina realized that there was someone standing near her, she stopped crying. Tears sparkled in her eyes and the gold-chain around her neck glittered in the sunlight. The man was delighted. He knelt down beside the child and tickled her under her chin. She smiled. He took the chain off her neck and tucked it in his tehmad. Then he picked her up and walked back the way he had come.

The man's companion was also happy with what he had found in Qasim's house.

"Let me go home now, Sardarji. I have found what I wanted," the man said.

"What have you found?" the Sardar asked. When he saw the child in the man's arms, he said, "She won't help you ease your hunger. Steal a few more things while you have the chance. There's still time. You'll regret it later. There are still lots of houses left to loot."

"No, Sardarji, let me go now. My conscience doesn't permit me to steal anymore. She is hungry."

"A girl?"

"Yes."

"You are lucky. She must be Qasim's daughter."

"Can I leave now?"

"As you wish. You can still take a few clothes for your wife."

"You know my wife. She curses me everyday for being a thief. She thinks that it is because of my sins that we still don't have a child. Besides, she'd rather have this child, than have new clothes."

"Go, take her home. Leave my horse at the haveli on your way back."

The Sikh was a zamindar in a village nearby. That man was his servant. He was a Muslim. It was with the man's help that the Sikh zamindar had looted many houses in the area. When all the other Muslims had fled from the village a few days ago, the Sikh had persuaded the man to stay back. "No one will dare to touch you," he had assured the man.

When the man reached home, his wife opened the door and turned away without looking at him. The man entered, shut the door behind him and said, "Don't you want to know what I have brought?"

"What could you have brought me? Lots of money to last me a life-time?" the woman replied without looking at him still.

"Don't talk nonsense. At least come and see," the man said, as he uncovered the child's face.

"O my God," the woman exclaimed, as soon as she saw the child. "Did you kill her poor mother?"

"I don't know whose child she is. I found her abandoned under the lasuda tree behind the zaildar's house," the man said. Then he pulled the gold-chain out of the folds of his tehmad and said, "I found this around her neck. I hid it because I didn't want anyone to become jealous."

The woman took the child in her arms. Kissed her. Blessed the gods. She didn't pay any attention to the gold-chain.

"You must be hungry, very hungry. You couldn't have had anything to drink throughout the night. I'll give you something, have patience." She fetched some milk. Asked her husband to hold the child and began feeding her milk out of a small cup. The child drank it greedily. The woman wiped the child's mouth with the hem of her shirt and said, "Strange are the ways of rasool. I didn't have a child of my own. I am grateful. Don't you leave me now."

The man and his wife were ecstatic. They spent many happy days playing with the child. The woman made the man promise that he would never steal again. "She'll not be a burden on us. Even I'll be able to earn enough to feed her."

But hardly two weeks had gone by, when the people in the village began talking about them. Refugees from Pakistan had occupied the village. They were not even willing to hear the name of a Muslim, leave aside tolerate his presence in the village.

One day the Sardarji came to the house of the man and the wife and said, "Moula, I am ashamed of myself, but I can no longer protect you. Your lives are in danger. The best thing for you to do would be to leave at once. It is still dark outside. I'll accompany you upto Rania. You can easily cross the border there."

"Whatever you say. We are under your protection."

"The situation here is bad. That's why I must ask you to leave."

"We are grateful to you."

"Leave tonight. I don't know what will happen tomorrow. It is dark and the ditch running alongside the fields is dry. No one will be able to spot us walking in it. But you'll have to leave the child behind."

The woman clung to the child in fear. She turned pale and exclaimed, "No, Sardarji. Don't ask me to do that. The lovely smell of her tiny hands has become a part of my very soul."

"I said that for your safety. You will have to walk for six miles. If the child cries on the way, you'll be killed. No one will listen to me. Thieves are on the prowl everywhere."

"I shall leave everything to God. I'll risk death, but I'll not leave her behind."

"As you wish. I'll help you as best as I can."

After the evening meal, the village was silent and its lanes were deserted. The Sardar and Moula lifted their bundles onto their backs and picked up their sticks. The woman held Mubina in her arms. They left the village as fast as they could. They began walking in the dry ditch along the wheat fields.

They had covered only a short distance when Mubina began to cry. At that very moment, they heard the sound of horses coming in their direction. It seemed as if Death was riding towards them. Terrified, Moula and his wife, clung to the side of the ditch. Suddenly, the Sardar had an idea. He quickly grabbed Mubina from the woman's arms, signalled to them to sit down quietly, and scrambled up the side of the ditch.

The horsemen hailed the Sardar and asked him who he was.

"It's only me. I am not a stranger."

"Who is that? O, Zail Singh?"

"Yes."

"What have you got in your arms?"

"I was out hunting. I had heard that a rich Muslim family was trying to escape."

"That's what we had heard also. We didn't come across anyone."

"They certainly passed this way. It seems they were afraid that the child would cry and betray their presence. That is why they abandoned her here."

The horsemen rode away in the direction of the village. The Sardar helped and encouraged the husband and wife along the way. Soon they managed to cross the border.

The next day, they reached Lahore. Tired and hungry, they found shelter in a refugee camp. The living conditions there were difficult, but the woman was happy that their lives were no longer in danger.

"Her parents are not alive," she said to herself. "No mother would abandon her daughter."

But a few tents away from her tent, Mubina's mother was lying delirious. No doctor could help her.

"I am not a mother," she wailed repeatedly. "I am a demon."

"Don't cry like this, daughter," someone said, trying to comfort her.

"It would have been better if I had been killed. I abandoned my own child...Jackals must have eaten her...Her tiny hands must have been crushed under the hooves of horses...She must have died of hunger...Someone must have buried her..." No one could bear to hear her lament.

Zeenat's brother was a government officer. He managed to get a permit for an army truck from the Deputy Collector and drove back to Zeenat's village. There he learnt that Moula had taken Mubina to Manavala. At Manavala, he was informed that Moula had made inquiries about a relative of his in Shekhupura.

Zeenat's brother went back to Lahore. There it was decided that he should go to Shekhupura. Zeenat insisted on accompanying him. He tried to dissuade her, but she was adamant. Finally, he agreed to take her with him.

Moula had, indeed, gone to Shekhupura and was staying with Saadat. Zeenat and her brother found him. But they didn't find either his wife or Mubina. Moula told them that he had recently come back from Wande. They took Moula to the police station. He stuck by his story that he had found Mubina, but that she had died of hunger on the way. They had hurriedly buried her. Neither Zeenat's pleas nor money made him change his story.

They found his wife the next day and took her to the police station also. She didn't seem to be afraid. She repeated Moula's story word for word.

At first, Zeenat lost heart. But when she looked at the woman's face, she requested the police to let her talk to the woman in private.

When they were alone in a room, something about Zeenat's face touched her heart, and she recollected that moment when the Sardar had asked her to leave the girl behind. "Maybe the sweet smell of the child's hands have become a part of her soul too," the woman thought to herself. But she at once pushed her moment of weakness aside and continued to tell lies to Zeenat.

"Are you telling the truth? Did you bury the child?"

"Yes, Bibi. I poured dust over her body with these unfortunate hands."

"Did she have a gold-chain around her neck?" Zeenat asked as her voice trembled.

The woman pulled the gold-chain out of her blouse pocket and handed it to Zeenat. "This belongs to you," she said.

When Zeenat saw the gold chain, she screamed. When people rushed into the room, they saw that Zeenat had fainted.

Now even the thanedar was convinced that the man and the woman were telling the truth. After all the gold chain would have provided them with food for a few months. He decided to let them go.

Everybody was busy looking after Zeenat. When the doctor arrived and heard the story, he wanted to talk to the woman himself. But the man and the woman, finding themselves in the way, had left.

The doctor examined Zeenat and said, "There is nothing t fear. Let her be as she is. Maybe she'll say something which wi help us to find a cure."

Zeenat lay in a faint for a few minutes. Just as the doct decided to help her, the woman reappeared. She was carrying child in her arms. She placed the child on Zeenat's boso Qasim screamed, "Mubina!"

The woman then placed the child's hands on Zeenat's fa The doctor moved forward to pick up the child, when the wom said, "No. I am holding the child. Maybe the sweet smell of the child's hands will help wake her up."

Zeenat opened her eyes. She noticed that a pretty child was lying on her body. She mumbled, "What sweet smell is this? Whose hands are these?"

"Your Mubina's!" Qasim said.

"No, my Sakina's," the woman said, contradicting him.

Zeenat kissed Mubina again and again. Mubina began to cry. The woman took her in her arms and comforted her.

Zeenat turned to the woman and asked, "Tell me, if she is my Mubina or your Sakina."

"You gave birth to her, I saved her life. I named her Sakina — If she is my Sakina, then you are her massi. I'll make day and night one to look after her. I'll do whatever you ask me to do for her. She'll marry whomever you want her to marry."

Zeenat thought that the woman looked like an angel. She felt that the woman had a greater claim on Mubina than she had herself.

She kissed Mubina and placed her in the woman's lap. Then she said, "She will always be your Sakina. You are her mother and I am her massi. But you must do me a favour."

The woman was not Mubina's mother. Yet she was the centre of attention of everyone. She had never felt herself to be so kind, good and rich. "Yes, sister. I'll do whatever you ask me to do. I am beholden to you. What favour can I do for you?"

"Mubina's mother and father must henceforth live in our house," Zeenat said, as she extended her arms towards the woman. The woman put her arms around Zeenat. Their tears mingled. With their arms around each other, it became difficult to tell the mother apart from the massi.

Original in Punjabi.
Translated by B.M. Sagar
and Alok Bhalla.

GULAM ABBAS

AVTAR: A HINDU MYTH

1

Prithvi took the shape of a cow and went to the court of Indra - the court of the Gods. She stood before Indra and pleaded, "May Indra Maharaj be praised. Maharaj, there is no religion left anywhere in the world. The darkness of sin has spread over it. In every city, in every town, in every village, innocent people are being slaughtered. Villages have been reduced to ash. Unborn children have been plucked out of the wombs of pregnant women, impaled on spears and brandished in the air. Breasts of women have been cut, noses of men have been chopped off, people have been roasted alive in fire. Human beings have become more ferocious than the beasts. I can no longer watch such horror, Maharaj. Permit me to leave this hell and sink into the nether world."

Indra Maharaj is the Lord of the Heavens. He rides a white elephant whose name is Iravat. Indra Maharaj is the God of the rains and of the crops. Thunder, lightening and the rainbow are his weapons. Prithvi's complaint disturbed and saddened him. He sat for a long time deep in thought. After a while, he sent for Ganeshji. Ganeshji is the son of Shiva and Parvati, and he has the head of an elephant. He is the god of knowledge and wisdom, and can solve all difficulties.

Ganeshji advised Indra Maharaj to call the assembly of the Gods. Amongst the gods present were Agni, the god of fire, Vayu, the god of wind, Basant, the god of the seasons, Madan, the god of the mountains, Surya, the sun god, Somdev, the god of the moon and many other gods. They didn't know what to do. Therefore, Indra Maharaj went with all of them to see Brahma.

Brahma had created the earth. His colour is red. He has four heads, eight ears and four hands. He holds a bow in one hand, a necklace of skulls in the other, a bowl of water in the third and the *Vedas* in the fourth. Saraswati, the goddess of wisdom, is his wife.

Indra Maharaj repeated Prithvi's tale of woe to Brahma. He, too, couldn't find a solution and console her. He decided to go with the gods to see Mahadev.

Mahadevji is also known as Shiva. He has five heads, four arms and three eyes. The third eye is on his forehead. He looks like a sadhu. His long hair is matted, his body is smeared with ash from funeral pyres, he wears a necklace of hissing snakes around his neck and wanders from one forest to another. Whenever he is drunk, he dances in mad ecstasy the Tandav dance with his wife, Jagdamba. Then the earth shakes and trembles. He knows how to put an end to evil in the world.

But even Shiva could find no solution to Prithvi's sorrow. He, therefore, went with all the gods to meet Vishnuji, who was resting with his wife, Lakshmi, on the coils of the snake, Sheshnag, on the waves of the sea.

Vishnu Bhagwan can transverse all the worlds in three strides. He rides the big bird, Garuda. The Ganga springs from his feet. He is a graceful, young and kind-hearted man. He always honours the pleas of those who are in distress.

He was woken up from his sleep by the gods. They stood before him with folded hands and began to sing his praises, "Maharaj, Adhiraj, who can sing your praises! In your incarnation as a fish, you saved the whole world and rescued the *Vedas* from out of the flood-waters. In your avtar, as the tortoise, you lifted the mountain on your back during the great churning of the sea by the gods and the demons; as a pig you lifted the earth out of the bottom of the sea with your teeth; as Narasingha, with a lion's head and a man's body, you appeared in the world to save Prahlad from his cruel father; as a dwarf you fooled Raja Bal. You appeared as Parashuram twenty one times in the world and destroyed the kshatriyas so that the brahmins could establish their kingdom. Your avtar, Ramchandraji killed the most vicious of the rakshasas, Ravana. And your avtar Krishna Bhagwan killed the cruel king of Mathura, Kamsa. As Gautam Buddha, who was also your avtar, you spread peace and happiness throughout the world.

Nathji, whenever there has been unendurable evil and suffering in the world, you have gone down to the earth to defend the innocent and the bereaved. Today, once again, the darkness of sin and evil has spread over the world. The earth is red with the blood of men and women. Prithvi has come to the court of the Gods to plead for help. She says that she has never witnessed such cruelty and barbarity before. Unable to endure it, she wants to sink into the nether world.

Nathji, we have come to request you to turn your attention towards the earth once more. Help men and women to live in peace once more. Only you can do it.

Kind-hearted Vishnu was deeply moved by the plea. His face was clouded with sadness. He sat lost in thought for a long time. Then he suddenly cast a loving glance at his wife and disappeared.

2

Sambhal is an old town in Moradabad District. It is not different from the other towns in India. It has the same narrow lanes, the same dust and beggars, mud hovels and small red-brick houses. The only thing that distinguishes it from the other towns is that it has a large number of temples.

Before the Partition of India, the population of Sambhal was made up of Hindus and Muslims. But during the days of the Partition, storms of violence raged through this town also. Hindus, who were in the majority in the town, began to systematically kill the Muslims who lived in it. Armed gangs of Hindus attacked Muslim localities, burnt down their houses, butchered countless men, women and children. Those Muslims who survived the massacre, fled from the town.

A few miles outside Sambhal, hidden from the roads that led into the town, there was a deserted valley. A few Muslim families, who had survived the carnage, sought shelter in that valley. Most of those who managed to reach its safety were women and children. A few men, who had been badly injured by the Hindus, also managed to drag themselves there.

The entire country was in flames. Death awaited the Muslims everywhere. Those who had reached the valley decided that it would be best for them to hide there for some time. At the slightest sign of danger they would move further into the valley. For days on end they survived on leaves and grass. Down at the very bottom of the valley they discovered a small stream. Water from it quenched their thirst.

In Sambhal itself, the rage of the Hindus subsided after sometime. Most of the Muslims who used to live there had either fled or been killed. The Hindus had also taken possession of the houses, shops and other properties of the Muslims. Satisfied with their success, they had given up the idea of pursuing the Muslims who had fled.

Slowly, over time, the situation in the country began to improve. Religious leaders and heads of different sects, got together to form peace committees and tour every village and town. They made attempts to rehabilitate those Muslims who had been forced to leave their homes.

One of these committees happened to reach the valley where the Muslims of Sambhal had found refuge. The members of the committee consoled these Muslims and tried to persuade them to return. They, however, refused to do so for they were terrified of living with the Hindus of Sambhal again. The committee, unable to do anything more for them, left them to look after themselves as best as they could.

When the Muslims began to feel a little more confident of themselves and the danger to their lives receded, they cleared a bit of the land around the valley and built a few houses of mud and grass to live in. Over time, other Muslim families, who had been wandering in despair in the area, joined them and established a small colony of about one hundred and fifty people.

Amongst the Muslims who had escaped the night of the massacre in Sambhal and had taken shelter in the valley, was an iron smith named Ibrahim. He was a hard working and a decent man. He had a small house in Sambhal and he used to live in it with his father and three sons. His elder brother, Ishaque, used to work with him. His other two brothers, who were very young, used to study in a school.

When a group of armed Hindus set fire to his house, all the members of the family were inside. The moment they tried to run out of the house, they were attacked with spears and knives by the Hindus. The men had put up a brave fight. They had snatched a few knives from the attackers and had killed some of them. But the Hindus were in greater number and they couldn't resist them for long. Finally, Ibrahim's father, his elder brother, Ishaque, both his younger brothers, Ishaque's two young daughters who had fought the Hindu goondas alongside their father and uncle, and Ibrahim's youngest son were all martyred. Thanks, however, to their resistance, Ibrahim's wife and sister-in-law managed to escape.

Ibrahim had been badly wounded fighting the Hindus, but his injuries were not fatal. He escaped with his life. After wandering through the lanes of the town for a while, he was fortunate enough to find his wife and sister-in-law. The three of them, under the cover of darkness, fled from the town. On the way, they met other Muslims who had also escaped the massacre.

Ishaque's wife, Bilquese, had managed to save her eight month old daughter. Ameena, Ibrahim's wife, had seen her two year old innocent son, Ashar, slaughtered. She was paralysed with fear and sorrow. It was an experience which could not be forgotten easily. When she discovered that there were many others who had suffered like her, she began to turn to them for consolation and support. The pain in her heart became more endurable.

There was an old and dilapidated temple near that valley. Its roof had caved in and none of its walls were intact. The archaeological department had removed the idols from it a long time ago and placed them in a museum. There was an unused well outside the temple. Bats had begun to live in it. The refugees made a rope out of grass, got hold of an old tin can and began to draw water for their use from the temple well.

Since the refugees had no money or jewellery with them, they were not afraid of dacoits. There were, however, a few young Hindu hoodlums who did not even want them to live like untouchables in the colony they had established. They often sneaked in at night and set fire to their huts. People of the colony almost always managed to control the fire quickly enough to prevent extensive damage. But once the fire was so fierce that it burnt more than half of the huts in the colony. That incident upset the Muslim refugees, but they controlled their anger and decided to act with patience and circumspection. They built a boundary wall of mud and stone around their colony. That wall protected them, at least to some extent, from the mischief-makers.

Necessity forced the Muslim refugees to learn new skills. They learnt to make ropes, baskets, mats, brooms, clay pots and toys. They sold them cheaply to the small shopkeepers in the town. In the course of time, they learnt to spin cotton and weave bed covers. Some of them began to keep goats and hens, and sell meat and eggs to the people in the town. They fed their children goat's milk.

A majority of the women in the colony had lost their husbands in the massacres. Circumstances, had thus, forced them to come out of purdah and labour along with the men. They learnt to weave cloth and make clay-pots. They also took upon themselves the task of fetching water from the well.

Ibrahim's wife and sister-in-law also did their share of work. Bilquese had no desire to live after the martyrdom of her husband and two children. But she was forced to carry on with the task of life because of her little daughter, Sara. The music of her daughter's laughter sometimes made her forget her sorrow.

Even Ameena's sadness had diminished a little. The anticipation of giving birth to a child and becoming a mother again had helped her to endure the pain of loss. The strange thing was that as the time of delivery approached a glow, a joy appeared on her face. She felt neither fatigue nor heaviness, inspite of her rough and hard life. She did her work and if someone tried to stop her, she would say, "I have found a new source of strength. These tasks seem light and easy."

Nine months after the Muslims of Sambhal had built their colony, a child was born in Ibrahim's hut. It was born a little past midnight. The fourteenth day moon had already completed its journey across the sky. Ibrahim's hut looked beautiful in its light. When a new sound of life broke the silence of the colony, Ibrahim rushed inside the hut. He saw Ameena lying on a mat, and Bilquese cleaning the blood-stained body of the child with rags. The moment Bilquese saw Ibrahim, she said, "Congratulations, Bhai, you now have a son."

Ibrahim's eyes began to glow with delight. He looked at his wife's face. She was moaning softly. As soon as her eyes met his, a slight smile appeared on her lips. Ibrahim sat down cross-legged on the mat. Bilquese wrapped the child in a clean cloth and placed him in his lap.

The child was beautiful to look at. His head was covered with golden curls and his face was glowing with a bright golden light. Ibrahim looked at him with wonder and awe. After sometime, he handed the child back to Bilquese and knelt down to pray.

Ibrahim named the child, Hamzah. Despite Ibrahim's poverty and the unsanitary conditions in the colony, the child remained healthy. To protect him from the evil eye, Ameena used to cover his head with a black cloth.

Hamzah began to grow up very quickly. Soon his lovely laughter could be heard in the huts all around. In a few months, he learnt to walk. And he wasn't even a year old when he began to babble. He spent his day playing with Sara, who was older than him. He was a good-natured and happy child who neither whined nor threw tantrums.

At the age of five he began to go to the school which a kind hearted maulvi had started in one of the huts of the colony. Hamzah was so intelligent that he learnt the *Bagadadi Kaida* in a few days and began to read the first stranger of the *Holy Koran*. Noticing his intelligent and keen interest in learning, the maulvi began to pay him special attention.

Hamzah was a generous boy. If his mother ever gave him anything special to eat, he would take it to school and share it with his class-mates.

Before he was eight years old, Hamzah had read through the *Holy Koran*. To celebrate that occasion his father distributed ladoos to everyone in the colony.

Hamzah was not only good in his studies, he also surpassed all the other students in sports. By the time he was ten years old there was no boy in the colony who could beat him at wrestling, kabbadi or racing. He could climb tall trees with such agility that his friends would watch him in wonder.

During that period an event occurred which became the topic of conversation in the colony for several days. What had happened was that Hamzah, as usual, had climbed a very tall tree. The upper branches of that tree were weak. As soon as Hamzah tried to catch one of them, it broke and Hamzah fell about twenty-five feet to the ground. All the other boys ran away in panic. But Hamzah merely laughed as he dusted his clothes and stood up. He didn't even have a scratch on his body.

After Hamzah had acquired a knowledge of Urdu and mathematics, along with that of the *Koran*, his father pulled him out of school in order to teach him the family craft. Ibrahim had opened his iron-smith's shop under a thatched roof. Both the father and son laboured there morning and night. Hamzah used to keep the fire going and hammer iron bars into shape, and Ibrahim used to make agricultural tools and other useful things.

Thus, ten or twelve years passed peacefully for the refugees in the colony of Sambhal. But those years weren't peaceful for the Muslims in the rest of India. The life of the refugees was undisturbed because they were very poor. They, too, were contented with their lot, because they believed that God wished them to live a life of poverty. They were grateful for his blessings, and rarely ever left their colony. When the Hindu traders from Sambhal and the neighbouring towns came to buy their goods, they treated them with courtesy and never gave them any cause for complaint. Their handiwork had improved considerably. They had also begun to supply milk to the neighbouring towns.

The Muslim refugees of the colony had preserved their Islamic ways. A big hut in the middle served as a mosque where they offered prayers five times a day. Apart from this they also celebrated Id and Bakra-Id. But they did so quietly.

During one such festival, Ibrahim closed his shop early. Hamzah, having nothing to do, wandered far into the valley alone. He saw signs of habitation, but without paying them any attention, he continued to walk. Soon he reached an open field where he saw some children playing. Some were playing cricket, some kabbadi, and some were practicing wrestling tricks. He watched them for some time with curiosity and interest.

The open ground lay just outside Sambhal. When the children saw Hamzah they were curious about him because he was dressed like a villager. He told them that he lived in a village nearby, because they couldn't ever imagine that a Muslim boy from the refugee colony would ever dare to come that far. When they invited him to join them, he readily agreed.

In a short while the Hindu boys of Sambhal realized that no one could match Hamzah's speed, cunning, strength or wrestling ability. Jealous that he had defeated each of them, they pounced on him together. Hamzah, however, was not perturbed. He tossed them into the air as if they were puffs of cotton. After he had defeated them, they stood around him at a distance and asked him to leave the field.

Upon returning home, Hamzah didn't narrate the incident to his parents or his friends because he was afraid that the news would reach the people in Sambhal and they would seek vengeance on the colony at night.

At the age of eighteen, Hamzah was a tall, handsome and well-built young man. His features were sharp, his skin fair, his large eyes were like half-opened lotus flowers, and hair seemed to be made of spun gold. If ever a girl caught sight of him, she could never erase his image from her heart. And Sara was willing to sacrifice her life for him.

Sara herself was a small and delicate woman. Her smiling face was like a flower and her eyes seemed intoxicated with joy. Together they made an ideal couple. And whenever someone in the family said that there was no need to look for a match for them, Sara would lower her head and blush. All the girls of the colony were envious of her good fortune.

As a child, Hamzah had seen the terrible conditions under which his parents and the other refugees in the colony had struggled to live. He knew they had accepted their fate. However, when he grew up he became acutely conscious of the degradation and the humiliation of the Muslims of the colony. He had heard horror stories about the massacre of the Muslims in Sambhal. He knew that Hindu goondas had forced his parents to abandon their comfortable home in Sambhal; that his uncle, his cousins had become martyrs while defending themselves against the Hindu hooligans; he also knew that his brother, Ashar, had been cruelly beheaded before his mother's eyes. He had heard of similar atrocities perpetrated on other families. Whenever he recalled those stories, he couldn't suppress his rage. He also saw how hard the men and the women of the colony worked to feed themselves and their children, while the Hindus treated them as untouchables. What hurt him most was the continuous effort by Hindu goondas to burn down their huts and drive them away.

The more he thought about all these things, the more perturbed he became. He began to brood and withdrew into himself. He even stopped eating. When Sara and other family members asked him why he had changed, he refused to give them a reply. Sara was deeply troubled by the change that had come over him. Even her love for him couldn't mitigate his sorrow.

After spending several days in despondency, he went to his parents and said, "I no longer feel like staying in this place. I want to go away. I shall earn my living wherever I am. I shall go disguised as a Hindu, so that no one will do me any harm. Please do not worry about me."

Ibrahim and his wife looked at each other with surprise. Without any sense of modesty, Sara caught him by his shirt, and wept and pleaded with him, "How can you go without me? I can't live without you."

"Don't worry, Sara," he said, trying to console her. "I shall return soon with beautiful clothes and ornaments for you."

"I neither want clothes nor ornaments. I only want you to take me with you."

But he did not listen to her pleas. His parents and Bilquese tried their best to stop him. He made a small bundle of clothes and left the same day.

Days and weeks passed, and Hamzah did not return. When the members of his family didn't see his face for six months, they were convinced that someone had recognized him and killed him. The three women remembered him and wept for him bitterly. His father walked about in the colony like a shadow with his head bowed. He neither talked to anyone nor answered anyone's questions. His shop seemed deserted.

A year after he had left home, Hamzah suddenly reappeared one night. His parents couldn't believe their eyes. They embraced him. Bilquese, Sara and his mother wept. Ibrahim kissed his forehead. Hamzah, however, stood like a statue. There was neither a smile on his lips nor a glow in his eyes.

His family noticed that he had grown thin like a thorn; his eyes had become lusterless like extinguished coal. It seemed as if he had been seriously ill. They asked him numerous questions, but he didn't answer a single one. It was as if he hadn't heard anything. His mother placed a plate of food before him, but he didn't even raise his eyes to look at it.

There was a broken cot lying in a corner of the hut. He lây down on it and soon afterwards went to sleep. His family heard him groan in his sleep throughout the night.

When he woke up the next morning, he seemed calmer. His mother offered him a glass of goat's milk. He drank it without any hesitation. His family again asked him many questions. At first he remained silent, then he took a deep breath and began narrating all that had happened to him during his absence.

"After taking leave of you, I wandered through many cities. I worked hard during the day and spent the night outside a sarai or a temple. Apart from dressing like a Hindu, I also learnt a few Hindu idioms so that no one discovered my real identity. No one suspected that I wasn't a Hindu.

I discovered that the Muslims everywhere in India were neglected, victimized and helpless. They always seemed to be afraid of something. Their mosques, their graves, the tombs of their apostles had been destroyed. They were too weak to protest and to defend themselves. Hardly a single day passed without there being an attack against the Muslims in some city or the other of India. In these attacks thousands of men, women and children were killed. The homes of the Muslims were looted and burnt. Those Muslims who survived were subjected to the worst kinds of atrocities and were forced to live a life of misery and degradation. God alone knows how much blood of the innocent Muslims has mingled in the waters of the Ganga, Jamuna, Narmada and Tapti.

Once I went to work as a labourer at the railway station of a big city. There I met an old man who was also working as a labourer. He was an emaciated looking man with sunken eyes. I had not seen a more pathetic figure. Although he wore his dhoti like a Hindu, I suspected that he was a Muslim like me. So I took courage and greeted him as a Muslim. The old man began to tremble with fear and look around him apprehensively. After I reassured him, he confessed that he was a Muslim.

He was once a successful trader. He had many sons and daughters. When the anti-Muslim riots broke out in his city, his house was surrounded by Hindu goondas. He was tied with ropes and his virginal daughters were raped before his eyes and cruelly butchered. His sons too were slaughtered. Still not satisfied, the Hindu goondas sprinkled kerosene around the house and set it on fire. His old father was buried under the debris. But the man himself somehow survived. Now he lives like a labourer and pretends that he is a Hindu.

I not only heard about such incidents, I also saw them with my own eyes. The faces of the tormented and the butchered are always before me. I can never forget their agony and their horror.

I have come back just to reassure you that I am alive. But I will not be able to stay here for long. There is a voice within me which is urging me to move on. I don't yet know where I'll go, or what I'll do. But I feel as if I have been chosen to perform an important task."

Ibrahim, Ameena, Bilquese and Sara heard Hamzah's tale without saying anything. When they woke up the next morning they discovered that his bed was empty.

The forces of evil which had lain quietly for so long in Sambhal suddenly rose up again. Someone spread the rumour that the Muslims had been drawing water from the sacred well of the Hindus and had polluted it. The rumour was used by the orthodox Hindus, who couldn't tolerate the presence of the Muslims on Indian soil, to incite a protest movement against the Muslims. The result was that a large crowd of Hindus gathered around the temple well and began to tease the Muslim women who had gone there to fetch water. They forced the women to leave without water. Later they set up guard over the well. Hindu volunteers took turns to keep watch over the well till midnight.

This was a serious matter for the inhabitants of the colony. They could put up with all sorts of hardships, but they couldn't survive without water. Muslim women were forced to go to the well after midnight to fetch water. Life went on like this for a few days, but when the Hindus heard that Muslim women were going to the well after midnight to fetch water, they decided to ambush them. They hid near the temple and when the Muslim women came for water, they pounced upon them like hungry wolves and began to rape them. They cut off the breasts of those who tried to resist.

When the screams of the women, mingled with the laughter of the goondas, reached the colony, the men rushed to their aid. They carried axes, rods and sticks with them. At first, the Hindus were frightened and thought of running away. But when they saw that there were no more than twenty-five Muslims who had attacked them, and they were supported by at least a hundred members of their own community, they turned back to fight the Muslims.

The Muslims fought bravely and killed a number of the Hindus, but how long could a handful of them have fought a large crowd? After a brief fight many Muslims became martyrs while defending their women. Those who were injured and tried to escape were quickly overpowered by the Hindus. Ibrahim was amongst those who were caught. He was wounded and was bleeding profusely.

The Hindus tied the Muslim men and women with ropes. Along with the eight or ten Muslims who had been killed, twenty or thirty Hindus too had died. In their frenzy for revenge for the death of the Hindus, the goondas decided to light a big pyre and burn the infidel Muslims alive along with the corpses of the Hindus.

Many of the Hindus rushed to the town to bring back cart-loads of wood. In a short while a big pyre was lit in front of the temple. Its flames leapt high into the sky.

Sara, who was tied with a rope to her mother and her aunt and was lying on the ground, looked around with fear in her eyes for her uncle. When she saw him writhing on the ground with blood oozing out of his body, she screamed hysterically. Ibrahim heard her scream and raised his head with a great deal of effort. Sara and he looked at each other in utter hopelessness.

Soon the Hindu goondas began to prod the captured men towards the fire. Ibrahim was the first one they pushed towards it. He had become so weak that he couldn't move. So a few of the volunteers picked him up and threw him into the fire. Sara let out a heart-rending scream.

The moment she screamed, there was a deafening burst of thunder in the sky. The earth shook and the fire was extinguished. The Hindus were terrified and began to run blindly in all directions. Just then a comet appeared in the sky. It was so bright that the entire earth and sky were illuminated. The comet rushed towards the temple at great speed. The nearer it came, the brighter it seemed. It so dazzled the eyes of those who looked at it, that they covered their eyes with their hands. It suddenly stopped over the heads of the Hindus and hovered over them for sometime.

Those who did manage to open their eyes and look at the source of light, saw a handsome young man standing in its midst. He rode a white horse and carried a long burning sword in his right hand. He wore a golden crown studded with rubies, diamonds, emeralds and other precious stones on his head. He wore necklaces of pearls around his neck. His horse, too, was gorgeously adorned with gems and plumes. The forelegs of the horse had long and colourful wings.

Seeing the strange horseman, the Hindus were paralysed with fear. They prostrated themselves on the ground and began to plead for mercy with folded hands.

On the other hand, the Muslims who had not been harmed by the fire looked at the horseman and couldn't take their eyes off him. Sara, too, stared at the horseman in wonder and awe.

The horseman then addressed the Hindus in his sombre, but sweet voice, as follows :

"I am the avtar of Kalki whose coming has been announced in the *Vedas*. I am the tenth and the last avtar of Vishnu Bhagwan. I was to appear at the end of Kalyuga, whose duration was supposed to be four lakh and thirty-two thousand years. But the earth is already so shrouded with evil and faithlessness that I have been forced to appear now.

I am Vishnu. Whenever the earth is threatened by evil, I leave my abode in Devlok and come here to protect the good and the innocent, and punish those who do evil. I have appeared on earth nine times before. But the evil I see now makes me shudder. You are not human beings. You are worse than jackals. The earth which has given birth to you and sustained you, is so fed up with your deeds that it wants to sink into the nether world. Even the Gods above curse you, although you claim to worship them.

You have violated every law of goodness. You have ignored the commandments of the *Vedas* and tarnished the name of Hinduism. Hindu religion considers life so sacred that it even condemns the killing of an ant. Yet you have spilt so much blood in its name. You have raped women; stripped them naked and paraded them through the streets of the city; chopped off their breasts and noses; burnt them alive. You have pierced their children with your spears and flung them in the air. You claimed that you committed these crimes in the name of your religious duty.

What crime had your victims committed? That they believed in a different form of worship than yours? That their style of life was different? Is that such a big crime that they should be exterminated?

Don't you know that the final goal of all religions is the same? That every human being is a pilgrim who follows his own path to reach the same destination.

Ramchander, Krishna and Gautam Buddha were my avtars. They had taught you to be truthful, just, humble, tolerant and patient. They had preached against nurturing hatred towards anyone. In the eyes of the Enlightened One, all living things are equal.

But you have become the slaves of pride and luxury, greed and envy, bigotry and hatred. Ignorance has blinded you. You have mistaken poison for nectar and fire for flowers. You have forgotten that the world is an illusion. It is like the sky, the moment you attempt to touch it, it vanishes.

Truth, honesty, decency are not granted to one community only. Gods protect the entire universe. It is to prove this, I have decided not to be born as a Hindu this time, but as the son of a poor iron monger."

Original in Urdu.
Translated by Vishwamitter Adil
and Alok Bhalla.

KRISHAN CHANDER

THE PESHAWAR EXPRESS

I heaved a sigh of relief as I pulled out of the Peshawar railway station. My carriages were packed with passengers, all of them Hindus. They had converged here from Peshawar, Hoti Mardan, Kolhat, Char Sada, the Khyber Pass, Landi Kotla, Bannu, Naushehra and Mansahra. Overcome by a sense of grave insecurity in Pakistan, they were trying to escape to India. The railway station was under heavy military guard, the soldiers were constantly on the alert. The refugees who had taken shelter with me, felt greatly relieved when I slowly started moving towards the beloved land of Punjab. Fair, hefty and loose-limbed, clad in salwar and kameez and wearing kullaed turbans, they looked like Pathans and spoke Pushto or rugged Punjabi. Two soldiers had been deployed in each carriage for their protection.

They were Baluchi soldiers. Flaunting plume-like turras on their turbans, they carried new rifles and smiled indulgently at these Hindu Pathans and at their women and children, who looked on fear-stricken, anxious to get away from the land where their families had lived for countless generations. Its rocky soil had toughened their sinews and they had drunk deep from its ice-cold fountains. Today the same land had forsaken them, refusing to shower its bounty on them. They were bidding good-bye to their homeland with heavy hearts and conjuring up visions of a new home. They were grateful that they were still alive and that their womenfolk had escaped molestation.

I sped on while the people sitting in the carriages cast the last lingering looks at the high rocky cliffs, the green fields and the happy valleys with fruit-laden orchards — if only they could tuck the scenery into the folds of their dresses and carry it along with them! I felt so weighed down under their cataclysmic grief that it slowed down my speed.

People looked depressed, the very picture of woe till we reached Hasan Abdal. There were a large number of Sikhs who had congregated at the station. They had come from Punja Sahib, carrying long kirpans. Their faces were tense with fear and their women and children looked around apprehensively. As they got into the train they heaved a sigh of relief and started talking to the other Hindus and Sikhs in the train. The houses of some of them had been burnt down and all that they had left were the clothes they stood in. But there were others who had been able to retrieve even their broken cots and other petty belongings. The Baluchi guards stood in the doors, holding rifles at the ready. Full of self-importance, they looked at their companions from the corners of their eyes and gave meaningful winks.

I was stranded for a long time at the Taxila railway station, and wondered what was this long wait for. Maybe there were more Hindu refugees who were going to join us from the neighbouring villages.

The passengers took out their food and started eating. The children, who were earlier dumb with fear, began to chatter and laugh. Girls peeped out of the windows and old men got their hookahs going.

Soon they heard some noise in the distance mingled with the booming of drums. So the Hindu refugees were coming at last. The long procession came into sight. The drums boomed and the processionists raised slogans. The people in the train quickly hid their faces behind the windows for a ghastly sight greeted their eyes. Every Muslim in the procession was carrying the corpse of a Hindu on his shoulder. They had been caught while trying to escape. Two hundred corpses. Arriving at the station the Muslims, with great solemnity, entrusted the corpses to the care of the Baluchi guards, enjoining upon them to escort the corpses with every care across the border. The Baluchi guards gleefully promised to carry out their wishes. They put ten or fifteen corpses in each carriage. That done, the processionists fired in the air and ordered the station master to allow the train to move out of the station.

I was about to start. But no, there was another signal for me to stop. The leader of the procession told the Hindu refugees that with the departure of two hundred Hindus their villages looked empty which would spell ruin for their business and trade. In lieu of the two hundred Hindu corpses that were going away they would like to have a similar number picked out from the train. The Baluchi soldiers praised them for their wisdom and foresight. They pushed a few Hindus out of each compartment and entrusted them to the care of the mob.

"Line up, you kafirs!" the leader of the mob thundered. He was the biggest landlord of the area and notions of jehad echoed in his head.

The kafirs stood like statues. They were picked up one by one and made to stand in a line. Two hundred men. Two hundred living corpses, their faces drawn, their eyes pricking them like arrows.

The Baluchi soldiers went into action. Fifteen people fell.

This was the station of Taxila.

The place once boasted of the leading university of Asia, where thousands of students flocked from distant places to study civilisation and culture.

Fifty more people fell.

The museum of Taxila housed unique images and inimitable jewellery, representing the finest examples of ancient art.

Thirty more collapsed to the ground.

Here the great King Kanishka held sway and enriched the people as an exemplar of beauty, bringing prosperity to one and all.

Twenty-five more people met their final doom.

Here Lord Buddha preached the gospel of non-violence and his monks showed the people the true path to peace and salvation.

And then came the turn of the last among the group.

Here for the first time on the border of India had flown the flag of Islam — the flag which stood for brotherhood and equality among men.

They were all killed. Allah-O-Akbar!

The railway platform had turned red with the blood of the victims and when I pulled out of the station my wheels seemed to be slipping from the rails. I feared I would derail, bringing disaster to those who were hiding in the carriages.

Death had stalked through every carriage. There were corpses in the middle of each carriage, surrounded by living corpses over whom the Baluchi guard stood smiling. Somewhere a child whimpered, an old mother sobbed, a young wife moaned for her dead husband. Shrieking and whistling, I tore through the distance and stopped at the Rawalpindi railway station.

Here no refugees got into the train except for a few young Muslims carrying rifles and accompanied by burqa-clad women. Into one compartment, they loaded arms and ammunition — machine guns, pistols, rifles and cartridges.

I had left Jhelum and was on my way to Gujarat when they pulled the alarm chain and brought me to a stop. They ripped off the burqas of the veiled women. "We are Hindus, we are Sikhs!" the women cried. "These people have abducted us." But the young men only laughed and dragged the women off the train. "We are going to have our way with these women," they shouted. "Come, if any one of you has the guts to stop us."

Two young Hindu men, belonging to the Frontier, jumped down from the train. The Baluchi guards blithely marked them with their rifles and shot them dead. More young men came out. They were knifed to death by the Muslim mob. A wall of flesh cannot compete against bullets and knives of steel.

The Muslim youths dragged the Hindu women into the jungle. Belching dark hideous smoke from my mouth I sped on. It appeared the whole earth was covered with the dark forebodings of Doomsday. My breathing became stilted as if something had stuck in my chest which would tear it apart and the red flames which lay within me would erupt and engulf the whole jungle which had just now swallowed those fifteen women.

When we reached near Lalamusa, the corpses started emitting such a terrible stench that the Baluchi guards were forced to throw them out of the carriages. They would order a young man to get up and carry a dead body to the carriage door. Then would push the young man and the corpse out of the carriage. In no time all the dead bodies, along with those who had carried them, had vanished leaving sufficient space in the carriages for the people to stretch their legs in comfort.

I reached Wazirabad — the place known for its knives and daggers all over India. This was the town where the Hindus and the Muslims had for centuries celebrated Baisakhi together. The railway platform was littered with corpses. Perhaps this was a new way of celebrating the festival. Smoke billowed up from the city and near the station one could hear the sound of an English band to the accompaniment of cheering and clapping by the crowd. In a few minutes, the crowd had surged over the railway platform, dancing and singing, villagers forming the vanguard, followed by a concourse of naked women ranging from old grannies to young virgins. They were Hindu and Sikh women and Muslim men and together they were celebrating the most gruesome Baisakhi. The hair of the women was untied, their bodies were marked with wounds, yet they walked erect as if the death had already cast its dark shadow on their naked bodies.

A roar went up from the crowd, "Pakistan Zindabad! Islam Zindabad! Quaid-e-Azam Zindabad!"

The dancing feet suddenly receded and the crowd surged forward towards the train. The women in the carriages pulled the veils over their faces and hurriedly put down the shutters.

The Baluchi guards objected. The windows must not be pulled down. They felt suffocated for want of proper ventilation.

But the women paid no heed to them. They went on pulling down the shutters. Infuriated, the Baluchi guards opened fire. But by then not a single window had remained open. Only a few refugees had to pay the price for it with their lives.

The naked women were made to sit among the refugees. I bid farewell to the place to the shouts of "Islam Zindabad! Quaid-e-Azam Zindabad!"

A child crawled to an old woman. "Ma," he asked, "why are you sitting naked?" He wondered if she was returning from her bath.

The old woman forced back her tears. Today,the sons of her land had given her a sinister bath.

"And your clothes,where are they?" the child asked.

"My clothes were a sign of my married bliss," the old woman replied. "They have taken them away to wash out those signs."

Two young girls, sitting utterly naked, jumped out of the window. But unmindful of this calamity, I sped on and did not stop till I had reached Lahore.

I was made to stop on Platform No. 1. Another train from Amritsar had been received on Platform No. 2. She was carrying Muslim refugees from India. No sooner had I stopped, when Muslim volunteers made a thorough search of all the carriages and took away all the gold, silver and other valuables from the passengers. After this pillage they pulled out 400 passengers from the train and lined them up on the platform. They were the sacrificial lambs, for the Muslims had just discovered that there were 400 passengers missing from the train from Amritsar and fifty Muslim women had also been abducted from the same train. So to square up the loss, 50 Hindu women were hand-picked from my train and forced down onto the platform. To complete the tally, 400 Hindus were also butchered on the platform. The population parity between population of India and Pakistan had to be maintained.

The Muslim volunteers pulled out their daggers and formed a circle. With great alacrity, one Hindu at a time was pushed within the circle and was swiftly done away with. It was all over in a few minutes. The fatal counting was complete. I was allowed to pull out of the station.

By now I had started detesting, each and every part of my body. I felt utterly polluted as if I had been thrown out of Hell.

As I reached Attari, I sensed a change in the atmosphere. The Baluchi guards had been taken off at Moghulpura and their place had been taken by Dogra and Sikh guards. On reaching Attari, the Hindu refugees saw so many dead bodies strewn all over the place that they went delirious with joy. They knew they had crossed the boundary line between India and Pakistan, otherwise how could their eyes have been greeted by such an enchanting sight? When I arrived at Amritsar, the joyous cries of the Hindus and Sikhs shook the earth. Corpses of the Muslims were piled high. The Hindus and the Sikhs peeped into every carriage, asking if there were any Muslims travelling incognito.

Four Brahmins got into a compartment. Shaved heads, long tufts, they were wearing Ram-nam dhotis and declared that they were bound for Hardwar. A couple of Hindu Jats and Sikhs, armed with rifles and spears who were going into the interior of East Punjab for Muslim-baiting, also got into the same compartment.

One of them became suspicious. "Holy Brahmin, where are you going?" he asked.

"To Hardwar on a pilgrimage," the Brahmin replied.

"Good man, are you going to Hardwar or Pakistan?"

"Ya Allah!" the 'Brahmin' blurted out.

The Jat laughed. "We've got you," he said. "We'll remember our Allah together."

He pierced the 'Brahmin's' chest with his spears. The other 'Brahmins' tried to escape but the Jats got hold of them. "Brahmin Gods!" they said blithely. "You must submit to the trouser test. The trouser test is a must for all who want to go on a pilgrimage to Hardwar."

They got down to ascertaining if their victims were circumcised. The four Muslims who were trying to pose as Brahmins failed the test and were done to death on the spot.

I proceeded on my journey.

On my way, I was stopped in the thick of a jungle and some of the people from the train disappeared into the jungle. I thought a big contingent of armed Muslims was lying in wait to ambush the refugees. But what I saw froze my blood. A large number of Muslim peasants along with their women and children were hiding in the jungle.

The Muslim peasants were quickly encircled and the jungle rang with the cries of "Sat Sri Akal!" It did not take the attacking party more than a half hour to hunt the Muslims down and kill them. A Jat impaled the body of an infant on his spear and jubilantly flung it in the air.

A Pathan village this side of Jullundur caught their attention. The Hindus stopped the train and rushed into the village. The Pathans put up a spirited fight but they were outnumbered by the invaders and were soon put to the sword. With the men and the children out of the way, it was now the turn of the women to be annihilated.

In those very fields, where barns were brimming with the golden wheat, where the mustard flowers smiled, where young women, fed on the love legends of Heer-Ranjha and Sohni-Mahiwal, bent like tender stalks under the loving gaze of their husbands, the marauders hastily improvised temporary brothels under the peepal and rosewood trees. Here fifty women were made to serve five hundred ravishers. Fifty sheep and five hundred butchers. That day Punjab died. Warris Shah's *Heer* had suddenly became mute and his songs were silenced for ever. A million curses on our leaders for seven generations for tearing the beautiful Punjab into pieces and burying its pure soul deep into the earth!

I was struck dumb with terror as the Sikhs, Dogras and Hindus returned, carrying the dead bodies of Pathan men and women. The rail tracts lay over a canal bridge. As I passed over the bridge, I was forced to stop quite often to enable the people to dump the dead bodies into the canal. When all the dead bodies had been disposed off, people took out bottles of country liquor and drank to celebrate. I proceeded on my journey stinking of liquour and the blood of the innocent.

At the Ludhiana railway station, the vandals got down from the train and made for the town where they ransacked the houses of the Muslims and returned loaded with the booty. Till they had ravaged and plundered to their heart's content, and indulged in all sorts of savagery, they would not let me resume my journey. My soul was riddled with scars and my body stank to the skies, so polluted was it. I desperately felt the need for a bath. But I knew it was a vain hope; they wouldn't let me have it.

Around midnight when I reached Ambala Cantonment, a Muslim Deputy Commissioner got into a First Class compartment with his family, under military protection. A Sardar Sahib and his wife were also travelling in the same compartment. I had nearly traversed ten miles when I was made to stop. Some people smashed the window panes and forced their way into the compartment and made short work of the Deputy Commissioner, his wife and children. Then they stood facing his young and beautiful daughter, a college student, whom they had marked out for attention at the end. They quickly got hold of her box of jewellery, forcing her down from the train and dragged her and proceeded towards the jungle. The girl was holding a book.

They went into a huddle, undecided whether to spare the girl's life or do away with her.

"Don't kill me," the girl said. "Convert me to Hinduism. I'm prepared to embrace your religion. I'm also willing to marry one of you. What good will it do you to kill me?"

"Yes, she's right," one of them said.

"But I know of a better way," another man said thrusting a dagger into her stomach. "And now back to the train. We have no time for idle gossip."

The girl lay writhing in agony on the carpet of grass and died a tortured death. Her book was soiled with her blood. The title of the book was *Socialism: Theory and Practice,* and the writer's name, John Strachey.

The girl must have been an intellectual, harbouring the desire to serve her country and its people. She was the central figure in nature's mystery and gave meaning to the creation of the world. But now her dead body lay in the jungle, to be preyed upon by jackals, crows and vultures.

I have returned to Bombay after a long time. I have been given a thorough wash and stalled in a shed. My compartments are now neither stained with blood nor do they reek of liquour. I do not hear the echoes of wild laughter. But as I stand here in the stillness of the night ghostly figures seem to come to life and the shrieks of the wounded fill the air. I would never go on such a horrible journey again. I only wish to pass through a land studded with barns of golden wheat, and swaying mustard fields on both sides of the track. I want to hear, the Hindu and the Muslim peasants together sing the love legends of Punjab while they sow the fields, while their hearts brim with love for each other, and they are full of reverence for women.

I am a lifeless train — a structure of wood and steel, devoid of feelings. But even I hate to carry a cargo of blood and flesh dripping with hatred. I will haul food grain to famine-stricken areas. I will carry coal, oil and iron-ore to the mills, and ploughs and fertilisers to the farmers. I will carry groups of prosperous peasants and happy workers in my carriages. The pious and simple women, secure in the love of their husbands, would cast loving glances at them, and the children, their faces radiant like the lotus in bloom, will not cower before death but greet the life to come with mounting confidence. Then there will be no Hindus and no Muslims. There will only be workers and human beings.

Original in Urdu.
Translated by Jai Ratan.

N. G. GORE

A MOUTHFUL OF WATER, A MOUTHFUL OF BLOOD

1

In the sky not even a cloud as large as the palm of one's hand could be seen, and the whole firmament glowed like a will o' the wisp. Outside was sunlight, yellow, yellow and harsh and humid, and from the cracked earth were emerging puffs of steamy air. Our train, like a fly that has emerged from gur-syrup and might drag itself slowly, was scraping its way along towards Allahabad. In our carriage, of course, there was no small crowd, but still one was able to go over to the toilet at least, stepping on fellow passengers' luggage or even their feet. But every traveller knew that once the crowd of people gathered at Allahabad station pushed their way into the carriage, one would not even have that kind of room. So once the train moved forward, having passed the outer signal cabin at Allahabad, and the rattle of the rail points could be heard, every passenger gathered himself together in his place and sat tight. Passengers near the windows brought down the shutters. And, the way soldiers in a forward battle position sit facing the expected enemy, we took our positions. How was this new kinship formed in an instant among the hundred passengers already crammed into that carriage?

Just then the train arrived at the Allahabad platform. Even before the train stopped with a jerk, our carriage was besieged by soldiers in dirty green uniforms. It was as if the entire platform was covered by these soldiers, running about here and there in their boots, which clacked and clattered because of their inch-thick soles. At the door of our carriage was a vast-bodied Marwari, who had spread just as large a bedroll on which he had been lounging since we left Moghalsarai. Now, the door having been flung open, he was squeezed within and he started yowling like a fox with its leg in a trap. All of us too started squealing pathetically, in Hindi, sentences like — "Don't enter, there's no room here!" But who cared about our yelping and squealing? Bearded and moustached Sikh soldiers, Punjabi and Jat soldiers wearing berets with crests — they all blundered and banged their way into the carriage. Right away they pushed up the shutters of the platform-side windows with a clatter; and then they began to shove in through the windows such quantities of baggage —! Rifles, kit-bags, bedrolls, great hulking trunks — they piled up a veritable mountain of these in the carriage. Here their gear was coming in through the windows, and there the soldiers through the door. And all of us passengers inside were quite irritated. Already our clothes were stinking mostly of sweat and a layer of coal dust gathered on our faces and arms. The train already delayed by three or four hours — we were really quite tired and sour. And now, besides, this swarm of locusts had descended. Losing my temper at this state of affairs I spoke with some irritation.

"Why has this misfortune come to us, goodness knows! Why didn't they blunder into the military van!"

"They are military men. Who's to question them? Consider yourself fortunate that they haven't flung you out of the carriage!" said an old Muslim, sitting on the bench across from me, rolling a tobacco-laden gob of spit around in his mouth.

"You spoke quite true, Baba," supplemented a middle-aged woman from behind a burqa, drawn down over her face. "The military men are quite a barbarous 'caste'! They don't feel any pity or compassion, do they?"

All of us older passengers in the carriage, were saying similar things amongst ourselves about these new passengers. But they paid no attention to that. They were absorbed in stowing away their gear. Placing their heavy trunks on the floor, they put their kit bags on top of them, and somehow squeezed out sitting space for themselves. The sweat that had broken out on their bodies was visible even through their clothes. We were of course drenched in sweat. We were flapping-and-fluttering and chittering like cocks grabbed by the butcher's hand. Just then a broad, well-built Sikh among them, with three stripes, stood up and said in his broad voice,

"Done with stowing the gear?"

"Yes, Sardarji."

"Then relax now —," saying this he loosened the buckle on the belt about his waist, and said to himself as he was sitting down, "The war's over, at last! About to see the sight of home after five years!" This sentence had hardly emerged from his mouth, which was covered with a forest of beard and whiskers, when his eyes suddenly filled with tears, and stooping forward a little, he sat without moving.

A tall Punjabi man sitting next to him, pushing up the curling ends of his moustaches with the back of his hand, said, "Don't worry, yar. That we've returned alive from hell is Khuda's mercy! God willing, everything will come out right here on!"

Who knows to what extent the Sardarji's heart perked up at his friend's reassurance! But he sat up straight again, and, fondling his beard, he muttered, "Waheguru! Waheguru!"

Just then, from the back of the bench a fair little hand fell on Sardarji's shoulder, and someone in a sugary and innocent voice, said "Chachaji! Chachaji!" All of us started to look on. A fair child, with pale mischievous eyes, and hair like the red-brown beard of a head of corn, was talking, his little hands, like a rabbit's soft paws, were on the Sikh soldier's shoulders,

"Chachaji! Uncle!"

Turning around, the Sikh took both the child's hands in his own, and held them for quite some time. The child was staring at him boldly, cheekily, and he at the child, for so long. Such a great big soldier, like a boulder, was thawing within, it seemed, from that delicate contact, melting. Yet not a word broke out from his mouth. The awe created at first in the mind of the child by the Sardarji's huge presence, his military uniform, thick jungle of beard and whiskers, disappeared in a moment. And hooking his pink little fingers in his beard, he bubbled with laughter, "Look, Ma, a lion!"

Sitting beside him in her burqa, his mother said to him in tones of intimidation, "Anwar! You are such a shameless child!"

But it appeared that Sardarji had appreciated Anwar's joke. Placing a finger on the child's cheek, he laughed and said, "So, I am a lion; what are you then? A rabbit, right?"

We were watching all this with fond admiration. But I was thinking to myself, where have this mother and child come from?

That woman and the boy hadn't been in our carriage before Allahabad. Then how did they even enter through that mad rush of people? We were surprised. These two must have been flung in willy-nilly, having got entangled in the flood of people. We were looking in curiosity at the soft and round boy like a baby-rabbit, and he was asking Sardarji question after question —

"When will our train start?"

"It'll start in a moment."

"Why have you got on these clothes?"

"We soldier folk have to wear such clothes."

"What do you do with this bundook?"

"Shoot a bullet at some people — Bang!"

"Who?"

"People."

"Why?"

"Because they trouble you!"

Knowing that Anwar's questions will never end, his mother said, "Anwar, how much longer will you chatter! Sardarji will say, that Anwar is a very naughty boy, he troubles us greatly!"

To show his mother that he wasn't going to give in before her threat, he kept his hands on Sardarji's shoulders, and leaning towards his mother he said, "And then Sardarji will shoot me with a bullet?"

Sardarji quickly drew him close to himself, and lovingly pinching his cheek, he said, "Fool — see how he talks! No one would shoot a chirruping Bulbul like you, would he?"

And, wanting to turn his talk in another direction, he said, "Well, what goodies do you want, come on, tell!"

Anwar said carelessly, "I don't want goodies." And then suddenly he remembered that he was thirsty. He turned to his mother and shoving himself into her arms he began to nag, "Ammi, give me water! I am thirsty!"

Offering the empty mug of water to him, the mother said, "You know, don't you, that in the rush of people a while ago, all the water spilled? Now don't you nag me about water! Now you'll get water only after reaching Lucknow...nothing before that."

Sardarji stood up quickly and said, "Behnji, give me the lota, I'll fill it and bring it back in a moment."

Saying this he took the mug, and shoved half of his body out of a window! His mate was saying, "Udham Singh, hey, it's time for the train to leave. I'll give you some from my water bottle, don't you go."

But, saying, "I'll fetch it in a jiffy —" Udham Singh leapt onto the platform and ran towards the water tap. After a minute or so, giving a long whistle, the train moved. Passengers near the windows were leaning out to look. His companions were yelling to Udham Singh, who had started running like the wind to get to his carriage, "Come back at the next station"; and some were saying, "Come, run a little faster!" Anwar was astonished at all this fuss. Did I do something wrong? Did 'Chachaji' fall out of the train? Because of this uncertainty, the mischief in his eyes had curdled. His thirst and the hot sun had put a burnt-red veneer on his face. The train had begun to gather speed. Saying, "He won't come now," the Punjabi Muslim soldier held before Anwar, his own water bottle. Even before Anwar had taken a couple of sips from it, we heard from the door the Sardarji's voice,

"Anwar, see, I brought the water!"

The moment he heard these words, Anwar quickly pushed away the water bottle, and started to drink from the mug which Sardarji offered him. Sardarji was holding the mug with one hand, and the thick fingers of his other hand were caressing Anwar's silky hair.

Admiring this sight, the Punjabi Muslim soldier put his water bottle back in its place. And one of the Jat soldiers who was watching this vision curiously, said, smiling a little, "See what a commodity love is!"

Wiping off a trickle of water from Anwar's lip with the tenderness one might use in picking off a dew-drop from a rose petal, Sardarji only said, "My Lachman too must have grown just like this boy by now!"

Before this utterance ended, Sardarji's eyes had filled like a pond in the monsoon, he was unable to say more.

2

Two, two-and-a-half years passed after this.

The first Independence Day! In the Jamia Millia School in Karol Bagh, preparations were being made for celebrating the Independence Day. The entire school building had been decorated with creepers and leaves. The joy and eagerness of the school children knew no bounds. I wandered about from room to room. I looked at the charts the children had made with great expenditure of effort. I saw the pictures and the toys. The children were themselves looking after their canteen, they were cooking all the food in it. Here were being created the new, young, citizens of Hindustan. It was as though we were looking at fresh seedlings growing in the dream-garden of Dr. Zakir Hussain and his companions. Then the bell rang, and the teachers who had come to show us around the school, suggested that as the dress rehearsal of the children's entertainment programme was about to begin, we might go there to see it.

First was sung the flag-song of Jamia Millia. Then were presented some performances that usually take place in primary schools. I was about to rise, having become somewhat bored by these activities of predictable pattern, when came to my ears the words of Iqbal, the great poet, "Sare jahan se accha..." so I decided to sit for a while. Who was this student singing the poem in clean and chaste Urdu? A visage as fresh and healthy as a white rose, eyes as pale as flax. The lad was singing,

"Hum bulbulen hai uski, woh gulistan hamara!"

— "We, we are its Bulbuls, and it is our garden!" Bulbuls? And the fair, fair visage? Pale light eyes? — my memories began to trace their path back into the past. On the stage the lad was saying —

"Ei aabru de Ganga, woh din hai yaad tujko,
Utara tere kinare jab karvan hamara!"

— "You, Ganga, who gives soul-restoring water, do you not remember that day...?" Well, then, how can I not remember? Where had I seen him? Where?

"Hindi hain hum, vatan hai Hindustan
hamara!"

When he ended his song with these words and a roar of clapping began, not being able to hold myself back, turning to the teacher who had been with me, I asked,

"Who is this student?"

"This chap? Anwar Hussain. He is among the brightest of lads in the school."

"From Lucknow?"

"Yes, from Lucknow. Where did you get to know him?"

Only smiling a little I said, "No, I don't know him, really!"

Anwar! Now I did recognize him. When I came out, having taken leave of the organizers of the school, I was filled with the joy one experiences when one finds at hand some priceless object that has been out of sight for days. Having become light as a bird's feather, my mind was floating, drinking in the air. That time, the dread hour of the summer afternoon, the crowd in the train, those soldiers thirsting after a homecoming, Anwar, his mother, and the eyes of that Sikh soldier, trembling with tenderness — for a moment I felt as though I was in fact sitting in that train again!

3

The driver of a bus going from Karol Bagh to Barakhamba, gave me warning to move out of his way by blowing his horn loudly and vigorously, but I didn't even hear it. At last, the driver put on his brakes and came to a screeching halt. With a piercing screech the monstrous big bus came to a stop almost touching me. And a Sikh shop-owner from the corner ran towards me saying, "Arrey, Babuji, Babuji... " I had no idea what a great risk had been averted for me. The driver glanced at me once contemptuously, and then having seen my clothes, he started his bus again, muttering but refraining from swearing! That massive Sikh caught hold of my arm and asked half-teasingly, "Did you intend to commit suicide?"

I too said, smiling, "No!"

"You barely escaped, sir! What dream were you lost in?"

I made no effort to answer him. Instead, I suddenly asked him, "Udham Singh, how is it that you are here?"

Hearing me address him by name, he was quite flustered. "Um, sir? How is it that you know me? What a fool I must be! I don't recall ever seeing you!" Thus blaming himself on the one hand, and on the other saying, "Come, Babuji! Forgive me for not recognizing you. Rest awhile in the shop!" he welcomed me into his shop. Brushing at the seat in the shop Udham Singh said to me, "Do sit down, Babuji."

As I was sitting down I said, "Your Lachman must be going to school now, mustn't he? Where is he?"

Now Udham Singh's surprise was extreme, and thinking that this strange visitor is asking such intimate questions, while he himself remembers nothing, he became very disturbed. I could see the pain this was causing him.

"Lachman, yes? He is in Pindi now — " he said absent-mindedly, and then he became quiet. I did not keep him in suspense any longer. I recalled our journey together for him, and then asked, "Do you remember that Anwar? He must be going to school in Jamia, where else?"

Udham Singh's response was merely superficial. I was watching his eyes, but I did not see in them anywhere even a shadow of affection! I felt, are these military folk like the rivers of our sorrow, overflowing in flood, and for the rest of the time, only pebbles and rolling stones! With the intention of finding out if the spring of affection might not start, if I were to dig deeper, I said, "A most lovable boy, wasn't he?"

Pushing a tea-cup towards me, Udham Singh said ironically, "Yes, doubtless. A golden lad, but a snake all the same."

Withdrawing the cup which I had taken towards my lips, I said in some shock, "Meaning?"

"Babuji, he is the progeny of a Musallman, don't forget!" Udham Singh smiled bitterly. I perceived that the edge of a dagger had flashed across his eyes.

4

The intoxication of Independence Day did not last long. How could it? The orchard should blossom, and then overnight should descend frosty cold and burn up all the blossom — now the situation was just like that. Even as the paeans of Independence Day were being sung, it was as if the roof of the marquee itself had caught fire. Amritsar, Lahore, Sialkot, one after another were the cities, towns and settlements burning — and the front of this unprecedented forest-fire was spreading in all four directions, just like a flood. The dancing step of the Destroyer, Rudra, fell here today, in some other place tomorrow. The profound, awesome beat of His drum was shaking the skies, embracing the minars of Delhi. His hideous laughter, falling upon our ears, was crippling our reason every moment that passed. The human layer on our bodies was dropping off. Instead, on them were sprouting wolfish eyes, tiger's claws, tusks of wild boars, and the he-goat's satyr penis! What has mankind held dear until now? The love of his sweetheart? What has he held sacred? A mother's tears? What has he considered sweet? Infants' smiles? — well, then, trampling all these loved, sacred, sweet things under the heel, drowning their desperate cries in our monstrous laughter, shamelessly displaying our hands lathered in our kin's blood, — we, who had become human beasts — having stripped naked, we were dancing, cavorting before this world on the day of the Flood; man had brought upon man the occasion to see, in broad daylight, the desecrating hand violating his mothers' breasts, his wives' thighs, his claws at his innocent children's throats!

Delhi had not yet caught fire, but it had begun to scorch in the heat of the news coming like wild-fire from Punjab, it had begun to flap about, to smoke! It had started to moan and groan! Into the eyes of Hindu and Sikh had begun to descend murder, and into the eyes of Muslims, the dark shadow of fear! Today, somewhere on Ferozeshah road a Dargah was razed, next day someone was stabbed in Sabzi-mandi, the day after, rocks were flung upon Muslim homes near Purana Quila — such things began to occur.

These were merely the first sparks of the wild-fire, the first drops of the raging storm. They slowly gathered momentum. And when from western Punjab, like a fuming hot wave of lava, came the flood of Hindus and Sikhs via Sonepat-Panipat and rushed into Delhi, then men's hearts were charred to coal; and these coals, having caught fire, became embers! Every word that came from the lips of these homeless people made the living hearts lose their reason; every tear dropping from their eyes deprived these irrational people of any trace of mercy! From the sea of people in Delhi rose just one roar — "Revenge! Vengeance! Justice!"

Slowly, at every junction began to gather groups of people. They'd whisper amongst themselves, seem to decide something, then dissolve out of sight. One felt that one was seeing people in Delhi whom one had not seen before. And even known persons began to look strange. Because from their known faces, familiar expressions had been erased. People were becoming taciturn, or else over-bold. I saw, however, that the movement of women and children had increased on the streets. They were hardly shoppers. Once I saw an exceptionally large gathering of people. Since having unexpectedly met Udham Singh, I had been peeping into his shop once in a way. Therefore, I went forward to see if anything out of the way had occurred. So I saw that Udham Singh was sitting still as a rock, and the rest were standing in a circle about him. No one was speaking. But, the way they say that an animal discovers another's state of mind merely by smell, I too imagined that some blazing red, dark, dark thought-matter must be bubbling in their minds. In my own mind, in some obscure corner, a spring of the same substance had begun to trickle; on my eyes too had begun to float a veil of some strange madness. I too had been transformed. I called to him softly, "Sardarji...Udham Singh!"

Separating his hands, which had been entwined together, he turned towards me eyes which had congealed to rocks. I asked him, "What's happened?"

Laughing with a strange dryness Udham Singh said, "What can happen? The same as happened in Rawalpindi, Sialkot, and in Multan, in all of Punjab, — the same thing's happened!"

"Meaning?"

"I have been wiped out, destroyed, Babuji!"

Udham Singh got up, and placing his hands, which were like iron claws on my shoulders, he said, "No matter." And then as though addressing not just me, not just the people gathered about him there, no — as though speaking to the lakhs of people who were standing in just such clusters from place to place all over Delhi — he said, "Tomorrow will come to Delhi, Judgement Day. All snakes will be crushed!"

And the truth is that the next day that broke over Delhi was the Day of Judgement at the end of Time! Groups of Muslim men began to move away with women and children wherever they found a way, their heads bowed. In broad daylight, right in the middle of public streets this began to happen. Houses started to burn with a crackle, collapsed with a bang. Into the air was mixed the faint trace of smell from these burning homes, and the sky seemed to be covered with a smoky film. Just as when the shepherd is away, wolves can choose the sheep they want from the herd, and carry them away, in the same way did things happen all over the city that day. And where was I? What was I doing? What were the thoughts coming to my mind?

Did I disapprove of these things? No. Honestly, no. I myself did not loot from anyone; didn't shove a knife between anyone's ribs; didn't drag any Muslim young woman into my house — that is true. But why? Only because I was faint-hearted, that's why! But what's the point in denying that I felt a sneaky joy in watching these neutering acts committed by others? That is why I was wandering through the streets, and I was watching each happening in this horrifying drama the way one watches scenes on the stage sitting in the front row, with fine discrimination. Don't the spectator's hands itch to see a trained Cheetah leap to the throat of a doe and dig its teeth into its soft throat? And how one grinds one's own teeth! Doesn't the blood heat in the veins of those who watch animals coupling, and does not a frantic urge to couple race through their minds? On this afternoon, I too had become just such a spectator. One who had merged with the aggressors before my eyes, one who experienced the joy of bravery by dipping his hands, in the imagination, in the blood they had spilt, feeling besides myself because of the thrill at seeing the fair, pale breasts of young women whom they had stripped, feeling that I was myself pressing my palms against them! In every one of their acts, I was their partner in imagination. Even if I did not participate bodily, I contributed in my mind to all of them!

It must have been about two o'clock in the afternoon. It came to my ears that there had been some trouble in the direction of Jamia Millia. Suddenly my stomach gave a lurch and I promptly turned in that direction. When I looked towards Jamia Millia, I saw that a column of brownish smoke was rising from the primary school building. Scorched leaves from nearby trees and squares of paper, crumpled, charred, were gyrating in the floating air. Scared crows and doves were flapping about on the roofs, and a mixed noise of people could be heard. At a time even two or three hundred Muslim men, women and children would walk by where I was. How can we say 'walk'? Because of their fear they were dragging their lame feet along! The crowd gathered around them was looking at them in contempt, uttering filthy language, cackling in laughter. But they had not yet become uncontrollable, had not begun to lay hands on those who were running away.

But when one group approached the corner at Udham Singh's shop, all this attitude changed. Fifty or so young men descended upon these pilgrims progressing in great trepidation and uncertainty. Crunching blows of staves and knives began to fall. Because of this attack the menfolk started to run, scurry about, and the women began to low like cows, holding their little ones to their breasts. On the tar road flowed runnels of blood, the way water flows from broken pots. Those who fell down would for a while flap their legs, moan and then become silent!

Just then I heard a screech, like the one uttered by a struggling little bird in the clutches of a falcon! What did I see? In the iron grip of his left hand, Udham Singh has caught one lad's hair, and the kirpan in his right hand, already thick with blood, has touched the boy's breast. The flames in the blue eyes of the lad have, it seems, died long ago, and his lips, pale with fright, are scrunched in some strange shape. He surely wants to utter something, but not a word comes from his lips...

Yes. I recognized the lad, it was Anwar, Anwar who had blossomed like a gladioli flower, who was soft as a rabbit, who glittered like a bulbul! No, he must not die. I wanted to gather all my strength together and shout, "Udham Singh, draw back your hand! Hey, that's our Anwar, don't you see?" But even before these words could be uttered, the edge of Udham Singh's kirpan has met the tender heart!

On that day, Udham Singh had fondled his brown silk-like hair; at a time of unbearable thirst he had given him water from his own hands; that rabbit, that bulbul, was now lying lifeless in the tarred Delhi street beside a handful of blood trickling away! The glow on his lips had returned. His cheeks were glowing in the rays of the declining sun once again, and his soft brown hair was glittering like skeins of silk. I felt that if Udham Singh were to go near him again, he would place those rabbit-soft hands on his shoulders, and call out lovingly to him —

"Chachaji!..."

Original in Marathi
Translated by Sudhakar Marathe.

VED RAHI

DEATH

1

The fog gradually became thicker and settled over everything. Soon, I couldn't see anything...anything at all.

The tonga moved towards the town. As it jolted me around, I strained to see where I was.

Gradually, I began to make out things. The scene began to acquire an outline and a shape. The figures I saw seemed as delicate as glass-dolls — as innocent as the words of children — and as truthful — but they were no longer a part of my life. They had slipped out of my hands forever. I could never hope to grasp them again.

A long time ago —

I sat spinning.

We were taught many things in that school — spinning, weaving, sowing and planting amongst other things. I loved to spin yarn. I was in the third class at that time.

Suddenly, I saw my teacher standing beside me. He was holding the hand of a new boy.

"This is Saleem," the teacher said. "From now on, he'll sit next to you. Teach him how to spin yarn."

Saying this the teacher left. I asked Saleem to sit beside me.

He was taller than I was. His complexion was fair, his face was broad and his hair was golden-brown. He looked exactly like the boy in the illustration opposite the following poem in our Urdu book : "I am a good boy, a good and a gentle boy."

I began teaching him how to spin yarn. Suddenly, I saw that his nose was running and I exclaimed, "Arrey!" He immediately sniffed the white snot back. I started laughing. He blushed.

2

"Madan," I heard Saleem calling me. I stopped. Turned to look back. I saw Saleem running towards me. He was being chased by four or five boys. As soon as he reached me, he clung to me and said, "They are trying to beat me."

I was the class monitor. When the boys saw me, they stopped. Mohan was leading them. If he wanted to, he could have grabbed us by our hair and banged our heads together.

"What did he do?" I asked them.

"He suddenly pushed me and sent me crashing against a passer-by," Raju said tearfully.

"That doesn't sound like a crime," I said.

"That man thrashed me," Raju said, and started crying.

"Why are you hiding? Come out," Mohan taunted Saleem.

Saleem moved even closer to me in fear.

I tried to assert my authority and said, "Look here, if you continue to fight like this, I'll report all of you to the teacher." Then I made a suggestion, "Don't hurt him, I'll take him to the teacher."

The boys agreed and left. I took Saleem to the teacher and said, "The boys in our class have become very mischievous. We need a second class-monitor. Please appoint Saleem as the assistant monitor."

The boys were very upset when the teacher announced that Saleem had been appointed assistant monitor of the class.

We were then in the fourth standard.

During the hot summer afternoons, under the scorching sun, we would slip out of our homes to bathe in the canal. We always saved the two paise, we got from home to spend in school, for those afternoons. I would buy a cucumber for two paise, so that we could play with it in the water. After playing for two or three hours continuously, we would be ravenously hungry. Saleem would then use the two paise he had to buy chana and rotis. We would eat them, along with the cucumber, with great relish.

Saleem was afraid of water and used to wallow in shallow water like a donkey. He never dared to go where the water was deep. That is why he still didn't know how to swim. I loved to dive into deep water. One day I got ready to dive into the water from the road which ran past the canal. Saleem stood on the bank and watched me. I don't know what got into me, but after diving, I began swimming underwater. When I surfaced again and looked back, I was surprised to see Saleem frantically splashing in deep water. I rushed towards him and, after some difficulty, saved him from drowning. He had swallowed a lot of water. After a long time, when he recovered his breath again, he said, "When you didn't surface for sometime, I thought that you had drowned. I jumped into the water to save you."

I laughed a lot.

Saleem was annoyed by my stupidity and didn't talk to me for many days.

3

A few days later the following incident happened.

Lots of us were plucking berries from the bushes growing on the banks of the river Tavi. We had filled our pockets with berries. Saleem and I had climbed high up a tree. We were about to climb down, when one of the boys suddenly screamed, "Snake!" All the boys vanished in an instant. It seemed as if they had never been around. Saleem and I couldn't get down the tree that quickly. Scared, we froze in our places. Our limbs turned cold like ice. We felt that if we even blinked our eye-lids, the snake would bite us. We didn't know where it was. After sometime, I noticed that a black snake was sitting coiled on a stone about six or seven yards away from the tree to my right. I was startled — but realizing that it was far away, I also gathered some courage. "Saleem!" I said in suppressed whisper. Terrified, Saleem looked towards me. I said, "The snake is over there. It is far away." Saleem looked nervously in that direction. Seeing that the snake was far away, he slowly moved to the branch I was sitting on. We sat next to each other. We gripped the tree with one hand and held each other with the other. Finding ourselves so close to each other, we were no longer mortally afraid. We looked carefully at the snake. We noticed that it had something in its mouth. Perhaps a small mouse or a lizard. We watched it with some interest. The snake was not looking in our direction, that gave us some consolation. Suddenly we heard a strange sound. We clutched each other in fear. But before we could find out what had happened, we fell down — the branch on which we were sitting, had broken. As we fell; we thought we were done for. Now the snake would lunge at us. We quickly jumped up, and unconcerned about our injuries, ran for our lives. We kept on running even after we had cleared the bushes. A black shadow of fear seemed to follow us. We stopped only after we could not run anymore and were breathless. We slowly climbed up the bank. But we were still afraid — perhaps about what people at home would have said if the snake had actually bitten us!

4

"Madan, why don't you come to my house?" Saleem asked me one day. At that time we were in the seventh standard.

"Adab," I said to Saleem's Ammi. She hugged me and kissed my forehead. How lovely she was! I couldn't take my eyes off her. She said, "Saleem talks about you all the time. I have asked him a number of times to invite you home. Now sit down, I'll get you some milk."

Saleem took me into a large room.

"Is he your friend?"

"Yes, Apa," Saleem replied.

His sister was sitting on a carpet in the middle of the room. She had a milky white cat in her lap.

"She is my elder sister, Madan."

I raised my hand in greetings. As I sat down facing her, she suddenly threw the cat sitting in her lap, on me. I jumped up in surprise. Saleem and she burst out laughing. I also joined in the fun. After that I met Saleem's younger brother and his elder brother. I liked both of them.

I went to Saleem's house almost everyday, but I could never invite him to my home. Saleem never asked me, why I didn't invite him to my house, but I felt very embarrassed. I was aware that my mother referred to the Muslims as melichas, and that when she walked on the road she was always afraid that either a

Muslim or an untouchable would brush past her. Once my elder brother had brought a Harijan friend of his into our drawing room and had asked for some tea for him, but mother refused to serve him any.

If ever Saleem accompanied me upto my house, he stood outside; only once in a while did he come into the drawing room. He never drank water in our house. Maybe I never offered him any. My helplessness always pained me.

"Madan, my father is going to admit me into a the Military School," Saleem said very sadly. Our seventh standard results had been declared that day. Both Saleem and I had passed.

I said, "I have to go to the High School."

"I too wanted to do that, but Abba has already enrolled me in the Military School in the cantonment."

That day we sat at the bank of the canal and talked for hours. The next day he went to the cantonment. Now he had to live there. When I went to his house a few days later, his mother held me to her breast and wept, "Son, now that Saleem has gone away, will you also stop visiting us?"

"I will come, Ammijan," I said. That day I found everyone in Saleem's house sad.

I continued to go there for sometime. One day when I went there, Saleem's mother put her hand on my head and said, "Son, you shouldn't visit us anymore."

"Why?" I asked, astonished.

Ammi held me closer to her and said, "Son, this is a Muslim locality and your coming here is not free from danger."

I kept quiet. I never went back there again. There were communal riots in the city. Two or three people were killed everyday.

The riots became worse by the day. The state of affairs deteriorated. Incidents of houses being set on fire began to increase.

It was during those days that the announcement of Independence and the formation of Pakistan was made. Fires began to rage all around. Groups of goondas, armed with naked swords, guns and pistols began roving through the streets, making it impossible for decent people to step out of their homes.

There were screams of terror and the sounds of gunfire all the time. I was concerned about Saleem. He was far away from his family. Had his father called him back? I wondered how his father was? And his mother? I was concerned about his brothers and sister. Did they get away to Pakistan?

I was miserable the day I heard that some Muslims had been lured away with the promise of helping them reach Pakistan, to a place where they could be easily slaughtered.

I was bewildered. I was very nervous, but I couldn't ever imagine that any harm could come to Saleem and his family.

Then, the tribals attacked Jammu and Kashmir. People began to flee. My family sent me to Amritsar with some neighbours who were running away. My uncle had fled to Amritsar with his entire family, after everything he owned had been looted.

Even there, I kept worrying about Saleem and his family.

When I returned to Jammu six months later, the city had completely changed. Instead of black caps one saw only red caps everywhere. A red flag with a plough on it, flew beside the flag of the Suryavamshi dynasty. People didn't get tired of shouting, "Long live the lion of Kashmir."

During that period my father had moved into a new house. As soon as I reached Jammu, I found out that Saleem was still in the hostel. My happiness knew no bounds, I hired a tonga at once, and went to the cantonment. The moment Saleem saw me, he came out of the barracks. We held each other's hands. Our eyes welled-over with tears — our hearts were heavy.

I asked Saleem about his family. He informed me that his father had succeeded in arranging for a jeep during the riots, and had managed to escape to Pakistan with the entire family. Theywere unable to reach the cantonment and take him with them. He had received a letter from his father, informing him that they had reached Sialkot safely.

I remembered how his mother had wept when Saleem had joined the school in the cantonment. I wondered what her condition must have been like when she had got into the jeep and left Saleem behind. A shiver ran through my body. I said to Saleem, "Why don't you come and live with us?"

"I am fine here. Besides, the arrangements for my journey to Pakistan are almost complete, and I may be asked to leave at anytime."

Saleem was right. I didn't persist. After sometime, he said, "Madan, before I leave for Pakistan, I would like to visit your house."

"Why don't you come today?" I said.

"No, I can't. Here one has to take permission in advance before going out. If you come back here the day after tomorrow, around this time, I'll go with you."

It happened to be a Saturday. We got into a tonga going towards the city. I was happy — very happy — because I was taking Saleem to my house. Saleem, too, seemed to be relaxed. We were sitting close to each other.

Saleem said, "Madan, I'll write to you from Pakistan. I hope you'll reply."

"I'll certainly reply," I said. "Write to me about everyone in your family. Tell your mother that I think of her often. Give my regards to your father. I am sure your sister has adopted a few more pet cats by now, and your brother still dreams of being a pilot."

When I looked towards Saleem, I saw that tears were flowing down his face. I placed my hand on his shoulder. He broke down and started sobbing loudly. The tongawalla turned back to look at us. After a while, Saleem regained control over himself. Embarrassed, he smiled at his own sentimentality.

"Madan, isn't your house in that direction?" Saleem asked, as the tonga turned into the lane where we lived.

"I forgot to tell you," I said. "We have moved into a new house. We had rented the previous one. This house, we have bought. A Muslim family used to live in it. The entire family was killed during the riots. Only one son, who was in Srinagar at that time, survived. Before leaving for Pakistan, he sold it to us rather cheap."

By then, we had reached the front door of our house. When I looked at Saleem, I was stunned. A dark shadow had covered his face. He stopped outside the door. I realized my mistake — but I didn't know what to do. Without thinking, I said, "Come — let's go in, Saleem."

Slowly, he followed me in. I didn't have the courage to look at him. I didn't know what was passing through his mind. Did his steps falter? I don't know. I was dejected. I felt as if there was a heavy burden on my heart — I felt suffocated. I felt guilty. I don't know why.

I took Saleem to the room upstairs. That day, my mother had gone to her village — I was, therefore, not worried about her. I had taken my sister into confidence, and she had promised not to tell my mother that Saleem had drunk tea in the house. She quickly made the tea. I ran to the market and brought back some things to eat. I had, perhaps, nourished the hope that Saleem's mother would be pleased when she hears that he had tea at my place. But, now, I had lost all my enthusiasm. I knew that I was deceiving myself.

I carried the tea and the food upstairs. Perhaps, the wind had shut the door. Carrying the tray in both my hands, I kicked the door open with my foot. Saleem was startled, as if there was an earthquake. He was perspiring badly.

We could barely drink half a cup of tea each. Saleem drank even that with great difficulty. Neither of us touched the food.

"Let's go now, Madan," Saleem said.

"Yes," I said, as I got up.

As soon as we came out of the house, Saleem started walking very fast. When we reached the main road, we got into a tonga. It took us an hour to reach the Cantonment, but during that hour neither of us uttered a word to each other. The silence was suffocating. We seemed to be surrounded by a heavy mist, through which nothing was visible. Our hearts were numb.

"I am going," Saleem said, as he got down from the tonga.

I continued to sit in the tonga. I didn't say anything in reply. Saleem got down from the tonga and looked towards me. He seemed frightened. We looked at each other for sometime.

"Madan," he seemed to have called me from somewhere far away.

I got down from the tonga.

He caught my arm, and asked in a terrified voice, "Madan, can you murder me?"

I stood like a statue.

Then he screamed, "No, no, you cannot murder me, Madan..." Still screaming, he ran towards his hostel. He went into the hostel. I stood there like a statue of stone for a long time. I didn't understand what had happened.

Original in Dogri.
Translated from Hindi
by Alok Bhalla.

<u>QURRATULAIN HYDER</u>

WHEN THE PRISONERS WERE RELEASED, THE TIMES HAD CHANGED

In 1939, after the Congress had made the historic announcement that it would not co-operate with the British to fight the Second World War, Iqbal Suhail Azamgardi had stood up in the U.P. Assembly and thundered :

Oppressors we shall face when they attack us,
 Let these days of fake kindness at least end;
Bandits we shall fight when they rob us,
 Let this loot by our protectors at least end;
Hawks we shall tame when they prey on us,
 But let this accursed imprisonment at least end.

During that period India was a vast prison-house.

A few years earlier when our ship, S.S. Maharaja, had sailed out of the Calcutta port, I was too young to have any idea about the different ways in which the struggle for freedom was being waged in the country. What violence and non-violence meant! Who the judges were and who their victims!

When the ship, with brightly sparkling lights (A Goanese band played 'Rule Britannia' on the ship's deck, and English men and women, determined to overcome their sorrow caused by the Great Depression, drank wildly and danced. After all, islands shaded by rustling palm and pagoda trees were still available as places of 'safe adventure' for the younger sons of rich English families. It was the fictional world of Somerset Maugham, Graham Greene and Evelyn Waugh. London newspapers had just printed photographs of Gandhiji, the 'naked fakir,' with his goat, and Katherine Mayo's *Mother India* had been published a long time ago), sailed into the Bay of Bengal, I was surprised to realize that the sea was so vast — "I wonder how many labourers had been employed to dig it?" I thought about it and then turned to watch the crowd leaning against the ship's railing.

A few days later, the island rose in the horizon. Coral rocks, clusters of coconut trees and green tropical hills. As we approached the port, row boats and motor-launches moved forward to meet us. The Union Jack flew over the building at the port; Anglo-Indian policemen and Indian soldiers stood at attention around it. An English sahib, in a white sola topee, marched up and down.

A 'brown sahib', in a white sola topee, walked up the gang-way and said to my father, "Welcome to Port Blair, Sir."

A few young men in handcuffs were marched off the ship. They had been brought there to serve out life-sentences in Asia's largest prison, the Cellular Jail.

Our house glowed on top of an emerald green hill. A road led up the hill to its outer gate. The road passed over a Japanese wooden bridge. The house was built on tall wooden stilts and was known as Bada Bangla. It was built out of wood, along with the armed guard, a small fire-engine and a few fire-fighters were always on duty downstairs. Behind the house, there was a hill covered with cashew trees. The District Magistrate lived in a house on top of that hill. The court building was also on that hill. The Chief Commissioner lived on Ross Island.

The Andaman Islands are a part of the Arakan Yoma range of Burmese mountains, and were formed after the eruption of volcanoes seven hundred feet below the sea. Made up of about two hundred small islands, they are rocked by frequent earthquakes.

Strange! We lived on the peaks of mountains which were entirely submerged under the blue sea.

The name, Andaman, is an English distortion of the Malay word, Hinduman. And Hinduman is Malay for Hanuman.

The *Ramayan* had a great influence in south-east Asia, especially on the cultures of Siam, Cambodia, Vietnam, Champa, Anam and others.

"Did Hanumanji and his monkeys travel this far?" my brother asked havaldar Ramchander, who had a long and pointed moustache, and had perhaps come here from Faizabad.

"Yes, Baba, it is likely that they had hopped and jumped this far while constructing the bridge to Lanka! After all, what can one say about the whims of Bajrang Bali! He may have even punched these volcanoes down under the sea with his fists!" Ramchander replied, running his hand over his moustache and looking at us kindly.

That very evening, my brother read in his geography book that the arrogant Aryans had treated the dark-skinned inhabitants of the south rather contemptuously, and used to call them monkeys. These dark-skinned people had negroid features and could be found in the Sindhu valley, the southern parts of India and as far down as Australia. The tribes of the Andaman and Nicobar Islands were the descendents of those ancient settlers. I, however, preferred havaldar Ramchander's story about Hanumanji.

The reality, of course, was that we had a house on top of a volcano.

The English rulers are peculiar! They create gardens wherever they go!

Neither before the rise of European powers, nor afterwards, did the Moghul Emperors of Delhi or the Nawabs of Bengal or the Kings of Malay, think that a naval force was important. Imagine, for example, that the Moghul rulers had established a small force on the Hinduman Islands and stuffed the English, Dutch or French ships sailing by with straw...

What happened, instead, was that Mr. Blair, a cartographer with the East India Company, explored the islands in 1798 and claimed them as a part of the Empire. How could these distant islands, which nobody had even heard of, have offered any resistance, when the rest of the country, from Kabul to Kanyakumari had come under the rule of the firangis. The English, however, had to pay a heavy price for their conquest of these islands. The tribals of the Andaman and Nicobar Islands, with their poisoned arrows and murderous spears, had put up a stiffer resistance to the foreign invaders than had the red Indians of America, the negroes of Africa or the bushmen of Australia.

What can one say about the pomp and show of these Islands now? They were now a part of the colonial splendour of the Indian Empire. The scenic beauty of Port Cornwallis, Elphinston Harbour and Port Campbell reminded the sahib log of Ireland and the Lake District.

There wasn't a single school on the Andaman Islands, not even in Port Blair. That is why a young Burmese used to come home to teach my brother. Sometimes he would gaze at the sea with dreamy eyes and tell us stories about the history of Burma. "Do you know why the Scottish love to settle in Bengal and the eastern parts of India? Because they used to die of hunger in the barren mountains of Scotland!" He was an enthusiastic young Burmese. "There is a scientific explanation for everything — cause and effect..." When he grew tired because my brother couldn't understand the big words he used, he would either stare at the sea or tell us about the adventures of Arkanese pirates who had their hide-outs on these islands more than two hundred years ago.

"Let me tell you about Port Campbell..." he would begin excitedly. "Do you know what happened? A hundred years ago, brave Burmese rebels fought the British in the plains of Chittagong. Just as they were making preparations to attack other British garrisons, the British declared war against Burma, and General Sir Archibald Campbell set out with a large force. The Commander of the naval fleet was the Victorian novelist, Captain Marryat. We were defeated and by the end of the nineteenth century had joined the company of slaves..."

After the Mutiny, many of the rebels were exiled to the Andamans, and these islands were governed by a Chief Commissioner. In 1874, Lord Mayo, the Viceroy of India was assassinated by a brave prisoner called Sher Ali while he was inspecting the Cellular Jail, which is popularly known as the Silver Jail.

By 1906, the national movement had spread throughout India and the freedom fighters of East Bengal were deported to the Andamans without trial. It was impossible to escape from here. Yet, prisoners, hid gold coins in their mouths in the hope of using them, if they ever managed to escape. Of course, no one ever succeeded.

These islands are famed for their wealth. Dense forests provided wood for export to Europe and America. Thousands of prisoners worked as bonded labourers in the fields to cultivate coffee, tea and manila fibre. The public was satisfied. The volcanic mountains were dormant.

Whenever the telephone in the glazed verandah rang, I would climb on the stool to speak into the mouthpiece — "Hello...hello...Yes, I am speaking from Bada Bangla..."

Throughout the night the path which ran past the garden echoed with the footsteps of the guard — Khat, khat khat...left-right — "Halt, hukum sadar," (Halt, who comes there?) the guard would shout.

The sweeper, with a white handkerchief tied around his head, would appear at the central staircase early in the morning. Noor Mohammad could be heard sneezing in the pantry. Noor Mohammad was from zilla Jhang. He was here because he had killed his wife and her lover with an axe. He was a very gentle and kind-hearted man. To everything one said, he replied, 'baun janab', which was a variation of 'bahut acha janab'. There were other prisoners, too, who had committed murder for money, love and land. Most of them were courteous and simple young men, middle-aged and old men, or Muslims, Sikhs, Punjabis as well as from the other regions of the country — 'They were all equal under the reign of the British!'

The dog's name was a problem. He was a lovely alsatian we had inherited from the previous English officer who had named it Tipu. "We'll call him Wellesley..." my brother said, making a dangerous decision. But the dog was used to the name, Tipu, and merely wagged its tail like a fool when it was called Arthur or Wellesley. Since everyone had been warned not to call it Tipu, it wandered namelessly from person to person looking at their faces with surprise and hope.

My father was assigned to the revenue department. Apart from him, and Mr. Kaytur of the agricultural department, there were no other Indian officers on the Andaman and Nicobar Islands.

In order to get some fresh air in the evenings, we often wandered far into the forests. The bright lights of Port Blair and the neighbouring town, Aberdeen, would vanish in the darkness. If I ever expressed the desire to drink coconut water, while walking through a valley, some tribal child passing by would climb up a coconut tree, pluck a coconut and climb down again fast as a monkey.

The tribal population had been reduced to a few thousand. They still hunted with bows and arrows in the forest. There were a few clans which had no spoken language and communicated with each other by making signs; some had no knowledge of fire.

To get to a forest, we had to pass through coffee gardens. The sea breeze sighed and groaned as it beat against the rocky shore.

Suddenly, the moon would emerge to light the way.

"Why does the moon follow us?" I often asked in wonder.

"It wishes to offer its salaams to you!" my father would reply. Bright moonlight filled the entire island, covered the tar trees and fell on the mountain peaks. Bamboo groves rustled in the wind. The wind, too, was my friend.

Once, walking through the garden of the Chief Commissioner with Havaldar Ramchander, I saw a pair of high boots through the window. They seemed to have climbed up the wooden-frame. "They are Mr. Anderson's legs which he has left behind in his house," I thought to myself fearfully.

One day there was a lot of commotion on the island. The nationalist prisoners in the Silver Jail had gone on hunger strike to protest against the ill-treatment of the inmates. The security around Bada Bangla had been doubled.

That evening, I saw Mr. Anderson wearing his high boots and sitting in a car parked under the Japanese bridge. Mr. Anderson was also the Chief Superintendent of Police of the penal settlement.

The next morning, I saw one of the nationalist prisoners being carried down the road on a stretcher.

"Sudhir Kumar Bose..." Prakash Chander, the cleaner, whispered to the Burmese teacher. Everyone leaned over the balcony to watch him being carried away. I looked through the lattice-frames of the verandah.

"Bose Babu is a brave man...Yesterday, the Bade Sahib went into his cell to kick some sense into him. Sudhir Bose may have looked thin and weak, but he stood up to fight him. The Bade Sahib quickly ran out."

"Mr. Anderson ran out because he had taken his legs with him!" I said with complete self-assurance.

"But Sudhir Bose will die," Noor Mohammed whispered softly as he wiped his tears and ran his hand over his white beard.

Then he called, as he walked away, "Come Tipu...Oh, no, no, God forbid, Arthur...Come, Arthur, it's time to eat..."

The days of my shameful ignorance soon came to an end.

One day my father was sitting in the verandah reading something. I was squatting on the floor turning the pages of some Urdu magazine when my attention was caught by a interesting photograph either of Samarkand or of the Alif Laila Bazar in Cairo. There was something written in bold letters under the photograph. I took the magazine to my father and asked him what was written under the picture.

He looked at me with surprise and said, "If you continue to live here, you'll remain an illiterate. You should learn how to read."

The very next day, Maulana Rab Nawaz, who had a French beard, was summoned. The Maulana was a clerk at the courts and was also the Pesh Imam at the mosque. He wore a silk turban with a tall plume and a golden band, a salwar and a frock coat, as well as a tie! When he came and sat in the verandah, Noor Mohammad kissed his hand with great reverence. Then he quickly served him tea and said, "The girl is four years, four months and four days old." The Maulana made his inquiries and announced that he would bring a qaida next Friday.

Ignorant as I was, I thought a qaida was a doll's house. Of course, there has to be a limit to stupidity. I knew that the Maulana had come to teach me, yet I assumed that a qaida was a doll's house. How could I have guessed the relation between a qaida and a doll's house?

The next day my brother called me, "Come along, your qaida has arrived."

I sped like an arrow towards the verandah.

What I saw, however, was a thin, dully printed book with drawings of a mango, a goat, a kite etc. on the first page.

There was no bismillah ceremony performed before I began how to read, because my mother had participated in various reform movements in the past and had abandoned all ritual practices.

Anyway, I sat at the French window of the verandah, watched the seagulls wheel in the sky above, and the Duke of

Wellington or Lord Arthur Wellesely chase squirrels in the garden, and took my first dip in the ocean of learning.

"Bismillahir-rahmanir-rahim...Let us begin..." Maulana Rab Nawaz said, as he swayed back and forth, and pointed his finger at the first page of the alphabet book.

"No, let me begin..." I objected.

"Alright, alright, you begin..."

The nationalist struggle became more intense throughout the country, but it was particularly strong in Bengal, U.P. and the border states. Thousands of satyagrahis were arrested.

"Terrorist activities in Bengal made the position of the Congress particularly difficult. The terrorists had created such an atmosphere that it had become very hard for the Congress to carry out its peaceful protests. The tough measures adopted by the government affected both the violent and the non-violent activists alike. The police and the local government, used the legal and administrative measures which had been created to deal with terrorism, against Congressmen, workers and peasants.

"The Chittagong affair was the most serious. The shooting of a Muslim police Inspector by a terrorist, resulted in Hindu-Muslim riots. It was obvious that there was no relation between the terrorists' act and communalism. The terrorists had assassinated a police Inspector, and not a Hindu or a Muslim, but the act had cleared the way for Hindu-Muslim riots. One curious aspect of the riots was that even the Anglo-Indian community had taken part in them.

"Terrorism had been condemned from many points of views...but one of its possible consequences had always especially frightened me, and that was the danger of sporadic and communal violence spreading in India...When people murder in the name of religion, or to reserve a place for themselves in Paradise, it is a dangerous thing to accustom them to the idea of terroristic violence. Political murder is bad. And yet the political terrorist can be reasoned with and won over to other ways, because presumably the end he is striving for is an earthly one, not personal but national. Religious murder is worse, for it deals with things of the other world, and one cannot even attempt to reason about such matters. Sometimes the dividing line between the two is very thin and almost disappears, and political murder, by a metaphysical process, becomes semi-religious.

"The Chittagong murder...and its consequences, made one realise very vividly the dangerous possibilities of terroristic activity and the enormous harm it might do to the course of Indian unity and freedom. The reprisals that followed, showed us that fascist methods had appeared in India. Since then there have been many instances...of such reprisals, and the fascist spirit has undoubtedly spread in the European and Anglo-Indian community...It is a curious thing, but the terrorists themselves...have also this fascist outlook...Their nationalist-fascism faces the imperialist-fascism of the Europeans, Anglo-Indians, and some upper-class Indians...

"...In all these meetings I discussed the question of terrorism, and tried to show how wrong and futile and harmful it was...I did not abuse the terrorists, nor did I call them...'cowardly', after the fashion of some of our countrymen...It has always seemed to me a singularly stupid thing to call a man or woman, who is constantly risking his life, a coward...

"On my last evening in Calcutta, a little before I was due to go to the station for my departure, two young men called on me. They were very young...with pale, nervous faces and brilliant eyes...They were very angry with me for my propaganda against terroristic violence. They said...they could not tolerate my intrusion in this way...they warned me finally that if I continued to misbehave in the future they would deal with me as they had dealt with others...

"...As I lay in my berth in the train that night I was long haunted by the excited faces of these two boys. Full of life and nervous energy they were; what good material if only they turned the right way! I was sorry that I had dealt with them hurriedly...and wished I had had the chance of a long conversation with them. Perhaps I could have convinced them to apply their bright young lives to other ways of serving India and freedom, in which there was no lack of opportunity for daring and self-sacrifice. Often I have thought of them in these years. I never found out their names, nor did I have any other trace of them; and I wonder sometimes, if they are dead or in some cell in the Andaman Islands" (From Jawaharlal Nehru, *An Autobiography*).

People throughout India had heeded the call for satyagraha. Those who had supported the hunger strike by the prisoners on the Andaman Islands and had protested against their deaths in prison, had been arrested. When Jawaharlal Nehru was released from prison in September 1933, and before he was rearrested, he had published an appeal, which was signed by Rabindranath Tagore, C.F. Andrews and others, demanding that the freedom fighters incarcerated in the Andaman islands be treated well and that they be moved to jails in India. The British Home Member had taken strong exception to the appeal and had declared that in Bengal, the expression of sympathy for the freedom fighters imprisoned in the Andaman islands was a crime.

A few days after our return to Dehra Dun from the Andaman Islands, we were driving to the station to see off a guest, when our car passed an old building on the roadside. My mother pointed towards it and exclaimed, "Look, there is Jawaharlal Nehru sitting on the front verandah."

Jawaharlal Nehru was sitting in an easy chair, his hands behind his head, and was gazing at the distant mountains. He stood up when he saw the car stop. My brother and I got down from the car and, quite instinctively, ran towards him. But the prison wall stood between us. Jawaharlal Nehru looked at us for a few moments and then sat down in his chair again.

"For fourteen and a half months I lived in my little cell or room in the Dehra Dun Gaol, and I began to feel as if I was almost a part of it...I had better cells in other prisons, but in Dehra Dun I had one privilege which was very precious to me. The gaol proper was a very small one, and we were kept in an old lock-up outside the gaol wall, but within the gaol compound. This place was so small that there was no room to walk about in it, and so we were allowed, morning and evening, to go out and walk up and down in front of the gate, a distance of about a hundred yards. We remained in the gaol compound, but this coming outside the walls gave us a view of the mountains and the fields and a public road at some distance. This was not a special privilege for me; it was common for all the A and B class prisoners kept at Dehra Dun...Only a prisoner who has been confined for long behind high walls can appreciate the extraordinary psychological value of these outside walks and open views...It was my good fortune that...I should gaze at these mountains that I loved. I could not see the mountains from my cell, but my mind was full of them and I was ever conscious of their nearness, and a secret intimacy seemed to grow between us...

"Spring was very pleasant in Dehra Dun; and it was a far longer one than in the plains below. The winter had denuded almost all the trees of their leaves, and they stood naked and bare. Even the four magnificent peepal trees, which stood in front of the gaol gate...dropped nearly all their leaves...Suddenly there was a stir both in the peepals and the other trees, and an air of mystery surrounded them as of secret operations going on behind the scenes; and I would be startled to find little bits of green peeping out all over them...And then, very rapidly, the leaves would come out in their millions and glisten in the sunlight and play about in the breeze...The monsoon rains were welcome, but it was not pleasant to sit cooped up in a little narrow place trying to avoid the water dripping from the ceiling or rushing in from the window...Autumn again was pleasant, and so was winter, except when it rained. With thunder and rain and piercing cold winds, one longed for a decent habitation and a little warmth and comfort. Occasionally there would be a hailstorm, with hailstones bigger than marbles coming down on the corrugated iron roofs and making a tremendous noise, something like an artillery bombardment" (From Jawaharlal Nehru's, *An Autobiography*).

December 1959. At the World Agricultural Fair, there were pavilions from each state of India. Each hall was designed to present the culture and history of a region. My glance fell on a large house which was surrounded by tropical plants and was built on stilts in the middle of an artificial pond. The board outside it read — Andaman and Nicobar Islands. I climbed the steps and went inside. The walls were covered with posters showing the progress the islands had made since Independence in industry, education and agriculture.

Two Bengali girls, wearing white sarees, stood behind the counter. The counter had samples of the latest handloom and handicraft work done on the islands.

"Were these things made by the prisoners in Silver Jail?" I asked.

"Silver Jail...?" the first girl repeated. The other girl moved closer.

"Silver Jail was shut down a long time ago. Andaman is no longer a penal settlement. New and free Andamanese live there now."

"New Andamanese...?"

"Yes, after the Partition, refugees from East Bengal were settled there. The two of us are from East Pakistan." The girl's voice had the same touch of sadness which I was to catch a few years later in the voice of a Sindhi sales girl in Sri Lanka when she told me, "I used to live in Karachi."

"The Andaman Islands are a tourist paradise," the first girl said.

"There is a weekly air service from Calcutta to Port Blair. Come there sometimes..."

"I shall," I replied politely and turned to look at the photographs of a few tribals dancing. There are only about twenty-three tribes left on the Islands now. There are some tribes which only have about a hundred members. Although primitivism is still a part of the consciousness of civilized man, there are almost no primitives left in the forests.

I turned to look at the other side, when I suddenly saw a very large photograph of Bada Bangla. "Bada Bangla!" I was startled and I stood silently before the photograph. Bada Bangla, which was now the office of some government department, was still intact and stood as before on wooden stilts on top of the hill. As I looked at it, the glass windows of its French porch glittered, as if they were glaring back at me in reply.

The tall rubber plants were still growing in front of Bada Bangla, but Arthur Wellesely no longer played under their shade. Havaldar Ramchander, Maulana Rab Nawaz, Noor Mohammad, Prakash Chander and Mr. Anderson were not there either. My father used to sit out on the porch in the morning and read his newspaper. Silver waves still beat against the lower slopes of the garden.

Life, I realized, always flows on, only the times change.

The person standing before that photograph at that moment was no longer the same person who used to either skip and play in those rooms, verandahs and gardens, or cry loudly, or hide with the cat under the dining table. I had changed, changed utterly.

Bada Bangla continued to stare at me, as if it was asking me — "You have come after such a long time. What do you have to say to me? What have you learnt in life in all this time?"

In order to escape its scrutiny, I turned towards the counter. The 'new Andamanese' sales-girl presented me with a bag woven out of pineapple fibre.

If I had told that girl that I had once lived within the walls of that house in the photograph, she wouldn't have believed me.

She belonged to a different race, and she had already endured all the pain her generation was destined to suffer. She was a member of the new generation of free India and Pakistan. The people who had fought for independence during the last fifty years thought that they had their feet firmly planted on the soil on which they were born and that they knew whose freedom they were fighting for. But the earth had already slipped from under the feet of the generation to which that sales-girl belonged.

Bada Bangla continued to stare at me.

Perhaps, the old wooden house had understood that I was still the same foolish girl who had looked at the world with wonder and had trusted it.

I quickly walked out of the pavilion.

November 1961. There was still some time left for the national music festival to begin at the Lalit Kala Kendra in Calcutta. A jaltarang player was testing cups full of water on the stage and, in the green room, some girls were softly humming one of Kazi Nasrul Islam's thundering songs. The hall was still empty and the ushers were idly walking up and down the aisles. The group I was with, was standing under the staircase and gossiping. I walked into the hall, put the programme brochure down on my seat and looked around. I suddenly noticed that there were paintings hanging on the walls. There must have been hundreds of them. "Is this a portrait gallery?" I wondered and walked upto them to have a closer look at the portraits of young men and women.

Who were those people with restless, searching eyes, calm and gentle eyes; with sad faces, nervous and thoughtful faces; with peaceful and self-assured smiles; with proud and dignified expressions? Curious, I began to read the names engraved on small metal plates under the pictures :

Satyendernath Bose	Hanged	1908
Khudiram Bose	Hanged	1908
Prafulla Chakki	Committed suicide in prison	1908
Ashfaqullah Khan	Hanged	1928
Bhagat Singh		
Pritilata Vadeda	Committed suicide	1932
Rajinder Singh Lahri	Hanged	1927
Gopinath Saha	Hanged	1924
Yateesh Guha	Killed by the police	1930
Devi Prashad Gupta	Shot to death	

There was a painting of an old woman!

Hazara Bibi	Shot to death by the police	1942
Sudhir Kumar Bose	Died while on hunger strike	

Suddenly I felt that someone was standing behind me.

When I turned around I saw a thin man in ill-health, with a sprinkling of grey hair. He walked upto me and said, "You seem to be looking at these paintings with keen interest. You have even taken down their names. Are you a reporter?"

"Ay...Come on honey..." a fair, handsome young man, who was wearing sharply pointed shoes, and stood between me and the paintings, called out to his girl-friend who was looking for their seats at the other end of the hall.

"Hey dope...come on here!" the girl, who was wearing a very tight salwar and an even tighter shirt, shouted back at the boy in pointed shoes. Pointed shoes danced back towards her, in his tight black trousers, and a silver belt around his delicate waist which shimmered in the light.

The Bengali gentleman began talking to me again. "My elder brother and I were terrorists. We spent half our lives in prison..." he said sadly. "Are you planning to write an article...?"

"Maybe, I don't know..."

"My name is Probodh Kumar Bose. I am from the zilla Mymen Singh which is now in East Bengal...When my elder brother was sent to the Andamans, I was still in school. My mother died lamenting for my brother. As soon as I left school, I joined the freedom movement. I was caught at Jessore and spent years in Alipore Jail. I was freed after Independence — but by then my village had become a part of the other country. My family was killed during the riots. And I..."

Pointed shoes walked past us quickly once again. He was accompanied by three American beatniks, one of whom was wearing a dark sherwani, churidar pyjamas and a silver bracelet. The second beatnik wore a Bengali kurta over khaki shorts and his long hair hung loosely over his shoulders like a yogi. The third beatnik seemed satisfied with his western clothes, but walked and behaved like a girl. The American girl with them was dressed like a boy. In order to get past the freedom fighter, the Indian boy, in pointed shoes, pushed him aside and walked away with his American friends.

At that very moment a long line of fat businessmen, society ladies, professional intellectuals and culture-vultures entered the hall through the door. I looked around for the freedom fighter. I wanted to tell him that he should tell me his story and the story of his elder brother. I wanted to tell him that I longed to write the story of India. But that one borrowed life was not long enough to tell it, besides would there be anyone who would listen to that story? I wanted to ask him if his elder brother wasn't that fiery young man who had gone to see Punditji...but that unknown terrorist, who had suffered so much, had vanished into that careless, carefree and self-satisfied crowd.

The jaltarang artist had begun to play on the stage.

Original in Urdu.
Translated by Vishwamitter Adil
and Alok Bhalla.

NOTES ON THE AUTHORS

Gulam Abbas: Was born in 1909. He worked for many years for the B.B.C. He published a large number of short stories in Urdu. His best known collections are *Anandi, Jarrey Ki Chandni* and *Kan Ras*. He died in 1982.

Mulk Raj Anand: Born in 1905, in Peshawar, Pakistan. He is a well-known novelist in English and a major art critic. His novel *Untouchable* is considered to be a classic. He was the Chairman of the Lalit Kala Akademi and was given the Sahitya Akademi Award in 1970.

Upendranath Ashk: Born in Jullunder in 1910, he worked for the All India Radio for many years. In 1965, he received the Sangeet Natak Akademi Award for his achievements as a playwright. A prolific writer in Urdu and Hindi, he has published many well-known novels, short stories and plays.

Dipendranath Bandyopadhayay: Born in 1933, in Calcutta. He has, thus far, published a number of volumes of short stories and a few novels in Bengali.

Samaresh Basu: Born in 1924, in Dhaka, Bangladesh. He lives in Calcutta and has published more than a hundred volumes of novels and short stories in Bengali. His best-known novels are *Prajapati* and *Samba*. He was given the Sahitya Akademi Award in 1980.

Krishen Chander: Born in 1914, in Poonch, Kashmir. He studied at the Forman Christian College in Lahore. He became famous with his first collection of short stories, *Tilasam-e-khayal*. He worked for sometime with the All India Radio. He is considered to be one of the most important of the progressive writers Urdu literature has produced. He died in 1977.

Ismat Chugtai: Was Born in 1925, in Badayam, Uttar Pradesh. She studied at Lucknow University. A highly regarded Urdu writer, she published seven novels (*Ziddi*, is considered to be the best) and numerous collections of short stories during her lifetime. Some of her stories were the basis of the famous Hindi film about the Partition, *Garam Hawa*. She died in 1992.

Kartar Singh Duggal: Born in 1917, in Rawalpindi district, Pakistan. He worked for the All India Radio for many years, and later served as member of the Planning Commission. He has published numerous novels, short stories and plays in Punjabi. His collection of stories, *Mhaja Nahin Moya*, was given the Sahitya Akademi Award in 1965.

Asif Aslam Farrukhi: Born in Pakistan in 1959, he teaches medicine at the Aga Khan University at Karachi. He has published three collections of short stories in Urdu and has translated a volume of contemporary Urdu poems into English (with Francis Pritchett) entitled, *An Evening of Caged Beasts*.

Intizar Husain: Born in the 1920's, in U.P., India. He migrated to Pakistan after the Partition. Considered to be one of the most important writers in Urdu, he has, thus far, published six collections of short stories, three novels (*Basti* is considered to be a classic), and a volume of essays. Recently, he was given the first Yatra Literary Award.

N.G. Gore: Born in 1907, in Ratnagiri district, Maharashtra. A politically active man, he joined the Quit India movement in 1942. He was elected to the Lok Sabha. A prolific writer of fiction in Marathi. He died in 1993.

Qurratulain Hyder: Born in 1927 in Aligarh. She studied at Lucknow University, and worked as an editor of *Imprint* and *The Illustrated Weekly of India*. After the Partition, she lived for a while in Pakistan, but chose to return to India. She has won the Sahitya Akademi and the Jnanpith Awards.

Saadat Hasan Manto: Born in 1912 in Ludhiana, he migrated to Pakistan in 1947. He died in Lahore in 1955. A major Urdu writer, his collected works have been recently published in five volumes. Apart from writing short stories, he also wrote film-scripts, radio plays and essays.

Gurmukh Singh Musafir: A well-known Punjabi poet and novelist, he was born in 1899 in Udhawal district, Punjab. He took an active part in the Indian nationalist movement, and later became an important figure in the political life of Punjab. He died in 1975.

Sultan Jamil Nasim: Born in 1935 in Agra, he was educated at Agra, Lahore and Karachi. He works in a bank and has, thus far, published two collections of short stories.

Ved Rahi: Born in 1933 in Jammu, he has worked as a film-director for many years. Thus far, he has published a variety of novels, stories and plays in Dogri. He was given the Sahitya Akademi Award in 1977.

Amrit Rai: Born in 1921 in Kanpur, he was educated at the University of Allahabad. He was the editor of *Nayi Kahaniyan*. He has published many novels and short stories in Hindi, as well as, an acclaimed biography of his father, Premchand. He received the Nehru Fellowship in 1977.

Mohan Rakesh: Born in Amritsar in 1925. He studied at the Oriental College, Lahore, and taught at Elphinstone College, Bombay, and D.A.V. College, Jullunder. Associated with the "Nayi Kahani" in Hindi, he published two highly acclaimed novels (*Adhe Adhure* is regarded as a classic), plays (*Ashard Ka Ek Din* has been performed repeatedly) and a few collections of short stories. He received the Nehru Fellowship and the Sangeet Natak Akademi Award. He died in 1972.

Bhisham Sahni: He was born in 1915, in Rawalpindi, Pakistan. He studied at the Government College, Lahore. After 1947, he taught in a college in Delhi. Thus far, he has published numerous volumes of short stories, novels and plays in Hindi. *Tamas*, his novel about the Partition, won the Sahitya Akademi Award in 1971.

Maheep Singh: A respected Hindi writer, he was born in 1930 in Unnao, Uttar Pradesh. At present, he teaches Hindi at the University of Delhi.

Aga Sohail: Born in 1933, in Lucknow, he migrated to Pakistan after the Partition. At present, he teaches at the Forman Christian College in Lahore. A prolific writer of Urdu fiction, his best known works are *Badalta Hai Rang* and *Asman*.

S.H. Vatsayan 'Ajneya': A celebrated Hindi writer, he was born in 1911, in Kusinagar, Uttar Pradesh. He published four novels (of which *Shekhar: Ek Jeevani* is the most famous), collections of short stories and more than twelve volumes of poems. He won the Jnanpith Award in 1978. He died in 1989.

GLOSSARY

Abba	Father
Abbajan	Father
Afimi	Opium-eater
Afsar	Officer
Agni	Fire
Ajwain	Oregano
Alam	Banner
Ameen	Amen
Amma	Mother
Ammi	Mother
Angeethi	Stove
Azan	Call for prayers
Babu	Respectful term of address
Bade Abba	Grandfather
Bade Bhaiya	Elder brother
Badi Amma	Grandmother
Badi Bitiya	Elder daughter
Bahaman	Brahmin
Bahen	Sister
Bahu	Daughter-in-law
Baisakhi	Harvest season
Basti	Town
Batter	Quail
Behist	Paradise
Bhai; Bhaiya	Brother
Bhajan	Religious singing of the Hindus
Bharjai	Sister-in-law
Bhatijay	Nephew
Bigha	A measure of land
Bismillah	In the name of Allah
Bundook	Gun
Chacha	Father's brother
Chachi	Father's brother's wife
Chandan	Sandal-wood powder or paste

Chillum	Earthen pot of a hookah in which tobacco is burnt
Choti Bahu	Younger daughter-in-law
Choti Bitiya	Younger daughter
Choti Khala	Mother's younger sister
Chunni	Cloth draped by women over their heads and shoulders
Dholak	Drum
Dulha Bhai	Brother-in-law
Fakir	Beggar; mendicant
Gharara	Loose pyjama worn by women
Goonda	Hooligan
Granthi	Priest in a gurudwara
Gur	Jaggery
Haldi	Turmeric
Huzoor	Master
Imambara	Shia sanctuary
Jehad	Holy war
Ji	Yes
Kafir	Infidel
Kameez	Loose shirt
Khalsa	Sikh
Kirpan	Dagger
Kothi	Large house
Kurta	Loose shirt
Mama	Mother's brother
Mandi	Market
Manjlay	Second son
Massi	Father's sister
Masterji	Teacher
Maulvi	Muslim religious teacher
Mehndi	Henna
Miyan	Respectful way of addressing a Muslim man
Mumani	Mother's brother's wife
Paan	Betel-leaf
Paandan	Box for keeping betel-leaves

Pani	Water
Prashad	Offering in a temple
Prithvi	Earth
Purdah	Veil
Qaida	Urdu alphabet book
Rasool	Messenger of God
Sabeel	Water served during Moharram
Sabzi	Vegetables
Sadhu	Ascetic; mendicant
Salaam	Greetings
Salwar	Loose pyjama
Sardar	Leader; chief
Seth	Rich businessman
Sherwani	Long coat
Sihani	Sikh woman
Sindoor	Vermillion
Surya	Sun
Tahsildar	Officer of a district
Taya	Father's younger brother
Tazia	Replica of the shrine of Imam Hussain at Karbala carried during Mohurram
Tehmad	Lungi
Thana	Police station
Tilak	Mark on the forehead applied by brahmins
Tonga	Horse-driven carriage
Tongawallah	Driver of a horse-driven carriage
Toppe	Hat
Tun ki karni hain	What are you doing
Tun kithe gayin sen	Where had you gone
Tun kithe hain	Where are you
Turra	Plume
Vayu	Wind
Waheguru	God of the Sikhs
Yakka	One horsed carriage
Yar	Friend
Zamindar	Landlord
Zindabad	Long live